Behavioral Science for Social Workers

Behavioral Science for Social Workers

Edwin J. Thomas, *editor*

Foreword by FEDELE F. FAURI

THE FREE PRESS, *New York*

COLLIER-MACMILLAN LIMITED, *London*

Foreword

The infusion of behavioral science into social work has been one of the most significant developments in social work education in recent years. We now observe the influence of behavioral science in many areas of social work education. Increasingly, we find knowledge from behavioral science employed in all areas of professional curricula. More and more faculty members having competence in one or another of the behavioral sciences are being added to social work faculties, and schools are valuing and making effective use of scholars and researchers whose training and interests involve a fusion of behavioral science and social work. In the community of professional education, the relevance of behavioral science to the many problems of social welfare is no longer denied.

The many changes that have brought about this receptivity to behavioral science are impressive when one realizes that the climate of opinion was very different as recently as two decades ago. In 1948 the new general director of the Russell Sage Foundation, Donald Young, said,

> As the Foundation sees the situation, both social science and social practice have made great advances in recent decades, but as they have progressed there has been a costly failure by each to maintain sufficiently close liaison with the other. Research needs to be kept realistic by contact with the practitioners who use its results; the practitioners need to keep informed about the frontiers of research knowledge bearing on their techniques. Responsibility for the current lack of adequate attention to this fact lies not chiefly with either the social scientists or the practitioners. . . . The problem seems to be that it has been almost no one's accepted responsibility to develop and maintain the needed liaison.[1]

Since 1948 the Russell Sage Foundation has devoted an important portion of its energies and funds to the means by which this liaison could be implemented.

It would be difficult, in this Foreword, to trace the many significant changes that we have witnessed in this area in the last two decades. It

1. Russell Sage Foundation, *Annual Report 1947–1948*, p. 14.

would not be inappropriate, however, to highlight some of the landmarks that occurred at The University of Michigan School of Social Work during this transition period. Many of the developments in the School necessarily mirror national trends. Similar developments are being planned elsewhere, or have their counterparts in the activities of other schools throughout the country.

There were at least four early activities at the School that laid the basis for subsequent developments.[2] The first was the reconnaissance study of evaluative research in social work carried out by David G. French and sponsored by the Michigan Welfare League and the James Foster Foundation. The study was located in the School and, during the period of the study, five faculty members from various University units served on the advisory committee.[3] We then accepted the invitation of the Russell Sage Foundation to conduct systematic discussions of the problems involved for a year. This was the second development. The ensuing faculty seminar (The Research Basis of Social Welfare Practice) met in 1953–54 with Mr. French as its executive secretary. In addition to breaking down the barriers to communication between social work and various other disciplines, the seminar fostered interdisciplinary research and established the climate of opinion necessary for planning a more substantial liaison between social science and social work.

Among the significant recommendations of this Seminar was that the University set up the Coordinating Committee on Social Welfare Research, representing the appropriate social science departments, professional schools, and social research units. The establishment, in 1955, of the Committee within the Social Science Division of the University, with Mr. French as its secretary, was the third significant development. Under the guidance of this Committee, interdisciplinary research was fostered and, more significantly, the basic planning was undertaken for a program of advanced training and research in social work and social science.

The three elements of the proposed program were as follows: (1) Advanced training at the doctoral level to equip persons specifically for the task of bringing together the approaches of social science and social work in practice, teaching, and research; (2) Research designed to produce findings of significance for both practice and scientific theory and to provide advanced students with experience in interdisciplinary work; and (3) The extension of social science knowledge and theory in the professional social work curriculum. The proposal was submitted to the Russell Sage Foundation, and funds were granted to support the program in 1956. These funds were renewed again in 1961 for another five-year period. The funding of this program and its establishment in The Uni-

2. These developments are described and appraised in greater detail in Robert C. Angell, "A Research Basis for Social Welfare," *Social Work Journal* (October, 1954), 145–51.

3. Some of the results of this effort were reported in David G. French, *An Approach to Measuring Results in Social Work* (New York: Columbia U. P., 1952).

versity of Michigan School of Social Work marked the fourth significant step in our efforts to coordinate social work and social science.

As important as these early developments were, however, they served mainly to provide the basis for the difficult tasks of concretely implementing and expanding a program. Since 1956, all features of the program have been developed. Many social scientists with interests and competencies in social work have been added to the faculty. We now have specialists in psychology, social psychology, and sociology, all of whom teach in the advanced and professional curricula and, along with most of their colleagues in social work proper, engage in interdisciplinary scholarship and research. Many of the writings of this specialized group, as well as of others on the faculty, are among the selections gathered together in this book.

The emphasis of this book is almost exclusively upon the contributions of behavioral science to social work because it is directed toward an audience of social workers and others in related fields. The relationship of behavioral science to social work is not a one-way proposition, however. Social work makes important contributions to behavioral science. The practical problems met in social work, when attacked in terms of current behavioral science understanding, provide an important field test that helps us learn what is useful in behavioral science and what is merely academic. Areas that require additional basic research are made conspicuous, and, by collaborating with social workers, behavioral scientists often carry out such additional inquiries in social welfare settings. Research on applied problems of social work is one of the many types of behavioral science research relevant to social welfare, and more than a few of the selections in this book are precisely of this type. Furthermore, the many practical innovations of change indigenous or particular to social work contribute to a basic understanding of behavioral and social change when studied by behavioral scientists. Behavioral science and social work are thus reciprocally interrelated. As each enriches the other it will be more difficult to draw a hard and fast line between them.

The professional schools of social work and the universities of which they are a part have crucial responsibilities for fostering the proper interpenetration of behavioral science and social work. In the future, the achievements in knowledge and practice in social work will be very intimately related to the place of the university in society, to the linkages of schools of social work to the relevant parts of the university at large, and to the responsibilities of the schools themselves. John W. Gardner, the Secretary of Health, Education, and Welfare, has discussed these topics in his projections made for education and social work of a quarter of a century ahead. His comments are penetrating and challenging.

First, the universities will have established themselves as immensely important nerve centers of society. The inner city of the university will concern itself with the basic fields of science and scholarship at both undergraduate and graduate levels. And that inner city will be ringed with great and powerful professional schools which serve as the bridge between the university and the rest of the community, between basic and applied knowledge, between the idea and its uses.

Among these professional schools, the school of social work will be one of the most important. We cannot be sure that it will be *called* a school of social work, nor can we describe the curriculum. But it will be a legitimate lineal descendant of present schools.

Like all of the great professional schools of 1990, it will have extremely close ties with the basic fields of science and scholarship in the university—in this case, with the behavioral and social science fields. Indeed it will not be ranked as a distinguished school of social work unless it is associated with an institution in which those fields are strong.

Over and above the basic research activities in the university, the school of social work will *itself* carry on extensive research, both basic and applied. It will conduct its own appraisal of social needs and problems. It will look into the methods by which social services are delivered as well as the institutional arrangements through which the needs of people are met.

Just as the medical schools found it necessary not only to establish ties with the basic biological fields but to develop their own biomedical research centers, the schools of social work will find that certain lines of research will prosper *only* under their own sponsorship. Standing, as all professional schools must, with one foot in the basic fields and one foot in practice, they will find themselves posing questions that may not even interest investigators in the basic behavior sciences.

In short, the great complex of gleaming buildings that make up the university social work center of 1990 will have many laboratories for social research.[4]

FEDELE F. FAURI

4. Remarks delivered at the Fourteenth Annual Meeting of the Council on Social Work Education, New York, January 25, 1966.

Preface

Knowledge is being developed in today's world at a tremendous rate and all spheres of social life are increasingly confronted with the prospects of consequent change. In social work and related professions the "knowledge explosion" is perhaps best exemplified by the rapidly expanding body of behavioral and social science knowledge relevant to professional endeavor. I am referring to knowledge in which scientific approaches are employed to understand human behavior and social life, this knowledge being included in the disciplines ordinarily covered by the terms "behavioral science" and "social science." (To avoid the cumbersomeness of referring to both behavioral and social science every time I wish to talk about this knowledge, I shall simply use the term "behavioral science," which is to be construed generically.) For over a decade now, the profession of social work has been particularly receptive to the contributions of behavioral science. However, because the profession had not followed closely all pertinent developments in behavioral science during the years prior to the last decade, it has had the problem of catching up with existing knowledge. Despite a growing literature on behavioral science addressed expressly to social workers and published in forms easily accessible to them, there are still pockets of behavioral science knowledge that have yet to be assimilated. Furthermore, the lag in assimilation threatens to become longer rather than shorter because of the increasing proliferation of behavioral science writings.

Every year thousands of articles appear in scores of behavioral science journals, to say nothing of the publication of hundreds of books in behavioral science. These writings pertain to behavioral development, perception, learning and thinking, motivation, the family, small groups, organizations, institutions, social stratification, ethnic relations, mass communication, opinions, attitudes and beliefs, the society, and culture—to say nothing of the various areas in political science and economics. After reviewing the research relating to these specific topics, Berelson and Steiner, in their *Human Behavior: An Inventory of Scientific Findings,*[1] report

1. B. Berelson and G. A. Steiner, *Human Behavior: An Inventory of Scientific Findings* (New York: Harcourt, 1964).

1,045 generalizations about human conduct. In the field of small groups—a specialization that did not exist twenty years ago—we find 1,385 references in Hare's *Handbook of Small Group Research*.[2] Well over half of these references were published after 1950, and additional writings are appearing at the rate of about 152 per year. March's 1,247-page *Handbook of Organizations*[3] includes 28 specialized reviews which draw upon hundreds of recent studies done in diverse subfields of behavioral science. The new field of behavioral therapy and behavioral modification has not been recognized as relevant in social work at this time, yet in the past few years over twenty books have been published on this subject along with hundreds of articles. With this increasing volume of behavioral science output, the task of assimilation is indeed formidable.

The field of social work has responded in diverse ways to the challenges posed by behavioral science. There has been an encouraging increase in articles in *Social Casework, Social Work,* and in the *Social Service Review* having theoretical and conceptual references and pertaining to verifiable content.[4] The recently established *Abstracts for Social Workers* reviews selected, current behavioral science literature relevant to social welfare. I have gathered the impression in recent years that the percentage of articles in social work journals devoted to behavioral science for social workers has been gradually increasing. Social role, deviance, social power, social class, ethnic and cultural factors, small-group processes and leadership, political processes, and economic analyses are among the more common topics addressed in such articles in social work journals.

Considering the sheer volume of what is pertinent to social work, however, the percentage of such articles is still relatively low. In a bibliography of sociocultural works published in nine North American social work journals, 163 titles were listed for the years 1956–1963.[5] I judge that approximately 100 of these references truly reflect and build upon the substance of behavioral science. This figure is to be contrasted with a total estimated output of 2,784 articles published in these same journals for the eight years in question. Using these figures, one may reckon that between 3 and 6 per cent of the articles in the professional social work journals have been devoted to sociocultural subjects. This comes down to 1 to 3 articles per journal per year—a most modest contribution.

Slightly more encouraging are figures from Silverman's recent analysis of the major subjects treated in 107 articles on group work found in recent issues of major social work journals and in compilations of papers relating

2. A. P. Hare, *Handbook of Small Group Research* (New York: Free Press, 1962).

3. James G. March (ed.), *Handbook of Organizations* (Chicago: Rand McNally 1965).

4. Merlin Tabor and Iris Shapiro, "Social Work and Its Knowledge Base: A Content Analysis of the Periodical Literature," *Social Work,* **10** (1965), 100–107.

5. Benjamin Schlesinger, *Socio-Cultural Content in North American Social Work Journals—1956–1963* (Toronto: University of Toronto School of Social Work, 1964; mimeographed).

to social work practice.[6] The articles were classified into one of eleven possible categories on the basis of the subject matter treated. Seven per cent fell into "applications of social science," and 4 per cent each into "innovations in practice theory" and "research and surveys." If we combine these percentages, we obtain a total of 15 per cent of the articles that reflect the more diverse, general contributions of behavioral science. These figures contrast markedly with the two single categories containing the largest percentages of articles; "descriptions" of group work contained 30 per cent of the articles and "areas of practice" 25 per cent.

The surveys cited above, however, probably underestimate the influence of behavioral science on the knowledge in social work. Some information on this problem is provided for group work in Silverman's analysis. The books cited in the articles were classified by profession and discipline. As might be expected, the largest percentage was for social work books— 44 per cent. However, books in behavioral science followed closely behind; 36 per cent were classified as sociology and social psychology and 12 per cent as psychology and psychiatry. Although we do not have at hand comparable data for casework writings, my guess is that the figures there would be lower for behavioral science, with perhaps somewhat higher reliance upon writings from the allied professions of psychiatry and psychoanalysis.

The trends apparent in the above characterization of the periodical literature in social work are sharpened when we add to this analysis the books in social work. Consider those on behavioral science that have been addressed to social workers. Here we find an influential but small set of books. Wilensky and Lebeaux,[7] Stein and Cloward,[8] Coyle,[9] Coyle and Hartford,[10] Pollak,[11] Ross and Hendry,[12] Zald,[13] Kogan,[14] and Riessman,

6. Marvin Silverman, "An Assessment of Knowledge in Social Group Work through a Review of the Literature," *Social Work*, 11 (1966), 56–63.

7. Harold L. Wilensky and Charles N. Lebeaux, *Industrial Society and Social Welfare* (New York: Russell Sage Foundation, 1958).

8. Herman D. Stein and Richard A. Cloward (eds.), *Social Perspectives on Behavior: A Reader in Social Science for Social Work and Related Professions* (New York: Free Press, 1958).

9. Grace Longwell Coyle, *Social Science in the Professional Education of Social Workers* (New York: Council on Social Work Education, 1958).

10. Grace Longwell Coyle and Margaret E. Hartford, *Social Process in the Community and the Group* (New York: Council on Social Work Education, 1958).

11. Otto Pollak, *Integrating Sociological and Psychoanalytic Concepts: An Exploration in Child Psychotherapy* (New York: Russell Sage Foundation, 1956); and Otto Pollak and collaborators, Bertram J. Black, Dorothy Dunaeff, Yonata Feldman, Bernice Wolf Frechtman, Maurice R. Friend, Lia Knoepfmacher, Bettina Lehnert, Frederika Neumann, and S. R. Slauson; *Social Science and Psychotheraphy for Children* (New York: Russell Sage Foundation, 1952).

12. Murray G. Ross and Charles E. Hendry, *New Understandings of Leadership: A Survey and Application of Research* (New York: Assn. Pr., 1957).

13. Mayer N. Zald, *Social Welfare Institutions: A Sociological Reader* (New York: Wiley, 1965).

14. Leonard S. Kogan (ed.), *Social Science Theory and Social Work Research* (New York: National Association of Social Workers, 1960).

Cohen, and Pearl [15] are among the authors or editors of significant volumes containing substantive contributions. Polansky [16] has edited a book on social work research that reflects portions of the methodological knowledge of behavioral science. Hearn [17] has explicated some of the conceptual and theoretical tools of behavioral science in his *Theory Building in Social Work*. There is also a more extensive monographic literature which reflects variously the substantive, methodological, and conceptual contributions of behavioral science to social work. I am speaking now of the monographs in which we mainly find evaluations of practice, services, and programs.

The significant texts on casework, group work, community organization, and administration highlight most vividly the lag in the consumption of behavioral science. The texts differ from the periodical literature in these areas in one noteworthy fashion: with only a few exceptions, the texts either ignore the relevant contributions of behavioral science or, at best, there is passing and sparing allusion to the thoughts of a particular seminal thinker in behavioral science or to the possible pertinence of a selected body of literature. It is probably not unfair to say that at this time the texts on the practice methods of social work have been mainly untouched and uninformed by the large corpus of knowledge in behavioral science. The fact that these texts have generally been based upon practice wisdom and codification of experience—as of course they should be—does not compensate for their having failed to incorporate the relevant material from behavioral science.

To improve practice, the knowledge of behavioral science must be diffused throughout the social work community, it must be assimilated and, after appraisal and selection, it must be systematically incorporated into the knowledge of social work proper. Everything considered, these tasks have only just begun. The large magnitude of the efforts required indicates that work must proceed on many simultaneous fronts.

This collection of readings was prepared so that a sample of current and germane writings in behavioral science would be available to social workers and members of related professions. Although many of the selections also represent contributions to behavioral science, which are generally inspired by problems of social welfare, the primary audience for the book is the social work student and educator. Practitioners and administrators in social work, and members of allied professions who work with problems similar to those in social work should find the book useful as well. Because the collection reflects a particular community of thought at this time, it is something of a progress report to be assimilated and

15. Frank Riessman, Jerome Cohen, and Arthur Pearl (eds.), *Mental Health and the Poor* (New York: Free Press, 1964).
16. Norman A. Polansky (ed.), *Social Work Research* (Chicago: U. of Chicago Press, 1960).
17. Gordon Hearn, *Theory Building in Social Work* (Toronto: U. of Toronto Press, 1958).

incorporated, as appropriate. Meanwhile, other efforts to help the profession keep abreast of recent developments in behavioral science will inevitably continue.

The community of thought that has informed the writings brought together in this book is representative of the national climate of opinion on questions of behavioral science and social work. (The main themes in the community of thought are developed in the first paper: "Types of Contributions Behavioral Science Makes to Social Work.") Nevertheless, any collection of readings necessarily presents only a particular sample of many possibly relevant contributions. Because most of the authors were engaged in aspects of a common enterprise involving behavioral science and social work, the writings in this book were drawn from selected publications of the professors and researchers affiliated with The University of Michigan School of Social Work. (Every article or selection from a book included here had at least one author associated with the School at the time the volume was edited.) Compelling limitations of space made it impossible to include pertinent writings on the social services proper, on research methods and techniques applicable to social work, and on conceptualizations of practice in the various methods of social work. Consequently, these contributions emphasize some themes more than others.

First, all the writings reflect, somehow, the scientific stance of behavioral science—a pervasive "scientific rationality" as it were. Second, there is a heavy weighting toward the substantive contributions that behavioral science makes to social work. Selections are addressed to the behavioral and social factors pertaining to individuals, groups, families, organizations, communities, and selected societal processes. Most of the relevant substance in many areas of behavioral science is covered, and the contributions are directed toward understanding the clients, the workers themselves, and particular services, programs, and policies of welfare. Third, the contributions of the "conceptual tools" of behavioral science are amply represented. Thus, the reader will find numerous examples of the conceptualization of problems particular to social work, among these being the one-parent family, the treatment organization, agency interrelationships, and various types of social deviance. He will find research inquiries on welfare problems guided by conceptual analysis, and papers reflecting conceptual analyses of various features of the very process of applying behavioral science knowledge (e.g., selecting knowledge from behavioral science, developing practice principles). Fourth, the methodological contributions, although not discussed per se, are to be found in every empirical study. The methodological contributions are perhaps most apparent in the research studies conducted on therapeutic processes and outcomes.

I am indebted primarily to my colleagues who have helped in so many ways to make their writings available for the collection. I should mention particularly Robert D. Vinter, Henry J. Meyer, Paul Glasser, and Jack

Rothman, all of whom provided helpful comments on drafts of this preface and the first paper ("Types of Contributions Behavioral Science Makes to Social Work") and, along with Rosemary Sarri, provided editorial counsel at various points of choice. Dean Fedele F. Fauri and Dr. Vinter, in his capacity as Associate Dean, provided the essential administrative support required to bring this book into being. Valuable secretarial assistance was provided by Neva Mastin, Marian Iglesias, and especially Diane Etzel who helped convert the selections to the proper form. The diligent and competent proofreading of Howard C. Myers was invaluable. I am grateful also to Andea Greenberg, who helped with the final reading of proofs, and to Roy Gaunt, Marsha Fisch, and Vivian Thomas who helped me prepare portions of the index. The numerous publishers who have so kindly given permission to reproduce the various selections are acknowledged specifically where the selections appear.

Ann Arbor, Michigan   E. J. T.

List of Contributors

HARVEY BERTCHER, M.S.W., D.S.W., Assistant Professor of Social Work, The University of Michigan School of Social Work.

EDGAR F. BORGATTA, Ph.D., Professor of Sociology and Chairman of the Department of Sociology, University of Wisconsin.

HARVEY E. BRAZER, Ph.D., Professor of Economics and Research Associate, Institute of Public Administration, The University of Michigan.

WILBUR, J. COHEN, Ph.B., L.H.D., LL.D., Under Secretary, Department of Health, Education, and Welfare.

MARTIN H. DAVID, Ph.D., Assistant Professor, Department of Economics, University of Wisconsin, and Director, Center for Household and Labor Market Research, Social Systems Research Institute.

RONALD A. FELDMAN, M.S.W., Ph.D., Assistant Professor, School of Social Welfare, University of California, Berkeley, California.

PHILLIP A. FELLIN, M.S.W., Ph.D. Associate Professor of Social Work, The University of Michigan School of Social Work.

M. DAVID GALINSKY, Ph.D., Associate Professor of Psychology and Director, Clinical Training Program, University of North Carolina.

MAEDA J. GALINSKY, M.S.W., Ph.D., Assistant Professor of Social Work, University of North Carolina School of Social Work.

LOIS N. GLASSER, M.S.W., Ann Arbor, Michigan.

PAUL H. GLASSER, M.S.W., Ph.D., Professor of Social Work, The University of Michigan School of Social Work.

JESSE E. GORDON, M.A., Ph.D., Associate Professor, School of Social Work and Department of Psychology, The University of Michigan.

SAUL I. HARRISON, M.D., Associate Professor, Department of Psychiatry, The University of Michigan School of Medicine.

WYATT C. JONES, B.D., A.M., Ph.D., Associate Professor of Research, The Florence Heller Graduate School for Advanced Studies in Social Welfare, Brandeis University.

JANE A. KAMM, M.S.W., Chief of Social Service, Genesee County Services, Pontiac State Hospital, and Instructor in Field Work, Wayne State University.

JACOB KOUNIN, Ph.D., Professor of Educational Psychology, Wayne State University.

EUGENE LITWAK, Ph.D., Professor of Social Welfare Research, The University of Michigan School of Social Work.

JOHN F. McDERMOTT, M.D., Assistant Professor, Department of Psychiatry, The University of Michigan School of Medicine.

DONNA L. McLEOD, M.A., Madison, Wisconsin.

HENRY J. MEYER, Ph.D., Professor, School of Social Work and Department of Sociology, The University of Michigan.

JAMES N. MORGAN, Ph.D., Professor of Economics and Program Director, Survey Research Center, The University of Michigan.

ELIZABETH NAVARRE, M.A., Research Associate, The University of Michigan School of Social Work.

NORMAN A. POLANSKY, Ph.D., Professor of Sociology and Social Work, The University of Georgia.

CHARLES N. POSKANZER, Ph.D., Professor of Health Education, School of Education, State University of New York, Cortland, New York.

FRANK RAFFERTY, M.D., Director, Child Psychiatry Service, The Psychiatric Institute, University of Maryland.

JACK ROTHMAN, M.S.W., Ph.D., Professor of Social Work, The University of Michigan School of Social Work.

ROSEMARY C. SARRI, M.S.W., Ph.D., Professor of Social Work, The University of Michigan School of Social Work.

WALTER E. SCHAFER, Ph.D., Assistant Professor of Sociology, University of Oregon.

JULES SCHRAGER, M.S.W., Director, Department of Social Work, University Hospital, and Assistant Professor of Social Work, School of Social Work, The University of Michigan.

DOROTHY SCHROEDER, M.S.W., Professor of Social Work, The University of Michigan School of Social Work.

HARRY SHARP, Ph.D., Professor of Sociology, University of Wisconsin.

EDWIN J. THOMAS, M.S.W., Ph.D., Professor of Social Work and of Psychology, The University of Michigan.

ROBERT D. VINTER, Ph.D., Professor of Social Work and Associate Dean, The University of Michigan School of Social Work.

PAUL T. WILSON, M.D., Principal Investigator, Information Processing Project, American Psychiatric Association.

Contents

Part I

Background

Introduction

What is the nature of the contributions of behavioral science to social work? What are the distinct features of social welfare to which aspects of behavioral science may contribute useful information? Surprisingly, writings on the relationship of behavioral science and social work have not adequately dealt with these important questions. In attempting to detail answers to these quesions, the first selection also provides a general frame of reference for the various contributions of behavioral science to social work represented by the selections that follow it.

1 Types of Contributions
Behavioral Science Makes
to Social Work

Edwin J. Thomas

Behavioral science is not a monolithic entity with uniform contribution. It is a complex amalgam of thought, practices, and products—of philosophy, methodology, and knowledge.[1] These different features of behavioral science are relevant to diverse aspects of social work. It is important to distinguish the separate contributions of behavioral science to social work so that we may appreciate the depth, scope, and limitations of its offerings and make better use of its particular contributions.[2]

Despite the increasing receptivity to behavioral science in social work and the growing literature on the interface of these two fields, the types of contributions behavioral science makes to social work have not been elaborated. In general, the social workers who have written on the use of behavioral science have tended to assume that the contributions were understood, or to emphasize one type of contribution and to ignore others. It would be unfair to criticize these writers too severely, however, because the many diverse contributions of behavioral science to social work are only now becoming apparent. These separate contributions must be inferred from an examination of many scholarly and empirical inquiries. My colleagues might not agree with this interpretation of the contributions in all details, and there are bound to be differences in emphasis to which, of course, I am not immune.

Although the major portion of this paper will be devoted to a discussion of the types of contributions behavioral science makes to social work, an important related topic will also be treated. This is the question of the component features of social work to which aspects of behavioral science may be applicable. We turn first to the types of contributions.

This paper was prepared especially for this volume.

The Types of Contributions

There are at least four specific components of behavioral science, each of which offers a distinctively different contribution to one or another aspect of social work. Each of these may be regarded as a type of contribution.

First, behavioral science contains a perspective concerning human behavior and how it is to be understood. We may call this perspective the *scientific stance* for it contains the principles of science as they are applicable to the understanding of human behavior. According to this stance, human behavior is naturally determined rather than governed by supernatural or mystical factors; it is represented and known naturally, i.e., through man's senses, and it is orderly and predictable, not random or capricious. Truth is known with approximate certainty; hypotheses are correct and valid with given degrees of probability as are the observations upon which generalizations are based. Knowledge must be verifiable and, to this end, impartial and objective observations are made, definitions of phenomena are made concrete, procedures of inquiry are made public and repeatable, and judgment is withheld, retaining scepticism until there has been proper corroboration. The approach is cumulative and systematic so as to build toward an organized body of verified generalizations. The objective of understanding, explaining, and predicting human behavior pervades this attitude.

The scientific stance is applicable to the development and use of knowledge in social work despite the fact that social work, in contrast to behavioral science, has the primary objective of achieving control as do most applied fields. The objective of understanding, explaining, and predicting behavior, as transmuted in social work, serves to enable social workers to attain their practical objectives better. The view that behavior is naturally determined enjoins social workers to examine the full range of behavioral determinants of their own action as well as the behavior of those with whom they work. Individual, group, organizational, occupational, community, and societal factors—indeed, the entire social fabric—consequently become proper objects of analysis. The emphasis upon verifiable knowledge enjoins the separation of value and fact and, more generally, cautions practitioners against adhering to knowledge that has little substantiation and, at the same time, encourages an active search for verified information. On balance, the scientific stance, as employed in behalf of social welfare objectives, infuses a scientific rationality into the use of knowledge and into the actions taken.

A second component of behavioral science is its approach to the conceptualization of phenomena, the *conceptual tools* of behavioral science. We are speaking here of the behavioral scientist's mode of thinking, as distinct from the scientific stance, the research methods, or the substantive knowledge that derives from the use of all of these. In this limited context, it is difficult to characterize something as complex as the way in which the behavioral scientist manipulates symbols and concepts in his quest for understanding. We are all familiar with concepts, hypotheses, theories, and models that are among the products of the conceptualizing activity. Given the limitations of this context, however, some of the salient features of conceptualization may be briefly indicated.

There are various elements of conceptualization, among these being the concept, the operational definition of the concept, the hypothesis, the theory, and the model. (For some writers, the metaphor, the construct, and the analogue should be added as well.) At least some of these are present in any effort to conceptualize behavioral phenomena. Three of these—the concept, hypothesis, and theory—will be discussed later in detail.

In the use of conceptual tools, the process is as important as the particular elements entering into it. Hearn's [3] elaboration of the theory-building process in social work serves us well as one explication of the conceptualizing process. The steps of this theory building process are as follows: (1). The preliminary phase, during which a domain of inquiry is isolated; (Merton [4] has recently added a useful treatment of "problem-finding" in which he specifies such factors as originating questions, the rationale, and specifying questions); (2). Identifying inadequacies in present theory; (3). Making explicit one's value orientation; (4). Selecting appropriate constructs and models; (5). Developing the constructural framework; (6). Formulation of hypotheses; (7). Testing hypotheses; (8). Formulating theory; (9). Concretizing (i.e., "translating theory back into practical terms"); and (10). Empirical testing and utilization. Hearn views this as a continuous circular process.

When these steps are examined closely, at least four different activities may be identified. The first step we may call problem formulation. It includes isolating a domain of inquiry, identifying inadequacies of present theory, and making explicit one's value orientation (Hearn's steps 1 to 3). The second step is the tying of concepts to real-world referents. This makes possible empirical testing on the one hand and practice concretizing on the other hand. (This clearly includes Hearn's step 9 and is presupposed for steps 7 and 10.) The third step is the interrelating of concepts, either as single hypotheses or as logically or topically related propositions. These latter are commonly called theories. The fact that the concepts are logically related enables the user to make predictions of forthcoming events or explanations of past events. When such predictions and explanations are considered in research, they make possible the testing of hypotheses. When considered in practice, they facilitate prognosis (in the case of predictions) and diagnosis (in the case of explanations). (Hearn's steps 5, 6, and 8 are obviously exemplary here, and 4 and 10 are activities in which the interrelationship of concepts would be implicated.) The fourth activity is the empirical testing of the hypotheses and theories. (This is clearly specified in Hearn's steps 7 and 10.)

Most behavioral scientists would recognize the relevance of these four activities to conceptualizing and the importance of the first three. Many scientists would exclude the last one, empirical testing, from conceptualization proper, though they would recognize nonetheless that empirical testing is generally pertinent to the validation of the propositions involved.

Conceptualization has many valuable functions when prudently undertaken. In his discussion of the functions of the theoretic paradigm, Merton [5] has pointed out that it serves to provide "a compact parsimonious arrangement of central concepts," an explicit framework upon which knowledge may be built and made cumulative, a basis for systematic analysis rather than mere description, a guide to qualitative and quantitative analysis, and a means to avoid making hidden or logically irresponsible assumptions. These are functions of conceptualization in social work no less so than in behavioral science. The adverse consequences, for their respective endeavors, of failure to conceptualize properly are just as great in social work as in behavioral science.

The need for conceptualization of social work knowledge has been expressed by many writers in social work; among them are Bartlett,[6] Boehm,[7] Gordon,[8] Greenwood,[9] Hearn,[10] Kadushin,[11] Kahn,[12] Loeb,[13] and Maas.[14] Most of the dissatisfactions voiced about the existing state of social work knowledge attest to the relative absence of conceptualization. Kadushin's [15] observations are not atypical. In his discussion of the current state of knowledge development in social work, he said that there have been few attempts to validate social work knowledge, that the lack of consistent efforts to conceptualize the knowledge has been accompanied by theories that were either excessively specific or so general as to be inoperative, with little falling in the middle range, and that, in general, the knowledge has not been sufficiently cumulative.

Practice theory is the phrase commonly employed to refer to one of the significant products of conceptualized social work knowledge. Greenwood [16] has observed that practice theory differs from scientific theory in at least three ways: it is oriented toward the objective of control rather than that of understanding alone, it tends to be value laden rather than value free, and it is prescriptive as well as descriptive. But the elements and processes of conceptualization in behavioral science, as alluded to before, are directly relevant to the task of developing principles of practice in social work. As applied to social work, conceptualization involves the particular objects of analysis germane to social welfare. These generally are the practices, services, and policies of the field. It employs the conceptual tools in behalf of the objectives Greenwood has described as particular to practice theory. While such conceptualization would necessarily entail the collation of practice wisdom and experience, the codification of relevant elements (such as techniques of change and change objectives), and the explication of behavioral and value assumptions, the conceptual tools involved and the entire process, as we have indicated, are precisely those already so self-consciously developed in the behavioral sciences.

There is another focus of conceptualization in social work that is sufficiently important to merit separate emphasis. I am speaking of the very process of utilizing behavioral science knowledge. Both the increasing knowledge of behavioral science and its selective applicability to social work necessarily compel a conceptualization of what contributes to social work and what does not. (To a limited extent this very essay on the contributions of behavioral science to social work is illustrative.) Behavioral science knowledge must be selected for use, assimilated by educators and practitioners, amalgamated into the larger fabric of social work knowledge, introduced into educational and agency contexts, and subsequently evaluated and tested. This process, which begins with selection from the heartlands of the academic disciplines of behavioral science and terminates in the front lines of practice in the social-work profession, is a complex intellectual, practical, and institutional transition in the engineering of behavioral science knowledge. This "engineering transition" is just beginning to receive the analysis it deserves.[17]

The third type of contribution of behavioral science to social work is perhaps the most widely recognized. This is the contribution of the *substantive knowledge* about human behavior and social forces. Such knowledge of individuals, groups, organizations, communities, societies, and culture indicates the scope of this substance. Whatever the substantive domain, however, the knowledge takes only a limited number of forms. Of these, I shall mention three.

The first and most elementary is that of the concept. Concepts have designating terms and defined meaning, the latter of which may be connotative or denotative. Some concepts (those called constructs) refer to complex hypothetical states. The ego, self, internalized norm, alienation, and affect are examples of constructs. Some concepts are little more than metaphors (e.g., taking the role of the other, or altercasting), while others imply mechanical, hydraulic, or biological analogues (e.g., social system, tension, homeostasis, cathexis). Still others, such as the operational definition, serve denotative ends, and some function to sensitize one to particular relevant associated phenomena (e.g., family of orientation, culture, ethnic group). But whatever its nature, concepts are the building blocks of the substantive knowledge in behavioral science, and those pertaining to the same subject matter constitute the analytic vocabulary by which the phenomena thus designated are categorized and thereby made amenable to symbolic manipulation.

Essential as they are, however, concepts alone are not enough. That is, in order to predict and explain behavior, we must at least have an hypothesis. This is the second knowledge form of which I spoke. The hypothesis is a statement that relates concepts to one another so as to imply causation or concomitant variation of the phenomena to which the concepts pertain. "Behavior that is punished tends to be suppressed" is an example of an hypothesis from psychology. Hypotheses range from the plausible speculation, which lacks empirical support, to the fully supported proposition, which is often called a law in the physical sciences. When hypotheses are employed to account for future events, we typically speak of them as predictions; when hypotheses are employed to account for past events, we generally refer to them as explanations. Without hypotheses, the prognoses and diagnoses of social work practice would be impossible, and knowledge in both behavioral science and social work would be desperately impoverished.

Theories are built upon hypotheses and generally provide for much more predictive and explanatory power than does the single hypothesis. A theory, a third form in which substance appears, consists of hypotheses that are topically and logically related. There are theories of reinforcement, social power, cognitive dissonance, punishment, organizational decision making, stress, attitude change, and adult socialization, to name but a few. Many theories in behavioral science today are relatively weak because the logical interrelationships are not well developed and the component hypotheses have not been fully corroborated. Such sets of hypothesis may nonetheless be very useful, however, for they often contain many topically related hypotheses relevant to problems commonly met in social work. These hypotheses are generally greatly superior to nonscientific knowledge. Parts of those fields loosely called role theory, small-group theory, organizational theory, and social-systems theory are examples. Some theories are better developed logically, and if they have proper empirical support, they are the preferred form of behavioral science knowledge. There are such theories of stress, perception, learning performance, decision making, social mobility, population growth, and behavioral modification, to name a few.

The fourth and last distinguishable contribution of behavioral science to social work consists of its *methods of research*. Although research in social work is typically addressed to the applied problems of the field, and many of the techniques and methods of research are either indigenous or particular to social work, the problems of research design and of gathering and processing data are sufficiently similar in the two areas to make the technology of behavioral science the single most important outside contributor to the methodology of social work research.

The empirical technology of behavioral science may be conveniently divided into three categories. The first might be called data-gathering designs (this is often referred to simply as methods). There are the experimental designs—which include experiments in natural, field, and laboratory contexts—and the nonexperimental designs which include the case study, the field study, and the sample survey. The second aspect of the research technology consists of the data-gathering techniques (or simply techniques). These include the interview, the questionnaire, projective devices, sociometric tests, observation, literature review, and the use of documents in general. The third feature of the technology consists of the data-processing techniques. Statistical methods, mathematical and analytic models, and computer simulation, among others, should be mentioned here.

In contrast to research methods traditionally identified with social work, it is fair to say that altogether the armamentarium of techniques and methods in behavioral science is more diverse and better developed. If selected properly, methods of behavioral science may be adopted with great benefit in social work. Consider, for example, the data-gathering designs. As compared with behavioral science, social work research has made sparing use of experimental designs, and when these have been employed, they have usually taken the form of demonstrations. Considering only the uncertainty-reduction objectives of such demonstrations and not the change objectives usually built into them, the researcher might substitute for the demonstration a genuine field experiment or even a natural experiment, a laboratory experiment, or an experimental analogue. Many recent studies indicate that researchers are increasingly selecting more diverse experimental methods. Even case analysis has experimental possibilities. The tendency to conduct fewer and fewer case studies in social work has been accompanied, ironically, by a greater use in the behavioral sciences of samples (often small ones) of subjects whose behaviors are monitored through time in response to diverse conditions of change. This analysis of cases thus converts case analysis from an essentially qualitative, nonexperimental approach to a quantitative, experimental method.[18] Such case analysis has great promise for teaching us more about the processes and outcomes of planned change. The nonexperimental methods of the field study appear to be more frequently employed in social work research, although the sample survey has been used little outside of the national and state welfare agencies.

Let us turn now from the designs and consider briefly the data-gathering techniques. It would appear that two such techniques have been the main work horses of past social work research. One has been the interview and the other the use of documents (e.g., case records, reported statistics, historical writings). However, there has been a noteworthy increase in the use of such techniques as the questionnaire and projective and sociometric tests. The direct, systematic observation of behavior still appears to be relatively uncommon, and systematic reviews of the theoretical and research literature are now rarely found in social work.

There tends to be a lag also in the consumption of data-processing techniques. The fine-grained analytic and mathematical models by which the behavioral scientists often order their data have barely touched social work research, although recent statistical tests and computer programs are increasingly being employed in social work research. There is every reason to believe that the data-processing techniques of the behavioral sciences, as well as those of science in general, will eventually be adopted for operational as well as research purposes in social work. Thus, many of the routine data-processing and decision-making requirements of social work agencies could be automated by being programmed for the computer.

Now that the four components of behavioral science have been elaborated, it is appropriate to compare them briefly in terms of how they have been employed in social work. Although the scientific stance is not often made explicit, this is perhaps the single most common feature of behavioral science to be found in social work. The reason for this is not so much that the scientific rationality has significantly pervaded the core of the field but rather because the other features of behavioral science presuppose a scientific stance and, to some extent, are built upon it. It is simply difficult to conceptualize, engage in research, and employ the substantive knowledge of behavioral science without adhering to the scientific stance. But taken by itself, the scientific stance has implications for the activities of practice that writers have just begun to consider.[19]

There seems to be a trend to employ the other component features of behavioral science singly rather than in combination. That is, we find that the conceptual tools are engaged, but not the substance or the research methods of behavioral science, that substance is adopted more or less by itself without conceptualization of the problems to which the substance presumably applies, or that research methods are employed to evaluate social work services where such services are not conceptualized in detail, to say nothing of being established on the basis of substantive knowledge in behavioral science. As behavioral science becomes more thoroughly employed in social work we would anticipate that there would be more uses of many rather than single components of behavioral science. To apply behavioral science appropriately it is unnecessary to engage all components at once, for each component, as the earlier comments have endeavored to make clear, has its own particular applicability. It would be shortsighted, however, to adopt only one component for handling a problem when the other components are also pertinent.

Objects of Analysis in Social Work

Social work, like behavioral science, is also a complex amalgam of thought, practices, and products. One does not simply apply behavioral science to social work in general. One applies some specific aspect of behavioral science to some component feature of social work. Many of the components of social work that constitute the separate objects of analysis were interwoven into the earlier discussion, but the various topics of concern were not considered by themselves. We now turn to these various features of social work that may constitute the foci of attention when applying behavioral science.

These objects of analysis consist of the following:

1. The clientele of social welfare services.
2. The social workers and related professionals.
3. The programs of welfare.
4. The services provided, including direct practice.
5. The agencies and organizations through which services are offered and programs are implemented.

6. The education and training of welfare workers.
7. The research in social work.
8. The knowledge of the profession of social work.
9. The institution of social welfare.

These topics of concern were derived from an informal analysis of writings on behavioral science and social work. Although the topics cover reasonably conventional and cohesive subjects in social work, one must acknowledge that other groupings could readily be evolved. Most of the writings in this area may be easily placed into one or another of the nine categories. The categories are those that appeared to be the objects of analysis commonly found in the writings on behavioral science and social work, but they are not all mutually exclusive. Two categories are conspicuously more inclusive than the others. One is knowledge of the profession of social work, which is inclusive of the knowledge in any or all of the first seven topics as well as the problems of professional knowledge development in general. The other category is the institution of social welfare, which includes many or all of the other topics as well as the entire institution of social welfare.

Such a listing of objects of analysis serves at least two functions. First, of course, it indicates specific topics upon which some work has been done and upon which future effort may be expended. Second, the objects of analysis, when combined with the four components of behavioral science that may contribute to social work, provide one set of analytic categories for explicating the many interrelationships of social work and behavioral science. (The reader will be spared a diagram that explicates the 36 categories of problems that result from combining the four components of behavioral science with the nine objects of analysis in social work, for this can easily be prepared if thought to be useful.)

The heuristic value of this way of thinking about the interfaces of behavioral science and social work will be illustrated for one component feature of behavioral science, namely, the substantive areas of knowledge in the discipline of sociology. Table 1-1 lists such exemplary areas of sociological knowledge for each of the nine specific topics of social work. While this is not proposed as a definitive ordering, it is clear that there are substantive domains of sociology relevant to all of the specific analytic areas of social work, that some substantive domains are either uniquely or most particularly associated with certain social work areas and not others, and that altogether a large portion of the knowledge of sociology bears upon one or another aspect of social work. Similar tables could be prepared for the substantive knowledge in such behavioral sciences as psychology, economics, and political science, among others. For all of the behavioral sciences, materials could also be ordered by the contributions of their methods, scientific stance, and of conceptualization. It will probably be necessary to elaborate these interrelationships as further work progresses on the problems of behavioral science and social work.

Table 1–1. Illustrative Substantive Areas of Sociology Ordered by Objects of Analysis in Social Work

Objects of Analysis in Social Work	Illustrative Substantive Areas of Sociology
Clientele	Social Stratification, Race and Ethnic Relations, Personality and Social Structure, Social Disorganization and Deviant Behavior, Family Sociology, Sociology of Mental Illness, Criminology, Social Movements.
Social Workers and Related Professionals	Professions, Occupations, Social Movements, Marriage and Family Counseling.
Programs	Political Sociology, Poverty and Dependence, Organizations, Institutions, Social Movements.
Services	Organizations, Institutions, Community, Ecology, Urban and Rural Sociology, Interpersonal Influence, Social Interaction.
Agencies and Organizations	Organizations, Institutions, Social-Systems Theory, Political Sociology.
Education and Training	Sociology of Education and Teaching, Professions.
Research	Sociology of Science.*
Professional Knowledge	Social Role, Small Groups, Family, Social Disorganization and Deviance, Community, Social Systems, Race and Ethnic Relations, Professions, Sociology of Science, Sociology of Knowledge.
The Institution of Social Welfare	Institutions, Values and Ideology, Social Movements, Political Sociology, Poverty and Dependence, Social Systems Theory.

* The research methods of sociology have been excluded here because the table lists only substantive areas of sociology. Any consideration of the methodological contributions of behavioral science would of course include the contribution of the methods and techniques of research for the behavioral science in question.

Summary

This paper is an attempt to explicate the specific contributions that behavioral science may make to social work. Four separate components of behavioral science were discussed: the scientific stance, the conceptual tools, the substantive knowledge, and the methodology of research. Examples of the particular problems of social work to which these four components of behavioral science may contribute further understanding were provided.

The last section of the paper was concerned with a more detailed exposition of the classes of problems in social work to which a behavioral science analysis may be addressed. These nine objects of analysis were the clientele of social welfare services, social workers and related professionals, the programs of welfare, the services provided, the welfare agencies and organizations, the education and training of welfare personnel, research in social work, the professional knowledge of social work, and the institution of social welfare. An example of the heuristic value of these categories was provided by ordering illustrative substantive areas of sociological knowledge by the objects of analysis in social work to which the areas of knowledge most clearly related. It was concluded that the particular relationships thus illustrated on the interface of behavioral science and social work were but a portion of the many specific interrelationships that will eventually require elaboration.

Part

Problems of Social Role

Introduction

As an emerging specialization in the behavioral sciences, role theory contributes a valuable perspective and mode of analysis to understand behavior. The perspective of role theory emphasizes the social determinants of the patterned behavior of individuals and of the members of social positions. Its analytic vocabulary contributes essential terms and concepts for helping to identify and conceptualize such behavior. Although there is no single theory of role, there are diverse hypotheses and miniature theories in its body of knowledge. These provide the propositions to aid in the prediction and explanation of patterned behavior. The selections in this section are illustrative of all of these aspects of role theory as it applies to selected problems of social work.

The first selection, by Thomas, Feldman, and Kamm, presents selected concepts of role theory. Using the methods of programmed instruction, such basic concepts as position, role expectation, role, role performance, and role conception are developed. These concepts are then elaborated as they pertain to common problematic conditions of role, such as role ambiguity, role conflict, role conflict resolution, coping, role discontinuity, and role strain. To make this mode of conceptualizing problems more concrete, an analysis of a case record of family difficulties is programmed for the concepts.

The next selection, by Schafer, offers a role-theoretical interpretation of deviance in the public school. In this analysis of school malperformance, an interactional conception of deviance is presented in which the deviance-defining process, in contrast to an individual psychology of the genesis of deviant behavior, is stressed. The social definition of the deviant position, the enforcement of norms in defining deviance, and the labeling of the deviant act are among the phenomena discussed. The nature of the deviant role is explicated along with some of the unintended consequences of the early identification of deviant behavior and of sanctioning and labeling deviant acts. While not denying individual difficulties, this emphasis upon the social factors entering into the definition of deviance indicates some of the ways in which the social fabric in which deviance occurs may serve unwittingly to generate and maintain the very deviant behavior which a system avowedly wishes to correct. A central practical implication is that deviant acts may be altered by changing the various social factors operative in the deviance-defining process.

The physically and mentally disabled constitute a particularly important type of deviant group in social work. In the selection by Thomas, the problems of disability are analyzed from the perspective of role theory. Five component "roles" of the disabled are elaborated: the disability comanager, handicapped performer, helped person, disabled patient, and public relations man. This is followed by an analysis of the role problems characteristic of the disabled, such as role conflict, role continuity, and difficulties of role synchrony and asynchrony. Because of the importance of these latter problems, six problematic types of synchrony are presented, along with defining conditions and clinical examples. In the final portion of the paper, the conditions underlying the various problems of synchrony are discussed. Role optionality, the extent of the disability, the visibility of the impairment, the acceptance of the disability, and selected societal and personal factors are emphasized here.

In the last selection, Glasser and Glasser report on a study of the role problems of aged parents and their children. It was found that among the 120 aged cases who applied for social service assistance in a family service agency, there were relatively close social and affectional ties with the children and that the problems presented in these cases were unrelated to the class status and mobility accomplishments of the children. The problems displayed, however, reflected a structural strain characteristic of the contemporary American family. Although the aged clients were members of their own nuclear family, they were also members of the families of their children as well. The cultural emphasis upon the independence of the conjugal family combined with increasing dependence of the aged upon their children places both the aged and their children in role conflict and leads to a reversal of roles of the parents and children. It is clear that the problems of these aged clients would be improperly understood without considering the role conflict and reversal generated by these sociocultural factors.

2 Concepts of Role Theory

Edwin J. Thomas and Ronald A. Feldman, with the assistance of Jane Kamm

Introduction

This selection consists of programmed questions which will enable the user to instruct himself in some of the elementary concepts of role theory. Part A introduces selected concepts of social role, Part B presents particular problematic conditions of role, and Part C applies these concepts to concrete instances in a case of marital difficulty. The three parts together constitute an introduction to this subject from which the user should gain an understanding of the specific phenomena to which the concepts pertain and of the promise that these role concepts offer for the analysis of social phenomena. The programmed case analysis in Part C is focused mainly on specifying concrete examples of the concepts and problems, using the case as a vehicle for this type of application. Because of this emphasis on concept illustration in the case analysis, less attention is given to "explaining" the problems in terms of role phenomena or to highlighting the possible approaches to change. After completing this chapter, the reader may therefore wish to consider the analysis of problems, using cases or real-life examples, in which the objectives are expressly to use role concepts for purposes of complete problem appraisal and for achieving change. The reader may also wish to turn to the literature on role which treats the more complex concepts, the research findings, and the theoretical statements.

Programmed instruction was employed here as the vehicle by which the concepts were to be learned on the premise that it would be as efficient and effective for this subject as it has been for the learning of many others. In the absence of a teaching machine, a program such as this may be used. In both the teaching machine and the book form there are generally common elements: each item (or frame) is presented almost automatically; the user reads the item and responds in writing, after which the correct response is uncovered for comparison; the user then moves to the next item. The model for programming employed here was the book of self-instruction called *The Analysis of Behavior*, by J. G. Holland and B. F. Skinner.[1] *The Analysis of Behavior* also presents some of the principles of behavior upon which such programmed instruction is based, namely, operant conditioning and shaping. We were attentive particularly to the following principles: (1) At any point in the program, the response of the user must have a relatively high probability of being correct. (2) The questions posed should progress from the simpler to the more complex, moving gradually by successive approximation toward the desired terminal responses. (3) The reinforcement for a response should be immediate and strong. Thus, in this program the user finds out immediately whether his response is correct or incorrect. And throughout, the items were constructed so that the user attends to and understands the critical idea before responding. *Because this form of instruction is so different from reading a text, the user must read the instructions carefully before beginning the program.*

Instructions [2]

In this chapter every part begins with *an exhibit that should be read carefully* before beginning the programmed material that follows it. *The user should turn to the first question* (put in a box called a *frame*), *read it, and write his response in the blank(s). After writing his answer, the user turns the page where the correct answer is given in the left-hand margin of the page*, immediately preceding the next frame. If the user's response is incorrect, he marks an "X" beside it. (The purpose of tallying errors is to be explained shortly.) *Then*, whether his answer was correct or incorrect, *the user goes on to the next question*, this to be found in the frame to the right of the answer to the prior question and it will be numbered appropriately; the question is answered and the user again turns to the next page for the answer. *The order is always the same: a question on one page and the answer on the next.*

It is essential that each answer be written and that it be recorded before looking at the correct answer. The vague, unwritten guess should be avoided as well as casual glances ahead to see what is coming. Learning will be more effective if the recommended procedure is followed.

Each item should be completed in its turn. The sequence has been carefully designed so that each item is part of a gradual progression, and the occasional repetitions have been inserted intentionally. *All questions should be answered, none skipped.* If the items are easy, the student may simply work more rapidly, but he should always work carefully. And if there is undue difficulty, he should repeat the set before going on to the next. If the number of mistakes made in a part exceeds the *mistake limit* indicated in the last item of the part, the user should probably repeat the set. The number of mistakes indicated in this limit, however, is merely a guide, not an authoritative standard. If the user begins to make errors because of fatigue or inattention, he should stop to rest before continuing.

Various conventions are used. Each item has one or more blanks, the number of blanks indicating the number of words required for the correct answer. A one-word response is thus indicated as "_____," whereas a two-word response is "_____ _____." The abbreviation (TT) after a blank, e.g., "_____(TT)," calls for a technical term; when it is used, a nontechnical term is incorrect. Technical terms are identified in the exhibits by having (TT) after them.

When determining whether or not a response is correct the user should realize that often there are several reasonably equivalent responses, especially when the response is nontechnical. In such cases it would have been a waste of time to have listed all possibilities, but occasionally some are given and are called *acceptable*. The user should employ his best judgment in deciding whether his response is synonymous with the printed one. If it is , it is scored correct.

Because there are only three parts it was unnecessary to prepare additional parts for review and summary. The user who completes the chapter and, after a lapse of time, desires to review the material may find that a rereading of the exhibits for Parts A and B is adequate. But in addition to this he may complete Part C again, for much of it is review as well as application.

Part A: Selected Concepts of Social Role

Exhibit

Instructions: READ THIS EXHIBIT AND REFER TO IT AS NEEDED.

A. <u>Position</u> (TT) is a collectively recognized category of persons who are similar in some respect.[3]

B. <u>Role</u> <u>expectation</u> (TT) is an idea held by a relevant individual concerning how the occupant of a position should perform the rights and duties of that position.   Expected behavior may involve something that a person is expected to "do," an expected <u>action</u> (TT); or may involve how a person is expected to "be," an expected behavioral <u>attribute</u> (TT).

   1. We may have expectations concerning our own position(s).

   2. We may have expectations concerning others' positions.

   3. Others may have expectations concerning our own position(s).

   4. Others may have expectations concerning others' positions.

C. <u>Role</u> (TT) is the set of role expectations held by relevant others concerning how the rights and duties of a position should be carried out.

D. <u>Role</u> <u>performance</u> (TT) is the behavior of an individual in a given position.

E. <u>Role</u> <u>conception</u> (TT) is how a member of a position thinks others expect him to perform in his position.

DO NOT BEGIN THE PROGRAM UNTIL INSTRUCTIONS AT THE BEGINNING

OF THE CHAPTER HAVE BEEN READ CAREFULLY.

Program

---

1. A boy who works in an office is called a(n) _____ boy. (For answer, turn to left-hand column, same row, next page.)

A-1

---

collectively
recognized
category

7. The advent of motorized vehicles has all but eliminated occupational _____(TT) such as harnessmaker and carriagemaker that evolved in connection with transportation relying mainly on horses and horse-drawn vehicles.

A-7

---

expects
role expectation

13. An idea held by a relevant individual concerning how the member of a position should perform the rights and duties of that position is called a(n) _____ _____(TT).

A-13

---

attribute

19. Role expectations for the behavior of position members often pertain both to expected _____ (TT) and _____(TT).

A-19

---

role conception

25. An individual's role performance in a position may be determined partially or fully by the _____ _____(TT) of relevant others, by the _____ _____(TT) he applies to himself, and by his conception of the role expectations of others, for himself, i.e., by his _____ _____(TT).

A-25

Positions
role performance

31. It is common for _____ than one individual to have a role expectation for a position occupant.

A-31

office	2. In respect to other boys who work in offices, the office boy is _____ to other office boys. "Office boy" furthermore is a name for a collectively recognized _____ of persons. A-2
positions (acceptable: roles)	8. Rapid social and technological changes often _____ certain positions. A-8
role expectation	14. When an expectation concerns how someone should perform in a position it is called a(n) _____ _____(TT). A-14
action(s) attribute(s) (ANY ORDER)	20. Although positions may be rapidly created and destroyed, the role expectations associated with them often remain relatively _____. A-20
role expectations role expectations role conception	26. An individual's role performance may be determined by his particular personality characteristics and by social influences other than role expectations. "Role theory" emphasizes, among other factors, the social determinants of role performance, especially the influences of _____ _____(TT) of relevant others. A-26
more	32. A role is the set of _____ _____(TT) held by relevant others concerning how the rights and duties of a position should be carried out. A-32

similar category	3. A(n) _____(TT) is a collectively recognized category of persons who are similar in some respect. A-3

alter
(acceptable:
  change,
  eliminate,
  create)
	9. It may be said then that society creates and destroys _____ (TT).
	
	A-9

role expectation	15. Role expectations are concerned with how the member of a(n) _____ (TT) should perform the rights and duties of that position. A-15

unchanged
(acceptable:
  unaltered,
  static, stable,
  constant)
	21. _____ _____ (TT) often change more slowly than do their concomitant positions.
	
	A-21

role expectations	27. A role expectation is an idea held by a relevant individual concerning how the occupant of a position should perform the rights and duties of that _____ (TT). A-27
role expectations	33. A role is a set of role expectations. The set of expectations, or role, is applied specifically to the _____(s) of a _____(TT). A-33

position	4. It may be said that an office boy holds the _____(TT) of office boy. A-4
positions	10. It is possible for a position to have many, some, one, or _____ individuals occupying it. A-10
position	16. _____ _____ (TT) is the behavior of an individual in a given position. A-16
role expectations	22. A professional helper may have _____ _____(TT) for his clients, and his clients may have _____ _____(TT) for the professional helper; also, the professional helper may have role expectations for _____ as well, and the clients may have role expectations for _____ as well. A-22
position	28. The person who occupies a position in a social structure is called a(n) _____ of that position. A-28
occupant position	END OF SET How many did you miss in this part? _____ (If you missed more than 5, go back and re-do all the questions.) NOW, take a break, and then proceed to Part B, page 27.

position	5. The terms postman, physician, housewife, friend, outcast, leader, enemy, teacher, social worker are words having reference to _____(TT).
	A-5

no	11. When a person thinks a member of a position should act in a certain way it may be said that he _____ the occupant of that position to act in a certain way.
	A-11

role performance	17. If an industrial employee is expected by his fellow workers to fit parts together rapidly with his hands, the role expectations pertain mainly to what he is expected to "do", an expected _____(TT).
	A-17

role expectations role expectations himself themselves	23. Thus, any given individual may have role expectations for _____ as well as for _____, and others may have role expectations for _____ as well as for _____.
	A-23

occupant (acceptable: member)	29. A role expectation is an idea held by a relevant _____ concerning how the _____ of a(n)_____(TT) should perform the rights and duties of that _____(TT).
	A-29

positions

6. A position is a(n) _____ _____ _____ of individuals who are similar in some respect. (Turn to page 21.)

(Turn to page 21.)

A-6

---

expects

12. A mother often _____ that her daughter should dry the dishes after dinner. The mother has a _____ _____(TT) concerning how her daughter should behave. (Turn to page 21.)

A-12

---

action

18. If a person is expected to be pleasant and calm, the role expectations pertain mainly to how he is expected to "be," an expected _____(TT). (Turn to page 21.)

A-18

---

himself) ANY
others ʃ ORDER
themselves) ANY
others ʃ ORDER

24. What an individual occupying a position thinks that others expect him to perform in his position is that individual's _____ _____(TT). (Turn to page 21.)

A-24

---

individual
(acceptable:
  person, other)
occupant
(acceptable:
  member)
position
position

30. _____(TT) are occupied, whereas _____ _____(TT) is the behavior of an individual in a given position. (Turn to page 21.)

A-30

Part B: Selected Problems of Role

Exhibit

Instructions: READ THIS EXHIBIT AND REFER TO IT AS NEEDED.

A. Role ambiguity (TT) is a lack of clarity of role expectations about the
    rights and duties of a given position.

B. Role conflict (TT) is the opposition of role expectations for a position
    such that a position member cannot perform in terms of all of them at the
    same time.[4]

   1. There are two basic types of role conflict:

      a. Intraposition role conflict (TT) arises from occupancy of one
          position in which there are opposing role expectations with
          respect to what the occupant of that position should do.

      b. Interposition role conflict (TT) arises from the occupancy of
          two or more positions, each with attendant expectations, and
          which together place role expectations upon the individual such
          that he cannot perform in terms of all at the same time.

   2. Solution strategies:

      a. Resolution (TT) of role conflict is the role performance of the
          position member in role conflict which is determined in terms of
          whether the performance is inconsistent or consistent with the
          performance advocated by one or more of those placing role
          expectations on the position member.

         (1) Preferential selection (TT) is role performance in role
              conflict which is consistent with one set of the opposing
              role expectations.

         (2) Compromise (TT) is role performance which is partly con-
              sistent with all sets of opposing role expectations, but not
              fully consistent. Compromise can occur serially, in which
              case an individual will perform consistently with one set of
              expectations for a brief period of time and then perform in
              accordance with another for a different period; or, in rare
              instances, may be evidenced as behavior which lies some place
              between the competing sets of expectations, being somewhat
              close to all.

         (3) Avoidance (TT) is role performance in role conflict which is
              fully inconsistent with all sets of role expectations placed
              upon the individual.

    b. <u>Elimination</u> (TT) of role conflict is an alteration of the conflict situation for the individual such that the conflict no longer exists for him. This change may come about by (1) <u>achieving consensus</u> of the role expectations, (2) <u>removing the individual from the position</u> in which there is role conflict, (3) <u>eliminating the position</u> and its attendant role expectations.

    c. <u>Coping</u> (TT) consists of all of the individual's "psychological" reactions in conflict not classifiable as resolution or elimination.

C. <u>Role discontinuity</u> (TT) exists when there is lack of correspondence between the role expectations concerning one position that an individual has held and the role expectations associated with a different position he now has or has held.[5]

D. <u>Role strain</u> (TT) is the experienced difficulty of a position member in performing in that position.[6]

Program

	1. Sometimes the role expectations concerning the rights and duties associated with a position are ambiguous. An occupant of such a position is in a situation of role _____(TT). B-1
role strain	8. When something has been temporarily (or permanently) interrupted or stopped, we may say that it has been temporarily _____ – ued. B-8

opposition
role expectations
position
occupant
  (acceptable:
    member)
all
	15. Role strain is the experienced difficulty of a position member relating to performance in that _____(TT). B-15

social worker one two role expectations	22. Interposition role conflict arises from the occupancy of _____(USE A NUMBER) position(s). Associated with each position are certain attendant _____ _____(TT) which are in conflict such that one cannot _____ in terms of all at the same time. B-22
a. preferential selection b. compromise c. avoidance	29. Both basic types of role conflict, _____(TT) role conflict and _____(TT) role conflict, can be resolved (but not eliminated) by any of the three modes of resolving role conflict. B-29
role performance inconsistent role expectations	36. In contrast to resolution, the elimination of role conflict implies a genuine termination of the role conflict. Elimination of role conflict is an _____ of the conflicting situation such that the conflict no longer _____. B-36

ambiguity	2.	If it has not been made clear to a secretary whether or not she should file papers and take part in bookkeeping we may say that the role expectations for her position are _____. She is in a situation of _____ _____(TT). B-2
discontin	9.	When a person must change from one position to another, each with differing role expectations, he undergoes role _____(TT). B-9
position	16.	When an individual is exposed to role conflict, it is more likely than not that he will experience role _____(TT). If so, it may be said more specifically that he is experiencing difficulty in fulfilling the set of _____ _____(TT) associated with his position. B-16
two (or more), or more than one role expectations perform	23.	The two basic kinds of role conflict are _____(TT) role conflict and _____(TT) role conflict. B-23
intraposition interposition (ANY ORDER)	30.	The three modes of resolving role conflict are: _____ _____(TT), _____(TT), and _____(TT). B-30
alteration exists	37.	Consider a case involving marital difficulties where the husband has expectations concerning his position that oppose the expectations which his wife has concerning his position. Since, in this example, the husband occupies only one position, he experiences _____(TT) role conflict. There are two ways to eliminate his role conflict. (a) The husband and wife can come to an agreement concerning how he should perform. That is, they can achieve _____. (b) The man could also eliminate the role conflict by obtaining a divorce, that is, by leaving the _____(TT) of husband. The third form of eliminating role conflict is impossible since neither person is capable of eliminating the _____(TT) of husband. B-37

ambiguous (acceptable: unclear) role ambiguity	3. When an individual experiences difficulty in carrying out the role performance in his position, we may say that the person has _____ _____(TT). B-3
discontinuity	10. The transitions from childhood to adolescence and from adolescence to young adulthood are relatively abrupt for most persons; such transitions between positions are termed _____ _____ (TT). B-10
strain role expectations	17. Which prefix roughly means "between"? _____. (Use "intra" or "inter".) B-17
interposition intraposition (ANY ORDER)	24. If a married man has a child he holds the position of _____ besides that of husband. B-24

preferential
  selection
compromise
avoidance
  (ANY ORDER)
	31. Resolution of role conflict is the role _____(TT) of the position member in role conflict, determined in terms of whether the performance is inconsistent or consistent with the performance _____ by one or more of those placing _____ _____(TT) on the position member.
	
	B-31

intraposition consensus position position	38. _____(TT) is the term used to describe such reactions as pertain to the degree of anxiety of the individual, his use of defense mechanisms, and so forth. A coping reaction alone does not _____(TT) the role conflict, for the role conflict still exists; similarly, a coping reaction is not a mode of _____ (TT) role conflict, for it does not pertain to the consistency of the role performance with the sets of conflicting expectations. B-38

role strain	4.	Role strain is the experienced difficulty of a _____(TT) member relating to performance in that _____(TT).
		B-4

role discontinu-ities	11.	Like role ambiguity, role discontinuity may lead to _____ _____(TT).
		B-11

inter	18.	Which prefix roughly means "within"? _____. (Use "intra" or "inter".)
		B-18

father	25.	The previous example indicates three positions occupied by the person: they are _____, _____, and _____.
		B-25

performance advocated (or suggested, expected) role expectations	32.	Preferential selection is role _____(TT) in role conflict which is _____ with one set of the opposing expectations.
		B-32

coping eliminate resolving	39.	Although it is not always possible in practice, the hypothetically ideal way to reduce role strain generated by role conflict is achieved by _____ role conflict.
		B-39

position position	5. Role ambiguity can lead to role _____(TT). B-5
role strain	12. Role Conflict is the opposition of _____ _____(TT) such that a position member cannot perform in terms of all of them at the same time. B-12
intra	19. Intraposition role conflict arises from the occupancy of _____ (USE A NUMBER) position(s). In this type of role conflict the individual occupies only _____(USE A NUMBER) position(s) but faces _____ expectations regarding how an occupant of that position should perform. B-19
father husband (accept- able: spouse) man (ANY ORDER)	26. If the child expects much attention from the father and his wife expects excessive attention from him, the father will be exposed to _____(TT) role conflict. This is because he occupies _____(USE A NUMBER) position(s) each with attendant expectations, and these expectations _____ each other. B-26
performance consistent	33. Suppose a client faces opposing expectations concerning his role performance from both his social worker and his wife. By entirely fulfilling the expectations of one <u>or</u> the other he is resolving his role conflict by means of _____ _____(TT). B-33
eliminating	**END OF SET** How many did you miss in this part ? _____ (If you missed more than 5, go back and re-do all the questions.) NOW, take a break, and then proceed to Part C, page 36.

strain	6. Role strain is the _____ _____ in performing in a _____(TT).
	B-6

role expectations	13. Role conflict is the _____ of role expectations such that a position member cannot perform in terms of _____ of them at the same time.
	B-13

one
one
opposing
  (acceptable:
  conflicting,
  differing)
	20. If a social worker has been taught to act permissively towards a client but is urged, by his supervisor, to act strictly towards the client, he is likely to experience role conflict; this is _____(TT) role conflict.

	B-20

interposition
two
oppose
  (acceptable:
  conflict with)
	27. In the previous example, the two positions of the person experiencing opposing expectations are _____ and _____.

	B-27

preferential selection	34 _____(TT) is role performance which is partly consistent with both sets of opposing expectations, but not _____ consistent.
	B-34

experienced difficulty position	7. A person who does not experience difficulty in performing in a position cannot be said to have _____ _____ (TT). (Turn back to page 29.) B-7
opposition all	14. Role conflict is the _____ of _____ _____ (TT) such that a _____ (TT) _____ cannot perform in terms of _____ of them at the same time. (Turn back to page 29.) B-14
intraposition	21. The important point in the previous example is that the conflict attends only one position, that of _____ _____. The social worker occupies _____ (USE A NUMBER) position(s) but faces _____ (USE A NUMBER) opposing _____ _____ (TT). (Turn back to page 29.) B-21
husband father (ANY ORDER)	28. Let us consider further the example of interposition role conflict faced by the man. (a) If he chooses to give the child a lot of attention and not his wife (or vice versa), he is resolving the role conflict by means of _____ _____ (TT). (b) He can also resolve the role conflict by giving some attention to his wife and his child, giving each somewhat less than they expect. This means of resolving role conflict is called _____ (TT). (c) If the man gives no attention whatever to either his child or wife he is resolving his role conflict by means of _____ (TT). (Turn back to page 29.) B-28

Compromise
fully (acceptable:
  entirely,
  wholly)
	35. Avoidance is _____ _____ (TT) in role conflict which is fully _____ with all sets of _____ _____ (TT) placed upon the individual. (Turn back to page 29.)
	
	B-35

Part C: Case Analysis Using Role Concepts

Exhibit: The Case of Mr. and Mrs. Allen

Instructions: READ ALLEN CASE AND REFER TO IT AS NEEDED.   YOU MAY ALSO
REFER BACK TO EXHIBITS FOR PARTS A AND B.

Re: ALLEN, Jack, born 2-14-29   Married in January, 1954
          Lois,   "   4-15-31
          Jane,   "   4- 4-54   SSE: 1- 6-54 University Clinic #2;
          Mary,   "   4- 7-56   5-11-54   "   "   Jane

Referral. 11- '57 Mr. and Mrs. Allen referred themselves to Family and Child
Service for help with their marriage problems. They had read various advice
columns in the newspapers and marriage counseling problems in the Ladies' Home
Journal, and from that had looked up the name of our agency and then referred
themselves.

Their marriage problems included:

> 1.   Many arguments over trivial affairs.
> 2.   Financial problems.
> 3.   Taking out their tempers on their children.
> 4.   Mrs. A's dislike of Mr. A's place of employment.
> 5.   Mr. A's feeling that Mrs. A. should improve her
>   housekeeping standards in their trailer home.

Background Information. Mrs. Allen, now 27, was born in a thriving midwestern
city, following the forced marriage of her parents. Her father works for himself in real estate (A). At the time of the application, her mother was employed in a Civil Service position (B) at an air base and had been in this same
type of job with frequent promotions for over 25 years. Mrs. Allen is the only
child in this family.

Mrs. Allen's father is described as a weak-willed kind of man of Scotch descent,
dominated by his wife. He is said to be penurious and his wife has stated that
she had to go to work soon after Mrs. Allen was born because her husband would
not give her enough money for food and clothes for the family. During her childhood, Mrs. Allen's father often made promises of toys, etc. to Mrs. Allen, which
he did not keep. She feels that she could never rely or depend on him. He is
not very handy around the home and he is often belittled in this regard by his
wife and by Mrs. Allen. Mrs. Allen believes that a good father should be dependable and handy around the house (C).

Mrs. Allen's mother reportedly rejected her from infancy on. She is a narcis-
sistic woman of English background, who has resented growing older. She dresses
and acts as though she were Mrs. Allen's younger sister (D). She has always been
flirtatious; has had many affairs with different men. She is selfish and has
never been able to give much of herself. She claims that her friends, articles
in women's magazines, and even television commercials say a woman should always
act youthful (E). But Mrs. Allen says everyone she knows thinks her mother should
"act her age" and be more thoughtful of her family (F).

Mrs. Allen grew up in a home with a succession of people hired to take care of her. She remembers only one warm relationship with one helper and her grief when that woman left the home.

Mrs. Allen completed high school and had 18 months of nurse's training. She had performed well as a student nurse (G) and her nursing supervisor urged her to consider taking a job with that hospital (H) following graduation six months later. However, at this time, she was pregnant and her parents were demanding that she marry Mr. Allen (I). She didn't want to give up a promising nursing career and seriously considered an abortion (J). At this time, also, she became so despondent that she claims to have considered suicide (K). However, she finally decided to give up a nursing career and to marry Mr. Allen with the hope that she might continue nursing at a later date. She immediately quit nursing school in order to marry Mr. Allen. Shortly thereafter she became a mother. (L)

Mrs. Allen had been fairly popular with boys, one or two of whom she liked because of their warm, loving and giving mothers. She met Mr. Allen at her mother's place of occupation. At that time, he had been restricted to the base because of financial debts, which had been incurred in this small, mid-western city. She remembers "sticking by" him when her parents and others of his acquaintance had let him down. Her parents at one time had been opposed to the marriage, her mother especially, since she felt that Mr. Allen was "spineless," and couldn't manage his finances well enough.

Mr. Allen was born in a suburb of Chicago and was the youngest of five children. His father was born in Slovenia in Yugoslavia, and his mother was born in Vienna. Both came to this country as children, met in Illinois and were married. Mr. Allen's father died when he was five. Mr. Allen's mother had quite a struggle keeping the family together, until her remarriage when Mr. Allen was about ten. Mr. Allen remembers that she was poor, but the home was always neat and clean. The second time she married a rather rigid man, who had been born and raised in Czechoslovakia. They had a daughter by this marriage and shortly after her birth Mr. Allen's mother became ill and died when Mr. Allen was thirteen (M). For a short while an older sister stayed home from school and cared for the baby, but after a time she left to obtain a job in Chicago. This left Mr. Allen at home from the age of thirteen to sixteen with his stepfather and a baby half-sister. A baby sitter came while Mr. Allen attended a military school as a day student. He came home each night to housekeeping chores (N) for his stepfather and smaller half-sister. Mr. Allen resented his stepfather's attitude of insisting that he, Mr. Allen, perform the household tasks (O). The stepfather had had a very strict upbringing, which included working hard on a farm at an early age and attending school as well. Mr. Allen began to truant from school (P); was brought to the attention of the Juvenile Court and placed on probation; then obtained a job ostensibly to help out at home; was returned to Juvenile Court and then placed with an older brother, who was married to an efficient housekeeper, an excellent home manager and cook. Here, he worked at an outside job and was taken care of, feeling that his sister-in-law was more like a mother than a sister-in-law to him.

Mr. Allen's first job was as a stock clerk in a department store. He was not satisfied with this job because of the low pay, so after his period of probation was over from the Juvenile Court, he got a job in the same company where a brother worked as a driver of a semi-trailer truck. He had to lie about his age in order to obtain this job, and this preyed on his conscience so that he gave up this job after a short while. Next he attended school for three months to learn how to be an insurance salesman but <u>felt that he didn't have the right personality for selling insurance</u> (Q). Then he obtained a job selling oil but did not have "good enough money sense" to know that he should buy back into the company for more oil. There followed a brief period as a clerk in a 5 and 10¢ store. Then he was drafted into the Army, where he was never able to save any money and finally, had financial difficulties while stationed at the base near the thriving midwestern city. He now rationalizes by saying that he was glad he was able to live so recklessly then because now he feels more ready to be careful of money. (One of the reasons this family came to the agency, as noted above, was because of their financial problem.)

Sometime following the birth of their first child, Mrs. Allen had a spontaneous miscarriage at three months. She then went to work at the Army base where her mother worked to help pay off some of the bills which Mr. Allen still had at the time of their marriage. She stopped working when she was pregnant with her second child several months later. Mr. Allen attended the local city university part time on his G. I. Bill, majoring in business engineering. At the present time he has about 15 credits left to complete for graduation. He also obtained a part time job with an engineering company and has become intensely interested in the diesel section of this company. He now has a supervisor interested in him, who is trying to help him get ahead. Mr. Allen dropped school at the end of the spring semester 1958 because the pressure of mounting debts, time required for school as well as learning the routine of business was so great that he became almost ill with worry. Thereafter, he was employed full time but his income was not much increased when the G. I. Bill money was dropped.

<u>Mrs. Allen kept pressuring Mr. Allen to return to school</u> (R) to obtain his degree and then to change jobs to a company which would offer a better salary. <u>His supervisor said that Mr. Allen should worry about providing for his family at the present time</u> (S), and the best way to do that would be to stay on the job full time. Mr. Allen liked his work and felt that there was a future in it for him.

In May, 1958, Mrs. Allen confided that she had been having an affair with a married professional man, 7 years her senior, for the last two years. This man is a strong, muscular man, with a determined will. He is successful in his profession, has set goals for himself and is excellent at keeping his own financial records straight. She contrasted this man with her father by saying that as a child, her father would never take her to any sports event, nor was he interested in them, whereas this man was very much interested in sports and is, himself, good at them. She contrasted his strong will with both her father and her husband, and contrasted his management of finances with her husband's lack in this regard. She has also talked of the fact that this man is considerate in his sexual relations with her, whereas her husband is cold and sometimes repels her advances in love making. She feels that she has to push her husband or he won't be ambitious enough, whereas she would prefer to be dependent on him and to be cared for by him.

In the fall of 1958, the Allens realized that their income was not meeting their outgo or expenses, and as Mrs. Allen became more and more frantic with 'phone calls and letters from bill collectors, Mr. Allen withdrew into his shell and would not talk. (T) He would answer her questions about bills with "Yes, I'll pay that tomorrow." As Mr. Allen seemed to be becoming panicked and close to some kind of a mental breakdown, I finally said to Mrs. Allen, "I think you should get a job right away before this makes Mr. Allen too much more upset." She then obtained a job as receptionist and secretary for a successful local surgeon. She had many fears of failure in this job since the surgeon was thinking of also requiring some secretarial training and bookkeeping (U), which she had not had. But she seemed to feel that my saying that I was sure she could do it was reassuring and she has been successful and has already received a raise. We helped the family plan for day nursery care for Jane and Mary, their two children, who are ages four and two.

There has been some discussion and friction concerning the household chores since then, but they have finally sat down and discussed what each could do best, so that they would both finish at about the same time each night. Mr. Allen's large fear was that he would be stuck with all the housework and chores and become the "housewife," since Mrs. Allen had never relished housewifely chores and had always used "a messy home" as a weapon when she became angry with Mr. Allen, knowing he gauged the amount of love he received from her by her housekeeping standards.

The bills are being paid off but more slowly than Mrs. Allen had anticipated. Mr. Allen finds it difficult to try an efficient bookkeeping method and so Mrs. Allen is trying to practice some of the bookkeeping procedures she is learning at her work.

The affair with the professional man has cooled off somewhat for Mr. Allen is now jealous of her relationship with her employer.

Mr. Allen's Diagnostic Material. We feel that Mr. Allen lacks ego maturity because of the parental losses in his childhood and adolescence. He seems to precipitate situations where he will be mistreated. He is fearful of being cast in a role of housewife by his wife (V) and this is associated with his resentment against his stepfather, who forced this role on him during his early adolescence (W). He would rather be taken care of in housekeeping matters. He feels that his choice of place of employment was a wise one and a satisfying one to him and that monetary rewards will come slowly and later. However, because of his wife's attitude toward his engineering company, he sometimes questions his value as a wage earner (X). He may have a neurotic involvement with money, since he has sometimes paid bills with checks that have bounced and has had various financial difficulties ever since he has become an earner.

Mrs. Allen's Diagnostic Material. We feel that Mrs. Allen has suffered from her parents' rejection and therefore believes that she, herself, is an unworthy person. Her affair may be an attempt on her part to prove her femininity to herself, because she is experiencing competition with her mother. She also has a need for acceptance from her mother; she wants to be loved and needed to prove to herself that she is worthy. The role of housewife does not appeal to Mrs. Allen because her mother never accepted that role and it has not been a family

pattern. <u>Her parents have placed education and business success above home</u>
<u>management success for her and she is always striving to prove herself suc-</u>
<u>cessful in their eyes. Mr. Allen does not approve of Mrs. Allen's career</u> (Y)
feeling that this depreciates him in her eyes and in the eyes of her family as
a dependable member of the family. However, he has also recognized that Mrs.
Allen is now fulfilling a need to be successful at something and accepts her
working on that basis. Mrs. Allen feels, on the one hand, that she would
rather be dependent on Mr. Allen as the dominant member of the family and,
yet, on the other, she fears his "spinelessness" and feels also that she is
accomplishing something worthwhile by working. Therefore, she is confused
about her role as well as about her identity.

<u>Goals in Treatment</u>.

1. To try to help this family return to a kind of balance, as in the first
   few months of their marriage, without the need for arguments, etc.

2. To help them try to live realistically within their income and to encourage them to work on a plan cooperatively.

3. To try not to involve Mrs. Allen's family in any planning, financial or
   otherwise, because they always let the Allens down.

4. To encourage Mrs. Allen in her attempts to prove herself worthy, both on
   the job and in her housekeeping areas.

5. To encourage Mr. Allen in his business pursuits and to help Mrs. Allen
   accept Mr. Allen's plans for himself.

6. To try to explore with each partner his and her own feelings concerning
   taking responsibility for his own role and to help each to accept the
   other in his role.

It is our feeling that this marriage may never be a completely successful one
but it is one that could be happier than it has been in the past.

The above material is a summary of the highlights from the exploratory period
upon which we based the diagnostic material in the case.

ogram

1. Position is a collectively recognized _____
   of individuals who are _____ in some
   respect.

   C-1

et
ole expectations
osition

11. (See line F.) According to Mrs. Allen and her
    acquaintances, the role of a mother is to "_____
    _____ _____" and be _____ _____
    _____ _____ _____.

    C-11

ole expectation
ole expectation
tudent nurse

21. However, at this time Mrs. Allen became pregnant.
    In line I we see that Mrs. Allen occupied another
    position, that of unwed pregnant _____ of her
    parents. She became subject to the expectations of
    both her parents (and of middle class society in
    general) that an unwed mother should _____.

    C-21

tudent
wo
ole expectations
nterposition
role conflict

31. Thus the death of Mr. Allen's mother eventually led to
    _____ _____ _____(TT) for him since
    it opened up a position in the household which he was
    expected to assume.

    C-31

ne
osition
ole expectations
osition

41. The role conflict Mr. Allen experienced between
    expectations to progress educationally and to be a
    good provider, along with the attending low income,
    caused Mr. Allen to withdraw more and more (line T).
    Mr. Allen's withdrawal is an indication of
    _____ _____(TT).

    C-41

ole conflicts
ole

51. Read the treatment goals listed on page 22. To the
    extent that the social worker introduces her own
    expectations into the picture to implement treatment
    goals, the worker will be placing additional _____
    _____(TT) on the marital partners.

    C-51

category similar	2. Doctor, lawyer, and Indian Chief are all names for _____(TT). C-2
act her age more thoughtful of her family	12. We use the term _____(TT) because we are referring to a <u>set</u> of _____s(TT). If we were to refer only to an idea held by Mrs. Allen concerning how her mother should behave, we would speak of her _____ _____(TT). C-12
daughter marry	22. With regard to her membership in the positions of student nurse and unwed mother-to-be, she thus occupied _____(USE A NUMBER) position(s), each with attendant _____ _____s (TT) which _____ with each other. This is an example of _____(TT) role conflict. C-22
interposition role conflict	32. In the last example, Mr. Allen was also subject to another role conflict. Mr. Allen's stepfather held the expectation that he perform household chores typically associated with the feminine position of homemaker. But there are also general societal expectations concerning the male role. Societal expectations were in _____ with those held by Mr. Allen's stepfather. C-32
role strain	42. In line U we see that the surgeon possibly did not clarify the rights and duties associated with the _____(TT) of secretary. To the extent that the role expectations were unclear, this illustrates role _____(TT). C-42
role expecta- tions	52. Treatment objectives 1 and 4 involve helping the Allens to _____(TT) with the role conflict, among other things. C-52

positions	3.	Mrs. Allen's mother (see line B) held the position of _____ _____ employee.
		C-3

role role expectation role expectation	13.	(See line E.) Mrs. Allen's mother thought that her friends and such media as the women's magazines and television, expected her to act _____. This was her role _____(TT). (See line D.) In this case, her role _____(TT) was consistent with her role conception.
		C-13

two role expectation conflicted interposition	23.	There are _____(USE A NUMBER) basic modes of resolving this role conflict: _____ _____(TT) of one or the other alternative, _____(TT), and _____(TT).
		C-23

conflict	33.	(See line P.) The fact that Mr. Allen began to _____ from school helps to illustrate the role strain which he was undoubtedly experiencing. Role conflict often creates _____ _____(TT).
		C-33

position ambiguity	43.	As indicated by Mrs. Allen's fears of failure in this job, role ambiguity can often lead to _____ _____(TT).
		C-43

cope	53.	In treatment goals 2, 5 and 6 there are references to such activities as "to encourage them to work on a plan cooperatively," "To encourage Mr. Allen in his business pursuit and to help Mrs. Allen accept Mr. Allen's plans for himself," and ... "to help each to accept the other in his role"; to various degrees, all of these activities imply efforts to achieve greater _____ concerning role expectations through changing role expectations for the self and the other, and thereby to _____(TT) role conflicts.
		C-53

Civil Service	4.	With respect to the fact that she was a Civil Service employee, she was _____ to all other Civil Service agents. And, the category called Civil Service employee is collectively _____. C-4
youthful (accept- able; young; like Mrs. Allen's sister) conception performance (acceptable: expectation)	14.	In the previous item, "role conception" is the appropri-ate answer for the second blank since Mrs. Allen's mother conceived her role in terms of what she thought relevant _____ expected of her. However, her role expecta-tion for herself need not necessarily be shaped by her role _____(TT). C-14

three
preferential
  selection
compromise
avoidance
  (ANY ORDER)
	24.	(See line J.) If Mrs. Allen had had an abortion she would have been able to continue her career in nursing. By pursuing her nursing career she would have adopted the mode of resolving role conflict called _____ _____(TT). Mrs. Allen's decision to give up her nursing career to marry Mr. Allen was the alternative chosen, illustrating _____ _____(TT) of the other performance alternative. C-24

truant role strain	34.	In line Q we note that Mr. Allen did not feel adequate as an insurance salesman. By "not having the right personality for selling insurance" he felt unable to meet the set of _____ _____(TT) associated with the rights and duties of the position of insurance salesman. C-34
role strain	44.	Role ambiguity is the lack of clarity in the role expectations concerning the _____ and _____ associated with a given _____(TT). C-44
consensus eliminate	54.	The application of only _____(TT) concepts to this case cannot account for all of the phenomena noted in the record. Other concepts would be required to develop a more complete diagnostic formulation in this case. C-54

similar recognized	5. In line A we can note two positions held by Mrs. Allen's father, that of _____ and _____ _____ _____ . C-5
others conception	15. A role conception is what an occupant of a _____(TT) thinks _____ expect of him in performing the rights and obligations of a position. C-15

preferential
  selection
preferential
  selection
	25. In line K, Mrs. Allen contemplated suicide which in this instance would have <u>resolved</u> the role conflict by _____(TT), and would have <u>eliminated</u> the role conflict as well by vacating both _____(TT).
	
	C-25

role expectations	35. Experienced difficulty in performing a role is called _____ _____(TT). C-35
rights duties position	45. (See lines V and W.) Mr. Allen's present fear of being cast into the position of homemaker may be traced back to early _____ _____(TT) caused originally by the death of his mother and his stepfather's subsequent role expectations for him to perform the duties of homemaker. C-45
role	END OF SET How many did you miss in this part? _____ . (If you missed more than 5, go back and do all the questions over again.)

father real estate agent	6.	In line C Mrs. Allen holds a _____ _____ (TT) concerning how fathers should behave. C-6
position others	16.	The way a person behaves in a position is his _____ _____ (TT). C-16
avoidance positions	26.	Mrs. Allen gave up nursing and married Mr. Allen. However, although she had selected this mode of resolving her role conflict, she still hoped eventually to pursue a nursing career. Thus she intended through time to use _____(TT) to resolve role conflict. C-26
role strain	36.	In line R we note that Mrs. Allen kept pressuring Mr. Allen to _____ _____ _____. C-36
role conflict	46.	In line X we note that Mr. Allen questioned his value as a _____ _____. C-46

role expectation	7.	She holds the role expectation that her father should _____ _____ _____
		_____ _____ _____ _____.
		C-7

role performance	17.	With regard to the youthful behavior of Mrs. Allen's mother, we may illustrate three role concepts. The fact that she thought others expected her to act youthful exemplifies a _____ _____ (TT). She then held the idea that a mother should be youthful; this exemplifies a _____ _____(TT) which one holds for the <u>self</u>. In this case, she also behaved youthfully, which exemplifies _____ _____(TT).
		C-17

compromise	27.	When Mrs. Allen gave birth to a child, she entered the position of mother. (See line L.) Previously her position was that of wife. This change is an example of role _____ (TT), since the role expectations between the two positions are not fully in correspondence.
		C-27

return to school	37.	Simultaneously, (see line S) Mr. Allen's _____ told him that a good husband should worry about providing for his family.
		C-37

wage earner	47.	This experienced difficulty in performing the _____ (TT) of wage earner is termed _____ _____(TT).
		C-47

be dependable and
handy around
the house

8. A role expectation is a(n) _____ held by a
relevant individual concerning how the occupant
of a(n) _____(TT) should _____ the
rights and duties of that _____(TT).

C-8

---

role conception
role expectation
role performance

18. (See line D again.) Mrs. Allen's mother acted in
a _____ful manner. She actually _____
(USE "was" OR "was not") a youth.

C-18

---

discontinuity

28. (See line M.) The death of Mr. Allen's mother
left open the _____(TT) of homemaker in his
family.

C-28

---

supervisor

38. Assuming that only the position of husband was
involved here, Mr. Allen was thus faced with
_____(USE A NUMBER) set(s) of opposing role
expectations.

C-38

---

role
role strain

48. Early role conflicts can often lead to _____
_____(TT) in adulthood.

C-48

idea
  (acceptable:
   expectation)
position
perform
position
	9.	Throughout the case record Mr. Allen, like Mrs.
		Allen's father, does not fulfill Mrs. Allen's role
		expectation of being _____-able.
		
		C-9

youth was not	19.	In line G, we note that Mrs. Allen held the position of student _____. C-19
position	29.	(See lines N and O.) Mr. Allen's stepfather demanded that he assume the position of _____ in the household. C-29
two	39.	Thus interpreted, the situation just cited is an example of _____ _____ _____(TT). C-39
role strain	49.	Role strain and defective role performance are possible consequences of early _____ _____(TT). C-49

depend	10.	A role is the _____ of _____ _____(TT) concerning how the rights and duties of a _____(T' should be performed. (Turn back to page 41.)
		C-10

nurse	20.	Her nursing supervisor, as we see in line H, had the _____ _____(TT) that Mrs. Allen would continue a nursing career and take a job with the hospital following graduation. This _____ _____(TT) applied to Mrs. Allen while she held the position of _____ _____. (Turn back to page 41.)
		C-20

homemaker (or housekeeper)	30.	At the same time that he was forced to assume the duties and obligations of the homemaker's role, Mr. Allen was a _____ at a military school. He therefore held _____(USE A NUMBER) position(s), each with attendant _____ _____(TT) which opposed each other. This is an example of _____ _____ _____(TT) (Turn back to page 41.)
		C-30

intraposition role conflict	40.	Intraposition role conflict arises from occupancy of _____(USE A NUMBER) _____(TT) in which there are opposing _____ _____(TT) with respect to what the member of that _____(TT) should do. (Turn back to page 41.)
		C-40

role conflict(s)	50.	Lines Y indicate how early and contemporaneous _____ _____(TT) can lead to role strain and defective role performance. Most of the problems in the same paragraph can be considered as some of the ultimate consequences of earlier difficulties involving _____(TT). (Turn back to page 41.)
		C-50

3 Deviance in the Public School: An Interactional View

Walter E. Schafer

Introduction

The past decade has seen increasing attention given to problems centering around the failure of the school to educate effectively a sufficiently large proportion of youth.[1] These problems include the tendency of some students to drop out of high school before graduation, underachievement and academic failure among students believed to be intellectually capable, and misconduct that disrupts classroom procedure and school discipline.

It is the contention of this paper that the solutions found, and, indeed, the very questions posed about these problems, depend on the conception held about these forms of deviant behavior. The thesis is that underachievement, misbehavior, and early school leaving are properly to be seen as adverse school-pupil interactions and not simply as individual acts, carried out by students as natural responses to damaged psyches or defective homes. An advantage of this view is that attention is directed toward, rather than away from, one of the partners in the interaction, namely, the school itself.

Deviance as Interaction

The starting point of an interactional approach to deviance is the observation that there is nothing inherent in an act making it deviant.[2] It becomes so only as a label is applied to it by others. This in turn happens when that act is defined as a violation of some social norm. Howard S.

This chapter was written especially for this book. It is based upon research conducted on a project sponsored by a curriculum development grant from the Office of Juvenile Delinquency and Youth Development, Welfare Administration, U.S. Department of Health, Education, and Welfare in cooperation with the President's Committee on Juvenile Delinquency and Youth Crime.

Becker, perhaps the most persuasive exponent of this view, has put it this way:

> Social groups create deviance by making the rules whose infraction constitutes deviance and by applying those rules to particular people and labeling them as outsiders. . . . The deviant is one to whom that label has been successfully applied.[3]

Deviance is the product of an exchange between an individual and some other individuals, who represent or claim to represent the interests and standards of a particular group. It is not properly to be seen simply as action engaged in by an individual, but rather as a characteristic of an interaction between persons. Moreover, deviance is a process rather than an event or series of events at isolated points in time.[4] Therefore, the process of interaction must be the target of attention in attempting to understand deviance. Both parties—their orientations, actions, and responses to each other—must be included in any adequate conceptualization of deviance.

This paper is an attempt to show some of the consequences of viewing deviance in the school from an interactional perspective. New light can be shed on the so-called dropout problem when the events which usually lead up to early departure are viewed in this way. Perhaps the major insight is that the so-called dropout problem quickly becomes at least in part a force-out problem.

Problematic Issues in the School

"Underachievement" and "Misconduct" as School-Defined

A behavior in the classroom may or may not be deviant, depending on whether it is or is not judged to be in violation of normative prescriptions. The first issue which becomes problematic, then, is this: what are the norms which regulate pupil conduct and performance and by which pupils are judged?

Three sets of norms are always found, although they may vary in salience and tolerance limits. First, all schools are legally bound to require attendance until some specified age, usually sixteen or seventeen. Second, pupils are expected, once in attendance, to perform at their highest possible levels in their schoolwork. This means that goals of academic success are to be internalized and pursued by all youngsters, the height of those goals to be limited only by the innate capability of the student. Third, all students must adhere to some minimum standards of conduct within school boundaries. These behavior norms serve requirements for social order and for the maintenance of control by teaching personnel over the various activities that occur within the school, especially within the class-room.

In order for deviance to occur, not only must a certain act be engaged in and there be a norm prohibiting such action, but also that norm must be enforced. Neither the mere existence of a norm pertaining to smoking nor the violation of that norm by a pupil need necessarily result in that act being deviant. The norm must also be enforced and the act judged intolerable.

Conditions under which Norms Are Enforced

What are the conditions under which adverse judgment is passed and a label applied to an act indicating it is deviant? In a certain sense, it is useful to regard each norm as having tolerance limits: behavior which is acceptable to the group falls inside those limits while behavior which is unacceptable and produces sanctions falls outside. Yet, according to M. B. Clinard:

> . . . the concept of "tolerance limit" (is) misleading for it implies that there is a definite and absolute point at which norm violations will involve a reaction. Actually the relation between norm violation and the (group's) reaction is not as simple as this and may depend on the nature of the situation or on the social status of the deviant.[5]

In short, there are factors and conditions extraneous to the particular nature of an act—a behavior or level of academic performance in this case —which have important bearing on whether it is placed inside or outside tolerance limits by those who do the judging. Examples of such factors are the value orientations and goals of the school, the class composition of the student body, characteristics of the teacher or other norm enforcer,[6] and characteristics of the student himself, e.g., his past reputation, his social class and racial background, and his status in the school. The fact that a student is identified and labeled as deviant implies as much about the situations in which he finds himself, and particularly about those who judge him, as about himself and his actions.

Since the school defines the conditions under which particular behavior becomes deviant and particular students take on the label of deviant, a proper understanding of deviance requires that attention be given that definition. For the researcher who is looking at rates of deviance, it is imperative, in comparing rates of so-called underachievement or misbehavior, to recognize that there may be qualitative differences among the kinds of behavior that are considered. For the change agent, the setting of change targets for ameliorative or corrective efforts requires an awareness of what the expectations are that are being violated. Attempts to change internal, psychological conditions or even overt behavior may lose their effectiveness unless simultaneous efforts are made to articulate behavioral change with the expectations and standards with which the student must conform.

Nature of the Deviant Role

ROLE ENTRY. The deviant individual is one to whom a label has been applied indicating he is somehow different and thus deserving of special treatment of one sort or another. Upon receiving such a label, the individual in essence enters a new role—the role of deviant. This fact has consequences at at least three levels. First, the individual takes on a new public identity. Henceforth, he is not just a pupil, but a pupil of a slightly —or greatly—different sort from most pupils: he is a poor student, a troublemaker, or a potential dropout. Second, the formal status of the student may change: he is now a student who is on probation, who is ineligible for the football team, or who is placed on a "remedial" or "personalized" academic program. Third, there are consequences for the career and career chances of the pupil. Thus, for instance, the probabilities increase that one will be seen and judged in the future as a deviant should be seen and judged—as a troublemaker, a hood, a disrupter.

The school finds itself in at least two dilemmas with respect to the identification and labeling of underachievers and pupils who experience behavioral difficulties of one sort or another. On the one hand, it is to its advantage to label and publicly identify those pupils who violate school regulations, inasmuch as norms thereby receive continual reinforcement. But on the other hand, public identification has the outcome of establishing pupils as confirmed outsiders or deviants in the eyes of both teachers and other pupils.

A second dilemma has to do with early identification. It is often argued that the heart of the drop-out problem is lack of early identification of deviants and potential deviants.[7] But it is not often recognized that early identification also has the consequence of early and continuing confirmation of the deviant identity, with all that means in terms of how one is perceived and how one perceives himself.

Along with the advantages of early and public identification of deviant pupils there are some important disadvantages, then, all centering about the fact that a self-fulfilling prophecy may be set in motion. A pupil is defined as being somehow different, inferior, or bad; he is treated as such pupils "should" be treated; he increasingly sees himself as this kind of person; and, sure enough, the likelihood is great that his future behavior will substantiate the label he wears. Particularly in the case of the marginal deviant, the public label may be all that is needed to swing the student away from a conforming orientation and to entrench more deeply his deviant motivation.

SCHOOL RESPONSES TO DEVIANTS. What sanctions or other responses are evoked when misbehavior occurs or when academic performance is labeled as too low? There are, of course, a wide variety of sanctions open to teachers and other school personnel. In terms of academic underachievement, responses may range from punitiveness to helping efforts inside the classroom to referral to someone outside the classroom for special assistance—e.g., remedial-reading teacher, social worker, speech correctionist, counselor—to referral to a disciplinarian for a talk, placement on probation, or suspension. When responses are made inside the classroom to behavioral deviance, they may be in the form of public criticism, persuasion, changing the seat, corporal punishment, or referral to someone outside the classroom, e.g., to a disciplinarian or to someone such as a counselor or a social worker who, presumably, will attempt to change the behavior by means other than negative sanctions.

Neither the frequency nor the nature of such responses is likely to be random. Rather, both tend to be patterned according to the interplay of a number of other variables: assumptions about the nature and source of the act itself; characteristics of the student (sex, race, social class, curriculum, reputation); characteristics of the teacher or other staff member (sex, race, age, experience, goals); situational factors (type of classroom situation—gym and shop as compared to English and physics; characteristics and behavior of others in the classroom); available resources and so-called administrative style. In short, what happens to a student once he is defined as deviant depends not only on what he did, but also on who he is, what his past record is, who saw and judged him, and where it occurred.[8]

EFFECTS OF SCHOOL RESPONSES. What are the effects of school responses to deviant inclinations on the future behavior of the same individual? Deviance in the school is most profitably to be seen as a process over time, involving a series of exchanges between a pupil and teachers, counselors, or others. The youth acts, he is responded to—in ways which may more deeply entrench him in a deviant direction or which may nip deviant tendencies in the bud—and he reacts to those responses.

In order to understand how school responses differentially effect deviant tendencies, it is necessary to understand why students engage in behavior that may be defined as deviant. It is our contention that there are three individual (or internal) factors that may result in behavior or performance likely to be defined as unacceptable by the school: low innate capability, low commitment to school goals, and low acquired capabilities. First, the school is obliged to take on all comers, regardless of capability, skill, or orientation, except under unusual circumstances. Some students do not possess the intellectual equipment necessary for meeting school standards. Second, either academic or behavioral deviance may occur in the absence of positive commitment to school goals and norms, even if innate capability is adequate. Partly as a result of the enrollment of youngsters of all backgrounds and aspirations and partly because of the adverse effects of past and continuing failure, some pupils are simply not very concerned with whether they do well academically or conform to school standards of conduct. Third, deviance may result from a lack of what we may term acquired capabilities which consist of academic and social skills necessary for successfully completing academic and other required tasks and for sustaining adequate relationships. If any of these three sets of factors is low, there is a high likelihood of deviance resulting, although the actual occurrence of deviance, as we have seen, depends not only on the motivation and behavior of the student but also on the existence and enforcement of norms.

In order to be maximally effective in alleviating or heading off future deviant behavior, social responses must not only control, contain, or cut off immediate deviant behavior, but must develop commitment or acquired capabilities, as the case may be.

Little research has been done on the actual effects of various kinds of sanctions on students' future behavior.[9] Common sense does, however, furnish us with certain guidelines. Thus, while sanctions that are highly coercive or degrading (suspension, corporal punishment, excessive long stays after school) may have the immediate outcome of curbing deviant behavior, it is likely that their result in the long run will be further deterioration of the student's educational commitment or, in other words, further alienation from school personnel, ideals, and norms. Such unintended by-products of sanctioning practices may in fact contribute to the very problems that the sanctions are designed to alleviate. Thus, the school itself may, through its own activities, sustain or even generate the deviance it seeks to reduce.

These unwitting outcomes may be intensified even further by the fact that considerably fewer deviants than supposed have difficulty because of low commitment. Our research has repeatedly made clear that more often than not students in trouble differ little if any from nondeviants in the extent to which they are concerned about succeeding in school as well as in later life. At the same time, however, we have continually observed that teachers, disciplinarians, and others frequently proceed on the false assumption that low commitment lies at the base of the problem and thus gear their responses toward increasing motivation and concern about success, rather than toward developing skills.

ROLE EXIT. The label of deviant may be extremely difficult to shed. One is not just a temporary, passing occupant of the role of deviant. Regardless how drastically the behavior of a deviant may shift, there are mechanisms over which he has no control which may serve to block the road back to full acceptance in the conventional world.[10] As is well known by the ex-convict, the discharged mental patient, the reformed delinquent, or, in the school, the former "goof-off," the ceremony of entry into the role of deviant is substantially more public and, as a consequence, more long-lasting in its effects on identity, status, and career-chances than the transition out of the role.[11] Thus, even if a student shows improved tendencies in motivation, behavior, and performance, he may continue to find himself perceived, addressed, and treated as a deviant because of a label once received, an identity once acquired—a "hood," a "dumb kid," a "troublemaker," or a "sick child." The problem of being locked in the deviant role may be the greatest difficulty facing the deviant on his way back; just as great, perhaps, as changing his own motivation, if this is low.

Once again, then, attention is drawn to the school's involvement in the deviant behavior of its students. We are at once led to ask, what are some of the processes affecting the permanence and irrevocability of the deviant label? In what ways, in other words, may the individual student be locked in once he has been placed in the role of deviant?

First, there are certain formal, official means by which students' deviant identities may be confirmed and, in fact, transmitted and diffused. Perhaps the most important means is the official record-keeping or informational system. A student's current reputation (and, as a result, how he is seen and judged) may be as often founded on what he has done in the past as on how he is currently behaving or performing, in part because his biography trails him like the proverbial shadow through the channels of official records.[12] Once again the school is in a mild dilemma: on the one hand, it must identify students with unusual talent and those needing "special attention." On the other hand, however, a consequence of this practice for the latter type of student is that career chances may be unalterably hampered.

Perhaps the answer is more limited access to such records, if not a decrease altogether in their use. But whatever the extent of their use, modification of their content may be called for whereby more use be made of positive entries that denote official exit from the role, to offset the frequency of negative entries that indicate entry into and continuing occupation of the role of deviant. At the very least it seems desirable to provide means in the records to note that individuals are no longer behaving in deviant ways, or that there has been improvement in their conduct and achievement.

Second, there are less formal means by which deviant identities are confirmed and transmitted. Very frequently, the teacher's coffee lounge is the burying ground of students' career chances. For it is here—or wherever teachers meet informally—that reputations are often confirmed and spread: "Do you have that little so-and-so too?" "What about that John Jones. He's been giving me a bad time since the first of the year. You too?" Awareness of this danger prompts some schools to adopt a deliberate policy proscribing informal communication about students' reputations or behavior. All too often, however, perceptions and judgments of students are founded on what has been *heard* about reputations or current behavior in other settings.

Implications

Two sets of implications follow from what has been said. First, consider educational practice. We have tried to make clear that the school itself may maintain or even generate the very malperformance it seeks to eliminate, by offering limited opportunity for educational attainment for some students, by judging students adversely because of certain of their characteristics which are independent of their actions, by undermining existing motivation through unwise use of discipline practices, and by making it exceedingly difficult for the student to find his way back once he has been defined as deviant. To the extent that this is in fact the case, efforts to decrease underachievement and misconduct must be directed toward the school as well as toward the student.

The second implication relates to research. In order for educators to design their operations in such a way as to cope effectively with problems of malperformance, much greater understanding must be gained of the nature of the student-school interaction. What are the variable effects of school structural arrangements, belief systems, and discipline and other coping practices on students' orientations and chances of success? What are the organizational conditions under which the most effective school responses to deviance can be made? Answers to questions such as these, we believe, will contribute greatly to effective modification of student-school interactions, and, hence, to more efficient and complete development of human resources.

4 Problems of Disability from the Perspective of Role Theory

Edwin J. Thomas

Introduction

The disabled are a mixed lot; all sorts of conditions—psychological, sociological and economic—are to be found among them, and the impairments that medically define these individuals as disabled are also remarkably diverse.[1] In her concluding comments concerning an assessment of the field of somatopsychology, Beatrice Wright has captured what is perhaps the heart of the matter for the case of the disabled. She said "... *somatic abnormality as a physical fact is not linked in a direct or simple way to psychological behavior.*"[2] In support of this is the sobering fact that the scholars who have reviewed the scientifically reputable studies concerning the effects of disability upon adjustment have not found that there is presently any known, general, deleterious effect upon adjustment attending disablement.[3] That is, there is no evidence that an impaired physique results in any general maladjustment or that there is an association between types of physical disability and particular personality characteristics, such as tolerance for frustration or feelings of inferiority. Future research, of course, may force a revision of these observations. In any case, these results do not deny another equally important generalization, one that is based upon personal accounts of disabled persons, the observations of practitioners who work with the disabled, and the rehabilitation literature in general. This conclusion is that there are significant behavioral correlates of disability for given impairments and for given individuals, and that disability often profoundly affects the person's life.[4]

One must therefore turn to the underlying psychological and social conditions responsible for these different reactions in order to gain a richer understanding of the problems of disability. It is here that role

From the JOURNAL OF HEALTH AND HUMAN BEHAVIOR, 7 No. 1 (Spring 1966). Reprinted with the permission of the author and the journal.

theory is useful. Its concepts make possible a consistent, general description of the behaviors of the disabled and of those with whom he relates, and this perspective helps predict and explain the strains and adjustmental difficulties that may attend disablement.[5]

This paper focuses upon problems of role that are linked to the behavioral changes associated with disability or to the behavioral changes deriving from the reactions of others to the disabled. The problems of role that disabled individuals share with the nondisabled and that do not, therefore, distinguish their condition particularly, will not be discussed here. Because of this emphasis upon the disability-linked factors, only portions of role theory will be employed.[6] Also, the problems of role associated with an individual's disability may not always create severe adjustmental difficulties. The disability-related role problem may contribute little or much to an individual's overall adjustment, depending upon the entire complex of personal and environmental pressures in his life. This is true despite the fact that role difficulties to be treated here generally have undesirable adjustmental consequences, assuming all other factors are equal.

The Roles of the Disabled

Because of the great diversity of impairments characterizing persons designated as disabled, and because of their almost infinite conditions of psyche and environment, is it meaningful at all to talk about the *roles* of the disabled? Are the behavioral repertoires, or roles, of the disabled and the repertoires of those with whom they interact sufficiently distinct to be singled out, analyzed, and labelled? The answer is decidedly affirmative. Whether he is disabled from birth or suffers the disability later in life, the disabled person has some segment of his behavioral repertoire that is different from that of his normal fellow humans. The difference may derive from any or all of the following: some responses may be lost, some regained, some may be substitutes, or some simply different or new.

Five disability-related roles have been singled out for analysis: disabled patient, handicapped performer, helped person, disability comanager, and public relations man. The names are but convenient designations for particular aspects of the disabled person's behavioral repertoire or for the behaviors of others with whom he interacts. The behavioral repertoires so labelled are really complex clusters of conceptions, rules, and performances. The behaviors associated with each role, however, are descriptively similar and are different from, and independent of, the behaviors grouped as belonging with another role. Although these roles, hopefully, capture the essential differences between the behavioral repertoires of the disabled and of those with whom they interact, all five roles are not necessarily applicable to every disabled individual. One or more of the roles, however, should apply to every disabled person.

Disabled Patient

At the onset of the impairment—and later, too—the disabled individual is typically a patient, and is thereby exposed to a characteristic set of expectations. To quote from Parsons' seminal discussion of the sick role:

> The first of these is the exemption of the sick person from the performance of certain of his normal social obligations. Thus, to take a very simple case, "Johnny has a fever, he ought not to go to school today."
>
> . . . Secondly, the sick person is, in a very specific sense, also exempted from a certain type of responsibility for his own state. . . . He will either have to get well spontaneously or to "be cured" by having something done to him. He cannot reasonably be expected to "pull himself together" by a mere act of will, and thus decide to be all right. . . . The third aspect of the sick role is the partial character of its legitimation, hence the deprivation of a claim to full legitimacy. To be sick . . . is to be in a state which is socially defined as undesirable, to be gotten out of as expeditiously as possible. . . .
>
> Finally, fourth, being sick is also defined, except for the mildest cases, as being "in need of help.". . . He . . . incurs certain obligations, especially that of "co-operating" with his physician—or other therapist —on the process of trying to get well.[7]

In addition, most disabled persons are also hospitalized at some point. The expectations placed upon hospital patients are partly those relating to the sick role and partly those attending the particular subculture of the hospital. King has described this particular set of expectations for the hospitalized as follows:

> The first general expectation is that of *dependence*, of compliance by the patient to hospital rules and regulations, to the daily routine, to the decisions that are made for him by physicians or nurses. The compliant patient is therefore likely to be perceived as the good patient by hospital staff, whereas the patient who tries to exert authority will be perceived negatively. . . .
>
> In line with dependence, the patient is expected *not to fulfill his normal role responsibilities*. This is one of the prerequisites of the sick role . . . and a factor that receives strong support from hospital expectations. The patient is encouraged not to worry about cares of family or job and to concentrate on the process of getting well. . . .
>
> A third expectation concerns the *de-emphasis on external power and prestige* which the patient carries in his life outside the hospital. The taking away of patients' clothes is a symbol of this loss, all patients being rendered as naked as the day they came into the world, and supposedly as innocent. Indeed, there is nothing quite so deflating to

an individual's sense of prestige as his own nakedness in public. A positive function is also served by this action and expectation, that of emotional neutrality and fairness. . . .

Suffering and pain are to be expected and should be borne with as much grace as possible under the circumstances, so goes the general expectation. Hospital personnel know that rarely do patients come without pain or malaise and often the suffering is intense. Furthermore, the procedures involved in curing sickness in themselves often produce pain. . . .

Finally, *the patient should want to get well* and do all he can to aid the process. Again, this expectation grows out of the definition of the sick role and is an aspect of the role that is subject to rewards and punishments. The faintest hint of malingering can be picked up quickly by nurse or physician and is a sign that the patient is not living up to his obligations. If malingering can be clearly established, it acts to release the hospital from its obligations and brings about attempts to get rid of the patient as quickly as possible. . . .[8]

We add to these the expectation that there be tolerance for prognostic uncertainty. With most medical problems there is a period between the recognition that there may be something wrong medically and the time following a diagnosis when there is relative certainty concerning the prognosis for the individual. During this period the illness or disability must be followed to see how it develops, and time is required to gather the information and to make decisions about the case. In addition to this time required to reach a medically sound prognostication, there are other factors that prolong the period of uncertainty. This is well illustrated in Davis' analysis of this problem for polio victims.

. . . As we have seen, medically there is a pronounced shift from prognostic uncertainty to certainty after the first six weeks to three months following the onset of the disease. Yet nothing approximating a commensurate gain in the patients' knowledge of outcome probabilities occurred then or for a considerable period thereafter. Thus, "uncertainty," a real factor at the beginning of polio convalescence, came more and more to serve social-managerial ends for treatment personnel. Instead of openly confronting the parents with the prognosis—by then a virtual certainty—that the child would be left with a disability, treatment personnel sought to cushion its impact by hedging, evading questions, and acting as if the outcome were still uncertain. Thus they tried to spare themselves the emotional scenes that outright utterances of the prognosis would probably have entailed. . . .

. . . we must . . . not lose sight of the possibility that in many illnesses, especially those of a chronic or permanently incapacitating nature, "uncertainty" is to some extent feigned by the doctor for the

purpose of gradually—to use Goffman's very descriptive analogy—
"cooling the mark out," i.e., getting the patient ultimately to accept
and put up with a state-of-being that initially is intolerable to him.[9]

One consequence of this prognostic limbo is that the patient and those
closest to him lack authoritative opinion with respect to which realistic
levels of performance may be set. Without the moorings of definite expert
opinion, the patient and others may easily entertain unrealistically high
or low expectations.

Another expectation held for patients is that they define themselves
as sick. This requires that the individual acknowledge the unalterable fact
that he is ill, injured, or otherwise impaired, and that his assumptive world
and actions be structured accordingly.[10] For the disabled, this, of course,
is represented by beliefs and behavior commensurate with the premise that
the individual in fact has a disability. The hospitalized and nonhospitalized
patient alike are expected to conceive of themselves as sick, although the
entry into a hospital is likely to impress this fact more emphatically upon
patients.

There will be wide variations in the forms that the patient role takes
for given disabled persons, depending upon the specific nature of the
disability. But to the degree that the impairment is permanent, most of
the elements of the patient role are extended or made enduring. The
exemption from responsibility for the impairment may be granted for the
duration of the disablement; the period of prognostic uncertainty, rather
than being a matter of days or weeks, may be months or even years; the
exemption from ordinary social responsibilities, as it takes form for the
particular person and disability, may be permanent.

The expectation that the patient should want to get well, however, is
not merely extended for many disabled. Rather, it is elaborated in complex
detail, as is revealed in present-day rehabilitation practice and philosophy.
Thus, the disabled is encouraged to make the most of his capacities, within
the restrictions set by the impairment. Motivation is the key word and
has reference to a major theme in much of the rehabilitation literature.
The expectation that the disabled realize his potentialities is manifested in
numerous services, these variously providing counsel, therapy, training
and education, prosthetic devices, employment opportunities, and money.

This philosophy also informs us that the disabled must accept his
impairment, the acceptance being nearly a necessary condition, one
gathers, to the proper realization of his capabilities. Acceptance of one's
disability typically requires at least that the disabled conceive his limitations
and promise realistically, and that rules for performance be made commensurate with his true degree of handicap, his capabilities, and the environmental opportunities. The rationale attending the idea that acceptance
is important for the disabled is a specification, in the context of disability,
of the expectation mentioned earlier that patients conceive of themselves
as "sick."

Handicapped Performer

Because of the disablement there will very probably be an attending handicapping of performance. The impairment, of course, may range from complete loss of function, at one extreme, to a very minimal loss, at the other. As a consequence, some portion—large or small—of the normal individual's behavioral repertoire is somehow circumscribed, limited, or eliminated. All this is well known, of course.

But there are important ramifications deriving from having this more limited behavioral repertoire. First, the disabled person may be less able to care for himself physically: he may not be able to feed himself, dress, or move around, to select common instances. Second, the impaired function may be one which is requisite to the performance of normal social roles. For all adults there are at least three key roles or role clusters: one is the individual's sex role, either as a female or male; another is one's occupational role; and the third is the individual's family roles, as son, daughter, father, mother, or spouse. The disability may reduce the level of performance for these roles or make it variable and unpredictable. In the extreme case, of course, repertoires required for all these roles may be essentially lost, resulting in the removal of the person from the main avenues society provides for accomplishment, reward, and a sense of personal identity. A third and related point is that the disablement may preclude the fulfillment of normal responsibilities to others. Thus, if disabled, the father may no longer be able to be the breadwinner or the mother may have to relinquish homemaking and child-care activities. And fourth, the disabled may simply hinder others; for example, the family members of the disabled may be constrained to forfeit vacations, educational advancement, social and recreational opportunities—all because of the added drain on the family resources of time, money, and effort consequent to the impairment.

The behavioral repertoire of the disabled person is not merely less complete than that of his nondisabled counterpart, it is also a partial collection of behaviors that are substitutes for those lost because of the impairment or for those which the person never had in the first place. The blind learns to read and write with braille, the deaf comes to read lips and use a sign language, the extensively crippled find devices to aid their physical locomotion, to mention common illustrations of essentially substitute behaviors with which disabled individuals may embellish their repertoires and thereby increase their effective functioning.

It is in all of these ways that the individual with an impairment may be said to be a handicapped performer.

Helped Person

All persons receive help from others from the beginning of life to its end, and the amount of aid is generally much more than is usually realized or acknowledged. The person with an impairment usually receives more help than does his normal counterpart, of course. His physical needs may have to be ministered to and the responsibilities he ordinarily shouldered may have to be taken on by others. The disabled is thus on the receiving end of helping acts, and he must adjust, accommodate, and respond to being an object of aid; he is thus a helped person. The help received may be relatively small or large but it is nonetheless sufficient generally to constitute a deviation from cultural standards of self-reliance and independence so esteemed and revered even now in the United States. The implications of this will be discussed further at a later point.

Disability Comanager

The disabled person often becomes an active participant in the decisions and regimen of living attending his impairment and rehabilitation. He may participate in the selection of an artificial limb, may assume responsibility for giving himself injections, taking medication, following a diet, taking exercises, or following a schedule of rest and activity. In all these ways, he may thus be said to be a disability comanager, following Beatrice Wright's terms.[11]

Public Relations Man

Nondisabled persons conduct a large share of the business of living in institutionalized roles and in the context of widely shared understanding relating to expected behaviors. As a consequence, it is not common that a person has to explain his role to others. How often does a man, for instance, have to explain his role to a woman, or vice versa? The disabled, in contrast, typically has a particular impairment, the understanding of which is not provided for others by such a widely held, common store of knowledge. The relative uniqueness of the particular person's impaired condition and the associated ignorance of others place a burden of explanation and interpretation upon the disabled over and above that which the nondisabled carries. The necessities to educate others are of at least two sorts. The first is mainly unsolicited in which another person behaves toward the disabled so as literally to force him to account for his problem. Thus the blind individual is asked what it is like to be blind or his arm is grasped by the well-intentioned sighted person who believes that he needs to be led across the street. The other set of occasions necessitating explanation, in contrast to the gratuitous, may be regarded as the relevant and legitimate. Consider these: the blind job applicant is called upon to indicate how he would perform with this handicap; the potential mate requests information about how the marital relationhip will be affected by the other's disability; the prospective student is asked how his impairment will affect his ability to perform academically.

The information conveyed ranges over many themes: explanations of the nature of the disease, injury, or birth condition; the extent of disability and handicap; the regimen of rehabilitation and disability management. All these pertain to the disability itself. There are also those features relating to the indiivdual's attitudes, beliefs, and life philosophy developed in relationship to his condition. Rich examples are provided in the rehabilitation literature of the diverse ways in which disabled persons handle these themes of public relations. At one extreme there is the educator, the one who dispassionately conveys the facts pertaining to his particular disability; and at a different extreme are those people who perform the function more as propagandists, apologists, defeatists, or deceivers. Erving Goffman has described a particular variant of explanation in his notion of apologia. In this respect he says:

> First, in many total institutions a peculiar kind and level of self-concern is engendered. The low position of inmates relative to their station on the outside, established initially through the stripping processes, creates a milieu of personal failure in which one's fall from grace is continuously pressed home. In response, the inmate tends to develop a story, a line, a sad tale—a kind of lamentation and apologia—which he constantly tells to his fellows as a means of accounting for his present low estate.[12]

The fact that the person's disability is particular, if not unique, for him, and because of the absence of a uniform corpus of common knowledge pertaining to that disability, great latitude is provided for personal differences to shape the explanations given to others.

Patterns of Disability Roles for Individuals

As observed earlier, a given impairment does not necessitate all of the behavioral changes identified with these five roles, but most disabilities implicate most if not all of them. A given person will characteristically display his particular pattern or profile, through time. Some roles may be engaged in for longer periods than others. At any moment, some persons may manifest two, three, four, or all five of the roles; and the sequence of going from one role to the others may also vary from person to person.

Beyond these individual differences is the question of when the disablement occurs in the person's lifetime. If the person has an impairment from birth or one acquired early in life, he must learn the behavioral patterns associated with these five roles in the course of growing up, where these behavioral patterns—with the possible exception of portions of the patient role—are not common with those of the population at large. The socialization of such a disabled person is, therefore, partially deviant. The person disabled later in life also has to learn these new behaviors, but in addition he must unlearn other behaviors no longer possible or appropriate. For these persons the task is that of resocialization into a deviant social category and, of course, this may be gradual or rapid. A large proportion of disabilities occur relatively suddenly and this therefore poses the occasion for rapid resocialization.

Problems of Role

We turn now to the problems of role which attend disability. These difficulties arise partly because of the role changes just described and partly because of general societal conditions, to be referred to shortly.

Role Discontinuity

Ruth Benedict introduced the concept of role discontinuity to characterize the lack of order and smooth sequence in the cultural role training of the life cycle.[13] She documented how various primitive cultures provided for more continuity in the training for responsibility, dominance, and sexuality than was characteristic in the United States. The storm and stress of adolescence so often attributed only to physiological changes, she concluded, was in fact caused by the particular discontinuities resulting from prior role training.

This seminal conception is sufficiently important to merit elaboration and extension. First, although Benedict used the term in connection with age-graded transitions universal for all mankind, it is but a simple step to realize that discontinuities may occur also for specific groups and individuals whenever there is a transition from one position to another in which the role behaviors associated with each are different. Such is the case with large numbers of the disabled.

Second, the elements requisite to continuous role training need specification. There are at least these five: (1) There should be congruence of the expected behaviors between the new and the old positions. (2) The person should have the capacity to acquire the new behaviors. (3) He should be properly motivated for the transition. (4) He should have been socialized in anticipation of the impending transition through prior rehearsal—either imaginative or actual—of the new behaviors. (5) The rate of change in moving from one position to the next should not be too rapid.

On most of these counts a disability that occurs later in life involves discontinuity. An abrupt, sudden change probably serves to exacerbate the effects of the other factors. Even a gradual, progressive change may never eliminate a basic incongruence of expected behaviors, rectify the possible absence of capacity to perform the new and different behaviors, or achieve proper motivation to change. A gradual rate may (but will not necessarily) make possible anticipatory socialization. Thus, even disabilities that involve gradual deterioration are mainly discontinuous role transitions, considering all of the requisites of role continuity here proposed.

Role discontinuity may result in confusion, anxiety and stress for the individual, and we assume that these effects will be more probable to the extent that there are many rather than few discontinuous junctures.[14]

Role Conflict

Whether or not the person's disability is attended by role discontinuity, there are various conflicts of expectations that are disability related. An expectation is a statement that defines given behavior as obligatory, forbidden, or permitted. Role conflict exists when there are two opposing expectations held for the behavior of an individual such that he cannot perform consistently with both at the same time. Role conflict may take many forms. Others may hold different expectations for you as compared with those which you hold for yourself; thus the child with a heart disorder may hold expectations for himself as if he were normal, whereas his parents may hold expectations requiring restriction of activity and rest. Another variant of role conflict occurs when others who prescribe behavior for the individual disagree between themselves; for instance, a parent, in attempting to deny a child's disability, may prescribe expectations for his behavior which do not take into account the disability, whereas the child's physician may advocate expectations more commensurate with the degree of impairment. A more subtle variant of role conflict occurs when the two conflicting expectations reside within the same skin, that is, are held by the same person for his own behavior; consider the father who has had a heart attack and who experiences conflict between his understanding of the doctor's orders that he care for himself properly and the expectations he has learned as a middle-class male that he be achieving, hard working, and successful in his work. Conflicts of role may result in stress for the individual, particularly to the extent that the conflicts are strong, enduring, or numerous.

Conflict of Role Definitions

Role definitions are in conflict when contradictory role conceptions are held for the same person. In the case of disability, the conceptions most likely to be conflicting pertain to ideas that the disabled person is normal or disabled. Thus the person may view himself appropriately as disabled in a given area, whereas selected others may view him as normal. More specifically, conceptions that the disabled hold for themselves may disagree with the conceptions others hold for them in any or all of the five disability-related roles described earlier. Consider, for instance, the youth with a serious heart condition, the visibility and significance of which is not apparent to the casual acquaintance. When meeting such a person for the first time it is not likely that others will conceive of him as disabled. The parallel problem involving the possible conflict of conceptions for the individual with a highly visible disability, such as blindness, is that the casual acquaintance is likely to conceive of him as more handicapped than he in fact may be. Conflicts of role definitions, at the very least, result in confusion and asynchronous behaviors of individuals vis-a-vis one another; more seriously, such conflicts may result in anxiety and stress, again to the extent that they are strong, recurring, or numerous.

Nonfacilitative Interdependence

Because of the impairment and the resulting inability to care for himself, the disabled person is usually less able to help others, yet others are constrained to act helpfully toward him. This helplessness and non-facilitative relationship with others departs from the dominant cultural emphasis upon self-reliance and independence. The person may have been well trained to be self-reliant, autonomous, and independent in the course of his social learning prior to the advent of the disability. Robin Williams, in his perceptive analysis of the values and beliefs in American society, has described achievement (success) and activity (work) as major value orientations in America,[15] and he has noted further that Americans esteem active mastery more than passive acceptance. The psychological needs for achievement and autonomy may be regarded as individual dispositions which derive in part from these highly esteemed cultural values.[16] The disabled may depart from this cultural standard of self-reliance and inde-pendence on many counts, and, as a consequence, there may be various psychological effects. First, the individual may experience what Bertha Reynolds called the poignant "hurt" associated with the receipt of assist-ance when he is unable to repay others for the help received.[17] Second, the individual may experience a drop in his self esteem.[18] Third, the help offered is likely to be apprehended ambivalently or even negatively.[19]

Role Strain

All these role problems—role discontinuity, role conflict, conflict of role definitions, and nonfacilitatively interdependent relationships—con-spire, either singly or in complex combinations, to create role strain, i.e., to affect the experienced difficulty that an individual has in performing his role.[20] This strain differs from anxiety and stress in general only by virtue of its particular association with the problems attending one's social role.

Special Problems of Role Synchrony

In addition to the role difficulties already discussed, there is a special set of problems relating to the synchronization or meshing of the behavior of the disabled with that of others with whom he interacts. Because the problems of role synchrony are subtle and complex, they deserve more extended comments.[21] Let us begin with an example.

Consider the blind person about to catch a train in a subway. Through practice and the use of the cane he has become proficient at navigating steps and turnstiles and knows the correct moves required to get on and off subway trains and, as a consequence, he is able to locomote relatively independently from one section of the city to another. In only one respect is this person unable to be totally self-reliant in his travels: he must inquire of others concerning whether the forthcoming train is the one he wishes to board. As he hears the distant roar of a forthcoming train, he asks this question: "Pardon me, is this an E train?" "Oh, yes!," comes the startled reply, "I've got you—" and the man to his left takes a firm grasp on his arm. In attempting to free himself, the blind person says, "That's all right, I can make it. . . ." "It's no trouble at all," he protests, and then taking the blind man's arm, the other says "This way," and the train is boarded. Although the blind man is now able to fend for himself, his guide announces that there don't seem to be any seats, in a distinctly audible voice, whereupon one of the passengers looks up and says "Here, he can have my seat." After the blind man is seated the guide inquires shortly after, in a voice louder than is required by the roar of the train, "Where are you going?" Pausing briefly, the blind man replies, "I'm getting off at Forty-second." "Oh," says the guide, "Well, I get off here. Good luck. Maybe someone else will help you." [22]

All that the blind individual needed was information regarding which train was coming, yet by virtue of the unsolicited help provided by the guide, he was treated as more handicapped than he was. The excessive handicap that was presumed was thus invalid. Furthermore, the blind person went along with the guide, this presumably being the course of least resistance, and he thereby fictitiously feigned a handicap that he did not have. The role behaviors of each were synchronic, however; the behavior of each meshed with that of the other, both sets of behaviors apparently being based upon the same behavioral assumptions. Thus, in this example we have *role synchrony* between the disabled and the other, but it was essentially invalid because the behavior of both presumed a handicap that in fact was not present—a *fictitious handicap*, as it were.

Now for another example. Fred is a ten-year-old boy with a mildly handicapping heart disorder. He does not choose to recognize his disability, however, and consequently he does not rest appropriately and, when he plays with others, he participates altogether too vigorously. Fred does all of this in spite of the admonitions and advice of doctors, parents, and even his friends.

In this example, Fred has ignored his disability and consequently he behaves essentially as if he were not handicapped. His behavior is thus invalid with respect to the true degree of handicap. Others behave toward him much more realistically, however, in that their behavior is commensurate with the true degree of handicap that exists. Because Fred's behavior does not mesh with that of others in respect to the degree of handicap, we may say that there is *role asynchrony* between him and others. The source of the asynchrony is *self originated*, for Fred has chosen essentially invalid behavioral options. This particular variety of role asynchrony, in the context of disability, might be termed *autistic normalcy*.

Valid Role Synchronies

The significance of role asynchrony and of invalidity is highlighted by considering the typical role relationship characterizing the interactions of most persons, namely, that of valid role synchronies. The nondisabled person typically behaves in a normal fashion with others, and he thus may be said to be performing validly; and others relate to him on the assumption that he is normal, and their behaviors vis-a-vis him are appropriately complementary. This might be called *true normalcy* and is a valid role synchrony which characterizes the large majority of the normal interaction encounters of nondisabled persons and, of course, it is characteristic for nondisabled persons prior to their disability (see Table 4–1). The problem posed by the advent of disability is that the valid role synchrony of true normalcy becomes less common and, in certain cases, is virtually ruled out.

Table 4–1. Varieties of Synchrony of Repertoires of Role Behavior for Self and Others

	Behavioral Options of Others	
Behavioral Options of Self	Behaviors Appropriate for a Handicapped Self	Behaviors Appropriate for a Normal Self
Handicapped Behaviors		
Correct for Self	I. True Handicap	II. Imposed Normalcy
Incorrect for Self	III. Fictionalized Handicap	IV. Autistic Handicap
Nonhandicapped Behaviors		
Correct for Self	V. Imposed Handicap	VI. True Normalcy
Incorrect for Self	VII. Autistic Normalcy	VIII. Fictionalized Normalcy

The ideal interaction encounter, from the perspective of role theory, is the valid role synchrony. Because the synchrony we have called true normalcy is generally precluded for the disabled person, the appropriate valid role synchrony for the disabled is therefore that which might be called *true handicap*. This is defined by behavior on the part of the disabled person commensurate with the true degree of handicap, and by related behavior of others also commensurate with the actual degree of the disabled person's handicap (see Table 4-1).[23] Interaction contexts in which this form of valid role synchrony is most likely to occur are the hospital, where the disabled person is on a ward with similarly disabled individuals cared for by a perceptive and competent staff, and in the disabled person's own family, assuming of course that he and his family members behave realistically. Interaction encounters outside of these more protected contexts have a greatly increased likelihood of being either asynchronous or invalid synchronies.

Invalid Role Synchronies

There are two varieties of invalid role synchrony to which the disabled are peculiarly subject. The first is characterized by a form of mutual denial of the disability in which the disabled performs in a manner implying or indicating less handicap than truly exists, coupled with the behavior of others toward him which analogously is appropriate for the absence of the handicap (see Table 4-1). This might be called *fictitious normalcy*. In his analysis of polio victims and their families, Davis has described an extreme case of what he termed normalization.[24] This was the case of six-year-old Laura Paulus, the most handicapped child in his group of nine study participants. Laura wore full-length braces on both legs, a pelvic band, high orthopedic shoes and had to use crutches. From a purely physical standpoint, she was extremely limited in what she could do. Her energetic mother was determined, however, to make Laura "normal." She was registered in the school that she attended before her illness, and took a regular city bus to school; parties, games and other festivities were held for her and she was enrolled in a Brownie troop. By joining willingly with her mother in this normalization, Laura was entering into fictitious normalcy. If the situation of fictitious normalcy is enduring and his health and rehabilitation depends upon how well he cares for himself, the disabled may of course expose himself to unnecessary hazards. The excessive striving, in any case, may greatly increase role strain.

The second invalid role synchrony is the *fictitious handicap*. This, too, involves a pluralistic deception, for the disabled and others jointly adopt invalid behaviors in terms of the disabled person's true degree of handicap; but fictitious handicap also involves behavior on the part of the disabled and others that exaggerates the actual degree of handicap. Many of the examples of so-called overprotection cited in the literature on disability would be illustrative here (see Table 4-1).

LD was a 40-year-old insurance salesman married to an aggressive, strong-willed woman at the time of his first heart attack. The attack proved to be a mildly disabling condition which left the patient with shortness of breath when performing physical labor over an extended period of time. Thorough medical examination revealed he was able to continue with his work on a reduced schedule. Mrs. D, however, was fearful that continued work of any nature would result in further attacks, or even death, in spite of medical reassurance to the contrary. She earned an adequate income to support both herself and her husband, and convinced him without difficulty that he should not return to work. Both refused repeated offers to help.[25]

The difficulty with ficitious handicap, clearly, is that as long as such a situation exists the disabled person will perform at a lower level than is necessitated by his disability.

Role Asynchronies

Role asynchronies occur when either the disabled person or the other adopts invalid behavior with respect to the true degree of the disabled person's handicap. We have already made reference to autistic normalcy in our example of Fred. Another self-originating asynchrony is *autistic handicap*. Here the individual displays more handicapped behavior than the disability actually warrants while others behave toward him in a fashion commensurate with the true degree of handicap (see Table 4–1). This is a variety of hypochondriasis for the disabled, as it were.

HB, a 35-year-old married Southern Missouri sharecropper with five children, had a brain infection five years prior to being referred for social casework help. The infection left him with a mild shuffling gait and general slowed ability to move hands and arms. Formerly an unskilled laborer, he quickly settled into apathy and developed a passive attitude toward various rehabilitative efforts which were attempted with him. His wife was unable to convince her husband that he should take more responsibility in helping himself since he believed he had a more serious and incapacitating illness than the doctors advised. The patient and his wife went on public assistance, and subsequent efforts toward re-employment became feebler with the patient finding numerous reasons why he could not work.[26]

Both autistic handicap and autistic normalcy are self originating, i.e., they derive from invalid behaviors and assumptions on the part of the disabled person himself. All kinds of personal and environmental conditions may generate these particular autisms, as the clinical examples in the rehabilitation literature amply demonstrate. Emotional difficulties are most patently likely to be operative in such cases.

In contrast to these asynchronies, there are two others that arise from the invalid behaviors of others. For this reason these have been called the imposed role asynchronies. The first, an *imposed handicap*, occurs when others behave toward the disabled person as if he were more handicapped than he actually is, while the disabled behaves validly (see Table 4–1).

> Joe was a 19-year-old plumber's apprentice when he was critically injured in an automobile accident resulting in what was at first considered severe brain damage. Gradually and unexpectedly, he improved to the point where he was considered medically capable of continuing in his previous occupation in spite of some clumsiness and a slight tendency to lose balance. Although both the patient and his employer were eager for him to resume work, his parents vigorously resisted and successfully interrupted his return to work. They had nursed him back from a critical illness, "protected" him to the extent of doing for him needlessly, and were fearful he would "get hurt" on the job and that it would be their "fault" if anything further should happen to him.[27]

An enduring imposed handicap may clearly eventuate in a fictitious handicap. In response to the extreme solicitousness, in other words, the disabled individual may succumb, lowering his performance to a level less than that of his true handicap.

The second asynchrony is that of *imposed normalcy*. Here the others who relate to the disabled person behave toward him as if he were less handicapped than he truly is, while the disabled maintains valid behavior (see Table 4–1). The case of Laura Paulus cited earlier would illustrate imposed normalcy had Mrs. Paulus foisted the normalization on Laura against her wishes. An imposed normalcy probably exists early in the development of fictitious normalcy, especially when the disabled are children. One apparent difficulty with imposed normalcy is that the disabled person is constrained to perform above the level appropriate to the true degree of his handicap.

These are the eight varieties of role synchrony for the disabled. The details of their exposition should not obscure the two basic points. The first is that disability generally restricts the possibilities for valid role-synchronic encounters, and the second is that the particular problems of role synchrony characteristic of the disabled appear either as an invalid role synchrony or as a role asynchrony. The particular problems of synchrony may be complexly patterned in the life of any given disabled person. The more enduring contexts of human encounter—such as home, school, and work—may involve one or more varieties of synchronic difficulty, and the more fleeting, casual encounters may involve different and possibly highly diverse confrontations.

Underlying Conditions

A basic condition that gives rise to these problems of role synchrony is that society has not provided a social niche for the disabled that is as clear, predictable, and as guiding as that which the nondisabled enjoys. There simply are not uniform, clear rules for disabled persons in the same way that there are rules for the performance of nondisabled persons, and the rules and conceptions that are held for these persons are generally diverse and lacking in agreement. Furthermore, an uncommon ignorance pervades the situation for the disabled. There is a widespread lack of public knowledge concerning the various types of disabilities, and there are many stereotypes concerning the disabled that substitute for genuine knowledge and operate along with ignorance. Contributing to the uncertainty is the disabled person himself; unless he is known rather well, he presents an ambiguous stimulus, as it were, in human form. The individual encounter with a disabled person is fraught with uncertainty about the conditions of his particular impairment, combined with ignorance of the individual personality and of how he has coped with his disability.

This lack of tradition, consensus, and knowledge—of institutionalization in general—surrounding the social niche of the disabled, has a singular consequence: the customary social moorings that control the choice of behavior in human encounters are weakened. The disabled and those who behave toward them consequently have more choices of behavioral alternatives. Speaking more generally, there is *role optionality*, a condition that is defined by the existence of two or more behavioral repertoires, each of which (1) attaches to a different social position, (2) has different implications for the person behaving and for the others with whom he interacts, and (3) lacks definition by the society and culture as preferred over other alternatives.

The main axis with respect to which the optionality exists for the disabled concerns that of normalcy versus disability, these being the central, opposing behavior repertoires. The disabled may behave so as to imply a greater or lesser handicap than he has, or he may behave consistently with the true degree of handicap. If he behaves consistently with the true degree of handicap, he may be said to be performing validly, as we have observed. And the other person (or persons) who interact with him may behave in analogous terms; i.e., they may perform so as to imply a greater or lesser degree of handicap than actually exists, or they may behave consistently with the actual degree of handicap. If the other (or others) behave toward the disabled commensurate with the actual degree of his handicap, then the performance may be said to be valid. Without a condition of role optionality for the disabled or for those with whom he interacts, problems of role synchrony would not exist.

Now, given these behavioral options the question is what factors determine which choices will be made. In short, what conditions determine whether the disabled will choose valid or invalid options and analogously, what affects the selection of options when others behave with a disabled person? There are a few conditions that immediately come to mind.

The first is the very degree of disablement. The nondisabled person obviously has little occasion to perform as if he were handicapped, and others are most unlikely to relate to him as if he were handicapped. Also, the person who is nearly totally handicapped in all areas of functioning is going to have little role optionality with respect to performing as a nondisabled person. Others, however, may or may not perform toward him as if he were as severely handicapped and thus even the totally disabled may face problems of role synchrony. Thus we see that occasions for invalid role options—and the consequent difficulties of synchrony—are more likely to be posed for persons who are partially, rather than more extensively, disabled.

Visibility of the disability also affects the behavioral options, especially those of the others who relate to the disabled person. The casual encounter with an individual with a visible impairment may cause others to behave toward him as if he were more disabled than he actually is, thus creating the occasion for what we have called an imposed handicap and possibly fictitious handicap as well. The situation is different for the disabled with an essentially nonvisible impairment, for cues are generally not present to signify disablement and, for that reason, others frequently behave toward him as if he were normal. Under these conditions, for the nonvisibly disabled, we would therefore anticipate that there would be problems of role synchrony involving either fictitious or imposed normalcy.

The disabled person's acceptance of his disabled condition is still another factor which influences behavioral options. If he fails to acknowledge his impairment and behaves accordingly, his denial clearly increases the probability that his encounters with others will involve the particular asynchrony called autistic normalcy. Analogously, if the person accepts his disability with resignation and denigration his behavioral options may well be biased toward excessive handicapping. This creates the conditions for the particular asynchrony called autistic handicap. Only when acceptance involves a realistic appraisal of one's impairment along with behavior commensurate with this viewpoint on the part of the disabled person are the conditions established for averting asynchronies that derive from invalid, self-originated behaviors. Although the proper acceptance of the disability by the disabled person does not guarantee, of course, that others will adopt valid options in their encounters with him, the disabled person's genuine acceptance of his impairment, when communicated to others, may greatly increase the chances that they will similarly adopt valid behaviors when interacting with him.

The society and culture also shape the choice of options, directing them mainly toward normalization. The design of society is based on the premise that its members are not disabled. As many writers have observed, the society has been created and is run for the benefit of the normal person. Also, the cultural values in the United States—stressing self-reliance, independence, and autonomy as they do—bias choice toward behaviors that would be designated as normal. Independence is esteemed, and there is still some stigma, generally covert and subtle, which attaches to most every disability.

These pressures toward the normalization of behavior are to be pitted against essentially countervailing conditions that constrain the disabled to select the invalid options of excessive handicapping. I am thinking particularly of the factors that give rise to self pity, to secondary gains from disability, and to the solicitude of others in general. Humanitarian mores constrain others to err generously rather than niggardly in the public treatment of the disabled, and the pain and stress of disablement conspire, along with various personality factors, to make the disabled accept and sometimes to exploit these opportunities for attention, love, and care.

Summary

The perspective of role theory was employed in this analysis of the disabled. Two general topics were discussed, the first being that of the roles of the disabled. Five disability-related roles were described: the disabled patient, handicapped performer, helped person, disability co-manager, and public relations man.

The second topic concerned the problems of role that may attend disablement. These problems were those of role discontinuity, role conflict, conflict of role definition, nonfacilitative interdependence, role strain, and the special difficulties of role synchrony. In addition to the synchronies of true normalcy (precluded for the disabled by virtue of the impairment) and true handicap (an ideal and sometimes uncommon encounter), the asynchronies of imposed normalcy and imposed handicap and of autistic normalcy and autistic handicap were discussed, as were the invalid synchronies of fictionalized handicap and fictionalized normalcy. Defining conditions and clinical examples were elaborated.

The conditions underlying the various problems of role synchrony were discussed, among these being role optionality, the extent of disablement, the visibility of the impairment, the acceptance of the disability, and selected societal and personal factors.

5 Role Reversal and Conflict Between Aged Parents and Their Children

Paul H. Glasser and Lois N. Glasser

Introduction

The purpose of this paper is to explore some of the problems between aged parents and their adult children in the light of the experiences of one counseling agency and previous research and theory in family sociology. Recent population statistics and projections, which indicate that there is and will continue to be a rise in the number of the aged in the United States, have been receiving increasing attention. One recent report states:

> . . . Persons 65 and older in the United States quadrupled between 1900 and 1950. There are in the country now approximately 16 million individuals aged 65 and over. . . . It is anticipated that 9 per cent of the population will soon be over 65 and that the percentage will level off at about 10 per cent by 1975. By then it is estimated that there will be approximately 22 million "aging" or "aged"; and about 30 million by the year 2000. . . . Barring a major catastrophe, about one out of every three Americans who are now 25 or older will be living in the year 2000.[1]

That this change in the composition of our population will have increasing effects upon child-rearing families and family life in general seems unquestionable. This problem has already been reflected in our social agencies, many of which have found it necessary to set up special departments to work with the increasing number of aged clients and their married children. However, specification of the types of problems they

From MARRIAGE AND FAMILY LIVING, 24 (1962), 46–51. Reprinted with the permission of the National Council on Family Relations and of the authors.

present, and the relation of these problems to the social system of the family remain unclarified. The evidence from earlier studies is not always consistent, and not necessarily in agreement with prevailing theory.

Collection of Data

The study was done at The Jewish Family and Children's Service of Detroit. The Aging Department serves those clients who are 60 years of age and over, and is staffed by one full-time social caseworker, two part-time caseworkers, and a graduate student in training. Volunteers are also used, on occasion, as friendly visitors to supplement counseling services.

The study population consists of all cases handled by the Department of Services to the Aging, in which one spouse was 60 years of age or over, there was at least one living child in the family, and in which there was a request for service between January, 1958, through June, 1959. These dates were picked because the period included the most recent cases seen at the agency in which there was present in the record the information the researchers were seeking. The cases were found by going through the daily intake reports starting with June, 1959, and going backward in time, until a total of 120 cases was reached. Data gathered from process records, summary records and the face sheets for each case were placed on a schedule, which was then used for analysis.

While material on the aged clients was usually complete, data on all of their children were sometimes not, especially if the aged parents had a large number of children, some of whom lived in another city. However, it is our impression that data were available on the great majority of the aged parents' living children and their families.

Description of the Aged

In 43 per cent of the cases both spouses were living. In 51 of the 120 cases the husband was dead; in 18 cases the wife was no longer alive. The mean age of men in the study was the study was 70.9; of women 68.3.

The estimated median income of the sample studied was between $2000 and $2500. The income was derived from the following sources in descending order of frequency: children, social security, savings, employment, Old Age Assistance, income property, retirement and pension funds, and a variety of other sources.

Grouped by occupation or former occupation of the male wage earner, 8 of the 120 men can be considered to have been in the upper class, 48 in the middle class and 64 in the lower class. The scale used in the collection of the data is a modification of the Edwards scheme, used by the United States Government for the 1950 census.[2] The ten-item scale was divided in the following way:

Upper Class (8)

1. Professional, technical and kindred workers 5
2. Owners of large companies 0
3. Managers and officials of large corporations 3

Middle Class (48)

4. Small business owners 31
5. Salesmen 12
6. Clerical and kindred workers 5

Lower Class (64)

7. Craftsmen, foremen and kindred workers 28
8. Operatives and kindred workers (unskilled)................. 11
9. Service workers 16
10. Laborers 9

This class division is used throughout the rest of the report.[3]

Half of the aging lived in rented quarters. A fourth owned their own homes; 20 per cent lived with their children in homes owned by their children; 5 per cent were in institutions. The great majority (99 out of 120) lived in a predominantly Jewish neighborhood.

Of the 69 living male spouses, the researchers evaluted 24 as in good health, 22 in fair health, and 23 in poor health. Of the 102 living female spouses, the records indicate that 37 were in good health, 30 in fair health, and 35 in poor health.[4]

Thirty-seven per cent of the aged clients had 2 children; 28 per cent had only one child; 21 of the clients had 3 children; and 11 clients had 4 children. The larger families of 5, 6, and 7 children included only 8 per cent of the 120 cases.

In many cases several presenting problems were interwoven. The following is an illustration:

> Mrs. C, a widow with 2 married sons, had recently been discharged from the hospital following an operation. When she got home she found that she had been evicted from her three-room apartment because her Old Age Assistance had been discontinued on the basis that the apartment was too large. She was instructed to move into a two-room apartment. Mrs. C. was willing to cooperate, but the Welfare Department refused to pay for her moving. One son was presently unemployed, and the other was failing in business, so they could be of no financial help. By the time Mrs. C. arrived at the agency she needed help in finding an apartment, paying for her moving and getting back on Old Age Assistance, as well as supportive casework to help strengthen her will to live.[5]

Despite this overlap, the researchers selected what was in their judgment the predominant problem. Using this subjective means of selection, the following was found:

Problem	Percentage of Cases
Housing	41
Planning re: illness	27
Financial aid and/or planning	18
Counseling on marriage or parent-child relations	13
Other	2

Description of the Children

Edwards' scale also was used to distinguish among the occupations and social class of children of the aged. The data did not include a list of all of their children, nor all of the children's occupations, so that it was necessary to use only the information on those children for which the data were available. The occupation of each child was assigned the number according to the Edwards scale. These were then added and divided by the number of children for which data were available in each family, giving a mean occupational score for the children in each family, and a mean social-class status for the children in the family. It might be noted that very few families had a wide dispersion of occupations among children, or in other words, the mean and mode in each family were closely related. The status of the children in 27 cases was upper class; in 60 cases middle class, and in 28 cases lower class. There were 5 minor children in school.

Among the children for which data were available, 50 per cent lived in predominantly Jewish neighborhoods; 10 per cent lived in mixed or non-Jewish neighborhoods; 18 per cent in varied neighborhoods (some children in Jewish neighborhoods, some in non-Jewish neighborhoods, or out of town); and in 18 cases all of the children lived out of town.[6]

Limitations of the Sample

In the discussion that follows, two important limitations of the population under study must be kept in mind. First, the study deals with a distinct cultural group that tends to live in homogeneous neighborhoods in a large metropolitan area. Secondly, *all of the families in the sample requested help from a social agency.* Thus, the sample is representative of the aged who request help from this agency. Generalizations to other cultural groups and "non-problem" families are not methodologically legitimate. Nonetheless, insights gained from this group of clients may be useful for other studies and in the general accumulation of knowledge about different population groups in the United States.

Industrial Society, the Family, and the Aged

Until recently there was a tendency in family sociology to characterize the rural family of the last century and the modern urban family in dichotomous categories. The latter has been described as an independent, nuclear, neolocal group in which vertical class and geographic mobility were emphasized as adjustments to the industrial society.[7] The assumption has been that this has left the older person isolated and without a legitimate role in society since he is separated by space and intergenerational conflict from his family of procreation, and he no longer fits into the productive economy. His children have independent conjugal groups of their own, and his association with them is limited.[8]

This does not seem true for the group of clients in this study. Among the 120 cases, there were 45 in which the elderly were living with their children; there were 61 in which the aged were receiving financial assistance from their children; in 27 cases the aged were living with their children and receiving financial assistance from them; and in 77 cases the older people were receiving financial aid from their children or living with their children.

This finding seems consistent with a number of other recent studies which indicate parents maintain somewhat close social and affectional ties with their children and the families of their children. Albrecht found this to be true for 85 per cent of her aged respondents.[9] Streib and Thompson found that 75 per cent of their aged respondents saw their children often. They summarize their findings with the statement:

> Family orientation primarily encompasses the family of procreation of the older generation, and only in a much smaller way does their own family of orientation serve as the focus of family relationships.[10]

The authors attempted to test the Burgess and Parsons hypothesis further. Following their argument, the authors assume that there is conflict between striving to get ahead by children and care for their aged parents. Further, it is the middle-class group which has the strongest mobility strivings.[11] Thus, one might expect upper-class children (those who made it) and lower-class children (those who have given up the fight) to be more concerned about their aged parents than middle-class children (who continue the more active striving). This does not turn out to be so. There is no significant relationship at the .05 level between social-class status and living with parents or in independent households $(P > .30)$.[12] Even when the lower class and the upper class are combined, the relationship turns out not to be significant $(P > .95)$. Taking the hypothesis one step further, the authors attempted to test Burgess' statement that "the greater the cultural difference between the older and younger generation, the greater will be the distance and points of conflict between them."[13] The children of aged parents were classified as upwardly mobile, stable, or downwardly mobile according to their movement or nonmovement among the three classes, comparing the social class of sons and sons-in-law with that of aged parents. Once again the findings are negative. There is no significant relationship between social-class mobility and living with parents or in independent households ($P > .20$). There is no significant relationship between social-class mobility and the giving of financial aid to aged parents ($P > .30$). If the downwardly mobile are eliminated because of their own financial necessity, the results are the same ($P > .80$). Thus, neither social-class status nor social mobility tend to influence whether children give help to their parents.[14]

Further evidence for this point of view is indirectly revealed by the data on religiosity. While there is no significant association between religious affiliation of children (Orthodox, Conservative, Reform Jews and no religion or non-Jews) and the giving of financial aid to their parents ($P > .30$), children who are less orthodox than their parents in their religious orientation are more likely to give financial aid to their parents than children who have the same religious identification ($P < .05$). Since children who move up the social class ladder through increased income tend to become less Orthodox Jews and more acculturated to American society, it can be hypothesized that it is the more mobile children who are more likely to give help to their parents. Since these mobile children are more likely to have the financial means to be able to do so, this is expected, but this finding is also inconsistent with the Burgess and Parsons hypothesis.

Role Reversal, Role Conflict, and Personal Problems

Evidence from this study and a number of others indicates that class differences do not seem to be the primary cause for personal problems among the aged. The aged do not seem to be isolated and cut off from social ties with their family of procreation. If this is so, then what brings aged clients to social agencies in increasingly larger numbers?

Some clues may lie in the nature of the major problem for which the client requested help. In more that 40 per cent of the cases the predominant problem seemed to be that of housing. Thirty-seven and a half per cent of those living with adult children had housing problems, while 44 per cent of those living independently had this problem. In 19 per cent of the cases the request was for financial aid or help in financial planning. Fifteen per cent of those living with children requested this aid, while 22 per cent of those living independently requested such help. More than a third of the aged were classified as being in poor health, although none had an acute illness requiring immediate hospitalization. In 28 per cent of the cases the client wanted aid in planning regarding illness. This included 32.5 per cent of the cases in which the aged were living with adult children and 26 per cent of the cases in which they were living alone. This must be seen together with the fact that in 63 per cent of the cases the aged were receiving some kind of material aid from their children.

Each of these 3 types of problems requires a decision by the aged and/ or their children about a societal norm which may require a disruption of the personal lives of the children and their families. Should the adult child take the aged parent(s) into his own home, especially since the parent's income is likely to be low and his housing inadequate? Should the adult child contribute to the financial support of his aged parent(s) at the expense of his own personal comfort and/or the standard of living of his own conjugal family? Should the adult child contribute time, energy and money to help care for his sick parent(s)?

While a number of studies indicate that aged parents and children are expected to maintain close psychological relationships, especially through visiting patterns, and do so, the independence of each of the conjugal family units is considered sacred. Streib and Thompson report:

> . . . maintaining ties with children is considered of first importance and that expecting children to share their experiences by keeping in close contact is a social norm held by the overwhelming majority of older persons.
>
> At the same time, the kind of contact which the older person feels should be maintained is strictly of the "hands off" variety. In nearly a hundred interviews, almost without exception, independence and noninterference were stressed as the key to successful intergenerational relationships.[15]

At one level, the evidence suggests a cultural lag. While the present normative structure of society emphasizes the independence of the conjugal family unit, society has not adequately provided for the aged to make this possible. In some ways it continues to function as if the strong mutual-aid patterns of the rural farm family were still in existence. The result is a gap between expected patterns of behavior and reality, leading to role conflict for aged parents and their children expressed in the personal problems they bring to our social agencies.[16]

At another level, the problem is one of role reversal. Aid to elderly parents by their children in the classical extended family was buttressed by the maintenance of the power and authority of the parents in the extended family group. This was supported by the economic security of the parents through land ownership. In the modern nuclear family this is no longer true. Parents who are required to turn to their children for material aid are defined as dependent upon them. Further, this dependency is similar to the way in which their children were dependent upon them—for housing, financial aid, and convalescent care when ill. This seems like a clear example of role reversal. Children tend to become like parents to their elders, and elders become like offspring of their children. For many children and parents this may be a psychological threat, leading to and intensifying role conflict and personal problems.[17]

Conclusion

The authors have attempted to explore some of the sociological facets of personal problems of Jewish clients who requested help at a social agency in a large metropolitan area. Their findings are consistent with other studies which suggest that social-class differences between parents and children are not responsible for such problems. The modern American family fits neither the stereotype of the classical extended family nor that of the isolated nuclear family. While parents and children are expected to maintain close psychological and emotional ties, children are not expected to provide material support for their aged parents, especially if this may disturb the independence of their own conjugal family group. Since society has not yet provided adequately for all of our aged, there is a gap between the expectation and reality, leading to role conflict among parents and children, and personal troubles. Changing societal norms have also pushed many of the aged into dependency roles in their family of procreation, a reversal of the roles they played with their own children, intensifying conflicts which may already be present.

The findings of this study are meant to be only suggestive. The distinctive population and small sample considerably limit generalization.

Part

Group Processes and Relations

Introduction

Primary groups are among the most significant groups in social life. A large portion of every person's entire life is lived in one or another small group. Families, neighborhood groups, gangs, and treatment groups are among the significant primary groups affecting the lives of clients, and staff groups, professional groups, and peer groups are among the significant primary groups having impact upon professional helpers. The selections in this section are oriented toward achieving greater understanding of the group processes that affect the behavior of group members and of the group as a social system. (Selections on the family are reserved for the next section.)

The themes in small-group theory developed by Thomas in the first selection are based upon an overview of the significant conceptions and research findings in the field. Among the topics developed are the conceptions of the primary group, factors influencing membership in groups, disruptive and cohesive group forces, and six specific types of group influences upon individual members.

Although the group may have a significant impact upon the reactions of individuals, research on communication and small groups reveals the highly contingent nature of such influences. In the second selection, Litwak discusses the policy implications in communications theory, with emphasis on such group factors. Specific social-psychological processes through which the group operates are elaborated. Attention is given to these processes as they are mitigated by known facts involving the self-selectivity in listening, and in the interpretation of persuasive communications and of the findings that indicate that there is no necessary relationship between knowledge and action. Research and theory are reviewed here with an eye toward identifying practitioner policies and practices conducive to achieving effective change in group contexts. This analysis has implications for achieving change at the interpersonal as well as at the organizational, community, and societal levels of intervention.

The gang is a particularly important type of client group because of its relationship to delinquency, crime, addiction, and violence. Rafferty and Bertcher, in the next selection, analyze the formation of gangs among disturbed children between the ages of ten and sixteen in a day-care treatment institution. The authors found that the gang is best characterized as intermediate between a total absence of organization and the more complex, rule-guided division of labor characteristic of a well-defined group. The organization of such gangs was found to be based largely upon the establishment of a status hierarchy of physical dominance. The relatively primitive type of organization and its relationship to antisocial destruction and the direct gratification of basic needs are emphasized as the cornerstones for the cohesiveness of such groups.

In the final selection, Rothman discusses the important topic of minority-group status and its relationship to mental health and intergroup relations. Minorities such as Negroes, Puerto Ricans, Mexican Americans, Italian Americans, and Jews are groups whose identification involves a social-psychological relationship between the minority-group member's family, his minority group itself, and larger aggregates such as the majority group and the nation state. Starting with Kurt Lewin's influential thesis that the minority-group problems of Jews and others might best be mitigated by strengthening identification with the minority group, the author reviews research and theory to show that strong minority-group identification is not necessarily conducive to good mental health, to the reduction of an alleged self-contempt, or to favorable out-group attitudes and interrelationships. Among the significant policy implications is that positive out-group relations should be treated as problems in their own right and that, rather than to rely upon minority-group identification as a means to achieve favorable out-group attitudes and interrelationships, specific programs must be implemented toward these ends.

6 Themes in Small Group Theory

Edwin J. Thomas

Conceptions of the Primary Group

The literature of sociology and social psychology is filled with definitions of the small group. The definitions typically specify the characteristics which distinguish the small group from large ones, on the one hand, and assert the qualities which must be present to differentiate the small group from noninteracting aggregates, on the other hand. To illustrate problems posed by the proliferation of definitions of the small group, we review the refinements made in the conception of the primary group since Cooley's classical statement. Cooley said: [1]

By primary groups I mean those characterized by intimate face-to-face association and cooperation. They are primary in several senses, but chiefly in that they are fundamental in forming the social nature and ideas of the individual [p. 23].

Edward Shils has criticized Cooley's formulation because it does not distinguish between the essential elements of the primary group as contrasted with possible antecedent conditions.[2] Thus, the proximity of individuals in a face-to-face relationship and small size, Shils argues, are not essential properties but rather possible preconditions of the primary group. For Shils, the essential qualities are:

. . . a high degree of solidarity, informality in the code of rules which regulate the behavior of its members, and autonomy in the creation of these rules. The solidarity involves a close identification of the members with one another and with any symbols of the group which might have grown up [p. 44].

Abridged from "Theory and Research on the Small Group: Selected Themes and Problems," in L. Kogan (ed.), SOCIAL SCIENCE THEORY AND SOCIAL WORK RESEARCH (New York: National Association of Social Workers, 1959), pp. 91–103. Reprinted by permission of the author and the National Association of Social Workers.

In addition to eliminating possible antecedent conditions from the definition, Shils has taken out the possible effects of the primary group.

Broom and Selznick have conceived of the primary group as consisting of individuals who have *primary relationships* with one another.[3] Following a lead from Ellsworth Faris,[4] who years ago noted that the personal, spontaneous, and emotional relationships were more significant than whether group members were in a face-to-face relationship, Broom and Selznick identify three characteristics of the primary relation: (1) response to whole persons rather than to segments, (2) communication that is deep and extensive, and (3) personal satisfactions that are essentially noninstrumental for obtaining immediate utilitarian objectives. A group is primary to the extent that there are primary relationships among the members. One implication of this conception, if adopted, is that the group's solidarity, the informality of its rules, and freedom to create them would be either possible preconditions leading to primary relationships or possible effects of the existence of such relationships, but would not be essential qualities as Shils has regarded them.

What do these metamorphoses in the conception of the primary group show us, other than a rare instance of progressive refinement of a significant concept? They highlight the different directions for theorizing which follow from adopting one conception rather than another. The elements of one definition may be possible dependent or independent variables from the perspective of another. Viewed as a conceptual problem rather than as an empirical one, the most useful definition of the primary group is therefore the one which places concepts in a meaningful relationship to one another so that strong, consistent predictions may be formulated. If one's task is to delimit an area of discourse rather than to develop theory, the best definition is simply the one which differentiates a given subject matter from other topics.

If the view is taken that the problem is not one of definition but of fact, it is apparent that the above considerations are relatively unimportant. In one of the first papers reporting a study attacking the problem empirically, Cattell and his associates state: [5]

> It has astonished the present researchers that many serious writers are apparently prepared to indulge in verbally involved theories without having investigated the first essential fundament in these relations, namely, . . . the dimensions along which the attributes of any group are to be quantified [p. 331].

A more complete statement of the empiricist creed is that of Borgatta, Cottrell, and Meyer,[6] who state:

> When it becomes possible to arrange all collectivites on a meaningful set of orthogonal (independent) dimensions, the definition of groups and the discrimination of group from not-group become arbitrary

matters of convenience and not issues of critical debate. As a preliminary to any other objectives, this should save time and energy otherwise wasted searching for the best definition of *a group* by trying to
fit alleged groups in some definition. Similarly, this should circumvent
the problem of developing valid criteria for determining when a collectivity is a group and when it is not [p. 223].

In a preliminary attempt to order the dimensions of group behavior,
these authors compared the factors derived from three factor analytic
studies of groups, and found five converging factors. Using the names for
the factors given by Cattell and his associates, these were: (1) vigorous
unquestioned purposefulness, (2) immediate high synergy, (3) democratic explicit procedure orientation versus horde urgency, (4) high intrinsic
synergy, and (5) democratic *savoir faire* versus lack of self-possession.
There was lack of convergence of many factors found in the three studies,
some factors being found in one and not another. Although it is not presently possible to state what the dimensions of groups are, the empirical
approach to the problem offers promise of eventually isolating a set of
dimensions along which interactional fields may be ordered.

Another empirical approach to the problem has been formulated by
Donald Campbell,[7] who addresses himself to the problem of how to determine the "entitativity" of social aggregates. Campbell suggests that rather
than positing that social aggregates are *systems,* deserving of investigation
at a social psychological and sociological level, the aggregates should be
subjected to empirical examination to see whether they in fact have the
properties of systems. He suggests that the boundaries of possible systems
may be discerned by developing empirically based coefficients of common
fate, similarity, and proximity for the elements under scrutiny. The challenge of Campbell's approach is that if a given aggregate has low coefficients on these criteria, and thus lacks entitativity, then the next lower
level of system analysis might be used. The wisdom of Campbell's suggestion that groups having low entitativity be analyzed at the next lower
level is borne out incidentally by findings of Cattell and his associates. In
a study of the dimensions of formally leaderless groups in their first three
hours of existence, these investigators found eight group dimensions in
which population personality factors had high or substantial loadings, suggesting that the behavior of the members was primarily determined by the
pregroup personality of the component individuals. Another provocative
implication of Campbell's approach is that the "level" of theory used to
account for behavior might parallel the degree of entitativity of the group.
Thus groups with high entitativity might be analyzed largely at the group
level, groups with moderate entitativity with group *and* psychological
concepts, and groups having low entitativity with psychological concepts.

It is apparent that further research and thought must be given to the
issues discussed above. Those who take as axiomatic some definition of the
primary group and the assumption that groups are emergent phenomena

worthy of analysis at a sociological level should reconsider their beliefs in light of possible empirical solutions to such problems. Meanwhile, in the absence of pertinent factual guidelines, we must proceed as best we can.

The present task of reviewing selected theory and research on the small group requires that a definition of the small group be adopted which limits the topic to manageable proportions. For present purposes *it is convenient to view the small group as a collection of individuals who are interdependent with one another and who share some conception of being a unit distinguishable from other collections of individuals.*

Factors Affecting Membership in Groups

Individuals enter groups in essentially two ways: nonvoluntarily or voluntarily. Entry by ascription here concerns us less than voluntary entry. Voluntary group membership involves joining groups in order to be with particular individuals, such as a marriage partner or a given friend, or entering groups to obtain ends which only the group can mediate.[8] Because many factors affect voluntary entry, the problem is necessarily complex. We review some of these factors, giving particular emphasis to the theoretical basis of principles that have been formulated concerning selective entry.

There is impressive evidence that *propinquity* is one of the significant determinants of group membership. Stated simply, the principle of propinquity says that individuals who are close together physically come to like one another and form groups more often than physically distant persons. Thus marriage partners are much more likely to come from the same block, neighborhood, or area than from more distant locations.[9] Festinger, Schachter, and Back [10] found in a housing project that individuals living in the same courts, where they were likely to come into frequent contact with one another, were much more likely to like one another than were individuals who came from differing courts. Corroboration for the principle of propinquity was found in a study by Newcomb [11] of 17 students who lived together in a rented house. In attempting to set up roommate pairs who had minimal and maximal attraction, Newcomb assigned individuals to roommates on the basis of background information that was assumed to affect attraction among the members. The attempt to create minimal and maximal satisfaction was a failure, however, because the mean level of attraction between roommates from the very beginning of their living together through each of the succeeding 15 weeks was higher than for all nonroommate pairs.

The principle of propinquity is a descriptive generalization that explains little, even though it has the virtue of simplicity. Clearly something happens when people are spatially proximal and this something is that the individuals *interact* with one another. From the perspective of Homans' [12] theory, the principle of propinquity could be stated simply as follows: "Persons who interact frequently with one another tend to like one another [p. 111]." Homans' proposition is probably correct more often than it is incorrect, although he did not distinguish between conditions of interaction that could bring about dislike instead of liking. Nonetheless, viewing the problem as Homans does is an improvement over the principle of propinquity in two respects: (1) a more specific condition—interaction—is identified as a possible antecedent condition, and (2) a specific consequence of interaction is noted—attraction.

The concept of interaction, although manifestly useful, is in some respects global in the same way that the concept of propinquity is. In his work on the prediction of interpersonal attraction, Newcomb has attempted to formulate the psychological mechanisms involved in interaction. He stresses the principle of *reward and reinforcement,* making two assumptions: (1) that when persons interact, the reward-punishment ratio is more often such as to be reinforcing than extinguishing, and (2) that on the whole rewarding effects of interaction are more apt to be obtained from those with whom one interacts most frequently. To these principles Newcomb adds the notion of *generalization* along the dimensions of stimulus similarity. This principle states that if interaction opportunities are equal, you will tend to like the individual who most resembles some other person whom you have liked in the past. Thus the client comes to like the caseworker who most resembles a liked parent of the client. Newcomb observes that the contribution of the principle of generalization lies in enhancing the probability that interaction will follow with persons resembling those toward whom one is already attracted, thereby opening up opportunities for reward and reinforcement in the interaction.

When persons interact, two forms of *reciprocal reward* are possible according to Newcomb, both of which provide gratification as well as reinforcement of future interaction. The first is reciprocal reward derived from *common interests.* Thus if you like to play cards and someone else does also, both of you receive reward from playing as well as reinforcement for continuing to play. The second form of reciprocated reward concerns *complementary interests* (as opposed to similar ones) and these require interdependent behavior. For instance, an assertive spouse prefers a receptive mate to a similarly assertive one, as suggested by the findings of Winch in his research on marital compatibility.[13] One of the significant findings growing out of Newcomb's attempt to predict interpersonal attraction is that perceived similarity of attitudes tends, on the whole, to be highly associated with attraction; the more perceived similarity of attitudes between individuals, the more likely it is that they will like one another.

Whether or not one appreciates Newcomb's attempt to reduce the concept of interaction to principles of learning, it is clear that possibilities for increasing the accuracy of prediction are greater when one can stipulate whether the interaction is rewarding or is not. Interaction which is not rewarding would on the whole result in dislike or affective neutrality, whereas interaction that was reciprocally rewarding (which is seemingly what Homans assumes in his general hypothesis relating interaction to liking) would on the whole result in liking.

Newcomb's theory not only suggests the mechanisms which may be operating when people interact but also provides a basis for discussing the properties of groups that should be conducive to attraction. What properties of groups are likely to be rewarding? We need not speculate from scratch on this problem, fortunately, for ready-made in the literature is a formulation of the sources of attraction to the group based upon psychological assumptions largely identical with Newcomb's. In their chapter on group cohesiveness, Cartwright and Zander [14] propose two major sources of attraction to the group. The first is the group itself as the object of the need. Thus, one may be attracted to a group because he likes the people who are in it. Friendship and leisure-time groups would be examples. One may also be attracted to the group because he likes the activities available in it. Joining a card club or a bowling league would be examples. A special case of this source of attraction is when an individual joins a group because of the high value he places upon its purposes. Groups with objectives to bring about change or to improve civic conditions would be examples.

The second major source of attraction is the group as an instrument for satisfying needs outside the group. Many committee groups and work groups would be examples of groups joined in order to attain some end which can be satisfied only through membership in such a group.

Basic to Cartwright and Zander's formulation is a *need* theory which states that attraction to a group varies directly with the strength of the needs to be satisfied in it and the perceived probability that the needs will be satisfied. An individual should be most attracted to the group, according to this reasoning, when the needs satisfied by it are intense and when the perceived probability is high that gratification will ensue from membership. Both Newcomb and Cartwright and Zander stress reward in their theories, although Newcomb says nothing about expectancy of reward as do Cartwright and Zander. The support for the principles of learning is of course much stronger than for the need theory of Cartwright and Zander. While many would regard the theory of Cartwright and Zander as being axiomatic, and thus unnecessary to test, I think that this is a mistake. In fact, only partial support for the theory has been found in the few studies which relate to it. Two studies will be cited which bear on the theory. The first, by Ross and Zander,[15] investigated 169 women who resigned from a large private utility. These women were compared with a matched group who remained on the job. It was found that those who resigned from the company were much more likely than those who stayed to have received less gratification of needs for recognition, achievement, and autonomy. Consistent with the theory, this study suggests that the more the group (in this case a large organization) provides gratification of the needs of the members, the more likely it is that they will remain in the group.

Another aspect of the theory of Cartwright and Zander was examined in an experiment by Deutsch [16] on factors affecting membership motivation in groups. In this experiment, Air Force personnel worked on five problem-solving tasks under conditions of extremely high and extremely low probability of winning prizes. Contrary to Deutsch's prediction, it was found that the probability of winning the prize had no effect upon membership motivation. One recalls that Cartwright and Zander argue that the greater the perceived probability of reward in the group, in general, the stronger the attraction. Thus Deutsch's finding that membership motivation (which included a direct measure of attraction to the group) was not related to the probability of winning the prize fails to support this part of the theory. Although Deutsch argues that the prizes offered were not as attractive as he had hoped, the study is a direct test of the proposition of Cartwright and Zander and suggests the necessity for further experimentation on this part of the theory. Moreover, tests of the theory should be performed with problems of group entry as well as with those relating to remaining in the group.

Cohesive and Disruptive Forces

The topic of selective entry into groups leads naturally into the question of why individuals remain members of groups and what binds individuals together in the group. The nature of the group bond was given serious attention by many early thinkers. Durkheim argued that small, simple, homogeneous groups held together by what he called "mechanical solidarity" were able to exercise strong and impelling influences on their members. The stuff unifying groups was for McDougall "group spirit," for Freud "libido," and for Comte "consensus."

The most significant contemporary conceptualization of cohesiveness is that of Cartwright and Zander, who define it as the resultant of all forces acting upon members to remain in the group. Groups with high cohesiveness have forces acting on members which exceed forces to leave the group. Cartwright and Zander assert that cohesiveness is based upon the attraction of the members to the group.

Cohesiveness is significant because it is probably one of the major dimensions along which groups vary. Although it is not clear whether cohesiveness may be regarded as a unitary dimension in the factor analytic sense, factor analytic studies [17] have isolated dimensions which strongly resemble the concept. Many studies have shown that cohesiveness has relatively potent effects upon the behavior of group members. We turn now to some of these effects.

Groups high in cohesiveness appear to be more conducive to the *security* of the group members than groups low in cohesiveness. In a study of 228 industrial work groups, Seashore [18] found that there was an inverse relationship between the anxiety workers experienced in connection with their work and their group's cohesiveness. A factor analytic study by Cattell et al,[19] provides indirect support for the relationship between cohesiveness and security. In a factor labeled "immediate high synergy vs. low motivation" there was found to be loading on the following: low degree of frustration, high degree of we-feeling, low amount of nervous tension, low level of worrying and suspicious anxiety, and lack of paranoid suspiciousness.

A second effect of cohesiveness is *pressures toward uniformity*. Festinger [20] has proposed that pressures toward uniformity vary directly with the cohesiveness of the group. Since the initial work on this problem by Festinger and associates,[21] in which evidence was presented consistent with this hypothesis, more direct corroboration has been obtained. For example, Back [22] created groups high and low in cohesiveness and found that in the highly cohesive groups there was a more intense rate in the discussion and more frequent attempts to exert influence than in the less cohesive groups. The significance of pressures toward uniformity is that the amount of change in opinion resulting from receiving a communication will increase directly with the magnitude of the pressures.[23] Although this related hypothesis was supported in a laboratory experiment by Festinger and Thibaut,[24] using two group discussion problems, an experiment by Downing [25] showed that conformity to conceptions of autokinetic movement did not vary with the cohesiveness of the groups. This latter finding, if supported in further research, suggests that Festinger's hypothesis concerning pressures toward uniformity may not apply to all matters of opinion.

The hypothesis concerning pressures toward uniformity applies to performance as well as to opinion. In an experiment to determine the relationship between cohesiveness and performance, Berkowitz [26] created high and low cohesiveness as well as high and low group standards for performance. Performance was found to be highest in the groups with high cohesiveness and high standards for performance, and lowest in groups with high cohesiveness and low standards for performance. Seashore's [27] study of industrial work groups also indicated that the cohesiveness of the groups was related to the uniformity of production. Thus cohesiveness is directly related to the uniformity of performance. The *level* of performance, however, appears to be determined largely by the group's standard.

A third major effect of cohesiveness is *resistance of the group to disruption*. Although one may assert this effect axiomatically, since it follows from the conception of cohesiveness, its significance is sufficient to give it special attention. Resistance to disruption may be considered with respect to external as well as internal threats. Pertinent to resistance to external threat is an experiment by Pepitone and Reichling [28] in which groups with experimentally created variations of cohesiveness were exposed to threat from the experimenter, who acted in an unjust, arbitrary, and insulting manner. It was found that the highly cohesive groups expressed hostility toward the experimenter more directly and more frequently than the less cohesive groups. In interpreting the results, the investigators argue that cohesiveness enables the group better to overcome restraints that impede the removal of threat or that impede the movement of the group toward its goal.

Experiments done on the ability of groups to resist internally instigated threat have been concerned largely with the capacity of cohesive groups to bring about pressures on members whose opinion is deviant from the others in the group. The pressures toward uniformity, in turn, may bring about change of opinion of the deviant, change of opinion of those who are not deviant, and rejection of individuals who hold deviant opinions. Schachter [29] set up an experiment which largely excluded the first two possibilities, allowing only for the possibility that the deviant might be rejected from the group. It was found that the highly cohesive groups more often rejected individuals taking a deviant position than did groups low in cohesiveness. Schachter observed, however, that to the extent that the members of the group are highly dependent upon the individual holding a deviant opinion, they will be less likely to reject him from the group. Another alternative to rejecting the deviant, especially when his opinion is valued, may therefore be acceptance of the individual as a deviant group member. [30] Such a deviant may of course be less threatening to the group and, indeed, may change the opinions of others. The evidence thus far clearly supports the contention that rejection is one of the consequences of deviation in highly cohesive groups, although much work remains to be done on other ways in which cohesiveness may be related to coping with internal threats to the group.

The research on the antecedents of group cohesiveness has been less extensive than that concerned with the effects. The frequency of interaction among group members should increase member attraction (assuming that the interaction is rewarding rather than punishing) and thereby increase group cohesiveness. The study by Festinger and his coworkers done in a student housing project, the study by Newcomb conducted also in a student residential setting, and a study by Bovard [31] performed with students in a classroom situation, all showed that persons who interacted frequently came to be more attracted to one another than students who interacted infrequently. Interdependence among individuals is another probable antecedent of group cohesiveness, but only if the interdependence facilitates rather than hinders the need satisfaction of members. Deutsch [32] found in his study of cooperative and competitive groups that the members of cooperative groups were more friendly and evaluated their group and its products more favorably than the members of competitive groups. In an experiment I conducted on facilitative interdependence, [33] it was found that cohesiveness increased with the extent that interdependence was facilitative for the group members, although the relationship for this dependent variable was not strong. It is probable also that a common threat, if a group solution to the difficulty is possible, may increase the group's cohesiveness.[34, 35] The results of these studies are generally consistent with the theory of Cartwright and Zander, but like their theory of attraction to the group there is also evidence which fails to support parts of the theory. For instance, in a study by Pepitone and Kleiner[36] concerning the relationship between threat and frustration and group cohesiveness, it was found that a reduction in the expectation of status loss tended to increase cohesiveness, but that an increase in the expectation of gain did not produce an increase in cohesiveness, as would be predicted.

Much less research has been done on the disruption of groups than on their cohesiveness and integration. The few investigations that relate to the problem of disruption indicate that a reversal of some of the conditions that bring about cohesiveness tend to bring about disruption of the group. Thus Sherif and Sherif[37] found that established groups of young campers having a high proportion of ingroup sociometric choices could be destroyed by placing the boys who were not previously friends into recomposed groups in which members interacted frequently in performing common tasks. After a period of time, the newly created groups were tested again sociometrically and were found to make almost all of their friendship choices within the newly composed groups, ignoring former friends who were members of the original groups. This study suggests that by destroying a meaningful basis of interaction among individuals, the solidarity that existed previously will dissolve. Less extreme conditions tending to disrupt groups have also been studied. Thus an unstable reward structure,[38] frustration,[39] and group defeat,[40] to varying degrees, may threaten the existence of a group.

Threat to the group may be disruptive as well as integrative, as we have seen. Under what conditions will threat to the group be disruptive? A significant clue comes from an experiment by Hamblin[41] who exposed some groups to an insoluble crisis by changing the rules of an involving game so that no group solution for the crisis could be achieved. These groups, as compared with control groups which performed uninterruptedly with known, consistent rules, displayed markedly decreased integration, as shown by less mutual aid among members and by high self-oriented need behavior. Hamblin suggests that a crisis will weaken the integration of groups to the degree that the group is unable to meet it with a collective solution. But if the group can mediate a solution to the problem, he claims that then the threat will most probably increase the group's integration.

Although much remains to be learned about group disruption, studies of groups under stress (in which complete disruption was not accomplished) suggest minor forms of disintegration which might contribute to a group's eventual total disruption. Symptoms of disintegration that have been noted are: (1) self-oriented need behavior, such as interpersonal aggression,[42, 43] (2) escape from the field,[44] (3) development of factions,[45] and (4) dislocation of the group's status structure.[46]

Some Effects of the Group on the Individual

Broadly speaking, the small group is significant because it performs important functions for the individual, for the large organization, and for society generally. The mediating function is double edged, in that small groups may or may not facilitate the attainment of individual goals, of organizational or societal objectives.[47] Implicit in this view is the assumption that the small group has a profound impact upon the individual. One of the contributions of research on the small group is that it uncovers some of the specific ways in which the behavior of individuals is affected by group membership, thus clarifying and giving more substance to the claims of social theorists who have long maintained that groups either mold individuals directly or set a general pattern for behavior.

Some of the specific types of influences upon individuals which arise in small groups are discussed, focusing largely on problems of conformity. Space does not permit complete appraisal of the large literature on this topic or a discussion of controversial issues. It has been convenient in ordering these effects to distinguish *passive* from *active* influences. Passive influences are those that tend to arise regardless of the intentions of group members, whereas active influences arise out of the more self-conscious intentions of individuals. Some of the effects discussed, of course, involve both types while others are more clearly one or the other. The more passive influences to be discussed below may exist in groups with minimal integration, whereas the more active influences presuppose some interaction and interdependence among the members.

Passive Group Influences

The first effect is *social facilitation,* a phenomenon noted by F. H. Allport [48] in his early experimental work on the effects of working together versus working alone. Stated simply, social facilitation refers to the effects upon individual performance and thought arising from the sights and sounds of others doing the same thing. These effects are a releasing of reactions for which the individual is in readiness and increasing these reactions once they have been initiated. Individuals working together as compared with individuals working alone performed more vigorously on thought and motor activities, although the quality of work was not improved in the "together" situation. It is noteworthy that Allport's "together" situations did not involve interaction; subjects merely sat together reacting in a parallel fashion to some nonhuman stimulus. The stimulation of others in this situation was regarded as contributory rather than direct.

A second passive influence may be identified as *taking the role of the other.* When an individual is in a social situation, he tends to react toward himself in the same way that he thinks others would react to him. The flavor of this type of influence may be garnered from one of G. H. Mead's [49] passages on the self. He said:

The individual experiences himself as such, not directly, but only indirectly, from the particular standpoints of other individual members of the same group, or from the generalized standpoint of the social group as a whole to which he belongs [p. 138].

Research on the small group has suggested some of the specific ways in which behavior is influenced by taking the role of the other. We refer to such effects in three areas: individual judgment, public opinion, and change of opinion.

In Allport's early work on the nature of the group effect he found that individuals made less extreme judgments when in the group as compared with making such judgments alone. He compared the extremeness of subjects' judgments of odors and the heaviness of weights when alone as well as in a coacting group situation. The reluctance of individuals to make extreme judgments when sitting together as compared with the alone situation was an unwitting process involving the avoidance of extremes of all kinds. Allport summed up his conclusions as follows: "To think and to judge with others is to submit oneself unconsciously to their standards. We call this *the attitude of social conformity*" [p. 278].

A similar effect was noted by Gordon [50] in a study of opinions toward Russia of members of a cooperative. This investigator obtained measures of private and public opinion, and of the individuals' conceptions of what the group's opinion was. The significant finding was that the individual's opinion, as given openly before others, tended to fall someplace between his private opinion and his conception of the group's opinion. In short, the person's conception of the opinions of others appears to restrain him from stating a public opinion which is as extreme as his private one, although the public opinion tends generally not to correspond perfectly with the conception of the public opinion.

The above findings suggest that if an individual is actively impelled to take the role of the other, he will more likely reflect the opinion of the other than if he can take this role passively. Janis and King [51] conducted an ingenious experiment which shows that this is probably correct. In one condition of their study the subjects were asked to read orally a statement reflecting a position which was not their own, and in another they were asked to give an informal talk from an outline calling for the sincere advocacy of an opinion that was not their own. Opinion changed more for subjects who actively played a role than for those who passively gave the oral statement.

Referring to these effects as the result of taking the role of the other is by no means an explanation. However, it is a convenient way to label influences in groups arising from one's conception of what others think. It would appear that the impact of what others think affects opinions and judgments more strongly when the individual is made acutely aware of the conceptions of others, as in the studies by Gordon and Janis and King, although the conceived reaction of others affects thought and judgment with only the minimal arousal of such conceptions.

A third type of influence derives from the *norms of groups of which the individual is not a member*. Such groups are passive influences in that the individual does not interact with members nor do the members attempt to achieve the particular individual's conformity to their norms. Such reference groups can serve comparative functions for the individual.[52] Thus the norms and standards of the group serve as a comparison point against which the individual's behavior is evaluated. This type of effect can be illustrated by findings (unpublished) from one of the studies I conducted in the Aid to Dependent Children Program. In a questionnaire phase of the study aimed at obtaining information about the training needs of ADC workers, we inquired of the workers as to whose standards they were most likely to use in evaluating their performance: the profession of social work, the clients whom they served, informed lay citizens, or supervisors in public assistance. We also obtained information on the extent to which the workers experienced role conflict on the job, the poles of the conflict being the requirement that they determine eligibility versus requirements to provide time-consuming services to families. It was found that the workers who experienced the most intense role conflict were those who used as their point of comparison the profession of social work; those who used their own supervisors in the organization for comparison experienced the least conflict. Of particular note is that none of these workers was in fact a member of the professional association, yet some of them apparently adopted the standards of the profession for evaluating their work. To the extent that they used these standards, they experienced role conflict in the organization.

Active Group Influences

When the individual is a member of a group which serves as a point of reference for him, the group norms are likely to be more visible and more effectively reinforced than when the individual is not a member of a reference group. Moreover, the norms of membership groups are probably more potent than are the norms of nonmembership groups.[53] We turn now to the more active forms of influence; these are found typically in groups of which an individual is a member.

The first is labeled *informational social influence*, following the terminology of Deutsch and Gerard.[54] These investigators define informational social influence as influence to accept information obtained from another as *evidence* about reality. The classic experiments of Sherif [55] and Asch [56] have dealt with this type of influence. In Sherif's experiment the perception of autokinetic movement for naïve subjects is influenced by the standard established by the subjects collaborating with the experimenter. In Asch's experiment judgments of the length of lines may be influenced by a unanimous but incorrect majority opinion. Both studies involve situations in which the judgments of others establish social validation for one's perceptions of the physical world. Deutsch and Gerard note the following concerning this type of influence:

> It is not surprising that the judgments of others (particularly when they are perceived to be motivated and competent to judge accurately) should be taken as evidence to be weighed in coming to one's own judgment. From birth on we learn that the perceptions and judgments of others are frequently reliable sources of evidence about reality. Hence, it is expected that if the perceptions by two or more people of the same objective situation are discrepant, each will tend to re-examine his own view and that of the others to see if they can be reconciled [p. 635].

Informational social influence may occur, as in the Sherif and Asch experiments, with only a rudimentary group situation. In these experiments the subjects sat together in *ad hoc* groups, did not interact freely, and were dependent upon one another only in their judgments of the experimental stimuli. When members of groups interact freely and are interdependent, *normative social influence* is likely to arise. This second type of influence has been defined by Deutsch and Gerard as an influence to conform to positive expectations of another, where such expectations refer to those whose fulfillment by another leads to or reinforces positive rather than negative feelings and whose nonfulfillment leads to the opposite, to alienation rather than solidarity.[57] The experiments by Festinger and his coworkers referred to earlier are examples of studies in which normative social pressures are operating. In these studies there is typically some established or inferred group standard, free interaction among members, active exertion of influence upon members to conform to the standard, and implicit or explicit punishment for failure to conform. The pressures toward uniformity which we have discussed earlier are assumed to arise when there is some ambiguity as to the nature of the physical world (a condition which existed in the Asch and Sherif experiments), and also if group locomotion toward a goal may be facilitated by uniformity within the group.[58] We shall not take up the presumed causes and effects of pressures toward uniformity because we have referred to some of this material in the earlier discussion.

The final active type of influence to be discussed is *interpersonal power*. Social power has been relatively neglected in social psychological inquiry, although some sociologists and political scientists have long had an interest in power on a broad scale. Most of the studies of interpersonal power conducted in the last ten years have followed Lewin's view that power is potentiality to exert influence. Lippitt, Polansky, and Rosen,[59] in their pioneering studies of power in a camp setting, define social power as "the potentiality for inducing forces in other persons toward acting or changing in a given direction" [p. 39]. An implication of this conceptualization is that it stresses *potential influence* rather than accomplished influence. The single term influence has customarily been reserved for actualized power.[60]

The study by Lippitt, et al., referred to above, demonstrated the utility of this concept for tentatively ordering influence phenomena and set the stage for much subsequent research on the problem. These investigators studied the power attributed to children in summer camps in relationship to the behavioral success of the campers in attempting to influence others. The attributed power of the campers was found to be positively related to the contagion of the power figure's behavior to others, and to the frequency and success of intentional attempts to influence others. There was also an initial examination of the characteristics of the campers which were associated with attributed power, noting for example that high-power boys in these settings tended to have physical superiority and to be knowledgeable of campcrafts.

In work on social power investigators have distinguished between power and the personal properties of individuals which contribute to their ability to influence. Thus, it is asserted that personal properties of individuals, such as intelligence and physical prowess, when *valued* become *resources* and thereby increase the likelihood that the possessor of resources will be able to induce others to change. Indirect support for the proposed relationship between resources and power was found in a study by Gold,[61] who studied the resources of elementary school children with respect to expertness, coerciveness, and social, emotional, and associational qualities. Gold found that almost without exception the children with high attributed power were characterized as possessing these resources as compared with those with low attributed power.

One consequence of viewing power as being based upon personal resources is that new directions are opened up for theory and research on the differential effects of types of resources in social influence. Following along this line of thinking, French[62] has distinguished five possible bases of interpersonal power: *attraction, expertness, reward, coerciveness,* and *legitimacy.* We review briefly some of the speculations and research relating to the differential effects of influence based upon these types of resources.

Attraction power is power based upon the attraction of the influencer to the person being influenced.[63] It has been speculated that attraction power, when exerted, will result in relatively independent change which is not contingent upon the presence of the influencer after the initial influence attempt. Both covert as well as overt change are presumed to follow from the exertion of attraction power.

Expert power has been conceived as ability to influence based upon the superior knowledge of the influencer.[64] Like attraction power, expert power, when exerted, is assumed to result in both private and public change. Unlike attraction, however, the resource of expertness may be consumed, or used up, because it can often be transferred from the influencer to the person being influenced, and therefore eventually cease to be a basis of influence.

Reward power is power based upon the influencer's ability to mediate rewards for the person being influenced.[65] Raven and French have speculated that reward power, when exerted, tends to result in public change of opinion, although continuation of the change is assumed to be dependent upon the continuation of the reward.

Coercive power is power based upon the influencer's ability to mediate punishments for the person being influenced.[66] As one would expect, coercion has been found to result in public rather than in private change.[67]

Legitimate power is power based upon the individual's belief that the influencer has the right to prescribe his behavior or opinions.[68] In an experimental test of the hypothesis that legitimate power would bring about more private and public conformity than nonlegitimate power, Raven and French [69] found that only part of the hypothesis was supported, that is, that legitimate influence would bring about more private conformity than nonlegitimate influence. Public conformity was found to be equally great under legitimate as well as nonlegitimate conditions.

Research on problems of social power has just begun. Only a few of the significant predictions formulated by theorists have been experimentally corroborated, and even though there is presently more theory than research on this problem, many conceptual problems remain also.

7 Policy Implications in Communications Theory with Emphasis on Group Factors

Eugene Litwak

The Problem and Purposes

This paper is designed to discuss developments in communications theory which may be of some use to the field of social work. There is one major limitation, i.e., there is no single theory of communication but rather an impressive array of theories ranging all the way from elaborate general systems [1] to *ad hoc* "middle range" propositions.[2] What characterizes these theoretical concepts is that they suffer either from a lack of logical persuasiveness or systematic documentation. As a consequence, any attempt —such as this—to derive policy implications from communications theory must be accepted with proper caution. The particular concepts selected can only be viewed in the nature of good bets. They cannot be accepted as being completely or thoroughly verified by the studies in the field.

There are many aspects of communications theory which could be studied. The nature of this paper will be delimited and will concentrate on two areas; first, a concentration on the problem of persuasion; and second, an emphasis on the role of the group in communications theory. These limitations are based on both the author's area of competence as well as on his estimate of what may prove of interest to social workers.

General Findings from the Initial Period of Research

In the initial stages of research in the field of communications it was assumed that man was basically a rational person. All that had to be

Abridged from EDUCATION FOR SOCIAL WORK, PROCEEDINGS OF THE SEVENTH ANNUAL PROGRAM MEETING (New York: Council on Social Work Education, 1959), pp. 96–109. Reprinted by permission of the author and the Council on Social Work Education.

done was to broadcast the facts of the situation—i.e., provide knowledge—and the individual would presumably look at the facts, evaluate them, and then act accordingly. Hyman and Sheatsley, in summarizing the literature on this subject,[3] pointed out the incorrectness of this particular position. Three findings seemed to occur in a universal enough form to dash any hope that communications theory might rest on the assumption of the rational man. These findings were:

1. Self-selectivity in listening
2. Self-selectivity in interpretation
3. No necessary relation between knowledge and action

In order that these points may be clear, each will be briefly illustrated.

Self-Selectivity in Listening

Self-selectivity in listening means that people will rarely listen to messages which present a viewpoint which differs from their own. Educational programs on television are unlikely to raise the educational level since generally the only people who listen to them are those who are highly educated.[4] Information about the United States Bill of Rights is unlikely to sway people very much since the people who tend to listen to it are those who are already favorable to the United States.[5]

Self-Selectivity in Interpretation

The findings of empirical research further undermine the assumptions of man's rationality by revealing that, even where individuals holding opposing views are reached, the message very seldom converts them. This is true because of the process of selective interpretation. Individuals take the facts and select only those which are consistent with their previous opinions and ignore the rest. Or they tend to reinterpret the message so that it has a different meaning than that which was intended.

No Necessary Relationship between Knowledge and Action

Even if a message avoids the first two pitfalls, there is some evidence indicating that people who are exposed to and accept facts which conflict with those they originally held will not necessarily act on these facts. Thus, Wiebe, in a study of the Kefauver-Costello hearings, was able to show that people listened, that they absorbed the message and were emotionally involved, and yet they did not act.[6] Bogart demonstrated that a person's knowledge about America could be increased without his opinion being changed.[7] Janis showed that increased knowledge about tooth decay did not necessarily lead to increased efforts to take care of one's teeth.[8]

There were three reactions to these empirical findings. The major reactions, which dominated communications theory until recently, were that formal means of communication are not as effective in converting people as they were thought to be,[9] and, second, that a much more complex theory of personality than the simple assumptions of rationality is needed. A third reaction, which has recently developed and to which the major portion of this paper will be devoted, is the systematic introduction of the concept of the group into communications theory and research.[10]

Group Structure and Communication Processes

If, in fact, it is true that the group mediates any communication, then it becomes apparent that any theory of communications must include some theory of group processes as well. What is of greatest importance to us today is that the analysis of group might provide clues to communications policy which might otherwise not occur when the analysis is made on the individual level alone.

The recognition of the group as a factor in modern communications theory rests on several empirical findings. In various studies, where the investigators sought to determine which of several media were most influential in the communications process, they were surprised to discover that other people, rather than formal media of communication, were the source of information. Where the majority of individuals receive their messages via their group memberships, such attributes of the group as its manner of enforcing norms, the position of the individual in the group, the individual's reference orientation toward the group, may all affect the nature of the communication and must be incorporated into any theory of communication.

The Social Psychological Process through Which the Group Operates

Once it is granted that the group plays a role, it can then be argued that the group is influential because it defines reality to the individual. This reality may develop through two processes—direct or instrumental.[11] The first section of this paper will be devoted to pointing out how previous studies which discussed self-selectivity, selective interpretation, and action without knowledge might be reinterpreted in terms of group reality processes. The second part of the paper will be devoted to the policy implications of these reinterpretations.

REALITY PROCESS—DIRECT AND INSTRUMENTAL. The viewpoint that the group provides *direct reality* for the individual has been conceptually expressed by such men as Cassirer, Mead, and Sullivan.[12] The basic assumption which is clearly illustrated in Cassirer is that there is an infinite set of sense data to which an individual may be exposed. The criteria for selection from this infinite set are the categories of language. The categories of language are, in turn, defined by the group and vary with different groups. Thus, what one group thinks to be evil another thinks to be good, and what is insignificant for one group is of great importance to another group. From this point of view it is quite clear why individuals who are exposed to a message tend to interpret it to suit their prior opinions. They may not have caegories of speech which permit them to make alternative interpretations. Or their categories of observation may be such as to make alternative explanations seem trivial. If this is so, it should be clear that any attempt to alter these people must involve altering their groups as well—i.e., the development of new concepts or the change in the weights of importance assigned to old concepts involves not only changes in the individual but also in his group.

The instrumental view of reality assumes two things: first, that there are many people who, because they belong to several divergent groups or because they are newcomers in the group, hold concepts which are different from those of any particular group with which they are affiliated. The second thing implied by instrumental processes is that most of man's goals must be met through cooperation with other people. Granted these two assumptions, the instrumental point of view argues that individuals will tend to conform to the group's values because they view such conformity as maximizing their chances for achieving their individual goals.[13] In this case, as in the case of direct reality, the investigator would have to know something about the group before he could assess how the individual would react to any given communication. In order that the functions of group reality may more clearly be understood, the previous discussion, which indicated that communication is empirically characterized by self-selective listening, self-selective interpretation, and action without knowledge, can now be re-analyzed in terms of the two processes of reality.

REALITY FUNCTIONS AND SELECTIVE INTERPRETATION. The evidence presented by Katz and Lazarsfeld,[14] that group reality may lead to selective retention of information in communication, may be reviewed and elaborated. There is evidence that individuals are very much influenced by the group in their perception of events.

There have been several studies which indicated that, when the individual holds an opinion different from one held by the group, he tends to change it to conform to the group. For instance, in political behavior, Berelson, Lazarsfeld and McPhee have shown that the persons most likely to change are those who hold views divergent from those of their families or friends.[15] Lewin and his group were able to demonstrate, in a series of areas dealing with food, changes in occupational evaluation, and changes in child care, that the greatest change occurs when an individual knows that there is explicit group support for such a change.[16]

GROUP REALITY FUNCTIONS AND SELF-SELECTIVE LISTENING. If it is assumed that the group provides the categories of reality, then there is a good explanation for selective listening as well as for selective interpretation. A hypothetical illustration from the controversy over the [1958] economic recession will help to clarify this point. There was considerable difficulty among economists in determining whether it was a recession or an inflation. Once there was some agreement as to whether there was a recession, there was considerable disagreement as to the correct procedure to cure it—cut taxes for the businessman and stimulate production or cut taxes for the worker and stimulate consumption. What typifies these disputes was the fact that they involved experts and that these experts had a legitimate area of dispute.

With the experts unable to decide among themselves with any degree of confidence, it is plainly nonsense for the average man to think that he can make a decision after listening to both sides of an issue.

In such an instance, one of two processes might operate. Once the average man knows that he cannot decide the issue on the merits of the case, he must then decide upon the nature of the people involved or the immediate consequence to his group. Thus, the working class man in such a situation of ambiguity may well decide that the man who is telling the truth is the one who suggests immediate tax benefits for the working class man. First, it is of most direct relevance to his own problem and his group's survival, and secondly, such men may have in the past looked to the interest of his group and been acknowledged by the group as experts. If this much of the argument is granted, it is then reasonable to assume that the rational man who seeks further information will tend to be attuned to the one who advocates a position which is favorable to his group.

Even where individuals feel that they are experts in the field and are in a position to decide certain issues, they may still attend only to the communications which are consistent with their group norms. This is true because of the second notion of reality—the instrumental one. Thus, in the South, the white person who attends an integrationist meeting or who purchases integrationist literature stands an excellent chance of becoming a social and economic outcast. Not only is a person punished for listening to messages which are hostile to the group, but he is also rewarded for listening to information which is favorable to the group. One study, which highlights the effects of the group on self-selective communication, is that by Katz, Menzel, and Coleman.[17] This study of doctors is especially interesting because it deals with scientific knowledge, an area which is generally least susceptible to group influence.

GROUP REALITY FUNCTIONS AND THE LACK OF RELATION BETWEEN KNOWLEDGE AND ACTION. Two of the three empirical generalizations have been dealt with which have emerged from early empirical work in communications theory. Attention should now be turned to the third point—

that communications which change states of knowledge do not necessarily lead to changes in action or opinion.

From the point of view of group reality functions there are two things which may be said about the lack of relation between knowledge and action. First, categories for gathering information may be considerably different from categories of expressing opinion or actions. Unless the communication expresses both, the listener may be in no position to take action. Second, opinions and actions are generally much more public than the processes for gathering information. Therefore, a group might exhibit differential tolerances for these processes.

To make this clear, Wiebe's analysis of the Kefauver-Costello hearings might be further explored. He points out that, in order to effect any change in the crime situation, it is necessary for the listener to engage in common group endeavors which would be highly organized.

From the instrumental point of view of reality it can be shown that the attainment of knowledge is generally a much more private form of behavior than the expression of opinion or action. Thus, a person might read literature or hear messages which indicate that the Negro is not biologically different in any significant manner from the white man. His fellow group members may not be aware of this, nor may they care, as long as this information is not translated into an opinion that there should be no segregation, or into an action which supports integration. Because of this differential group pressure in knowledge and action, it is quite possible that people may change their states of knowledge without changing their actions or their opinions.

Group Reality, Selective Listening, and Their Policy Implications

Thus far the discussion has been of a diagnostic character. The attempt has been made to show that major empirical findings—self-selectivity in listening, self-selectivity in interpretation, and the divorce of action from knowledge—can be explained in terms of group reality functions. If this diagnosis is to have any value, it should lead to some distinctive communications policy, by stating some of these policy implications. Wherever possible, communications policies which have some empirical support have been used, though none of these policies has been definitively verified. They can only be justified by the fact that some policy will be made and these considerations are the best bet, granted the limitations of research.

Since the concern is with policy in all that follows, a separate analysis must be made for groups which are hostile and those which are friendly to the communication. Different polices may well be recommended depending on which of these groups the communicator faces.

Self-Selectivity and Structure of the Message

Where an individual is communicating to a hostile group, the first problem he generally faces is getting the attention of the group. There is a study by Hovland, Lumsdaine, and Sheffield which indicates that, when one is dealing with people who are hostile to the message, it is best to include both sides of the issue—their point of view and the position to which it is desired to convert them.[18] A study by McGuire indicates that people are most likely to accept a negative message if it is preceded by a message they view favorably.[19] It is suggested in a study by A. R. Cohen that people are most likely to change if they are first emotionally involved before they are given informaiton, rather than given information and then emotionally involved.[20]

If all these principles are considered together, they would seem to provide evidence that, where one is seeking to convert a group and at the same time avoid the dangers of selective listening, one should initiate the communication with a message which is central to the group and with which they can positively identify. Once the group's attention is caught, one should turn to messages which may not be favorable to the group. The same principle applies to the nature of the communicator. In one experiment the communicator, who identified himself as being sympathetic to the group's views but in fact delivered a message which was not favorable, was able to change opinions much better than the same man with the same message who identified himself as hostile to the views of the group.[21]

When dealing with groups which are favorable, a somewhat different policy is called for. Where the group is uneducated, the evidence presented by Hovland would seem to indicate that an insistence on the positive aspects of the message with no mention of the other side of the argument seems to be called for. For the educated group, the two-sided message is again called for.

Self-Selectivity, Selective Interpretation, and Group Crisis

If the group plays a major role in enforcing self-selectivity and selective interpretation, then it is of some advantage to communicate messages which are unfavorable to the group when the group norms are least likely to be enforced. Berelson, Lazarsfeld, and McPhee presented evidence in election studies that people are most likely to diverge from their friendship and family groups in their vote intention between elections and most likely to converge during the heat of the campaign.[22]

This leads to one of the greatest paradoxes in modern communications behavior. It is generally at periods of crisis, when it is most difficult to reach and convert people, that the biggest efforts are made to do so. For instance, it is most difficult for Republicans to reach and convert Democrats during the campaign period preceding the election, yet it is at this period that they make their greatest efforts. The same thing can be said about psychological warfare. It is during periods of war scare that our propaganda agencies are most likely to receive funds for additional broadcasts, but it is generally during these periods that they are least likely to reach or make converts. (This is a historic problem in family counseling where the social worker seeks to communicate on matters of reconciliation when the family group is most heavily geared to resist such messages.)

If the foregoing analysis is correct, the best time to reach and change political opinions of people is in the period between campaigns. It is at this point that their group norms are weakly enforced.

In contrast, a completely different picture emerges if one is attempting to reach a group which is friendly. It is precisely when the group is under greatest threats from the outside that it is likely to speed up messages which support the norms. Thus, the Democrat is much more likely to get an audience from Democratic groups during election time than between elections. Furthermore, his messages tend to reinforce the norms of the group.

In short, when the communicator seeks to convert members of a hostile group, he is most likely to encounter the problems of selective listening and interpretation if he broadcasts his messages during periods when the group is under attack. This is the worst time to communicate. Just the opposite is true for those seeking to reinforce group norms.

One further suggestion might be made which derives from the view that group enforcement of norms plays a role in the communication procedure. Where the group is truly well organized and hostile to the communicator, he might spend his initial efforts in attempting to break down relations between the group members. This may have nothing to do with the message he will eventually send. It is merely a way of weakening enforcement of norms which are barriers to an eventual message.

Self-Selectivity—Authority Structure

Aside from the question of the kind of message and the conditions under which the message should be broadcast, there is a real question as to the group member to whom the message should be directed. The initial assumptions regarding group structure were simple—there was a leader and there was a group. For those who have messages which are hostile to the group the answer seems somewhat clear. The leader is usually the major communicator in the group. If the message could be drawn to his attention, he could do a much better job of spreading the information than an outside communicator could. However, this is a deceptively simple assumption. Though the leader is most likely to hear messages from the outside—hostile as well as friendly—he is also most likely to support the group norms. He may, therefore, perform a role with regard to hostile messages which is analogous to the lightning rod and lightning. He attracts hostile messages but is least likely to channel them on to the group.

These considerations suggest that, when one is seeking to reach a group which is unfriendly, it may well be that messages should be addressed to isolates or to people who are in the process of leaving the group. They are not as likely to be influential in disseminating the message through the group but they are more likely to do so than the leader.

Cohen, in a study dealing with status, power, and mobility differences, revealed other aspects of group structure which affect communication behavior.[23] Thus, he provides some evidence that people, who live in a society where there is an overall norm for mobility and who find their mobility curtailed, are likely to pass on hostile or irrelevant messages to their superiors. Such people would be much more open to communications which are hostile to the group norms.

Where the communicator faces a friendly or indifferent group his problem is quite different. He should actively seek out the leader and permit the leader to spread his messages. This point was dramatically illustrated in a study by Leighton. He studied the Japanese who were put in relocation camps during the war.[24] He reported that it was not until the camp authorities utilized the natural Japanese community leaders that messages were properly communicated.

In short, the principle stressed is that groups can be structured in many ways. The question as to who will be most susceptible to communication depends on the nature of this structure. Therefore, one of the first tasks of the communicator is to attempt to diagnose the pertinent structure of the group.

Group Reality, Selective Interpretation, and Policy Implications

The policy discussions thus far have been listed under the rubric of selective listening and selective interpretation. For the most part, the same considerations which hold with regard to selective listening also hold with regard to selective interpretation. Yet there are some processes that seem more directly related to problems of selective interpretation.

Selective Interpretation and Multiple Group Affiliations

Once the communicator has the group's attention, he must determine the extent to which the group is characterized by people with multiple group affiliations. According to some theorists there are two things of importance which characterize modern urban societies. First, division of labor leads to multiple group affiliations, and, second, there is frequently a disparity in values among the groups. Usually societies provide institutional saeguards to keep such groups isolated.

Where the communicator is faced with the problem of converting a hostile group, his task is then to break down these safeguards whenever possible. In doing this the communicator may succeed in converting the hostile group by pointing out that other groups of which the target is a member would approve the message. This point is clearly illustrated by the analysis of the German army made by Shils and Janowitz.[25] They revealed that the morale and the will to fight of the German army were very directly related to the primary group cohesion at the platoon and company level. So powerful was this group force that the soldiers fought on even though they knew the war was lost. The Allied propaganda to surrender never persuaded the individual soldier until the primary groups were destroyed by virtue of rapid wholesale replacements. However, Shils and Janowitz pointed out that the one factor which did tend to weaken these groups was the information that the families of the men were suffering as a consequence of the war. In short, any propaganda which could highlight the difficulties of the family would put the soldier under cross-pressure and in turn heighten his vulnerability to surrender messages.

Pretty much the same analysis can be made if one considers that groups usually have multiple value systems. In this connection, Tumin showed that segregationists in the South frequently have a conflict between their educational values and their segregationist policy or between their segregationist policies and their value of law and order. Communications which highlight these conflicts are likely to dissuade a considerable number of people from segregationist policies.[26]

Needless to say, where the group is friendly just the opposite considerations hold. The communicator does everything to prevent hostile multiple group affiliations from becoming evident to the respondent. Or he tries to segregate conflicting group values within a single group.

Selective Interpretation and Group Participation

Where the investigator has the attention of the group, there seems to be some evidence that he can produce change in the group by allowing the group to participate in the decision and communication process. Thus, many studies [27] produce evidence showing that, where individuals can participate in the communication process, they are likely to feel committed to the message. This may be due to the fact that group participation is just another way by which individuals learn social reality. The general point which these studies suggest is that, where possible, the communicator should encourage members of the group to participate in the diffusion of the message.

Action Prior to Learning

The last kind of empirical generalization from communications research is that action is not necessarily related to knowledge. Festinger has developed a theory of dissonance which illustrates this principle and may well have some group implication.[28] He points out that, where people's public actions are different from their private opinions, there is a tendency for the private attitude to change to coincide with the public action. As such this is a theory which would seem to indicate that knowledge need not be related to actions.

Action Prior to Knowledge—Dissonance Theory

There is one study in particular by Brehm dealing with the *fait accompli* which had very interesting implications for communications which seek to convert. Brehm induced pupils to eat vegetables which they had privately indicated that they disliked by offering them a slight reward.[29] After they had eaten the vegetables, he then proceeded to inform one group that the information would be passed on to their mothers. To the other group he said nothing. By telling the pupils that their mothers would be given the information, he increased the discrepancy between the private attitude and the public action. Moreover, he did it in a way not anticipated by the pupils. Brehm then shows that it was those very students whose public and private attitudes differed the most who changed their private opinions to conform to the public actions.

If this type of information can be generalized, it would suggest that a person wishing to convert the group should seek some group action which has some implications which are negative to the group values. He should develop the maximum possible counter-group implications of this action, then should broadcast it as widely as possible. By doing so he presumably will set up some dissonance which would lead to change. The communicator who wants to support the norms should be careful not to broadcast any communications which show that a group's actions have gone counter to the norms. He should concentrate on the group actions which certify the norms. Messages which point out errors as a lesson of what not to do might actually boomerang on the communicator.

What, of course, characterizes this dissonance theory is the viewpoint that frequently action, not knowledge, produces change.

*Action without Knowledge—The Public Nature of
Action and the Private Nature of Knowledge*

Where the group is unfriendly, the communicator should, as much as possible, concentrate on individual action and involve the group as little as possible. For instance, on the segregation issue in the South, those seeking integration may advise their people to vote against the segregationists. This is a very private kind of action.

Where the communicator is trying to enforce the norms of the group, just the opposite advice might be offered. Thus, in the case of the Kefauver-Costello hearings it was suggested by Wiebe that people did not act because action involved the creation of a social organization and the communication provided no information on this problem. Thus, the communication increased knowledge about the infamy of crime without showing any line of action. The communicator must, therefore, stress actions in terms of institutional and organizational solutions rather than merely stressing information or private action because the group is friendly to his point of view.

Long Term Change and the Sequence of Communication

Much of the foregoing analysis operated under the implicit assumption of short term immediate change where the communicator has only a short opportunity to reach his goals. However, some entirely different considerations arise where the communicator can reach the group studied over long time periods. One of the most important ideas in this connection is the idea of sequence of communications. This can be illustrated in a hypothetical consideration of the attempt by the Chinese to convert prisoners of war during the Korean War.

Since groups are important determinants of reality and the Chinese were seeking to convert individuals, the first series of communications might have been aimed at producing group disorganization. To publish rumors of group members betraying each other, to publish rumors of invidious treatment between different strata of men, keeping communications between group members to a minmium, were all ways to create group disorganization. This could have been done without once seeking to broadcast any propaganda in favor of communism. Once the groups were fragmentized, then propaganda might be broadcast. Those who seemed most receptive to this message could then have been put into common groups and thus reinforce each other. When a sufficient number of such groups would have been formed, then the more recalcitrant members could be introduced into the group and the group-reality process used to socialize the newcomers. Once the majority of the prisoners were incorporated into a new group, all communication should be addressed to encouraging group cohesion.

The general point which should be made is that the communicator must plan the sequence of policies he will use and this will be a function of his problem and the group he is trying to reach.

Conclusion

First, developments in communications theory have emphasized the role of the group. Second, three empirical generalizations—selective listening, selective interpretation, and action without knowledge—can be reinterpreted in terms of group reality functions. Granted this, certain communications policy decisions seemed to follow depending on whether the group was unfriendly or friendly. These policy decisions had to do with (1) the structure of the message and the rational nature of group norms, (2) the group's relation to the outer society in terms of threat, (3) the internal structure of the group and to whom the message should be sent, (4) the extent to which multiple group affiliations or multiple values existed in the group, (5) the need for a group structured so as to permit all to participate in the communication process, (6) the fact that fortuitous or divisive group actions can be used to create dissonance and change, (7) the need to differentiate between actions which are organizational and nonorganizational and the need to recognize that categories for learning are frequently more private than categories for opinion or action, and (8) the need to take into account the sequence of action depending on the state of group organization.

It should be pointed up again that there is no pretense that the above lines of policy have a basis in a unified theory. As a consequence, future work might very well reveal they are not exhaustive or exclusive. They represent, as was pointed out, a deliberate delimitation of the topic to emphasize the group aspects of communications theory. There is empirical evidence which illustrates most of these mechanisms, but generally none of the evidence can be considered as definitive.

If these policies are to be related to problems in social work, there are some obvious implications. Problems in social work must be formulated to highlight the group aspect as well as the traditional personality variables. The social worker must be sensitive not only as to how he can help the individual to correct the problems but how the social worker can use the individual's group—family, friendship, work group—to aid him or at least prevent them from working against him. This means the social worker should become proficient in the diagnosis of group structure.

8 Gang Formation *in Vitro*

Frank T. Rafferty and
Harvey Bertcher

Since Thrasher's initial study, *The Gang,*[1] there has been interest in the sociological analysis of gangs found in underprivileged sections of large cities. Gangs are usually described as informally organized small groups. The gang has been of special interest because of its relationship to delinquency, crime, addiction, and violence. Special techniques have been developed by social group workers to attach themselves to gangs and to convert them to clubs with a different set of goals and values. Natural history accounts of existing gangs have been made through the process recording of these workers. These studies are limited by several factors: 1) observations are restricted by the requirement of the worker to be accepted by the gang; 2) the gang is studied *in situ,* i.e., as part of a neighborhood structure and tradition; 3) the worker usually begins his study at a midpoint in the gang's history with only a word-of-mouth account of its origin; 4) psychiatric studies of gang members are usually not available. The purpose of this paper is to report observations on the formation of gangs in what amounts to a laboratory setting, i.e., *in vitro.*

From 1958 through 1961, a program was under way exploring the treatment of poor prognosis adolescents and pre-adolescents between ages of ten and sixteen by the use of a day treatment program utilizing semiclosed groups, interacting five hours daily, five days a week over a period of approximately nine months.[2] A radical manipulation of the social structure of the institution was made to focus on the spontaneous development of social organization in disturbed children.[3] One important phase in the development of group structure was the formation of an informally organized group that had all the characteristics of a gang. This process took place openly and its dynamics were easily observed. The gang members were individually well known and each had complete psychiatric studies.

Abridged from JOURNAL OF NERVOUS AND MENTAL DISEASE, 137 (1963). 76–81. This study was supported by Special Project Grant OM-104, National Institute of Mental Health, U.S.P.H.S. and the University of Utah College of Medicine Department of Psychiatry. Reprinted with the permission of the authors and the journal. Copyright © 1963. The Williams and Wilkins Company, Baltimore, Md. 21202 U.S.A.

The following is a summary of observations on the formation of one of these gangs, the Cobras.

The Cobras' development began after approximately 450 hours of group interaction. Prior to this the group had gone through a stage of development characterized by active and passive aggressive behavior in an erratic, chaotic pattern. Gradually regular patterns of interaction had developed in which a hierarchal order of dominance, had been established. David W., aged 14, was the oldest, largest, strongest boy in the program with good athletic skills. Until recently he had been extremely withdrawn, conforming, and avoided group contact. Such behavior prior to admission had caused a serious learning problem, and David W. was a complete non-reader and functionally inadequate.

Jim R. had demonstrated the most uncontrolled, vicious, antisocial behavior of all the youngsters from early in the group history. He was physically large, bright and capable of good academic work but seldom productive. He was unskilled in games or sports. Only fear of physical hurt controlled him.

At this time a new boy was admitted. David B. was an excessively conforming, brilliant student, an exceptional athlete with seriously obsessional parents. He had become clinically depressed about six months before, reached a point of early schizophrenic disorganization and had been hospitalized. He had responded with a remission leaving a rigid school phobia that resulted in his admission to this program. As a new admission and as an over-controlled boy, David B. had started at the bottom of the dominance hierarchy, but his upward progress was rapid. Soon these three boys were constantly together and engaging in testing and anti-authority behavior. Jim R. supplied ideas and David W. carried them out. For example, David W., as a feat of daring, was able to crawl out a two-story side window, swing over a drain pipe and reach the roof of the front porch. Neither Dave B. nor Jim R. were able to follow.

A week later, the following typical behavioral sequence took place. The three boys were in the gameroom with the group worker. Jim and Dave B. were playing Canasta with the worker. David W. silently sat apart. The worker commented on his silence and lack of participation and invited him to join the game. David W. almost immediately got up and left. David B. quit playing and followed. In a moment Jim R. scurried out after them. The order of departure was directly related to status hierarchy.

The three boys began to avoid the morning class situation. They would remain downstairs and covertly smoke. A week subsequent to the above, the following occurred. Whitey and Mark, two boys of still-lesser status, were working on the school newspaper with the teacher. David W. and Jim came in, interfered and effectively stopped all productive effort. The five boys then proceeded to leave the school grounds, climbed on the roof of a nearby nursing home and caused some property damage.

David W. became more openly destructive each day. The more defiant toward authority he became, the more apparent and accepted his leadership status became. The staff first learned of the name "Cobras" in a conversation between Dave B., Jim and Mark and the group-leader, in the gameroom. David W. was present but sat apart silently. The purpose of the gang as defined by the boys was to smoke, throw snowballs at passing cars and to plan the day's activities. David W. terminated the conversation by leaving and the others followed. A short time after this Whitey was observed trying to suggest various delinquent activities to the group, but was ignored and withdrew to read.

The Cobras now met daily in the garage until class was over. Then they usually returned to the main building in a provocative way. Several days after the above, the lock on the gameroom was broken and the room was "captured" by David W. and Mark (a child of lesser status aspiring for membership). The door was barricaded with furniture. Jim and David B. were admitted, and the room was released only after a small fire was started in a chair. The gang was led to attack in another direction by Whitey, who broke into the basement and began scattering some cotton stored there.

Mark, the lowest-status member, had become extremely excited over the past few weeks and was being used by the others to initiate and carry out destruction. The staff decided that he had to be hospitalized for his own protection. Jim and Whitey, in protest, again broke into the basement and began flooding it by opening the hot water heater. The staff had to set limits at this point. Dave B. responded. David W. and Jim and Whitey could not stop and were confined in the Detention Home over the weekend.

The Director met with the boys in detention, encouraged their interest in a club and suggested that they make use of the group worker to help them. It was also suggested to David W. that he had a responsibility as Cobra presndent to keep their behavior under control. At the beginning of the next week, club jackets were discussed by David W. with the group worker. Whitey brought a catalogue of jackets. David W. did act as a positive controlling authority and kept horseplay under control. In particular, he kept Jim R. in check. Jim R. had clearly moved into the number-two spot, displacing Dave B. The latter had apparently lost status by not going along with the ultimate in vandalism. He now became the most openly defiant in testing the staff.

At this time the boys, with Whitey providing ideas, began to talk about fixing up the garage as a clubhouse. Whitey was the most intelligent boy and was most able in planning and completing a task. But he was a poor, frightened fighter. As a result he constantly occupied the lowest status and served as a supplier of ideas and materials such as matches, razor blades, cigarettes, wine and such. Mark was the young-est and smallest, but most ferocious, and had gained position by sheer force of his hostility toward the staff.

Whitey, Jim and David W. began work cleaning up the garage. Mark and the group worker arrived on the scene. There was a discus-sion of whether the worker could stay. Jim said that it was their club-house, and they didn't want the worker. The latter supported the state-ment that it was their clubhouse and started to leave. Jim then said he was only kidding, and the worker's presence was not questioned after this.

Mark was invited to join, and he immediatly began to think of ways to remove two old pumps from the concrete. The group goal was soon lost, however, in his desire to sell the pumps for scrap iron.

Whitey continued to look for new things to do such as sweeping and moving old doors. He frequently verbalized rules which were ignored by the others. Jim floated around with a hammer using it to smash locks rather than to build or repair. David W. (the president) was quiet, passive, did very little. He soon lost interest and left the area. Mark and Jim got in a fight over the hammer, Whitey went to get David W. saying, "You'll have to kick Mark out. He's been violating rules. He's breaking things, and we don't want him." By now Mark was furious and began throwing rocks at everyone.

With minor variations, the above process was repeated three times with three different groups of youngsters in essentially the same social setting. *The basic conclusion derived from these observations was that a gang is an intermediate stage in the evolution of social organization from a point of no regularity of social interaction to that of a well-defined group.*

A gang is not a mere collection of individuals in the same area acting on the basis of individual motivation. On the other hand, this gang was not a stable group in a strict sense. A group can be defined as two or more individuals interacting in relationship to common motives, manifesting differential effects on the participants, resulting in the formation of an organization consisting of roles and a hierarchal status; a demarcation from non-members; and the development of values or norms which regulate relationships and activities of consequences to the group.[4]

Common motives were not the reason for organization. But the gang could be observed looking for motives for existence. The gang structure developed out of a previous stage of social organization characterized by chaotic, purposeless aggression between individuals that resolved itself into a hierarchy based on physical dominance. Motivating forces for the development of the dominance relationships were obscure. This form of social behavior has been studied most intensively in animals. Presumably a dominance relationship reduces conflict and functions as a principle in the distribution of scarce items such as food, territory, mates and the like.[5] To some extent this appeared true in this situation. The dominance relationship did control access to certain geographical territories, to tools, the bathroom, adults. But these items could hardly be considered as scarcities. The program was amply supplied with equipment, space, food and people. *Indeed the drive toward dominance seemed to come from the same organismic sources as does aggression.*

After the dominance relationship was established, there seemed to be a vacuum of goals. The primitive gang was not capable of a coordinated effort to perform tasks of even a minimum degree of complexity, as in the attempt to fix the garage. With only a dominance social structure without differentiated roles, any task which required a division of labor was not possible for the gang. This was true even though a few individuals had been previously capable of complex role differentiation. David B., for example, had played team sports with some distinction. Whitey had performed acceptably in a Scout Troop. However, Jim R. and David W. were almost devoid of group role skills.

As the primitive gang sought goals it turned as a gang to struggles with the staff group and individuals for territory and dominance. Examples of this were the escape of the gang from territories such as school and the gameroom where the staff was dominant, to fringe areas such as garage, attic and porches where staff dominance was minimal. On occasion the gang captured staff territory, as in the gameroom incident. Defiance of staff dominance as a gang was apparent in the many acts of destructiveness which seem purposeless unless viewed as a test of staff dominance and motivation for group formation. This behavior occurred concomitantly with various degrees of individual acceptance of care, affection, authority, and instruction from staff members. In none of the children did this occur to a normal degree. In Jim R. such behavior was almost totally absent.

Of the thirty children studied, only one child failed to participate to some extent in gang behavior as here defined. This means that in the particular social structure described, gang behavior occurred in the children of varied ages, both sexes, various psychiatric diagnosis, different degrees of health, and varying individual dynamics. The child who did not participate was a thirteen-year-old boy who had had a diagnosis of childhood schizophrenia since the age of four and had been treated unsuccessfully in a residential program for four years prior to admission to this unit. After ten weeks in the program he seemed isolated from the others by his confusion, disorientation, delusions and bizarre behavior. He was removed because of fear of increasing his disorganization.

Another childhood schizophrenic with bizarre appearance and behavior, mannerisms and overwhelming anxiety, but with more intact intellectual ability, was able to participate and achieved a good clinical result. Several children with a more adult type of depressive and/or schizophrenic symptoms lost their symptoms relatively quickly, as did David B. Both withdrawn and acting-out children participated. Withdrawn children had to be drawn into the behavior by the acting-out child, but as in the case of David W., could become very active, influential gang members.

It seemed as if gang formation was the resultant of the interaction of two complex variables: 1) psychopathology in the youngsters; and 2) the absence of firmly defined, enforced social structure. Comparison of this setting with reports from other programs such as training schools and adolescent units in state hospitals would seem to support the idea that disturbed youngsters can be handled without the manifest formation of gangs provided there is a sharply defined and rigidly enforced social structure with peer-group authority kept to a minimum. There is always a tendency to gang formation and most often a covert delinquent subculture.[6]

The terms psychopathology in view of our findings of lack of correlation with specific diagnostic syndromes must be redefined. Since gang behavior for us was defined as the relative absence of complex role differentiation, we looked for this as an ego characteristic in our patients. We found an absence of complex role differentiation provided we accepted two categories of absence. In one category role differentiation was absent as a result of lack of enculturation, e.g., Mark and Dave W. In the other category, role differentiation was absent as a result of an aggressive rejection of a significant object relationship, e.g., mother or father. In order to preserve a consistent hostile relationship to the object all identifications with the object with respect to roles and values must be denied. In effect, the child rejects a role model and consequently rejects the repertoire of roles available through identification with the model. In most situations we dealt with a mixture of the two types in varying quantities. This seems to be a distinction that could resolve the problem of distinguishing between the normal or social delinquent and the sick or mentally ill delinquent.

The social structure of the setting which permitted development of gang organization was characterized by an atmosphere of plenty. There was no deprivation of any significant degree. A social structure was present and visible. Participation in it was suggested and encouraged, and required performance in a role context, acceptance of authority of staff person, a reciprocity of acceptance by peer group, and the like. The one crucial absence in this setting was that of conformity pressure. During each five-hour session the children were offered an opportunity to engage in the full range of academic, recreational, arts and crafts and relationship activities. But they were free to choose their activity, their spatial orientation, their inanimate and human object orientation with a minimum of influence by adult authority. A child could reject any activity or relationship. Hostility was accepted to the greatest extent possible without counter-hostility. Destructiveness was ignored whenever possible except to repair. There were no sanctions administered. Physical punishment, isolation, deprivation of privileges or love were never deliberately used until late in the gang history. In order to prevent misunderstanding, it must be stated that these observations in no way suggest that conformity pressure and strict application of sanctions are a solution to delinquency. The transition of a child from a dominance social structure to a role-oriented structure is a more complicated process.

The clinical material presented was derived from the early stages of the gang formation. As the history of the gang continued, a process of development of roles in relationship to simple tasks was observed. Role is used to define mutually expected behavior between two or more individuals as their functioning becomes differentiated in the performance of a common task. It is the writers' impression that Kobrin's [7] description of gang structure refers to a later stage, when some role differentiation is present yet the organization around physical dominance and territory is still the most influential social structure. The delinquent tradition of some neighborhoods seems related to the long-term self-perpetuation of this type of organization. This would imply that the achievement of a role-oriented social structure is a slow, difficult process. The experience with these gangs indicated that roles developed very slowly, spontaneously. Influence of the staff members was a vital factor in the development of appropriate role functioning.

When the constant care-giving aspects of the staff began having a significant effect, the staff was forced, and chose, to develop dominant roles in a variety of ways. Aggression and hostility by the staff were kept to an absolute minimum. But invariably at this stage some one or more gang leaders would be expelled from the program. In this year's activities David W. and Dave B. were returned to the public schools and later Jim R. was surrendered to the courts to enter the State Training School. After the exclusion of the gang leaders, the gang continued with an established dominance order and the same primitiveness of role organization. There appeared a new acceptance of dominance by the staff, however, and the help of the staff was utilized in learning and developing roles.

In addition it should be pointed out that David W. and Dave B. were discharged at the height of their antisocial activity to the public schools. Their antisocial activity did not continue in the new setting, however. Dave B., after a few apprehensive days, returned to his premorbid, superior social and academic performance and finished the year at the top of his class after spending fully two-thirds of the year without functioning in the student role. David W. was able to remain in school for a few weeks, but then returned to his previous withdrawn state and refused to attend school.

It is frequently stated in the literature that peer-group relationships are of more significance to adolescents than relationships to parents or adults. This concept is obviously only partly true. It recognizes that in surface behavior the adolescent will very often take his peer society as a reference group rather than his parents. Psychotherapy has of course demonstrated repeatedly the significance of the parental relationships even when they are being denied. The present study adds another dimension. Adults live in a social structure oriented to extremely complex roles, particularly in middle-class socioeconomic groups. The ability to function in a complex role seems to be an internalized skill, learned as a result of the social shaping of biological drives. A teenager is expected to have a certain repertoire of these role skills, but many children arrive at this age without having learned them. Such children then find it difficult to participate in the social structure of the community. They seek more simple, directly gratifying tasks which are of interest only to other adolescents. At other times he must function on a more primitive level of social evolution and relate to other individuals according to principles of territoriality and dominance. For the most part significant adults are not available for this kind of interaction. The dominance patterns manifested by the hostile-aggressive father or teacher without the acceptance of reciprocal roles only stimulates increased conflict and escape of the adolescent from the adult's sphere of dominance. Domination by another adolescent is more thoroughly established because of the sharing of directly gratifying activities and because there is less social inhibition in the other adolescent to directly exerting his dominance.

Conclusion

Experience with this project has led to the conclusion that the phenomena of gang formation and gang membership have significance far beyond the implications of the existence of gangs in slum neighborhoods. The gang is apparently a transition phase in the evolution of social organization. When disturbed individuals are brought together as strangers and permitted to interact intensively, the early stages of organization are based on primitive principles including aggressive testing and the establishment of physical dominance. Only much later do definitive social roles based on a division of labor develop. The gang is intermediate in this process. A status hierarchy based on physical dominance is the basic organization of the gang. The gang then seeks common motivating tasks which are simple enough to be accomplished by this primitive type of organization. Antisocial destruction and direct gratification of basic instinctual needs are the easiest goals that provide cohesiveness. The gang, operating on the theory that might makes right, is at a different level of social organization than that of the rule of law governing the majority of the communiy. The setting of legal limits, the enforcement of law, the judgment and punishment of the offender, represent a very complex differentiation of roles to perform a community function. It would be our hypothesis that many individuals have internalized patterns of social organization much more primitive than this and literally function within an alien subculture.

9 Minority-Group Status, Mental Health, and Intergroup Relations

Jack Rothman

A member of a minority group growing up in American society has a difficult adjustment to make. He must develop a suitable mental attitude and pattern of social relationship with regard to both his minority ingroup and the outgroup comprising American society as a whole. Such a coming to terms, including a determination of which of these two major reference groups should receive his chief loyalty, is not an easy task for most individuals. Stonequist, in his classic study of marginality, describes the individual in such circumstances as "poised in psychological uncertainty between two (or more) social worlds; reflecting in his soul the discords and harmonies, repulsions and attractions of these worlds." [1]

The way the individual comes to view his affiliation with the minority ingroup is undoubtedly a key factor in resolving his state of tension, and has been increasingly recognized as such. However, whatever mode of identification the minority individual strikes in regard to his ingroup must be seen, as is being intimated here, in the context of his ability to participate in the broader society, and in the context of favorable interrelationships among all groups making up that society.

A multitude of sociologists and psychologists have addressed themselves to this subject. They have produced recommendations ranging from heavy emphasis on ingroup participation and identification [2] to almost complete disregard for the ingroup along lines of assimilation into the majority culture. [3]

Perhaps the most prominent and widely accepted of the theoretical

Abridged from THE JOURNAL OF INTERGROUP RELATIONS, **3** (1962), 299–310 and from JOURNAL OF JEWISH COMMUNAL SERVICE, **37** (1960), 91–93. Reprinted by permission of the author, THE JOURNAL OF INTERGROUP RELATIONS, the JOURNAL OF JEWISH COMMUNAL SERVICE and the National Association of Intergroup Relations Officials. Support for this research was provided by a Harry L. Lurie Research Felllowship of the Council of Jewish Federations and Welfare Funds.

formulations produced in this area is that of Kurt Lewin. Lewin used the Jewish group as the basis for his writings, and he maintained that in order for the Jewish child to form a positive self-image and to be able to relate to outgroup members, it was first necessary for him to develop a clear and firm sense of identification with the minority ingroup. While the Lewin formulation is extensively discussed and referred to and, incidentally, conscientiously put into application within some minority groupings, its exact structure and rationale are not often carefully examined. It is the point of view of this writer that upon critical analysis the Lewin thesis will be found lacking in a number of vital respects. Further, until this is recognized, work in this area will be unnecessarily retarded. This paper, accordingly, will consist of two major portions: (1) a factual summarization of the Lewin formulation and; (2) a critique of the formulation.

The Lewin Thesis

For a somewhat detailed statement outlining what Lewin actually postulated in connection with minority-group adjustment we will draw upon his book, *Resolving Social Conflict,* which is a collection of five previously published articles conveying the essence of what Lewin had to say on the subject.[4] Lewin himself, in different articles, varied the development of a particular theme and the stress on various elements within the theme. In the interests of a meaningful analysis and discussion it will be necessary to pull the materials together and fabricate them into some kind of cohesive whole which seems to be consistent with his underlying approach.

Lewin begins by noting that minority group members often are found to suffer from insecurity, fear, inferiority and maladjustment (pp. 169–170; page numbers refer to Lewin, *op. cit.*). This occurs because the individual in large measure accepts the stereotypes which the majority culture holds toward his group (pp. 193–194). Further, since belonging to the minority group causes disadvantages with regard to meeting social and psychic needs and improving conditions of life, some individuals—negative chauvinists—attempt to disaffiliate and move outward into the majority culture. They are *blocked* by the outgroup in this, and as a result build up frustration and finally aggression.

Since the majority group is omnipotently powerful and prestigeful this aggression is turned inward upon the self and upon the minority group (pp. 191–192). Tension is further built up by the fact that in a modern and relatively free society the boundaries between ingroup and outgroup are not clearly demarcated and rigidly enforced. As a result, the individual becomes highly conflicted in regard to whether he should attempt to slip over the sociological boundary line into the realm of the majority group. This conflict accounts for much of the restlessness and extremes of behavior found among minority-group members (p. 156).

Within any minority-group member, Lewin goes on, there are a composite of forces, some of which attract and tie him to the ingroup, some of which propel him toward the outgroup (p. 190). Whether the individual remains in the ingroup or leaves it depends on the *balance* of these forces. When the balance of forces is on the negative side, that is, when those directed toward the outgroup predominate, the individual experiences self-hatred, based on hatred of his group. The group represents for such a person a block to the attainment of his goals for the future. "It is easy to see how such a frustration may lead to a feeling of hatred against one's group as the source of that frustration (p. 189)."

In the face of self-hatred and as a result of numerous counterbalancing forces, the minority-group individual may find himself in a marginal position. These individuals, "eternal adolescents," become confused and tense, unsure of their moorings and of their sense of belonging. Typically modern man belongs to a multiplicity of groups and plays many roles without undue difficulty. It is only when one is marginal in the sense of having no feeling of belonging to any group that the situation becomes psychologically intolerable (p. 146).

Lewin's Solution

With this theoretical foundation laid, Lewin proceeds to offer his remedy concerning what can be done to safeguard the minority individual against poor mental health. In the first place, and most important, the parents should provide for the child "a clear and positive feeling of belongingness" to the minority reference group (p. 183). This is so because "the group to which a person belongs is the ground on which he stands, which gives or denies him social status, gives or denies him security and help (p. 174)." The child should be encouraged to identify with the minority group at an early age so that he will be prepared to cope adequately with prejudice and rebuff. The parent should not underplay or deny his belonging to a minority group since he will learn about it soon enough and it should not come as a shock to him. This is similar in principle to preparing an adopted child for acceptance of his actual status through providing him with knowledge about his true place in the family in his earliest years (p. 183).

Lewin maintains that one cannot approach this problem through elevating the general self-esteem of the child because he will suffer discrimination and rejection not as a human being, but as a member of a minority group. He should be aware of his group belongingness and the meaning of this in terms of what to expect from some members of the outgroup (pp. 171–172). In connection with this, the child should not be induced to combat prejudice through exemplary personal behavior. This only places an additional burden on him and increases psychic tension. It is his group membership, not his specific actions, which leads to the rejection directed against him. Unusually high-level performance may only serve to intensify resentment and rejection by the outgroup (p. 162).

The ultimate solution of the problem, Lewin holds, will be achieved only when the status of the minority group is elevated to that of the majority group. "Only then will enmity against one's own group decrease to the relatively insignificant proportions characteristic of the majority group's (p. 198)." Until this sociological parity of groups is achieved the minority-group member must be given a strong sense of ingroup identification and pride in order to counteract potential feelings of inferiority.

Through emphasizing and enhancing the minority group, intergroup relationships may be helped to improve. It represents a step in the direction of placing the social status of the groups on a somewhat more even level. Further, an individual who emphasizes his minority ingroup through identifying firmly with it will ward off harmful stereotypes and find emotional strength within the group. Hence, he will be secure and at peace with himself, and as a well adjusted individual will be able to relate well to the many individuals and groups in the outside culture. "Neither a group nor an individual that is at odds with itself can live normally or live happily with other groups (p. 214)."

Furthermore, members of the majority group respond in a more friendly manner to those minority-group members who demonstrate clearly their true status than to those who hide it. One who emphasizes his ingroup affiliation makes the situation clear from the start and does not put majority individuals, who generally frown on full assimilation, in the uncomfortable position of having to reject him for his attempt to steal over the line separating the two groups. The Gentile, says Lewin, will be suspicious of the unidentified Jew and will feel safe only with the Jew who is firmly identified and acts out this identification in clear behavior patterns (p. 182).

Wide Acceptance of the Thesis

This, then, constitutes a telescoped representation of Lewin's point of view on minority-group status. It is important to note that Lewin conducted no empirical studies of the propositions enumerated. Still, Lewin's work is viewed as the final word in this area by some social scientists and within some minority groups. In the Jewish community, for example, Lewin's writings have come to embody quasi-official doctrine for the group in orienting itself to the training of the young and to intergroup relations.[5] The preeminence of the Lewin formulation and its pervasiveness as social theory as well as social policy makes all the more compelling a realistic evaluation of its merits.

Critique

Group Identification and Mental Health

1. There is no evidence establishing a clear positive relationship between minority-group identification and good mental health. As a mat-

ter of fact, quite to the contrary, Radke and Lande after a penetrating investigation in depth of sixty Jewish college students reported: "Comparisons of scores on the (Psychological) Insecurity scale by subjects high and low on Group-Belongingness Scales showed no significant differences between the two groups." [6] Various other investigators have reached similar conclusions.[7, 8, 9, 10]

Self-Hatred and Belongingness

2. Accepting Lewin's premise that minority-group members suffer from self-hatred, it is not altogether clear that the highly identified suffer less or in a way more conducive to good mental health. We would here postulate that self-hatred is to a large degree pervasive and generalized in a disadvantaged minority group—which is in actuality not out of keeping with Lewin's point of view. When negative stereotypes toward a minority exist and flourish in the broad society, it is an inevitable consequence that these stereotypes will be internalized to a greater or lesser degree by the broad base of members of the minority group. Social scientists from various disciplines have demonstrated that an individual growing up in a particular society incorporates the norms and values which impinge on him. The work of Bogardus [11] reveals that there is a rather stable hierarchy of psychological acceptance and rejection of socio-cultural groupings within American society. His studies further show that all groups, including minority groups, more or less adopt the common rating scale, with the exception that the minorities raise the relative standing of their own particular group to some degree.

Radke and Lande found that expressing anti-Semitism and avoiding identification as a Jew correlated positively in the same individuals with the clearly opposite reaction of Jewish chauvinism. The authors conclude:

> These findings indicate that the individual who "thinks" his group is best also accepts many of the stereotypes directed against it and "hates" it; and on occasion, resists identification with it. This suggests that the ethnocentric person, who must utilize so much of his energy in demonstrating that his group is best, is really not convinced that his group is worth belonging to, and achieves no more genuine satisfactions from the group than the egocentric person achieves from the self.[12]

Brennman's [13] study of Negro women, Radke's [14] study of a Jewish fraternity and a Zionist group, and Meyer Greenberg's [15] study of Jewish students at Yale all reveal similar results—negative and positive ingroup attitudes residing side by side in the same individual. Psychoanalyst Antonia Wenkart offers a useful psychological explanation for this phenomenon. She indicates that opposing tendencies—differences, contradictions, polarities—exist and coexist in the normal personality and that they are beneficial as an aid in attaining self-acceptance.[16] The individual must eventually accept himself for all the things he is and not deny any genuine facet of his being. Did not Walt Whitman express the same thought succinctly in "Song of Myself?"

> Do I contradict myself
> Very well then I contradict myself
> (I am large, I contain multitudes).[17]

Role of Family Group

3. Assuming that mental health or personal security is a key factor in determining intergroup attitudes and relationships, is not the family group of greater moment in developing positive mental health than the minority group to which one belongs? Lewin himself suggested this when he wrote, "One of the important constituents of the ground on which the individual stands is the social group to which he 'belongs.' In the case of a child growing up in a family, the family often makes up his main ground." [18] In their study of outgroup preference patterns, Brodbeck and Perlmutter [19] discovered that self-acceptance is an important factor to consider regarding such preferences. But they go on to assert that self-acceptance itself is determined primarily by relationships with parents.

In supplement to the above, we would hold that the child's basic self-image, his fundamental sense of security, may be fashioned in its major dimensions prior to the point at which minority group considerations enter the picture. Every investigation of the subject shows that children do not become aware of belonging to a minority group until the age of three and one-half or four at the earliest.[20] Richard Trent in his study of self acceptance in Negro youth develops the point as follows:

In order to reach mature, healthy adulthood, the Negro child in America must first accomplish . . . (a) acceptance of himself as a person; (b) acceptance of himself as a Negro . . . The child first accepts or rejects himself as a person. At a later date, when a child is more mature physically, mentally, socially and emotionally, he becomes aware of the fact that his family belongs to a particular ingroup, nationality or race. The child's acceptance or rejection of himself as a Negro is primarily influenced by his (previously fashioned) self concept. . . .[21]

Here we find a reversal of the Lewin proposition. Whereas Lewin asserts that the child's self-acceptance is determined by acceptance of his ingroup, Trent holds that acceptance of his ingroup is determined by acceptance of himself, and that self-acceptance itself is in turn primarily influenced by the family situation in which the young child finds himself.

Personal Security and Outgroup Attitudes

4. Nevertheless, there is no evidence available which proves that possession of a secure personality leads to more favorable outgroup attitudes. Personal security may contribute to ability to make relationships with those to whom one wishes to be related. Specific attitudes are a different matter and may vary, based on manifold considerations, in individuals with similar levels of personal security. Often it is the relatively insecure person, the individual with greater sensitivity due to a dissatisfied, searching disposition who has the inclination to dissent from circumscribed ingroup norms and empathize with members of an outgroup. This very person, however, may have personality limitations or distortions which may inhibit his capacity to transform his favorable outgroup attitudes into positive outgroup relationships.

One is reminded of David Riesman's point that it is in the marginal individual who is not necessarily securely and unmistakably nestled in a definite social ground that "the intellect is at its best and its ethical insights are at their best." [22] With ethical insight comes the ability to see the other fellow's point of view and to conceive of him as a worthwhile person in his own right regardless of his minority- or majority-group affiliation. Overcommitment to a specific ingroup may make for a narrow personality type.

5. Lewin's conception of what goes into making outgroup attitudes seems particularly oversimplified and one-dimensional. While outgroup attitudes may be influenced by feelings of minority group belongingness, they are also influenced by a whole host of other factors. These factors include among others: psychic security; strength and wholesomeness of the family constellation in infancy and childhood; the specific outgroup attitudes of the parents; intergroup attitudes prevailing in the community where the child grows up and which are reflected in such institutions as the school and church; attitudes of peers and of significant adults outside the immediate family circle; concrete outgroup encounters which the child experiences, including being subjected to prejudice and discrimination; the climate of intergroup relations which exists in the broad society; etc. It would be the interrelationship of all these factors and their total impact which molds the outgroup orientation of a minority-group member; the factor of minority-group identification may be included among this list of variables, but it is not the key and overriding consideration. An empirical investigation completed recently by the writer bears this out. In his study of some two-hundred Jewish adolescents there was found to be no correlation between ingroup identification and either outgroup attitudes or outgroup associations. [23]

As a corollary, it may be assumed that the total impact of outgroup factors will have a greater influence than the impact of ingroup factors on one's outgroup orientation. This is a conclusion reached by Fishman in his investigation of Jewish children receiving different types of religious training.[24] Dean, following a national survey of associational patterns of Jews, hypothesized that *contacts with the outgroup* is the key element in leading to outgroup socialization and friendship.[25]

A critical factor in the development of outgroup attitudes is the opinion held and conveyed by the parents regarding the outgroup, particularly to the very young child. Accordingly, the attitudes of the parents toward the outgroup will count more in determining the outgroup orientation of the child than the attitude of the parents toward the minority ingroup.

Conclusions

There may be valid, even compelling reasons for a minority group to emphasize ingroup identification and belongingness. However, evidence adduced here suggests that among these reasons should be excluded that of improving intergroup relationships. As a matter of fact, it should be recognized by minority-group agencies and officials that with heightened identification comes the sociological risk of deteriorated intergroup relations caused by separation and social insulation of groups.

A second conclusion, related to the first, has to do with practice on the part of minority-group agencies. If such agencies consider that constructive intergroup relationships are of value to their members and to our society as a whole, they must deal with this as a distinct and prominent problem with those they serve. It is not enough to foster strong ingroup identification on the supposition that this will somehow evoke positive outgroup relatedness. Proper outgroup attitudes must be treated as a weighty subject in its own right. Activities with intergroup content and bearing on issues of general community welfare should be stimulated as well as programs which bring ingroup and outgroup together in close association. This might mean a smaller proportion of time devoted to ingroup identification, or a goal of only moderate or balanced identification for the individual rather than total commitment.

Part IV

Family Processes and Problems

Introduction

Because most individuals are exposed to family influences during their most formative years and it is in this group that most individuals have the longest direct exposure, the family is perhaps the most influential of all social groups. Considering its impact upon the individual, the family mediates need satisfactions of its members, is the source of many personal problems, and is a promising vehicle for purposes of achieving planned change. Standing as it does between the individual and the social system at large, the family also serves to purvey the culture, to link individuals to schools, neighborhood groups, occupational groups, and other social units and, in many other ways, to mediate more general societal functions. Processes and problems of families of particular importance for social workers are found in the selections in this section.

Significant features of the contemporary American family are discussed in Fellin's reappraisal of changes in American family patterns. Stereotypes and professional misconceptions are re-examined and the effects of social, geographical, and occupational changes on the family are described. With respect to its structure, it is observed that rather than being either an extended family or an isolated nuclear family, it is best to view the contemporary American family as a modified extended unit linked to the social structure by friendships and kin contacts. Various mechanisms of the family and neighborhoods that serve to mitigate the effects of occupational and geographic mobility are identified. The suitability of the modified extended family for coping with nonuniform idiosyncratic tasks is discussed as a family function. Throughout, the author identifies the implications of his analysis for policies in the field of family services.

The remaining selections in this section treat characteristics and processes of particular problem families. In the first of these, Glasser and Navarre explicate the structural problems of the one-parent family. In addition to casting the vulnerabilities of one-parent families in bold relief, the analysis incidentally illuminates structural weaknesses of many families that are intact. The effects for parents, children, and the family as a complete unit are examined in terms of the structures of tasks, communication, power, and affection. Many of these effects are adverse and, as the authors acknowledge, may be attributed either to variations in the age or sex of the parent and the children, or to limitations of human resources. Many families seen in social work are precisely of this type. Indeed, one-parent families constitute more than one quarter of the group classified as poor. In their discussion of the implications for social work practice, the authors identify new as well as existing services required to meet the problems of such families.

Glasser reports on changes in family equilibrium during psychotherapy in the next selection. In this detailed study of three families having one member in intensive psychotherapy, evidence is adduced to refute the naive notion that family interaction improves and that there is simply a gradual re-establishment of the prior equilibrium as a consequence of continued psychotherapy. The interaction processes and role changes that accompany psychotherapy of one member disclosed three stages of family equilibrium accompanying the psychotherapeutic process. A period of re-equilibrium following the patient's initial improvement was found in the first phase. In the second, however, there was a period of disequilibrium that the author identifies as a family crisis. This period corresponds to the improvement of the patient as a consequence of intensive treatment. In the third phase, the author found that prior to the termination of treatment there was the emergence of a new equilibrium in the family. Among the implications for practice, the author indicates the foci for family diagnosis prior to treatment and identifies important considerations for the role of the worker during the treatment process.

The social and psychological factors in status decisions of unmarried mothers are examined in the next selection by Jones, Meyer, and Borgatta. Possible determinants of whether an unmarried mother will surrender her baby for subsequent adoption or will keep it are highlighted in this study and, contrary to some prevailing views, much more is involved in these decisions than individual psychological characteristics of the unmarried mothers. From their review of past research, the authors conclude that an unmarried mother is much more likely to surrender her child for adoption if she is white rather than Negro, young rather than old, more rather than less highly educated, and of non-Catholic religion. The authors discuss these factors as being indicative, in various ways, of cultural norms of dominant or deviant groups in the population. They argue also that one may adduce evidence that increasingly there will be a general cultural norm prescribing the surrendering of the baby and forbidding keeping it. Supplementing their review, the authors report on a study of 113 unmarried mothers who were clients at a private social agency. The racial and background characteristics mentioned above were again found to be predictors of the mother's decision. In addition, some personality characteristics of the unmarried mothers were found to be predictors. Specifically, the diverse personality characteristics suggested that immaturity was associated with retaining the baby and that intelligence, independence, and emotional stability were associated with surrender. Although the social factors were not controlled in this analysis of personality predictors, the authors' interpretation is that personality factors may be understood in part as being indicative of cultural conformance and nonconformance.

In the final selection, Litwak discusses divorce law as a means of social control. The breakup and estrangement of families constitute a significant form of family disorganization for social workers and this article identifies how court procedures and law may be employed to prevent various types of family breakup. The punitive, therapeutic, and educational features of the legal system are discussed as they apply differentially to four types of family breakup. The conclusions of the author's analysis bear upon the types of laws that should be passed concerning marriage and divorce, the establishment of court services for treating family and divorce problems, and upon how generally to counsel members of estranged families.

10 A Reappraisal of Changes in American Family Patterns

Phillip Fellin

Changes in American society have influenced the patterning of American families. The subject of this article is the implications of these changing family patterns for the practice of social work. More specifically, two questions are examined here: What is the nature of the impact of our changing society on the structure and functions of the family? What is the role of professional social services in relation to family functions? In this discussion the family is viewed not as an isolated phenomenon but as a unit of a complex society. Emphasis is placed on the strengths of the family that its members can utilize to cope with the demands of a changing society.

The rapid and extensive changes that have taken place in the structure of American society over the past century have been well documented.[1] The two major processes that have brought them about are urbanization and industrialization. The population has been shifting from a rural to an urban environment, intercity and intracity mobility have become commonplace, and a bureaucratized occupational structure has been created. Thus the growth of today's urban industrialized American society has been characterized by social, geographical, and occupational mobility.

While there has been considerable agreement among social scientists about the nature of these changes, some controversy has developed about their effect on the family. Most of the earlier statements concentrated on the negative aspects of social change. It was pointed out that as the extended family was replaced by the nuclear family, there was an increase in family isolation and a loss of mutual aid among family members. Family functions were said to have been taken over largely by formal organizations, with the family becoming a weak, unstable social unit lacking con-

Abridged from SOCIAL CASEWORK, 45 No. 5 (1964), 263–268. Reprinted by permission of the author and the Family Service Association of America.

trol over its members. Extensive mobility was said to be disrupting family life, leaving the family loosely integrated with society, and affecting its mental health and stability.

This account of what has been happening to the American family is familiar to most social workers. Later statements, however, based on empirical social research, have begun to throw doubt on the earlier formulation. For example, Sussman, Litwak, and Miller and Swanson have pointed up ways in which the family can maintain viability within the present structure of American society and have suggested the need to reappraise the impact of the structure on it.[2] Such a reappraisal is of special relevance to social work, since the sociological base of professional knowledge must be brought up to date if workers are to understand and deal appropriately with the needs of families.

Family Structure

It has been said that the extended family has been replaced by the nuclear family because it cannot operate efficiently in a modern democratic society.[3] The contrast generally made is between the classic extended family and the nuclear family. The classic extended family is characterized by geographical propinquity, occupational integration (nepotism), strict authority over the nuclear family, and emphasis on extended rather than nuclear family relations.[4] Bell and Vogel define the extended family as "any grouping, related by descent, marriage, or adoption, that is broader than the nuclear family." [5] In contrast, they define the nuclear family as a group "composed of a man and a woman joined in a socially recognized union and their children." [6]

Extensive examination of these two structures by Litwak suggests a third type, the modified extended family. Unlike the classic type, the modified extended family does not demand geographical closeness, occupational integration, or strict authority relations.[7] Nor does the concept of the modified extended family replace that of the nuclear family. In the modified extended-family system each nuclear family is one of a series of such families bound together on an egalitarian basis and providing significant aid to one another.[8]

The important question is whether the nuclear family is part of a modified extended family network or is structurally and functionally isolated from kin families. The isolation of the nuclear family in urban society is a major assumption in most considerations of contemporary family structure. Perhaps the only sense in which it is true, however, is if isolation is defined in terms of the nuclear family's living apart from other kin groups. It may be more meaningful to think in terms of *structural* and *functional* isolation. The former, having to do with the geographical distribution of kin units, becomes extreme when no two kin groups live in the same metropolitan area; the latter exists when there is no communication or aid between kin units.

This is how Sussman has defined isolation, and the empirical evidence of his study indicates that most urban nuclear families are neither structurally nor functionally isolated from kin units.[9] Litwak also found that the modified extended-family pattern exists among middle-class urban families,[10] and there is some indication that it exists among lower-class families. There is thus some evidence that a major potential source of strength for the urban nuclear family is the existence of the modified extended-family structure. In addition to kindred, family friends also strengthen the family. Zimmerman and Cervantes noted the significance of friend families for successful family living. In their work they linked family stability with the degree to which families surround themselves with other families having similar values.[11]

The modified extended-family and the friend-family systems serve to support the stability of the nuclear family, to exert social-control pressures to keep it together, and to regulate the behavior of the children. The families are bound together in a social relationship that makes it possible for members to request aid from one another in crises. Finally, these systems serve as reference groups that provide models of behavior for members of the nuclear family.

The fact that help from the modified extended family is available and is used by a large segment of our society indicates that the goals and objectives of social work should not be based on the assumption that most nuclear families are isolated. The modified extended family helps to meet the needs of the nuclear families within its circle, and social work must deal with the issue of when aid can appropriately be granted from within the extended family and when it should be granted by a social institution such as a social work agency. Sussman found, however, that approximately 24 per cent of the families in his study were in fact isolated.[12] Therefore, social workers must ask, What groups operate with an isolated nuclear family structure? What occupational experiences lead to isolation? What social-class groups or ethnic groups remain isolated? What programs are necessary to cope with problems of urban isolation and anomie?

Mobility and Family Structure

The conventional view is that in the United States the most functional family structure is the nuclear because it meets the demands of a mobile society, and that the family becomes disrupted if its structure is not suited to societal demands. According to Litwak's theory, however, mobility need not lead to a lack of extended family relations.[13] Its disruptive effects can be alleviated by means of the modified extended family, which does not depend on geographical or occupational proximity. Within a modified extended-family system, mobile nuclear families are given economic, social, and psychological support. The members of the extended family want the nuclear family to be successful, and thus mobility is legitimized. Of course, geographical mobility is encouraged by the extended family only when the move is occupationally rewarding. Thus, even though mobility results in fewer face-to-face contacts among members of the extended family, this type of family structure may in fact be more functional in coping with a changing society than the isolated nuclear-family structure.

In addition to the modified extended family, other resources, such as neighbors, are helpful in lessening the untoward effects of mobility. It is assumed that rapid integration into a new neighborhood helps alleviate the disrupting effects of mobility upon members of the family. Current studies indicate that families become integrated into new neighborhoods more quickly when there has been training for integrating under condtions of change.[14] The social policy question is whether social agencies can provide clients suffering from mobility problems with training or experience that is a substitute for the kind gained in occupational settings characterized by ordered change.

Some procedures have been found useful in the integration of families into new neighborhoods, and these might be employed by social agencies. An agency might, for example, organize local voluntary groups, since such groups are found to facilitate rapid integration. If it can develop neighborhood structures through which newcomers are offered a welcome, they can be integrated with little difficulty. Programs that include both husband and wife also ease integration problems. Since integration occurs easily when individuals are oriented toward discussing personal problems with neighbors, the agency may need to stress the values of neighborliness and casual friendships. In short, social workers need to take into account some of the mechanisms that serve to overcome the disrupting factors of mobility.

Social workers maintain that in planning with the client the extended family is always considered. When the nuclear family is separated geographically from the extended family, however, the assumption is made that it can no longer be called on to provide family support. The extent to which social workers can use the modified extended-family or the friend-family system as a resource for emotional, economic, and social support of the nuclear family is yet to be demonstrated. In one empirical study of housing-project and slum residents, it was demonstrated that these people looked not to the social agency but to their extended kin groups for help. Furthermore, most of them had kin groups available to them within the community.[15] Thus our present society may offer the working-class city dweller a place of regular employment in a community where he is surrounded by kin and friends on whom he can rely for aid and social relations. That this pattern is not present among most social work clients does not mean that the urban structure does not allow for it. It may mean that social workers must take responsibility for creating and supporting ways in which the pattern can be developed.

Family Functions

In discussing changing family patterns, it is imperative to consider the nature of family functions. The family may be seen as a social unit performing certain functions for its members, for other social institutions, and for the wider social system. Some of the functions the family performs for its members are likely to coincide with those it performs for the society at large. For example, the function of reproduction serves both to maintain the family as a group and to replace the members of society. Again, the family's economic and status-placement functions both serve its members and provide for the distribution of power and property for the society. Finally, the family has certain responsibilities to society for the behavior of its members that are carried out through the functions of socialization, emotional maintenance, and social control.[16]

One important issue is the extent to which family functions have been transferred to other social institutions. Litwak's excellent review of the different points of view regarding family functions is particularly helpful.[17] Ogburn holds that, with the one exception of emotional support, the functions of the family have been taken over by large formal organizations and that this has resulted in a weakened family.[18] A view shared by several sociologists is that though the family has lost some of its functions, the loss has been compensated for by more intensive practice of the few that remain, such as the stabilization of the adult personality and the early socialization of the child.[19] These sociologists deal with the extent to which the family retains its functions; the impact of the change in its functions on its stability and strength, and also, explicitly or implicitly, the extent to which formal organizations have taken over family functions.

The question must be raised concerning which tasks or functions can best be performed by the family and which by formal organizations. This question also alerts us to the issue of when formal organizations can best supplement the functions of the family. The assumption can no longer be made that the family is the best-equipped social unit in our society to perform all the functions required by society and family members. It is unlikely, however, that society can allow families to become completely dependent on social agencies or other social institutions to perform their traditional functions.

Maximum benefit for the family and society is most likely to result from co-ordination of the efforts of formal organizations and primary groups. Such formal organizations as nurseries, social agencies, and mental health clinics can grow at the same time that the family continues to carry out socialization and stabilization functions for its members. Few theories have been advanced about how the relationship between primary groups and formal organizations should be structured. Litwak has taken an important step in this direction by suggesting that formal organizations take responsibility for certain uniform and repetitive tasks and the family take responsibility for most nonuniform idiosyncratic tasks.[20] For example, family, neighbors, or friends can provide immediate first-aid health care; the hospital staff can handle the treatment of serious illness; and the primary group can take care of posthospital needs. The achievement of goals in most areas of life—economic, leisure-time, educational—requires an interaction between a series of social units: the family, the neighborhood, and social institutions. The family has the structure to deal with everyday management of its members; if their needs and problems are more serious, professional services such as those performed by social workers must be developed. In this scheme the goal of the family service agency is to help the family as a social system become equipped to handle nonuniform tasks, since the social worker cannot always be present and the agency cannot give all its time to serving only a small group of dependent families.

Conclusion and Summary

The changes in American society have resulted in changes in the extent to which the family continues to discharge what were formerly considered its traditional functions. These changes have also resulted in a growth of social institutions that take responsibility for performing some functions and for complementing the performance of others. The family need not be a weak social unit, even though it has lost some of its former functions. A problem occurs when the family cannot fulfill its functions of emotional support, socialization, and social control and formal organizations either do not or cannot assume the responsibility. Both social agencies that attempt to carry out the economic function for the family and those that try to deal with the tasks of socializing children or stabilizing adult personalities are faced with the problem of dependency, which may limit the services that could otherwise be offered to a larger number of families. Whenever possible, the goals of the organization in both situations must be the same: to provide complementary services to the family on a nonpermanent basis.

The focus of this article has been on a reappraisal of the ways in which changes in American society have affected the family. The urban family is likely to be part of an extended family group, rather than an isolated family. Various mechanisms serve to help the family function with minimum disruption under conditions of mobility. The family has not retained all its traditional functions; in some it has been supplanted by formal organizations and in others it is complemented by such organizations. Social services are a source of strength when they complement the functions of the family.

11 Structural Problems of the One-Parent Family

Paul H. Glasser and Elizabeth Navarre

Introduction

Recent concern about the problems of people who are poor has led to renewed interest in the sources of such difficulties. While these are manifold and complexly related to each other, emphasis has been placed upon the opportunity structure and the socialization process found among lower socioeconomic groups. Relatively little attention has been paid to family structure, which serves as an important intervening variable between these two considerations. This seems to be a significant omission in view of the major change in the structure of family life in the United States during this century, and the large number of one-parent families classified as poor. The consequences of the latter structural arrangements for family members, parents and children, and for society, is the focus of this paper.

One-parent families are far more apt to be poor than other families. This is true for one-fourth of those headed by a woman. Chilman and Sussman [1] summarize that data in the following way:

> About 10 per cent of the children in the United States are living with only one parent, usually the mother. Nonwhite children are much more likely to live in such circumstances, with one-third of them living in one-parent families. Two-and-a-quarter million families in the United States today are composed of a mother and her children. They represent only one-twelfth of all families with children but make up more than a fourth of all that are classed as poor. . . .

From JOURNAL OF SOCIAL ISSUES, 21 No. 1 (1965), 98–109. Reprinted by permission of the authors and Society for the Psychological Study of Social Issues. The conceptualization in this paper grew out of work on Project D-16, "Demonstration of Social Group Work With Parents," financed by a grant from the Children's Bureau, Welfare Administration, Department of Health, Education and Welfare.

Despite the resulting economic disadvantages, among both white and nonwhite families there is a growing number headed only by a mother. By 1960 the total was 7½ per cent of all families with own children rather than the 6 per cent of ten years earlier. By March 1962 the mother-child families represented 8½ per cent of all families with own children.

When these demographic findings are seen in the context of the relative isolation of the nuclear family in the United States today, the structural consequences of the one-parent group takes on added meaning. It may be seen as the culmination of the contraction of the effective kin group.[2]

This "isolation" is manifested in the fact that the members of the nuclear family, consisting of parents and their still-dependent children, ordinarily occupy a separate dwelling not shared with members of the family of orientation. . . . It is, of course, not uncommon to find a (member of the family of orientation) residing with the family, but this is both statistically secondary, and it is clearly not felt to be the "normal arrangement."

While families maintain social contact with grown children and with siblings, lines of responsibility outside of the nuclear group are neither clear nor binding, and obligations among extended kin are often seen as limited and weak. Even when affectional ties among extended family members are strong, their spatial mobility in contemporary society isolates the nuclear group geographically, and increases the difficulty of giving aid in personal service among them.[3,4]

Associated with the weakening of the extended kinship structure has been the loss of some social functions of the family and the lessened import of others. Nonetheless, reproduction, physical maintenance, placement or status, and socialization are still considered significant social functions of the modern American family although they often have to be buttressed by other institutions in the community. At the same time, however, the personal functions of the family including affection, security, guidance, and sexual gratification have been heightened and highlighted.[5,6] These functions are closely and complexly related to each other but can serve as foci for analysis of the consequences of family structure. In the one-parent family neither reproduction or sexual gratification can be carried out within the confines of the nuclear group itself. But more importantly, the other personal and social functions are drastically affected also, and it is to these that this paper will give its attention. A few of the implications for social policy and practice will be mentioned at the end.

While it is recognized that all individuals have some contact with others outside the nuclear group, for purposes of analytic clarity this paper will confine itself to a discussion of the relationships among nuclear family members primarily. Two factors will be the foci of much of the content. The age difference between parent and children is central to the analysis. Although it is understood that children vary with age in the degree of independence from their parents, the nature of their dependence will be emphasized throughout. The sex of the parent and the sex of the children is the second variable. Cultural definitions of appropriate behavior for men and women and for girls and boys vary from place to place and are in the process of change, but nonetheless this factor cannot be ignored. Since the largest majority of one-parent families are headed by a woman, greater attention will be given to the mother-son and mother-daughter relationships in the absence of the father.

Structural Characteristics of One-Parent Families and Their Consequences

Task Structure

The large majority of tasks for which a family is responsible devolve upon the parents. Providing for the physical, emotional, and social needs of all the family members is a full-time job for two adults. If these tasks are to be performed by the nuclear group during the absence or incapacity of one of its adult members, the crucial factor is the availability of another member with sufficient maturity, competence, and time to perform them. The two-parent family has sufficient flexibility to adapt to such a crisis. Although there is considerable specialization in the traditional sex roles concerning these tasks, there is little evidence that such specialization is inherent in the sex roles. It is, in fact, expected that one parent will substitute if the other parent is incapacitated and, in our essentially servant-less society, such acquired tasks are given full social approval. However, in the one-parent family such flexibility is much less possible, and the permanent loss of the remaining parent generally dissolves the nuclear group.

Even if the remaining parent is able to function adequately, it is unlikely that one person can take over all parental tasks on a long term basis. Financial support, child care, and household maintenance are concrete tasks involving temporal and spatial relationships, and in one form or another they account for a large proportion of the waking life of two adult family members. A permanent adjustment then must involve a reduction in the tasks performed and/or a reduction in the adequacy of performance, or external assistance.

In addition to limitations on the time and energy available to the solitary parent for the performance of tasks, there are social limitations on the extent to which both the male and the female tasks may be fulfilled by a member of one sex. If the remaining parent be male, it is possible for him to continue to perform his major role as breadwinner and to hire a woman to keep house and, at least, to care for the children's physical needs. If, however, the solitary parent be a female, as is the more usual case, the woman must take on the male role of breadwinner, unless society or the absent husband provides financial support in the form of insurance, pensions, welfare payments, etc. This is a major reversal in cultural roles and, in addition, usually consumes the mother's time and energy away from the home for many hours during the day. There is little time or energy left to perform the tasks normally performed by the female in the household and she, too, must hire a female substitute at considerable cost. The effect of this reversal of the sex role model in the socialization of children has been a matter of some concern, but the emphasis has been upon the male child who lacked a male role model rather than upon the effect of the reversal of the female role model for children of both sexes. In both cases, the probability seems great that some tasks will be neglected, particularly those of the traditionally female specialization.

The wish to accomplish concrete household tasks in the most efficient manner in terms of time and energy expenditure may lead to less involvement of children in these tasks and the concomitant loss of peripheral benefits that are extremely important to the socialization process and/or to family cohesion. Some tasks may be almost completely avoided, especially those which are not immediately obvious to the local community, such as the provision of emotional support and attention to children. A third possibility is to overload children, particularly adolescents, with such tasks. These may be greater than the child is ready to assume, or tasks inappropriate for the child of a particular sex to perform regularly.

Females are often lacking in skills and experience in the economic world, and frequently receive less pay and lower status jobs than men with similar skills. The probability of lower income and lower occupational status for the female-headed household are likely to lower the family's social position in a society which bases social status primarily upon these variables. If the family perceives a great enough distance between its former level and that achieved by the single parent, it is possible that the family as a whole may become more or less anomic, with serious consequences in the socialization process of the children and in the remaining parent's perception of personal adequacy.

Communication Structure

Parents serve as the channels of communication with the adult world in two ways; first as transmitters of the cultural value system which has previously been internalized by the parents; and secondly, as the child's contact with and representative in the adult world. Except for very young children, the parents are not the sole means of communication, but for a large part of the socialization process, the child sees the adult world through the eyes and by the experience of his parents, and even his own experiences are limited to those which can be provided for him within whatever social opportunities that are open to his parents. More importantly, to the extent that the child's identity is integrated with that of the family, he is likely to see himself not only as his parents see him but also as the world sees his parents.

Since sex differences have been assumed in the ways men and women see the world and differences can be substantiated in the ways that the world sees men and women, the child can have a relatively undistorted channel of communication only if both parents are present. Therefore, whatever the interests, values, and opinions of the remaining parent, the loss of a parent of one sex produces a structural distortion in the communications between the child and the adult world and, since such communication is a factor in the development of the self-image, of social skills, and of an image of the total society, the totality of the child's possible development is also distorted.

The type and quality of experiences available even to adults tend to be regulated according to sex. In the two-parent family not only is the child provided with more varied experiences, but the parent of either sex has, through the spouse, some communication with the experiences typical of the oposite sex. Thus, the housewife is likely to have some idea of what is going on in the business or sports worlds even if she has no interest in them. The solitary parent is not likely to be apprised of such information and is handicapped to the extent that it may be necessary for decision making. The female who has taken on the breadwinner role may be cut off from the sources of information pertinent to the female role as she misses out on neighborhood gossip about the symptoms of the latest virus prevalent among the children, events being planned, the best places to shop, etc.

Finally, the solitary parent is likely to be limited in the social ties that are normal channels of communication. Most social occasions for adults tend to be planned for couples and the lone parent is often excluded or refuses because of the discomfort of being a fifth wheel. Her responsibilities to home and children tend to never be completed and provide additional reasons for refusing invitations. Lone women are particularly vulnerable to community sanctions and must be cautious in their social relationships lest their own standing and that of the family be lowered. Finally, the possible drop in social status previously discussed may isolate the family from its own peer group and place them among a group with which they can not or will not communicate freely.

Power Structure

Bales and Borgatta [7] have pointed out that the diad has unique properties and certainly a uniquely simple power structure. In terms of authority from which the children are more or less excluded by age and social norms, the one-parent family establishes a diadic relationship, between the parent and each child. Society places full responsibility in the parental role, and, therefore, the parent becomes the only power figure in the one-parent family. Consequently, the adult in any given situation is either for or against the child. Some experience of playing one adult against the other, as long as it is not carried to extremes, is probably valuable in developing social skills and in developing a view of authority as tolerable and even manipulable within reason, rather than absolute and possibly tyrannical. In the one-parent family the child is more likely to see authority as personal rather than consensual, and this in itself removes some of the legitimation of the power of parents as the representatives of society.

Even if benevolent, the absolutism of the power figure in the one-parent family, where there can be no experience of democratic decision making between equals in power, may increase the difficulty of the adolescent and the young adult in achieving independence from the family, and that of the parent in allowing and encouraging such development. Further, the adult, the power, the authority figure, is always of one sex, whether that sex be the same sex as the child or the opposite. However, in contemporary society where decision making is the responsibility of both sexes, the child who has identified authority too closely with either sex may have a difficult adjustment. The situation also has consequences for the parent, for when the supportive reinforcement or the balancing mediation which comes with the sharing of authority for decision making is absent, there may be a greater tendency to frequent changes in the decisions made, inconsistency, or rigidity.

Affectional Structure

The personal functions of the family in providing for the emotional needs of its members have been increasingly emphasized. There is ample evidence that children require love and security in order to develop in a healthy manner. Although there is nearly as much substantiation for the emotional needs of parents, these are less frequently emphasized. Adults must have love and security in order to maintain emotional stability under the stresses of life and in order to meet the emotional demands made upon them by their children. In addition to providing the positive emotional needs of its members, the family has the further function of providing a safe outlet for negative feelings as well. Buttressed by the underlying security of family affection, the dissatisfactions and frustrations of life may be expressed without the negative consequences attendant upon their expression in other contexts. Even within the family, however, the expressions of such basic emotions cannot go unchecked. The needs of one member or one subgroup may dominate to the point that the requirements of others are not fulfilled, or are not met in a manner acceptable to society. To some extent this danger exists in any group, but it is particularly strong in a group where emotional relationships are intensive. Traditionally, the danger is reduced by regulating the context, manner, and occasion of the expression of such needs.

Family structure is an important element both in the provision and the regulation of emotional needs. The increasing isolation of the nuclear family focuses these needs on the nuclear group by weakening ties with the larger kin group. Thus, both generations and both sexes are forced into a more intensive relationship; yet the marital relationship itself is increasingly unsupported by legal or social norms and is increasingly dependent upon affectional ties alone for its solidity. Such intense relationships are increased within the one-parent family, and possibly reach their culmination in the family consisting of one parent and one child.

In a two person group the loss of one person destroys the group (Table 11–3). The structure, therefore, creates pressure for greater attention to group maintenance through the expression of affection and the denial of negative feelings, and in turn may restrict problem solving efforts. In a sense, the one-parent family is in this position even if there are several children because the loss of the remaining parent effectively breaks up the group. The children have neither the ability nor the social power to maintain the group's independence. Therefore, the one-parent family structure exerts at least some pressure in this direction.

However, where there is more than one child there is some mitigation of the pattern, though this in itself may have some disadvantages. In a group of three or more there are greater possibilities for emotional outlet for those not in an authority role. Unfortunately, there are also greater possibilities that one member may become the scapegoat as other members combine against him. In spite of the power relationships, it is even possible that the solitary parent will become the scapegoat if the children combine against her. This problem is greatest in the three person family as three of the five possible subgroups reject one member (Table 11–2). The problem is also present in the four person family, although the possible subgroups in which the family combines against one member has dropped to four out of twelve (Table 11–1). The relation of group structure to emotional constriction has been clearly expressed by Slater: [8]

> The disadvantages of the smaller groups are not verbalized by members, but can only be inferred from their behavior. It appears that group members are too tense, passive, tactful, and constrained, to work together in a manner which is altogether satisfying to them. *Their fear of alienating one another seems to prevent them from expressing their ideas freely.* (Emphasis is ours.)
>
> These findings suggest that maximal group satisfaction is achieved when the group is large enough so that the members feel able to express positive and negative feelings freely, and to make aggressive efforts toward problem solving even at the risk of antagonizing each other, yet small enough so that some regard will be shown for the

feelings and needs of others; large enough so that the loss of a member could be tolerated, but small enough so that such a loss could not be altogether ignored.

Subgroup Choices among Groups of Varying Sizes *

Table 11-1: The Four-Person Group

1. A,B,C,D	5. B,C,D	9. B.D
2. A,B,C	6. A,B	10. A,D
3. A,B,D	7. C,D	11. B,C
4. A,C,D	8. A,C	12. All persons independent; no subgroup

Table 11-2: The Three-Person Group

1. A,B,C	3. A,B	5. All persons independent; no subgroup
2. B,C	4. A,C	

Table 11-3: The Two-Person Group

1. A,B	2. Both persons independent; no subgroup.

* Persons designated by letter.

Interpersonal relationships between parents and children in the area of emotional needs are not entirely reciprocal because of age and power differences in the family. Parents provide children with love, emotional support, and an outlet for negative feelings. However, while the love of a child is gratifying to the adult in some ways, it cannot be considered as supporting; rather it is demanding in the responsibilities it places upon the loved one. Support may be received only from one who is seen as equal or greater in power and discrimination. Nor can the child serve as a socially acceptable outlet for negative emotions to the extent that another adult can, for the child's emotional and physical dependency upon the adult makes him more vulnerable to possible damage from this source. The solitary parent in the one-parent family is structurally deprived of a significant element in the meeting of his own emotional needs. To this must be added the psychological and physical frustrations of the loss of the means for sexual gratification. In some situations involving divorce or desertion the damage to the self-image of the remaining parent may intensify the very needs for support and reassurance which can no longer be met within the family structure.

The regulation of emotional demands of family members is similar in many ways to the regulation of the behavior of family members discussed under power structure. As there was the possibility that authority might be too closely identified with only one sex in the one-parent family, there is the similar danger that the source of love and affection may be seen as absolute and/or as vested in only one sex. Having only one source of love and security, both physical and emotional, is more likely to produce greater anxiety about its loss in the child, and may make the child's necessary withdrawal from the family with growing maturity more difficult for both parent and child. Again, as in the power structure, the identification of the source of love with only one sex is likely to cause a difficult adjustment to adult life, particularly if the original source of love was of the same sex as the child, for our society's expectations are that the source of love for an adult must lie with the opposite sex.

One of the most important regulatory devices for the emotional needs of the group is the presence and influence of members who serve to deter or limit demands which would be harmful to group members or to group cohesion, and to prevent the intensification of the influence of any one individual by balancing it with the influence of others. Parental figures will tend to have greater influence in acting as a deterrent or balance to the needs and demands of other family members because of their greater power and maturity. The loss of one parent removes a large portion of the structural balance and intensifies the influence of the remaining parent upon the children, while possibly limiting the ability of this parent to withstand demands made upon her by the children. There is also a tendency for any family member to transfer to one or more of the remaining members the demands formerly filled by the absent person.[9] There would seem to be a danger in the one-person family that:

1. The demands of the sole parent for the fulfillment of individual and emotional needs normally met within the marital relationship may prove intolerable and damaging to the children, who are unable to give emotional support or to absorb negative feelings from this source, or

2. The combined needs of the children may be intolerable to the emotionally unsupported solitary parent. Since the emotional requirements of children are very likely to take the form of demands for physical attention or personal service, the remaining parent may be subject to physical as well as emotional exhaustion from this source.

When emotional needs are not met within the family, there may be important consequences for the socialization of the children and for the personal adjustment of all family members. Further, fulfillment of such needs may be sought in the larger community by illegitimate means. The children may exhibit emotional problems in school or in their relations with their play group. A parent may be unable to control her own emotions and anxieties sufficiently to function adequately in society. When there are no means for the satisfaction of these demands they may well prove destructive, not only to the family group and its individual members, but to society as well.

The consequences of the problems discussed above may be minimized or magnified by the personal resources or inadequacies of the family members, and particularly the solitary parent in this situation. But, the problems are structural elements of the situation, and must be faced on this level if they are to be solved.

Implications for Social Policy and Practice

The Introduction describes the growth of the number of one-parent families during the last generation. Chilman and Sussman [10] go on to describe the financial plight of many of these families.

> The public program of aid to families with dependent children (AFDC) that is most applicable to this group currently makes payments on behalf of children in nearly a million families. Three out of every four of these families have no father in the home. Less than half of the families that are estimated to be in need receive payments under the program and, ". . . with the low financial standards for aid to dependent children prevailing in many states, dependence on the program for support is in itself likely to put the family in low-income status. . . . The average monthly payment per family as reported in a study late in 1961 was only $112. . . .
>
> "The overall poverty of the recipient families is suggested by the fact that, according to the standards set up in their own states, half of them are still in financial need even with their assistance payment."

There is increasing evidence that both the one-parent family structure and poverty are being transmitted from one generation to the next.

> A recently released study of cases assisted by aid to families with dependent children shows that, for a nationwide sample of such families whose cases were closed early in 1961 more than 40 per cent of the mothers and/or fathers were raised in homes where some form of assistance had been received at some time. "Nearly half of these cases had received aid to families with dependent children. This estimated proportion that received some type of aid is more than four times the almost 10 per cent estimated for the total United States population. . . . [11]

If poverty and one-parent family structure tend to go together, providing increases in financial assistance alone may not be sufficient to help parents and children, in the present and future generation to become financially independent of welfare funds. Under the 1962 Amendments to the Social Security Act states are now receiving additional funds to provide rehabilitation services to welfare families, and these programs have begun. Creative use of such funds to overcome some of the consequences of one-parent family structure is a possibility, but as yet the authors know of no services that have explicitly taken this direction.

A few suggestions may serve to illustrate how existing or new services might deal with the consequences of one-parent family structure:

1. Recognition of the need of the mother without a husband at home for emotional support and social outlets could lead to a variety of services. Recreation and problem focused groups for women in this situation, which would provide some opportunities for socially sanctioned heterosexual relationships, might go a long way in helping these parents and their children.

2. Special efforts to provide male figures to which both girls and boys can relate may have utility. This can be done in day-care centers, settlement house agencies, schools, and through the inclusion of girls in programs like the Big Brothers. It would be particularly useful for children in one-parent families to see the ways in which adults of each sex deal with each other in these situations, and at an early age.

3. Subsidization of child care and housekeeping services for parents with children too young or unsuitable for day-care services would provide greater freedom for solitary mothers to work outside the home. Training persons as homemakers and making them responsible to an agency or a professional organization would reduce the anxiety of the working parent, and provide greater insurance to both the parent and society that this important job would be done well.

More fundamental to the prevention of poverty and the problems of one-parent family status may be programs aimed at averting family dissolution through divorce, separation, and desertion, particularly among lower socioeconomic groups. Few public programs have addressed themselves to this problem, and there is now a good deal of evidence that the private family agencies which provide counseling services have disenfranchised themselves from the poor.[12] The need to involve other institutional components in the community, such as the educational, economic, and political systems, is obvious but beyond the scope of discussion in this paper.[13] Increasing the number of stable and enduring marriages in the community so as to prevent the consequences of one-parent family structure may be a first line of defense, and more closely related to treating the causes rather than the effects of poverty for a large number of people who are poor.

Summary

One-parent families constitute more than a fourth of that group classified as poor, and are growing in number. Family structure is seen as a variable intervening between the opportunity system and the socialization process. The task, communication, power and affectional structure within the nuclear group are influenced by the absence of one parent, and the family's ability to fulfill its social and personal functions may be adversely affected. Some of the consequences of this deviant family structure seem related to both the evolvement of low socioeconomic status and its continuation from one generation to the next. Solutions must take account of this social situational problem.

12 Changes in Family Equilibrium during Psychotherapy

Paul H. Glasser

This report summarizes one section of a larger study of the ways in which role changes occur in a family when a parent is mentally ill and undergoes psychotherapy. A large number of case records from the Psychiatric Clinic at North Carolina Memorial Hospital were examined following a review of the literature on family-crisis studies,[1] marital-adjustment studies,[2] family-development theory,[3] role theory,[4] and social psychiatry.[5] Out of this survey and from beginning contacts with study families, an investigation emerged which focused upon the equilibrium of the family as a small group [6] in the following areas: How internal stresses within the family arise, what changes take place in the behavior of family members, and what changes take place in group methods for handling problems. This paper discusses primarily the intrafamilial processes which accompany the psychotherapy of one member of the family group.

During the psychotherapeutic process, three stages of family equilibrium were delineated: (1) re-equilibrium following the patient's initial improvement, (2) disequilibrium (family crisis) during intensive psychoanalytically oriented treatment, and (3) the emergence of a new equilibrium prior to termination of treatment. Each stage is associated with a seres of factors related to (1) the therapeutic technques used and the depth of the transference relationship at different periods in the treatment process, (2) the reactions of family members to the patient's new behavior patterns, his changing symptom picture, and his treatment, and (6) other situational factors (hospitalization, loss of income, etc.). At the second stage, these elements lead to inconsistent expectations between the patient and other members of the family; that is, a serious crisis. Changes in the

From FAMILY PROCESS, 2 (1963), 245–264. Reprinted by permission of the author and the journal. This investigation was partially supported by a National Institute of Mental Health Training Grant through the University of North Carolina Institute for Research in Social Science.

patient's behavior and expectations require other members of the family to change also. This change process in the family group is described in detail in the body of the paper. A final section of the report discusses implications for social work practice, emphasizing particularly the need for family diagnosis even when the patient is receiving individual psychotherapy and the important part the worker can play in facilitating treatment and in keeping the group together by seeing other members of the patient's family.

Research Method

Since this was an exploratory study which attempted to shed at least some light on the ways in which families change and the causes for this change in order to generate new and insightful hypotheses, the decision was made to use the case-study method. Three families in which both spouses (one of them the patient) and at least one child under the age of eighteen were living at home were chosen for study. Each of the patients was either under, or expected to begin, intensive psychotherapy over a long period of time with a staff or resident physician. These families were followed carefully for a period of about thirteen months. Four types of data were collected in the study:

1. Interviews with individual family members, most often with the patient's spouse.

2. Observations and interviews with the family as a group during home visits.

3. Data collected in conferences with the psychiatrists treating the patients. These conferences were held at fairly regular intervals (two to four times a month for each case).

4. Psychiatric and social work records and identifying data sheets, which included information not found in the first three sources.

A total of at least 153 contacts concerning the families in the study was made. More than 204 contacts with individuals either singly or in groups occurred. Thus, the researcher got to know these families and their methods of functioning extremely well.

Process records were written or dictated soon after each contact with one or more family members or the patient's psychiatrist. As the data were gathered, the records were read and reread for new insights into the material. These were set down in rudimentary form and in progress reports and checked again through another reading of the material and later interviews. At this point some insights were discarded, revised, or embellished.

Once all the data were collected, a role framework was used as the basis for a content analysis of all of the record material in order to check the earlier insights and find new understanding in a more rigorous manner. Each paragraph, sentence, or even phrase which related to one of the seven role areas was identified with a number and letter indicating in which of the six stages of family organization the behavior occurred, and to which of the seven role areas it applied.[7] In this way a description of the role of each family member in each of the seven role areas during each of the six stages was written. Role conflicts, role confusions, role gaps, and role dissatisfactions were more clearly discerned by reading through all of the material in each role area during each stage. The content which follows is based upon an analysis of the above material.

The Return to the Familiar

Following the patient's initial contact with the psychiatric clinic, there appear to have been vigorous attempts by each of the families to return to the old ways of doing things. Each family member tried to resume the roles used before the family disequilibrium which appeared during the stages of the patient's mental illness. There are numerous reasons why this seems to have occurred.

The onset of treatment in itself served to give the family some sense of relief. There was the hope that the intervention of a professional outsider would interrupt the downward spiral of family disequilibrium. Some family members felt that matters could not get much worse, so that with psychiatric aid they were bound to get better. Knowing no other method of family adjustment which had been satisfying to them, family members attempted to return to old patterns.

Hospitalization early in the treatment sequence tended to reinforce hopes and aid members in their return to old roles.[8] Familiar with the analogy of physical illness, family members believed that the patient would return from the hospital in a greatly improved state of health. Further, removal of the patient from the home had a number of positive consequences. It permitted the family some relief from the patient's symptoms and interpersonal difficulties. There was time to reorganize the family along the old lines with the patient absent, and members were able to assert their strengths in the adjustment process. Spouses and children tended to recall the patient's strengths and the once satisfying interpersonal relationships, repeating stories of the happy times they had had together. There is a chance to love the patient for what he once was like when the reality demands of his difficulties are removed. While the patient's absence from the home is not always easy to handle, the positives seemed to outweigh the negatives at this point in the family's history. Since the patient is expected home soon, the threat of continued absence and its consequences is minimized, and as the family members move into the old role structure, the patient's roles tend to be preserved for him until his return home.

Visits to the hospital tend to reinforce the expectation of re-equilibrium and the return to the old family pattern. The patient seems calmer, better behaved, easier to get along with, and more relaxed. For the first time in months or years, in the controlled environment of the hospital, spouses are able to discuss important matters together and even make some decisions without getting upset. Promises are made to behave in the same way when the patient returns home and to return to the old ways of handling problems, which seem much more satisfying in comparison with the turmoil that took place during family disequilibrium while the patient was acutely ill. There seems little awareness of the causes for family demoralization or mental illness.

A sense of relief is also expressed by the patient and his family when they know what is wrong, despite a diagnosis of psychiatric illness and the fear attached to this. The concreteness of the label seems to provide more security than uncertainty and the suspicion of mental illness. With the addition of a supportive and warm response from the psychiatrist, the social worker, and others, the patient and his family feel reassured that the group will be able to return to the former level of equilibrium.

Often there is an expectation by the patient, his family, and the therapist that the patient will respond positively to treatment and get well. In the eyes of the patient and his family this means that he will be as he was before the illness and so they can all assume their old ways. Many of the individuals in the study saw in psychiatry a magical component, believing that something the physician will do will change the patient's behavior and enable him to recover. It is only after the patient has been in treatment for some time that he is able to give up this belief. Until this occurs the family is encouraged to believe that there will be a return to the good old days.

When there is some improvement in the patient's behavior and symptoms—and there generally is in the protected environment of the hospital and/or when treatment first begins—these hopeful expectations about the patient and psychiatry are confirmed. There is the feeling that now the patient is almost his old self again, that members can pick up where they left off before his illness began. The self-fulfilling prophecy has been fulfilled. Neither the family nor the patient seem to understand that separation from the family, the sense of relief associated with diagnosis and treatment, the expectation that the patient will get well, and the therapeutic environment of the hospital, have all contributed to the patient's temporary relief of symptoms, and that in time these same or other symptoms are likely to return after the patient leaves the hospital.

This flight into health and the family process associated with it was particularly noticeable in two families. Mr. O gave up alcohol for some time after hospitalization. Mrs. U gave up many of her somatic complaints while at the hospital, and her behavior became somewhat more tolerable to the nuclear and extended family members for the first few months after discharge. Since the patients generally show improvement in the hospital, the family eagerly awaits the patient's return home.

When the patient does return home, family morale is high. There is less need to hide the patient's behavior since he has improved, and sometimes his hospitalization has made this impossible.[9] Thus, one source of pressure has been removed. The patient is better, which gives the family reason to rejoice. The family itself has reorganized somewhat during the patient's absence, enabling its members to better tolerate and handle the patient's deviant behavior, if some of this remains. The family has preserved the patient's roles in its structures, and his return home in an improved state leads them to believe that he will assume these roles in the very near future. This pushes the patient to conform to the pressure of these expectations. He does attempt to assume his old roles in the family. The husband returns to his job, takes his wife out socially, does repairs around the house, and resumes some responsibility for the children. The wife returns to cooking and cleaning, caring for the children, etc. This is reason for further rejoicing.

High morale contributes to the avoidance of arguments and the expression of discontent. Since the underlying causes for family disequilibrium and mental illness have not yet been handled, role dissatisfaction continues to exist, but it remains below the surface. There are persistent attempts by the spouses of the patients and other family members to avoid arguments and to conceal discontent with expected behavior in fear of encouraging the return of the patient's symptoms. The result is less effective communication than before the patient's illness began, while at the same time the family has the illusion that things are running smoothly. Mrs. O verbalized these fears to the researcher a number of times. For example she said that she was afraid to express any of her hostility. Mr. O seemed to remember weeks and months later what she might say in anger, and he would bring it up. This was one reason why she was afraid to express herself. Secondly, she was afraid he would react at the moment, and that this would upset him further. She didn't want to undo the work of the psychiatrist.

Finally, the process of psychotherapy also indirectly encourages this family process. Treatment at this early stage is primarily directed at catharsis, relief of guilt, and emotional support. The effect is to reduce the patient's anxiety, which results in the relief of some symptoms, with the consequences described earlier. The family appears to be functioning in the same manner as before the onset of family disequilibrium and the patient's symptoms.

A Second Period of Disequilibrium

The previous method of family organization had not worked successfully in the past, either because it did not satisfy personal needs or was inadequate to handle problems facing the group, or for both of these reasons. Thus, after the initial rejoicing following hospitalization and/or the beginning of treatment, the process of family disequilibrium gradually began once again. The rapidity with which this process became apparent to members of the family depended upon many factors in the family and treatment situation. In each of the study families, however, there was a recurrence of symptoms in the patient concurrent with the second period of family disequilibrium.

There were many pressures towards disequilibrium in addition to the important ones stated above. First of all, the family and its members were not really the same after treatment began as before the onset of the patient's symptoms. Many events had occurred in the interval which made a difference in the reactions of family members to each other and the external system. The group had gone through one crisis, mental illness of the patient, during which interpersonal relationships had been markedly strained. One of the members of the family had become acutely ill. While some of the patient's symptoms had been removed after treatment had begun, sometimes the more prominent ones, other symptoms generally remained. The crisis had been a learning experience in itself so that individuals in the family were no longer the same as before the crisis, and they could no longer play the same roles as easily as before. Their psychosocial reactions to each other were different.

Family members were aware that these changes had taken place but found it difficult to be specific about them. These changes provided motivation for more change. If Mr. O could pick up his daughter Ann at the home of her girlfriend for the first time, why couldn't he do this more often, especially when Mrs. O most needed this kind of help? If Mrs. U could face up to her mother's anger once, why couldn't she do this consistently? Members of the family found it difficult to put these feelings into words, but they felt them nonetheless. The results seemed to be role confusion and ambiguous and unclear expectations. Behind this lay role dissatisfaction which gradually arose to the surface and began to get expressed.

Another cause for role dissatisfaction and role confusion was that the role gaps created by the patient had been filled by other family members during the crisis. It was not always clear to the family which roles were played by which members, and even if it was clear, some members were reluctant to give up some of these new tasks. Mrs. O, the wife of a minister, was not certain what responsibilities she had had in her husband's church before his illness, but she knew that she enjoyed many of her present responsibilities. When her husband pressured her to give up some of these responsibilities while he was in intensive psychotherapy, she became upset. When the onset of family disequilibrium and the patient's symptoms is more rapid than in the O family, this seems to be less of a problem.

Further, when there is a considerable period of time between the onset of symptoms and the beginning of psychiatric treatment, as in the O family, the group may face new developmental problems. Over a period of more than five years, from the beginning of illness to the end of treatment, Ann changed from a latency age child to an adolescent who had acquired dating patterns and other new interests. This caused a good deal of disruption in household routines and was the focus for discussion between Mr. and Mrs. O. The family faces new types of problems and has to find new ways of handling them.

Another cause for disequilibrium in the family at this period is related to the increased pressure on the patient to conform to family roles and tasks. The patient's ability to assume some of his old responsibilities, and his improvement after hospitalization and the beginning of treatment, lead the family to believe that the patient is fully recovered much before this is really so. If he can do some tasks then he should be able to do all, is the reasoning of many spouses and children. Since the patient is not ready nor able to do so, he may become increasingly upset under this pressure and there will be a return of some or all of his symptoms. The secondary gain from such symptoms seems rather important in this situation.

Often, after the onset of treatment, the patient begins to perform his basic tasks in the family, as is expected of him. As stated above, the pressure to do so is great. In the past he may have expressed his frustration and anger by refusing to do so. Now, however, the family and his therapist keep him reality-oriented. The avoidance of such tasks is no longer considered as legitimate after hospitalization and the beginning of treatment as before. Frustration and anger may be expressed in new ways; new symptoms may become prominent. Mr. O, who never before had expressed his hostility except through drinking, exploded at his wife and child at the breakfast table over a burned piece of toast. Mrs. U no longer neglected the care of the home and her children and complained much less about somatic difficulties, but became much more argumentative with her husband over little things and blew up at the children a few times a day. To some family members, the old symptoms seemed easier to handle than the new ones. At least they had experience with the former. They may have even indirectly encouraged a return to these old symptoms in the attempt to help the patient give up the new ones.

Reality orientation had another important effect in increasing pressure towards disequilibrium. It seemed much more socially acceptable to act out within the confines of the nuclear family than in situations outside the family. Mrs. U exploded at her mother and grandmother, and in-laws much less often, but argued vigorously with her husband whenever they were alone together. In the confines of her home she also frequently exploded at the children. Aware of this, Mr. U attempted to get her and the children out of the house and in social relations with friends and family as much as possible. Similarly, Mr. O was much more effective as a minister following hospitalization and the beginning of therapy, especially since he was not drinking, but he exploded within the home much more often.

This type of pressure in itself is difficult for family members, and tends to be more so because there is less acting-out behavior outside the home at this period. To members of the extended family, friends, and neighbors, the patient appears to be normal and functioning well. Thus, difficulty within the family cannot be explained to others as easily. The spouse is less able to confide in others. She and the children tend to blame themselves more for interpersonal difficulties with the patient. This increases anxiety and tension in them, and the second downward spiral of disequilibrium continues.

Finally, the psychotherapeutic process itself indirectly encourages family disequilibrium. If the patient does not withdraw from treatment once the most prominent symptoms are removed, the therapist begins to focus upon the understanding of present behavior in terms of the past. Old wounds are reopened for the patient. Once more he becomes anxious and this may revive old symptoms or bring out new ones. The consequences for the family have been noted.

As intensive insight treatment begins, the patient may begin to test out new behavior within the nuclear family. This is not consistent with former expectations and becomes the focus of considerable stress for the group. Since the patient does not know what will be effective and what will not, this behavior is very variable. In Mrs. U's attempt to become more autonomous, she refused a vacation with her husband and children, often changed her mind suddenly after decisions and plans had been made, and sometimes refused to visit her parents and in-laws, but at other times visited them unexpectedly. Mr. O sometimes relied heavily upon his wife for aid in making social calls, as he had in the past, but occasionally he showed an ability to function well in this area independently. This situation was confusing and difficult for spouses and children. Thus, it seems necessary that there occur a breakdown in the old organization accompanied by family disequilibrium before and during the evolvement of a new equilibrium.

Re-equilibrium

This new crisis during treatment may be more difficult for the family to cope with than the disequilibrium precipitated by mental illness. In some families the threat of divorce is persistent throughout this period despite many years of marriage. The personal needs of the family members can no longer be successfully met in the old ways. The old methods for handling family problems are no longer effective, and a new organization of the family is required. In addition, there are new needs and new problems. In their interaction together family members force changes upon each other during the development of a new role structure.

Role dissatisfactions become expressed during the crises, resulting in role expectations placed on an individual which are in opposition, or role conflict. This leads to many open disagreements and arguments in the family. While each of the families characterized this period as very difficult and unpleasant, there was a great deal of pressure to change. There was also an increase in communication over the preceding stage, as family members tended to have it out. This led to the acceptance of new patterns of behavior.

In this climate, there was a gradual clarification of those patterns of behavior which provided more personal satisfaction for the patient and for the other family members as well. Roles which enabled the group to handle its problems more effectively were also evolved. Through trial and error new behavior was tested out within the nuclear group. Some behavior was abandoned; other ways of acting developed into a successful and effective pattern. While the patient may have been the first to test out new behavior, encouraged by the therapeutic process, this in turn forced changes in behavior upon the other family members. Their response to the patient becomes different and old symptoms may be handled in new ways. In this atmosphere of experimentation, the upward cycle of new organization and re-equilibrium begins.

For example, Mr. O. learned that he enjoyed spending time with his daughter and participating in the purchase of a gift for her. At first, his wife resented her husband's interference in what she thought was an exclusive relationship between Ann and herself. However, she found that her husband provided her with new satisfactions. He bought her gifts for the first time also. She found that Mr. O could be quite helpful in handling Ann's sometimes difficult behavior. She thus came to expect him to take a much greater interest in their daughter. In a much oversimplified way, this illustrates the process that took place.

Similarly, in the U family, Mrs. U resented her husband's out-of-town business trips. These trips not only forced her to be alone but also seemed very exciting compared to her dull life at home. On the spur of the moment, Mr. U invited her to go along with him one day. At first fearful, she finally agreed. She enjoyed the trip so much that Mr. U was also pleased and gratified. He promised to take her along again. One source of role dissatisfaction is lessened through a new pattern of behavior.

As the incidents above indicate, these changes in the patient's behavior may place the spouse and children in a difficult position. While it may be inconsistent with their expectations, they cannot always define it as sick behavior. Some new behavior may be defined in this way, but it is discouraged. Some new behavior may be very pleasing to the family, and this is encouraged. Some new behavior which did not meet expectations may be confusing and result in role conflict for spouse and children.

Mr. O, a man known for his even temper, had explosive outbursts at his wife and child during this period. Mrs. O's negative reactions conveyed to him her dislike of this type of behavior. On the other hand, when he arranged for a special gift of flowers for her birthday, she was overwhelmed and pleased, although this too, was quite unexpected. However, when he arranged for her to give up her secretarial services at the church, she was confused and unhappy. This was not sick behavior, especially since she occasionally complained about the burden of work. Nonetheless, she enjoyed this responsibility and was reluctant to give it up, just as she was reluctant to give up many other church duties. She could either argue this decision with her husband, or conform to these new expectations. Sometimes she took the former choice, and often the result was clarification of the problem and compromise. Sometimes she took the latter choice, attempting to find substitute gratifications. Neither choice was easy for her to handle, but both led to changes in patterns of behavior and new role relationships.

This, in turn, encourages the spouse and children to try out new ways of handling the patient and his symptoms. It was during this same period that Mr. O made an obvious attempt at suicide, similar to the half dozen attempts which brought him to psychiatric treatment. Instead of indicating concern, sympathy, emotional support, and becoming upset, Mrs. O let her husband know that she did not consider this behavior appropriate and acceptable. He quickly got over his sulking and they were able to discuss the causes for his recent depression.

Many such critical incidents occurred in the families during this period. While they were sometimes very emotionally upsetting to family members, that behavior which seemed more effective than old ways of handling similar situations tended to be repeated. Thus, these new patterns were reinforced through time and tended to replace the old ways. Furthermore, success in one role area encouraged family members to try out new behavior in other areas. As negative contagion occurred during family disequilibrium, positive contagion occurred during re-equilibrium. It also led group members to expect more and more changes from each other, changes which would be more personally satisfying to them and enable the family to deal with their problems more effectively. If Mrs. U enjoyed the out of town business trip with her husband, she might also enjoy going along with her husband to sports events away from home. If Mr. O can respond more naturally and spontaneously to his wife during the sexual act while under the influence of alcohol, he ought to be able to do so while sober. Gradually, the content of roles changed and a new type of organization evolved. An upward cycle or re-equilibrium replaced the downward spiral of disequilibrium.

In addition, these new patterns were reinforced by members of the external system. Some changes were noted by extended family members, friends, and neighbors. This was especially true as role conflicts began to diminish and family disagreements occurred less often. Members became more satisfied with family life and the group became more cohesive. For example, parishioners commented about the improved job Mr. O was doing as minister of the church. Friends and family noted Mrs. U's new ability to handle her children. Members of the nuclear family were pleased about such comments, which reinforced their wishes to continue using these new patterns.

Once again, there is a close tie between this stage of family organization and the therapeutic process. Insight therapy helped the patient to understand better the causes for his own behavior, to perceive reality more clearly, and to behave in a manner more appropriate to this reality. New, more appropriate patterns of behavior became established, and the patient's interpersonal relationships and his social functioning in general improved.

To the therapist, these were strong indications that the patient was getting well, and the need for therapy decreased. The therapist began to think of termination.

The final stage in therapy before termination involves the interpretation of the transference relationship between the therapist and the patient, and the consolidation of gains made by the patient through emotional support and the understanding of recent events in the light of current reality.

In less technical language, the therapist helped the patient to understand better the therapeutic relationship in the same way that he had helped him to understand his relationships with others. This allowed the patient to be less dependent upon the therapist. In addition, the therapist encouraged the continuation of newly established, more appropriate patterns of behavior, thus acting as another reinforcement agent. Thus, these new patterns tended to persist. As the focus on insight therapy diminished, the pressure for the patient to change his behavior diminished, enabling new behavior patterns and their concomitant expectations to become established.

As new roles are seen to provide greater psychosocial satisfactions for family members and to be more effective for handling family problems, there is internal pressure to reduce testing out and behavior change. The new role structure becomes clarified and the new equilibrium more firmly established. There is internal role consistency, consistency of family roles and norms and actual role performance, and compatibility of family roles and norms with societal norms. There continues to be change to meet new demands, but it occurs much more slowly. There is a new type of family organization, the crisis is over, and the family is in a period of equilibrium once again.

Implications for Practice

This study has many complex implications for practice in the helping professions. Only a few of the more important ones will be discussed in this paper.

The need for, and the utility of, family diagnosis prior to the beginning of treatment for the patient and/or other members of his family is one of the more obvious and significant practice considerations that grows out of this research project.[10] This is necessary before the therapist can make two vital decisions regarding the patient and his family:

1) What is the treatment of choice for this patient? This becomes particularly vital if intensive insight therapy is considered as one method which might be helpful to this patient since it has significant effects upon the rest of the family group, effects which may well hinder the progress of therapy or result in family disequilibrium, separation, and even divorce. Are the efforts directed at one person worthwhile if it may have major detrimental effects upon other members of the family group? [11] This is

partially a value decision, but also should be a decision based upon knowledge.

2) If the patient is to receive some form of individual psychotherapy, how much and what kind of help will the spouse and children require? As is implied above, this requires an evaluation of the effects of individual psychotherapy for the patient upon other family members and the family as a group. Included must be some anticipation of the degree of disturbance psychotherapy might cause for other family members. In addition, the therapist must evaluate the extent of disequilibrium and the type of disorganization in the family that may result from any treatment method.

These decisions require knowledge of the types and depth of interaction patterns (dyadic role relationships) between the patient and other members of his family. What are the strengths and limitations of other family members, and are role relationships interlocked in such a way that changes in behavior of the patient or his expectations for others will be resisted by them, tend to result in personality disorganization in others, etc.? Thus, family diagnosis requires an evaluation of the personality dimensions of each of the family members.

But further, family diagnosis requires a knowledge of the family as a group, particularly the ways in which it handles its problems as a social system.[12] Knowledge of the parts and their interaction should be supplemented by knowledge of the whole (the Gestalt). Finally disequilibrium need not be accompanied by personality breakdown. Psychotherapy may not lead to psychopathology in other family members but may lead to inefficient family functioning and even the breakdown of the family as a group. We have much more to learn about this aspect of the treatment process.

A second implication has to do with the role of the worker during the treatment process. Two periods of disequilibrium in the family were identified in the larger study: (1) during the acute phase of the patient's illness and (2) during the period in therapy when the patient is focusing on the development of insight through the recall of significant material in his life history, and he is testing out new patterns of behavior, primarily within the nuclear family group. It is at these times that the patient's spouse often needs and seeks help and a professional person can be especially helpful.

During this first diagnostic period the family tends to experience a sense of relief about getting the patient some help, which they often feel he desperately requires. For this reason they are often willing and anxious to cooperate in any way possible. However, they are also quite fearful about the meaning of mental illness and psychiatric treatment. It is an unknown to them which is confusing. In addition, these same reactions in extended-family members, friends, and neighbors may reinforce their own reactions, and many times these members external to the nuclear family will pressure spouse and children not to permit the patient to undergo psychiatric treatment. While the nuclear group tends to align itself with the patient against the external system, this causes internal conflict and anxiety for each member.

The fear of mental illness and psychiatry will diminish if the family has some contacts with the clinic, and if they have been informed of the diagnosis and treatment plan by a warm, friendly, supportive person. This concrete material, given in this manner, reinforces their hope that the patient will get better, and they are willing to make many sacrifices, financial and other, to see this goal accomplished.

The therapeutic stage in which the patient is developing insight into his problems is a very difficult period for the family group. Unfortunately, the optimism present in re-equilibrium during the previous stage of family life leaves the family unprepared for the hardships and tasks they must face.

The return of the patient's symptoms and the development of new symptoms is a threatening experience to the spouse and children. Since the patient is continuing treatment, they find it difficult to understand. The magical component of psychiatric treatment is shattered, sometimes rather abruptly, and they don't know what to expect next. Further, they feel they have no way of finding out.

As the patient begins to test out new behavior inconsistent with the family's former expectations, some of which they may interpret quite negatively, the group members become confused and angry. They don't know where to place the blame for this as well as the recurrence of the patient's symptoms. They alternate in placing responsibility upon themselves (guilt), others outside the family, and the therapist. They find it difficult to handle the patient's new behavior, and even if they wish to change, they are confused as to how to behave. Further, they don't know where to turn. The patient's behavior outside the family often continues to show improvement, which makes the spouse feel that relatives and friends will not understand. Traditionally, the therapist has refused to see the spouse during this therapeutic stage in fear of damaging his relationships with the patient.

This situation is complicated by the deep transference relationship between the patient and the therapist. The patient tends to lean a great deal less upon his family for the gratification of a variety of psychological needs, and a great deal more upon the therapist. He often discusses serious problems and decisions with the therapist and not with his spouse. Further, he tends to see the therapist as an ideal spouse, one which a spouse in real live could not live up to. The result is that the relationship between spouses may grow more distant and cold, and meaningful communication between them may reach an all-time low. The spouse feels left out of the therapeutic system, which has become more meaningful to the patient at this point than any other experience in his life.

Family members may thus become envious, competitive, hostile, and frightened. It is then that there are threats by the patient and the spouse to break up the marriage. The spouse's inability to change and the dis-agreements between marital partners may confirm the patient's belief that his spouse is no longer for him. Neither patient nor spouse understands what is happening, but both tend to become bitter and angry. In the study families, there were two prominent reactions to this situation. The spouse may feel in need of treatment for herself and make demands to see the therapist or another staff person for help with her problems, for the prob-lems she is having with the patient, or for both reasons. The second re-action is to put pressure on the patient to withdraw from therapy. Both of these reactions can sometimes be handled if the spouse can be seen by an-other therapist. By seeing the spouse, the worker can give her some oppor-tunity for catharsis which is badly needed at this point in the family's history. It also brings the spouse into the therapeutic system, if even in-directly, by enabling the spouse to better understand the causes for her husband's reactions at home and some of what he is going through in therapy. Further, the worker can give the spouse reassurance and support, pointing up that this is probably a temporary situation, and the long his-tory of marriage may well be built upon a firm foundation which can stand this type of stress.

This exploratory study investigated one aspect of the social situation in which the psychiatric patient finds himself, that is, the family. As the most important primary group for children and adults in our society, the family seems to have a significant influence on the patient, his illness, and his therapy. This paper presents some generalizations which we hope will be meaningful for theory, practice and future research.

13 Social and Psychological Factors in Status Decisions of Unmarried Mothers

Wyatt C. Jones, Henry J. Meyer, and Edgar F. Borgatta

In prior studies the association of background characteristics—such as race, religion, and education—to the decisions of agency samples of unmarried mothers to surrender or keep their babies has been examined.[1] Some findings were sufficiently striking to suggest that further study might establish empirical relationships that would make it possible to identify persons in terms of their likelihood of making a particular decision. This might alert practitioners serving such clients to differential problems, especially where decisions appear to differ from those predicted. The first purpose of this paper is to examine another set of cases and to suggest in more general terms the implications of the empirical relationships that now appear to be reasonably stable.

A second purpose is to report associations between a series of personality and attitude measures and the decision to keep or surrender the baby. In the prior studies certain personal characteristics rated by caseworkers appeared to have some association with the decision. Here we report relationships based on test-response data obtained before the birth of the baby. Such information, not usually available, has intrinsic interest and adds as well to knowledge about the unmarried mother's decision.[2]

Background Characteristics and the Unmarried Mother's Decision

The empirical relationships found in the series of studies can be interpreted briefly by reference to general theories about American soci-

Abridged from MARRIAGE AND FAMILY LIVING, **24** (1962), 224–230. Reprinted with the permission of the authors and the National Council on Family Relations.

ety. In broadest terms, the relationships can be viewed as reflecting a conflict between the dominant values and mores of American society, on the one hand, and opposing values of relatively unassimilated subgroups or subcultures and of deviant individuals, on the other hand. The dominant values of American society, phrased simply, include a negative view of births outside of wedlock. To illustrate from one subgroup, Negroes in America can be assumed to support the ideal of having children within the legally constituted family unit, but this ideal is apparently not so strongly held as it is within the society as a whole. Such an assertion is not totally circular (i.e., Negroes hold the ideals less strongly because there is more illegitimacy) since it rests on evidence of historical tradition and also on analysis indicating that, even when such important factors as education and socioeconomic class are controlled, some aspects of behavior are left unexplained and must be attributed to the *culture* or common behavior of the group. Raising economic and educational levels of any group may constitute an important change, but it does not automatically change the values of the group in regard to such things as orientations of pleasure, friendship, dating, courtship, and marriage. However, as the subculture becomes more integrated, its values may be expected to approximate the dominant values of the general society. This explanation would fit the experience at one social agency [3] in respect to decisions of its Negro clients. In 1954, 83 per cent of the Negro clients kept their babies. In 1956, the proportion was 76 per cent. In the 1957–1959 sample, the percentage had fallen to 62. During the same period, the proportion of white clients who kept their babies fell from 38 per cent in 1954 to 21 per cent in the current sample. Over a five-year period, the differential between Negro and white clients was reduced by 3 per cent. Other explanations, such as changes in agency policies and increases in adoption outlets, are also possible, of course.

As decreasing association between subgroup membership and deviance occurs, predictions for the general society may be expected to apply equally for Negroes. Such is not the case at present, and we therefore consistently find that Negro unmarried mothers, in comparison to white mothers, keep their babies rather than surrender them. The explanation for this difference need not assume any innate peculiarities of these Negro mothers. The status of the Negro in the total society produces a number of compelling social pressures. Thus, even if a Negro girl wishes to surrender her baby for adoption, in addition to subcultural norms imposed on her or internalized by her, social, economic, or legal barriers may make it impossible for her to do so. Our only assertion is that it is efficient, at this point in history, to predict that Negro unmarried mothers will keep their babies to a greater extent than white unmarried mothers.

Our earlier studies found four background variables most useful for predicting the disposition decision of white unmarried mothers: age, education, and religion of the mother, and marital status of the putative father —the male involved in the relationship. Agency clients who were young, more highly educated, and of non-Catholic religion tended to surrender the baby for adoption. It also appeared in these earlier studies that when the putative fathers of the babies were unmarried, the mothers tended to surrender, but this appears to be a less relevant variable for predictive purposes than the other background characteristics.

Consideration of the marital status of the putative father was suggested by the theory that when a girl has relationships with a man who is unavailable for marriage, she will, upon becoming pregnant, perpetuate her deviance for the same psychological reasons that led to her situation by tending to keep rather than surrender the baby. In the absence of consistent evidence for this theory, however, we prefer to give attention to more direct social and psychological variables.

Although by no means invariant, there is a consistent relationship between the Catholic religion of an unmarried mother and the tendency to keep the baby. Our data are insufficient to explore why this is so. Like Negro girls, Roman Catholic girls might be considered to come from a cultural subgroup of American society. We might speculate that girls from Catholic backgrounds have accepted obligations of natural motherhood as more compelling than restoration of single status. Perhaps this reflects strong religious beliefs associated with sex, marriage, and motherhood, or with retribution and responsibility. Perhaps it reflects differential ethnic values deriving from national origin because Catholics are more likely to be of recent immigration than Protestants. Our previous studies do not, however, support the interpretation that the association between professed Catholic religion and keeping the baby is a reflection of socioeconomic status because it occurs even when social class is held constant. Whatever the explanation, the empirical relationship has persisted throughout the series of studies and constitutes a predictor, even though not a determiner, of the decision about the baby.

Education, particularly at the college level, is associated with surrendering the baby. A direct and obvious interpretation of this relationship might suggest that keeping the baby constitutes a handicap to continuation of a normal education, occupational, and marital career. Surrender of the baby represents the only means by which a girl, socialized through years of education, can remain consistent with general American values of marriage and motherhood.

Younger ages are associated with surrender of the baby. At the youngest ages, subadult status minimizes individual choices and subjects the unmarried mother to the imposition of adult control more likely to conform to the general value system. The older the unmarried mother, the more free she is to express subcultural or personal values by keeping the baby. Similarly, the younger the unmarried mother, the less likely that the attributions of adult independence will occur to inhibit a return to the more normal nonmother status.

In the historical sense, these predictive variables are almost certainly transitory. With secularization of knowledge, any subcultural values that may exist for Catholics with respect to unmarried motherhood are likely to change in the direction of the more general value system. A similar change can be expected for Negroes. If values become more homogeneous, it appears that in the long run most unmarried mothers will return to their nonmother status by surrendering their babies. If this is the trend, race, religion, age, and education will eventually have but trivial potency as predictors of the decision. It may simply be predicted that unmarried mothers will seek to surrender the baby.

It may be further suggested that reduced insulation of subcultures will lessen whatever satisfactions might be obtained from conformity to subcultural values. If the basic proposition is accepted that, in general, conforming behavior yields more total satisfaction—social as well as psychological—than nonconformity, the general societal norm will be more widely accepted. When norms conflict, in the absence of subcultural isolation, it is more likely that the general norm will be accepted. If surrendering their babies becomes recognized by the unmarried mothers as a general norm, keeping the baby can be expected to become less and less satisfying.

We postulate surrender of the baby as a general norm for a number of reasons. In the first place, there is little evidence that the status of unmarried motherhood is more acceptable now than formerly. Further, widespread acceptance of contraception may be expected to reduce further any tolerance for accidental pregnancy among the unmarried. We would presume also that other means—such as abortion—of returning to nonmother status would become more widely acceptable. The trend toward secularization, as already mentioned, would point in the same direction with respect to surrender of the baby as the general norm. Accompanying this, emphasis on individual careers, rather than on continuity and maintenance of family and communal traditions, would discourage unmarried mothers from keeping their babies. Finally, there appears to be sufficient infertility among married couples to provide a ready market for adoption of babies surrendered by unmarried mothers.

Although we postulate the general norm of surrender, we do not imply that subcultural, family, and individual factors may not result in some deviant behavior in respect to the unmarried mother's decision. What we insist is that until there is, in actuality, such a general norm, background factors now associated with the decision are likely to predict better than more individual or psychological variables. As a consequence, studies of psychological factors associated with the decision should be interpreted with caution unless background factors—especially race, education, religion, and age—are taken into account. Put another way, psychological factors may more appropriately be interpreted for the light they throw on general and subcultural norms than as psychological explanations for the decision.

The Present Sample

Over a three-year period, the unmarried mothers who were clients at a nonsectarian, private social agency in New York City were studied. The agency offers casework services to adolescent and young adult female clients. Most of them were known to the agency for one to four months prior to delivery of the baby. Information was obtained for a large proportion of these clients, as well as from caseworkers, through tests administered both before and after delivery. The clients for whom information is lacking appear not to differ from the usual clientele of the agency. The sample, obviously not representative of all unmarried mothers, is composed of persons from a wide range of socioeconomic levels and a variety of geographical and subcultural backgrounds.[4]

Prediction for Background Criteria

Of the total sample studied (113 clients), 20 per cent were Negro and 80 per cent were white. The proportion of Negro unmarried mothers keeping their babies was 62 per cent, smaller than our earlier studies found but nevertheless significantly greater than the 21 per cent of whites who kept their babies.[5] Thus, in accord with prior experience, we may conclude that the prediction that Negro girls will keep their babies can be made with some confidence.[6] The small number of cases here precludes detailed examination of other characteristics of the Negro unmarried mothers in our sample and hence our subsequent analyses will be confined to whites only. Furthermore, the prior studies have not yielded factors that would improve the prediction for Negro unmarried mothers.

Using the 90 white clients who constituted our sample for this analysis, we have made a test that includes the variables of age, education, and religion. For this purpose, young age (under 17 years of age), non-Catholic religion (rather than Catholic), and some college education (rather than less education) are taken as predictors that the unmarried mother will surrender her baby. While the fact of being white is a substantial predictor in itself, since 71 of the total 90 in the sample surrendered, a more efficient prediction can be made for such groups of the sample using these additional variables. Thus, if two or three of these criterion variables are present, 23 out of 24 unmarried mothers surrendered their babies. If none of these variables is present the probability is 40 per cent (8 out of 20) that the baby will be kept. If only one of the criterion variables is present, the results are more ambiguous, 36 surrendered and 10 kept their babies. These results are consistent with our previous studies.

Personality Characteristics and the Decision to Keep or Surrender

Unlike information about background characteristics, prior quantitative data based on personality or other psychological variables have been scarce. Only recently, for example, has Vincent published some data using the C. P. I.[7] We therefore examined such variables in our study to see which differentiate unmarried mothers, prior to the birth of their baby, with respect to the decision. For the 90 white clients, responses to a sentence completion test (MAST),[8] the Cattell 16 Personality Factor Test,[9] and a checklist of items about feelings and problems have been analyzed for this purpose.

Personality Characteristics Measured through the MAST

Of the 11 MAST scoring categories, only one discriminated between the mothers who surrendered and those who kept their babies. This was the scale indicating paranoid responses (MAST 1). Significantly more mothers who kept their babies had scores above the median cutting point for the variable. With scores of zero to three, 41 of 71 mothers surrendered; with scores of four or more, 14 of 19 mothers kept their babies.

Several other scoring categories seem to indicate differences, but none achieved the significance level.[10] The largest additional difference is an association of MAST 8, Anxious, with keeping the baby.

The Cattell 16 Personality Factor Test

Five of the personality factors were significantly associated with the decision to keep or surrender the baby. Scores for girls who kept their babies would characterize them as "insecure, anxious" (o score), "tense, excitable" (Q_4 score), "emotional, unstable" (C score), "dull, low capacity" (B score), and "submissive, mild" (E score). In contrast, those who surrendered their babies could be described as "confident, unshakeable," "phlegmatic, poised," "mature, calm," "bright, intelligent," and "dominant, aggressive." Thus, unmarried mothers who kept their babies, in comparison with those who surrendered them, tended to be: (1) lower in intelligence, (2) lower in ego strength or emotional stability, and (3) more submissive.[11]

Discussion of Personality Characteristics

The constellation of personality characteristics describing the unmarried mother who keeps her baby implies general immaturity, and this is the same conclusion suggested by earlier examination of caseworker ratings of unmarried mother clients in another social agency.[12] Those who ultimately surrender the baby can be described as exhibiting greater intelligence, independence, and emotional stability, less anxiety and tension, and less feeling that others make things difficult. These are characteristics that might be associated with greater competence than the contrasting characteristics of those who kept their babies.

The idea that those who surrendered were, on the whole, somewhat better adjusted or felt more competent in the face of their situation is supported by responses to a short checklist of attitudes toward problems and other circumstances. When asked the simple and direct question: "How do you feel?," 46 of the 90 clients answered "very well" or "excellent," but among those who eventually surrendered their babies, the proportion giving these responses was slightly higher (although not statistically significant) compared to those who eventually kept their babies. Similarly, those who surrendered gave somewhat more favorable responses when asked if they felt better at present than two months earlier, but, again, the difference did not achieve statistical significance. Likewise, those who ultimately surrendered were slightly more likely than the other category to say that they were getting along very well with family and friends.

Table 1 may be interpreted in keeping with the idea that surrender of the baby is associated with maturity and competence, and that this in turn

Table 13-1. Relationship of Disposition Decision to Responses on Selected Cattell Scores and Self-Assessed Problem Status, White Only

Responses	Scores	Surrender	Keep	Totals
Emotional	LM	42	17	59
stability (C)	H	29	2	31
Anxiety	LM	48	7	55
(O)	H	23	12	35
Tension	LM	50	7	57
(Q₄)	H	21	12	33
Intelligence	L	27	13	40
(B)	MH	44	6	50
Dominance	L	39	17	56
(E)	MH	32	2	34
Number of prob-	Many	28	11	39
lems indicated	Few	43	8	51
Ability to take	Well	52	5	57
care of problems	Trouble	19	14	33
Totals		71	19	90

is related to conformance with the general norm of surrendering the baby so that legitimate nonmother status is restored. The proportion of those who indicated that they had many problems was smaller for those who surrendered than for those who kept their babies. A higher proportion (statistically significant) of the group who surrendered also expressed confidence in their ability to take care of their problems in the future. These findings suggest more secure and confident attitudes on the part of those who surrendered than of those who kept. Realistically, those who surrender have fewer problems to face in the future precisely because keeping the baby constitutes continued and visible deviance as well as increased economic and other responsibilities. The more mature may be expected to recognize this.

When we ask whether variables associated with the disposition decision are those to be expected from the general theory of subcultural deviance, we conclude that this is a plausible interpretation. Because of the small size of our sample, we cannot examine personality and attitudinal variables holding constant the social background characteristics found to be predictive of the decision. But we would surmise that the differences in personality measures would reflect the background characteristics we consider indicators of subcultural variation.

Conclusion

This paper has briefly reviewed current research about social and psychological factors in status decisions of unmarried mothers. Cumulative evidence appears to show considerable consistency in findings on background factors such as race, religion, education, and age and some consistency also for psychological variables. The findings lead to the tentative conclusion that the phenomenon of unmarried motherhood may be appropriately interpreted, at this stage of available research knowledge, through analysis of subcultural values. Such values may be exhibited in differential intrafamily relationships, in differential peer relationships especially those involving dating and other heterosexual activities, and in differential cognitive orientations, attitudes, and self-images internalized during the socialization of girls who have babies before they are married. However, until subcultural variations can be taken into account, it would seem premature to interpret status decisions of the unmarried mother, such as the decision to keep or surrender the baby, primarily as manifestations of individual, psychological dynamics.

Studies available to the present time have been based on relatively small samples of agency clients. The selective bias of agency samples limits generalization and the small sample sizes limit the detail of analysis that is now possible. Replication of the gross findings lends support to a subcultural hypothesis and suggests that it is timely now to develop comprehensive research on the factors affecting the status decisions of unmarried mothers.

14 Divorce Law as a Means of Social Control

Eugene Litwak

Problem

This paper will address itself to the problem of law as a means of social control. More specifically the question is: To what extent can divorce law be used to prevent *de facto* family breakup, i.e., the situation where marital partners are separated formally or informally. This paper will not concern itself with an equally relevant problem: Is breakup good or bad?

Types of *De Facto* Breakups

If law is to act on human behavior, it should provide an environment which will enable the deviant or potential deviant to internalize the values embodied in the law or it should provide an environment which will force the deviant to conform by systematically placing blocks in his achievement of his deviant values, whenever he violates the law.

In searching for environments both social and psychological which lead to breakup one is confronted by an impressive number of items which have been related to breakup.[1] Though the list is long it is thought that all of these factors actually act upon the family members in one of four ways. These have been called *de facto* breakup by conflict, *de facto* breakup by indifference, *de facto* breakup by opportunity, and continuance by fiat.

Breakup by conflict can be exemplified by the case in which the husband was raised with the value of leisure as paramount and the wife with the value of status. The wife might view the husband as a shiftless time waster, while the husband might view the wife as a vain status striver. Other things being equal, this will lead to a higher probability of breakup.

Abridged from "Three Ways in Which Law Acts As a Means of Social Control: Punishment, Therapy, and Education," SOCIAL FORCES, 34 (1956), 217–223. Reprinted with the permission of the author and the University of North Carolina Press.

Breakup by indifference has been most thoroughly discussed in connection with Ogburn's theory [2] that the family is losing its functions. The less the husband and wife depend on each other the greater are their chances of splitting up.

Breakup by opportunity refers to the number of contacts between members of the opposite sex. Thus, where the husband's job throws him into contact with women (e.g., traveling salesman), where husband and wife are separated (e.g., during wars, etc.) a high probability exists for one of the spouses to meet other potential spouses. Other things being equal, this is likely to lead to breakup.

The fourth mode is that which is called continuance by fiat. It refers to the fact that a high value is placed on marriage per se. In our society the Catholic considers marriage a sacrament and therefore places a great value on marriage per se, and, other things being equal, the very religious Catholic would be less likely to divorce.

These four modes are thought to encompass all of the factors which relate to family breakup. At the same time they are sufficiently different so that the same law might have entirely different effects depending on which of these four modes characterizes the family. Laws will be analyzed as mechanisms of social control in terms of their ability to affect these four modes of marriage breakup and stability.

Three types of law will be discussed: that which we have called law as punishment, law as therapy, and law as education.

Law as Punishment

Punishment is defined in this paper as the deliberate and public blocking of the deviant's ability to achieve his goals if he violates those embodied in the law. The law as punishment might act in three ways. It might deter the deviant by threatening the values he holds dear; it might act as a learning device and force the deviant to internalize the values of the law; and it might serve through the publicity of punishment to reinforce the values of the nondeviants. The law as punishment, by definition, stresses the first but it also affects the others. [3]

Historically the idea that divorce is a punishment seems to rest on the general Christian doctrine that marriage is a good per se, which can be broken only by a sinner. [4] Today the idea of divorce as a punishment for guilty parties is maintained in the divorce law of some states. This is exemplified by laws which say that the amount of alimony should be based on the extent of guilt, [5] that the disposition of the children should be decided on the basis of who is innocent, [6] that the guilty party should not be able to remarry for given periods of time (sometimes for life), [7] and by forcing the prosecution of the guilty party in a criminal action rather than in a civil action. [8]

Table 14–1. Ways in Which Types of Law Affect Different Kinds of Family Breakup

Types of Breakup	TYPES OF LAW		
	Law as punishment	Law as therapy	Law as education
Breakup by Conflict	Penalties are so great that people have an incentive to reconcile their conflict.	Allows fundamental conflicts to breakup; other conflicts are settled through the process of therapy.	Seeks to develop personal abilities so that individuals can deal with conflicts or will be less likely to marry people who conflict with them.
Breakup by Indifference	Forces one spouse to depend on the other as a condition of breakup; forces the guilty spouse to depend on the innocent for seeing the child.	Attempts to point out areas of mutual need.	Attempts to develop the ability to share oneself with others without fear of losing one's identity.
Breakup by Opportunity	Provides penalties if the guilty party remarries; forces the guilty party to wait before remarriage.	Does nothing.	Does nothing.
Breakdown of Fiat	Does nothing except insofar as publicity of punishment increases the strength in which a value is held.	Does nothing except point up value of marriage per se if the client holds it.	In the hands of a social system which holds the value of marriage per se it inculcates this value.

Conditions under Which the Law of Punishment May Fail

What are the possible limitations of the law as punishment for affecting family breakup? Six possible situations will be discussed. These are as follows:

1. The punishments established by the law cannot reach basic values of the deviant.
2. Where the society has conflicting values the innocent as well as the guilty suffer by punishment.
3. Where there is a deviant group rather than a deviant individual, punishment might lead to a martyr effect and boomerang, causing further deviation.
4. Under certain value systems punishment is by definition not apropos, which leads to the refusal of the innocent party through collusion, perjury, etc., to press the punishment.
5. The simple learning theory implied is not sufficient to bring about changes in values of the deviant.
6. The punishment law will not act as a deterrent where the deviant feels there is little chance of getting caught no matter how efficient the law might actually be.

The law as punishment might fail where it is unable to provide sufficiently serious blocks to the deviant's values. This point is quite easily seen in political deviation and has been virtually sloganized by Patrick Henry's famous "Give me liberty or give me death." Insofar as the maximum block the law could bring was death, and insofar as liberty was a greater value than life to Patrick Henry, the law as punishment would have been ineffectual in deterring him from initiating deviant behavior. In the field of divorce the law fails to act as a means for preventing break-up insofar as people feel that they would prefer the penalties of paying a little more alimony, waiting a longer time to remarry, or even having their children taken away from them than live in a marriage which violates their values of love, companionship, and freedom of choice.

A second interrelated point and one reason why the law cannot find blocks to deviant values is that, ideally, punishment should only be directed at the deviant and never at the nondeviant if it is to achieve social control. However, where individuals have conflicting values, punishment of the criminals many times rebounds on the innocent as well. For instance, the criminal who is thrown in jail has to be supported out of funds which the conforming member would like to use for such things as better schools, leisure time activities, health, etc. In this sense the punishment of the criminal is also felt as a punishment by the conformist.

In our society, the value that marriage is a good per se has gone together with such values as marital chastity, good treatment of children, preservation of health, etc. Where there is a clash in these values, the cost of maintaining the value that marriage is a good per se is (after a certain point) greater than the rewards of maintaining the value. For instance, should the husband be a drunkard who cannot make a living, then any divorce law which seeks through punishment to keep the marriage together will uphold the value of marriage as a good per se but it will also result in violations of other values. It not only punishes the husband but might also punish the innocent wife. It forces her to live in poverty or in danger of her life, etc. Insofar as the law as punishment punishes the innocent (conformist) as well as the guilty (nonconformist) it will not be effective as a means of social control.

Another factor which enters into the consideration of the effectiveness of punishment is the extent to which the deviant is an isolate or a member of a deviant group. In a society such as ours which is made up of groups having some overlapping values and some conflicting values the concept of the deviant group is quite a propos. For instance, the Catholic Church is at odds with most of the populace on the question of divorce, yet in other matters such as foreign policy, interracial freedom, etc., it might be in complete harmony.[9] In some states Catholics are a deviant group as far as marriage values are concerned and in others they are the nondeviant group.

Where deviant groups rather than individuals are being considered, the mechanism of control which Durkheim and Mead [10] refer to might work in reverse. They point out that publicity of punishment provides an opportunity for the conforming members of the society to reaffirm their values publicly. This public confirmation in turn leads to greater reaffirmation of these same values. However, where there is a deviant group, a member of which is punished publicly, it is recognized, particularly in political deviation, that such public punishment leads to the martyr effect. In short, it provides an opportunity for the deviant group as well as the conformist to affirm their values publicly. The public punishment boomerangs. It promotes greater cohesion within the deviant group and, thus, a breakdown of social control.

It is possible that the public punishment administered in divorce cases might lead to reaffirmation of marriage as a good per se. Lichtenberger points out that at the turn of the century concentrated attention on the rising rate of divorce led to changes in the law which made them even more stringent. This would seem to fit the Mead-Durkheim thesis. Yet a more commonsensical assertion, which seems to fit our social situation more completely, is that the more people heard about divorce, the more people got divorced, the more they accepted divorce as legitimate. This is especially true where the divorces come from the power groups of the society.[11]

Still another factor is interrelated to the above. The idea that divorce is punishment for the guilty rests to a great extent on the notion that marriage is a sacrament and therefore a good per se. However, if marriage is considered as based primarily on love, companionship, and freedom of choice, and only secondarily on being a good per se, punishment becomes literally a meaningless concept to the married couple. Thus a wife who might not want her husband to leave but feels he has a moral right to, might not want to take advantage of the law as punishment to demand the maximum alimony she can get; she might permit the husband to visit the children, even though he has no right to under the law, etc. Where the person who is defined by the law to be the innocent party refuses to recognize punishment as a legitimate mode of orientation in marital separation, then punishment loses all threat to the guilty spouse.

Also, under these circumstances, as pointed out by many lawyers, the rules of litigation, condemnation, collusion, actually serve to prevent reconciliation, and reduce the effect of law as a means of social control.[12]

Another factor which mitigates against punishment as a means of control is where the violation is due to a personality element which is a consequence of long and constant social interaction. In such a situation the simple conditioning theory of change which law as punishment implies would not be enough to affect the behavior of the deviant. Rather constant punishment would be required in much the same manner and with as much energy as the Chinese displayed in their treatment of American prisoners to get them to change their basic orientations. Thus the ability of a man to control his temper will not be increased by a threat of paying alimony to his wife.

Somewhat in the same vein is the assertion that it is not always possible for the "guilty" person to correctly assess the possibility of getting punished. He is quite willing to do something which might bring about punishment if he *feels* that the chances of being punished are small or that the punishment is not severe. The fact that he will have to pay alimony without having any of the privileges of marriage will not act as a preventive if the husband cannot visualize prior to his decision the consequence to his standard of living, being without his children, etc.

Ways in Which Punishment Operates to Prevent Breakdown

Despite the various limitations mentioned above about the possible utility of punishment as a means of social control it is not the intention to say it cannot act as such. There are too many cases, such as the agrarian laws of Russia, our own tax laws, etc., where the law can and does act as a means of social control. If the situation is crucial there is no reason why some of the limitations mentioned above might not be altered by society. Even the data of Lichtenberger indicate the effectiveness of laws which are extremely severe.

The divorce laws strive to achieve control through reduction of the four modes of breakup: breakup by conflict, breakup by indifference, breakup by opportunity, and breakdown of marital fiat.

The law of punishment only indirectly faces the problem of breakup by conflict. If the married couple realize that it is very difficult to get a divorce and that they must stay together, then they will attempt much harder to reconcile their conflicts. In this sense the law promotes a harmony of values.[13]

The law of punishment controls breakup by indifference in several ways. It basically tries to link several values to the marriage relationship. For instance, it might make the guilty spouse completely dependent on the innocent one for the privilege of being with his children.

The law as punishment seeks to control breakup by opportunity directly by refusing the guilty party the right to remarry.[14] This reduces his opportunity of finding another spouse. The law as punishment will prevent the breakdown of marital fiat only in the sense that the Meadian theory would hold—that public punishment serves to strengthen the values of society and where society places a value on marriage per se.

Law as Therapy [15]

A basic premise of law as therapy is that people seek divorce because of serious emotional problems. Therefore, any legal procedure seeking to control divorce should provide that the spouses see a therapist. What are the advantages and disadvantages of the law as therapy? In the previous section we have outlined six conditions which if present might lead to ineffectiveness of the law as punishment. Therapy by definition avoids several of the conditions which make law as punishment ineffective. It does not worry about finding blocks for deviant values, since it focusses on internalization of societal values. It reduces by definition the problem of trying to treat interpersonal relationships in terms of guilt and punishment when it has no such meaning to the participants. By taking the marital dispute out of the public court and putting it into the private chambers of the therapist, it reduces both the boomerang character of the martyr effect as well as the reenforcing effect on social values suggested by Mead et al. It very definitely attempts to meet the objections of trying to bring about change in the deviant's basic pattern by use of a simplicistic psychological theory.

The major contribution of the law as therapy is that it brings to bear upon the deviant a more focussed kind of pressure for internalizing the values of society. It provides a highly trained social worker to replace the former personality expert—the judge. And presumably it brings along more effective psychological techniques roughly called therapy. It presumably affects breakup by indifference and by conflict directly. It does this by clarifying the source of conflict and ways of evading further conflict, and by developing the personality of the individuals so that they can share emotionally with each other. This is especially important in view of the fact that affection is, according to some schools of thought, the major bond holding the western industrialized family together.

The second major area of contribution by therapy is that it assumes that marriage is primarily based on the values of love, companionship, and freedom of choice, and only secondarily based on the notion that it is a good per se. Operationally this means that conciliation—and if that fails, arbitration—are the techniques used rather than litigation. People can meet together and talk out their differences without fear of collusion or need for perjury.

In the hands of a religiously oriented therapist it might even prevent the breakdown of marital fiat. The law as therapy has little to do with preventing marital breakdown by opportunity.

Law as therapy has several shortcomings. In a report of the Swedish divorce law, which includes many of the ideas of the law as therapy, several major evasions of the law were noted.[16] The basis for these evasions is that the law as therapy usually goes into operation only after the couple have really committed themselves to their hostilities or to new spouses. This means they will not cooperate with the therapist. Since much of modern therapy, to be effective, requires cooperation of the clients, much of the therapy session advocated by law becomes perfunctory. Secondly, when people do not believe in therapy, they view it as a punishment, and evade it in the same manner as other forms of punishment. Thirdly, the law as therapy is rather expensive and ineffectual in cases of fundamental personality factors which lead to conflict, or inability to share one's self with another. The policy under the law as therapy is usually to allow breakup where major changes in personality are required.

The difficulties mentioned above are not considered fundamental. It is conceivable that new developments in the methods of therapy might remove them as problems. The fundamental objection to the law as therapy is that it tends to locate deviation within the individual. It fails to recognize that the faults of marriage need not lie within the persons involved but might well be a product of the regular societal system of socialization.[17] For instance, it has been pointed out that in our middle-class culture men and women are systematically raised with conflicting concepts of their roles and those of their future spouses.[18] These conflicting concepts of role are a basis for marital conflict. Ogburn [19] has pointed out that in our regular societal development the increasing tendency for families to lose their functions lays the basis for breakup through indifference. These facts have meant that the social system has produced spouses who systematically have a high probability of developing conflicts, being indifferent, meeting new spouses, and who place a low value on marriage per se.

The Law as Education

The law as education is one type of law which is designed to meet this objection. It, in a sense, recognizes that the individual's ability to handle himself is a consequence of the regular institutional processes. Unlike the other two types of law it does not wait until the deviant act has occurred before becoming operative. Illustrations of the law as education exist in many areas of life. Most licensing laws are law as education.

For instance, the laws which demand that doctors have a certain amount of eduction and pass certain examinations before they can practice would illustrate the law as education. The marriage licensing laws insofar as they view minimum age limits as being an index of a person's competence might be thought of in terms of law as education.

In considering the law as education it becomes apparent that certain factors which affect family breakup would be rather difficult to alter by law. Or, put somewhat differently, the environments the law presents cannot compete so easily against such factors as urbanization, industrialization, wars, and depressions. Any law as education would have to take such factors as a given.

If one takes a modern industrial society as a given, then the systematic development of individual capacities is one area in which the law as education might play a major role. Law as education is basically concerned with developing environments which allow individuals to internalize given values.

In the past, the law as education has been thought of as a panacea. For any ills in the society the answer has been education. However, usually a very narrow viewpoint has been taken of the educational processes—they have been thought of primarily in terms of the traditional classroom lecture systems. It has been assumed that exposure to facts is tantamount to their acceptance. Because the notion of education has been so closely tied to the lecture method of information exposure there is a historic backlog of failures.

It is only when looking at recent investigations into learning processes that one gets a sense that incorporation of facts for use in real life situations is far more than mere exposure to those facts.[20] Much greater use should be made in education of those processes which sociologists have called socializing processes. It is the learning which takes place gradually, imperceptibly, and informally through participation in common group endeavors.

With this in mind courses in family living can be thought of as applied courses in social psychology. Each course is in this sense a study in personality development. The technique for evaluation of this change and for bringing it about should be far more sophisticated than straight lectures and factual examinations given at the end of the class, as is now the case in most schools.

One socio-psychological theory which might be incorporated into the processes of education is that of Foote and Cottrell.[21] It rests fundamentally on the proposition that the individual's personality is a function of his interaction with others and is not fixed but capable of infinite development and variation. There is reason to believe that such a systematic development of interpersonal competence might have an effect on family breakup [22] since it takes as a given condition a rapidly changing environment which is one of the chief characteristics of the industrialized urban community in which we now live and which is thought to be the chief institutional source of breakup. Moreover, it suggests types of learning environments which approximate the regular socializing experiences and which are at the same time capable of systematic mass disseminations.

Insofar as the law requires all individuals to attend schools and insofar as school systems have courses in family living and insofar as these courses take cognizance of modern social psychological developments on learning behavior, these laws might become the most powerful aids in preventing family breakup.

If the law as education is successful, it does everything other types of law will do plus locating responsibility in the institutional structure. Its chief limitation in the past was that the learning environments it presented to the individual have never seriously been able to compete with the other environments to which they were exposed—job, family, peer groups, etc.

Conclusion

Although the law has been discussed as being either that of punishment, therapy, or education, in actual fact laws have elements of all of these. Furthermore, different occasions might at any given time make one more effective than another.

The present discussion has been limited to presenting the law as a means of social control in terms of six conditions. It has not, for instance, discussed the interaction between the enforcement agents and the deviants. It has not considered systematically the effects of various ways into which society can be organized into power structures and the differential effects of these power structures on the enforcement of laws. Yet these would provide crucial limitations on some of the generalizations made in this paper.

The intent of this paper has been to indicate two things. First, that a single set of laws—divorce laws—have different ways of effecting social control—through punishment, therapy, and education. Secondly, that the dependent variable which the law seeks to control, family breakup, is complex. There are different kinds of breakup—breakup by conflict, indifference, opportunity, and of marital fiat. The matching of type of law and type of breakup will lead to the maximum form of social control.

Part V

Organizational Factors in

Service Agencies

Introduction

It is popularly alleged that this is an era of the organizational man, of red tape, and of bureaucracies. Much truth is implicit in these simplistic and sometimes denigrating phrases. In social work, virtually all professional work is done in and through a welfare organization and these agencies have rules by which the services are provided. Moreover, the social work agency is itself typically a large organization, part of an extended, complex organizational system. Welfare organizations greatly affect the quality and quantity of services provided. Taken together, they constitute the web and structure of the social welfare system. They are purposefully created administrative forms for achieving service objectives and it is through the deliberate actions of administering their day-by-day activities that the service objectives are implemented. For all of these reasons we are enjoined to study carefully the types of organizations in welfare, the effects of relevant organizational variables upon staff and client relations, the structural features of organizations, the issues and dilemmas pertaining to them as well as the interrelationships between and among the organizations. The selections in this section pertain to these problems.

Vinter's discussion of the social structure of service, in the first selection, is an organizational analysis of the common dilemmas and issues posed by the provision of welfare services in organizations that serve a clientele directly. Here we find stressed some of the noncomplementary and conflicting features of the bureaucratic and professional structures. The effects for clients and staff of organizational size and of interrelated factors are treated and, in the discussion of the structure of authority, the author presents problems relating to hierarchies of personnel, official policies, rules and procedures, and problems of supervision. Complementing these themes, the author emphasizes the intended as well as the unintended consequences of administrative action. Practitioners who work directly with clients, as well as administrators of agencies and those who plan organizational and service structures, will benefit from this penetrating analysis.

In the next selection, Vinter presents an analysis of treatment organizations. This type of organization is conceived as one type of "people-changing" organization, the other type being the socialization agency. The characteristics of people-changing organizations are outlined, as are differences between schools and youth-serving agencies as socialization organizations, and prisons and mental hospitals as treatment organizations. Varieties of treatment organizations are then discussed in terms of differences in the change technologies employed, the extent of reliance upon professional personnel, the ways in which professional behavior is controlled, as well as difficulties and consequences for clients. Some of the problems in evaluating effectiveness in different types of treatment organizations are discussed as well. More than illustrating the fruitfulness of a sociological perspective in the study of welfare organizations, this analysis indicates both the limitations and the unique suitabilities of these various types of organization.

The relationship between self-image perspectives of delinquents in custodial and treatment institutions is reported in the selection by Sarri. By considering organizational goals, the structure of authority, and staff perspectives and behavior, the five institutions studied are ordered in terms of their relative emphasis upon custody and treatment. The major hypothesis is that the extent to which attitudes and the perspectives of inmates are positive will vary directly with the degree of emphasis in the institution upon treatment versus custody. Contrary to what many might have expected, it was found that the social backgrounds and personal characteristics of the inmates were relatively similar in the five institutions. Length of stay in the different types of institutions was found to have an influence upon perspectives and behaviors. Furthermore, the attitudes toward conformity and the change and therapeutic goals differed as anticipated among the five institutions, but the differences were less marked in the extent to which the self-images were positive. The findings reveal in general that the different goals of custody and treatment, as reflected in the subjective reports of the inmates, appear to have been attained. The significance of organizational factors as preconditions for change is particularly highlighted in this study.

The next selection, by Galinsky and Galinsky, complements the analysis of Sarri by examining the organization of patients and staff in three types of mental hospitals. In this review of published research, there is a systematic comparison of custodial, individual-treatment, and milieu-treatment hospitals. The authors compare the range and frequency of interaction of the patients, their hierarchical structure, group cohesion, and membership in elite groups, and the staff practices, staff hierarchical structure, belief systems, and physical resources. The effects of organizational goals and practices are again emphasized as they relate to the extent to which the institution provides a facilitating or a constraining context for the achievement of therapeutic change.

In contrast to the prior analyses, the last selection is focused upon relationships external to the organization. Litwak and Meyer present a theory of the coordination between bureaucratic organizations and external primary groups. This framework has direct implications for community organization, administration, and direct practice, for in all of these areas there are problems of linking client groups—as well as of cadres of professional helpers—to the organizations and agencies through which services are provided. The objective of the authors' analysis is to explicate the proper relationship, for purposes of achieving social control, between bureaucratic organizations (such as schools and hospitals) and social agencies and primary groups (such as families and neighborhood groups). The authors isolate and describe eight diverse coordinating mechanisms (e.g., detached expert, opinion leader, common messenger) by which formal organizations can seek to influence an external primary group. The advantages and limitations of these mechanisms as communicative and influence-inducing mechanisms are appraised in terms of the extent of organizational initiative they afford, the intensity of relations they provide for the primary-group members, the necessity to communicate expert knowledge, and the extent to which the influence reaches all members of the primary groups. Because coordinating mechanisms also depend upon various types of bureaucratic organizations, the authors describe four distinct types which they then relate to the most effective mechanisms for coordination with various primary group. Finally, the authors consider the coordinating mechanisms that would be most effective for achieving social control, depending upon whether the primary groups in question are deviant or congenial. Running throughout the exposition are the criteria of balance which the various coordinative relationships achieve.

15 The Social Structure of Service

Robert D. Vinter

Attention will be directed toward certain issues posed by the transaction of welfare services through administrative organizations. It is maintained that commitment to the agency as *the* means for providing health and welfare services has had significant consequences for professional social workers, for the social goals embodied in the services, and for the clients to whom the services are directed.[1] Emphasis is given to dilemmas and events that are salient for social workers, but this is not to suggest that all organizational effects are problematic. These dilemmas and conditions are discussed under two major headings: bureaucratic structure and professional culture, and the structure of authority. Such interrelated topics can be separated only arbitrarily for purposes of analysis.

The extremely broad range of organizational types in the social welfare field presents difficulties in any discussion of agency structure. Social welfare agencies may be national in scope or limited to a small community; they may be governmental units or voluntary associations. Some are direct-service agencies, others are engaged in planning, coordinating, or forum activities. Furthermore, certain agencies have existed over several generations and some are oriented toward sectarian values. These wide variations are directly pertinent to organizational patterns, yet make it almost impossible to speak of *the* social agency. Attention is directed to relatively common features of social welfare agencies, but with particular reference to those providing services directly to clientele.

Bureaucratic Structure and Professional Culture

Bureaucracies and the professions are consequences of similar forces in Western society. Both are expressions of general trends toward division of labor and specialization that characterize complex and highly techno-

Abridged from Alfred Kahn (ed.), ISSUES IN AMERICAN SOCIAL WORK (New York: Columbia U. P., 1959), 242–270. Reprinted with the permission of the author and the Columbia University Press. Copyright © 1959 Columbia University Press, New York.

logical societies. Yet not all bureaucraries are professionalized (e.g., the post office), that is, staffed by independently trained professional personnel. Nor are all professions bureaucratized (e.g., lawyers), that is, conducting most specialized effort through administrative structures. Bureaucratization has advanced further in the social welfare system than has professionalization, although the orientations of the trained career professionals are widely diffused, and this group maintains a dominant position. Stated differently, all social work is provided through bureaucratic organizations, although not all social welfare agencies are wholly or even largely staffed by professional social workers.[2]

The fact that not all professions are committed to administrative structures leads us to inquire into the nature and effects of the association between agencies and social work profession. It seems that the ideology and standards of the profession are generally compatible with the requirements of the agency as an administrative organization. For example, the norm of professional discipline (affective neutrality toward the client or client group) is largely consistent with the tendency toward impersonality found in administrative bureaucracies. The staff member is thus enjoined by profession and agency to regard clients with a certain detachment and without injecting his personal feelings into the service relationship. Similarly, the social worker's preference for discharging his professional function through a definite and circumscribed role complements the organization's assignment of activities among personnel as official duties. Agency goals and professional service aims are derived from the same overarching humanitarian value system. Many of the specific tasks agency workers perform are therefore perceived as contributing to attainment of ends sanctioned by their professional reference group. These and other convergences between the agency and the profession facilitate practitioners' harmonious functioning within welfare organizations.

Not all features of profession and agency are complementary, however, and several major sources of strain may be identified. It should be recognized that quite different organizing principles underlie agency and profession, although both are consequences of similar historical trends. The bureaucratic principle of efficiency impels agencies toward the best possible use of resources (including personnel) in attainment of their goals. The highest values of the profession incline practitioners toward mastery of technical skills and dedicated, selfless service. Limits of these orientations for the professional are stated in terms of competence and ethical commitments. But limitations on service imposed by the agency are of a different order, introducing administrative considerations of policy, rules, budget, and so forth. What constitutes the best possible use of resources for an agency in pursuit of its proximate goals is often at variance with orientations toward skill and selfless service. That professionals are generally able to work effectively in administrative structures attests to both the flexibility of these structures and the adaptabiliy of professionals.

Strains are usually manifested as role conflicts when the imperatives and constraints of profession and agency are not congruent.[3]

A pervasive type of role conflict arises from discrepancies between agencies' limited service goals (the "function" of each agency) and the profession's relatively unlimited commitments. As an agency employee, the social worker must often refuse service because the prospective client's needs do not assume the form appropriate to a given agency; he is deemed "ineligible." Such conflict can be especially acute as the practitioner becomes immediately aware, in the process of determining eligibility, of individual's pressing (but inappropriate) needs, and as he must himself be the agent of refusal. Some of this conflict is expressed as staff dissatisfaction with "restrictive" agency policies, and is partially relieved by heavy emphasis on referrals and by attempts to expand the service jurisdictions of agencies. It seems probable that continuous growth of the social welfare services assuages some of the frustration of professionals, as they are inclined toward the optimistic belief that if people cannot obtain all the help they need here and now, they may there or later.

A second type of role conflict is generated by discrepancies between specific agency goals or practices and professional values. Social workers tend to concentrate in agencies whose means and ends are most compatible with the profession's codes and standards, and to avoid those where major incongruities are perceived. Thus, disproportionate numbers of the professionally trained are found in all types of psychiatric settings and family service agencies, but very few in correctional and public assistance agencies.[4] Workers are sometimes required to perform tasks not perceived as commensurate with their training and professional images; they may experience constraints in the full utilization of core technical skills, or find little organizational support for their distinctive values and practices. These conditions may exist in any agency at a given time, but are believed to be more prevalent in certain sectors of the field not yet fully professionalized. Ohlin has documented the processes by which value differences induce stress and high turnover of social work personnel in correctional settings.[5]

One approach to reduction in this type of conflict has been to redefine the situation so that the agency and professional value systems may be perceived as congruent. This can be achieved in part by stressing the compatible elements in both systems. For example, recent statements have presented assertions that professional aims are germane to correctional services, and that use of authority by the professional probation or parole officer need not contravene social work values.[6] Similarly, it is maintained that the determination of eligibility and giving of funds in public assistance require the exercise of professional skills consonant with social work principles.[7] Another approach has been to introduce enough professional personnel to secure modifications in the practices and climate of agencies. Perhaps the most promising solution is to attempt modification of certain features of professional culture which are especially discrepant with organizational realities. For example, declining emphases on professional subspecializations (e.g., psychiatric social work) will serve to lessen status problems and strictures on practitioner roles to which these distinctions have contributed among agency personel. The same trend toward generic preparation of professionals will permit a more flexible and extended utilization of practitioners in accordance with agency necessities. Agency field training as an integral part of professional preparation serves both to ameliorate and to increase the practitioner's role conflict. The graduate student in social work becomes acquainted with agency structure primarily by direct experience in it as a student worker. Accommodations to the agency as the context for practice are probably achieved at an early career point. On the other hand, most students are assigned to agencies largely permeated by the professional culture, while academic study emphasizes organizational features that are compatible with professional norms and values. Strain between profession and agency is thus accentuated for novice practitioners first employed in agencies whose characteristics are less than ideal. However, an essential point to be made is that orientations of the profession do not necessarily ensure more effective service to clients than do the patterns of specific agency structures.

Another type of conflict between professional and agency role demands is that arising from inherent differences between the administrative structure and the professional culture. The profession values skill rather than procedure, and service rather than routines. The agency, in contrast, interposes a variety of requirements relevant to the operation of a complex organization. Records must be written, files maintained, requisitions prepared and routed, directives adhered to, and so on. Furthermore, the worker must participate in a more or less elaborate system of informal relationships; he must get along with colleagues and be a good member of the team. Some of these operational realities provide satisfactions; for example, case conferences frequently offer gratifying opportunities for the symbolic exercise of professional skills. Some provide frustrations; for example, the status problems experienced in teamwork with psychiatrists.[8] These events are intrinsic to the operation of the agency as an organization. When the net balance of satisfaction-dissatisfaction from such sources becomes adverse, workers tend to depart.[9] Continuity of service to clients is thus enhanced or diminished by the organizational circumstances of professional practice.

Organizational Size

Questions often arise about the most desirable size for client groups, departments, staff committees, boards, and even whole agencies. There is general awareness that various effects depend upon the number of personnel grouped together in work units, but more precise knowledge is lacking. Although size has been an important consideration in administrative designs, relatively little empirical study has been given to it. Some knowledge of the effects of size is available from small-group studies, however, and can be briefly reviewed. It has been found that an increase in group size is accompanied by lessening of member participation and satisfaction; consensus among members also decreases, while leadership requirements increase. There is a tendency toward specialization of functions and roles within groups as they become larger and endure over periods of time. The number of potential relationships among members increases rapidly with increments in group size, yet the intimacy of relations among all members is reduced and factionalism emerges. Larger groups are able to undertake tasks impossible for smaller groups, but efficiency and size are not invariably associated; optimum group size depends partly on the type of task at hand.

These generalizations about the effects of size are substantiated by a number of studies,[10] but caution must be exercised in applying them directly to organizations. Most of these findings are derived from studies of small independent problem-solving groups, created for brief experimental periods, and lacking administrative structure. They are, however, suggestive of effects to be anticipated with variations in the size of organizations or their subunits. These findings also suggest that there is no ideal group size. Instead, differences in group size are accompanied by particular effects, some of which may be desired, such as greater efficiency or specialization. Other effects may be undesirable, such as reduction of participation. The administrative problem is one of determining what size achieves a net balance of desired effects.

The significance of size for administrative structures can be most clearly seen by examining the effects of increasing the number of personnel. Enlarging the size of the staff generally presents greater requirements for coordination and control. More supervisors are needed with added workers; at some point it becomes necessary to introduce a division head or supervisor of supervisors. Direct positive relationships have been found between the number of employees and the number of vertical ranks in comparable welfare units.[11] Extension of the vertical chain of command is not the only impact of size on the structure of coordination, however. Activities that are broadly distributed among personnel in smaller units become segregated in the large agency and are assigned to specialized roles: accounting, consulting, statistical control, and so on. Greater efficiency is obtained for the total work unit when such specialization occurs on the line (e.g., intake interviewers, program specialists, home-finders). And tasks impossible for the smaller, less specialized agency can be accomplished. But increments in number of personnel and the degree of specialization require that larger proportions of organizational resources be devoted to central administrative tasks.[12] This phenomenon is commonly referred to as increased overhead costs.

Communication problems are another consequence of larger size. In a small office or agency workers usually have direct access to each other and to the executive. Problems can be explored and decisions shared by word of mouth. Conformity to policy and standards of performance are readily apparent, and can be reinforced by direct friendly relations among all personnel. In the larger agency, with many workers and several administrative levels, interaction among personnel takes on a more formal quality. Communication by memorandum and directive supplants contact between executive and practitioner. The larger number of people, who cannot all be known intimately, and the elaboration of the agency formal structure also contribute to greater social distance among personnel. The executive becomes a remote figure, contacts among workers at different levels or from different sections assume a more businesslike and reserved character, and many co-workers remain relative strangers. Under these circumstances intimacy and informality may continue to characterize relations among workers in the same subunit, but factionalism and interunit rivalry often develop.

Increases in the number of administrative levels, in highly specialized roles, and in the total number of personnel, also lead to more routinized procedures. Many persons are involved in each decision and phase of operation; they must be kept informed and their efforts coordinated. These requirements are typically met by standardizing activities which, under other conditions, remain less circumscribed. Manuals, job descriptions, multiple staff conferences, and administrative audits are among the devices used to ensure predictability of behavior.

The larger agency is, thus, in certain respects a different place in which to work than the smaller agency, although many of the particular tasks are the same. For some persons these are less satisfying conditions, and personnel turnover may increase. While the larger organization can efficiently undertake service responsibilities impossible for the small unit there may also be reduced effectiveness in terms relevant to social work objectives. The study of Aid to Dependent Children workers conducted in various sized units by Thomas revealed important differences in staff role conceptions and quality of performance.[13] Workers in smaller units, as contrasted with their peers in larger units, evidenced more consensus with their supervisors about important worker functions, greater breadth of role conceptions, and more commitment to the ethics of social work. Similarly, their performance was more effective, as measured in terms of diagnostic acuity and the appropriateness of treatment plans.

This analysis suggests that much of what is known through experimentation with small groups has relevance for social welfare administrative structures. However, other factors intervene in the relationship between organizational size (as number of personnel) and the consequences noted. Cloward points out that certain emphases in professional practice (e.g., controlled relationships) contribute to formalized relations even in the small agency.[14] The extent to which social relations and staff member behavior may be related to differences in the *kinds* of persons employed in small and in large welfare organizations deserves intensive study. Agency and community size frequently vary together, and personnel available to agencies located in small towns and rural areas are different from workers available to large agencies in the big cities. Differences in personal characteristics of staff members in large and small units of the same state welfare department are related to differences pertaining among urban and rural residents.[15] It may be found that variations in these personal characteristics account for much of the observed dissimilarities among various sized agencies.

The impact of administrative or service unit size on clientele has received no systematic study. It has, however, been a matter of concern in the composition of different sized groups in, for example, group work practice and in the design of living units in residential settings. For child-caring institutions there is general recognition that smaller units provide greater intimacy and informality in relations among staff and clientele. Similar considerations have guided social group workers in composing small groups for various purposes, particularly when serving disturbed clientele. Most of this knowledge is derived from practice experience; it is often vitiated by the intrusion of other administrative considerations, as well as pressures to serve more clients. The disadvantageous effects of formalized staff-client relationships, due in part to increased agency size, have been reviewed by Cloward with respect to client recruitment, turn-over, participation, and so on.[16]

The impact of agency size on clients can be seen most clearly by considering child-caring institutions. The small agency permits all clients and staff members to know each other and to develop intimate relationships. These patterns of interaction are especially crucial to attainment of agency service objectives. Decisions about clients and agency operations can be made by those immediately familiar with the individuals and the situational details. The development of such intimacy and familiarity is very difficult in the large institution. There are too many people to know them well, and decisions are made at levels more distant from both clients and line staff. The larger number of workers presents problems for the maintenance of consistency in treatment of clients and application of rules. Contending factions and dissimilar perspectives may develop.[17]

It is not asserted that these differences can be entirely attributed to size, or that largeness is undesirable. But there can be little question about the significance of size for the functioning of social welfare organizations. Without a body of tested knowledge, administrative decisions about the optimum size of organizational units must be made on the basis of intuition and experience. There is a high risk that the effects intended by administrative design are thwarted by unintended consequences which follow on unit size.

The Structure of Authority

All organizations create means for ensuring that cooperative action is oriented toward desired objectives. To avoid a state of anarchy among participating personnel, an explicit structure of authority and responsibility is defined in every social agency. However rudimentary this structure, it seeks to ensure predictable behavior of workers in conformity to policy. It coordinates individuals and their manifold activities within the agency. And it guides decision-making, resolves overt conflicts, and orders new issues and problems that emerge through time. Such controls are especially important to social agencies that spend other people's money. In addition, policies and practices of governmental agencies are imbued with sociopolitical meanings of significance to many interest groups. The responsibility, accountability, and sensitiveness of social welfare agencies, therefore, pose special requirements for the maintenance of organizational controls.

The agency's structure of authority typically takes the form of a hierarchical ordering of personnel in official positions. Every position is subordinate to some position, and superior to others, with differential responsibility and authority being allocated to each. This ordering of personnel denotes command authority, as superior-subordinate relations between levels are based on administrative sanctions; it may also denote functional authority if special competence is required for occupancy of superior positions.[18] Both types of authority often characterize differences between position levels in social agencies. Staff members exercise their responsibility for the activities of personnel at lower levels through decision-making, giving advice and instruction, communicating information, and reviewing performance. Production in social agencies is directly accomplished by practitioners, who constitute the second lowest administrative level (above clerical staff) in the hierarchy of employed personnel.

An agency's official system of policies, rules, and procedures comprises another dimension of its authority structure. This system establishes patterns of expectations that direct and proscribe staff members' activities. Furthermore, the official structure becomes elaborated and supplemented with informal patterns: work norms develop and persist, subordinates in one department are granted more discretion than in another, or warm and friendly relations rather than cool formality exist between administrative levels.

This statement of the structure of authority provides only a very general description of agency reality. In particular agencies there may be two or many levels of authority, with diverse patterns of responsibility, and differing rule systems. Aside from such specific variations, there are common features of agency authority structures which distinguish them from certain other types of organizations. Reference has already been made to the operational relevance of norms and values originating in the culture of professional social work. Thus, social agencies are characterized by a strong emphasis on harmonious and satisfying relations among co-workers; ability to form positive relationships with co-workers is perhaps more valued in social agencies than in many other organizations. The proliferation of specialized personnel outside the chain of command (e.g., consultants of all kinds) poses added problems in achieving coordination of effort.[19] New means for integrating influences and perspectives and for arriving at decisions, are necessary when the functional authority of the specialist is segmented from the command authority of the supervisor. The administrative level at which certain types of decisions are made about service and clients may substantially condition the nature of these decisions. Janowitz and Delany have shown that individuals' positions in the administrative structure condition their knowledge and their perspectives.[20] Accuracy of knowledge about clients depends partly on degree of contact with them; workers at lower levels develop somewhat different perspectives toward clients, with whom they interact frequently, than do higher administrative personnel, who interact more frequently with the general public. Further study is needed to explore the consequences for decision-making stemming from the perspectives of diverse agency personnel.

The nature of a social agency task conditions the type of authority structure that can be established. When tasks are complicated, require deliberation, and cannot be concretely defined in advance, greater authority must be delegated to personnel in the lower ranks. When appropriate action can be specified in advance, rule systems are more likely to emerge, and authority retained at higher levels.[21] The prevalence of technically trained personnel in an agency's lower ranks also tends to produce a downward delegation of authority.

The significance of agency authority structure can be seen by examining supervisor-practitioner relations in social work. The professional literature reveals great emphasis on the role of the supervisor. Some of this emphasis characterizes all production organizations: objectives are tangibly achieved at the practitioner level and administrative control must be exercised at the next higher level, the supervisor. Similarly, the foreman is the focus of concern in manufacturing organizations. A high proportion of untrained personnel in the field of social welfare impels administrative attention to supervision. But professional considerations appear to reinforce administrative concerns regarding this single aspect of the authority structure. Thus, supervision has afforded one means of upgrading practice, thereby validating the profession's claims to technical competence.[22]

The traditional status of the supervisor involves a combination of prestige, power, and expertness. Supervisors in many agencies are chosen because of their knowledge and skill, thus enhancing the prestige and authority officially invested in the position. The power of the supervisor accrues from the informational vantage point provided by the position, and from whatever special competency is possessed, as well as the authority to make decisions, offer rewards, and evaluate performance. In these respects supervision in the social agency does not differ markedly from the patterning of authority in many other types of organizations. Yet a distinct note of disquiet can be discerned in the literature, suggesting special strains are associated with supervision. Discrepancies between professional orientations and administrative requirements seem to be one source of difficulty. All occupational groups claiming professional stature assert the competence and ethical commitment of their members (or of the profession's right to certify and enforce conformity with its standards). Professionals take considerable pride in their technical skills and prefer initiative and self-direction in the use of these skills.[23] Limits are placed on practitioner initiative and autonomy through supervision, however able the supervisor may be in exercising her authority.[24]

This analysis suggests that claims to autonomy are greater among fully trained and experienced practitioners. Under such circumstances it is expected that strain between professional and administrative orientations increases, and alternative arrangements are sought. The literature tends to confirm this inference, indicating most doubts refer to the supervision of fully trained and experienced practitioners.[25] Terms employed in referring to the problem are suggestive of the extent to which close supervision is perceived as a denial of professional autonomy: "emancipation," "independence," and "self-dependent practice." When male practitioners are assigned to female supervisors it seems probable that additional stress develops in the authority relations. As Caplow points out, this situation traverses the social norm that women should not be in positions of authority over men.[26] Furthermore, because success and achievement aspirations are more strongly held among men, the presence of a female supervisor in the promotional chain may be especially stressful.[27]

Strain also arises from juxtaposition of the nonauthoritarian ideology of social work and the exercise of authority and control within the administrative context. Valuation of autonomy and self-determination for the client has pervaded the administrative structures of social welfare, reinforcing distinctively professional claims to independence. Other conditions may contribute to authority and control problems: larger agencies include more separate functions, roles, and units to be coordinated; and higher proportions of untrained or inexperienced personnel reduce assurances that performance will meet acceptable standards. Under these conditions controls must be increased through closer supervision and more elaborate rule systems. Staff resistance to more tangible controls is partially attenuated by the obvious coordination requirements posed by the larger agency. And among untrained and inexperienced personnel, according to this analysis, professional autonomy values are less fully developed. It is in the small agency with a high proportion of skilled personnel that the traditional pattern of close supervision is expected to create greatest strain. And it is precisely for such agencies that alternative patterns are proposed in the literature.

The more prominent of these alternatives, consultation-supervision (not to be confused with consultation of the specialist), may be examined in the light of the foregoing analysis. Consultation as a mode of practitioner supervision seems intended to minimize the former educational focus, to share some of the supervisor's power with the practitioner, but to maintain the administrative authority of the supervisor. Reduction of the educational focus may be interpreted as removal of an implication that, because he has more to learn, the practitioner has not yet achieved full professional status. Strain between administrative procedure and valuation of professional competency is thus minimized. Modification of the supervisor's role only in these terms would probably have little salutary effect, however, since the worker is restive not only with the assertion that he has more to learn, but with the process which reduces his autonomy. This second objection is met by redefinition of the supervisor's role as "consultative," inducing a more advisory and collaborative relationship with the practitioner. This redefinition, if effected in supervisors' functioning, probably distributes power more equitably between supervisors and workers, as the latter obtain a greater share in decision-making. Maintenance of the supervisor's administrative authority presumably is intended to exercise, at least minimally, the responsibility to review performance, and so on. If the proposed changes have been correctly interpreted, consultation-supervision seems designed to reduce the strains in present supervisory limitations on professional autonomy. Educational supervision, effective during a period when upgrading of practice was a crucial task, is now a hindrance to professional morale and self-esteem where both are well developed and substantiated.

Difficulties which may result from such changes deserve brief mention. A significant downward shift of decision-making power reduces the effective authority of the supervisor and thereby alters the existing structure. Changes of this order sometimes have extensive effects neither intended nor anticipated in the initial design. One such effect may be to reduce the esteem and gratification of the supervisor. The emphasis in the literature on supervisors being "ready" for these changes can be interpreted as meaning they must be able to tolerate such deprivation. Another effect may be delegation of decision-making to a level below that required for effective communication and coordination in a given agency. For example, the breadth of information reaching supervisors through the present structure may be curtailed by the consultative pattern. The accumulative effects of this change could be to deny supervisors the flow of information essential to coordination between units and among staff specialists.

Attention should be given to the status of the client in the authority structure, and its effects for him. Three significant features characterize the relation of clientele to social agencies. First, many social agencies have an absolute or near monopoly of the services they render. Since clients can seldom "shop around," their preferences do not have the same weight as in a competitive market. Furthermore, individuals have little or no control over whether they shall remain as clients of some agencies (e.g., correctional institutions and mental hospitals). Second, the specificity and duration of client relations vary among agencies, usually being dependent upon the type of service. Relations with some agencies require only limited participation and involvement, the service being relatively specific and the contact transitory (e.g., administration of unemployment compensation). For other agencies (e.g., most residential settings), extensive involvement and commitment are characteristic, the service being diffuse.[28] Third, clients usually comprise the lowest status level, having no authority over others in the organization.[29] The consequences of low status and no authority will have greatest import for the client who participates maximally in the agency, and who has little choice of agency or even whether he shall remain a client.

Much more happens to clients than is denoted by the activities specifically designated as service or treatment. Moreover, even these activities are themselves conditioned by the entire character of the organization. The diverse influences operating on the client may be partially discerned by consideration of his status and the expected role behaviors associated with this status.

The phenomena of low status and no authority are impressed on clients by several features of agency organization. There exists a distinct and caste-like cleavage between staff and clients. The recipient of service may not aspire to the status level of professional personnel, though he may move upward within the hierarchy of clients. Many agency decisions affecting clients involve considerations relatively incomprehensible to them, and are made at distant levels. The rules and routines of an agency frequently occasion delays and denials for clients; these may be viewed as unfair and as negations of the agency's service goals. Interpretations by staff are helpful but often involve reasons irrelevant in the client's perspective.[30] The potent sanctions agencies may employ provide further confirmation of the client's subordinate status and relative powerlessness. Service may be denied or privileges withheld from the uncooperative client. On the other hand, the cooperative client (like the model patient) may receive many symbolic rewards or praise and recognition, in addition to actual privileges and services.

Permanency of lower status, exclusion from decision-making, and application of powerful sanctions are circumstances (stated in extreme form) usually regarded as unattractive in other areas of life. Customary responses to these conditions are alienation and disaffection, withdrawal, submissive dependency, or covert rebellion. None of these responses is considered desirable for the effective use of social services, yet all are evidenced in various degrees among agency clientele. Nonparticipation and dropouts from the leisure-time services, non-returns to the family casework agencies, and prisonization and covert hostility in the correctional setting, are familiar phenomena. Furthermore, it is well known that many persons and groups who may need the services most are often least willing to become clients. The fact that the rates of such behavior are not greater suggests that compensatory conditions exist. Several of these may be identified.

First, in an era of large bureaucracies—governmental, commercial, educational, and even religious—citizens have become accustomed to client status. They may comprehend the nature of the organization and have developed response patterns that vitiate the negative consequences of such status. They *expect* to be treated as they are. Some of the findings presented by Maas and his associates substantiate the notion that client expectations of being authoritatively dealt with are widespread and do not result in service failures.[31] The transitory and specific nature of many client-agency relations minimizes the negative implications of this pattern. Indeed, it seems primarily when the client role pervades the client self-image (i.e., permanency of low status and diffuseness of involvement) that the pattern becomes problematic.

A second compensating condition is created by practitioners' mediation of the adverse effects of agency structure on clientele. Professional dicta to be friendly, interested, and responsive in relations with clients are probably crucial in offsetting the arbitrariness of rules and administrative decisions, and the impersonality of agency routines.[32] Also significant is practitioner emphasis on service rather than procedure, even at points where this may conflict with official agency practices. To ignore or cut through rules is professionally disapproved, yet is probably frequently done.[33] The actual incidence of such mediation by practitioners is not known. And it should not be assumed, as noted earlier, that all professional norms serve to ameliorate negative structural effects.

A third and potentially more promising compensatory pattern is now emerging. This is an explicit recognition of the effects of organizational structure on service, and deliberate modification of agency patterns to resolve the dilemmas encountered. The concept of a therapeutic milieu being developed in mental hospitals is, in large part, movement toward designing organizational arrangements so as to enhance rather than hinder service effectiveness. This approach seeks to reexamine every feature of the institutional structure, and the interrelations among staff and clients which are governed by it.[34] Specific modifications envisioned in this approach are directed at minimizing the status differentials between higher professionals and lower echelon staff and patients, reducing the powerlessness of the patients, and increasing their participation in decision-making. Particular attention is given to the roles of all participants in the institutional system in order to maximize the therapeutic contributions of each. This leads to assessment of the actual and potential influences of every echelon of staff (e.g., from psychiatrists to ward attendants)[35] on patients, and of the influences of patients on each other. Similarly, every policy and procedure—even physical arrangements—must be reexamined with regard to criteria of both therapeutic effectiveness and administrative efficiency. It is important to note that such an approach requires attention not only to particular organizational conditions, but to the interrelation and integration of all components. Among the more problematic conditions, from this viewpoint, have been the segmentation of treatment personnel and their services, and the emergence of informal patterns (among and between staff and clients) which conflict with official therapeutic purposes and procedures.

The rationale that, in so far as possible, the whole of organizational operation should be governed by the criterion of therapeutic or service effectiveness can be applied to every type of health and welfare agency. It is most relevant for those agencies which have the characteristics of small communities, such as mental hospitals, child-caring institutions, and residential camps. In such agencies client involvement is typically extensive and diffuse, and the client's role pervades his self-image. But the central focus of this paper has been to indicate some of the ways in which structural features are relevant to all agencies, however limited or transitory the client's contact. The notion of a therapeutic milieu suggests, although in limited terms, the utility of organizational analysis. With this perspective it becomes possible to comprehend more adequately the structures of social welfare, and their conditioning of social work services.

16 Analysis of Treatment Organizations

Robert D. Vinter

In this statement organizational analysis is applied to direct-service health and welfare organizations, which are given the general term "treatment" agencies. We begin with consideration of the larger category of people-changing organizations and the two major types that compose this category: socialization and treatment agencies. We then examine the distinctive features of treatment organizations. Finally, we address certain problems that confront treatment and other complex organizations, namely, use of human relations technologies, reliance on professionals, consequences for clients, and evaluation of performance.

People-Changing Organizations

Treatment agencies are part of a larger class of organizations responsible for changing people. The university and military academy, guidance clinic and mental hospital, probation office and correctional institution are all examples of organizations in this general class. Viewed broadly, the major functions of people-changing organizations are socialization and social control. In each instance a specific population is dealt with in ways calculated to insure the preservation of dominant values and patterns.

Organizations in this general class can be distinguished from all others on the basis of their substantive goals. To some extent every organization must bring about certain changes in those who participate in it: newcomers must be socialized into appropriate behavior patterns, proper loyalties and attitudes must be induced, persons must be managed, their activities coordinated, and so on. These changes are, however, essentially instrumental and incidental to the main purposes of most organizations; they are necessary but do not in and of themselves constitute goal achieve-

Abridged from SOCIAL WORK, **8** No. 3 (July 1965), 3–15. Reprinted with the permission of the author and the National Association of Social Workers.

ment. For schools, mental hospitals, prisons, and the like, the major goal *is* that of changing persons in ways distinctive to each, and the extent to which the organization achieves such change is a primary criterion of its effectiveness.

The nature of the change sought, as well as its primacy as a goal, also differentiates these from other organizations. A scope and permanence of change is customarily attempted that pervades the behavior of persons and endures beyond the period of their affiliation with the organization. People-changing organizations are usually concerned with effecting new and diffuse modes of behavior, new self-images or personalities—in sum, with altered persons in changed statuses. Finally, the behavioral modes or altered personalities sought by people-changing organizations are invested with a moral quality that does not infuse the limited modifications sought by other organizations. Thus, the proper education of youth is imbued with quasi-sacred meanings, while the rehabilitation of criminals or the mentally ill touches on basic societal values.

Question can be raised about whether certain organizations included in this analysis, particularly the prison or custodial mental hospital, are concerned with people-changing. Substantive goals serve as the basis of our classification, not whether organizational strategies are judged as likely to achieve lasting change or the rates of change are actually achieved. The latter are questions of effectiveness and should be addressed in empirical terms. The author asserts that an organization has people-changing as a goal under one or more of these conditions: (1) when such a mandate is specified by its goal-setting agents, (2) when changing clientele is professed as a goal in the organization's formal statement of purpose, (3) when a significant proportion of organizational resources is allocated to the tasks of changing its clientele or to the personnel assigned to such tasks. More often than not all these conditions, in various balances, are met by specific treatment organizations.

The goal of changing clientele need not be the agency's only (or even its dominant) goal, since complex organizations typically possess a hierarchy of goals whose priorities change over a period of time. Most adult prisons adhere to deterrence as a primary goal (i.e., confinement and punishment of inmates in order to forestall future offenses by these or other persons), yet there is ample evidence that they are increasingly committed to the goal of rehabilitation. Insofar as custody and confinement are aimed at preventing future commission of offenses by felons, the prison is engaged in the task of changing people. The prison's coercive and archaic practices of inducing change are not assumed, on an a priori basis to vitiate the goal itself. Distinctions must be made, therefore, not only between goals and effectiveness but also between ends and means. This mode of analysis has the benefit of directing attention to the *consequences for the organization* of treatment as a goal: publics pose different expectations of achievement, new élites contend for dominance, and ideologies and strategies must be redefined. Failure to accomplish the goal, or even persistent reluctance to implement its imperatives, subjects the organization to new strains.[1]

Socialization and Treatment Organizations

The two major types of people-changing organizations, socialization and treatment agencies, can be differentiated in at least three ways: the presumed nature of their clienteles, the changes they seek, and the contrasting valuation accorded each by the larger society. Socialization organizations, primarily schools and youth-serving agencies, seek to prepare individuals for adequate performance of their social roles. The persons worked with are perceived as moving along normal developmental gradients. It is generally assumed that these persons are motivated to change and that the essential task is to provide appropriate learning opportunities. Other conditions in most of their life situations are generally presumed to be benign and unlikely to impede change.[2]

Treatment organizations, in contrast, seek to resolve problems of deviance; they serve persons who have demonstrated that they are *not* moving along normal gradients and, for one reason or another, are not adequately performing conventional social roles. Delinquents and criminals, emotionally disturbed persons, and the chronically unemployed are regarded as possessing defective attributes or as improperly motivated and oriented. Their behavior is disapproved; conditions in their past or present life situations are believed to be adverse and likely to impede change efforts.

These distinctions, while stated in very broad terms, characterize dominant views shared among the general public about the clientele and tasks of these two types of organization and underlie differences in the valuation and resources each receives. Schools enjoy legitimation and resources in far greater measure than those awarded to prisons, mental hospitals, and the like. This seems due in part to the persistence of adverse public sentiment regarding various forms of deviance. Concern for public safety, revulsion with many types of misconduct, and fear of the bizarre are responses often directed at the behaviors of treatment organization clientele, especially criminals and the mentally ill. In former eras such problems were dealt with by scourging, harsh repression, exile, or even death. Persons who persisted in deviant behavior were excluded from the community, which then closed ranks against them.[3]

The rise in humanitarianism has muted these more extreme attitudes of past eras. Harsh and repressive measures for coping with deviant behavior are less often utilized, while insistence on protection of the community has been balanced by a new optimism about the potentials of rehabilitation. These trends have significantly altered the societal mandates given treatment agencies, although they still enjoy a far less favorable status than do socialization organizations.

Public attitudes toward specific deviancy patterns are, of course, highly differentiated. The degree of jeopardy for others, the age and sex of the deviant, and the normative areas in which behavior violates expectations are among the conditions that shape public response to the deviancy. In an important sense, however, the many forms of deviance are perceived as alike. In this society, largely oriented toward individual achievement, fulfillment of conventional roles tends to be regarded as the responsibility of the individual. Conformity and deviance, like success and failure, are seen as matters of personal volition and as somehow inhering in the character and willfulness of each individual.

Negative attitudes toward the behavior to be changed are easily expanded to include the organization responsible for the changing. Rehabilitation goals are consequently more precarious than educational goals, and the treatment organization must expend greater energy in justifying its programs and gaining support for its purposes. Persisting belief that the deviant *intentionally* violates expectations produces a continuous strain toward punitive and exclusionary measures and a reluctance to allocate generous resources in support of the treatment organization. Differences in resource allocation between socialization and treatment agencies also derive from more rational considerations about gains and losses for the community: the conditions of survival may be seen as set more by the effectiveness of education than of treatment.

These elements in belief and valuation serve to define the essential nature of the client populations and the mandates for change. They provide not only the cultural context but also the restraints and imperatives that shape organizational effort. And finally, these perspectives are deeply intertwined in the technologies utilized by treatment organizations.

Change-Oriented Technologies

The means for change utilized among organizations concerned with deviance range all the way from coercive repression to manipulative persuasion. Organizations at both these extremes use human relations technologies and emphasize that the basic task of people-changing is accomplished through *deliberate structuring of staff-client relations*. The operational strategies of each, however, are based on quite different assumptions about the causes and cures of deviance, how much of what kind of change is possible, and how to achieve this change. The range of change-oriented strategies can be illustrated by comparing that used by the mental health clinic with that of the prison.

The technology of the clinic focuses on *manipulation of affect and cognition through persuasive communication*. Change objectives are ambitiously defined and refer primarily to intrapersonal modifications. Emphasis is placed on development of intimate interpersonal relations, on inducements, volition, and high communication between staff and clients.

Clients are perceived essentially as wanting to change, or only persons sufficiently motivated are selected for service. Despite the clinic's use of quasi-standardized diagnostic categories, its clients are seen as more different than alike, requiring careful assessment and individualized response to their unique attributes. The major personnel tasks involve ability to manage affect, to respond unconventionally in charged situations, and to maintain warm and trustful but impersonal relations. These nonroutinized tasks constitute an esoteric and complex technology, and the necessary staff competencies must be secured through specialized training.

The prison, at the other extreme, focuses on *coercion and the application of negative sanctions*. Change objectives are minimally defined; they emphasize secure containment and limited accommodations to the official system rather than intrapersonal reorientation. Relations between staff and clients (in this case inmates) are distant and formal, based on the principle of domination and submission. Since clients are perceived as more alike than different, they can be handled by use of standardized procedures and in large groups. Clients are typically seen as opposed to change and as united in solidary opposition to official purposes. Here, too, affect is a problem, but it is dealt with by means of constant supervision, forced deference, and a protective architecture. Personnel are expected to follow the rules and routines, to manage men without increasing their opposition, and to maintain social distance from the clients. Such basic capabilities can be found on the open labor market, and skill can be gained through experience.

Some of the beliefs underlying these contrasting strategies are traditional and include major elements of folklore; others are derived from newer behavioral theories and professional philosophies. Although more crystallized or sophisticated, these views are directly analogous to those cited as shared among the general public. Both public and professional belief systems tend to emphasize that *individual* attributes are at issue in deviancy patterns. Only recently and in small measure have these beliefs about the characterological bases of deviancy been infused by understanding of the situational and social forces that induce nonconformity. The target unit among most treatment organizations continues, therefore, to be the individual person, usually abstracted and sometimes removed from his local environment, rather than the immediate social conditions that may have generated or shaped his performance problems.

Treatment technologies can be considered in large part as action correlates of these prevailing belief systems. Thus, the classification and diagnostic systems utilized in treatment agencies have their origins in such beliefs and, in turn, they categorize clients for organizational effort.[4] As indicated, all treatment organization technologies assert the crucial importance of staff-client relations in achieving change. There are three major dimensions along which these relations vary, permitting notation of significant differences among agencies.

How Treatment Organizations Vary

Standardization of Procedures

Every treatment organization makes some differentiation among its clientele and adapts activity accordingly. These distinctions may be relatively crude and result merely in assigning persons to categories that are then handled uniformly and en masse. Segregation of prisoners among types of security units and separation of front and back ward programs are examples, respectively, among prisons and mental hospitals. At this extreme clients are subjected to the same general regimes and are expected to accommodate themselves appropriately. At the other extreme the organization may design its approaches with regard to the unique characteristics and needs posed by each client. Staff are then required to discriminate in their perceptions and actions, to encourage differentiated client behavior, and to respond accordingly.

Relative emphasis on client categorization rather than individualization —on universalistic rather than particularistic orientations—can be seen as conditioned by the balance of accommodations the organization is willing to make for, rather than demand from, the clientele. This balance, in turn, is often viewed as a consequence of organizational size and the pressure of managerial requirements, especially within residential institutions. The necessity of caring for and coordinating the activities of a large number of people on a twenty-four-hour basis does create pressures for routinization. Findings from a comparative study of juvenile institutions make clear, however, that the use of standardized group management procedures is not determined simply by size, but by choice among alternative technologies.[5] When clients are viewed as more alike than different they can conveniently be handled routinely and in the aggregate.[6]

Balance of Gratifications and Deprivations

In some organizations the stress on deprivations is such that the client has little to gain but much to lose. Pessimism about the degree of change that is feasible and belief that client motives are antagonistic support use of repressive means. In other organizations the stress on gratifications is such that the client has much to gain and little to lose. Material and social inducements are offered for compliance with the official system and willing participation in the processes of change. Rewards and inducements are more likely to be utilized when the client's motives are regarded as positive or when he can terminate affiliation with the agency of his own volition. The problem of developing and sustaining client commitment and compliance will be discussed later.

Complexity of Change Techniques

Treatment organizations vary in the range and complexity of techniques utilized to cause change among clients. Some present only a limited range of approaches, while others use a wide repertoire of techniques. Limited approaches are more likely to be utilized when the client personality is conceived in essentially simplistic terms or the deviance is not regarded as severe. Use of multiple measures and esoteric techniques serves to increase, respectively, the organization's coordination requirements and its dependence on specialized personnel.

The author's thesis is that treatment organizations may be differentiated with respect to these important technological dimensions: implications of each for staffing patterns as well as for clients have been hinted at. Before proceeding with consideration of these organizations' reliance on professionals, the indeterminateness of treatment technologies must be noted. The final section of this statement will deal with this problem; here it need only be observed that neither agencies nor professionals concerned with deviance have succeeded in creating technologies that achieve high levels of demonstrable effectiveness. This limitation has contributed to the precariousness of treatment organizations and has heightened their dependence on professional cadres.

Reliance of Professional Personnel

The rise of treatment agencies has been accompanied by the emergence of service professions concerned with the same problems of deviance and dependence. Treatment organizations increasingly rely on these professions to compose their élite cadres and to implement their goals. Social work, psychiatry, and clinical psychology have been the most numerous professions among organizational personnel, with psychiatric nursing, teaching, and a variety of counseling or therapy specialties also found in some contexts.

The most obvious reason for dependence on professionals is that they possess the technical competencies necessary for guiding interpersonal relations. Their expertise is directly relevant to the task of people-changing through staff-client transactions. Treatment organizations have also gained a relatively stable labor market by reliance on the professions.[7] The precarious goals and values of treatment organizations are defended by professional groups and additional legitimation is gained as the more or less prestigious professions are able to mediate directly with various public sectors in commanding resources for the organizations.[8] Finally, and most importantly, professionals are needed to certify that clients are able to resume conventional roles because they have been treated, rehabilitated, or the like.[9]

Reliance on the service professions has had other consequences than mere implementation of agency purposes. A question about who has captured whom arises once the primary tasks of the organization are defined as requiring professional expertise. Performance of these tasks may then become the exclusive responsibility of professionals, or at least subject to their direct control. When professionals can be induced to serve in limited numbers and in lower-echelon line positions, the general perspectives of the organization may remain relatively unaffected. When, however, professionals are present in large numbers and assume élite positions, dependence on them brings with it limiting commitment to particular ideologies and strategies of change. Alternative approaches are thus denied the organization except as these are mediated through the profession.[10] The risk is that the approaches defined by one or another profession may not be sufficient for achievement of treatment goals, yet the organization is no longer as free to pursue alternative means.

A second problem posed by reliance on professional cadres is that the treatment organization may become primarily a context for professional practice, which is something different from being a goal-oriented enterprise. Internal arrangements may be shaped to serve the interests or convenience of professional practitioners. The medical hospital is an example of a formal organization largely adapted to professional requirements; many of its problematic aspects and the criticisms directed at these are conditioned by this fact.[11]

The service professions are variously dependent on treatment organizations as contexts for practice. It would be expected that the broader the opportunities for practice—as among different organizations, or wholly outside any organization—the less a profession's dependence on and accommodation to a single type of organization. Thus, psychiatrists are better able than others to assert their claims with respect to the treatment organization: in addition to their greater prestige, psychiatrists are sought by many types of treatment agencies, while they typically maintain some anchorage in private practice. Social workers and teachers, however, are members of largely bureaucratized professions, and have few opportunities for practice independent of organizations. Being in relatively scarce supply, social workers are still able to influence some of the terms of affiliation with any particular treatment agency. One measure of this is their concentration in certain agencies considered as more favorable contexts for professional practice.[12]

It must be noted that not all treatment organizations have accepted professional claims to crucial competencies. Most of those in the corrections sector, and especially prisons, have refrained from a thoroughgoing commitment to the professions. Similarly, relatively few professionally trained social workers are employed within public assistance agencies. One explanation for these patterns may be that neither the prison nor the public assistance agency should be considered a treatment organization as it has been defined. If they are not concerned with changing people, they do not require these professional competencies. Another explanation may be that both organizations are, in fact, concerned with effecting change, but social workers do not have the appropriate skills. There is probably some truth in each of these statements. Many of the difficulties evident in the limited employment of social workers in these two contexts arise from the dominance of other than change goals (e.g., custodialism and deterrence in the prison) as well as from limitations in professional technologies.

As treatment agencies become more complex they tend to employ members of several—sometimes many—professional groups. This presents new problems in defining the appropriate division of effort and allocation of authority among these groups. Competing claims are presented with respect to the essential competencies, preferred tasks, and appropriate statuses within the organization.[13]

Controlling Professional Behavior

Finally, professionals in treatment organizations also assert the principle of autonomy in exercise of their special skills. They value independence and initiative in the use of these skills, especially in the primary areas of *decisions about and transactions with clientele.* The more complex and esoteric the technology utilized, the less possible it becomes to control behavior directly through administrative rules or close supervision. The treatment organization must, nevertheless, insure that staff behavior is in conformity with its general purposes, and that staff actions are coordinated. Certain mechanisms are developed, therefore, to achieve the necessary controls while respecting professional claims to autonomy. Four of these control mechanisms are:

1. COMMITMENT TO ORGANIZATIONAL GOALS. When the agency can neither precisely specify the task to be performed (because of its complexity) nor closely observe performance (because of autonomy claims), it can seek control by demanding greater commitment to its general purposes. Ideological conformity to the values and goals of the organization can be scrutinized among staff and taken as an approximation of direct control.[14] Thus, the organization can rely on members of a profession known to espouse similar values, select individuals who seem most committed to its particular ends, and encourage overt manifestations of staff dedications. Unfortunately, high ideological commitment tends to increase doctrinairism and parochial perspectives among treatment agency personnel. These, in turn, impede pragmatism and rationalism in organizational operation and innovation.

2. MAXIMIZING COLLEAGUE CONTROLS. Acknowledgment of the legitimate authority of officials primarily because they are in superior positions is not a tenet of professionalism, yet practitioners are strongly oriented to collegial relations. They value their reputations among members of their own profession, seek colleague support and advice, and respond to the judgments of those recognized as more expert than themselves. The organization, however, cannot always adjust its administrative hierarchy to parallel the gradations of competence accepted among its professional personnel. Even when this is possible, persons in higher posi-

tions tend to be viewed as *senior* colleagues, who can offer recommendations but should not issue directives.[15] The organization may, therefore, increase the opportunities for interchange among personnel with respect to crucial decisions and actions. While providing reassurance that the less proficient will be guided by the more expert, such interchange also supports ideological commitment and conformity. Staff meetings and case conferences are examples of decision-making procedures that increase colleague controls.

Emphasis on colleague controls presents several difficulties for the agency. Professionals may spend inordinate proportions of time in consultation with colleagues, weighing views on clients, considering alternative procedures, and reviewing processes of client change.[16] There are also difficulties in defining who should be included and excluded in such collective decision-making. Thus, the extension of equalitarianism contemplated by certain of the team practices and the therapeutic milieu philosophies must eventually encompass all operative personnel. Ultimately, the excessive communication requirements and the erosion of administrative authority may severely limit the organization's capacity to perform its basic service tasks.[17]

3. SEGREGATION OF TASKS AND ROLES.   Insistence on semi-independent performance is most characteristic of professional personnel, primarily with respect to activities involving their core competencies. Other tasks may be assigned to nonprofessionals, for whom conventional administrative procedures are more appropriate. Role separation as one approach permits the organization to differentiate its control procedures among personnel in accordance with the type of task. By establishing dual hierarchies of authority, one set of control procedures may be used for professionals, with another set for ward attendants, secretarial personnel, and so on. Furthermore, professionals are assigned many secondary activities that they do not perceive as requiring core competencies, and which can be governed by conventional administrative procedures (e.g., record-keeping). The latter pattern results in the establishment of dual lines of authority to control personnel in different *phases* of their work.[18] Thus, professionals in hospitals and universities seem willing to accept the exercise of administrative authority over certain of their activities, while relying on professionally defined controls for other activities. The problem with each of these dual authority structures, whether they divide only the tasks or both staff and tasks, is that of unclear and debatable boundaries between the phases of agency activity governed by each.

4. SUPERORDINATION OF PROFESSIONS.   Control of staff performance and coordination among professional subgroups has also been attempted by giving greater authority and pre-eminence to members of one profession. In general and mental hospitals all other groups are subordinated to the medical profession, whose members direct and oversee activities. This

arrangement can suffice only when there is one profession to whose superior knowledge and skill others defer, and when such deference within the organization is generally condoned among the professions. Nurses and social workers, for example, have long acknowledged the pre-eminence of medicine and have experienced less strain in being subordinated to control by physicians and psychiatrists. In contrast, clinical psychology has no tradition of subordination and acknowledges the superior wisdom of psychiatry in far less degree. Subordination of psychologists to psychiatrists is consequently accompanied by tension.[19] Similarly, there are challenges within the correctional field when other personnel are subordinated to social workers, while within courts social workers are often skeptical of the legal profession's pre-eminence.

The superordination of professions has only transitory usefulness for control of performance in treatment organizations. On the one hand, the press toward attainment of full professional stature impels each subgroup to affirm the authenticity of its own special knowledge and competence. On the other hand, enlargements in the knowledge base of each profession jeopardize continued dependence on another group.

Given the contemporary status of professions and their relative monopoly of certain competencies, the treatment agency has little choice but to rely upon them, although this dependence has mixed consequences for organizational performance. Once professionals are introduced within the agency, special mechanisms are required for their coordination and control. Reciprocally, however, it is probable that the long-term development of the professions is shaped crucially by their movement into treatment agencies. At the very least the tenets of independent entrepreneurial professionalism must give way to the demands of practice within bureaucratic contexts. Study of such patterns among treatment organizations offers special opportunities for pursuit of more general questions about emerging forms of professionalized bureaucracies.

Consequences for Clients

Let us now turn our attention to clients, and to certain of the effects for them induced by the patterns of treatment organizations. It was noted earlier that the treatment agency seeks to modify the personalities, statuses, or behavior patterns of its clientele. Pupils, patients, and prisoners are simultaneously the raw material on which and with whom the organization works, persons whose interests must be served, and—in their changed condition—the products of organized activity. Clientele frequently sustain affiliation with these organizations over extended periods and acquire formal statuses within them, since change cannot be effected by means of transitory or peripheral involvement.

The essential strategy of all treatment organizations is the design of client experiences calculated to result in relinquishment of nonconformist patterns of conduct, disapproved values, and deviant identities. New and more acceptable modes of behavior must be presented to the client and he must be trained in them. Relations between staff and clients are crucial significance since the former must both *represent* the new modes to clients and directly *manage* the learning of them. A number of conditions may and often do adversely affect the desired relations between staff and clients, thereby curtailing treatment effects. Thus, persons may sometimes be involuntary client members of the organization, they may be opposed to the official change objectives and wish to remain deviant, and they may be alienated from many aspects of the organization.

One source of client resistance or alienation may be the various conceptions of them and of their problems that have previously been identified. These are, in balance, less than positive conceptions and may be resisted as they are made manifest through the person's experience as a client. Observers of correctional programs have noted, for example, the origins of inmate opposition in their attempt, by "rejecting the rejectors," to preserve at least minimally adequate self-images.[20] Acceptance of the fact that one's condition or behavior is disapproved by others and commitment to the objectives of treatment are made more difficult by the negative characterological implications associated with certain prevailing conceptions of deviance.

Difficulties in mobilizing client commitment to change may be aggravated by a client's initial experiences within the treatment organization. Although the goals of the agency are defined at least partially in terms of the client's well-being, he must assume a status in which he is accorded least power, least prestige, and fewest rewards. Acceptance of the client status and role may require a radical shift from the person's conventional situation. Furthermore, motivation and allegiance of persons at the lowest ranks cannot be maintained—as in many other types of organizations—through promotion and advancement opportunities for those who perform most capably. (Parenthetically, it should be noted that socialization organizations, such as schools and youth-serving agencies, typically promote their clientele through the ranks and actively recruit the most promising among these for eventual membership in the staff system.)

Adverse conceptions of clientele, nonvoluntary change, low status within the organization, and lack of advancement opportunities are problematic conditions that may be offset for persons if the remainder of their experiences as clients is essentially positive. It is at this point that the treatment technology becomes most important. If clients are handled in largely routinized ways that ignore or deny their individuality, and if they are subjected to deprivations rather than inducements, further resistance and antagonism would be expected. Under these circumstances is found, moreover, the crystallization of client resistance into a kind of collective opposition working against the goals of treatment. The custodial prison is often cited as a prime example of these adverse conditions, and the prison's change potentials, correctly, are questioned.

Most other types of treatment organizations present certain degrees of these problems, however, and their demonstrated success rates are also less than desirable. Thus, the use of standardized routines that vitiate individuality can be seen in the red tape associated with agency intake, decision-making, and referral processes; in the adherence to formal and often arbitrary rules and procedures; and in the lack of staff spontaneity and warmth in direct contact with clients.[21] Each of these conditions can be justified in terms of other organizational requirements, yet their net effect on clients must be regarded as dubious. Similarly, one may question whether the gratifications and inducements mediated through staff-client relations in many agencies are sufficiently potent to accomplish desired change. Evidence of how difficult it is to sustain a client's commitment to change, when he is free to disengage himself at will, can be seen in the high dropout rate of open treatment agencies.[22]

Evaluating Effectiveness

All treatment organizations—indeed, all people-changing organizatons—encounter difficulties in evaluating their effectiveness. Relatively speaking, it is much easier to judge the success of a manufacturing corporation, since it can be stated, for example, in terms of the quantity of goods produced and sold at certain levels of profit. Profit and production goals can more easily be translated into operational codes, and objective measures exist for assessing results. Direct comparisons can thus be made among many such organizations.

Treatment organizations cannot so easily refer, however, to numbers of persons changed with such and such degrees of success. The clinic can, of course, cite how many clients were served or the per-capita costs of this service. Yet these facts say little about effectiveness, and it is difficult to describe the ways in which clients have been helped or served. There is far less certitude in such statements, little agreement about the most appropriate terms, and even less public understanding of what is meant.

There are three basic sources of difficulty in judging success of treatment organizations: (1) The change goals of each are sufficiently ambiguous that they do not provide clear guides either for designing strategies or for assessing results. What precisely is meant by mental health, rehabilitation, or better social functioning? Change objectives that refer to people are perhaps necessarily ambiguous or statable only in very general terms. (2) Whatever the balance of particular purposes for a given treatment agency, specific operational implications are not readily derivable from the statement of tasks and therefore remain contentious. Treatment procedures and practices are as yet indeterminate and of uncertain validity. Practitioners of these healing arts can neither obtain nor offer clear guidelines for action, and the consequences of their efforts remain only partially demonstrable. Evaluation cannot, therefore, as in certain other enterprises, center on the operational processes of the agency without begging the question of outcomes. (3) Treatment organizations are largely deprived of information about a person's performance *after* termination of client status. This problem is aggravated for agencies that deal with persons removed from their local environments, such as mental hospitals, since there are fewer means for gaining knowledge about the client's behavior after his discharge. For all treatment agencies, however, the effects of the organization's interventions tend to be confounded with the influences of other social systems in which clients live. The resources necessary for follow-up studies are seldom available, and even when they are it is difficult to factor out the specific impact of the organization.

Limitations in objective assessment of effectiveness have important consequences for the treatment organization. They induce emphases on intra-organizational behavior, pressures toward goal displacement, and a tendency toward self-justifying doctrine rather than rational planning. Since follow-up or outside information is relatively unavailable, change in a client is assessed more in terms of his responses to agency expectations and his relations with other personnel than in terms of his capability for conventional social role behavior. The model patient or prisoner is one who conforms to the rules and routines; the model clinic client is one who keps his appointments and learns to reveal himself and to communicate using the language of therapy. Such organizationally valued changes may not merely be irrelevant to community performance requirements, but in extreme form may result in a client's trained incapacity to function adequately outside the agency (e.g., institutionalization in the mental hospital).[23] The task of the treatment organization is to define roles and changed modes of behavior for clients that directly intersect with performance requirements of conventional life in the community. This becomes more difficult insofar as clients are abstracted from their local environments and the agency ignores or lacks knowledge of their immediate social situations. Disjunctures between organizational experiences and community life reduce the relevance of change processes and increase the difficulty of clients' reintegration.

Displacement of goals may be evidence in two directions: one toward overconcern with means and the other toward emphasis on secondary objectives. Limited measures of achievement encourage an imbalance of concern between goals and the procedures that supposedly are instrumental to them. The risk, as has been noted, is that the treatment organization becomes essentially a context for professional practice rather than a goal-directed enterprise. Among agencies that do not rely upon professionals, goal displacement is more likely to take the form of overhauling organizational stability. Rule adherence, efficiency, administrative convenience, and preservation of good order become watchwords in the absence of independent measures of effectiveness.

These tendencies combine to engender a high degree of doctrinairism throughout the entire range of treatment organizations. Belief systems become self-validating, routines are not objectively assessed, and ideological commitment is pervasively inculcated. Charismatic leaders emerge since they offer coherence and guidance in otherwise ambiguous situations. Similarly, personnel in treatment organizations develop strong feelings that only insiders, immersed in the rhetoric and reality of the agency, can adequately appreciate its processes and accomplishments.

Deprived of confident knowledge about goal attainment, the treatment organization encounters difficulties in assuring external publics that it is both competent and effective. Defense of its precarious values becomes more difficult when these are transformed so that they can be fully appreciated only among the sophisticated. The capability of the agency to certify that its clients have been changed is reduced, as external publics maintain their closed ranks even against those who have been rehabilitated. Yet, paradoxically, the growing prestige of the service professions has made it somewhat easier to interpret organizational activity in terms of professional practice. Less professionalized agencies, however, experience new difficulties as support diminishes for the traditionalistic values they embody.

Perhaps a more serious problem is that of planned innovation and technological advance among organizations that are less oriented toward utilitarian criteria. Growing rationalism in the larger society has affected the treatment organization: its former stratagems are now less serviceable in the competition for scarce resources, and there is increasing public reluctance to accept its claims without objective evidence. Reasoned choice among alternative courses of action and development of more effective measures are thus rendered difficult when crucial knowledge about consequences is lacking.

17 Self-Image Perspectives of Delinquents in Custodial and Treatment Institutions

Rosemary C. Sarri

Introduction

Although there has been limited systematic investigation of methods for changing self-attitudes, there is growing evidence to suggest that changes in self-image occur as persons experience particular types of change efforts.[1] Furthermore, attempts have been made to relate the behavior of a given individual to his self conception and to the attitudes of others toward him. Self-attitudes appear particularly vulnerable to change at the adolescent level because of status ambiguity, rapid physical development, and because it is a time for making decisions about one's future life. Our interest here is to examine comparatively the attitudes of delinquents in different types of correctional institutions. Self-attitudes, as they shall be considered here, refer to the manner in which a person evaluates himself, his own situation, and also to his perceptions of the view of significant others toward him.

Many observers of correctional institutions have assumed that all or most inmates develop negative and oppositional attitudes toward the organization and the efforts of staff to achieve changes in attitudes and values. Explanations of the solidary oppositional model are variously attributed to the high level of commitment to criminal values among inmates, to the nonvoluntary nature of the inmates' participation, to prior negative experiences in other correctional agencies, and to the punitive handling of inmates by staff.[2] There is general agreement that basic psychological requirements of self-esteem, autonomy, and gratification are frequently

This paper was prepared especially for this book. An earlier version was presented at the Annual Meeting of the American Sociological Association, St. Louis, Missouri, August 29, 1961. This research was part of a comprehensive study of juvenile correctional institutions directed by Robert D. Vinter and Morris Janowitz and supported by NIMH grant M-2104. Appreciation is expressed to the staff associated with this project for their ideas, criticism, and support.

frustrated in juvenile correctional institutions.[3] Not only does the inmate enter the institution as a committed delinquent, but once there he is exposed to further status degradation in practices which involve deference rituals and sanctions disproportionate in severity for the deviant actions. Despite these conditions it is unlikely that one explanation is sufficient or adequate to describe a range of organizations varying in goals and practices.[4]

The structure of authority in the correctional institution defines the inmate role and the accompanying prescriptions and proscriptions of behavior, which are implemented through elaborate systems of rewards and punishments.[5] The inmate occupies the lowest echelon in the organizational hierarchy and often has little defense against perceived societal rejection other than to unite in covert opposition with peers to "reject the rejectors." [6] As a result peers become influential in modification of one's self-image, but this influence is often negative with respect to identification with socially accepted values. Numerous personal documents by offenders have repeatedly referred to the process of criminal self-definition through repeated interaction with offenders.[7] Differences in self-attitudes and other perspectives, however, have been observed to vary within and between organizations according to an inmate's length of confinement, his position in the informal system, and his perception of institutional goals.[8] Behavioral expectations and perspectives of staff can also be expected to influence inmates to maintain existing self-attitudes or to modify them in a positive or negative direction. Because of all the above factors it was expected that the experience of being institutionalized in a juvenile correctional institution would have an impact on the self-attitudes of offenders, but that varying organizational conditions would lead to quite different self-conceptions.

Organizational Goals

The frame of reference for this research was based on a goal-oriented theory of organizations. Attention was directed to the substantive aspects of goals since these specify the kinds of effects which the organization seeks for its primary members, in this case, juvenile offenders. Goals serve as determinants for the design and management of events within the organization and thus have both direct and indirect effects upon inmates' attitudes and behavior. In the case of the juvenile correctional institution, primary goals can generally be stated as the rehabilitation of the juvenile offender and the protection of society from certain types of disruptive deviant behavior.[9] Although these goals are not necessarily incompatible, when juxtaposed they present serious problems for stable organization functioning.

Analysis of goals provides a basis for ordering juvenile correctional institutions along a hypothetical continuum on the basis of the ratio of containment to treatment goals. Custodial institutions maintain traditionalistic views of rehabilitation, emphasizing obedience, deprivation, and protection of the community. On the other extreme, treatment institutions stress changing attitudes and values through high gratification and an individualistic approach to the situation of each inmate.

The institutions studied were selected nonrandomly to insure variation in goals, auspices, size, and other dimensions. Each was studied through interviewing of staff and clients, extended participant observation, analysis of official records, and administration of questionnaires to staff and inmates. Analysis of these data permitted us to identify tentatively five types of institutions which can be briefly characterized as follows: [10]

1. DICK (discipline). This was a large (225 males) public institution which defined its goals as training inmates in obedience and conformity. Boys were perceived in an undifferentiated manner and were handled en masse because staff believed that they were basically alike with respect to their delinquent behavior. Strong external controls and surface accommodations were emphasized. Numerous physical and social deprivations were employed with few gratifications except for certain individuals.

2. MIXTER (mixed goals). This was a large (375–420 males) public institution which focused on teaching good habits and training in conformity, but also attempted some individual treatment. Staff were observed to have differentiated perceptions of inmates, but they generally maintained a pessimistic view of inmate change potential and sought limited goals. Deprivations were numerous and gratifications few. Inconsistencies in staff practices were frequently observed; some staff were authoritative and distant while others attempted to develop warm and friendly relations with inmates.

3. REGIS (training). This was a small (45–60 males) sectarian institution which sought to train and educate and to change attitudes and values. Emphasis was placed on education, the development of resources, and the learning of new behavior. Staff were generally optimistic about change potential and maintained close relations with inmates. Greater consistency was observed in staff practices toward offenders than in the mixed-goals institution. Although there were sanctions for misbehavior, a high level of gratification was maintained. Staff were firm but also warm and friendly.

4. MILTON (milieu treatment). This was a fairly large (160–200 males) public institution which was concerned with the development of both individual and social controls. The treatment technology was complex and highly developed, with numerous and diversified programs. Staff were optimistic about inmate change potential and emphasized the maintenance of primary relationships between staff and inmates. Although the program was developed around the cottage as the central focus, and treatment staff were generally in charge, some bifurcation in effort between clinicians

and cottage line staff was observed. Gratifications were generally high and deprivations few but more severe than Inland.

5. INLAND (individual treatment). This was a medium size (60–75 males) private institution which focused on the development of individual control, insight, and understanding. Extensive changes in inmates' attitudes and values were sought. Staff maintained a complex view of human nature and were optimistic about the potentiality for change. Primary relationships between staff and inmates were emphasized with much stress placed on the two-person therapeutic relationship. Gratifications were high and deprivations were few and seldom severe. The treatment technology was highly specialized with an individualized approach toward each boy's needs and problems.

The above descriptions, although brief, point to marked differences between custodial and treatment institutions in goals, structure of authority, and staff perspectives and behavior. It was hypothesized that inmate perspectives would reflect these differences in the following ways:

1. Inmates in treatment institutions will maintain positive attitudes toward the institution, staff, and treatment; self-image perspectives will reflect positive character attributes and skills.

2. Inmates in custodial institutions will maintain negative and oppositional attitudes toward the institution, staff, and treatment; self-image perspectives will reflect behavioral traits related to superficial conformity and compliance.

Inmate Perspectives

The central task facing juvenile correctional organizations is that of devising treatment technologies that will bring about in inmates strong and stable adherence to acceptable social norms and values. It is assumed that the behavior and attitudes of inmates are a result of their previous experience, their experience within the institutions, and the interaction of these two factors. Therefore, to understand the behavior of any particular individual, one would have to investigate both his unique biography and his present situation in the institution. Personal characteristics of inmates (for example, age, race, IQ, community of residence, offense, psychological diagnosis, and so on) were studied, and despite the existence of some differences between institutions, we found that these organizations tend to recruit offenders who have similar backgrounds. Many differences within these institutions were as great as those between institutions, and many similarities were evident among the various inmate populations. Although the belief is widely held in the correctional field that individual attributes are related to inmate perspectives, we did not find that personal characteristics were uniformly related to important attitudes and behaviors. Where relationships were found between inmates' attitudes and behavior and their background characteristics, more often than not these could be traced to organizational conditions and staff perspectives about the meaning of the characteristic. In other words, organizational conditions have much to do with which attributes actually become significant. Length of stay was one variable which was observed to have important effects across institutions. Inmates in Milton and Inland developed more positive attitudes as they were retained by the organization over time. In contrast, boys in Dick and Mixter became increasingly negative with respect to several important attitudes the longer they remained in the institutions.

Considerable variation existed among the institutions with respect to the perspectives of inmates. In the custodial types at one organizational extreme inmates viewed the institution negatively, even hostilely at times. They remained socially distant from the staff, they did not perceive that they had received help with their problems, and they tended to maintain more negative self-images. At the other extreme inmates had far more positive views of the institution, they developed cooperative relations with the staff, they perceived that they had received help, and they tended to have more positive images of themselves. We did not find evidence to support the contention that the inmates are universally opposed to the organization and the efforts directed toward individual change.

Marked variations between institutions are apparent in Table 17–1, where findings are presented about inmates' perceptions of the institution as a place to help boys or a place to punish boys. In the treatment and training institutions the large majority of inmates responded that the institution was a place that helped boys in trouble, whereas, in the custodial institutions, the majority stated that it was a place to send or

Table 17–1. Inmates' Perceptions of the Institution [a]

| | CUSTODIAL | | TRAINING | TREATMENT | |
Percentage of Inmates Who Responded That:	Dick	Mixter	Regis	Milton	Inland
Institution is a place to help boys.	33	43	63	62	86
Staff have high level of commitment to helping boys.	42	45	73	53	82
N =	(208)	(379)	(56)	(175)	(65)

[a] Differences in proportion significant at .05 level between treatment and training, and custodial institutions. The assumptions required for the use of statistical tests of significance are violated by the design of this study, but they were primarily employed for heuristic reasons in deciding whether to deny predicted differences between treatment and custodial types of organizations.

punish boys. We also observed that boys in the treatment institutions more often perceived that their family and friends viewed the institution as a place to help boys. A similar question was asked of staff and the results were closely correlated with inmates' attitudes. Consistent and systematic differences among institutions were observed on a number of other items used to assess inmates' perceptions of the institution and its goals. The most stable patterns of responses were observed in those institutions classified at the extreme ends of the custody-treatment continuum. Inmates at Milton were less positive about the level of staff commitment. As we shall note subsequently, this was at least partly attributable to staff inability to deal with problems as they were defined by inmates and to particular uses of group psychotherapeutic procedures.

Observation of responses in Table 17–2 indicates that they directly reflect institutional goals. Inmates in the treatment and training institutions were far more positive about the ability of staff to provide treatment, about the extent and type of help received, and about probable future behavior after they left the institution. Superficial conformity or expressions of remorse for past deeds were avoided by these inmates as appropriate behavior guides. It is important to note, however, that a majority of inmates in all institutions except Regis stated that they needed help or treatment to avoid future delinquency. The emphasis on education rather than treatment per se appears to be the reason for this response by the Regis inmates.

The lack of explicit treatment focus at the custodial institutions is reflected in the pattern of responses by inmates at Dick and Mixter; only 6 per cent and 14 per cent respectively stated that learning to understand oneself was helpful in getting along there. Instead, the large majority reported that they had "learned their lesson."

Responses at Milton evidenced greater inconsistency than at Inland. In the latter case the organization was quite effective in implementing an individual-treatment model. Milton aspired to be a milieu-treatment model, but encountered considerable difficulty in successful implementation of its program. These data suggest that the majority of inmates at Milton recognized areas of change that were desired, but supporting relationships between staff and boys were less adequate than at Inland. The use of esoteric group psychotherapeutic techniques with a predominantly lower class population plus the inability to mediate the informal system effectively appeared to have provoked negative reactions from some inmates.

To evaluate other self-image perspectives, a series of nine projective measures were employed.[11] We did not attempt to measure self-image comprehensively, but tried instead to measure specific attitudes and characteristics likely to be affected by institutional experiences. We were interested in the inmate's view of himself, his perception of others' evaluation of him, his choice of ego ideals, and his attitudes toward misconduct. To ascertain the inmate's perception of his own characteristics and qualities, each was asked, "What do people like best about you?" and "What

Table 17-2. Inmates' Perspectives toward Conformity and Treatment, by Institution

Percentage of Inmates Who Scored Positive: [a]	CUSTODIAL		TRAINING		TREATMENT	P[d]
	Dick	Mixter	Regis	Milton	Inland	
Most boys are just getting by	29	19	25	31	52	N.S.
Perception of need for treatment	63	53	32	66	64	N.S.
Perception of staff ability to provide treatment	45	61	59	76	76	<.05
Perception of best way to get along	6	14	25	42	54	<.01
How much helped most boys	45	46	79	65	81	<.05
Reason why institution helped most boys	52	63	84	72	90	<.05
How much has institutions helped you	68	70	82	71	80	N.S.
Reason why institution has helped you	47	58	78	70	84	<.05
Perception of release criteria	28	23	48	65	65	<.05
Perception of chances to make good outside	38	39	40	48	65	<.01
Perception of future behavior	26	41	35	39	56	<.01
N =	(215)	(390)	(56)	(175)	(65)	

[a] Responses were classified as "positive" with respect to rehabilitative goals, optimism about prosocial future behavior, and ability of staff to assist in rehabilitation.

[b] The Kendall Rank Order Correlation statistic was used to compare the observed ranking of institutions with the predicted ranking on the custody-treatment continuum.

Table 17–3. Self-Image Perspectives, by Institution

Percentage of Inmates Who:	CUSTODIAL		TRAINING		TREATMENT	P^a
	Dick	Mixter	Regis	Milton	Inland	
Score high on positive character attributes	10	19	27	25	32	<.05
Score high on obedience[b] and conformity attributes	31	18	18	9	6	N.S.
Score high on positive self-characterization	12	10	18	20	23	N.S.
Score high on "prisonized" response[c]	39	36	39	25	20	N.S.
N =	(204)	(340)	(56)	(155)	(60)	

[a] The Kendall Rank Order Correlation statistic was used to compare the observed ranking of institutions with the predicted ranking.

[b] The specific item was (paraphrased): What do people like best about you? Responses were coded in several categories including character attributes, skills, virtuous habits, interpersonal relations, and so forth.

[c] The specific item was (paraphrased): Boys think different things about themselves. Check the item that comes closest to what you think about yourself: someone with a personal problem, trying to straighten out, who knows the score and how to play it cool, who got a raw deal, and who doesn't let anyone push him around.

do people like least about you?" Responses about inner qualities and traits were classified as more positive than those which suggested superficial compliance, conformity, or avoidance.[12]

In examining the findings in Table 17–3, it can be seen that boys in the treatment and training institutions more frequently mentioned internal traits or character attributes than did the boys in the custodial institutions. At Dick and Mixter inmates reported that others preferred them to be obedient, well-behaved, or to avoid trouble (31 per cent and 18 per cent at Dick and Mixter, respectively). In comparison, the proportions at Inland were 6 per cent and 9 per cent at Milton.

Some general observations can be made about the response patterns for all of the institutions. A large number of inmates stated that the possession of work and school skills was an important and desirable attribute. Most of these boys were seriously retarded in school, and the overwhelming majority were from lower socioeconomic status. They could anticipate encountering considerable difficulty in preparing for future occupational roles. In none of the institutions did we observe that staff were fully aware of this concern nor had they developed vocational and other educational programs that would prepare these boys adequately for current and future employment situations.

Some self-attitudes which were seldom mentioned supported other observations about differences in self-image between delinquents and nondelinquents. Inmates seldom referred to social-responsibility attributes or to rational action. On the other hand, there was evidence of prisonization attitudes in that a number of inmates (more in the custodial than in the treatment institutions) described themselves as follows: "I'm cool and don't bother anybody," or "I mind my own business and keep to myself." Although there were differences between institutions, a sizeable percentage at all except Regis gave negative, inappropriate, or unspecified responses. These findings suggest a lack of clarity about one's self-image, a negative evaluation, and inability to specify self-characteristics, and probably some negativism about responding to the questions.

Discussion

The findings on inmates' attitudes toward conformity, change, and therapeutic goals provide support for the general hypothesis of this study in that inmates in treatment institutions maintained positive attitudes toward the institution and reported that they had been helped to a greater extent to cope with problems and difficulties. Some support was also provided for the hypothesis that inmates in treatment institutions tend to develop more positive self-images, and that their attitudes imply greater acceptance of socially approved norms and values. The latter findings, however, did not differentiate as consistently between institutions as did attitudes toward treatment and change. Although appropriate substantiating data are lacking, these findings indicate, at least tentatively, that both custodial and treatment institutions tend to attain their stated goals. Custodial organizations sought to achieve obedience, containment, and conformity in varying degrees, and inmates' responses were in accord with these objectives. In contrast, treatment and training institutions variously sought to change antisocial attitudes, to increase self-understanding, and to develop personal and social controls. Responses of inmates generally corresponded with these aims. This report did not consider informal relations among inmates and their differential consequences, but these must be examined if we are to understand the situation more fully.[13]

Variations were observed between the treatment institutions, Milton and Inland, and they were such that they provoked more extensive examination of organizations' patterns and practices. Milton was less effective than Inland in presenting and reinforcing a positive model of inmate behavior. The reliance on group psychotherapeutic approaches in formal treatment services appeared to have serious limitations as did the failure to deal adequately with current problematical situations. Inconsistencies in staff practices toward inmates were observed more often at Milton, although they appeared less frequently than at Mixter.

In several instances it was observed that inmates' responses at Regis were more positive than would be predicted by its location on the custody-treatment continuum. The clarity and consistency of staff expectations, the emphasis placed on education, the relatively high gratification ratio, and the greater freedom of movement allowed inmates all appeared to be significant factors in producing these results.

Despite the differences between institutions, these findings suggest that there are a number of concerns that are common to at least some inmates in all of the institutions. The findings directly challenge the notion that delinquents do not view themselves as in trouble and in need of assistance with personal problems. With regard to self attitudes, we observed that a relatively high percentage of inmates were concerned about skills related to school and work performance. Since these inmates were all adolescents, this appeared to be a reflection of a more general concern. Adolescents in contemporary American society experience considerable role discontinuity with respect to adult occupational roles, and this problem is likely to be even more aggravated for lower-middle-class and lower-class persons. Erikson and Rosenberg have suggested that adolescence poses particular problems in this society because many young people encounter problems in clarifying their identity.[14] It is likely that this situation is particularly problematic for the majority of institutional offenders who suffer a severe loss of status in this stressful period.

These findings on inmates' attitudes have relevance in terms of preconditions for effecting the rehabilitation of institutionalized offenders.[15] If treatment goals are identified for inmates, if role expectations are clear, and if a positive model of behavior is articulated, boys will perceive the institution and its staff as helping agents and will respond positively in the evaluation of their experience. None of the data from this study permit us to comment directly on the long-term consequences of these experiences for the reduction of delinquent behavior, but it appears unlikely that those in the custodial institutions have been helped in ways that will aid them in successfully avoiding delinquency in the future. This research also points to the need for the development of viable treatment technologies that are specifically directed toward changing delinquent behavior. The majority of professional staff in juvenile correctional institutions today have been strongly influenced by clinical perspectives developed in the diagnosis and treatment of mental illness. Such approaches are not only inadequate, but often may be dysfunctional as the example of Milton illustrates. As institutions move toward implementation of treatment goals, group management problems become interwoven with problems in the integration of professional and nonprofessional staff in the performance of their specialized tasks. None of the institutions studied had completely resolved problems in the integration of staff effort, but our findings suggest that there are alternative patterns which could be adapted to facilitate the attainment of treatment goals for inmates.

18 Organization of Patients and Staff in Three Types of Mental Hospitals

Maeda J. Galinsky and

M. David Galinsky

Why patients in mental hospitals behave in the way they do is a question that has been raised again and again by both critics and advocates of different kinds of mental hospital organization. Yet there has been no comparison made of the effects of the varied formal organizations in mental hospitals on the development of patient subsystems. Studies of institutions have repeatedly confirmed the existence of a relationship between the way the institutions are formally organized and the behavior of clients in these settings. A recent study by Street et al.[1] of organizational goals and structures and of inmate social systems in juvenile correctional institutions has isolated variables that are relevant to an examination of mental hospitals as well. Variables such as power structure in an institution, and staff practices, sanctioning power, and belief systems appear to affect markedly the behavior of institutional members.

The present paper will examine and compare patient subsystems in three types of mental hospitals: custodial, individual-treatment, and milieu-treatment hospitals. First the differing patient behavior and informal structure will be described, then an attempt will be made to account for the differences noted in terms of variations in formal institutional structure and practices.

The information on which comparisons of institutions were based was gathered from a review of already published literature on mental hospital organization. The material available was uneven in the empirical evidence it provided. Some of it was the result of controlled observation and study, while other papers consisted of descriptive reports without very complete

This paper was prepared especially for this book. It is based on a paper presented at the Annual Meetings of the American Orthopsychiatric Association, March, 1964.

documentation. Moreover, in very few of the works cited was direct attention paid to the patient subsystem per se. Therefore, evidence was sometimes lacking for a particular aspect of patient organization and it was necessary to make conjectures about patterns of patient behavior. None of the studies to be cited dealt with more than one type of mental hospital nor provided any comparative material. Therefore, the conclusions drawn have to be considered as tentative.

Types of Mental Hospitals

The three categories of organizations to be compared were suggested by Parsons.[2] Institutions that have the custody of patients as their primary purpose concentrate on protection and physical care. Those whose major goal is therapy emphasize treatment techniques (either individual therapy or milieu therapy) that strive to restore persons to health or enable them to leave the hospital. When such restoration is not possible their avowed aim is to help patients to live as nearly normal lives as is possible within the institutional setting. Commitment to different goals for patients leads to different organizational practices for attaining those goals. Organizational practices in turn exert influences on the environment in which the patient subsystems develop. As Street[3] hypothesized, different types of patient subsystems develop in different organizational settings. The frequency and range of patient interaction, the degree of group cohesion and solidarity, the nature of the leadership structure, and the types of cliques formed are central characteristics of the patient subsystem and may be expected to vary in the three types of mental hospitals.

Patient Subsystems in the Custodial Hospital

In the custodial hospital, interaction among patients seemed to be quite limited. What we are calling interaction consisted almost entirely of verbal communication. During one period of study, Greenblatt, York and Brown[4] found that only 4 per cent of the patients on a women's chronic ward in a large state hospital could be classified as interacting with each other. In the hospital as a whole they noted that leaders could be found on every ward, but alert responsible patients were in a minority. The majority of patients had settled down to a minimum level of activity and almost no social interaction. In an earlier study of a similar hospital, Rowland[5] noted that there were three types of interaction on the wards—interaction with a maximum of insight, with a minimum of insight, and with considerable withdrawal from social contacts. Among the first group whose members were the high-status patients, there were a number of ingroup and outgroup identifications. The typical picture was one of small, closed friendship groups. Belknap[6] also described a small group of patients who engaged in most of the verbal interchange on the ward. Although some patients had much to say to each other in these hospitals, for the most part there was only a small amount of interaction among all patients. The patients in the hospital studied by Dunham and Weinberg [7] were divided into three categories: agitated, chronic, and hopeful. Those on the agitated wards were in poor contact with reality and had very erratic interpersonal relationships. As in the other hospitals, the chronic patients interacted with each other minimally. By contrast, however, patients on the hopeful wards, who were short-term inhabitants of the institution, engaged in a great deal of superficial interaction.

There was a definite hierarchy among patients in custodial hospitals, with those who assisted attendants in their ward duties at the head of it. Rowland referred to those in the top category in the patient hierarchy as the institutional cures. They showed improvement but could make a satisfactory adjustment only in the hospital environment. Belknap gave the most detailed description of the client subsystem in the custodial hospital. Patients were grouped by attendants into three categories: the privileged and cooperative, the partly privileged and neutral, and the unprivileged and dangerous, disturbed, or listless. This hierarchy of patients' statuses assigned by the attendants established the system of relationships among the patients themselves. The privileged patients were highest in the patient hierarchy, the partly privileged occupied a middle position, and the unprivileged were relegated to the lowest status. The privileged patients vigorously maintained their monopoly of privilege by sarcasm, ridicule, physical threats, and sometimes physical punishment. They were the most intelligent and most rational patients on the ward. Leaders were drawn from this group and informal cliques were established among them. They helped care for the ward and for the incoherent and untidy patients, and helped to control the disturbing patients, especially the troublemakers. Occasionally patients from the status level below theirs were allowed to move up. In general, however, the privileged patients excluded all of the lower status patients from their personal relationships.

In the custodial hospitals, for the most part, a definite system of patient organization existed. A hierarchy of patients was established, with the ward helpers heading the group. They were the ones most likely to form cliques and to maintain a high degree of interaction. Leaders were drawn from among them and as a group they received the most privileges. They constituted a cohesive group, but among the patients as a whole there appeared to be little solidarity. Patients who were not members of the ward elite might interact with each other, but their interaction was minimal. There were many withdrawn patients who usually did not participate in ward interaction at all.

Patient Subsystems in Individual-Treatment Hospitals

In the individual-treatment hospitals there was evidence of a greater degree of interaction among all patients. Here, too, there seemed to be an elite group of patients, but qualifications for inclusion in the elite were quite different from those in the custodial hospital. The reports of Stanton and Schwartz [8] and Polansky et al.[9] indicate that in each instance there was a group of patients who monopolized the attention of the ward and who interacted with each other most intensely. Stanton and Schwartz noted that there was a group of withdrawn patients that essentially was neglected, whereas Polansky mentions no similar group. Of the individual-treatment institutions, the one studied by Caudill [10] presented the most complete account of patient interaction. He described in detail a ward-collaborative activity that involved a great deal of patient interaction. The descriptions of interaction in the individual-treatment hospital suggest that it involved a larger proportion of the patients and a greater amount of communication among patients than in the custodial hospitals.

In the individual-treatment hospital there were elite groups who dominated the ward, but the types of leaders who emerged and the roles they performed were quite different from those in the custodial hospital. In none of the treatment hospitals was the extent to which patients participated in housekeeping activities important in determining their statuses. Rather, the ability to interact in the way one would outside the hospital was most important. For example, Stanton and Schwartz differentiated patients on the basis of the level of overt activity shown on the ward—the active, the intermediate, and the withdrawn—a classification scheme similar to those used by Rowland and Belknap. The active patients interacted mainly among themselves, while the withdrawn ones were generally ignored by other patients. The active group clearly formed a dominating and cohesive clique on the ward, known as the sewing circle. This clique lasted about four or five months and was the only informal patient group that persisted for so long a time during the period when the ward was studied. Patients in this group competed among themselves for staff attention or for the use of facilities, but rarely were they engaged in competition with patients outside the group, mainly because these could not measure up to their level of activity. Unlike the situation in the custodial hospital, the clique members were more tolerant of hostile behavior by patients not members of the clique. The clique was viewed by other patients as a unified collectivity which excluded them, or related to them antagonistically. No outgroup developed in opposition to the clique, but there were a number of individuals who openly opposed it. The clique in this ward dissolved when two of the five patients were discharged. Polansky described a similar patient structure. In the hospital he studied, a group of the most coherent patients formed a clique that deliberately restricted its membership. Caudill also observed the formation of a clique composed of the most dominant and aggressive ward members, as well as another more loosely structured group.

In the individual-treatment hospitals, then, elite cliques existed on the wards as they did in the custodial hospitals. The composition of these elite groups was based on the patients having characteristics which most nearly approximated "normal" behavior, rather than characteristics important to institutional maintenance. Characteristics such as clear, meaningful communication, little disorganization of behavior, and persistence and tenacity in seeking fulfillment of their wishes were prominent in the behavior of patients in the elite groups. These clique groupings, with the possible exception of the hospital described by Polansky, were not so impenetrable to other patients as were those found in the custodial hospitals. In the individual-treatment hospitals, cliques dissolved and new cliques developed. The patient structure in the custodial hospital was a more rigid one: cliques, once formed, remained quite fixed.

Patient Subsystems in Milieu-Treatment Hospitals

In the milieu-treatment hospitals interaction among all patients was greater than in either of the other types of institutions. In all of the hospitals that changed their orientation from either individual-therapy or custodial goals to those of milieu therapy there was an increase in interaction among patients. For example, Greenblatt reported that on a women's ward in a large custodial hospital, an increase in patients' constructive interrelations was noted after the initiation of a program designed to stimulate social interaction. Similar results were reported by Millier [11] and by Sivadon.[12] With the increase of patient interrelationships, there was also evidence of greater consideration and concern about each other among patients, as well as attempts to be useful to one another therapeutically. Greenblatt observed that patients related to one another more frequently when materials were provided for them to work with and when attendants and nurses encouraged their interaction. Moreover, in the course of patient government meetings, withdrawn patients were increasingly stimulated to greater participation. The interaction appeared to be quite extensive in "the therapeutic community" of Jones [13] designed to promote the development of a group culture. The patients in this hospital were mostly diagnosed as neurotic and might not have been as disturbed as those in the hospitals previously described. Therefore, the increase in interaction might be partially attributable to the less severe disturbance of the patients. In this hospital, group sessions were emphasized more than individual therapy was. Most patients participated in these sessions, and an effort was made to encourage group members to accept more useful social roles.

While the degree and range of interaction among patients in hospitals emphasizing milieu treatment is reported to be relatively large, the structure of the patients' relationships, clique formation, and leadership roles were largely neglected in the descriptions given of these hospitals. However, there is some information to show that, as in the case of the individual-treatment hospitals, there was an elite group of patients on the wards composed of the more verbal and "normal" patients, and that these patients formed cliques. Jones pointed out that in the group sessions that were held with one group of patients, "the proceedings were kept active chiefly by a nucleus of the more intelligent and understanding patients. They tended to prevent the intrusion of what appeared to them to be irrelevant material, and they even made tentative interpretation." On the wards in this hospital the group structure seemed to differ, depending on the composition of the patients. In one ward, where an aggressive psychopath ruled, a "tea group" monopolized the ward kitchen; this ward was contrasted with another where, in the words of one patient, everyone appeared to be happy and there was a family atmosphere. Greenblatt did not describe the patient organization in any detail, although he did mention that at times conflicts about activities (e.g., what music would be played) were settled by majority rule. Most of the patient behavior described in these accounts of milieu treatment involves formal efforts to influence group development. In the custodial and treatment hospitals no similar efforts were made. Nonetheless, one of the results of the staff efforts in encouraging patient interaction seemed to be an increase in the degree of spontaneous patient interrelations that went beyond the activities in which the hospital personnel were involved.

In milieu-treatment hospitals, then, there was some clique formation, leadership was based partly on characteristics desired outside of the hospital, and there was greater interaction among all patients rather than domination by an exclusive clique.

Table 18–1 presents a summary of the above discussion.

Organizational Variables

Now that we noted some of the differences in patient organization in the three types of hospitals, let us examine some of the features of the institutional system that might account for the kind of patient organization that emerged. The organizational variables that appear to have potent effects on patient subsystems are hierarchical structure, staff practices and sanctioning power, staff belief systems, and physical resources. Although the patient populations might have differed in the institutions examined, it does not seem possible to explain the variance found in client subsystems on the basis of population differences alone. Lower-class psychotics were present in both the custodial hospitals and the milieu-treatment hospitals. Treatment-oriented hospitals contained upper-class as well as lower-class patients, and neurotics as well as psychotics. It is true that the custodial hospitals were much larger than the treatment-oriented hospitals, both as a whole and on individual wards, and size is one of the organizational variables commonly considered to have an effect in sociological analyses of mental hospitals. However, the size of the hospital or of ward considered alone would not seem to account for the client subsystem that develops. A large institution may or may not have a higher ratio of personnel to patients, it may have a greater number of physical resources and a more humanitarian view of clients than a smaller hospital. Variables other than

Table 18-1. Characteristics of Patient Organization in Three Types of Institution

Type of Institution	CHARACTERISTICS OF PATIENT ORGANIZATION			
	Frequency and Range of Interaction	Hierarchical Structure	Group Cohesion	Elite Group
Custodial	Minimal interaction among patients as a whole; much interaction in small group of "institutional cures."	Rigid structure headed by "institutional cures" who assisted in caring for wards.	Little solidarity among patients as a whole.	Membership based on ability to help with ward care.
Individual Treatment	Some interaction among all patients; small groups of active patients interact most intensely.	High status associated with ability to act "normal." More fluid structure than custodial.	Participation in some activities by group as a whole, but apparently little solidarity.	Membership based on ability to act "normal."
Milieu Treatment	Considerable interaction among all patients.	Apparently rather equalitarian but higher status accorded more "verbal," "normal" patients.	Evidence of at least moderate cohesion, e.g., group decision making.	Membership based on ability to act "normal," but apparently less clique formation than in other types.

size alone would seem to affect the differences found among client sub-systems.

As we compare the three types of hospitals with regard to their particular characteristics that might relate to patient organization, we will discuss the following: staff beliefs about the efficacy of treatment, the duties of nurses and attendants, patients' access to physicians, nurses' and attendants' control over reward and punishment, the role of physical resources in the institution, and kinds of interaction between patients and personnel.

Organizational Variables in the Custodial Hospital

The belief system in the custodial hospitals emphasized custody rather than treatment of patients. Belknap viewed the latent belief system that lay behind the development of custodial hospitals as founded on the idea that the mentally ill would not respond to any treatment or rehabilitative effort. The only realistic course was therefore to provide minimum custodial care. Attendants' formal duties were to handle the custodial functions of running the ward, while physicians were responsible for medical and psychiatric matters. Patients had no easy access to doctors, who were few in number, because the hierarchy demanded that communication go rigidly upward from patient to attendant, and then either to nurse or to doctor, depending on which one supervised the attendant. Since custody was the primary function of the hospital, patients had no doctors to whom they were assigned for continuing treatment. Therefore, almost all communication between the patient and the rest of the hospital personnel passed through the medium of the attendant. Attendants had little official power to make decisions about patient treatment, but informally they had almost absolute power on the ward, where practically all patient care took place. There was, in reality, a split in authority. Physicians had nominal authority for patient care, but since the main business of the hospitals was custody, most power over patients was actually in the attendants' hands. Because attendants were scarce and help was needed to care for the wards, they divided patients into categories of "workability," i.e., cooperative, neutral, or uncooperative.

There was very little social interaction among attendants and patients, but the former had many rewards to offer for compliance with their wishes, rewards such as better rooms and beds, more privacy, allowing patients to leave the ward without supervision, luxuries like coffee on the ward, permitting patients to contact a physician, and treating patients with kindness and respect. A great variety of punishments were employed for not obeying the attendants' wishes. The attendants could suspend all the patients' privileges, ridicule or physically punish them, use the isolation room, put patients on the list for electroshock therapy, or threaten to transfer them to undesirable wards, and regularly assign them to unpleasant tasks.[14]

The patient subsystem that developed is understandable in view of the ward structure. Because materials were scarce and attendants had absolute power over them, and because patients had almost no access to personnel other than the attendants, the patients' only recourse was to follow the attendants' orders. An elite group developed that helped the attendants run the ward and, in return, received supplies. These patients in turn controlled the other patients. This rigid patient structure in part reflected the inflexibility of the hospital as a whole. Since all gratifications that were available in the rather deprived environment of the custodial hospital became the province of the elite groups of institutional cures, they, too, had a stake in maintaining the *status quo*. The only exception to this behavior pattern was found among the patients on the hopeful wards of the hospital studied by Dunham and Weinberg. These patients were oriented toward getting out of the institution, and, therefore, valued acting normal, conforming, and maintaining contact with people outside the hospital. Their behavior had more in common with patients in the treatment-oriented hospitals to be described below than with the rest of the patients in the custodial hospitals..

Organizational Variables in Individual-Treatment Hospitals

The environment in which patient subsystems developed in the individual-treatment hospitals was somewhat different. Although there was a definite hierarchy from doctors to nurses to attendants to patients, the patients had more access to treatment personnel, who were, in fact, concerned with treatment. The belief in these hospitals about the fate of patients was also different from that of the custodial hospital. The physicians held the belief that most patients could recover or improve greatly if they received adequate psychotherapy. The nurses also believed in the efficacy of psychotherapy, and so did the patients. It is interesting to note that in one of the hospitals, the one described by Caudill, the nurses doubted that the patients had any therapeutic influence on each other, and patients, for the most part, thought they affected one another positively. Nurses felt that their relationships with patients were therapeutic, but patients did not consider them so. The nurses generally did not interact with the patients informally with respect to needs and problems, but concerned themselves with ward management. Therapeutic care of patients and all decisions related to that care were administered by the doctors, and the custodial or ward-management activities were directed by nurses or attendants. In one hospital, a physician acted as administrator of the ward, but in actuality the nurses were more responsible for the management duties.[15] Attendants and nurses did have access to some rewards and punishments that they could administer to patients. For example, in the hospital described by Caudill nurses made decisions about when to call a patient's doctor and about which patients should attend occupational therapy. Nurses clearly did not have the power in these institutions that attendants in the custodial hospitals had. In the individual-treatment institutions the patients could appeal nurses' or attendants' decisions to their physicians, whom they saw frequently in individual psychotherapy. The physicians held many sanctioning powers, such as deciding when the patient would be allowed off the grounds, and who would go into seclusion. In addition, nurses' decisions were evaluated in staff meetings. Physicians, therefore, had a good deal of actual control over their individual patients. The physical and emotional resources to which patients had access were less scarce in these hospitals than in the custodial hospitals, partly because there was a greater ratio of staff to patients and because there were more material resources available. Patients had better living conditions in every respect, and they had constant recourse to and support from their therapist.

Therefore, in the individual-treatment hospitals the patient did not develop a subsystem designed primarily to obtain scarce resources from powerful persons. Nursing personnel were not so scarce in these institutions, and help was not needed with ward work. Attendants and nurses did not have the absolute sanctions to effect the formation of the kind of patient group they might consider ideal. The patients' values and norms partially reflected those of the physicians and of the hospital in general in their intense interest in psychotherapy and in their desire to understand the causes of their illnesses. Furthermore, because the patients looked forward to the time when they would leave the hospital, the elite groups that developed were based on characteristics that were considered desirable in the community outside the hospital. When an institution does not place unusual and rigorous demands on its inhabitants, the social norms they develop appear to approximate norms that they have been accustomed to in other life situations.

Organizational Variables in Milieu-Treatment Hospitals

In the treatment institutions emphasizing milieu therapy still another environment existed. In both of the institutions described (Greenblatt, et al., Jones), physicians had the most power and the ultimate authority in decision making. An attempt, however, was made in both hospitals to give attendants and patients a voice in ward and hospital management. The administrators, and later other staff, believed in the efficacy of treating patients along group and ward lines, especially through the group, rather than only in individual therapy. They believed in the potentially therapeutic effects of patients upon one another. Attendants, nurses, and ancillary personnel were given a formal treatment role with power to make decisions in the milieu-treatment hospital described by Greenblatt and his associates. Physicians interacted with the patients on the wards, and patients had access to many persons who were considered treatment personnel and dispensers of resources. It is not clear what sanctioning powers the attendants and nurses retained in these hospitals. They seem to have had greater power than in the individual-treatment hospitals because they were among the personnel who had therapeutic interaction with patients and, therefore, had more emotional and social resources to give and withhold. On the other hand, they had less power than in the custodial hospitals because they had less control over material resources. How material resources were controlled in these institutions is not clear, although patients were given access to their own clothing and were allowed to spend their own money. It seems, then, that patients had some control over resources. The physicians who headed the ward teams, however, had the most power over resources and action, although they tried to share power with other staff and patients.

In the milieu-treatment hospitals, then, patients were encouraged to take initiative, and there was an interest in their forming groups. The patient structure in these institutions showed that there was a greater inclusion of all types of patients in group activities and that, as present evidence suggests, no overpowering elites developed on the wards. Patients showed greater concern about one another's well being and attempted to take responsibility for each other. Their behavior reflected the distribution of power that was characteristic of the staff structure. The patients accepted the culture of the hospital and began to behave in accord with it in their informal interpersonal relations.

Table 18-2 presents a summary of the organizational factors for the three types of institution.

Discussion

The preceding has suggested that the organizational structure of an institution has a powerful effect on the development of patient subsystems. The kind of hierarchical structure that exists among patients seems to develop along parallel lines to that which is characteristic of staff relationships, e.g., the rigid hierarchy of the staff in the custodial hospital was repeated in the patient organization. Similarly, staff practices, attitudes, and beliefs are either directly or covertly communicated to patients and affect their attitudes toward themselves and their behavior toward each other. In this regard, there appear to be a number of striking similarities between staff and patient ideas about kinds of desirable interaction, preferred methods of treatment, and likelihood of patient improvement. The development of the patients' subculture seems to be strongly influenced by existing staff practices and attitudes.

A number of patient variables have not been discussed. Some others that may be supposed to have an effect on the more specific development of patient subsystems are personality characteristics and psychological diagnosis, age, size of ward population, IQ, and social class. The relationship of these factors to the nature of the patient organization that emerges needs further study. The effect of different patient subsystems on differ-

Table 18–2. Characteristics of Staff Organization in Three Types of Institution

Type of Institution	CHARACTERISTICS OF STAFF ORGANIZATION			
	Staff Practices	Hierarchical Structure	Belief Systems	Physical Resources
Custodial	Little or no therapeutic care; virtually all power over patient in attendants' hands.	Rigid hierarchy led by physicians; patients had little access to professional staff.	Mentally ill do not respond to treatment.	Extremely limited; controlled by attendants.
Individual Treatment	Therapeutic care in hands of physicians; ward management directed by nurses.	Definite hierarchy with physician at the head; patients had access to professional staff.	Patients could improve if they received adequate psychotherapy.	Adequate to good; controlled mainly by nursing staff.
Milieu Treatment	Physicians, nurses, and attendants all had treatment roles.	Physicians at head of flexible hierarchy; involvement of all staff in therapeutic care and decision making.	Patients could improve if they received proper treatment, including use of milieu; therapeutic effect of interaction among patients.	Adequate; patients had some control over resources.

ent types of patients also requires further study. There has been inadequate recognition, in most hospitals, of the effect of patients upon one another. These effects may be therapeutic, but they also may be deleterious, as evidenced in Caudill's description of the regressive effect on open-ward patients of introducing locked ward patients to their immediate environment.

Since many of the goals set for patients in mental institutions involve changes in social and interpersonal behavior, it has seemed reasonable to assume that the patient group itself could be a powerful device for achieving desired change in patients. In recent years, milieu-treatment approaches have been advocated as a panacea for all difficulties in treating the mentally ill. More recently, however, criticisms of the milieu approach by Cumming and Cumming [16] and Rapoport [17] have pointed to the diversity of meanings of the term, the contradictory aspects apparently inherent in milieu approaches, and their lack of orientation with reality. The most pointed criticism is advanced by Perrow.[18] He notes that it has been widely held that oppressive practices in large mental hospitals were caused by faults in their social structures and goal orientations. What has been called milieu therapy in these settings represents simple upgrading of the institutions to a more humane level, and not an introduction of a new kind of technology. He suggests that there is at present no well developed scientific methodology on which to base the development of milieu treatment, and that considering the milieu approach as a new technology can only encourage misleading generalizations. While Perrow's criticisms are rather strong, it is true that no well-articulated statements have been offered by advocates of milieu treatment about the relationship between hospital staff structure and patient change. For example, instead of blandly following the tenet that patient-staff and patient-patient interaction is a good thing, it would be far more useful to explore the effects of a variety of such interaction possibilities and suggest organizational changes to implement desired goals. Such research could make it possible to modify organizational structure by helping to create the kinds of patient subsystems which, in turn, could facilitate desired changes in the individual patient.

19 A Balance Theory of Coordination between Bureaucratic Organizations and Community Primary Groups

Eugene Litwak and Henry J. Meyer

The general problem we wish to discuss is how bureaucratic organizations and external primary groups (such as the family and neighborhood) coordinate their behavior to maximize social control. It will be argued in this paper that mechanisms exist to coordinate the two forms of organizations, and that these mechanisms of coordination can be systematically interpreted by what we will call a "balance theory of coordination." It will also be argued that this "balance theory" provides a formulation to account for current empirical trends more adequately than traditional sociological theories.

Present Theory of Bureaucratic-External Primary-Group Coordination

A number of sociologists have analyzed the characteristics of industrial bureaucratic organizations and primary groups such as the family and the neighborhood so as to imply that their relationships are antithetical. Thus Weber, in his discussion of China, suggests that one reason why a modern industrial bureaucratic system did not develop was because it was contrary to the strong extended family ties of the Chinese family.[1]

Abridged from ADMINISTRATIVE SCIENCE QUARTERLY, 11 (June 1966), 33–58. Reprinted with the permission of the authors and the journal. Acknowledgement is made to the Social Work and Social Science Program at The University of Michigan for financial support through the Russell Sage Foundation Grant during the exploratory phase of a research study of organizational factors and social control in the community, and to the U.S. Office of Education, Contract No. 3-10-033, Project 1796.

This is also an implication of Tonnies' remarks insofar as relations characterized as *Gemeinschaft* are viewed as dominated by primary-group ties, while *Gesellschaft* relations are characteristic of the bureaucratic organization.[2] Schumpeter is very explicit on the issue, and points out how the rationalistic elements of the work situation tend to undermine affective family bonds.[3] Only in partial contrast are the analyses of contemporary theorists such as Parsons and his associates.[4] They accept the view that the two types of organizations are antithetical, but also point out that the family has distinctive functions that cannot be performed by any other type of organization. Furthermore, these functions are necessary for the survival of a society. They argue that the bureaucratic organization and at least one type of primary group (the nuclear family) can exist in the same society provided they are kept relatively insulated from each other.

The positions seem to suggest that bureaucratic and external primary groups, unless they are isolated, tend to conflict with each other.[5] Coordination between them is not explicitly entertained in such a conclusion.

Relation of Present Theory to Empirical Trends

It is paradoxical that such theoretical formulations seem to overlook developments that may be observed in the most advanced bureaucratic organizations in American society. Thus, if the largest and most successful of the industrial bureaucratic organizations are examined, there is considerable evidence that they have in recent decades increased explicit efforts to establish closer ties with families and neighborhood groups.[6] This development in industry has had a double base. First, management of such large bureaucracies has come to recognize that work morale and productivity are closely tied to family and local community conditions. Second, it has been realized that these large organizations are increasingly exposed to public view. Decisions within these giant corporations that were previously thought to be private decisions of management have now to be reinterpreted in terms of the public welfare so that they are now as often political as business decisions (e.g., the fixing of prices in the steel industry now clearly involves public policy).

Furthermore, if diverse areas of social life are examined—such as the political, the educational, the military, delinquency control programs, and welfare fund raising—formal organizations involved can be found to exhibit deliberate concern for closer contact with external primary groups such as the family, neighborhood, or local community.[7] More to the point, it is our view that this concern grows with the final stages of bureaucratization within a society where the issues of power and control are especially crucial to the organization. Because they are subject to public scrutiny by virtue of magnitude, to industrial or political centrality, and to dependence on extensive markets, such organizations become sensitive to the need for organizing and maintaining grass-roots (primary-group) support.

Implicit Assumptions of Present Theory

Underlying the discrepancy between the theoretical position usually presented and the evident empirical trends are some assumptions of the theory that should be made explicit. Two will be stated in exaggerated form in order to expose what seems to us to be implied.

The first assumption is that the primary group and the bureaucratic organization have antithetical, mutually destructive atmospheres. Bureaucracies operate on an instrumental basis. They stress impersonality, specificity, the use of rules, professional expertness, etc. Primary groups operate on a kinship or affective system of evaluation, and stress diffuse, personal, face-to-face contact, etc.

The second assumption is that the activities of the primary group are, for the most part, directly replaceable by those of the bureaucratic organization. Thus, if the bureaucratic organization performs a task, there is no reason why the family should do so well. This assumption rests, in turn, on the premise that in a mass society bureaucratic organization is the most efficient way to achieve most social goals. As a consequence, in competition between the two types of organization, the bureaucracy will tend to supplant the primary group.[8]

An Alternative Assumption

The assumption that the two forms of organization have antithetical atmospheres can be accepted with some reservations, but nevertheless accepted. Much of the research of industrial sociology has sought to show that bureaucracies can be operated in a more "human relations" atmosphere than Weber would have anticipated. Nevertheless, there are some basic differences in atmosphere between the bureaucracy and the primary group such as the family. These differences are partly a matter of degree and partly a matter of quality. For instance, the family operates primarily on the basis of nepotism and permanence of membership, but industrial bureaucracy operates primarily on notions of merit and transitory membership.[9]

However, the assumption that bureaucracies and primary groups are alternative means for the achievement of most goals must be seriously questioned. Rather, it is suggested that these forms of organization are complementary and that each provides necessary means for achieving a given goal. This position does not deny that the family, for example, has unique social functions, but it does assert that both primary groups and bureaucratic organizations operate in most major task areas of life, and that they bring different attributes to bear on the achievement of a given end. From a structural point of view, instead of suggesting the isolation of primary groups and bureaucracies, the position we propose necessitates close communication between the two forms of organization.

Some of the very characteristics that have been ascribed to the formal organization and to the primary group lend plausibility to our view. One common observation notes that the bureaucratic organization is unable to deal with nonuniform or relatively unique events.[10] This inability is usually attributed to the necessity for a priori rules and standardized role specifications as well as to the amount of time required for the large organization to deal with an issue not previously defined. Thus, messages must move up and down long chains of communication before policy decisions can be made to meet nonuniform events. The strength of bureaucratic organizations, it is claimed, lies in the professional expertness they can provide as well as their capacity to deal with large numbers of people.

In contrast, the strength of the primary group is seen to lie in speed of adaptation and flexibility capable of meeting nonuniform situations.[11] The primary group is incapable of dealing with large numbers of people and is deficient in professional expertness.

Thus, the very virtues claimed for bureaucratic organizations are the defects of the primary groups; the virtues claimed for the primary group are the defects of bureaucratic organizations.

For optimum achievement of many social goals—i.e., for social control—it would appear necessary to have both expert knowledge and flexibility, both breadth of coverage and speed of reaction.[12] In short, bureaucratic and primary groups share in the achievement of functions in all areas of life. They are not necessarily competitive nor is there a division of labor which requires each to function independently.

A Balance Theory of Coordination

The dilemma that must be faced by a theory of interorganizational relations and social control is posed by these two propositions:

1. The contributions of both bureaucratic organizations and primary groups are frequently necessary to achieve maximum social control in a mature industrial society.

2. The characteristics of bureaucracies and of primary groups are such as to make them incompatible, if not antithetical, as forms of social organization.

A theory of coordination acknowledging both these propositions must avoid two kinds of errors. If the bureaucratic organization and external primary group are too isolated from each other they are likely to work at cross purposes and thus lose benefits of one or the other. However, if the two organizational forms are brought too close together their antithetical atmospheres are likely to disrupt one or both organizations, again leading to the loss of benefits.

This reasoning prompts a balance theory of coordinating mechanisms that may be stated as follows:

Maximum social control is most likely to occur when coordinating mechanisms develop between bureaucratic organizations and external primary groups that balance their relationships at a middle position of social distance where they are not too intimate and not isolated from one another.

This formulation requires recognition of the importance of a variety of mechanisms of coordination, ranging from those capable of bridging great social distances to those capable of increasing distance while maintaining communication.

The idea of variable social distances bridged by varied mechanisms of coordination becomes obvious once the empirical situation of any given large bureaucracy is examined. For instance, where school systems are involved with families in which parents are highly identified with the goals of the school (e.g., middle-class families with professional occupations), there is a minimum of social distance between the bureaucracy and the external primary groups. By contrast, where the schools are dealing with families ignorant of, or in opposition to, the goals of the school (e.g., low-income migrants from the Southern Appalachian Mountains with a fundamentalist religious position), there is likely to be great distance between the bureaucracy and the external primary groups. In the task of educating children, the schools frequently have to deal with both kinds of families. The same would be true of industrial concerns seeking to influence the families of their employees on matters relating to work conditions and worker productivity. They would need to relate to families that were identified with them as well as those that were initially hostile to them. Similarly, if the police seek citizen cooperation in law enforcement, they must deal with persons and groups that are hostile as well as those in sympathy with the purposes of the organization.

By acknowledging variability in social distance between bureaucratic organization and external primary groups, the balance theory provides a criterion for deciding which mechanisms of coordination will maximize social control. In the case of great social distance, such mechanisms should permit communication and reduction of social distance if a middle point is to be reached. In cases of little social distance, such mechanisms should increase social distance if a middle position is to be achieved.

Mechanisms of Coordination and Balance Theory

The theoretical consideration of issues involved in coordinating bureaucratic organizations with external primary groups is noticeably lacking in the literature on social organization.[13] However, because organizations are, in fact, very much concerned with maintaining communication with external primary groups, it is relatively easy to find, in the applied literature, many illustrations of mechanisms of coordination. From a review of some of this literature we have identified eight types that are reasonably distinct, although they are often found in combination.

For convenience, the mechanisms are viewed as approaches by which a formal organization might seek to influence external primary groups to adopt values and norms in keeping with those of the organization. The eight types are described as follows:

1. DETACHED-EXPERT APPROACH: Professional persons (such as social workers or public health nurses) act with relative autonomy, by direct participation, in external primary groups to bring group norms and values into harmony with those of the organization. They operate by becoming trusted members of the group the organization is seeking to influence. The use of "street-gang workers" to deal with delinquent groups is an illustration.[14]

2. OPINION-LEADER APPROACH: The organization deals with "natural" leaders in neighborhoods and local communities, and through them seeks to influence the members of the primary groups. The Shaw-McKay area approach to delinquency control illustrates this procedure.[15] Katz and Lazarsfeld [16] point out that those utilizing mass media may also inadvertently be using an opinion-leader approach as well. Analysis of community power suggests that the management of large industries frequently uses this procedure to exercise influence.[17]

3. SETTLEMENT-HOUSE APPROACH: A change-inducing milieu is provided through physical facilities and proximity and through the availability of professional change-agents. The approach combines the traditional community center with focused educational programs. One partial illustration is the work at Provo described by Empey and Rabow.[18]

4. VOLUNTARY-ASSOCIATION APPROACH: A voluntary association, which brings together members of the formal organization and the primary groups, is used as a means of communication between the two. The parent-teacher association in the schools is a typical case in point. The same kind of phenomenon can be seen among other types of bureaucracies. The police have various recreational groups for children, churches have many church-related clubs, hospitals have voluntary associations like the Gray Ladies, the Army maintains close ties to veteran's associations, and business firms and unions often sponsor recreational associations. In all instances it would be argued that the voluntary associations, whatever their explicit function, also serve to permit communication between the bureaucratic organizations and significant outside primary groups.

5. COMMON-MESSENGER APPROACH: Messages intended to influence are communicated through a person who is regularly a member of both the organization and the primary groups. The school child often serves as such a messenger for communication between school and family. Communication may be very explicit, as in the case of some large industrial organizations where employees are urged to go out and sell the idea of a better

business environment to their friends and families. On the other hand, it may be more subtle, such as a company's attempt to influence management wives by indirect socialization.[19]

6. MASS-MEDIA APPROACH: The formal organization tries to influence primary groups through mass communication media. The characteristics of communication through such media have been thoroughly considered in many studies.[20] Through the entire range of bureaucratic organizations—e.g., church, governmental, business, etc.—examples of the use of this approach are common.

7. FORMAL-AUTHORITY APPROACH: Legal or well-established norms are the basis for communicating with external primary groups. The truant officer, for example, links school and family and has a legal right to do so. There are certain agencies, such as the police, whose relations to the outer community are almost solely guided by legal power. There are other agencies, such as the schools, that utilize some legal and some voluntary forms of communication, and there are others, such as business and social work agencies, that depend almost solely on voluntary arrangements for communicating with outside primary groups.[21]

8. DELEGATED-FUNCTION APPROACH: The organization seeks to influence primary-group members through another organization that is assumed to have better access, greater expertise, more appropriate facilities, or greater legitimacy in the society. For instance, schools are frequently asked by other organizations, such as the fire department and safety councils, to pass information into homes through the children.[22]

Principles of Communication Involved in
Mechanisms of Coordination

Having briefly described these mechanisms of coordination, we wish to point out more explicitly some of their utilities and limitations for narrowing or increasing social distance.

For convenience, our analysis approaches the mechanisms as communications from the bureaucratic organization to the primary group. However, with relatively minor modification the principles noted can be restated so as to characterize communication in the other direction, i.e., from the primary group to the formal organization. The mechanisms will here be thought of as though they are deliberately purposive, intended to influence.

PRINCIPLE OF INITIATIVE.   Where there is great social distance between bureaucratic organizations and external primary groups, it is hypothesized that those mechanisms of coordination that permit the organization to take great initiative in contacting these groups will promote communcation. Without considerable initiative, selective listening may prevent the message from reaching the group for which it is intended.[23] Some of the mechanisms of coordination permit initiative on the part of the bureaucratic organization more clearly than others. Thus, the detached-worker approach is one in which the bureaucratic organization sends out its experts to make contact with the primary-group member, in his home territory if necessary. By contrast, the voluntary-association and the settlement-house approach are passive approaches requiring more initiative to be taken by the primary group. The mass-media approach requires organizational initiative even though it leaves the decision to accept the message almost completely in the hands of the target of the communication.

PRINCIPLE OF INTENSITY. To communicate across the boundaries of resistant primary groups, it is necessary to have intensive relations with primary-group members in order to surmount the barriers of selective perception and selective retention. Messages that reach a hostile primary group without strong support from a trusted member are likely to be put aside or distorted.[24] The opinion-leader approach, because it depends on pre-existing influence relationships, represents a mechanism of considerable intensity. So does the detached-worker approach. In contrast, the mass-media and common-messenger approaches exert a minimal degree of intensity in the coordinating process.

PRINCIPLE OF FOCUSED EXPERTISE. Much communication between bureaucratic organizations and primary groups involves simple information, such as times of meetings, announcements about speakers, descriptions of new programs, plans for the opening of new facilities, etc. Some communications, however, involve complex kinds of messages. For example, communicating to families a fundamental change in educational policy of a school; communicating to southern rural migrants the employment norms of the northern, urban factory; communicating to the family of a returning mental patient how they should act to help the patient; etc.

The principle of focused expertise implies that the more complex the information the more necessary for effective communication is close contact between a professional expert and the group to be affected. Where complex information is transmitted, an expert is required to convey it. Furthermore, the presentation of complex information requires the communicator to take account of unique problems any given group may have in absorbing the information and to adapt the communication accordingly. Thus, immediate feedback and response are necessary when the message is complex. Because of such factors as these, an expert in close touch with the group is called for.[25] The detached-worker approach, the settlement-house approach, and the voluntary-association approach are all procedures that may put the professional expert in face-to-face contact with the external primary groups. By contrast, the opinion-leader, the mass-media and the common-messenger approaches permit the expert only indirect access to external primary group members. It may be noted that great social distance usually implies that complex information must be transmitted and therefore suggests the need for focused expertise.

PRINCIPLE OF MAXIMUM COVERAGE.   Other things being equal, it is hypothesized that better coordination will occur when a procedure can reach the largest number of external primary groups. This is not only a principle of economy but also one of extensiveness. Procedures that reach more people without loss of effectiveness are preferred to those of limited scope. The detached-expert approach is limited in the number of primary groups it can reach at a given level of resources because it requires a one-to-one relation between expert and group. By contrast, the settlement house and the voluntary association can reach more people because, through these mechanisms, a given expert can deal with many groups at the same time. The common-messenger approach has an even wider scope, and the mass-media approach has the widest scope of all.

The enumeration of some of the major principles of communication governing the mechanisms of coordination is not intended to be exhaustive but only to suggest differences in efficacy of communication procedures. To summarize how these principles relate to the eight designated mechanisms of coordination, we have devised Table 19–1. This table applies the principles as criteria to evaluate the suitability of a mechanism of coordination for any given state of imbalance. Obviously, there are many logical combinations of principles which have not been considered here or represented in Table 19–1.

Balance Theory of Coordination Re-examined

From the preceding presentation of mechanisms of coordination and some of the underlying communication principles involved, specific predictions can be derived from the balance theory of coordination. To illustrate, we may examine the detached-expert approach in terms of the principles of communication. This approach has the following characteristics (see Table 19–1):

1. It requires great initiative on the part of the bureaucratic organization.

2. It involves intensive relations between change agent and external group.

3. It entails focused expertise, or close contact between professional and his target group.

4. It has limited scope.

With the exception of scope, all characteristics of this mechanism are highly useful for communicating across great social distance, i.e., achieving a balance when the bureaucratic organization must deal with hostile primary groups. Thus, when a school or a business seeks to communicate

Table 19–1. Underlying Principles of Communication Related to Mechanisms of Coordination between Bureaucratic Organizations and External Primary Groups

PRINCIPLES OF COMMUNICATION

Coordinating Mechanisms	Initiative	Intensity	Focused Expertise	Maximum Coverage
Detached Expert	highest	high	highest	lowest
Opinion Leader	moderate	highest	low	moderate
Settlement House	moderate to low	high	high	moderate
Voluntary Associations	lowest	moderate	moderate	high
Common Messenger	moderate	low	lowest	highest
Mass Media	low	lowest	lowest	highest
Formal Authority	high	moderate to low	high to low	moderate to low
Delegated Function	high to low	high to low	high to low	moderate

its goals and program to a hostile family, it must take the initiative, it must use intensity of interaction to penetrate primary-group boundaries, and it must make use of focused expertise to effect changes in social norms through messages that are very complex. In northern urban communities, migrant southern white families often seem to require such an approach to achieve balance between school and family on behalf of the educational motivation of the children. Unions seeking to organize in resistant industrial atmospheres or management seeking to sway strong labor groups have analogous problems.

In terms of balance theory, this same mechanism must be considered less effective for coordination where primary groups are overidentified with the bureaucratic organizations. In this case the bureaucratic organization does not require initiative since the primary group will take it. Intensive relations are unnecessary since there are no hostile primary-group boundaries to pierce and intensive relations in such circumstances may, indeed, evoke too much affectivity. School teachers, for example, might be tempted to evaluate children on the basis of their attraction to or fear of parents, whereas parents might evaluate their children too exclusively on the basis of their school performance. In the industrial situation, bringing the families too close may lead to nepotism and favoritism within the concern whereas, among the families, it may lead to undue evaluation of family members in terms of occupational success or utility. In either case it is likely to lead to a loss in effectiveness. Furthermore, the detached-expert approach is extremely wasteful where families already identify with the organization, since there are other procedures (mass media and voluntary association) that can communicate to such families and reach many more of them without running the danger of too much intimacy for effective balance.

By similar analyses, the balance theory of coordination suggests that where great social distance exists, mechanisms such as the detached worker, opinion leader, and settlement house are more effective than mass-media, common-messenger, formal-authority, or voluntary-association approaches. Where there is already great intimacy between bureaucracy and primary groups, the opposite prediction would be made. Needless to say, these statements are very general in character, intended to give only an idea of the broad principles of the theory. More precise hypotheses relating given mechanisms of coordination to different family types to maximize goal achievement for the organization depend on a more detailed analysis of the primary groups involved.

Bureaucratic Organizations and Balance Theory

Thus far, only two elements involved in balance theory have been considered in our formulation: mechanisms of coordination and external primary groups (e.g., whether they are deviant-hostile or conforming). Little has been said about the other element of our hypothesis, the bureaucratic organization. The theory of balance we are advocating should be able to take account of all types of bureaucratic organizations in industrial societies if it is to have general meaning.

As a general statement, balance theory must be formulated in the face of two empirical observations about bureaucratic organizations in our society: (1) that most bureaucracies must coordinate their behavior with that of outside primary groups if they are to achieve their goals successfully, and (2) that our society contains a bewildering variety of bureaucratic structures. Thus, the theory must encompass the relatively small, collegial bureaucracy of the private social work agency, the large legalistic structure of the police force, the large industrial bureaucracy with production and marketing goals, the school system, and the mental hospital, where requirements to conform to organizational rules may conflict with norms of professional autonomy.

Earlier in this paper we have argued the necessity for coordination with external primary groups if their contributions are to complement those of formal organizations to maximize goal achievement. We would further argue that apparent variations in the need for such coordination by different types of bureaucracies are related to varying degrees of legitimacy in our society accorded to organizational efforts to influence the public. Thus, welfare organizations, schools, hospitals, and churches can legitimately expose their efforts to affect the primary groups with which they are concerned. In contrast, industrial organizations and most governmental agencies do not have legitimate privilege to influence the primary groups that concern their successful performance and hence their coordinating efforts must operate less visibly and in camouflaged forms. For example, utilization of a detached-expert approach by the public relations department of an industrial concern might take the covert form of infiltration into social clubs and civic organizations. Nevertheless, this approach might not differ structurally from the overt use of the detached expert by a school.

We will use Litwak's conceptual scheme to describe the generic characterstics of bureaucracies so as to reduce the apparent great variety of such organizations to a limited number of types.[26] He points out that organizational structure and goal achievement are related, in part, to the nature of the organization's goals and the nature of its tasks in pursuit of the goals. Where goals are relatively unambiguous, criteria for their realization fairly determinate, and tasks relatively standardized and repetitive, the rationalistic structure of bureaucracy described by Weber would appear to emerge and become efficient. In contrast, where goals are ambiguous, criteria uncertain, tasks nonuniform and likely to require interpersonal techniques, a human relations form of bureaucracy is more likely to appear and to represent the more efficient structure. Finally, when organizational goals and criteria are mixed, tasks both uniform and nonuniform, and techniques both impersonal and interpersonal, a third bureaucratic type that combines both rationalistic and human relations elements would seem to emerge and constitute the more efficient form. This type has been called a professional bureaucracy since one of its most obvious features seems to be the conflict between organizational and professional modes of behavior by its members.

Adapted to the purposes of our presentation of a balance theory of coordination, the types of bureaucratic organizations may be described in somewhat more detail but by no means exhaustively:

Types of Bureaucratic Organization

1. The *rationalistic model* is characterized by impersonal social relations, detailed rules governing most actions, strict hierarchy of authority, job specialization, narrow delimitation of occupational duties and obligations, evaluation on the basis of merit (knowledge, training, success on the job). This is the model of bureaucracy described by Max Weber. This type is illustrated by government bureaucracy, which follows detailed legal regulations such as those involved in administering the income tax,

processing applications for licenses, etc. It is the type most familiar in industrial bureaucracies.

2. The *human-relations model* exhibits personal relations, general policies rather than detailed rules, colleague rather than hierarchical structure, broad definition of the organization's goals, as well as evaluation on the basis of merit. Except for evaluation (employment, pay, promotion) on the basis of merit, the human-relations model exhibits characteristics opposite to those of the rationalistic model. This type may be illustrated by small social work agencies, small scientific laboratories, small graduate schools, etc.

3. The *professional model* simultaneously incorporates rationalistic and human-relations elements. Where both standardized, recurrent tasks and tasks requiring interpersonal skills to deal with nonstandardized events are regularly faced—as in hospitals and schools—this type of organization may develop. Since it must reconcile contradictory administrative approaches, the professional style of organization develops internal arrangements to do so (such as parallel structures of authority, segregated departments, etc.).[27] This is illustrated by hospitals, school systems, industrial organizations with major involvements in research as well as production.

4. The *nonmerit model*, unlike each of the other forms, is characterized by significant intrusion of bases other than merit for evaluation of personnel and performance. Thus, criteria irrelevant to the achievement of organizational goals are introduced. Dependence on nepotism, personal friendship, discrimination on the basis of race, religion or social class, and excessive emphasis on personal rather than organizational goals illustrate nonmerit bases of evaluation. Although these conditions may appear, deliberately or unconsciously, in other types of organizations, when they predominate the result is distinctive enough to identify a separate organizational form. Most typical of small organizations, some large organizations as well nevertheless appear to aproach this model.

Types of Bureaucratic Organizations and Coordinating Mechanisms

At our present stage of knowledge, we believe that the relationship between bureaucratic structures and the mechanisms that link them to the outer community can be stated in a straightforward fashion if we make the following simplifying assumption:

When administrative style and mechanisms of coordination are structurally consistent, they will both operate most effectively.

Structural consistency is defined in terms of the dimensions of organization already suggested: hierarchical vs. colleague relations, impersonal vs. personalized relations, specific rules vs. policy, etc. Each of the mechanisms may be analyzed to see which of these attributes it demands in order to operate. The detached-worker approach, intended to change values or deal with hostile populations, and requiring integration into the primary group, is a mechanism that must permit localized decision making, affective rather than impersonal relations, internalization of policy rather than specific rules, and diffused rather than delineated duties. In contrast, sending messages through mass media is an approach that is highly consistent with centralized authority, specific rules, impersonal work situations, delimited tasks, etc.

The opinion-leader approach requires that the good will of the leader be obtained so as to make use of his primary-group attachment. This approach therefore demands affective rather than impersonal relations, localized autonomy (for the opinion leader), use of internalization of policy rather than specific rules, etc. Katz and Lazarsfeld have pointed out that, in fact, this approach is often an unrecognized aspect of the more rationalistic mass-media approach.[28] Our analysis would lead us to hypothesize that it is optimally effective (e.g., the bureaucratic organization has maximal control) when it is used by a human-relations administrative structure.

In contrast, agencies that use legal authority as their major means of communication must operate through rationalistic aspects of organizational structure. There are some countertrends among organizations using legal authority, such as the juvenile court's stress on treatment. However, permitting localized organizational discretion often tends to subvert one of the basic tenets of the law—due process. As a consequence the use of formal authority as a means of communication in our society puts very definite rationalistic restrictions on organizational structures.

The settlement-house approach, as we have defined it, stresses attitude and value change. As such it requires decentralized authority, affective relations, diffuse relations, and internalization of policies. Therefore, we would hypothesize that it is most consistent with the human-relations structure. In contrast, the voluntary association tends to deal with individuals who are already in sympathy with the organizational goals and who are often involved primarily in getting factual information or keeping informed. As such, they could well operate within the boundaries of a rationalistic administrative style. This would also hold for the common-messenger approach.

When effective coordination requires the use of the range of coordinating mechanisms—where the organization is confronted by both hostile and congenial primary groups—we hypothesize that the professional organizational structure would be more effective. Thus, a school might develop a detached-worker program for deviant families and, at the same time, promote a parent-teacher association for families who are congenial. The professional structure permits these mechanisms (with markedly different organizational demands) to operate within the same organization with minimal friction.

With regard to the fourth model of organizational structure—the nonmerit—we assume that none of the mechanisms of coordination will be consistent with this type of organization. To put it somewhat differently, any other organizational structure combined with any mechanism of coordination is more likely to effect coordination than a nonmerit type, regardless of the mechanism of coordination employed. This assumption rests on the belief that where the organization does not select or assign people in terms of its tasks it is less likely to perform as well as the organization that does.

This discussion can be usefully summarized by noting five significant combinations of coordinating mechanisms and administrative styles: [29]

1. Human-relations administrative style with detached-expert, opinion-leader, and settlement-house mechanisms.

2. Rationalistic administrative style with formal authority, voluntary-association, mass-media, and common-messenger mechanisms.

3. Professional administrative style with combinations of mechanisms from each of the above, e.g., detached-worker and delegated-function, opinion-leader and mass-media, etc.

4. Mismatched administrative style and mechanisms of coordination, e.g., rationalistic style and detached expert, human relations style and formal authority, etc.

5. Nonmerit administrative style and any mechanism of coordination.

Bureaucracy, Primary Groups, and Mechanisms of Coordination

With these combinations in mind, we are now in a position to state systematically the relationships between the three independent variables of our balance theory—the primary groups, the bureaucratic organizations, and the mechanisms of coordination—and to present hypothesized consequences for achieving balance and hence maximizing social control. These are presented schematically in Table 19–2.

Where the organization is confronted with deviant families or neighborhood groups (Column I), it must have some mechanism of coordination that permits communication over great social distance (initiative, intensity, and focused expertise). The use of such mechanisms are most consistent with a human relations organizational structure. Thus, in the first column of Table 19–2, we hypothesize that Row 1 would lead to maximum control (given the largest weight, 5). In contrast, where the organization is dealing with congenial primary groups (Column II), those mechanisms that permit wide scope and prevent too much intimacy are hypothesized to be most efficient (mass media, voluntary association, etc.). These are most consistently located in a rationalistic administrative structure. As is indicated in Column II, our hypothesis is that the second row would lead to maximum control. Where the organization must simultaneously deal with deviant and conforming primary groups (Column III), it requires both sets of mechanisms, and the organizational structure most

Table 19–2. Hypotheses Relating Primary Groups, Bureaucratic Structure, and Mechanisms of Coordination to Maximum Balance for Goal Achievement [a]

Bureaucratic Structure	Mechanisms of Coordination	I Deviant Primary Groups	II Conforming Primary Groups	III Mixture of Some Groups Deviant and Some Conforming
Human Relations	A. Opinion leader, settlement house, detached expert, delegated function	5[a]	3	3.5
Rationalistic	B. Common messenger, mass media, formal authority, voluntary association	3	5	3.5
Professional	C. Both A and B above	4	4	5
Either human relations or rationalistic	D. Mismatched, i.e., with A or B	2	2	2
Nonmerit	E. Any mechanism	1	1	1

[a] The larger the number in the cells, the more likely balance (and hence goal achievement) will occur. Numbers represent rankings within each column.

consistent with contradictory dimensions in the professional model. Therefore, in Column III we hypothesize that the third row will lead to maximum control.

It is assumed that where the organizational structure is mismatched with the mechanisms of coordination it will lead to less balance than where they are matched, because of the internal organizational conflict that such inconsistency implies. As was mentioned earlier, the nonmerit organizational model is always hypothesized to achieve the least balance and goal achievement.

Summary and Conclusion

A brief review of the major points we have presented may be useful. Current sociological theory generally neglects the problem of coordination between bureaucratic organizations and external primary groups because it has overemphasized their incompatibilities and underemphasized their complementary contributions to the contemporary social order. The unique function of each, rather than the shared character of their tasks, has been emphasized. Conclusions from such theory that see continuous tension or extreme insulation of bureaucratic and primary forms of organization do not seem to correspond to observable trends in American society. We therefore hypothesize that social control and goal achievement in modern society are accomplished through the shared contributions of both social forms in most areas of life, and that maximum control and achievement will obtain when these forms are in balance. Furthermore, we argue that balance between these forms is a function of coordinating mechanisms the most obvious of which we attempt to describe and to analyze in terms of underlying principles of communication.

Our presentation of this theory and some associated hypotheses is not meant to be exhaustive. Indeed, elaborations will be necessary in order to specify the data necessary to examine the theory empirically. We have intended our statement merely as a first attempt to open a neglected area of importance in the understanding of contemporary society. The approach we have proposed seems plausible to us, but it is research now in progress that must determine its utility and suggest modifications in the balance theory of coordinating mechanisms between bureaucratic and primary forms of social organization.

Part VI

Poverty and Dependency

Introduction

Poverty and the host of other problems related to economic dependency are among the most significant problems of our day. The formulation of welfare policy and legislation and the provision of services depend, in part, upon the availability of pertinent factual information relating to these problems. The first two selections in this section indicate how timely information on questions of poverty may be collected from national and local surveys and may be brought to bear on questions of welfare policy. The last selection, dealing with a selected sample of welfare recipients, combines the information derived from interviews qualitatively appraised with the application of information from sociological and psychological studies of problem families.

Morgan, David, Cohen, and Brazer discuss, in their selection, various features of poverty in the United States. The study upon which this selection is based drew upon a national sample of interviews held with 2,800 respondents combined with a supplementary sample of 300 low-income families with heads under age 65. An economic definition of the poor is provided along with information indicating that one-fifth of the population meet the authors' criterion of spending units having inadequate income. Among the subgroups isolated as likely to be poor are the aged, the disabled, single family heads with children, nonwhite individuals, farmers and self-employed businessmen. By predictive statistical analysis, the study also reveals a discrepancy between actual earnings and income predicted on the basis of economic and income correlates, suggesting the possibility that subtle psychological and social conditions, in addition to such factors as inability to work and lack of education, may contribute to poverty. Evidence is also provided for continued dependency between generations and for the contribution of downward mobility to poverty.

National health and medical service has been one of the most controversial public issues in social welfare. Some of the debate involves opinion about matters that are, in principle, questions of fact. But in general there has been a relative paucity of factual information brought to bear in this debate. A significant question is how receptive to governmental medical services the prospective consumers are. In the selection by Cohen, Poskanzer, and Sharp, the results from two surveys on attitudes toward governmental participation in medical care are reported. Attitudes toward governmental action to help finance low-cost medical care were found generally to be favorable, and a substantial portion of the respondents believed that the government was not doing enough in this area. It is of particular interest that the authors examined differences in receptivity to governmental participation in medical care, placing particular emphasis upon the responses of the aged, the poor, farmers, Southerners, Negroes, and Republicans and Democrats. The findings of these surveys correct many common misconceptions.

The mothers of children whose fathers are unemployed or are estranged from the mother constitute a sizable proportion of those having inadequate incomes. Such mothers and their children often become recipients of assistance in the federal program of Aid to Families with Dependent Children. In a study of this important group, Glasser and Navarre contrast the views of recipients and their workers concerning the problems of these families. To these views the authors add those of the social scientist, giving attention to sociological and psychological factors. In addition to detailing the similarities and differences of these views, the authors indicate directions for improving services to these families.

20 Poverty in the United States

James N. Morgan, Martin H.

David, Wilbur J. Cohen, and

Harvey E. Brazer

Because little is known about the causes of poverty, it is difficult to define remedial programs to combat it, or to determine the extent to which such programs can be effective. By studying the poor in a framework of over-all income distribution and degrees of economic well-being, their back-grounds, their attitudes and plans, and their outlooks for the future can be compared with those of the whole population. Through this process it may be possible to describe some of the factors responsible for poverty and determine whether these factors can be alleviated or eliminated through legislative programs and private concern.

This chapter describes and analyzes the problems of poor families—those whose incomes fall below a minimum standard of adequacy. The report describes the extent to which characteristics of the poor imply limited working ability and poor earning power in a competitive market, the possible permanence of poverty, and the degree to which it is trans-mitted from generation to generation. It also includes a discussion of the sources of income of poor families and the effect of transfers, particularly those provided by government income-maintenance programs.[1]

Definition of the Poor

In order to select for study a group of poor families, measures of income, need, and income adequacy are required.

Abridged from Chapter 16 of INCOME AND WELFARE IN THE UNITED STATES by J. N. Morgan et al. Copyright © 1962 McGraw-Hill, Inc., pp. 187–218. Used by per-mission of McGraw-Hill Book Company and the authors.

The Measure of Income

Gross disposable income was chosen as the most appropriate measure of income for a study of inadequacy and needs because it is a relatively comprehensive measure of the total resource flow of a family. In addition to money income, an estimate of the more important sources of income in kind is included; rental income on net equity in a home is imputed; and estimated Federal income tax liability is deducted.

The measure of income understates somewhat the resources of families who could use savings or realize capital gains; however, very few of the families with inadequate incomes have substantial savings, and it is unlikely that many had capital gains during 1959.

The Standard of Need

Family needs differ according to the size and composition of each family, and any indicator of the requirements of families must include some measure of these varying needs.[2]

The budget needs of each family and each adult unit in the sample were estimated according to data derived from a schedule prepared by the Community Council of Greater New York.[3] This schedule allows for variations in the size and composition of each unit, and for differences in food, clothing, and other requirements of persons of different ages. It also recognizes that the cost of clothing, transportation, and food is higher for persons employed outside the home than for those who are not.

An estimate of the budget requirements of each adult unit was prepared by adding the entry appropriate to each adult unit member in part I of Table 20–1 to the entry determined by the size of the unit in part II of Table 20–1. Thus, the budget costs of an adult unit containing an employed head, a housewife, and two children aged eight and eleven would equal $4,030 ($1,144 + 546 + 416 + 416 + 1,508). The estimates of the budget needs of families were calculated in the same manner as for adult units, except that entries from the rows entitled "other adults" were necessary in families where there were extra adult units.

These estimates of family budgets have several limitations. They make no provision for differences in the cost of living in different areas. The Bureau of Labor Statistics data indicate a range of about 20 per cent in the cost of living between the most and least expensive of the twenty largest cities in the United States in the fall of 1959. Similar variation can be expected between large cities and rural areas.[4] However, as no systematic data on rural-urban price differences have been collected since 1936, no adjustment was made for this bias.

The New York budget used in this study agrees fairly well with other attempts to measure the relative costs of maintaining families of different sizes.[5] The New York Council Budget is probably a low estimate of the cost of living, since it is used by private agencies in New York City as a

Table 20–1. Schedule of Estimated Annual Costs of Goods and Services

I. Food, clothing, and other personal costs
Head

	Employed or unemployed	$1,144
	Other (retired, disabled housewife)	676

Wife

	Employed	1,092
	Other	546

Other adults

Employed

	Age	
	18–40	1,196
	41 and older	988
	Other	546

Children

	Under 6	312
	6–11	416
	12–15	572
	16–17	676

II. Rent, utilities, and other costs

1 person in the unit	1,040
2	1,248
3	1,404
4	1,508
5	1,664
6	1,924
7	2,080
8 and more	2,184

Adapted from The Community Council of Greater New York, Budget Standard Service. ANNUAL PRICE SURVEY AND FAMILY BUDGET COSTS, OCTOBER, 1959.

standard for determining eligibility for assistance and free medical care. Also, the Council estimates are consistently exceeded by estimates prepared by the Bureau of Labor Statistics for New York City worker families in 1959.[6]

The Ratio of Income to Need

The ratio of gross disposable income to the estimated budget requirement was used to estimate the level of welfare enjoyed by each unit; this quantity is referred to as the *welfare ratio*. Table 20–2 shows the distribution of welfare ratios for adult units and families.

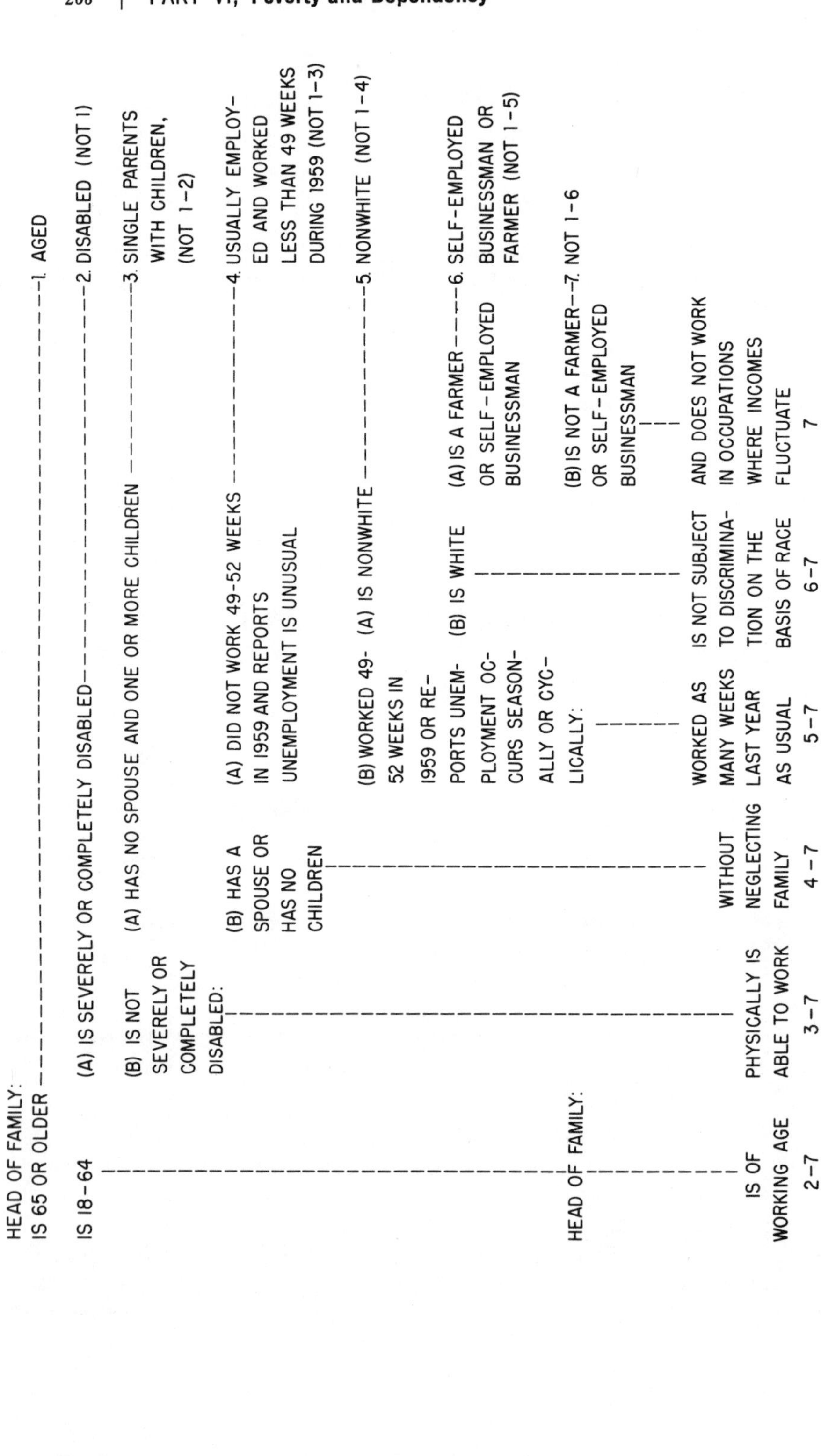

HEAD OF FAMILY:
IS 65 OR OLDER — — — — — — — (A) IS SEVERELY OR COMPLETELY DISABLED — — — — — — 1. AGED

2. DISABLED (NOT 1)

(B) IS NOT SEVERELY OR COMPLETELY DISABLED:

(A) HAS NO SPOUSE AND ONE OR MORE CHILDREN — — — 3. SINGLE PARENTS WITH CHILDREN, (NOT 1–2)

(B) HAS A SPOUSE OR HAS NO CHILDREN:

(A) DID NOT WORK 49–52 WEEKS — — — 4. USUALLY EMPLOYED AND WORKED LESS THAN 49 WEEKS DURING 1959 (NOT 1–3)
IN 1959 AND REPORTS UNEMPLOYMENT IS UNUSUAL

(B) WORKED 49– (A) IS NONWHITE — — — — — 5. NONWHITE (NOT 1–4)
52 WEEKS IN
1959 OR RE-
PORTS UNEM- (B) IS WHITE
PLOYMENT OC-
CURS SEASON- (A) IS A FARMER — — — 6. SELF-EMPLOYED BUSINESSMAN OR FARMER (NOT 1–5)
ALLY OR CYC- OR SELF-EMPLOYED
LICALLY: BUSINESSMAN

(B) IS NOT A FARMER — 7. NOT 1–6
OR SELF-EMPLOYED
BUSINESSMAN

HEAD OF FAMILY:

IS OF   PHYSICALLY IS   WITHOUT   WORKED AS   IS NOT SUBJECT   AND DOES NOT WORK
WORKING AGE   ABLE TO WORK   NEGLECTING   MANY WEEKS   TO DISCRIMINA-   IN OCCUPATIONS
                               FAMILY   LAST YEAR   TION ON THE   WHERE INCOMES
IS 18–64   AS USUAL   BASIS OF RACE   FLUCTUATE

2–7   3–7   4–7   5–7   6–7   7

Figure 20–1. Likely Causes of Poverty.

Families with inadequate incomes are defined as those whose incomes are less than nine-tenths of their budget requirements. The exact point which separates adequacy from inadequacy is, of course, a matter of judgment. Incomes were defined as inadequate when welfare ratios fell below nine-tenths in order to assure that this study's estimates of inadequate incomes would be conservative relative to the standards set by the Community Council, and to allow for some error in estimates of the cost of living in rural areas.

Table 20–2. Adult Unit and Family Welfare Ratios (Percentage Distribution of Adult Units and Families)

Welfare ratio	Adult units	Families
0–0.4	11	6
0.5–0.6	9	7
0.7–0.8	8	7
0.9–1.0	10	10
1.1–1.2	10	10
1.3–1.5	13	14
1.6–2.0	18	21
2.1 and over	21	25
Total	100	100
Number of units	3,396	2,800

Most of the analysis is based on the group designated as *poor families,* families with inadequate incomes who also have less than $5,000 in liquid assets.[7] According to these definitions, poor families comprise one-fifth of the nation's families.

Causes of Poverty

It is quite clear that both the family income and the number of its dependents vary in the course of the life cycle. This raises an important question concerning the interpretation of the welfare ratio for different families in the sample. For some the level of well-being indicated by the ratio may reflect a temporary situation, especially when 1959 income is not representative of the normal earnings of that family. For others the welfare index may be quite a suitable measure of long-run well-being.

The classification illustrated in Figure 20–1 was developed to distinguish families whose level of welfare is associated with long-run factors from those with temporary fluctuations of income.

For example, the aged are most likely to have stable, though low, incomes. The incomes of farmers and self-employed may rise or fall rapidly with innovations, short-term fluctuations in yield, and long-term changes in productivity.

The classification also offers a *sequential* analysis of factors which may lead to low earning power.[8] Thus old age and retirement (category 1) are sufficient to explain low incomes; a single parent with children is somewhat more likely to be able to work regularly, although such a situation would lead to low earning power; and the residual category (7) includes families whose heads have no obvious impediment to earning income on a regular basis.

The residual group (category 7) is composed of families which meet the criteria for poor families but which exhibit none of the characteristics classified as likely causes of poverty. The heads of many of these families are unskilled seasonal workers, for whom yearly unemployment is usual. Others are widows or single females under sixty-five with no work experience, students, and a small number of housekeepers or servants who live in their employers' households and work for room and board.

For a few of the families in the residual group, students or young couples just getting started, poverty is only temporary. For most families, however, the problem of chronic poverty is serious. One such family is headed by a thirty-two year old man who is employed as a dishwasher. Though he works steadily and more than full time, he earned slightly over $2,000 in 1959. His wife earned $300 more, but their combined incomes are not enough to support themselves and their three children. Although the head of the family is only thirty-two, he feels that he has no chance of advancement partly because he finished only seven grades of school. The plight of this family is typical of the situations faced by many in category 7. The possibility of such families leaving the ranks of the poor is not high.

The sequential classification also sorts families into groups which are significant from the point of view of remedial legislation and government programs designated to alleviate poverty. Without major changes in the labor market, most of the aged will retire and will have little chance of returning to the labor force. Their economic problem can be eliminated if they receive an annuity sufficient to meet their needs. The economic problems of the nonwhite population may be alleviated by fair employment practices legislation.[9]

Table 20–3 indicates that significantly more of the aged, the disabled, the single parents with children, the unusually unemployed, and nonwhite persons have inadequate incomes than is the case for the remaining groups of the classification. A parallel tabulation showing the welfare index of adult units would show the same pattern, but the proportion of adult units whose incomes are inadequate would be somewhat higher. (See the last two rows of Table 20–3.) Despite the relationship between the causes of poverty shown in the sequential classification and the welfare ratio, a majority of the families in each category of the classification have incomes that meet or exceed their needs. This fact indicates that the sequential classification does not predict which families have inadequate incomes. At best the classification serves to describe a part of the family's economic

Table 20–3. Family Welfare Ratio within Likely Causes of Poverty (Percentage Distribution of Families)

		LIKELY CAUSES OF POVERTY						
	Head of family is:		3	4	5	6	7	
	1	2	Single and has children (not 1 or 2)	Usually employed and worked less than 49 weeks during 1959 (not 1–3)	Nonwhite (not 1–4)	Self-employed businessman or farmer (not 1–5)	Not 1–6	All families
Family welfare ratio	Aged	Disabled (not 1)						
0.0–0.8	39	46	45	27	47	21	8	20
0.9–1.2	21	22	22	25	24	17	18	20
1.3–1.6	11	7	21	26	13	13	23	19
1.7–2.2	14	16	8	13	12	16	28	21
2.3 and over	15	9	4	9	4	33	23	20
Total	100	100	100	100	100	100	100	100
Number of families	384	116	157	177	216	299	1,451	2,800
Per cent of adult units with welfare ratios of 0.8 or less	48	57	48	26	55	23	17	28
Number of adult units	496	143	194	192	279	314	1,778	3,396

Table 20–4. Proportions and Aggregate Estimates of Heads of Poor Families Having Characteristics Related to Poverty within Likely Causes of Poverty (Proportions and Aggregate Estimates for Poor Families)

Likely causes of poverty	PROPORTIONS AND AGGREGATE ESTIMATES OF HEADS OF POOR FAMILIES HAVING CHARACTERISTICS RELATED TO POVERTY							Per cent with other indications of poverty
	Aged	Disabled	Single and has children	Usually employed, unemployed in 1959	Nonwhite	Self-employed businessman or farmer	None of these	
1. Aged	100% 2.8 mil.	32% .9 mil.	1% .04 mil.	2% .04 mil.	22% .6 mil.	17% .5 mil.	0%	65%
2. Disabled (not 1)		100% .8 mil.	15% .1 mil.	4% .03 mil.	26% .2 mil.	26% .2 mil.	0%	62%
3. Single and has children (not 1–2)			100% 1.1 mil.	14% .1 mil.	43% .5 mil.	4% .03 mil.	0%	60%
4. Usually employed, worked less than 49 weeks in 1959 (not 1–3)				100% .9 mil.	29% .2 mil.	0%	0%	29%
5. Nonwhite (not 1–4)					100% 1.4 mil.	14% .2 mil.	0%	14%
6. Self-employed businessman or farmer (not 1–5)						100% 1.0 mil.	0%	0%
7. Not 1–6							100% 2.4 mil.	0%
All	2.8 mil.	1.7 mil.	1.2 mil.	1.1 mil.	2.9 mil.	1.9 mil.	2.4 mil.	

problem. If a family is poor the classification tells something about the type of poverty and the chances that the family may be able to improve its situation.

Table 20–4 presents the relationships among the categories used to classify likely causes of poverty, and shows the extent to which poor families in each group exhibit more than one characteristic associated with poverty. For poor families which belong to two or more of the groups, the problem of poverty is compounded. For example, 29 per cent of heads of poor families who experienced unusual unemployment in 1959 are also nonwhite. Forty-three per cent of the poor single parents with children are nonwhite.

Earning Power of Poor Families

To determine in what way the characteristics of poor families limit the head's ability to earn a living, labor force participation rates, wage rates, and hours worked were derived from multivariate relationships. Each adjusted deviation from the analyses [reported earlier] was weighted by the proportion of family heads with that characteristic and with inadequate incomes; the weighted coefficients were added to give the average expected rates of labor-force participation, wage rates, and hours of work for the heads of families with inadequate incomes.

Table 20–5. Work Experience Projections

	Families with inadequate incomes	All spending unit heads
Proportion who worked during 1959	73%	86%
Wage rate earned	$1.63 *a*	$2.29
Hours worked	1,852 *a*	2,092
Estimated earnings (Product of lines 1, 2, and 3)	$2,204	$4,122
Number of cases	788	2,997

a Calculated on the unrealistic assumption that equal rates of labor-force participation apply to all groups of family heads whose incomes are inadequate. The assumption implies some downward bias in the estimated values, as aged and disabled heads that are least likely to work also have lower than average wages and hours.

Although the expected value of earnings for the heads of families whose incomes are inadequate is estimated at $2,204 (Table 20–5), the heads of these families *actually earned* an average only slightly more than $900. Both expected and actual earnings of the heads of these families fell substantially short of the national averages, and their actual earnings averaged even less than expected. The *gross disposable income* of families with inadequate incomes averaged only $1,886.

Many heads of families with inadequate incomes are aged, or poorly educated, or unskilled, or farm workers. The group includes a high proportion of female family heads, disabled persons, and families living in the South. All of these characteristics reduce the expected earning power of the group below the average estimated for all spending units, but they do not explain the very low actual earnings of the group. The difference between expected and actual earnings may reflect underlying variability in the determination of incomes. Alternatively, it may be associated with differences in ability, motivation, or other factors not adequately measured by the analyses [reported earlier].

Permanence of Low Incomes among the Poor

Of course, one year's income is not a complete measure of the economic status of the unit. Workers suffer from unemployment in some years, not in others. The self-employed have good and bad years. However, most people have to live out of their current income, including unemployment compensation, so that current income is important. Also, the analysis of those with low incomes in this chapter takes account of imperfections in one-year income by excluding from the group for most of the analysis those with substantial assets, and by looking separately at those who were unemployed in 1959 and are not unemployed every year, and those who were self-employed. The residual group of the poor thus contains no substantial number of temporarily poor.

The permanence of low incomes is inferred from a variety of findings. Data on the past earnings of the heads of the families suggest chronically low earnings. The meager assets held by the poor result from low incomes, financial disasters, or poor financial management in the past. Data on health insurance and pension rights suggest that the poor will continue to be hounded by financial difficulties, since they have little protection against future risks of poor health and involuntary retirement.

In many poor families the head has never earned enough to cover the family's present needs. (See Table 20–6.) The heads of poor families report they earned an average of $2,949 in the year in which they earned the most. Present needs of these families cost an average of $3,676. There are substantial differences in the highest earnings reported by poor families in the seven categories of the classification of likely causes of poverty. The unemployed and the farmers and self-employed businessmen report considerably higher than average past peak earnings. The level of peak earnings for those groups suggests the instability of their incomes. The peak earnings of the aged and disabled actually represent more purchasing power than the peak earnings for other groups because the aged and disabled earned their past incomes at a more distant time in the past than is true for other families.

Table 20-6. Highest Income Family Head Ever Earned within Likely Causes of Poverty (Percentage Distribution of Poor Families Whose Heads Have Worked)

				LIKELY CAUSES OF POVERTY					
	Head of family is:								
	1	2	3	4	5	6	7		
Highest income head ever earned	Aged	Disabled (not 1)	Single and has children (not 1 or 2)	Usually employed, and worked less than 49 weeks during 1959 (not 1-3)	Nonwhite (not 1-4)	Self-employed businessman or farmer (not 1-5)	Not 1-6	All poor families	All families
$1–949	13	14	32	12	19	11	9	14	4
$950–1,949	18	24	24	20	19	10	16	18	5
$1,950–2,949	18	16	24	16	17	14	20	18	7
$2,950–4,949	10	15	11	29	25	24	27	21	22
$4,950–7,449	2	8	0	13	6	18	15	9	33
$7,450 or more	1	4	0	1	0	10	4	3	21
Not ascertained	38	19	9	9	14	13	9	17	8
Total	100	100	100	100	100	100	100	100	100
Per cent who never worked	28	13	19	0	2	0	4	12	4
Mean highest income ever earned	$2,230	2,833	1,673	3,066	2,490	4,143	3,474	2,949	
Mean budget requirement	$2,401	3,801	4,359	4,161	4,144	4,446	4,033	3,676	
Number of families	137	65	86	65	128	91	183	755	2,800

Table 20-7. Year in Which Family Head Earned the Highest Income within Likely Causes of Poverty (Percentage Distribution of Poor Families Whose Heads Have Worked)

				LIKELY CAUSES OF POVERTY					
Year in which head earned the highest income	Head of family is:								
	1	2	3	4	5	6	7	All poor families	All families
	Aged	Disabled (not 1)	Single and has children (not 1 or 2)	Usually employed, and worked less than 49 weeks during 1959 (not 1-3)	Nonwhite (not 1-4)	Self-employed businessman or farmer (not 1-5)	Not 1-6		
1959	7	16	59	41	50	22	37	32	51
1958	1	7	1	22	10	10	10	8	9
1956-1957	1	10	13	16	10	19	14	11	10
1951-1955	10	18	12	12	9	11	17	13	10
1946-1950	15	16	2	0	7	18	6	9	6
1941-1945	18	16	6	6	3	11	5	9	5
Before 1941	16	7	0	0	5	2	3	6	3
Not ascertained	32	10	7	3	6	7	8	12	6
Total	100	100	100	100	100	100	100	100	100
Per cent who never worked	28	13	19	0	2	0	4	12	4
Number of families	137	65	86	65	128	91	183	755	2,800

276

Table 20–8. Amount of Savings within Likely Causes of Poverty (Percentage Distribution of Poor Families)

	LIKELY CAUSES OF POVERTY								
	Head of family is:								
	1	2	3	4	5	6	7		
			Single and has children (not 1 or 2)	Usually employed, and worked less than 49 weeks during 1959 (not 1–3)		Self-employed businessman or farmer (not 1–5)		All poor families	All families
Amount of savings [a]	Aged	Disabled (not 1)			Nonwhite (not 1–4)		Not 1–6		
$1,000–5,000	23	6	1	5	1	10	8	10	26
$500–1,000	9	5	3	3	4	6	7	6	14
Has none or less than $500 now:									
$500 or more in past 5 years	11	14	5	12	7	10	10	10	18
Less than $500 in past 5 years	45	31	50	36	41	37	36	41	28
Amount in past 5 years not ascertained	5	38	37	40	44	33	38	29	10
Amount now not ascertained	7	6	4	4	3	4	1	4	4
Total	100	100	100	100	100	100	100	100	100
Number of families	137	65	86	65	128	91	183	755	2,800

[a] Savings of the spending unit containing the head of the family.

Table 20–9. Mean Amount of Net Equity in Home or Farm, within Likely Causes of Poverty (for Poor Families)

Likely causes of poverty	Number of families	Proportion of each group who are home owners	Mean amount of net equity in home or farm
Head of family is:			
1. Aged	137	50	$ 3,300
2. Disabled (not 1)	65	53	3,600
3. Single and has children (not 1 or 2)	86	20	1,000
4. Usually employed, and worked less than 49 weeks during 1959 (not 1–3)	65	29	1,900
5. Nonwhite (not 1–4)	128	23	1,200
6. Self-employed businessman or farmer (not 1–5)	91	77	12,000
7. Not 1–6	183	37	4,300
All poor families	755	41	3,800

Almost a third of the poor families in this study report that 1959 was the year in which the head earned his highest income [Table 20–7]. Both the aged and the disabled are likely to report that the head earned the most in years prior to 1959. This finding is to be expected since few of these heads worked in 1959. Since the average age of aged heads of poor families is less than seventy-five years, the frequency with which peak earnings are reported for 1941 to 1950 indicates that a substantial number of the poor who are now over sixty-five suffered from a declining income even before a normal retirement age.

The distribution of assets among poor families identified by likely causes of poverty reveals relatively clear differences in income history. The nonwhites and single parents with children have accumulated the least reserves from their past incomes. Farmers and aged persons have accumulated some assets; but even those amounts are small.

To some extent these differences in assets reflect wide differences in the average age of family heads in the groups identified by likely causes of poverty. The disabled and the businessmen and farmers with inadequate incomes are largely aged forty-five to sixty-four. Families whose heads are sixty-five and older are included in a single category by definition. More than one-third of the single parents with children and nearly half of the unemployed family heads are under thirty-five. The aged have had a lifetime to accumulate savings; many of the unemployed have just begun. If the ages of heads of families with inadequate incomes are considered, the findings in Tables 20–8 and 20–9 suggest that nonwhites with inadequate incomes have had low incomes for a longer period of time than other groups. Nonwhite families include a substantial minority whose heads are over forty-five and who have had the time to accumulate savings; yet they report less savings than any other group. This probably results largely from lack of income in past years. No matter what the interpretations of the cause of their lack of assets, it is clear that the nonwhite families whose incomes are inadequate have almost no contingency reserves to meet future crises. The situation of the disabled, single parents with children, and persons who were out of work during 1959 is little better.

Table 20–10 offers another indication of the past experience of poor families. Families with unemployed or disabled heads used up a significant amount of savings during 1959. The amounts used are a small but useful addition to their incomes. Farmers and businessmen dissaved somewhat less: nonwhites and single parents with children reported almost no dissaving. Perhaps the unemployed and disabled became poor in the recent past and were able to maintain their living standard somewhat by living on savings.

Table 20–10. Mean Amount of Savings Used in 1959,[a] within Likely Causes of Poverty (for Poor Families)

Likely causes for poverty	Number of families	Proportion in group who used savings in 1959	Mean amount of savings used in 1959
Head of family is:			
1. Aged	137	30	$119
2. Disabled (not 1)	65	24	182
3. Single and has children (not 1 or 2)	86	12	24
4. Usually employed, and worked less than 49 weeks during 1959 (not 1–3)	65	30	160
5. Nonwhite (not 1–4)	128	14	24
6. Self-employed businessman or farmer (not 1–5)	91	26	125
7. Not 1–6	183	23	185
All poor families	755	23	$120

[a] Savings and liquid assets of spending units which contain family heads

Poor families have little protection against the costs of illness. Only one-third of the families in this group have hospitalization insurance which covers the entire spending unit containing the head of the family; three-

Table 20–11. Hospitalization Insurance Coverage within Likely Causes of Poverty (Percentage Distribution of Poor Families)

Hospitalization insurance [a]	LIKELY CAUSES OF POVERTY								
	Head of family is:								
	1	2	3	4	5	6	7	All poor families	All families
	Aged	Disabled (not 1)	Single and has children (not 1 or 2)	Usually employed, and worked less than 49 weeks during 1959 (not 1–3)	Nonwhite (not 1–4)	Self-employed businessman or farmer (not 1–5)	Not 1–6		
Everyone in the spending unit is covered	21	21	25	60	39	27	36	32	63
Someone in the spending unit is covered	3	8	12	1	8	3	5	5	6
No one in the spending unit is covered	74	67	63	38	51	70	58	62	30
Coverage not ascertained	2	4	0	1	2	0	1	1	1
Total	100	100	100	100	100	100	100	100	100
Number of families	137	65	86	65	128	91	183	755	2,800

[a] Coverage for spending units containing heads of families

fifths have no insurance whatever [Table 20–11]. This contrasts with the 63 per cent of the national population who have hospitalization coverage for the entire spending unit.

Poor families are similarly disadvantaged by lack of rights to public and private retirement pensions. Among poor families, only those whose heads are usually employed but who worked less than 49 weeks during 1959 are more completely covered by social security than the national population [Table 20–12]. In the case of private pensions a similar finding holds.

Table 20–12.   Public and Private Pension Coverage (Percentage Distribution of Poor Families and All Families Whose Heads Are 30 and Older and Not Retired)

Pension coverage	Social security and other government pensions [a]		Private pensions and annuities [b]	
	Poor families	All families	Poor families	All families
Covered	84	93	11	40
Not covered; coverage not ascertained	16	7	89	60
Total	100	100	100	100
Number of families	453	1,967	453	1,967

[a] Includes only family heads
[b] Includes family heads and wives

Clearly, short-run cash deficiencies and temporary loss of earning power are not the sole explanation for the economic difficulties of poor families; their difficulties also develop from inadequate long-term protection against those contingencies which are likely to curtail further their incomes in the future.

For persons fifty-five and older, the question of resources for the future is particularly critical. The incidence of both illness and unemployment increases for that age group, and the availability of a cushion of savings or insurance is important. Table 20–13 shows the welfare ratio of families which contain aged individuals within a classification of the individual's cushions of resources. The welfare ratio is the most comprehensive measure of individual income, since it includes nonmoney income and any help received through living with relatives, as well as the adjustment for need. Persons between fifty-five and sixty-one are shown separately from persons sixty-two and older, since persons can start collecting social security benefits at age sixty-two.

Table 20–13. Family Welfare Ratio within Savings, Health Insurance, and Age (Percentage Distribution of Persons 55 and Older)

	SAVINGS, HEALTH INSURANCE, AND AGE						
Family welfare ratio	$5,000 or more in savings		Less than $5,000 in savings, health insurance		Less than $5,000 in savings, no health insurance		All persons 55 and older
	55–61	62 & over	55–61	62 & over	55–61	62 & over	
(Income as a per cent of budget standard)							
0.0–0.44	1	1	3	6	17	12	7
0.45–0.84	2	12	8	15	19	34	18
0.85–1.24	8	11	12	18	25	25	18
1.25–2.04	25	28	35	42	25	22	29
2.05 and over	64	48	42	19	14	7	28
Total	100	100	100	100	100	100	100
Number of persons (in millions)	2.8	3.8	4.7	5.0	3.1	7.9	27.3

Neither the past earning experience nor the assets of the poor suggest that a large fraction were much better off in the recent past than they were in 1959. Their present level of savings and their rights to health insurance and pensions suggest that many will be worse off in the future. None of the poor can afford sickness or injury. Some will be unable to retire because they have no pension rights. This substantial long-term poverty suggests the need for an examination of the transmission of poverty from one generation to the next.

Transmission of Poverty between Generations

Many writers have suggested that poor families perpetuate their problems by raising children who cannot support themselves. Others have written about the freedom of opportunity that is the touchstone of success for anyone who chooses to work hard. Neither point of view can be disproved in this statistical study. The evidence is too indirect. Some of the poor have less education and less skilled occupations than their parents. Many of the children of the poor attain substantially better education than their parents. Those children who do not attain more education than their parents may repeat the history of their parents, finding it extremely difficult to earn the income they require to support their families.

Transmission of poverty between generations can be examined from two points of view. How are the characteristics of the poor similar to the characteristics of their parents? And to what extent do the poor transmit their own liabilities to their children?

The median educational attainment of fathers of all heads of spending units was less than eight grades in school. The median attainment of the heads themselves is slightly less than a high school diploma. According to Table 20–14 the heads of poor families had fathers with slightly less education than did heads of all families, although the differences are not great. However, the education of the heads of poor families is clearly less than the average for all heads of families.

Relative to their fathers, the heads of poor families either failed to go beyond their fathers' educational levels as much as most, or even slipped back. Table 20–15 shows that most failed to rise above their fathers' educational level. More than three-fifths of all spending unit heads whose fathers had less than nine grades of school, went beyond that level themselves. Among the heads of poor families, fewer than two-fifths did so.

Among the groups identified by the sequential classification of likely causes of poverty, family heads who were unusually unemployed during 1959 appear to have significantly more education than the remaining groups. In part this reflects the fact that this group was educated more recently than any other, at a time when standards were high. Similarly the low attainments of the aged and disabled reflect the fact that most were educated at a time when levels of educational achievements were considerably lower. Nevertheless, the unusually unemployed are the only

Table 20–14. Education of Family Heads and Their Fathers, within Likely Causes of Poverty (Proportions for Poor Families)

	LIKELY CAUSES OF POVERTY								
Education of family heads and their fathers	Head of family is:							All poor families	All families
	1 Aged	2 Disabled (not 1)	3 Single and has children (not 1 or 2)	4 Usually employed, and worked less than 49 weeks during 1959 (not 1–3)	5 Nonwhite (not 1–4)	6 Self-employed businessman or farmer (not 1–5)	7 Not 1–6		
Per cent of fathers with less than 9 grades	57	70	76	66	66	79	63	66	64
Per cent of family heads with less than 9 grades	75	78	60	49	65	55	58	64	32
Per cent of family heads with less than 12 grades	84	93	89	66	80	78	78	81	53
Number of families	137	65	86	65	128	91	183	755	2,800

group who attained relatively the same education as their parents; this fact suggests both greater ability and more motivation for the group than is typical of the remaining poor family heads.

Table 20–15. Education of Family Heads within Education of Their Fathers (Percentage Distribution of Poor Families)

Education of heads	Education of fathers		All heads of poor families [a]	All families
	0–8 grades	9 grades or more		
0–8 grades	65	23	64	33
9–11 grades	18	23	17	21
12 grades or more	17	54	19	46
Total	100	100	100	100
Number of families	500	72	755	2,800

[a] Includes 183 heads for whom education of father was not ascertained

In summary, the low educational attainments of heads of poor families result from a failure to improve educational attainments relative to the previous generation at the same rate as the remaining population. The data offer little support to the hypothesis that a majority of the poor failed to obtain education because of inadequate education on the parts of their fathers. It is quite possible that other children of these same parents may have attained more education and are in good economic positions.

Comparison of the occupations of the two generations, however, shows some correlation between the poor earning power of the present generation and the earning power of their fathers. The fathers of heads of poor families are more likely to have been farmers or unskilled laborers than are the fathers of all family heads [Tables 20–16 and 20–17]. This lack of skill is also typical of the heads of poor families themselves. Even when heads of poor families are compared to all family heads whose fathers were in the same occupations, the poor family heads show much less upward mobility. Indeed, it appears that a number of the heads of poor families have moved into less skilled jobs than their fathers had.

Thus the lack of education and skilled occupations among heads of poor families does not result solely from the unskilled and uneducated background of their parents. It also stems from the failure of these persons to improve their skills in the way that typical family heads have improved their skills over the past generations. Skills and education that were adequate for the last generation are marginal in today's labor market. Though no sweeping generalizations can be made on the basis of these few tables, they offer little support for a theory of poverty that rests entirely on intergenerational transmission.

Table 20–16. Occupation of Family Heads and Their Fathers within Likely Causes of Poverty (Proportions for Poor Families)

Occupation of family heads and their fathers	LIKELY CAUSES OF POVERTY							All poor families	All families
	Head of family is:								
	1 Aged	2 Disabled (not 1)	3 Single and has children (not 1 or 2)	4 Usually employed, and worked less than 49 weeks during 1959 (not 1–3)	5 Nonwhite (not 1–4)	6 Self-employed businessman or farmer (not 1–5)	7 Not 1–6		
Per cent of heads whose fathers were unskilled laborers and farmers	58	64	66	63	75	87	56	64	44
Per cent of family heads who are unskilled laborers and farmers	48	60	58	47	61	80	37	52	31
Number of family heads	137	65	86	65	128	91	183	755	2,800

Table 20–17. Occupations of Heads of Families within Occupations of Their Fathers (Percentage Distribution of Poor Families)

Occupation of family heads	OCCUPATION OF FATHERS				All poor families	All families
	White collar workers	Skilled and semiskilled workers	Unskilled laborers; farmers	Not ascertained; never worked		
White collar workers	34	9	11	3	13	37
Skilled and semiskilled workers	23	37	21	21	24	35
Unskilled laborers; farmers	28	45	59	51	52	23
Not ascertained; never worked	15	9	9	25	11	5
Total	100	100	100	100	100	100
Number of families	85	112	501	57	755	2,800

Transmission of Poverty to Children

To what degree do these families transmit their own liabilities to their children? The data offer two pieces of evidence on the extent to which children inherit the inadequate education of their parents.[10] Poor families have substantially lower aspirations for sending their children to college than is true for the national cross section [Table 20–18]. The usually employed who lost work in 1959 are the most aspiring group. Their expectations that incomes will improve in the near future and their relatively greater educational attainment may be responsible.

Table 20–18. Education Expected for Boys of Family Heads (Percentage Distribution of Heads of Poor Families, and All Families, with Boys 20 or Under)

Education expected for boys of family heads	Poor families with boys aged 20 and under	All families with boys aged 20 and under
Less than 12 grades	4	2
12 grades; 12 grades and nonacademic training	50	24
Some college	31	66
Not ascertained	15	8
Total	100	100
Number of families	343	1,211

For those whose children have finished school, the data offer a similar finding; 45 per cent of the children of poor families completed high school or more [Table 20–19]. Sixty-five per cent of the children of all families achieved that level of education. A substantial minority of the children of poor families thus obtain enough education to qualify for better jobs than those held by their parents. Unfortunately, more than one-third of the children have less than a grade school education and will probably perpetuate the poverty of their parents. The proportion of children who drop out of school before graduation is somewhat overstated by Table 20–19 for younger families whose children have not yet reached the last years of high school. Those who remain in school are not counted while those who drop out are included among those finished with school.

Of course, a study such as this gives an incomplete picture of social change, in that only those families who are poor at the present time are analyzed. Some of the present poor came from families which were not poor; likewise, some families that are not poor may produce children who will join the ranks of poverty of the next generation. Also, there are families in the present generation who are not now poor but will become so after retirement or following some catastrophe.

Table 20–19. Education Attained by Children Finished with School (Percentage Distribution of Poor Families and All Families That Have Children Finished with School)

Education of children finished with school	All poor families	All families
0–8 grades	34	14
9–11 grades	21	21
High school graduate or more	45	65
Total	100	100
Number of families	755	2,800

Summary

According to the estimates presented in this chapter, there are some 10.4 million poor families in the United States. Many of the families can be categorized by a classification of likely causes of poverty which stresses situational, involuntary factors that lead to low earning power:

The *aged* have retired and are unable to find work or are limited in their ability to work.

The *disabled* have a severe physical limitation; thus, they are unable to work.

Single family heads with children have the double burden of raising a family and earning a living. Inability to arrange for child care may keep the head from working.

Heads of families who worked less than 49 weeks in 1559 but for whom unemployment is unusual have an obvious explanation for their low incomes in that year.

Nonwhite persons may suffer from severe discrimination so that they are limited in their earning power.

Farmers and self-employed businessmen suffer from fluctuations in demand and may have low incomes as a consequence.

However, such situational factors do not describe the entire picture of poor families. The heads of poor families, on the average, have never earned as much as it would cost to support their present families at the levels specified by the New York Community Council budgets. This is true in spite of the fact that many of these heads were not always aged, disabled, or without a spouse. Poor education among all but a few heads of poor families is partly responsible; however, a careful analysis of the characteristics of families whose incomes are inadequate reveals that they should earn considerably more than they do on the basis of their education and other characteristics. The multivariate analysis indicates that heads of poor families should average $2,204 in earnings. In fact, heads of poor families earned an average of only $932 in 1959. The discrepancy may arise from psychological dependency, lack of motivation, lack of intelligence, and a variety of other factors that were not studied.

The expectation for most poor families is continued dependency or inadequate income. The poor have little protection against the costs of sickness or injury. The majority will receive social security when they reach retirement age, but few will have any other source of income to supplement what is likely to be a minimum payment.

Data on the education and occupations of the parents and children of heads of poor families indicate some transmission of poverty from one generation to the next. They also indicate that the poor include many who have slipped from the level of well-being enjoyed by their parents. The experience of all families implies that heads of poor families should have better education and better occupations than they have actually had. Whether the family environment or personal failures are responsible for the lack of advancement is not clear.

It is clear that rehabilitation, education, training, and substantial increases in financial support will be needed to alleviate the problems of poor families. Despite the many forms of assistance programs and social insurance programs operating in this country, nearly half of the families whose income are inadequate received no transfer aid during 1959. Only 23 per cent of all poor families received public assistance, although public assistance is intended to supplement the incomes of those families who do not receive sufficient income.

21 Attitudes toward
Governmental Participation
in Medical Care

Wilbur J. Cohen, Charles N.

Poskanzer, and Harry Sharp

Introduction

Financing the costs of medical care is one of the foremost domestic problems in the United States today. During the past forty years there have been attempts at both the national and the state level to enact governmental health insurance legislation in the United States. Arguments against public medical care plans tend to revolve about problems of possible governmental control of medical practice, the interposition of a barrier in the doctor-patient or hospital-patient relationship, and interference with the freedom of choice of physician or hospital on the part of the patient. Proponents of national health insurance argue that it is through some nationwide insurance system, applicable to our entire population, that the economic burden of illness can be met and a desirable degree of utilization attained of what medical science has to offer for the promotion and preservation of a healthy nation.

An important consideration in the determination of the means by which medical care needs can best be met is the opinion of the consumer of this care. Several surveys on health insurance coverage have been made in the past. In this paper we present the findings of a national and a local survey as they relate to opinions concerning governmental participation in the provision of medical care at low cost from doctors and hospitals.

Sources of Data

The data reported in this paper are taken from two surveys conducted in late 1956 and early 1957. The first study used a national sample

Abridged from HEALTH NEEDS OF THE AGED AND AGING, Hearings before the Subcommittee on Problems of the Aged and Aging, Committee on Labor and Public Welfare, U.S. Senate, 86th Congress, 2nd Session, April 1960. Reprinted by permission of the authors and the United States government.

of all U.S. residents 21 years old or older. The second study was based on a sample of all adult residents of Wayne County (Detroit), Mich.[1]

The national survey was carried out in 1956 and completed shortly before the presidential election of that year. This research employed a probability sample of all adults in the United States. The data from the national study which are reported here constitute only a very small part of that undertaking.[2]

The Detroit Area Study's survey was completed in early 1957, shortly after the national survey. This research used a probability sample of all adult residents of Wayne County. Similar to the national study, the Wayne County data discussed here only a small segment from a larger study of political behavior in Greater Detroit.[3]

Both the national survey and the Wayne County survey used a fixed-address sample designed by the sampling section of the Survey Research Center. In these investigations interviewers were assigned specific addresses at which to call. The respondent at each selected dwelling was chosen at random by a procedure over which the interviewer had no control. Substitution of dwelling unit or respondent was not permitted. Checks with U.S. Census data and with other independent criteria indicate that the samples are representative of their respective research universes.

Differences in proportions which are specifically mentioned in the text are statistically significant at the 5 per cent level or better.

The authors do not claim that this paper represents a comprehensive analysis of public attitudes toward governmental assistance in meeting the costs of medical care. Moreover, neither of the above studies was solely an investigation of this issue. Both investigations included an identical series of questions which dealt with attitudes toward the role of the national government with respect to medical expenses. It is the authors' hope that an analysis of these data may provide some useful insights on the way in which Americans as a whole and the residents of a single large metropolitan community view this issue. The authors realize that attitudes on this issue may be subject to change. However, these data are the most recent available to us and may provide a benchmark for future studies.

The paper presents some general conclusions of the analysis and then discusses some of the detailed findings. The conclusions presented are based on the tables [not presented in this paper: see the original report for the tables in question—Editor's Note].

The Questions Used

The three questions relating to medical care used in these surveys are as follows:

1. "Now I would like to talk to you about things that our Government might do. Of course, different things are important to different people, so we don't expect everyone to have an opinion about all of these.

First: The Government ought to help people get doctors and hospital care at low cost. Do you have an opinion on this, or not?" If the respondent had an opinion, he was asked: "Do you think the Government should do this, or not?"

2. Respondents with opinions on question 1 were then asked: "On the question of the Government helping people get doctors and hospital care at low cost, is the Government going too far, doing less than it should, or what?"

3. Again, respondents with an opinion on question 1 were asked: "Would the Democrats or the Republicans be closer to what you want on this issue, or wouldn't there be any difference?" [4]

General Conclusions

A majority of adults in both the United States as a whole and in greater Detroit favor governmental assistance in the provision of low-cost medical care. In view of earlier research, this finding is not surprising. Several national studies [5] and a 1952 survey of greater Detroit [6] have shown general support for some form of governmental action in the field of medical care.

A significant proportion of the population have no opinion as to the principle or extent of governmental participation. In view of the pervasiveness of medical care needs this lack of knowledge should be of public concern. Among those who do have an opinion, however, a slightly larger number would increase governmental aid than believe the current level of aid is correct. Very few adults feel that governmental aid should be reduced.

Both surveys indicate that among most of the general public the positions of the two major political parties on the role of government in medical care are difficult to distinguish. Many persons either do not know which party is closest to their own views on the issue, or believe that both the Republicans and the Democrats are equally close.

Summary of Major Findings

I

*A Majority of the American People and
the Residents of Wayne County Favor
Governmental Action to Help Finance
Low-Cost Medical Care*

Some 55 per cent of all adults in the United States believe the government ought to help people get doctors and hospital care at low cost; 25 per cent oppose such action; and 20 per cent are not sure or have no opinion on this issue. Stated somewhat differently, of those Americans who express a specific attitude, two persons are in favor of such government support, for every one who is opposed.

As compared with the United States as a whole, Detroiters are somewhat more likely to be in favor of the principle of governmental assistance (64 per cent). They also are less likely to be unsure of how they stand on the matter, or to have no opinion at all.

II

A Substantial Proportion of the American People
Believe Present Governmental Aid for
Medical Care Is Not Enough

Only a Very Small Proportion of Persons Expressing
an Opinion Believe Present Governmental Aid for
Low-Cost Medical Care Is Too Much

One out of every three adult Americans feels that the present extent of governmental aid in meeting medical costs is not enough. Only 2 per cent of our adult population believe the government is already going too far with such assistance. Almost one out of every four adults states that the present level of assistance is about right. And fully 4 out of every 10 persons have no opinion on the subject, or don't know.

Of those who express an opinion, not quite 6 out of every 10 Americans appear to be in favor of greater governmental participation, while no more than 3 per cent believe the government is already providing too much aid in meeting the costs of medical care. The remaining 39 per cent are satisfied with the present extent of governmental assistance.

Wayne County is quite similar to the Nation as a whole in the proportion of its residents who feel the government is not now going far enough. Detroiters, however, tend to be more likely to approve of the present level of governmental assistance than are the Americans in general. Conversely, the national population is much more likely to have no opinion on this issue than are Wayne County residents.

III

Aged Persons in the United States Overwhelmingly
Favor Government Aid for Low-Cost Medical Care

Over 6 out of every 10 Americans aged 65 or older favor governmental aid for low-cost medical care. In the age group 21–34, the proportion is 50 per cent. The likelihood of favoring assistance consistently increases with age. It should be noted, however, that the proportion favoring government aid is at least 50 per cent or more for every age group.

The results for the United States are as follows:

Attitudes toward the Principle of Governmental Assistance

Age group	Favor	Oppose	Not sure; no opinion	Total Per cent	Number of cases
21 to 34	50	27	23	100	576
35 to 44	53	28	19	100	485
45 to 54	57	27	16	100	367
55 to 64	56	25	19	100	257
65 and older	63	15	22	100	229

It is signficant that the general results presented above are similar to those of an independent survey taken in 1957 by the National Opinion Research Center of the University of Chicago in cooperation with the Health Information Foundation.[7] In the NORC study, Dr. Ethel Shanas reported that a majority of aged respondents (54 per cent) declared themselves in favor of government insurance paying doctor and hospital bills; a somewhat smaller proportion (43 per cent) of the older population were not in favor of this. Only 3 per cent of the sample used in the Shanas research, however, had no opinion on this issue.

Older residents with large medical care requirements clearly would benefit from any governmental program. The relationship between increasing age and increased approval of governmental aid which is discussed above is therefore not surprising. Of perhaps more interest, however, is the absence of this relationship in Wayne County. Detroiters over 65 years old are no more likely than are very young adults to be in support of, or in opposition to, the principle of governmental assistance in meeting medical costs. However, since the proportion of all persons under age 65 in the Detroit area favoring governmental aid was higher than those in comparable ages in the entire United States, it may be reasonable to assume that a 60 to 63 per cent favorable response represents the effective limit to favorable opinion on this subject. It should also be noted that the proportion without an opinion or not sure in the Detroit area was somewhat less than that for the country as a whole.

There is a tendency for political conservatism to increase with age in the Detroit area as elsewhere. The substantial proportion of the older groups in favor of some governmental participation in medical care is thus of significance. It indicates that older persons who might otherwise favor a smaller role for government in general make an important exception to this principle when it comes to financing medical care costs.

IV

Socioeconomic Status and Opposition to
Governmental Aid Are Directly Related

High-income groups, persons with higher occupational status, and Americans with a large amount of formal education are much more likely to be in opposition to the principle of governmental assistance in meeting medical costs than are persons at the lower income, occupational, and educational levels. This relationship holds both for the United States as a whole and the greater Detroit area.

The tendency for lower socioeconomic groups to be highly supportive of the principle of assistance is not unexpected; these population groups undoubtedly would receive the greatest improvement in the extent of medical care obtained from this type of governmental activity. The magnitude of the variation by socioeconomic status is sizable however. For example, one-tenth of the adults in Wayne County with less than an eighth grade education are against such assistance; residents who have had some college experience are almost five times more likely to be opposed to governmental aid.

V

Among the Middle Socioeconomic Groups the
Principle of Governmental Aid Has Wide Acceptance

Both nationally and in greater Detroit, the middle-class levels of the population are much more likely to favor than to oppose governmental participation in medical care plans. In fact, majority opposition to the principle of governmental assistance appears only among those residents of Wayne County whose incomes exceeded $10,000 in 1956. Slightly less than one-half of even the college-educated adults in the United States, or in just Wayne County, do not believe that the Government should help people obtain low cost medical treatment. Among the professional and managerial group, opinions were about equally divided as to whether they favor or oppose such aid.

VI

The Nation's Farmers Are in Strong Support of
Governmental Aid for Medical Care

Nearly two out of every three farmers in the United States state that they are in favor of governmental aid. Farmers are at least as much in support of this principle as are urban workers.

VII

The Tendency to Favor Greater Governmental Aid
Decreases with Increasing Socioeconomic Status

When only those Americans who have an opinion on the matter are considered, a majority of the lower- and middle-socioeconomic groups support greater governmental assistance; in contrast, about one-third of those Americans with a 1956 income in excess of $10,000 believe greater assistance is desirable. However, only 11 per cent of the nation's high income population feel that as of now the governmental assistance in the area is excessive. The comparable proportion for Detroit is 16 per cent.

VIII

An Extremely Large Majority of Negroes Are In
Favor of Governmental Assistance

The generally lower socioeconomic position of Negroes, as compared to whites, is consistent with the strong support which members of this race give to governmental participation in medical care plans. In the United States, and in Wayne County, 8 out of every 10 Negro adults are in favor of governmental aid.

IX

Slightly More Republicans Favor Governmental Aid
than Oppose It; At Least Three Times as
Many Democrats Favor It as Oppose It

Political party preference is strongly correlated with attitudes toward governmental assistance in meeting the costs of medical care. Republicans in the nation and in Detroit are considerably more likely than Democrats to be in opposition to aid. Even among the Republicans, however, the number of supporters of this principle is slightly larger than the number of opponents. But Democrats, either in Wayne County specifically or in the nation as a whole, are much more likely to approve than to disapprove governmental assistance. It may also be noted that among those with an opinion a rather large minority of Republicans (43 per cent in the United States and 37 per cent in Wayne County) feel that the present extent of governmental aid in meeting the costs of medical care is not enough.

There is not much significant difference by party preference with respect to those who believe government aid is excessive. Seven per cent of the Republicans in the nation think present governmental aid for medical care is too much, compared with 4 per cent of the Democrats.

X

The American People Do Not Think of Governmental
Aid for Medical Care as a Partisan Political Issue

Even though the political preference of an individual is strongly associated with attitudes toward governmental aid in this field, an overwhelming majority of Americans, 7 out of every 10, either do not know which party is closest to their own position, or feel that the Republicans and the Democrats are equally close. Fifteen per cent of the adults believe that the Democratic Party best represents their position on the issue; and a somewhat smaller proportion (11 per cent) feel that the Republican

Party is closest to their wishes. Thus, one-quarter of the nation's population can clearly distinguish between the Republican Party or the Democratic Party on this issue, and about one-half of the adults in the United States either do not know or have no opinion as to which party is closest to their own wishes. These findings for the nation apply almost equally well when only the Detroit area is considered.

In almost every socioeconomic and demographic segment of the population, the most common response of those who have an opinion on the subject is that no difference is discernible between the Republican and the Democratic positions on medical care programs. There is some evidence that adults at the upper income and educational levels are closer to the Republican Party on this issue than are others; conversely, lower socioeconomic groups tend to favor the Democratic Party's position to a greater extent. The major conclusion seems clear, nonetheless: Most Americans do not perceive medical care programs as an important partisan political issue.

XI

A Significant Proportion of the American People
Say They Are Not Sure or Do Not Have an Opinion
About Governmental Aid for Medical Care

Twenty per cent of all Americans say they are not sure or have no opinion with respect to governmental aid in meeting medical costs; about 40 per cent have no opinion or are not sure as to the extent of governmental aid. When asked "Are the Republicans or the Democrats closer to what you want on this question, or are they about the same?" about one out of every two Americans either has no opinion or is not sure of his position. The residents of Wayne County generally are more likely to state an opinion on this issue than are all adults in the United States.

XII

A Substantial Majority of People in the South Favor
Governmental Aid for Medical Care

Sixty-two per cent of all persons in the south favor governmental aid in meeting medical care costs; 21 per cent of the southerners are opposed. The northeast region of the United States is very similar to the south in this respect. In the midwest and far west, almost one-half of the adults support the principle of governmental assistance, while 30 and 27 per cent, respectively, are in opposition.

In all regions of the country, front 29 to 38 per cent of the population believe that the present level of governmental aid is not adequate. No more than 1 to 3 per cent of the residents of each region feel that the government is already providing too much assistance.

22 The Problems of Families
in the AFDC Program

Paul H. Glasser and

Elizabeth L. Navarre

Mrs. Smith is the 42-year-old mother of 13 children. Born and reared in the Deep South, she migrated to the Detroit area in late adolescence in search of work during World War II. Despite only a fifth-grade education, she readily found employment during this period of labor shortage and continued to work in an unskilled job until after the war ended and she began having children.

Her children range in ages from 3 to 25. The first six were born when Mrs. Smith was married to a man whom she later divorced because of his drinking. A passing flirtation led to the birth of her seventh child. However, the last six children are all the children of same father. This man, now no longer in the picture, has never contributed more than intermittently to the family's support.

Mrs. Smith receives the maximum allowance given in the Federal-State aid to families with dependent children program (AFDC) of the Michigan State Department of Social Welfare. This grant is supplemented by the general relief and surplus foods programs of the local welfare department. Nevertheless, Mrs. Smith still has a hard time making ends meet. The family lives in an old and crowded tenement building in need of repair, in a neighborhood where there is much crime and delinquency. The children are not always properly clothed or fed, and some of them are badly in need of medical or dental care. Often they do not have enough money for their school supplies and laboratory fees.

Poverty is obviously an omnipresent problem in the Smith family. But poverty in this family, as in many of the 9.3 million families in this coun-

From CHILDREN, **12** (1965), 151–157. A report based upon research sponsored by Children's Bureau Grant No. D-16. Reprinted with the permission of the authors and the United States Children's Bureau. This analysis is the responsibilty of the authors, and not of the Mchigan State Department of Social Welfare or its staff.

try with incomes under $3,000, is a reflection of a complex of other problems. Some of these have been noted in a congressional report:

> A closer examination of the statistics regarding poverty shows the scars of discrimination, lack of education, and broken homes. Of the poor, 22 per cent are nonwhite and nearly one-half of all nonwhites live in poverty. The heads of over 60 per cent of all poor families have only a grade school education. . . .[1]

While sharing the complex problems of poverty with a host of other families, the Smith family experiences these problems in its own ways, and has its own strengths and weaknesses to help or impede its effort to break out of the poverty chain. In addition to money, it needs services to tip the balance in favor of the strengths—services based on an understanding of the family's own perceptions of its problems and how these may be overcome, as well as on the perceptions of the experts.

In preparation for the development of a special service program for families in the AFDC program in Detroit, the University of Michigan School of Social Work has undertaken an exploration in the mothers' perceptions of their problems and how well these correspond with the view of the public welfare workers and social scientists. The undertaking is part of a project being carried out in the department by the school, with a federal grant from the Children's Bureau, to demonstrate the utility of the social group-work method in a public welfare setting.[2]

In this project, mothers in the AFDC program were invited to form discussion groups, each group to focus on one area, such as the mother's employment opportunities, the adjustment problems of families with incapacitated fathers, child-rearing difficulties, and school problems. The groups met weekly for 6 to 12 sessions. Leaders, drawn from the agency's personnel and students of the School of Social Work, were closely supervised by an experienced social group worker.

We quickly learned that in order to provide an effective service, we need to know more about the families' problems and their origins from the viewpoints of clients, workers, and social scientists. The following findings are based on preliminary data gathered during 1963–1964 and a review of the literature. More complicated data, gathered in 1965, are now in the process of analysis.

The Clients' View

We constructed an open-end, probe-type questionnaire eliciting information about the immediate problems of applicants for and recipients of AFDC (hereafter called clients) and their plans for solving them. Included were such questions as "What has worried you most during the past few weeks?" and "What have you been trying to do about this problem?" The questionnaire was administered to 16 applicants to the program after the completion of the regular intake interview. A similar questionnaire was administered during the same period to 17 mothers in the group sessions focused on the mothers' employment problems.

The problems mentioned by mothers in the two samples were similar, except that employment problems, as would be expected, were mentioned more often by those attending the group meetings.

As anticipated, many of the participating women described concrete problems. Fifty-eight per cent of the problems mentioned involved the need for money, either in general or for specific purposes such as medical care or school clothes. This percentage included the 16 per cent of the problems mentioned that were concerned with the mothers' own employment difficulties or those of their husbands, and the 13 per cent that were concerned with poor living quarters or the necessity of living with relatives.

One-quarter of all the problems delineated had to do with children. (Some of these were also included in the 58 per cent involving the need for money. Among the specific difficulties mentioned were dressing children adequately for school, locating a good baby sitter, and the effects on a child of living in a crowded home with quarreling relatives. In addition, a good deal of general anxiety about the children's future was expressed, especially in relation to the lack of a father in the home, the mother's inability to give children the things they needed or wanted, and fear of not being able to rear the children properly.

Somewhat less expected was the degree of concern about health, the focus of 19 per cent of the problems mentioned. Many women expressed worry about specific conditions and the out-of-reach cost of needed medical or dental care. Some mentioned their own and their husband's inability to work because of ill health, and some expressed worry about having nobody to care for their children if they became ill. Four of the women said they had a "nervous" condition. Women whose husbands were incapacitated saw problems in the effect of the man's illness upon relationships within the family and in their own ability to accept the role of household head and breadwinner.

Few of the respondents said much about marital problems, possibly because of the shortness of the interviews. In general, when marital problems were mentioned they were expressed as hurt over divorce or desertion, hope for reconciliation (though the husband may have been gone for several years), or unhappiness over the actions of an estranged husband. One woman said flatly that if she could remarry, all her problems would be solved.

While much anxiety was expressed about specific areas of social functioning, almost one-fourth (23 per cent) of the problems mentioned indicated the existence of a more or less generalized anxiety about the present or the future. Nevertheless, few respondents indicated having plans for alleviating their problems or any idea where they might get help with them. Even the few who said they had made plans or knew where they could get help expressed little hope of improvement. It may be that the client's very anxiety about her problems prevents her from doing anything about them. This is a hypothesis presently being tested.

In summary, our inquiry indicated, not unexpectedly, that the mothers involved saw the scarcity of money as their major problem. They apparently felt helpless about the situation they were in and knew of no way to get out of it. They revealed little awareness that a part of their problem might have been their own inability to call on the personal and situational resources at their disposal. However, they did show concern about the effects of their present circumstances on their children.

The Workers' View

Workers' perspectives are colored both by agency policy and the attitudes of the public at large. At times their views reflect the inconsistencies of both these frames of reference, particularly since the emphasis in the program is changing from income maintenance to rehabilitation.

In the study, the opinions of the agency's caseworkers and supervisors were sought in two staff meetings. The lists of problems turned in by the caseworkers, when recommending clients for participation in the social group-work meetings, constituted another source of information.

We found that the caseworker tends to see most clearly what the client sees least clearly: that in many instances the client's inadequacy in using her resources led to her present problems and are at least partially responsible for her inability to get out of the situation she is in. The caseworkers describe the clients as living from day to day, or even in the past, as if their ambitions and hopes had ended with the crisis that led to the application for public assistance. Some are described as immature, emotionally unstable, alcoholic, or unmoral, some as being pleasure-bent with little or no interest in their children, their homes, or employment. Others are described as tending to give their children excessive protection, but, paradoxically, seeming unaware that irresponsible behavior in other areas of life may also affect their children. Other problems mentioned were poor budgeting of funds, unwise buying, poor housekeeping, and carelessness in the physical care of children.

At the same time, the caseworkers recognized the fact that most of the women in the program have problems that are unrelated to their morals and values. They also recognized that those women with questionable values have never experienced, and do not now see evidence of, any other kind. They pointed out that many clients in seeking employment are handicapped by real problems, such as inadequate child-care facilities, transportation difficulties, poor personal appearance, chronic ill health, and lack of education and skills. They pointed out that, for many clients, employment offers no real economic advantages unless it is steady and secure and the money earned is budgeted for an unmet need rather than deducted from the assistance grant.

The workers expressed particular concern for the children in the program, most of whom are living in broken homes. They mentioned the lack of appropriate opportunities for male identification for boys in fatherless homes. They expressed somewhat less concern about the psychological effects that divorce, desertion, or illegitimate pregnancy may have upon the mothers themselves or about their difficulties in trying to do a job generally carried out by two persons. However, they did point out that the women in the AFDC program are lonely women who have few social outlets. One caseworker suggested that society may be expecting higher moral standards of these women than are common in the general population. Many others expressed concern not only for the children in the program but also for their mothers, and gave evidence of wanting to help them.

Sociological Factors

From the sociological point of view, a mother who receives public aid is a deviant in several ways. She is a member of the lower class in a society where middle-class values predominate. She is supported by public funds in a society in which self-support is the tradition. Unless she is one of the mothers who is in the program because her husband is incapacitated, she is rearing children without a father present in a society whose acceptance of the broken home is much stronger in print than in actuality. She is apt to be poorly educated and may be of less than average intelligence. With all these strikes against her, she is expected to live on an income which is no more than minimal by any standards and less than minimal by many.

Social scientists point out that one of the strongest determinants of an individual's chances in life is his position in the class structure.[3] In a sense, social class defines the individual's responses to the major social pressures. Lacking the partial protection that money, power, or personal influence can give, the child born into a family poor in money, education, and skills is more vulnerable than others to the vicissitudes of life. His chances for getting a good education are poor for several reasons. He receives less than normal encouragement and enrichment in the home, and possibly also less than normal in school, for cultural deprivation may give an appearance of stupidity even to a bright child. In addition, the school system may be dominated by middle-class values to such an extent that neither the content nor methods of the teaching are effective with a child from a different background.[4,5]

The poorly educated person finds few employment opportunities open to him, and these decrease as technological advances eliminate more and more unskilled jobs. Such jobs as are open to him are the least desirable ones in terms of pay, job security, working conditions relevant to health and safety, and fringe benefits, such as insurance and sick leave. Frequent layoffs are likely, and savings to tide the family over a crisis are almost impossible to come by.

Having less access to adequate medical care throughout his life than most people, the person of low socioeconomic status is more prone to illness. Since his employment often requires physical labor, he can become incapacitated by a physical condition that would not be incapacitating to persons in more sedentary work. His poor education and lack of skills make him less adaptable to new occupations after an economic crisis.[6]

The income of the families in the AFDC program is at the lower limits of low incomes. Housing is, of necessity, usually in cheap rental units where the condition of the building may create problems in housekeeping and in efforts to make the home attractive. Drab and deteriorating housing, depressing both adults and children, often discourages women from any effort to improve their homes. Overcrowding in the homes of relatives, not uncommon in families in the AFDC program, not only requires greater physical effort in housekeeping but also creates problems in family relations.

Thus, economic need affects every part of daily life.

Receiving support from public funds is not an unmixed blessing. This is particularly true for the mothers in the AFDC program, a program long the target of much public disapproval. The uniform minimum standards of need limit to employment expenses and a few unbudgeted items of need the amount of any additional income they may receive without having their AFDC payments reduced. Thus, a mother cannot raise her family's economic level above minimal standards unless she is able to take on the entire burden of the family's support.

Psychological Factors

Among the most pervasive effects of social class status are the attitudes and values instilled in children. Not only are differences in opportunity perpetuated in each succeeding generation, but a style of life and a value system commensurate with the realities of the position are also perpetuated. Many studies have shown class differentials in child-rearing practices,[7] health practices,[8] living patterns,[9] and attitudes toward sex.[10] Current theories of child development indicate that such differences experienced as children will produce psychological differences in adults, differences which tend to maintain adults in the socioeconomic status of their childhood.

Rainwater, Coleman, and Handel have studied the attitudes of women of lower socioeconomic status.[11] Presumably, the AFDC clients are similar to these women, with two important exceptions: the AFDC recipients must live on an income considerably below that of the women these investigators studied, and most of the women in the AFDC program have gone through marital crises.

The women studied by Rainwater and associates regarded themselves as acted upon rather than acting. They saw the world as unchangeable. Such a woman responds only when she is approached in terms that are "specific, clearly defined, and readily understood." She feels helpless in the face of a chaotic world; she does not reach out to it. Seeing what happens in life as based on luck or fate rather than on her own actions, she has a "fairly pervasive anxiety over possible fundamental deprivations."

Such a woman does not lack hope, for luck may also be good, but she does not expect to be personally successful against forces she cannot control. Her gratifications tend to come from her own limited world of husband and children. She likes to be "needed." Yet, again, she does not see herself as having effective power over her husband, and little over her children after their babyhood. She greatly fears loneliness.

What then must be the psychological state of the AFDC recipient who, divorced from or deserted by the father of her children, is in the midst of a crisis of the type most feared by women of low socioeconomic status? Surely the sense of a chaotic world, of personal inadequacy, and of anxiety over future catastrophe must be increased.

One may assume that the dissolution of a family unit is a traumatic experience whatever the emotional relationship of the adults involved. Regardless of any other emotions, the very fact that the relationship has failed tends to lower the self-esteem of both husband and wife. Social disapproval often complicates the adjustment. A woman who has been deserted or divorced against her will might be expected to have a sharp sense of personal failure and inferiority as well as a good deal of bitterness, which may be turned either outward upon the former spouse or inward upon the self. When the woman has to depend upon public funds for support, the sense of inadequacy may be aggravated and may, in turn, heighten the helpless and dependent attitudes fostered by the lifetime experiences encountered by persons of low socioeconomic status.

Mothers as Family Heads

The mother who has become head of the family through divorce, widowhood, or the incapacity of the husband is a focal point for many of the conflicts in the value system of society. Society's expectations of her, as well as her own, are apt to be confused and contradictory. A woman should work to support herself, rather than become dependent, but a mother should stay home and take care of her children. A woman should help her family in any way possible, but her role in marriage should be that of a dependent and relatively subordinate partner. A woman may work so long as her children are well cared for, but society is not obligated to help her arrange for the day care of her children. A woman alone must be strong enough to take over the paternal role of breadwinner and disciplinarian while maintaining her own role as housekeeper and mother; yet she must remain feminine enough to prevent her children from receiving a distorted conception of the feminine role in social relationships.

Women of low socioeconomic status who are heads of families face additional difficulties. Some have many children whose care leaves them little time for a companionable and educational relationship with them. However, such women are apt to look for gratification from their children in present affection rather than in future achievement.

Such women tend to be interested in broad categories of behavior such as "being good" and "being healthy," but feel helpless about influencing the details of their children's behavior. When there is no father in the home, their tendency to protectiveness, rather than the fostering of development, becomes further exaggerated. Since the home is the source of the woman's satisfaction, the attention once given to the husband may be transferred to the children. The paradox of overprotectiveness and extreme permissiveness often found in the homes of women of low socioeconomic status may be due to the passive attitudes of the mother toward life in general and toward the children's behavior in particular.[12, 13, 14]

Women of low socioeconomic status are not joiners; the world must come to them. Such tendencies toward isolation intensify the loneliness of the female head of the household. A woman without a man is a proverbial fifth wheel in many social activities. Yet a mother who goes out with a man must be extremely circumspect in her activities, particularly if she is a recipient of public aid, or the suitability of her home may be questioned. Even when the social activity is irreproachable, the problem remains of finding a baby sitter she can afford.

In addition, mothers in the AFDC program who are raising their children alone face the same problems confronting any woman in this situation. How can they provide male identification for their children? What priorities must they set upon their time and energies? In short, how does one play two full-time roles concurrently?

The conflicts implicit in the social role of a mother in the AFDC program, and the contradictory and often ambiguous demands society makes upon the woman who is rearing children without a father in the home, are likely to create a paralyzing level of anxiety in the individual. Studies have indicated that persons subject to conflicting forces are likely to react not with "goal-directed activity" but rather with "restlessness, a desire to leave the field, aggressive feelings, toward himself and others and so on." [15]

Such a level of anxiety may become a problem in itself. It may be the source of the tendency to live in the present, and of the pleasure-bent behavior noted by the caseworker in our study. It may prevent clients from making greater use of the resources available to them.

The Practitioner's Problem

The views of the client, the social worker, and the social scientist overlap, although there are differences in emphasis both within and among groups. Nevertheless, all three groups have the same goals for the family in the AFDC program: financial independence and emotional security.

The problem the practitioner faces is to find a way to help the family to achieve these interlocking goals. The clients' complex, interrelated problems cannot be reduced to a simple cause-and-effect formula. All of the major factors seem to be both causes and effects, like the chicken and the egg. However, the circular cause-effect relationship may well mean that changes accomplished by intervention in one area of life will, in turn, affect many other areas. Therefore, the practitioner needs an integrated view of the family, adding to his own observations the perspectives of the client and the social scientist.

With these perspectives, he will find that each family requires a somewhat different rehabilitation plan. He may need to deal with pressing situational factors by helping parents and children secure the clothing, housing, and medical care necessary for maintaining the kind of standard in their daily living under which they can build the self-confidence required to help themselves in other ways. He may need to help parents and children to improve their education and skills by referring them to training or retraining programs or working with school personnel. He may also find need to deal, through referral or directly, with the many psychological factors impeding the family's solution of its problem. Some mothers may require counseling through group-work and casework methods in order to change attitudes and values that are detrimental to themselves or to their children's development. Some may also need help in learning how best to carry out the dual role of mother and family head and in weathering the unusual stresses this entails. Some children may need special help with emotional problems.

This review suggests several foci requiring special attention. One is the problem of psychological passivity, which in so many families in the AFDC program not only inhibits efforts toward solving immediate problems, but also affects the quality of parental control over children and the quality of the self-image internalized by the children. Another is the need for helping families develop techniques of living in a manner acceptable to society and advantageous to the physical health and the well-being of the family, techniques their past experiences have not given them an opportunity to develop. A third is the need for defining the appropriate role for lone parents and for recognizing the structural limitations as well as the psychological elements in the one-parent family.

Effective intervention at the individual or family level requires a framework of appropriate public social policy. It must be adequate to the need and involve a strategy that takes account of the complexity of the problem. Whatever the nature of the problem it attacks—sociological, psychological, or social-psychological—the problem areas are so interrelated that intervention in any one can affect the others if it is planned from an all-encompassing perspective.

The important thing is to build on the family's strengths, for, with the help of appropriate community resources, many families in the AFDC program have succeeded in improving their situation. For example, let us take another look at the Smith family:

> Mrs. Smith gives her children the best physical care possible in her circumstances. Her oldest son is a college graduate and her two older daughters are presently in college. The family is closely knit. When told that he was not obligated to help his half-brothers and sisters, the oldest son said that he paid no attention to that: "They are my brothers and sisters and I will help them as much as I can."
>
> Mrs. Smith has been a member of one of our mothers' groups focused on helping parents maximize the school experience for their children. She has contributed generously to the formation of more useful attitudes on the part of other group members while receiving a good deal of support for her own efforts.

Part  VII

Practice Processes and

Outcomes

Introduction

Some form of direct practice with clients is common to virtually all social services. Although knowledge of the processes and outcomes of direct practice has been difficult to obtain, and existing information is incomplete, such information has been accumulating rapidly in recent years. Practitioners, administrators, and educators in social welfare are increasingly attentive to the results of inquiries into practice, for these results provide knowledge about the intended and unintended effects of practitioner action and thereby provide a factual basis for strengthening practice.

Three studies in this section involve processes related to practice. In the first, Thomas, Polansky, and Kounin report on an inquiry into the expected behavior of a potentially helpful person. What is the potentially helpful person expected to do? And is the expected behavior of so-called warm helpers different from that of so-called cold helpers? These were among the questions that motivated this exploratory experiment. In an analog of a helping relationship, these investigators employed college students who took the role of persons having personal problems. For one group of students, each was asked to assume that he was meeting a helper who was highly motivated to assist him and, in another group, each was to encounter a helper who had low motivation to help. Subjects were then queried specifically concerning the expected behavior of such potential helpers. Differences in the expected behavior were found for the initiation and maintenance of communication, in the sensitivity to and desire to reduce a client's tension in the initial interview, and in the ways in which the interview was structured. Furthermore, attributed willingness to help was positively associated with the subject's willingness to continue the relationship and to be influenced by the helper depicted. The correlates of conceived motivation to help suggest the actual behaviors that practitioners may engage in to achieve such conceptions, and what specific behavior clients with differing conceptions and motivation to help may anticipate of helpers.

In the next selection, Gordon reports on an examination of leading and following therapeutic techniques. Hypnosis was used to establish an analog of a miniature neurosis involving repression of an upsetting event combined with a therapist who was made to resemble the person who initially caused the upsetting event. It was found that there was no difference in the recall of repressed material for the two therapeutic techniques, but leading therapists had subjects who took less time than following helpers to verbalize repressed material. An adverse effect of the therapist's incorrect hypotheses about a client, as these affected his behavior in lifting the repression, was noted. Although therapist technique was unrelated to the amounts of different types of hostility to the therapist, the degree of extrapunitiveness was directly related to the speed of recognition. In discussing the implications of the results, the author emphasizes suggestions for therapeutic theory as well as for the use of hypnosis to create analogs of complex psychological states often found in therapeutic situations.

An important feature of the helping process involves the diagnosis of problems and the various social and psychological characteristics associated with diagnostic judgment. In the next selection, McDermott, Harrison, Schrager, and Wilson report on diagnostic correlates of social class, with special reference to blue-collar families. Using psychiatric evaluations of 263 children in a children's psychiatric hospital, these investigators divided their children into two groups on the basis of whether the father's occupation was skilled or unskilled. Systematic differences were found by diagnostic category for these two groups of patients, and the children whose fathers were unskilled, as compared with those whose fathers were skilled, displayed more malign symptoms, more often came from unstable and conflict-ridden homes, performed more poorly in their academic work at school, and incurred a greater lapse of time before receiving professional help. The many psychological and social differences between these two groups of children indicate clearly that patients in the blue-collar families will display more adverse social and psychiatric profiles. Because the unskilled group more clearly falls into a lower-class category than does the skilled group, the findings of this study are generally consistent with the results of other studies on the relationship between social class and mental illness. And the results of this study, like those of others to which it is related, raise questions about the extent to which the class-related differences are caused by biases of the professional community or by genuine differences attributable to the formative influences of a social-class environment.

The remaining studies in this section report on the outcomes of practice in three different service contexts. In the study by Thomas and McLeod, the results of the research evaluation of in-service training and of reduced workloads in Aid to Dependent Children are reported. In the first of two phases of inquiry, these authors report on an assessment of the training needs of public-assistance workers. The results served to guide the content for the program of in-service training instituted in the second phase of the inquiry. In the second phase, the experimental study proper, in-service training was provided for a sample of public assistance workers who also had their caseloads reduced appreciably. In a control group, workloads were reduced but in-service training was not provided. In the "as is" group, neither training nor reduced workloads was instituted. For all three groups, a before-after design was implemented for the assessment of the possible changes of internal processes and performance of workers. Following the experiment, changes in the areas of self-support and family life were determined for over 1,000 families seen by all of the workers in the various experimental conditions. Among the findings reported are data revealing that, for the workers, training resulted in selected changes in internal processes and in performance as displayed in an experimental interview with an actress portraying a welfare recipient. These changes were selective, however, and there were aspects of internal processes and performance that did not reveal changes in the training group at the termination of the project. The effects of reduced workloads, in contrast to those of training, were restricted to the families, not the behavior of the workers. Specifically, it was found that reduced workloads allowed the workers to have more contacts with their cases, to achieve more rehabilitative closures of cases, and more positive changes in the area of family life and in self-support. The implications of these diverse effects of reduced workloads and of in-service training for welfare policy were discussed by the authors.

Malperformance in the public school is the subject of the next evaluative study, by Vinter and Sarri. As a guide to instituting the services provided, the authors propose an interactional view of deviance in which the malperformance of pupils in the public school is conceived to be a resultant of the interaction of pupil characteristics and of the conditions of the school. Group-work services were provided in five schools and the experimental design included a matched as well as a random control group. On the basis of school grades, behavior ratings of the pupils, and interview data, the authors report preliminary findings on pupil characteristics, school conditions, and the role of the social worker in the public schools. The results generally confirm the authors' viewpoint that more than the characteristics of pupils must be taken into consideration in the efforts of social workers to interrupt deviant careers of school malperformers. Of particular relevance for practice is the discussion of the necessity for social workers to address more fully the social conditions of the school and not to limit their contacts exclusively to the malperforming pupils.

The last report in this section, by Meyer, Borgatta, and Jones, is a summary of an experiment in social work intervention directed toward potential problem girls in high school. With their preventative focus, the diverse casework and group services were oriented toward interrupting potentially deviant careers. In a comparison of nearly 200 girls with a like number of control cases, the authors examined school status, academic performance, school-related behavior, out-of-school behavior, personality changes, selected attitudes, and sociometric data as indicators of change. The use of a large battery of objective indicators combined with random assignment of potential problem girls to experimental and control groups makes this study one of the most methodologically rigorous evaluative studies in social work. The fact that there were no discernible effects of the diverse services provided or, at best, very modest positive effects, recommends this careful study as a most challenging evaluative study.

23 The Expected Behavior

of a Potentially

Helpful Person

Edwin J. Thomas, Norman A. Polansky,

and Jacob Kounin

Introduction

The focus of this study was to explore the specific behaviors of a potentially helpful person which a client associates with motivation to help. The question raised in this study may be stated as follows: Given a conception of the potential helper's (H's) *intensity* of motivation to help as high, what pattern of expected behavior of H is uniformly associated with this conception as compared with a conception that H's intensity of motivation to help is low?

This exploration is intended to provide suggestive leads toward answering two questions: (1) What behaviors of a potentially helping person are used as cues by a client in forming an impression of H's intensity of motivation to help? (2) Beyond this, is the conception of the intensity of motivation to help an organizing factor with reference to other dimensions of the client's cognitive field? We are especially interested in those dimensions that influence a client's decisions about maintaining the helping relationship with a particular helping person.

Method

1. Two sections of students enrolled in elementary sociology classes at Wayne University were the subjects for this study. A total of 56 subjects was involved in both sections—32 subjects in one section and 24 in

From HUMAN RELATIONS, 8 (1955), 165–175. This investigation was supported by a research grant PHS M-544 from the National Institute of Mental Health, U.S. Public Health Service, to The School of Social Work, Wayne University. Reprinted with the permission of the authors and the journal.

the other. Four-fifths of those in both sections were less than twenty years of age; about two-thirds were in their sophomore year of college. The two samples appeared to be quite homogeneous.

2. The experimental manipulation consisted of varying the conception of H's (the potential helper's) intensity of motivation to help C (the client). The conception of high intensity of motivation to help (hereafter abbreviated high M-H) was contained in the following clause of the initial instructions: ". . . *In the course of this you get the definite impression that this person is deeply concerned that you become a happier person in every respect.*" The conception of *low* intensity of motivation to help (hereafter abbreviated low M-H) was substituted for the above clause in the initial instructions: ". . . *In the course of this you get the definite impression that this person is really not very interested in you, and doesn't care whether you feel any better or not.*" One section of 24 subjects received the low M-H induction; the other section of 32 subjects received the high M-H induction.

3. The experiment began with a brief introduction to the subjects, after which hectographed forms were distributed to all in the section. The following instructions, also printed on the upper half on the first page, were read to the group:

> We are interested in the impressions people form of persons whose profession it is to advise, counsel and help others with problems. Put yourself in the situation of having an important personal problem of some nature. You are not able to solve this problem yourself and decide you will have to have help with it. You go to a person who by training, experience, and profession is qualified to help people with this kind of problem.
>
> Now suppose that you have gone to see this person for the first time and have talked about your problem. *In the course of this you get the definite impression that this person is deeply concerned that you become a happier person in every respect.*

(Instead of this italicized clause, the low M-H condition received the second italicized statement given *supra*, section 2.)

The subjects were then presented with ten incomplete sentences relating to their expectations as to what H might do at certain points in the interview situation. The specific incomplete sentences were selected as sufficiently representative of important aspects of the interview for C. The incomplete sentence method was employed because it provided for control over the areas from which the expectations were to be procured, yet allowed for individual variations of response. Each item was to elicit an expectation of *behavior* of H. The subjects were asked to be as specific as possible in completing the following sentences:

1. As I walked into the office, he/she. . . .
2. After I told this person what my problem was, he/she. . . .

3. While talking to this person, I had the feeling that he/she expected me to. . . .

4. When the secretary interrupted to say there was a phone call, he/she. . . .

5. When the person was informed that others were waiting to be seen, he/she. . . .

6. When I got off the point a little to bring in things about my total life situation, he/she. . . .

7. When I blurted out a remark which sounded stupid, he/she. . . .

8. When I had trouble making up my mind, he/she. . . .

9. When I hesitantly suggested something that would cause this person considerable effort, he/she. . . .

10. When I asked a question about the person's family, he/she. . . .

In the next phase the subjects were asked to indicate their attitudes regarding the anticipated willingness of H to do things for them (a validity check). Finally, we asked whether the subject had the same person in mind throughout, whether the person was real or imaginary, to what profession the person belonged, and the nature of the problem that he (the subject) had in mind.

4. The procedure up to this point was designed to provide answers for our questions: What behaviors of H are associated with a client's conception of H's high or low degree of motivation to help and along what dimensions might these be categorized? Following this phase of the questionnaire we attempted to devise some questions pertaining to the second question: Does this conception serve to influence other dimensions of the helping situation as seen by the client?

Here we are interested in what may be regarded as an important consequence of an initial interview: a client's decision about whether or not to maintain the relationship with H. This decision may be seen as consisting of two parts: (a) C's degree of willingness to see H again; and (b) C's willingness to be influenced in some way by this relationship. Having formed a conception of H's intensity of motivation to help in the initial contact, does C use this conception in making a decision about the future, in making a commitment about continuing the relationship and intending to be influenced by it?

In this phase of the study, and following the sentence completions, the subjects were asked to indicate their attitudes regarding: (a) anticipated desire to see H again; and (b) anticipated willingness to be influenced by H.

5. In coding the responses, they were transcribed to individual cards so that neither the experimental treatment nor the context of other responses was known to the coder. Unless specifically mentioned, intercoder reliability on any incomplete sentence may be assumed to be ninety per cent agreement or more on the first or second check with samples of twenty-five responses.

Results

"The Helper"

Over 90 per cent of the students reported having the same person in mind throughout; for over 80 per cent, H was male. A wide variety of helping professions was presented: psychology, social work, psychiatry, educational psychology, ministry, and so on. No one profession received a preponderance of mentions in either the high or low M-H group. Nearly all of the problems involved that category of difficulties which the layman labels "personal." Although a higher proportion in the high M-H group stated that they had a real person in mind, the majority in both groups labelled H imaginary. In a few cases there was specific evidence that this conception involved a composite of recalled and imagined experiences.

The Success of the Manipulation

A difference on the conception of motivation to help should be associated with C's expectations as to the willingness of H to do things for him. Check marks on the latter scale were quantified by measuring the distance from the low end of the scale with a centimeter rule. The mean score for the high M-H group was 12.66; for the low 5.16 ($P<.01$).[1] The high mean falls between the statements: "Would be very willing in general" and "Would be inclined"; the low mean falls between: "It would depend upon the request" and "Would be disinclined." It may be assumed that the conception of H's motivation to help was successfully manipulated.

Patterns of the Expectations

In the results to follow, an attempt will be made to show the patterning of behavioral expectations associated with high and low conceived motivation to help. For brevity, the responses to some of the incomplete sentences will be omitted or briefly summarized.[2]

Expectations Involving Communication

Many of the incomplete sentences involved responses relating to the anticipated ease of communicating with H. By ease of communication is meant the degree to which it is expected that H facilitates or hinders the communication between him and C. Such expectations can be of three kinds: (*a*) that H assigns importance to C's problem; (*b*) that H wishes to maintain or to continue communication; or (*c*) that H makes more areas accessible to communication with H. The incomplete sentences containing responses relating to both types of expectations about the ease of communication will be presented in this section. It will be noted, however, that occasionally some of the responses to these sentences also involve other dimensions. Specific attention will be directed to these particular responses in later sections of the results.

The first group of responses related to communication were those given in response to the following incomplete sentence: "When I told him what my problem was, he/she. . . ." A few typical responses were as follows: "Accepted my problem as important"; "Said that my problem wasn't significant." Fifty-six per cent (17) of those in the high group expected that H would accept the problem as important, as compared with 4 per cent (1) in the low group. On the other hand, 54 per cent (12) in the low group expected H to minimize the problem versus 6 per cent (2) in the high group ($P < .01$). The significant contrast is that H in the high M-H condition was expected to assign importance to C's problem, thus bringing it into the area of communication.

Two incomplete sentences produced responses concerning H's anticipated willingness to maintain communication. The first was, "When the secretary interrupted to say there was a phone call, he/she. . . ." Typical responses here include the following: "Excused himself politely and answered the call briefly"; "Continued the interview and had his secretary take the message"; "Answered the call and talked a long time with his wife." The responses to this item were coded in one of the following two categories: (a) Answers call with indicated interest in C or refuses to interrupt the interview; or (b) Answers call with indicated disinterest in C.

All but one of the 29 subjects in the high M-H condition said H would either refuse the call, or would handle it briefly and with indicated continued interest in C. Twenty of 24 of the subjects in the low M-H group thought H would answer the call with evident disinterest in C ($P < .001$). Although only a few (all in the high group) expected H to refuse the call altogether, the difference in manner of answering was noteworthy. The high group saw H as excusing himself reluctantly, and holding a brief conversation; the low group saw H's alacrity and lengthy conversation as indicating his desire to escape the interview situation.

Responses similar to those above were produced by the following incomplete sentence: "When the person was informed that there were others waiting to be seen he/she . . ." Twenty-six (81 per cent) of the completions in the high M-H group could be classified in terms of the various indications of willingness to maintain communication and of doing it without ambivalence. By contrast, in the low M-H group, 23 (96 per cent) expected H to show cues of wanting to terminate communication, or of being ambivalent about it, by rushing C, by fidgeting, or by other mannerisms indicative of conflict and discomfort ($P < .001$).

The significant trends and contrasts in the responses to both of these questions indicate that the subject expected H to be willing to maintain communication (or to regret not being able to) in the high group and to be reluctant, ambivalent about, or unwilling to maintain communication in the low group.

The next group of responses was more directly related to the extent to which it was expected that different areas of communication were accessible in the interview situation. The first incomplete sentence was "When I asked a question about the person's family, he/she. . . ." Twenty-nine (91 per cent) in the high M-H group anticipated a simple, direct answer; 13 (58 per cent) in the low group expected that H would not answer, or would answer grudgingly ($P<.01$). Thus, personal aspects of a person conceived as highly motivated to help are expected to be more accessible to communication than are those aspects of a person who is conceived as having low motivation to help.

The degree to which H is expected to admit more regions of communication into the interview is seen in the responses to the following incomplete sentence: "When I got off the point a little to bring in things about my total life situation, he/she. . . ." The predominant expectation in the high group (97 per cent) was that H would permit the digression and gradually refocus the interview and thereby, at least temporarily, extend the range of admissible items of communication. On the other hand, abrupt refocusing or impatience was predominantly expected in the low group (45 per cent), indicating an unwillingness on the part of this H to extend this range of communication ($P<.01$).

In summary, where H was conceived as having high motivation to help it was expected that: (a) He would assign importance to C's problem; (b) He would be willing and unambivalent about maintaining communication with C; and (c) He would be willing to admit more areas of communication between him and C.

Expectations Involving Concern about Tension States

There were some responses that either directly or indirectly indicated expectations about H's sensitivity to C's tension states. One incomplete sentence was designed specifically to secure such anticipations. It was as follows: "When I blurted out a remark which sounded stupid, he/she. . . ." Typical responses here would be: "Pointed out that everyone occasionally said such things"; "Told me I had blundered and corrected me." The classification of expectations may be seen in Table 23–1.

In Table 23–1 it can be seen that there was great anticipation in the high group that H would try to minimize the embarrassment ($P<.01$). On the other hand, disapproval of the remark was most often anticipated in the low group ($P<.001$). This significant contrast may be construed as showing that H's actions and intent to reduce C's tension during an initial interview belongs to the pattern of expectations associated with the intensity of a motivation to help.

Table 23-1. Expected Reaction of H to C's "Stupid Remark" [a]

Expectation	HIGH M-H N	HIGH M-H per cent	LOW M-H N	LOW M-H per cent
1. Tried to minimize embarrassment	15	47	2	8
2. Did not react	10	31	4	17
3. Indicated disapproval	2	6	14	58
4. Miscellaneous other	5	16	4	17
Total	32	100	24	100

[a] Inter-coder reliability was 80 per cent agreement on this incomplete sentence.

Expectations about Structuring

The expectations regarding the decision-making process were explored with the following incomplete sentence: "When I had trouble making up my mind, he/she. . . ." Typical responses here were: "Reminds me of the different alternatives that I have"; "Offers suggestions and advice"; "Waits and says nothing"; "Tells me to hurry up and make up my mind." The three types of expected behaviors are given in the categories of Table 23-2.

Table 23-2. Expected Role of H to C's Difficulty in Decision Making

Expectation	HIGH M-H N	HIGH M-H per cent	LOW M-H N	LOW M-H per cent
1. Helps structure situation	23	72	5	21
2. Remains neutral	9	28	8	33
3. Pushes C to decide	0	0	11	46
Total	32	100	24	100

Subjects in the high M-H group (Table 23-2) expected H to participate in the decision-making process by helping to structure the situation significantly more than did those in the low M-H group ($P < .01$). This consisted primarily of directive structuring (e.g., giving advice) and nondirective structuring (e.g., reviewing, restating). Expectations that H would not participate directly in helping to structure the situation were found only in the group of subjects in the low M-H group. Here H was expected to attempt to terminate the interview, to show irritation, or to urge C to hurry and decide. H's participation in resolving decision difficulties and in structuring the situation can then be said to be a part of the pattern of expectations related to the intensity of motivation to help.

The Effects of the Conceptions upon Commitments for the Future

One of the significant consequences of one's conception of H's motivation to help would be whether this had any effect on whether C wanted to see him again. The mean for the high M-H group was 12.51, between the statements: "Would want very much . . ." and "Would prefer to see *this person* again." The low mean (2.47) was between "Would be indifferent whether . . ." and "Would prefer *not* to see *this person* again" ($P<.01$). It can be concluded that the higher the conceived motivation to help the more likely it will be that C will make a decision to commit himself to continue the relationship with H.

Another significant consequence of one's conception of H's motivation to help is C's anticipated willingness to be influenced by H. The mean of the high M-H group was 10.61 and was closest to the statement "Would take advice very seriously." The mean of the low M-H group was 3.93 and was near the statement "Would *not* take advice very seriously" ($P<.01$). On the basis of this difference it may be concluded that the higher the conceived motivation to help the more likely it will be that C will be willing to be influenced in the relationship with H.

We may outline the chain of events as follows: Given a conception of H as highly motivated to help, this conception organizes C's expectations about H in the categories of H's initiation and maintenance of communication with C, H's sensitivity and concern about C's tension during the interview, and H's help in structuring the interview in moments when C has decision difficulties. These are the patterns which may be said to be C's conception of H's intent and commitment to help C. In turn, C uses this conception of H's commitment to help to make his decision about the future of the relationship. In this process, C makes commitments about his own intentions, namely, to continue seeing H and to be willing to be influenced by H.[3]

Summary and Conclusions

This study was a preliminary exploration of the behaviors expected by a client of a potentially helpful person acting in a professional capacity. Subjects given a conception that a potential helper was highly motivated to help them had different expectations of his behavior in an initial interview than did subjects given a conception that a potential helper had low motivation to help.

The evidence of this study suggests that the conception of a potential helper's intensity of motivation to help a client is effective in organizing the client's pattern of behavioral expectations of the helper. We studied three such patterns as they occur in an initial interview. These are:

1. Expectations involving the initiation and maintenance of communication between the client and the helper. The person highly motivated to help the client is expected by the client to do the following, and to do so without signs of ambivalence: (a) Assign importance to the problem the client has, thus bringing it into the area of communication; (b) Show willingness to maintain communication; (c) Show willingness to broaden the range of communications made accessible to both the client and the helper.

2. Expectations involving sensitivity to, and desire to reduce, a client's tension in an initial interview. A helper highly motivated to help is expected to attempt to reduce a client's discomforts in the interview situation.

3. Expectations involving the helper's role in structuring the interview situation. A helper seen as highly motivated to help is expected to engage in attempts to help structure the interview and to help the client overcome decision-making difficulties regarding the progress of the interview.

In addition, the data are further suggestive that two major decisions about, or commitments consequent of, an initial interview are also positively related to a client's conception of a helper's intensity of motivation to help. These are: (a) Commitments by the client about his willingness to continue the relationship; and (b) Commitments by the client about his willingness to be influenced by the helping person. We now hypothesize that these commitments on the part of the client are in part a function of his conception of the helping person's commitment to help him.

While we may conclude that this pattern of behavioral expectations is elicited by an established conception of a potential helper's intensity of motivation to help, we may not, at this time, conclude that the process is reversible: That these behaviors by a helper will result in the formation of this conception and its related consequences by a client.

24 Leading and Following Psychotherapeutic Techniques with Hypnotically Induced Repression and Hostility

Jesse E. Gordon

Psychotherapy research has in general been refractory to experimental methods. A set of procedures is needed by means of which laboratory research into the influence of a variety of patient, therapist, and outcome variables may be conducted. These procedures, however, must be such that results may be generalized to clinical practice. The ecological validity required of such research makes it necessary that subjects be permitted a wide range of responses, as are patients in therapy. Such requirements make experimental control and direct behavioral measurement difficult.

These problems are not so acute when the experimental variables are global ones such as directive vs. nondirective therapy, therapeutic success as defined by various criteria, and patient "maladjustment." However, systematic investigation aimed at building up a body of knowledge regarding therapeutic practices, instead of simply "proving" one school of thought to be superior to another, requires more refined control and manipulation of discrete, unitary variables rather than global ones. When a body of knowledge has been acquired in which the relationships among particular therapeutic practices and specific responses by patients are known, then a therapist may decide what effect he wishes to have on a a particular patient and select his therapeutic techniques accordingly.

From JOURNAL OF ABNORMAL AND SOCIAL PSYCHOLOGY, 54 (1957), 405–410. Reprinted with the permission of the author and the American Psychological Associaton.

Although this state of affairs may be an unattainable goal, it seems to be the only possible ideal at which the scientific therapist can aim.

With these considerations in mind, a set of experimental procedures was developed which seemed to possess ecological validity, which permitted a measure of control over the major client, therapist, and outcome variables, and which permitted the use of direct behavioral measures as well as psychometric methods. The experimental procedures involve the use of hypnosis to make normal subjects believe and act as if they had undergone a standard, mildly upseting experience. The S's have freedom to react to the experience in their own idiosyncratic ways. Reviews by Weitzenhoffer,[1] Hull,[2] and Rapaport[3] present much direct and indirect evidence to support the validity of generalizing from such hypnotically stimulated reactions to reactions actually encountered in clinical patients.

The use of a standard mildly upsetting experience, hypnotically induced, puts control over an important patient variable into the hands of the experimenter. This kind of control is practically and theoretically impossible in field research in psychotherapy. The acquisition of such control by the experimenter represents the major advantage of this type of research over therapy research conducted in the clinic with a patient population.

Instructions to the hypnotized S's were designed to make them believe that they had been bumped into by a physical education teacher in high school and unjustly blamed for the incident. These instructions were patterned after those used successfully by Counts and Mensh.[4] In addition, it was suggested to S that the therapist who was to interview him after he awakened bore some resemblance to the physical education teacher. Posthypnotic amnesia for the upseting experience was also induced. These hypnotic instructions are based on a neurosis model which characterizes neurotically inappropriate behavior as resulting from an unconscious identification of the patient's present situation with an unpleasant and often unremembered experience in the patient's past.

The independent variables of this experiment were therapist's Leading (asking questions, making suggestions, etc.) and the therapist's Following (restating, reflecting, clarifying). These two kinds of therapist verbal behavior were selected for experimental comparison on the basis of investigations which indicate that they reflect a basic split among schools of psychotherapy.[5] Roughly paralleling this split regarding the use of Leading and Following behaviors is a split in what is regarded as the important outcomes of therapy. Those who use Leading techniques tend to regard the lifting of repressions as the aim of therapy. Those who use Following techniques generally disclaim interest in the historical approach to therapy and focus instead on improvement in the patient's present interpersonal functioning as the aim of therapy. It seems appropriate, therefore, to employ measures of both types of outcome variables, repression and interpersonal functioning. The hypnotic instructions to forget the "traumatic" experience produce behavior analogous to repression, making possible the measurement of the lifting of repression. The inclusion in the hypnotic instructions of a suggested similarity between the teacher in the traumatic experience and the therapist provides a situation analogous to transference, and thus makes possible some measurement of the inappropriate, "neurotic" interpersonal behavior of S.

The specific purpose of the present research, then, was to test a set of procedures for the experimental investigation of psychotherapy by applying them to a study of the effects of therapist Leading and therapist Following on hypnotically induced repression and on neurotic interpersonal functioning.

Method

Procedure

Sixty-two male college students volunteered to participate in "an experiment on hypnosis." Two group and then one individual training and screening sessions were held, out of which 26 of the volunteers emerged as susceptible enough to obey a hypnotic suggestion to be amnesic for trance events. Of this group, the data on eight subjects were lost as a result of faulty recordings of the interviews. Thus, 18 S's remained in the two experimental conditions, Leading and Following. The S's were appointed for the individual experimental sessions following the third training and screening session. During this third session they were instructed, while hypnotized, to imagine themselves in a situation in high school in which a physical education teacher accidentally bumped into the S in a hallway, then blamed S for clumsiness and threatened reprisal. The S was instructed not to remember the incident after he was awakened and was told to have a daydream about it upon a signal. This served as a check on the acceptance of the hypnotic suggestions and as practice in covertly playing the role of an unjustly blamed person. Following this test, the graduate student "therapist" to whom S had been assigned was introduced to the subject. The S was then rehypnotized and told that the incident with the physical education teacher had actually occurred. In addition, it was specified that the physical education teacher looked "something like Mr. ——, the man who will be interviewing you soon." The instructions used to induce belief that the incident had actually occurred were those used with success by Erickson.[6] In addition to Erickson's instructions, it was further specified that though S would not be able to recall the experience when he awoke, it would bother him, and he could spend the interview hour trying to figure out what was bothering him. The instructions made it permissible to recall the experience during the course of the interview. Before being awakened, S's were made amnesic for the entire session, including the introduction of the therapist.

The *S* was then awakened and brought into the interview room for a 50-minute interview, which was tape recorded. Following the interview, *S* was again rehypnotized, permitted to recall the content of the previous hypnosis, and disabused of the experience.

The therapists were nine advanced graduate students in clinical psychology at the Pennsylvania State University. Each therapist was in possession of a statement describing the acceptable therapist verbal behaviors in the Leading and Following conditions. These were explained and discussed more fully in a group meeting with the therapists. However, the therapists were not told the nature of the dependent variables or that a paramnesia had been induced in the *S*'s. Each therapist appeared twice, once in each condition, in an effort to control intertherapist differences. The order in which each therapist appeared in the conditions was counterbalanced.

Typescripts were prepared from the tape recordings of the interviews. Therapist statements on all even-numbered typescript pages were categorized by the *E* as Leading, Following, and Miscellaneous as a check upon the extent to which the experimental conditions were realized.

REPRESSION. The content of the experimental "traumatic experience" had been broken down into meaning units, and criteria for scoring recall of the units were prepared. Three independent graduate student judges scored the typescripts, using these criteria to obtain scores for an Amount Recalled measure of the extent to which repression had been lifted. The means of the recall scores assigned by the judges constituted the scores on this variable. Agreement among the judges was high ($r = .94, .98, .93$).

The judges were also asked to indicate the statement in each typescript containing each *S*'s third scorable recall item. By locating these *S* recall statements on the tape recordings, it was possible to record the amount of elapsed time from the beginning of the interview, thus yielding a Recall Time score of the speed with which successful lifting of repression began to occur.

One other measure related to the lifting of repression was designated Recognition Time. To obtain this measure, the judges were asked to check the first *S* statement in each typescript which contained a verbalized awareness that the therapist, or someone like him, was familiar to *S*. Again, by locating the checked *S* statement on the tape recordings, it was possible to measure the elapsed time from the beginning of the interview to the point at which this kind of insight began to develop.

HOSTILITY. Hostility related behavior of the *S*s was measured by means of rankings. Verbal descriptions of three aspects of hostility were given to three graduate students in a course in therapeutic interviewing at the University of Wisconsin, who then ranked the typescripts on each aspect. These hostility variables were (*a*) Extrapunitiveness, in which S attempted to convey his hostility to the interviewer in a direct manner, (*b*) Passive Hostility, in which hostility was expressed through negativism, uncooperativeness during the interview, and general resistance to the therapist, and (*c*) Disguised Hostility, in which S's hostility was communicated in symbolized or other indirect fashion, such as discussion of hostile dreams, overemphasis on aggressive feelings toward others, etc. Coefficients of concordance revealed significant agreement among the judges in their rankings on the first two variables but not on Disguised Hostility, which was therefore not included in further statistical analyses. Each S's rank on the two hostility variables was the mean of the ranks assigned to him by the three judges. Kendall's tau was computed between the rankings on Extrapunitiveness and on Passive Hostility and was found to be nonsignificant. The two indexes were therefore regarded as independent.

Results

The results of the classification of the therapists' verbal behaviors are presented in Table 24–1 in terms of frequencies and proportions.

Repression

AMOUNT RECALLED. Significance testing was in terms of the differences between each therapist's Leading and Following interviews. Six differences showed greater Amount Recalled in the Leading condition with two differences favoring the Following condition and one of zero value. A randomization test of the differences, described by Moses,[7] indicates that this distribution of differences just falls short of significance at the 5 per cent level with a two-tailed test.

RECALL TIME. Analysis of Recall Time was again in terms of the differences between each therapist's Leading and Following interviews. Three differences showed faster recall in the Leading condition; five differences favored the Following condition, and one difference was zero. A randomization test of the differences indicates that this distribution does not depart significantly from chance ($P > .05$).

RECOGNITION TIME. The differences in Recognition Time between each therapist's Leading and Following interviews indicated more rapid recognition in the Leading condition five times, three differences favoring the Following condition, and one difference of zero. A randomization test of the differences indicates that this distribution does not depart significantly from chance ($P > .05$).

The correlation between Amount Recalled and Recall Time was − .78, between Amount Recalled and Recognition Time − .55, and + .50 be-

Table 24–1. Mean Frequency and Proportion of Therapist Leading and Following Statements in the Leading and Following Conditions

Measure	LEADING CONDITION		FOLLOWING CONDITION	
	Leading	Following	Leading	Following
Frequency:				
Mean	26.88	10.22	10.55	27.22
Sigma	12.22	8.48	10.93	13.64
Proportion:				
Mean	.64	.21	.20	.65
Sigma	.21	.16	.14	.19

tween Recall Time and Recognition Time. All three correlations are significant at the .05 level. The very high correlation between Amount Recalled and Recall Time probably represents the extent to which these variables measure S's ability to repress and to conform to the hypnotic suggestions. On this assumption, an analysis of variance of errors of estimate in the regression of Amount Recalled on Recall Time was carried out. In effect, this procedure partialed out intersubject variability in conformity to the hypnotic suggestion. The results of this analysis are presented in Table 24–2.[8]

Table 24–2. Analysis of Variance of Errors of Estimate in the Regression of Amount Recalled on Recall Time

Source	df	Mean Square	F
Between Treatment	1	62.94	12.87 [b]
Among Therapists	8	17.66	3.61 [a]
Residual	8	4.89	
Total	17		

[a] Significant at .05 level.
[b] Significant at .01 level.

Table 24–2 indicates that the errors of estimate in the regression of Amount Recalled on Recall Time were significantly larger in the Following condition when differences among therapists are eliminated from the comparison. It would appear that in the Leading condition, S's tended to verbalize the repressed material more nearly to the limits of their ability to recall, whereas in the Following condition, other variables beyond the basic recall factors entered into the determination of how much recalled material was verbalized, thus producing larger errors of estimate and less verbalized recall. Differences among therapists were also found to be significant, which probably reflects differences in therapeutic skill.

The interviews were divided into those which were the therapists' first interviews and those which were second, and then analyzed in order to test the effect of therapist experience in this sense. Randomization tests of the differences indicate that first interviews produce significantly more recall than second interviews ($P<.05$), but Recall Time and Recognition Time variables were not significantly different from first to second interviews.

All interviews were then combined and ranked in terms of the number of Leading statements, the proportion of Leading statements, and on the three repression variables. Kendall's tau statistic was computed between all pairs of independent and dependent variables. The only relationship found that approximated significance was expressed by a tau coefficient of .31, with an associated probability of .075, between Amount Recalled and proportion of Leading statements.

Hostility

Mann-Whitney U tests indicate that there was no significant tendency for Leading or Following interview S's to be ranked higher on either hostility variable. Chi square was computed between classification of the interviews as above or below the median rank on Extrapunitiveness and their classification in the same terms on Proportion Leading. The value obtained after correction for continuity was 3.56, just short of significance at the .05 level. Similar analyses between Extrapunitiveness and Amount Leading, and between Passive Hostility and Amount and Proportion Leading, yielded definitely nonsignificant results.

The rank order correlation between rankings on Extrapunitiveness and on Recognition Time was .44, which is significant beyond the .05 level. Passive Hostility was not significantly correlated with Recognition Time, and neither of the two hostility variables was found to be significantly related to the other repression variables. The relationship between Extrapunitiveness and Recognition Time would be expected on the basis of the nature of the experimental instructions regarding the similarity between the therapist and the teacher. An S who quickly recognized his interviewer would be expected to be, and was, more hostile toward him than one whose recognition was delayed. One cannot decide, on the basis of these data, whether the recognition led to the hostile expression or vice versa.

As in the analysis of the repression variables, the typescripts were divided into those for the therapists' first interviews and those for their second, and analyzed for any relationships between sequence and hostility. A Mann-Whitney U test yielded a probability of less than .01, indicating that S's were significantly more extrapunitive in the therapists' second interviews than in their first. It will be remembered that there was also significantly less recall in these interviews.

Discussion

The results of this experiment indicate that Leading therapist behaviors tended in the samples used to be more efficient in obtaining as much verbalization of "repressed" material as S was capable of. A review of the typescripts lends support to this interpretation; in the Following interviews one notes several instances in which S's failed to pursue what appeared to be a productive line of thought, ostensibly because of the lack of stimulation from therapist.

The finding that therapists' first interviews were more productive than second interviews, in terms of the amount of recall, appears contrary to what one might expect. Second interviews should have reflected the insights gained by the therapists in their first interviews, and therefore might have been expected to be more productive. A suggested explanation for the findings is that the poorer results in the second interviews arose as a result of generally incorrect hypotheses developed by the therapists on the basis of their experiences in the first interviews. None of the therapists were able correctly to identify the nature of the experiment or the role of hypnosis after the first interview. Considering the many things about which S's spoke in the interviews, it was highly probable that therapists would give undue weight to irrelevant verbalizations in forming hypotheses about the experiment and the S's. This may be a function of the relative lack of experience of the graduate students who served as therapists. If this interpretation is valid, the danger of premature diagnostic hypotheses becomes apparent.

The significantly greater Extrapunitiveness of S's in the therapists' second interviews is of interest. The relationship between Extrapunitiveness and Recognition Time indicates that the hostility is at least in part a product of the experimentally induced negative transference. The data do not permit a clear understanding of the relationship between this negative transference and the serial position of the interviews. It will be recalled that S's in the therapists' second interviews had significantly lower Amount Recalled scores. Possibly the direct hostility in these interviews inhibited the recall, but it appears equally plausible that the unresolved repressions in the second interviews produced tensions in S's expressed as Extrapunitiveness. Neither of these hypotheses was supported by the nonsignificant correlations between Amount Recalled and Extrapunitiveness. However, the experimental design used in the present research provides a method for testing these hypotheses more systematically in the future.

Many of these suggested conclusions stem from inferences drawn from relatively unreliable data. However, the experimental technique employed in the present study has demonstrated its usefulness in studying psychotherapy variables and generating new hypotheses. That these procedures bear striking similarities to clinical practice is demonstrated by the behaviors of the S's, who appeared genuinely anxious about the "repression."

They seemed highly motivated yet natural in their associations, defenses, topics of conversation, etc.

Of incidental interest in reviewing the typescripts are the chains of associations by which S's approached and eventually resolved the repression. These associations were natural, involving the telling of past experiences in the Ss' lives related to the "repressed" incident. For example, one S began the interview by describing his hostility and guilt when, as a small boy, his mother had punished him unjustifiably. She later overheard him expressing his anger toward her to a playmate. The relevance of this memory to the induced experience is obvious. It is interesting that this S eventually recalled most of the induced experience but could not correctly identify the relationship between the therapist and the physical education teacher. However, he did manufacture a plausible though incorrect reason for his feelings toward the therapist and experienced a real sense of relief when he hit upon this "reason." This observation suggests that true insight may not be a necessary prerequisite for relief from anxiety. It is quite possible that reasonable rather than accurate schematizations of experience contribute most to therapeutic effectiveness. Other interesting phenomena encountered in the interviews were dynamic determiners in word choice ("I'm sure we've *bumped into* each other somewhere or other") and the many ways in which hostility toward the therapists was expressed.

Other examples of realism in the interviews are provided by one S who spent the entire interview time "spontaneously" discussing difficulties in controlling frequent and intense anger. Another S experienced much embarrassment in relation to the therapist, whom he eventually discovered reminded him of his high school physical education teacher. He described the teacher as a father figure who disappointed him by not always behaving in the perfect way in which the S idealized him. The specific incident which S finally described as support for his disappointment was the induced one. Thus, there is considerable clinical evidence that the reactions of the S's to the induced experience were idiosyncratic and clinically realistic.

The procedures used here appear to be practicable, and they potentially provide reliable and quantifiable information on a number of important psychotherapeutic issues: the relationships between the lifting of repressions and transference and hostility, the effects of therapist experience, the interaction of therapist and client personalities, the effects of therapist's sex on male and female S's, etc. The procedures in their present form, however, are not without their limitations. The use of hypnotically susceptible S's places an important restriction on the extent to which experimental results may be generalized. The restriction of this kind of study to a single interview with each S makes it difficult to study such procedures as the free association method, which requires fairly extensive training of S. Further, the traumatic neurosis model implied in the experimental design does not take into account the observation that neuroses occur only as a result of many such experiences in persons of particular personality structures.

Finally, there are problems in controlling therapist behavior. It is fundamental to the present study that the independent variable is a unitary, easily defined verbal response of the interviewer. An attempt was made to select for study a verbal response similar to those frequently made during psychotherapy. However, psychotherapy cannot be defined strictly by such limited verbal behaviors. The purpose of the present research was *not* to study psychotherapy; rather it was to provide a framework for studying variables involved in psychotherapy. This is an important distinction, and one which makes it necessary to select meaningful but well-defined variables while controlling as many associated contaminating variables as possible. As long as experimental research is concerned with different kinds of therapy, it will suffer from such problems as those involved in having therapists artificially change their professional styles, difficulties related to the experience of therapists, etc. Such problems may be largely avoided when research is conceived as chiefly concerned with particular classes of verbal response in face-to-face interactions.

These considerations emphasize the apparently essential limitations of experimental research in psychotherapy in that complexity and richness may be sacrificed in order to obtain reliable answers. However, there is still much to be profitably learned about the kinds of variables included within the relatively wide limitations of these experimental procedures. Inasmuch as this method makes possible the reliable measurement of fairly discrete variables, it has value for current investigators. It may be important to find answers for the questions that can be confidently answered at present before going on to find less reliable answers to more difficult questions.

Summary

A set of experimental procedures for use in psychotherapy research was tested. These procedures involved the use of hypnosis for the induction of miniature neuroses in normal individuals. Therapist Leading and Following, operationally defined, were studied for their effects on hostility and on the lifting of repressions in one-hour therapeutic interviews.

The findings indicate that Therapist Leading is more effective than Following for lifting repressions. It was also found that therapist experience which might lead to the formation of incorrect hypotheses about a client has a deleterious effect on the lifting of repression and is also associated with stronger expression of transference hostility by the client. The usefulness and limitations of the experimental procedures in providing possibilities for better control and measurement of psychotherapy variables were emphasized.

25 Social Class and Mental Illness in Children: Observations of Blue-Collar Families

John F. McDermott, Saul I. Harrison,

Jules Schrager, and Paul Wilson

Introduction

In 1919 Freud [1] called attention to the implications of social-class differences when he predicted that it would be more difficult to treat lower-class patients. He felt that they would be less willing to give up their illness to face the hard and unattractive life which awaits them when they recover. Forty years later Hollingshead and Redlich [2] demonstrated that among the adult population of New Haven, Connecticut, there was, in fact, a definite relationship between social class and mental illness. We have come to accept these results and their implications, but the importance of class difference among children may be less easy to accept. Equality among children is a sacred American ideal. The implication that differences do exist and that these differences might possibly influence our attitude toward various groups of children challenges this sacred heritage.

In an attempt to explore the possibility that a relationship between social class and mental illness among children actually might exist we decided to examine the data available from our clinical experience at Children's Psychiatric Hospital over the past several years. A pilot study of these data as reported by Harrison, et al.,[3] found that there was indeed a distinct correlation between the father's occupation and the particular kind of psychiatric diagnosis and dispositional recommendation that we made. Most striking were the contrasts between the extreme ends of the

From AMERICAN JOURNAL OF ORTHOPSYCHIATRY, **35** (1965), 500–508. Copyright, the American Orthopsychiatric Association, Inc. Reproduced by permission.

social scale, for example, between the children of professional persons and those of unskilled laborers. There was, however, one finding that we had not anticipated regarding the children of the blue-collar group.

The blue-collar group was divided into two subgroups: children of skilled workers and those of unskilled workers. One might have expected that these two subgroups, being neighbors on the socioeconomic scale and presumably sharing overlapping cultural factors, would have been highly similar in terms of psychiatric diagnosis. Such was not the case. Our curiosity about the basis for differential diagnosis within the blue-collar group led to a further investigation and the attempted explanation to be described here.

Method

The records of 450 children evaluated at University of Michigan's Children's Psychiatric Hospital during the year July, 1961–July, 1962, were examined. Using the father's occupation as the indicator of social class,[4] 263 of these children were assigned to the blue-collar group. The blue-collar group was then further broken down into the categories of unskilled and skilled. The unskilled group was defined as those who were employed for tasks involving either no training or a very small amount of training, e.g., janitor or assembly-line worker. The skilled category was defined as consisting of those who were employed in a manual activity which required training and experience, e.g., machinist, self-employed small farmer.

One hundred forty-eight children fell into the unskilled group, and the remaining 115 into the skilled group. These two groups were matched for relevant variables (Table 25–1). Code sheets which had been filled out by psychiatrists and social workers at the time of the children's evaluation were then used. These forms were employed to compare the two groups in terms of diagnosis, symptomatology and historical data. Symptoms were assigned to the categories of "benign" or "malignant" as indicated in Figures 25–2 and 25–3. Assignments were based on our observation of the attitudes toward these symptoms prevalent among the mental health workers at our clinic. It is our impression that these attitudes are shared by many, if not all, clinics throughout the country.

Results

The variables listed in Table 25–1 (age, sex and the like) were found to be essentially constant in both groups.

Differences emerged in the diagnostic evaluations of the two groups (Figure 25–1). Most notably personality disorders, including borderline psychoses, were diagnosed significantly more often in the children of the unskilled workers ($x^2 = 3.93$, $df = 1$, $P<.05$). Furthermore there appeared to be a grouping of the symptoms indicated by psychiatrists. These symptoms, although not statistically significant by themselves, suggested a trend when viewed together. Overt hostility, impulsivity, paranoid reactions, affective disturbance and withdrawal were seen to be more characteristic of the unskilled group. Anxiety, obsessive compulsive behavior and somatic complaints were seen to be more characteristic of the "skilled" (Figures 25–2 and 25–3).

Table 25–1. Background Characteristics

Variables	Per cent of Unskilled Group (N = 148)	Per cent of Skilled Group (N = 115)
AGE—UNDER 4 YEARS	3	3
4–6 YEARS	14	15
7–10 YEARS	48	41
11–14 YEARS	35	41
SEX—MALE	70	74
RACE—CAUCASIAN	90	96
NEGRO	10	4
RELIGION—PROTESTANT	68	64
CATHOLIC	23	28
JEWISH	1	1
SIZE OF COMMUNITY (OVER 10,000)	52	47
NUMBER OF SIBLINGS		
NONE	10	10
1–2	44	44
3–4	30	34
WORKING MOTHER (PAST OR PRESENT)	34	30
PHYSICAL HEALTH ALWAYS GOOD	53	55

Children in the unskilled group were characterized by the evaluators as coming from unstable, conflict-ridden homes, in contrast to those of the skilled group ($x^2 = 10.29$, $df = 1$, $P < .005$) (Figure 25–5).

A comparison of the history of the groups pointed up the following factors. Although the families of both groups rated their children alike with respect to adjustment at home, they reported a marked difference in the children's adjustment to the academic standards of the school. The upper end of the rating scale (doing very well at school) was weighted by the skilled group ($x^2 = 5.45$, $df = 1$, $P < .02$) and the lowest (doing very poorly at school, failing grades) by the unskilled ($x^2 = 4.57$, $df = 1$, $P < .05$) (Figure 25–6).

In fact, general school maladjustment more frequently was considered the primary reason for referral to the clinic in the unskilled group ($x^2 = 5.90$, $df = 1$, $P < 0.25$). Home maladjustment was the chief complaint just as as often in both groups (Figure 25–4). Finally, it was found

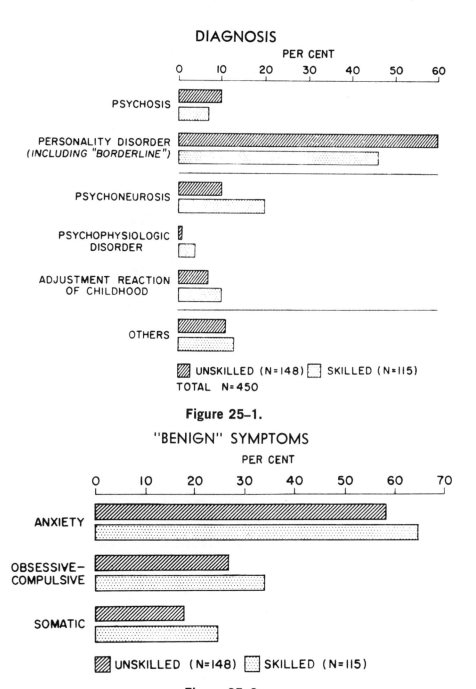

Figure 25–1.

Figure 25–2.

"MALIGNANT" SYMPTOMS

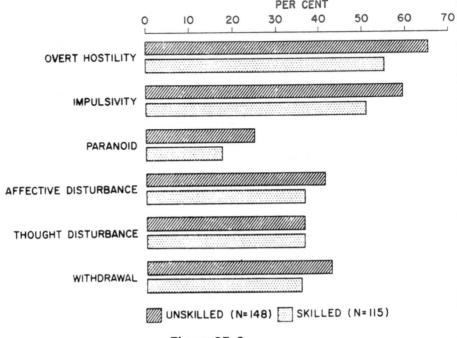

Figure 25–3.

HISTORICAL DATA

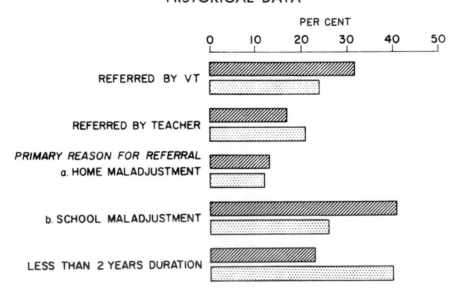

Figure 25–4.

HISTORICAL DATA (cont.)

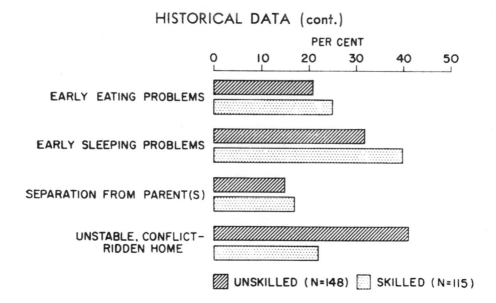

Figure 25–5.

HISTORICAL DATA (cont.)

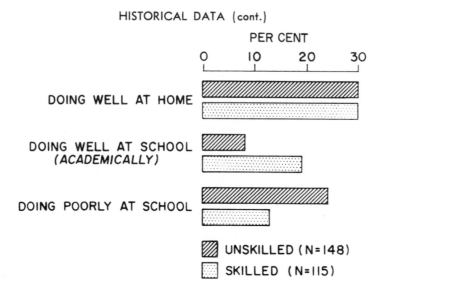

Figure 25–6.

that there was a significantly longer delay in referral of the unskilled group to the clinic from the time that their problems first became apparent ($x^2 = 6.70, df = 1, P < .01$) (Figure 25-4).

Discussion

How are we to account for the differences between the children of unskilled and children of skilled workers? One explanation may lie within the heterogeneity of the blue collar group itself.

In our complex and changing social system traditional class distinctions have become more difficult to identify and follow. Blue-collar workers no longer can be considered a homogeneous group. Hollingshead and Redlich,[5] in their development of an index which employs a five-point social scale were able to place the unskilled workers in one category without much difficulty. But they found that skilled workers spanned at least two positions on the social scale and were much harder to define according to education and residential area. Thus, the traditional blue-collar classification has become blurred, with the skilled worker absorbed into the other classes. Perhaps the change leaves the unskilled worker even more isolated from the main stream of American life.

Although the isolation of the unskilled might account for differences within their offspring, we have yet to speculate about the nature and direction of these differences. Should we conclude that weaker egos and lessened ability to check impulses (the significance often assigned to the diagnosis of personality disturbances and psychoses) actually exist in the unskilled group? If so, why should there be a correlation with the father's work skill?

Knowing the influence of such factors as loss or absence of primary parental figures, we look naturally to the home environment for clues to the development of disturbed object relationships. It often is assumed that the lower the socioeconomic position, the more frequent is disruption of the family unit by desertion, divorce or a generally inconstant makeup. Yet a similar, large majority of children in both of our groups were living with both parents at the time of evaluation. In fact, separation from parent or parents due to all causes including divorce was noted slightly more frequently in the upper, or skilled, group than in the lower group (Figure 25-5). On the other hand, in spite of the apparent intactness of the family units, the evaluators rated almost one-half of the unskilled homes as unstable and conflict-ridden (twice as many as in the skilled group). The subjective nature of this evaluation should be noted. The similarity of sleeping and eating problems also would seem to be inconsistent with psychopathological development of the children of the unskilled group.

What then accounts for our tendency to diagnose acting out disorders more often in the unskilled group? This question has implications, not only in terms of favorability of prognosis, but also in shaping future attitudes of the community and the kinds of help these children will be offered.

We must keep in mind that the assessment of ego strength is partially subjective, depending upon the examiner as well as the patient. Is it possible that those of us who appraise behavior as normal or abnormal unwittingly view the unskilled differently because of our own values? Perhaps what is described as withdrawal, paranoid thinking, hostility and impulsivity is partially the reaction of a child who is uncomfortable in our office. He is in a totally foreign setting equipped with unfamiliar objects such as desks and soft chairs, in which he is expected to talk about his problems or to express himself through toys and games with which he also is unfamiliar because of his background. It has been postulated that lower-class individuals have fewer alternatives available to them in adjusting to stressful situations.[6] There may indeed be cultural differences in the way in which reality is handled that do not reflect analogous degress of individual pathology. A psychological distinction, for example, must be made between a child's ego weakness and feelings of social inferiority, since in either case he might use projection and denial of his inadequacy.

The discomfort of the unskilled in the psychiatric setting would seem to have its counterpart in the school, where all children must meet the standards of the prevailing middle-class culture. It is not surprising then that problems centering around maladjustment in school were given as the primary reason for psychiatric referral 50 per cent more frequently in the unskilled group.

In addition to standards of behavior children react to the academic process itself in various ways. We might presume from the studies of several authors [7] that the lower-class children hear encouragement from their parents, who earnestly express a desire for their children to have the education they missed and who are said to be *more* concerned about their children doing well in school than middle-class parents. They consistently express the hope their children will finish high school to get good jobs, or even to go on to be professional persons (paradoxically, perhaps, often a doctor or a teacher). Yet our findings indicate a sharp difference in scholastic performance between the children of the skilled and those of the unskilled. Twice as many of the skilled group are considered to be performing well or very well academically. Twice as many of the unskilled perform "very poorly or are failing" (Figure 25-6). The discrepancy between the degree of presumed parental encouragement and actual performance may partly result from unconscious parental conflict. A father may claim to want his son to rise above his surroundings and have a better future than he, but is it *really* natural for a father to wish his son to succeed where he has failed, to surpass him as a man, when he himself is insecure in his occupational role, one aspect of manliness? It has been noted that lower-class families place great emphasis on masculinity. Physical force is commonly used by the fathers, and toughness is stressed. Introspection (the opposite of impulsive action), learning, and discussion of feelings and issues may be considered to be weak and unmasculine and may produce tension which cannot be tolerated. In any event, it is probable that educational ambition is a source of inner conflict for both father and son.[8]

And yet despite the greater difficulty of the unskilled in making a good school adjustment, a considerably longer time elapses before professional help is requested for them. (Twice as many unskilled as skilled were seen as having problems two years or longer prior to referral.) It may indicate that difficulties actually are identified by the teacher, or family or both, but early intervention is less likely to occur with children of the lower group. Yet we generally assume that serious problems can be prevented by early identification and early application of corrective measures. This finding also may contribute to the fact that more serious diagnoses are made for the unskilled group when they finally reach the clinic.

In conclusion, it would appear that the professionals of the community *do* view these two groups of children differently both in the psychiatric clinic and in the school. It may be that this actually reflects some degree of psychological difference acquired through life experience, which becomes even more pronounced because of current social forces. Yet there may be factors in us, the community of professionals, which also must be considered.

Summary

Two hundred sixty-three children of blue-collar families evaluated during a one-year period at Children's Psychiatric Hospital were divided into two groups on the basis of their father's occupation, i.e., skilled or unskilled. Historic and psychiatric data collected on these children were analyzed and compared.

The unskilled group was seen as having a significantly higher incidence of diagnosed personality and borderline states. School and home adjustment also were compared for the two groups. Although the home adjustment ratings were comparable within the two groups, the unskilled group was seen as presenting a significantly greater problem in school. Referrals for professional treatment nonetheless were found to be made relatively later for the unskilled.

Speculations concerning the above findings were made with special attention being given to the cultural implications of social class. A suggestion was made that subjective factors such as unwitting social biases within the professional community may be partly responsible for the differences in diagnosis characteristically assigned to the two groups.

26 A Research Evaluation of In-Service Training and of Reduced Workloads in Aid to Dependent Children

Edwin J. Thomas and

Donna L. McLeod

This paper reports some of the findings of a study aimed toward learning more about how to improve services, beyond those involved in determining eligibility for financial assistance, to families receiving aid to dependent children. It became evident in the early phases of the project that there were two promising means of improving services that were well suited to evaluation through research. One was a program of in-service training for workers carrying ADC cases, and the other a reduction of the work assignment in order to allow workers the time that might be needed to help families more adequately.

Training while remaining on the job has been viewed by many as an important way to provide upgrading of the worker's knowledge and skill without requiring a sustained absence from daily activities.[1] The high trust placed in the public assistance worker highlights the significance of maximizing the quality of his efforts. With respect to money alone, each ADC worker in Michigan, for example, has initial responsibility for granting around $100,000 per year if he handles only ADC recipients.

The worker similarly is charged with great responsibilities in matters of social and emotional life. Changes in the composition of caseloads through time suggest the magnitude of these responsibilities. Not only has the number of recipients of ADC been increasing nationally over a

From PUBLIC WELFARE, **16** (1958), 109–13, 132–34. Reprinted with the permission of the authors and the American Public Welfare Association. This study was sponsored by a grant from the legislature of the State of Michigan for research and service in the utilization of human resources. The costs resulting from the reduction of workloads were borne by the Michigan State Department of Social Welfare.

period of many years,[2] the trends disclose that the problems of families are becoming increasingly more difficult. As contrasted with the early 1930's, when widows from previously integrated families were typically the recipients of aid for their children, the recipient of today is beset by many social and emotional problems. More and more the cause of dependency resides in family estrangement, arising from such factors as divorce, separation, and unwed motherhood.[3] In addition to being in poverty, then, today's recipient very often has health problems, emotional disturbances, and lacks occupational skills and outlets for recreation and entertainment. If these problems are to be modified, the social worker must be able to recognize them and to assist families in getting needed aid, in addition to determining eligibility for the payment. For these activities, the worker should be knowledgeable, understanding, and skillful.

The question asked in this study was the degree to which a program of in-service training would better enable the public assistance worker to provide some of these needed services. The provision of services may also be facilitated by the amount of time workers are given to devote to ADC recipients. Indeed, some administrators and workers in public assistance have urged that reduced workloads would allow the worker to aid the ADC recipient in ways that are not now possible. The research was designed also to look into this question. Workloads were reduced not only to learn about their independent effects upon services given to ADC recipients, but also to provide the workers participating in the study with the added time necessary to put into practice what they had learned in the training program.[4]

The research lent itself to an ordered sequence of steps.

1. An assessment of the training needs of ADC workers in the state of Michigan to evolve a sound basis for the training program.

2. The establishment of an experimental program of in-service training for ADC workers. In addition to training, the experiment also involved a reduction of workloads for the workers so that it was possible, considering the entire scheme of the study, to infer the effects of training when workers had reduced workloads as well as the independent effects of reduction of workloads only.

3. An evaluation of the results of the experiment in terms of changes in workers as well as changes in families served by these workers.

Some of the highlights of the study are summarized here; a more complete presentation of the findings is given elsewhere.[5]

Training Needs of ADC Workers

The concept *training* was necessarily viewed quite broadly because of the task faced by the ADC worker. Beyond specific knowledge and skill the ADC worker should, desirably, possess appropriate attitudes, motivation to help people, certain ethical commitments, and an appropriate conception of his job. These serve as guidelines for the practical decisions the ADC worker makes. Training thus implied all of the ways in which an ADC worker might be changed to do a more effective job of helping people.

To infer suggestions about the focus for a training program, information was gathered at this stage of the study from the clients, the supervisors, and the workers. Only the findings for the supervisors and workers will be reviewed here. The method was to administer questionnaires to ADC workers and their supervisors in the large, medium, and small counties in Michigan. A total of 12 county bureaus of social aid participated, with 109 workers and 25 supervisors completing questionnaires. The results from the questionnaires provide a fairly representative picture for the state of Michigan, but there is a slight bias in the sample in the direction of overrepresentation of the larger industrial counties.

Although not delving into questions of eligibility for financial assistance, the questions asked on the questionnaires were designed to measure many things. They inquired into the ideas that workers had of their jobs; into the values, such as the ethical commitment of workers; into the attitudes that workers had, such as how positive or negative they felt about various policies, about the program, and about their supervisors; and into selected matters of knowledge relating to performance in public assistance. Every effort was made when administering the questionnaires to obtain truthful replies. Workers were assured that their response, as given individually, would be kept anonymous, and that what they said would never get into the hands of officials of the State Department of Social Welfare. This promise, of course, has been kept and the findings offered consist of trends in the data based upon statistical averages.

All workers participating in this first step of the study carried some ADC cases, although those in the larger counties often specialized in taking just ADC cases, and not others. The workers were predominantly female, and most of them were married. A majority had worked in public assistance for less than four years and 22 per cent had worked less than one year in this area. Seventy-four per cent stated that they had received college degrees, and of these, 9 percent mentioned that they had specialized in social work.

The results indicate that there were many areas in which the workers could benefit from training. The findings summarized below are a few of the main points:

1. Of all services for which the ADC workers indicated whether or not they could benefit from training, the most highly endorsed one was the area of how to motivate families. Seventy-two percent of the workers and 81 per cent of the supervisors checked this area.

2. ADC workers generally tended to see their jobs more in terms of determination of eligibility for financial assistance than in terms of promoting the social and economic rehabilitation of the families through specific services that could be given to them. For example, when asked about the purpose of their job, the workers were more inclined to indicate that it

was to determine eligibility for financial assistance and to employ various techniques for determining eligibility, than to help the children in the family become better citizens or to work toward some other social value.

3. The ADC workers did not show a high level of acuity in analyzing the problem of recipients. When presented with a test case of a family, the workers, on the average, were able to identify only a small proportion of the family's manifest problems. Moreover, the workers were not particularly adept at formulating rehabilitation plans for these families.

4. ADC workers were not as committed to the ethics of helping people as were those professional social workers who had had postgraduate training in a school of social work. On a test of ethical commitment, it was found that the ADC workers scored lower than their supervisors, and the supervisors earned lower scores than a sample of professionally trained social workers.[6]

5. ADC workers experienced conflict between the requirement of the job that they determine eligibility and the need of some families for time-consuming services. Eighty-one percent of those sampled mentioned experiencing conflict in this way and these, the intensity of the conflict was rated, on the average, as quite strong.

From these findings and many others the important training needs of the workers were inferred. It was apparent that some findings implied more clearly the content for training than did others. The following focus of training emerged after a careful weighing of the results by the training supervisor and the research staff: to motivate and to rehabilitate families in the direction of self support, where appropriate, and in the direction of a stronger family life. To accomplish this task, it was clear that there had to be a focus upon the principles of casework service, upon a knowledge of psychological functioning, upon the critical analysis of difficulties presented by families, upon treatment plans, and upon how to obtain information about the current situation facing the family. The results had shown that the workers could benefit from training in all of these areas.

The Experiment

The second phase of the research was the establishment of a program of in-service training that took place immediately following the assessment phase. There were three groups of workers in the experiment, all of whom participated in the study at the same time. The first was called the *training group* because it included the workers who received the program of in-service training (eight workers, two counties). Workloads were reduced by giving workers only 50 ADC cases, and no others, and by eliminating the necessity that they complete any applications for assistance. The second group was termed the *control group* because the workers did not receive in-service training but had their workloads reduced (seven workers, two counties). Workloads were reduced and made comparable to those in the training group. These workers also carried only ADC caseloads. The third group was termed an *as-is group* because everything remained the same as before. The five workers had an average of 53 ADC cases, 72 old age cases, 5 aid to the disabled cases, and 2 aid to the blind cases and, in addition, carried the normal flow of applications. One logically important group left out of the study was one having in-service training but no reduction of workloads. It was omitted because resources were not available to include it.[7] The experiment began in February, 1957, and ended in the middle of May, 1957, a period of three and one-half months.

Precautions were taken to see that the workers participating in all counties were sufficiently similar so that individual differences would not account for the results of the experiment. The available information shows that the workers in the groups of the experiment did not differ greatly. Hence, the essential difference between groups appeared to be what was introduced in them, not what the workers were like in the first place.

The content of the training program was planned and formulated by the training supervisor of the study in consultation with the research staff. The main themes of content in it were (1) The interpersonal relationship between the ADC worker and the recipient as a medium by which recipient change is brought about; (2) Matters relating to the worker's understanding of the families, such as psychological functioning, the current situation faced by the recipient, and analysis and identification of problems; and (3) Approaches and techniques to motivate individuals toward appropriate and attainable goals and the process of developing and evaluating treatment plans. During the training period the training supervisor met with the eight workers for four hours per week. The determination of eligibility on cases was left in the hands of the regular case supervisor of the workers and the training program, in turn, was conducted entirely by the training supervisor. The case supervisors were briefed throughout, as appropriate, about the material being covered with the workers. The measurement required for evaluation was left entirely in the hands of the researchers.

Effectiveness of In-Service Training and of Reduced Workloads

At the outset it is well to recognize that training is a complex phenomenon to evaluate. Workers are exposed to many experiences from within and without the program over a relatively long period of time. A consequent problem posed for the researcher is that he cannot be sure of exactly what ways the workers should be expected to change to show that the program was effective. In view of this uncertainty the approach used in the study was to obtain measures on more characteristics, as possible indications of effectiveness, than would have been necessary if the training program had been a simple clear-cut experience. The measures of possible effectiveness were of three types: those of internal processes, of performance, and changes in the families seen by the workers.

First consider some of the changes in internal processes as inferred from the worker's responses on questionnaires given before and after the project. The workers who had received the program of training were found to improve in analytic skill as evidenced in improved identification of problems in cases [8] and in motivation to help recipients. These factors were not found to be influenced by reduced workloads. However, there were areas in which training as well as reduced workloads were found to have no effect on the workers, but will not be stressed here because the reasons for failure to achieve a result are numerous and complex. Among the areas not showing change were knowledge as measured by the objective tests employed,[9] and commitment to the ethics of professional social work as measured by a validated test developed in the study.

The second general way that workers may change, or be modified, as a result of an experience in training is in their performance. A sample of the way a worker performed with a recipient was taken at the end of the experiment by the procedure of conducting what was called an experimental interview. In it the ADC worker had an interview with an actress who played, in a planful way, the part of a recipient. The actress, in fact, played her part so that everything she did was controlled and predictable because she was following a memorized script. The experimental interview, which was described to the worker as a role play, lasted twenty minutes for each worker, and was recorded on tape. The results were derived from an analysis of these tapes.[10]

The findings show that the workers who had received training more often took advantage appropriately of opportunities in the interview to reassure the client than did those workers who had not received training. A second way that training seemed to modify the performance of the workers was in what was called diagnostic acuity. Results revealed that those workers who had received training more often than those who had not had what was judged to be correct insights into the dynamics of the behavior of the recipient. In contrast to in-service training, reduced workloads were not found to be associated with either of these types of changes. Some areas in which workers in all groups of the experiment performed about equally well were in attempting to get and in obtaining information, and in skill to interview.

The changes in the families contacted by the workers were perhaps some of the more intriguing findings of the study. Information was obtained for 1,139 families who were seen by the 20 workers participating in the experiment by having the worker record on a special schedule for each family all the problems and the changes observed for members during the course of the project. The two broad areas were family life and self-support, each having numerous subcategories for recording that were defined quite explicitly. Since the workers were told that the purpose of recording was to obtain an accurate tabulation of the problems and changes for ADC recipients, they were not aware that the information was to be used also to evaluate their performance with recipients. A special check proved this conclusion to be correct.

Only a few of the findings relating to families can be presented. Details of analysis must necessarily be omitted.

The number of contacts between the worker and recipient was found to vary, as expected, with the size of the work assignment. The average number of contacts in the *as-is group* was .67 and in the other two groups approximately 2.00 per case. Reduced workloads thus clearly enabled the workers to have more frequent contacts with the recipients. It was found, however, that the increased case activity had no influence upon the proportion of cases closed, which in all groups of the experiment was approximately the same—a little over 10.

This result is deceiving, however, because it was found that some reasons for closure suggested a rehabilitative outcome for the families whereas others did not. Among the reasons for closing suggesting a rehabilitative outcome were the employment of the homemaker and support from an absent father. Among the reasons for closure classed as nonrehabilitative were unsuitability of the home and refusal to comply with regulations. Workers who had reduced workloads, regardless of whether they also received training, closed approximately two times as many cases for reasons classed as rehabilitative as for reasons classed as non-rehabilitative. In contrast, the closures of the *as-is group* were predominantly for reasons classed as nonrehabilitative. These and related findings suggested that the added time the workers were given to do their work resulted in productive rehabilitative efforts with families.

Now for the changes in families brought about during the period of the project. In the area of family life the percentage of families in which there was at least one positive change for a member and in which this change was inferred to be due to the efforts of the worker, was calculated; it was 16 in the *training group,* 11 in the *control group,* and 1 in the *as-is group.* Some areas of positive change for the *training group* were housing, housekeeping, patterns of conduct, and a sense of personal worth. Since reduced workloads was the factor common in the training and control group it appears that this is responsible in large measure for the positive changes observed in families. The measure of self-support of the recipients included instances of changes leading to an increased potential of self-support as well as those of actual self-support. Of positive changes in this area, the per cent was 6 in the *training group,* 7 in the *control group,* and 1 in the *as-is group.*

Implications

What do the findings suggest about in-service training in public assistance? They show clearly that without it the workers do not improve in any aspect of skill or ability. One recalls that neither in the *control group* nor in the *as-is group* did there appear to be any indications of improvement or change in the workers. The selected upgrading of the workers that was observed was confined exclusively to those who had received in-service training.

A natural query at this point is to wonder just how successful the training was. It is not easy to say. Generalizations must be limited to what has been learned about this program and ones similar to it. Generalizations are limited also by what the positive findings tell us because the negative ones tell us so very little. This point merits elaboration. It was found, for example, that training did not improve scores on the test of ethical commitment. Failure to find change here could have been due to any of the following possibilities: a lack of emphasis upon this type of content in training, some shortcoming of the test itself, or the difficulty of changing ethical orientations of persons.

One must be similarly cautious about interpreting the rather modest changes in families that were associated with in-service training. Failure to find greater effects of in-service training for families may have been due to the relatively short period of the training program, the relatively brief period of time allowed for families to show changes, or the relatively small number of contacts which were had with the majority of the families.

More is learned about how successful the training program was from the positive results because there are fewer possibilities for them to be invalid. Two of these findings deserve special emphasis. The remarkable improvement in analytic skill resulting from training needs highlighting because it was just this skill that was found in the assessment phase to be so badly in need of improvement. Workers were aided during training to improve this skill by discussions and exercises aimed toward the development of more precise thinking about the kinds of problems of families. It appears, in short, that a training program like the one employed in this study can enable public assistance workers to identify more accurately the problems of recipients.

The other finding of note is the high rate of appropriate reassurance given by the workers who had received the training. Past research suggests that appropriate reassurance is important in the casework interview because it facilitates the movement or change of the client in the desired direction.[11] Results from this study not presented here support this supposition. Since reassurance was not taught directly as a technique in the training program, it is probable that the high frequency of reassurance in the training group indicates that the quality of the treatment relationship of these workers improved as a result of training. There was unquestionably an emphasis in the training program upon the significance of the quality of the helping relationship between the worker and the recipient. One interpretation of these findings, therefore, is that a program of in-service training that stresses the quality of the helping relationship is likely to enable the workers to facilitate the movement of families receiving assistance.

What do the findings tell us about the effects of reduced workloads in public assistance? Although the reduction of workloads did not improve the skill or ability of the workers, it probably allowed workers to do, with the skill and knowledge they had, what they already knew should be done. Interviews with the workers not reported here revealed that the increased time freed workers to perform numerous activities that could not otherwise be performed. One recalls that reduced workloads were found to be associated with positive changes of families in both self-support and in family living. Thus it appears that the time given to workers by reducing their work assignment allows them to approach a more optimal use of their existing capacities and resources.

27 Malperformance in the Public School: A Group-Work Approach

Robert D. Vinter and Rosemary C. Sarri

A variety of approaches are being undertaken to resolve certain problems within the public school and to enhance educational attainments. These problems include the tendency of some youth to drop out before graduation from high school, underachievement and academic failure among pupils believed to be intellectually capable, and misconduct that disrupts classroom procedures and school discipline. This paper will describe the development of group services as one approach to such problems and will report preliminary findings from a systematic assessment of this approach.

The work reported here has involved innovations in group-work practice, in conceptions of pupil problems, and in adapting research designs to a comparative framework. Because of these complexities it is necessary to review study formulations and procedures before presenting the findings now available. The study is in its third and final year; although much data analysis remains to be done, the general direction of outcomes is already clear.

Let us begin by outlining the conception of pupil malperformance—and of its sources—used in this study. First, it is known that standards for academic achievement and for desirable conduct vary among schools, and even within the same school. These variations mean that such types of

From SOCIAL WORK, **10** No. 1 (Jan. 1965), 3–13. Reprinted with the permission of the authors and the National Association of Social Workers. Principal support for this research has been provided by a curriculum development grant from the Office of Juvenile Delinquency and Youth Development, U.S. Department of Health, Education, and Welfare in cooperation with the President's Committee on Juvenile Delinquency and Youth Crime, and by a research grant from the National Institute of Mental Health, United States Public Health Service.

malperformance as underachievement, classroom misconduct, and failure to adjust are not identically defined, since different standards and judgments are used from one school to the next, and to some extent among teachers in the same school. The aspects of pupil personality, performance, or ability presumably at issue in one situation are not the same, therefore, as those relevant in another.

Second, there are many differences among schools in terms of their curricula, resources, teacher competencies, student bodies, and school organization. These variations produce wide differences in pupil learning environments, in opportunities for achievement or adjustment, and in conditions that shape the meaning of the school experience.

Third, there are significant differences among schools with regard to their procedures for identifying and coping with pupil malperformance. Thus, in one school youngsters manifesting difficulty may become the targets for a full complement of facilitating services. In another school, however, youngsters exhibiting similar difficulty may encounter relative indifference; when attention is given, it may result in loss of status and privileges for such pupils, perhaps leading eventually to their exclusion from classes and even suspension from the school.

It is proposed here that malperformance patterns should be viewed as *resultants of the interaction of both pupil characteristics and school conditions.* Specific conditions of the school may interact with attributes of the student population to enhance or impede educational achievement. Indeed, certain aspects of school organization and practice may contribute, inadvertently and unwittingly, to the very problems they are designed to alleviate. Certain aspects of this issue will be discussed subsequently, but here it is sufficient to assert that, because of variations among schools, pupils at the same level of ability and performance have quite different experiences, depending on which schools they attend. The import of these variations is that any type of malperformance must be considered not as a unitary phenomenon, or as inhering primarily in the attributes of the pupils, but rather as a resultant of the interaction between school and pupil.

This general conception of malperformance leads us to view pupil difficulties as *social* in several important respects. They are manifested within the social context of the school through interaction with other pupils, with teachers, and with the academic tasks of the curriculum. These patterns assume major relevance as they are judged in terms of the social values and objectives of school personnel. Such problems have their origins in and are currently influenced by pupils' social relations and experiences in the school and elsewhere. Thus, once a pupil has been identified as an underachiever or as disruptive, this social recognition may significantly affect his public identity, his self-image, and his motivation to achieve. Such identification, furthermore, has important implications for how the pupil is subsequently dealt with by the school, for how his school career is shaped, and, ultimately, for his life chances.

In a sense there is nothing especially novel about these conceptions. School social workers have long recognized—certainly at the level of direct experience—that schools are dissimilar, and that some of Johnny's lack of success may be due to certain classroom teaching practices. Nevertheless, there has not been an explicit analysis of the essential ways in which schools and pupils interact. This study has attempted to assess both the characteristics of the pupils and the patterns of the schools that are associated with malperformance problems. There has been an attempt, furthermore, to develop means for modifying the latter as well as the former through school social work services.

Research Design and Procedures

Five public school systems have been included in all phases of this research.[1] Group work practitioners were assigned in each, as an integral component of school social work services, to assist malperforming pupils at the junior and senior high school grade levels, with elementary grade pupils also served in two systems. Pupils were identified and referred in all these schools for underachievement or disruptive behavior; the introduction of group services did not alter schools' criteria for referral. Detailed information was collected about each pupil, providing a basis both for study of pupil change and for comparisons between schools. An attempt was made to systematize the selection of pupils receiving group service by use of standardized referral procedures for teachers, examination of school records, and observation of pupil behavior within the school setting. Youngsters were screened out whom school staff judged as retarded, needing intensive psychiatric treatment, or so handicapped they could not participate with their peers.

A control-group design was utilized in the five school systems to assess the effectiveness of the group-service strategy. Referred pupils were carefully matched in pairs with respect to several characteristics; one of each pair was then randomly assigned to the service groups, and the other became a control who received whatever attention was customary within each school *except* the group service. Another sample was randomly selected from the rest of the student population at the same grade levels. The design of this study called for the use of a series of before-and-after measures, and comparisons between treatment groups and both matched and random control groups. The use of two control samples permits the study of outcomes that can be directly attributed to the group work service rather than to pupil maturation or factors of chance. Also, the design allows for attitudinal and behavioral comparisons at single points in time between malperforming pupils and a sample of the rest of the student population. During 1963–1964 approximately 400 pupils in the service, matched control, and random groups were thus closely observed in the five school systems. A smaller number of pupils from fewer schools were included in the research during the 1962–1963 academic year.

Several sets of before-and-after measures were used. (1) School grades, attendance records, and similar official school information provided one important basis for assessment of pupil change. (2) Teachers and other school personnel completed a behavioral rating form on pupils in all samples early in the school year and again at the end of the year. This standardized form elicited observational information about classroom performance and behavioral patterns, and was validated for use as a sensitive indicator of change. (3) Pupils completed questionnaires and were interviewed with respect to their attitudes, self-images, commitment to educational objectives, school experiences, peer relations, and so forth. All the above types of information had additional use in providing knowledge of the characteristics of malperforming pupils and of different school modes for identifying and responding to problem behavior.

These before-and-after measures of pupils served as the primary means for evaluating changes effected by group services. Means for assessing the *processes* of change included systematic review of practitioners' reports and service records, independent interviewing of treatment groups, and direct consultation with service personnel. To provide the necessary basis for comparability, services to groups were quasicontrolled through preparation of a practitioner's manual and regular group conferences with the research team.[2]

School patterns and practices were assessed through direct observation, interviewing of school administrators and teaching personnel, review of documents and file materials, and questionnaires administered to all school staff. These procedures permit measurement of operational differences among schools with reference to the ways in which school conditions affect pupil malperformance problems. Of particular interest have been the kinds of pupils and problem behaviors produced by each school's system for identifying malperformers. Through a series of group conferences with practitioners and another with school administrators there has been joint review of study procedures and preliminary findings. These have afforded opportunities to explore the meaning of results and of their implications for policy and service.

Group-Work Service

We turn now to a consideration of the group-work services provided in the five school systems. In each school pupils were routinely identified and referred for special services. As indicated, certain youngsters were screened out at this point. Each prospective member of a group was interviewed by the worker to review his school difficulties, to explain why he had been selected for this service and what would happen in the group, and to establish an initial contract for work together on his specific problems. Groups were typically composed of five to eight members and were homogeneous with respect to sex and grade level. Under the guidance of professional workers group sessions were conducted regularly during school hours and in school buildings. These group sessions were the primary means by which change was attempted, although individual service to the same pupils was provided as necessary and by the same professionals.

Within the groups there was explicit public recognition of each pupil's school difficulties and mutual assistance in resolving these. Group discussions and activities were focused on actual problems manifested in the school. Emphasis was placed on mobilizing pupil desire to change toward improved achievement and appropriate conduct. Pupils were helped to develop new skills and alternative methods for coping more effectively with certain stressful school experiences.

There were several primary targets of change through this group work approach: pupil values and goals, self-images, motivations and expectations, social interaction skills, and specific academic abilities. Pupil *values and goals* may be at odds with those of the school, especially as achievement goals become reduced because of past failure and difficulty. *Self-images* are often more negative than desirable, with loss of confidence in ability to achieve academically or to interact appropriately within the school. *Means and opportunities* for successful performance may be insufficiently perceived or known among such pupils, increasing their pessimism and reducing their chances for success. Indeed, opportunities for these students may actually be more limited than is either equitable or desirable. This problem requires intervention *on behalf of* the pupils with other school personnel, as well as work within the groups. Such students typically lack certain *social skills* essential for achievement and for adequate interaction with fellow pupils, teachers, and other school personnel. Lastly, these pupils are, of course, deficient in certain *academic skills*, some of which can be effectively improved within the group (e.g., study habits, efficient use of time, test preparation).

Groups were involved in a variety of activities, depending on the particular service goals set for them, the interests and characteristics of the members, and the development and movement of each group.

Problem-focused discussion predominated, but all groups also engaged in other activities to enhance pupils' learning and change. Study habits, test preparation, how to request assistance from teachers, how to obtain help from classmates, and how to carry out assignments were among the matters discussed and about which groups provided mutual assistance to each other. Group sessions sometimes included in-school creative or recreational activities, outside trips to use selected community facilities, and so on.

Although pupils tended to perceive the groups as pleasurable and rewarding, they were continuously aware of the serious purposes of this experience and its relevance to school performance. In part this was accomplished by encouraging them to report incidents and difficulties they were currently experiencing in the school—and for most participants there is no want of opportunities for such reports. The worker then involved the group in joint exploration of the situation, in consideration of the actual cause-and-effect sequence, and in discovery of more appropriate responses the pupil might have made. Because all pupils had witnessed or been involved in similar incidents, they were effective in curbing each other's tendencies toward denial or projection, and in proposing alternative ways for coping with situations. Sometimes group members used role-playing to recreate their stressful encounters and to test out different response patterns. At other times workers engaged groups in review of their grades and other indices of academic performance, with discussion of the barriers to achievement, and training in methods these pupils could use to improve their course work. These suggest some of the means by which the group sessions were directly related to school concerns and served as vehicles for problem-solving that benefited all participants.

One of the special advantages of working with such pupils in groups is that the powerful forces of peer pressure and judgment can be harnessed in the service of desired change, rather than covertly supporting deviance. The researchers noted, as have many others, that pupils identified as under-achieving or disruptive tended to seek each other out and to form associations that reinforced deviancy. A boy in one of the groups explained it in these words:

> It depends on who you hang around with. Some guys' idea of fun is to see who gets the lowest grades, skipping school, classes, smoking in the bathroom. I started hanging around with guys like that. . . . The only reason me or anyone else did things like skip school was to make an impression on your friends. They'd think you're chicken otherwise. I feel if you can't get good grades, then brag about getting away with it.

These findings make it clear that malperforming pupils have at least as many friends as do other pupils, and that they tend to associate with those experiencing similar difficulties more than other students do. These friends are not the strongest supporters of achievement standards, but such friend-ships are highly valued—perhaps for compensatory reasons. These peer influences, which may support either achievement or malperformance among pupils, are largely ignored by other types of special services and individualized methods.

The progress of each pupil in the groups was assessed several times during the school year to determine whether service should be continued, modified, or terminated, but most pupils were served for two semesters. School grades, attendance records, disciplinary reports, and conferences with classroom teachers provided the primary bases for practitioners' assessment of pupil change—or lack of change.

Group work supplements but does not exclude use of other, more traditional services to implement educational objectives. This approach is conceived as an integral phase of school social work services, and must be

supported by school personnel and closely coordinated with their activities. Group workers maintained frequent contact with classroom
teachers, advisers and counselors, and administrative personnel. They con-
ferred and consulted regularly about specific pupils, shared views on
individuals' behavior and progress, and exchanged information about
current developments. Much of the practitioners' efforts through these
contacts was to modify perceptions and practices toward malperforming
pupils on the part of school personnel.

Although several more months will be required to complete the study,
the nature of the conclusions has already clearly emerged. This statement
is neither inclusive nor final, and subsequent reports will present detailed
empirical materials. Findings of three kinds will be reviewed briefly,
having to do with pupil characteristics, school practices and conditions,
and practitioner roles.

Preliminary Findings: Pupil Characteristics

Intensive study of the referred pupils provides new understanding
of those who are identified as presenting malperformance problems. Although it seems widely believed that underachievement and misconduct
are generally alike among schools, study findings indicate that these behavior patterns are, in fact, shaped by the distinctive organization and
practices of each school. Thus, each school's particular system produced
somewhat different kinds of pupils and problem behaviors. There was a
congruence between the kinds and proportions of identified problems and
the dominant goal orientations of school personnel. When developmental
rather than academic goals were emphasized among teachers, for example,
pupils were more often referred for reasons of misconduct than for
underachievement.

Despite these variations among schools, certain commonalities became
apparent and achieved statistical significance. Most malperforming pupils
fell within the average range of innate capability. They had the intellectual
resources to achieve satisfactorily, but the large majority were performing well below their capabilities. Most were also manifesting serious behavioral problems, including disruptive conduct in the classroom or in
other school areas, poor interpersonal relations with adults and peers,
violation of school norms, or withdrawn and isolated behaviors. Nevertheless, these students were as highly committed to long-term educational
and community goals as were other pupils.

The malperformers were less committed, however, to short-term
academic tasks and behavioral norms. They appeared to lack effective work
and study habits—although they seemed to spend as much time on their
studies as other pupils did, they reported that they were unable to complete assignments or use their study time efficiently. They did not reject
the school or the system, but believed they were rejected by the school.
(Parenthetically it should be noted that many school personnel have been

surprised at some of these findings. Malperformers are often regarded as lacking in motivation and commitment to the school and to their learning tasks. Evidence derived from this study shows that most of these students do, in fact, possess sufficient motivation but lack the necessary means and skills to succeed.)

They were doubtful about their prospects for the future and pessimistic about their chances to change their reputations and to achieve. This pessimism about themselves and their future seemed especially important. It was accompanied by a frank and realistic recognition of their misconduct or inadequate performance. They knew they were not doing well, they doubted that they could do much better, and they seemed unable to take the steps necessary to succeed or conform. At the same time, these pupils believed they had poor reputations among teachers—as indeed they had—and suspected that teachers therefore tended to minimize some of their actual accomplishments. These pupils' negative but more or less accurate appraisal of their current situations and fateful predictions for the future seemed to account for much of the reduction in their investment in educational tasks and in their efforts to improve.

One tenth-grade student described his pessimism in these terms:

I don't want to drop out of school. I want to get a good job. I dropped out for a time in the fall—just didn't care. I wasn't getting good grades in the ninth grade. I figured since I wasn't getting good grades then, it wouldn't change so I just didn't care.

This is, of course, the classic frustration response, in which continued failure to achieve desired goals results in withdrawal, resignation, alienation, and may eventually lead to relinquishment of the goals themselves. In work with these pupils there was heavy reliance on the persistence of their commitment to conventional values—including achievement and success—and on their keen desire to reduce the adverse consequences of being regarded and handled as malperformers. Stimulating motivation to develop and use the abilities they actually possessed was emphasized. At least as important, however, was the creation or opening of opportunities for successful performance within the school. Only by finding ways to achieve, even in limited areas, could anticipations of continued failure be disrupted. Experiences within the group sessions offered some opportunities for success, together with supportive encouragement from others in the group, and the development of additional skills and tools for classroom accomplishment. The crucial condition, however, was the extent to which these pupils could also find opportunities for achievement in the classrooms and other phases of school activities, and could be appropriately rewarded for improved performance. The ways in which school practices and conditions may limit these opportunities was a focus of attention in this study.

Preliminary Findings: School Conditions

The writers have asserted that it is the *interaction* between certain aspects of the school and characteristics of the pupils that probably accounts for the observed difficulties. To clarify this relation, three features of the school will be considered: sanctioning procedures, record systems, and teacher perspectives.

Sanctioning Procedures

In addition to offering rewards and recognition to pupils for acceptable conduct or achievement, teaching personnel use a variety of negative sanctions to curb malperformance. Grades are, of course, the chief means for doing both: higher than passing grades reward exemplary performance, while lower than passing grades represent a net loss to the pupil. In the short run poor grades serve as negative judgments, and in the long run they curtail pupils' future opportunities. It was observed that students were frequently exposed to a kind of double—or even triple—penalty. Those who performed below a certain standard received adverse grades and might *also* be denied, as a direct consequence, a wide variety of privileges and opportunities within the school. They lost esteem among their classmates, they were seldom chosen for minor but prestigeful classroom or school assignments, and they were excluded from participation in certain extracurricular activities. This process, in turn, often subjected such pupils to negative parental responses, representing a third penalty.

The linking of secondary rewards and sanctions to grades may result in far more than reinforcement of academic criteria, since it denies the poor performer legitimate *alternative* opportunities for recognition and success. His motivation to continue trying and his commitment to educational objectives is thereby jeopardized at the very time when additional supports may be needed to stimulate effort. In these situations the underachieving pupil receives little support for his efforts to improve, as continued failure subjects him to new deprivations.

Record Systems

Schools' extensive files on students were found to be most detailed and reliable with respect to grades and other academic performance information. These files tended to be deficient or highly variable with respect to other kinds of facts, such as family characteristics, agency contacts, and so on. Whatever their differences, however, school record systems appeared alike in the retention of information that documented malperformance. Disciplinary actions, contacts with parents about critical situations, notice of probationary status, suspensions, and class absences were among the kinds of facts most often recorded in student files. These files followed students from grade to grade and from school to school.

The collection and retention of such information, together with grade records, appears to present a number of difficulties. First, it is much easier for pupils to acquire negative than positive formal reputations since, except for grades and at the upper high school level, good events are less often recorded (e.g., special classroom duties). Second, it is hard for the pupil to live down his past, especially when he moves upward to another school, since the record follows him and is examined there by teaching personnel. Third, there are few ways to certify in the record—except for an unusual improvement in grades—that particular pupils are no longer malperforming or having difficulties. Serious question must be raised about the emphasis on early identification when for so many youngsters it results not in service, but in the assignment of negative reputations that cannot easily be surmounted, even if subsequent behavior is acceptable.

Pupils were very much aware of these peculiarities of school file systems and of informal communication among staff that supplemented and extended the official record. They suspected that they were judged to some extent in terms of their reputations *apart* from the objective facts of their current performance. They felt burdened with their negative histories and overwhelmed with the likelihood that they had to do far better than simply behave themselves in order to cancel out the past. They became frustrated, finally, with the ambiguous means for clearly establishing that they were *now* conforming or making modest gains, since the evidence of this was less dramatic than that of being in trouble.

Interviews with pupils who were having difficulty illustrated their belief that past events would shape future chances:

> When you get in trouble, they never let up on you. They keep calling you in. Like you get caught for smoking and they suspend you. Then they watch out for you so they can catch you again.

> I have a bad reputation here. Last year in junior high I gave teachers a lot of trouble and I guess the record follows everywhere I go. Teachers here (in high school) have the record. They have to find out about all the kids.

Teacher Perspectives

Interviews with teachers early in this research suggested two aspects of pupil behavior that were of particular concern and that should become foci in group work service. Subsequent findings from teacher questionnaires and from their ratings of pupils have underscored the importance of these issues. On the one hand, teachers regarded pupil motivation toward academic achievement as crucial to either success or failure. They perceived malperforming students as being uncommitted to educational objectives, as lacking incentive to study, and as not trying to learn. These views provided the rationale for the double penalty system, since secondary rewards and sanctions were believed necessary to mobilize pupil concern. Because of these perceptions it has been difficult for school personnel to accept study findings that reveal relatively high levels of commitment and aspiration among malperformers, and that indicate the problem may be more one of means and skills than of deficient motivation. It is possible that student awareness of teachers' skepticism contributes to the pessimism and frustration evidenced among malperformers.

On the other hand, teachers showed much concern about maintaining desirable conditions within the classroom and effective control over their students. They shared an understandable belief that misconduct and disruptive behavior jeopardized the necessary learning climate and their own management of the classroom situation. Many, but not all, malperforming students were perceived as challenging teachers' authority and in some schools teachers were much more concerned about this problem than in others. Information from pupils manifesting difficulties and intensive work within the service groups indicated that most of these youngsters were deficient in the social skills needed for positive relations within the classroom. They did not know how to ask for help, how to accept constructive criticism, or how to withdraw from spiraling conflict situations. Partly because of their self-doubt and their suspicion that they were being singled out by teachers, they tended to misinterpret situations and could tolerate little stress. The escalation of minor incidents into major crises was to be expected, given these orientations among teachers and students.

Even though all these findings were not available to the practitioners, most of them focused their group sessions on resolving problem situations in the classroom. Had the results of the teacher questionnaire been fully anticipated it is likely that even greater emphasis would have been placed on helping pupils make manifest their positive attitudes, and on development of social skills relevant to the classroom and to pupil-teacher interaction. This would have been especially important in those schools where teacher perceptions and expectations were of most significance to malperformers. Impressive gains were achieved, nevertheless, as indicated by teachers' ratings of pupils before and after group work service. Those in the service groups, as compared to their matched controls, showed significant improvement in most areas of performance. Improvement was generally judged to be greatest in the areas of classroom conduct and academic motivation and performance.[3]

Preliminary Findings: Roles of Social Workers in Schools

The conception of malperformance as a resultant of interaction between school conditions and pupil characteristics had certain other implications for this study. It argued for attention to the ways in which special services (including social work) were oriented toward the particular circumstances of each school. It also impelled study of social work roles as these might be simultaneously addressed to changing features of school operation as well as attributes of malperforming pupils. The group-work practitioners were the main but not the only helping persons observed in these terms within the five school systems.

Social workers and certain other special service personnel were found to be engaged in several types of activities. Some tended to concentrate on one area of effort, while others concentrated on different areas. These variations in task patterns appeared related to the skills and preferences of individual professionals, to the specific definitions of the social worker role within schools, and to other features of each school's staff and organization. Although analysis of these variations is still incomplete, the preliminary findings are of interest.

Four major types of activities were undertaken by social workers in the schools. *Direct work* with pupils was obviously an important area of effort, involving service contacts with students singly and in groups. In some schools pupils worked with were primarily those whose behavior was disruptive of classroom management, sometimes they were pupils performing far below known abilities, or in other schools they were pupils manifesting both kinds of malperformance. *Mediation* with teachers and other school personnel was another important phase of activity, when staff contacts were focused on specific pupils in difficulty. Such mediation could take the form of information exchange, joint planning about how to handle individuals, or attempts to modify teacher practices on behalf of certain pupils. Social workers in the schools also served as *consultants* to teaching personnel, when attention was directed not so much at specific individuals as at improvement of classroom patterns, modification of teacher perceptions, or changes in school policy and procedure. Next, effort in some situations was devoted to *negotiating* with families and agencies in the community. The primary aim was usually to resolve a particular situation by helping the family or by obtaining agency resources for a pupil or his family. The intent was occasionally more general, such as participation in community planning for troubled children, attempts to change community practices, and the like. In the latter case, the professional served as a kind of lobbyist on behalf of such youngsters and services for them.

Most social workers in the schools engaged in each of these activities at one time or another, but among different schools there seemed to be definite patterns by which certain efforts were emphasized and others were minimized. It is apparent that social workers in schools might concentrate on working directly with pupils, working with teachers and other personnel within the school, or working with families and agencies outside the school. Whether social workers were assigned to more than one school appeared to be a significant determinant of their roles. Those who spent part time in several schools were less likely to be used to handle daily crises, while they also had less time for continuous contact with teaching personnel in each school.

Apart from direct work with the service groups there was no attempt to achieve uniformity in role patterns among the social workers who cooperated in this study. However, these service role differences are being taken into account in tracing out those patterns associated with improvement among pupils. The researchers' initial belief that school practices and conditions are a significant factor in malperformance has been buttressed by study findings. The implications of this view for the design of effective school social work patterns are worthy of note.

It appears essential that social work practitioners must address themselves more fully to the conditions of the school, and not limit their efforts to contacts with pupils. Unless the practitioner has intimate knowledge of teachers and their practices, classroom climates, and general school conditions, he cannot understand the particular circumstances that contribute to each pupil's problem situation. Unless there is close contact with other school personnel, the social worker cannot foster those opportunities for success and achievement here suggested as necessary for positive change. The pupil's motivation to learn and to conform that may not appear in the classroom becomes known to the practitioner and must be communicated to teachers. Lastly, and perhaps most important, when positive change does occur, in one area or another, and even in limited degree, the social worker must certify this improvement to teaching personnel. Because of the unintended negative bias of the official record system, the pupil–social worker–teacher informational channel is of central importance. Attempts to help malperforming pupils by treating them in isolation or as though abstracted from the context of school circumstances must be viewed with extreme skepticism. As has been indicated, group work offers a special opportunity to guide the informal peer influences that appear as another potent aspect of the school environment.

Because of their close acquaintance with malperforming pupils, and their knowledge of the conditions that impinge on these pupils, social workers in schools occupy a strategic location. They have the opportunity to assist teachers and administrators in identifying those school practices and arrangements that inadvertently contribute to malperformance, and that curtail learning and adjustment. As has been discussed, some of these problem conditions are integral to each school's system for identifying and coping with pupil deviance. If the social worker concentrates his energies mainly on helping *some* pupils accommodate to the school, he can do little to ameliorate the patterns that will continue to generate difficulties for many *other* students. If he addresses himself primarily to attributes of the pupil (or his family situation) which seem to be contributing to malperformance, the effectiveness of his helping efforts will be greatly reduced. It seems important, therefore, that the social worker retain dual perspectives, and attempt to resolve problem *situations* or *processes:* both pupils and school conditions should be targets of his interventive activity. He must find ways of serving specific individuals while simultaneously dealing with the sources of pupil difficulties within the school.

28 An Experiment in Prevention through Social Work Intervention

Henry J. Meyer, Edgar F. Borgatta,

and Wyatt C. Jones

Introduction

This report describes a portion of a study of the consequences of providing social work services to high school girls whose record of earlier performance and behavior at school revealed them to be potentially deviant. Over the course of four years girls with potential problems who entered a vocational high school in New York City were identified from information available to the school. From this pool of students a random sample of cases was referred to an agency where they were offered casework or group counseling services by professional social workers. A control group was also selected at random from the same pool of potential problem cases in order that a comparison could be made between girls who received service and similar girls who did not. Since all these girls were identified as potential problem cases, they may be considered latent or early detected deviants. Services to them consisted of efforts to interrupt deviant careers.

Youth Consultation Service (the agency in which this research was located) is a nonsectarian, voluntary social agency, in New York City, that has specialized in offering services to adolescent girls through a highly trained staff of caseworkers and group therapists for more than fifty years. The characteristic problems that bring troubled girls between the ages of 12 and 25 to YCS are out-of-wedlock pregnancy, school behavior prob-

Abridged and adapted from the authors' GIRLS AT VOCATIONAL HIGH: AN EXPERIMENT IN SOCIAL WORK INTERVENTION (New York: Russell Sage Foundation, 1965). Reprinted with the permission of the authors and the Russell Sage Foundation. Funds to support the research were provided by the Russell Sage Foundation and, to expand the services of the agency, by the Grant Foundation.

lems, chronic truancy, unmanageability at home, "immoral conduct," incorrigibility, and "runaway." At the time this research was undertaken, the agency served approximately 200 clients each year, of whom about two-fifths were unmarried mothers.

The major service offered to clients is casework, but since about 1952 the agency has developed a supplementary group-therapy program and has pioneered in group methods of treatment for unmarried mothers and adolescent girls with other behavior problems. In addition to the regular complement of psychiatric consultants, group-therapy consultants have been provided.

The research arose from a problem the agency had been concerned with for some time, namely, how to serve effectively the adolescent girl with types of problems that got her into difficulties at school and elsewhere. Previous experience had led the social workers to believe that intervention earlier than they had heretofore been able to achieve with similar clients might facilitate the establishment of meaningful treatment relationships that would, hopefully, decrease the likelihood of serious difficulties later. It was recognized that a preventive effort would present novel issues: general rather than specific presenting problems, uncertainty about and diversity of treatment objectives, the need for special efforts to involve girls who were not yet in severe difficulties, development of ways of working with the school that was the referral source, and uncertainty about criteria of effectiveness. But it seemed to attempt a preventive effort and to investigate its effects carefully.

The Research Design

The basic plan of the research was a simple experimental design requiring random assignment of adolescent girls with potential problems (1) as clients of Youth Consultation Service to constitute an experimental sample, that is, to receive treatment, and (2) as members of a group of control cases, with no treatment provided by YCS. The comparison of these two groups of cases after the former was exposed to the services of the agency will constitute a test of the effects of that service, since in other respects the two groups may be assumed to begin equally and to differ in experiences only to the extent that the control cases have not had the services of YCS. It is to be noted that these are assumptions and therefore require some empirical examination if they are to be accepted with confidence.

In order to check these assumptions, as well as to provide information additional to the experimental test, it was arranged that the total school population from which experimental and control cases were chosen would be tested prior to random assignment, and again periodically throughout the study, so that equivalence could be examined and change differentials noted. Similarly, it was arranged that the total school population, as well as the experimental and control cases, would be observed at a determinate follow-up point according to criteria that reflected a range of objectives contemplated by YCS in its services to the experimental sample.

Through additional procedures, including clearance with the Social Service Exchange and direct inquiry from both experimental and control subjects, an effort would be made to estimate whether YCS service did, in fact, constitute the primary variation in experience of the two groups of cases, or whether, for example, similar or comparable services might have been provided elsewhere for the control cases. In the strictest sense, therefore, the experimental test was not one of provision of service vs. withholding of service, but rather the known provision of service vs. unknown experiences excluding these specific services. This is a severe test of the impact of such services. But it is also a powerful one and the sort of question that is, in effect, asked of social agencies: "Have your services benefited clients more than no services or services provided on a casual and haphazard basis?"

Implementation of the Research Design

Selection of Experimental and Control Cases

The cooperating school—here called Vocational High—agreed with the agency that the girls selected for referral would be encouraged to accept the help of Youth Consultation Service and that the necessary home permission for the girls to go to the agency would be sought by the school in cooperation with YCS. Vocational High also agreed that the girls selected could fit into their school-day schedules the required appointments with caseworkers at the agency and (as group procedures developed) the scheduled group meetings. The school also accepted the condition that the project would continue through four years in order that the requisite numbers could be referred and observed throughout their high school years, normally the time between entrance and graduation from the school (tenth, eleventh, and twelfth grades).

It was established practice at Vocational High to review each entering student's prior record to assess academic preparation and plan programs, and also to identify problems that might require special planning by the school. The social workers at YCS and the researchers concurred that these records could be used to note aspects of the student's school behavior, personal characteristics, and home situation indicative of possible future difficulties. In this way an inclusive pool of girls with potential problems was identified from which referral and control cases could be designated. This procedure was relatively superficial but it represented the use of kinds of information the agency would have accepted as warranting referral for at least further diagnostic study. When subsequently asked, "Do you feel this client was really in need of treatment when she was referred?", the social workers answered "not at all or slightly" for only

6 per cent of the cases referred to YCS; 36 per cent were rated "somewhat or quite a bit" in need of treatment, and 58 per cent were judged to need treatment "to a considerable extent or very much."

The records of four entering cohorts of girls at Vocational High were screened and potential problem cases identified for each. Only those entering in the fall term were included in order to provide as long a time for treatment as possible. Approximately one-fourth of each cohort was included in the potential problem cases and from this pool a random procedure was used to select those to be referred to YCS, the number depending on the capacity of the agency to accept additions to its caseload. At the same time, and by the same random procedure, the control group was selected from the potential problem cases. Over the course of four years, 189 referrals and 192 control cases were selected and included in the experimental and control samples.

Referral from the School

When YCS indicated that it could accept a number of clients for the project, the names of those selected were drawn from the pool and given both to the school guidance department and to the agency. Neither the school nor the agency was given the names of other girls who had been selected as control cases, and they were not informed of the students who constituted the rest of the potential problem cases.

The girls selected for referral had to be approached with an explanation of the program and invited to accept help from YCS. They had to obtain parental permission to leave the school premises during school hours and arrange appointments with the agency within their school schedules. In addition, they had to be given some rationale for this unusual attention directed toward them. Furthermore, in keeping with the design of the research, the entire entering class of girls, including the potential problem cases, was given a series of tests and asked to fill out questionnaires so that uniform information would be available to describe the experimental and control samples.

The specific act of referral was handled in various ways by the Guidance Department. In general, it consisted in telling the girls individually that they had been selected because the school thought that they deserved the opportunity to have the extra assistance that YCS could give them with problems high school girls usually have. They were told that such opportunity was available only to a few of the students and they were encouraged to take advantage of it. There is little doubt that the warm and friendly interest of the administrative assistant in charge of guidance was a factor in conveying a positive attitude toward referral even if, as the caseworkers subsequently reported, some girls were uncertain and confused about the basis of their selection and expressed the fear that they were thought "crazy" or otherwise invidiously identified. The school's interest was emphasized by its willingness to permit the girls to go to YCS on school time and this, also, undoubtedly entered into the success with which referral was achieved. Whatever doubts the referred girls entertained, they did, for the most part, voluntarily accept the invitation and subsequently make contact with the agency. Of the 189 girls who were designated for referral, only 3 per cent failed to have at least one service contact with a social worker at YCS in addition to the interview in which the girl was invited. The median number of casework interviews or group counseling sessions that the total experimental group had with YCS workers was 16. Approximately 25 per cent of the girls had 36 or more scheduled treatment contacts, 50 per cent had between 7 and 35 contacts, and 25 per cent had 6 or fewer contacts.

Acceptance at the Agency

Just as the school had no choice, under the design of the project, with respect to which students among those in the pool of girls with potential problems it could refer to YCS, so, too, the agency relinquished its freedom to decide by its own criteria which of these girls it wished to accept and endeavor to treat. This restriction was accepted to protect the validity of the experimental results from unknown selective processes that would affect the equivalence of the experimental and control cases. In the interest of the preventive goal of the project, it is also to be noted that the agency thereby accepted clients without the overt presenting problems customary for its intake, which is a novel situation for a voluntary social agency. However, this constituted not only a challenge but a fruitful professional experience.

Although the agency agreed that the pool of potential problem cases consisted of the kinds of girls they wanted to try to help through preventive intervention, the requirement of arbitrary referral and acceptance created an experimental population that could be expected to differ in unknown ways from the usual clientele of the agency. One might speculate that Vocational High students were less motivated to accept help than clients who came entirely on their own initiative. However, adolescent girls were often seen by YCS under conditions not likely to encourage positive motivation. Despite the acute difficulties they often were experiencing, few of the usual clients were self-referrals; they were frequently brought in by parents or sent by schools, community agencies, or professional persons. They often had attitudes resistant or even hostile to adult help. When it had facilities, YCS attempted to work with such clients as long as it was deemed possible and useful. With project clients, the social workers were obligated to attempt service persistently and hence may have continued to see some girls they felt unable to benefit. Like other clients, Vocational High referrals were free to discontinue contact when they wished but the agency, on its part, undertook to see the girls as long as they were willing to come and considered in need of treatment.

Many of the arbitrary referrals from Vocational High might not have

been as visibly in need of help as some of the usual clients of YCS. However, as previously indicated, the preventive objective of the project
accepted this as the major question to examine: could help before problems
were clearly visible prevent them from developing? It was not the effectiveness of the agency with its usual clients that was in question, therefore,
but rather the effectiveness of its special effort with a determinate clientele
in an experimental project.

Research Data Obtained for the Study

With the focus of the research on evaluation of effectiveness by
comparing referred and control samples, data on criteria of success and
change were required.

For experimental and control cases alike, information was obtained
about school performance and behavior. Did the student finish school or
drop out? Was she ever suspended or expelled from school? Was she truant
from school? Did she pursue the vocational training program provided for
her? Was her attendance at school good or poor? Was her school conduct
satisfactory or unsatisfactory? Did she receive honors, awards, and good
ratings for school service? Did teachers regard her as outstanding or as
presenting a serious problem to them?

Some out-of-school behavior also is indicative of getting into trouble,
but this was more difficult to obtain without resources for an extended
field follow-up. Out-of-wedlock pregnancy, however, was one event that
became known to the school and represented unsatisfactory behavior, and
it was included among the criteria. Also, getting into trouble with police
or becoming known through delinquent acts was a relevant negative behavioral criterion, and an effort was made to obtain information about this
for experimental and control cases through use of the Social Service Exchange, in which contact with juvenile authorities as well as social agencies
is recorded. In general, it might be expected that out-of-school serious
trouble for a girl would result in her removal from school or impairment
of her school record, so that school continuity was considered a reflection,
at least in part, of the out-of-school situation.

It may be asked whether such objective criteria of appropriate adolescent behavior can be expected to reflect the type of treatment offered by
an agency such as YCS. From one viewpoint, the agency is not directing
its primary effort to achieving school continuity and good behavior, but
rather is seeking to achieve optimal functioning, healthy personalities,
satisfactory interpersonal relations, and the like. Therefore, a number of
clinical criteria of success were included.

Two direct measures of personality change were used, the Junior Personality Quiz [1] and the Make A Sentence Test.[2] The JPQ is a questionnaire containing items that have been selected through factor analysis to
reflect twelve personality dimensions. This personality test was expressly
developed for use with young adolescents between twelve and sixteen

years of age. Its dimensions have meaningful relationship in content to the more fully developed 16 Personality Factor Test that has been widely used in studies of adult personality.

An alternative method of reflecting personality was sought. It appeared that the sentence-completion form had more advantages and fewer liabilities than other projective tests. Responses to sentence-completion test items are capable of content analysis by standardized techniques, and such surface interpretation of content appears to be an important part of even the more subtle uses of projective tests. Other projective test approaches —the TAT and Rorschach, for example—appeared too demanding of language ability for group administration and prohibitive in individual administration. Therefore, the MAST was adopted after considerble developmental work. The scoring categories have been used reliably and have been shown to be correlated with apparently similar dimensions as measured by a number of objective personality tests.[3]

It may be argued that the type of treatment to which the adolescent girls referred to YCS were exposed cannot be expected to affect fundamental personality characteristics such as those presumably measured by these tests. Persons may not change basically from limited contact with social workers. This may very well be true but it is an open question and one on which light may be shed by examining these measures. Plausible differences to be expected from so-called healthier, more normal, less disturbed, better functioning persons may readily be hypothesized in terms of the categories of these tests. Therefore, they may suggest differences between treated and control cases that are in directions accepted as indicative of successful treatment.

A more superficial but nevertheless, clinically meaningful level of change for successfully treated girls might be expected. Therefore, a number of questionnaires were administered that sought to reflect general feelings the girls might have about themselves and their problems, their sense of the dynamics of behavior and the value of getting help from others, and their outlook for the future.

Another behavioral measure was used that might possibly have some relationship to changes induced by treatment and hence become available as an interpretable criterion of successful preventive treatment. This was a general sociometric questionnaire asking the student to list classmates who are "friends of yours, whom you pal around with." Several alternative hypotheses bearing on successful treatment experience might be investigated with such sociometric data. First, it might be hypothesized that casework treatment might reduce perception of social isolation at school or increase gregariousness. Second, it might be hypothesized that the healthier girls would be more often chosen than those with more manifest problems. Third, the hypothesis might be proposed that composition of the friendship circle might change, for successfully treated girls, toward greater association with those showing positive rather than negative characteristics. Thus, successfully influenced clients might be expected to have fewer "bad associates." In particular, changes through the years in the type of choices made and received might reflect trends in positive or negative directions that could be indicative of beneficial influence from YCS.

Validity of the Experimental Assumptions

Data were analyzed on social and family background characteristics of the total population of high school girls involved in the study, on some of their attitudes, and on their measured personality characteristics, in order to test the assumptions that experimental and control samples were initially equivalent and that both—constituting the pool of potential problem cases—differed from the remaining girls in their cohorts, the residual cases. Differences observed between potential problem cases and residual cases were generally in keeping with the intention of the project to identify for treatment a group of girls for whom future school and personal difficulties could be anticipated. It is clear that this intention was achieved, and it is to be noted that potential problem girls dropped out of school in greater proportion than their peers who were not so identified.

The data also indicate that the random procedure for selecting experimental and control cases among the potential problem population resulted in generally similar groups on which to examine effectiveness of social work intervention.

Treatment Experiences

The primary data for observations and judgments about the character of treatment experiences are the case records of the workers and the group records of the therapists. These individual and group records were reviewed regularly by the supervisors and served as the basis for periodic discussions with the appropriate consultants. The reports of these consultations were also incorporated into the permanent records of each case and group. In preparing summaries of this material for research purposes, a supervisor and the director of casework read the complete records of all individual cases. The senior group therapist and the group-therapy consultant read all of the group records. Each of these readers prepared an extensive analysis of the cases involved.

Individual Treatment

Insofar as the experimental setting would permit, the 53 cases referred for individual treatment in the first phase of the project were handled within the framework of the agency's normal intake processes. When these were not effective in reaching a girl, more intensive efforts were directed toward making contact with her and finding some way to involve her in the agency's program. In six of these cases, such efforts were of no avail and the girls were not seen at all. When the caseload was reviewed by the director of casework, a little more than half of the girls who were seen, twenty-seven, were not considered to be involved in treatment to any appreciable degree. The other twenty girls were judged by their caseworkers to have been treated significantly.

The 27 cases considered not appreciably involved in treatment were seen from 1 to 19 times by the caseworkers, but little or no progress was reported toward motivating the clients to use the agency's services constructively. Three of the girls were seen once, 1 was seen twice, 4 were seen 3 times, and 4 were seen 4 times. In contrast to these 12 short-term cases, 11 girls had from 5 to 8 interviews and 4 girls had from 11 to 19 individual sessions.

The other 20 cases referred for individual treatment were judged by the caseworkers to have been sufficiently involved in the relationship for it to have had some significant effect upon them. The number of interviews with these clients ranged from 1 client who was seen only 5 times, 15 who were seen from 10 to 15 times, and 4 who were seen from 60 to 90 times. The average for this group was about 35 interviews. This figure is approximately 1 per week for a school year of 9 months.

From Group to Casework Treatment

In the later years of the project, girls were referred from groups to the casework department for individual treatment when the group therapist and consultant thought this might be the preferred treatment technique, when there were special or unusual problems requiring individual attention and handling, or in order to clear the case for official closing by the agency for whatever reason. In the course of the project, 72 cases were so referred.

Group Treatment

The decision to try large unselected observation groups as a referral technique was made in the spring of 1957 when one group was activated. Four others were activated early in the next fall term and continued through the school year. With a change in group-therapy consultants, the entire group treatment program was reevaluated the following year and the decision was made to continue working with general discussion groups which, however, should be smaller in size—composed of 7 or 8 members instead of 13 as in earlier groups. The girls already in the program and the new referrals coming from the short-term orientation groups were reassigned to one or another of the specialized treatment groups designed to meet their particular needs.

In contrast with similar girls in individual casework, the girls in these groups were seen by the social workers as less tense and apprehensive and better able to ventilate their feelings, whether hostile or not, about unhappy and depressing facts in their lives. Whenever they did so, they seemed to gain reassurance by noting that others had similar problems. Each week a different girl emerged, presenting her own particular problems, and most of the girls in the group could relate to the material.

Although these first groups were large and unselective, the staff felt that a certain kind of constructive change occurred among the girls. The staff felt, however, that in unstructured groups of that size, many girls who might benefit from more deliberately structured group therapy could not be reached in a meaningful way. An attempt was made to meet this situation by developing new principles for the formation of groups. The new groups consisted of fewer members and an attempt was made to be selective about their composition.

The new series of small, selective groups was introduced by reassigning girls from the earlier unselective groups and adding new members from the current orientation screening groups that were subsequently formed for all new referrals. During the remaining part of the project, 13 selective groups, averaging seven members each, were formed. These consisted of five Observation Groups, two Family Life Education Groups, three Interview Treatment Groups, two Protective Groups, and one Activity Group. All of these were not in existence at one time, and many of the girls were in more than one group. Generally, girls who were placed first in the Activity Group were later put in other groups or referred for individual treatment.

In the most general terms, the group program tried to help adolescent girls who face crises "to add significantly to their repertoire of reality-based problem-solving techniques and thus improve their crisis-coping capacity for the future." [4]

Objective Criteria of Effects

The experimental and control cases were, as intended, essentially alike at the beginning of the experimental project. This was to be expected from the random procedure of assigning potential problem cases to experimental and control groups. The potential problem group itself (including both experimental and control cases) differed from the remaining girls in their school classes (residual cases) in the "negative" ways one would expect from the deliberate selection of potential problem girls to constitute the pool from which experimental and control cases were chosen. For example, a significantly smaller proportion of potential problems than of residual cases remained throughout the three high school years. We may be reasonably confident therefore, that the therapeutic program for experimental cases among the potential problem group was offered to girls who were less promising, girls who were, for the most part, "in need of treatment," as the social workers saw them. Almost all of the girls (95 per cent) received some treatment services, and half of these had 17 or more treatment contacts with social workers. The experimental cases as a group were clearly well exposed to the therapeutic program. In short, the experimental cases consisted of high school girls more likely to get into trouble, recognized by social workers as needing treatment, and actually receiving treatment.

Measures of effect are provided by the periodic testing procedures at the end of each school year and by the collection of terminal data about each potential problem case three school years after entrance into high school or as of a cutoff date in the summer of 1960. Four cohorts were subject to the experimental program, beginning with the cohort entering in September, 1955. Therefore, the normal threee-year period of the high school had elapsed for the first three of the cohorts by the terminal date in 1960. For the fourth cohort, only two years had elapsed. In the analysis of effects, where criteria are appropriately applied only to cases with the longer time span (for example, graduation from high school), the first three cohorts taken together will be examined. This group of cases had the longest exposure to the therapeutic program. Where lapse of time is less relevant (school grades or behavior ratings), the fourth cohort will be included and the total potential problem sample examined. For all cohorts the random selection procedure resulted in equivalent duration of time for experimental and control cases when measures of effect were taken.

The samples used in the analysis may be summarized as follows:

Table 28–1. Amount of Elapsed Time from School Entrance, for Experimental and Control Cases

Elapsed Time from School Entrance to Terminal Date	Experimental Cases	Control Cases	Total Cases
Cohorts with three years elapsed time	129	132	261
Cohorts with two years elapsed time	60	60	120
All cohorts	189	192	381

Completion of School

SCHOOL STATUS AT THE END OF THE PROJECT. Identical proportions of all experimental and control cases had graduated from high school by the termination of the project: 29 per cent of each. Equal proportions had left school without graduation or were in school, either in their normal grades or below normal grade. Success—in the sense of graduation or achieving normally expected grade—was the school status of 53 per cent of both experimental and control cases, and lack of success—in the sense of dropping out of school or being behind normal grade in school—was the school status of 47 per cent. [For purposes of brevity, where the text is relatively explicit, tables have been selectively omitted.—Editor's note.]

When only those girls are considered who could be observed over three full school years, 48 per cent of both the experimental and the control cases had graduated or were in normal grade. By way of contrast, 65 per cent of the residual cases who could have graduated actually did finish high school.

Clearly the treatment program had no discernible impact with respect to the criterion of graduation from high school.

HIGHEST SCHOOL GRADE COMPLETED. Graduation is the formal symbol of completion of high school. Nevertheless, girls who complete their senior year of high school, whether they formally graduate or not, represent a higher level of success when compared to those who do not remain in school as long. Each successive grade completed is that much more education. Proportionately more of the experimental cases than of the control cases completed higher grades of school, although the differences between the two groups are not statistically significant.[5] Among experimental cases, 49 per cent completed the senior year whether they graduated or not, compared to 42 per cent among control cases. Seventy-three per cent of the experimental cases and 64 per cent of the control cases completed at least the junior year. None of the experimental cases, compared to 4 per cent of the control cases, failed to complete at least the freshman year of high school.

Concerning the number of years attended by those girls who might have attended any high school at least four years by the terminal date of the project, 56 per cent of the experimental cases and 49 per cent of the control cases attended four or more years of high school, and 83 per cent, compared to 75 per cent, attended at least three years. The distribution for residual cases indicates that significantly more of them (73 per cent) than either experimental or control cases attended high school four or more years.

A smaller percentage of experimental cases (52 per cent) than of control cases (56 per cent) were suspended or discharged from school during the period of the project but, again, the difference is not statistically significant. When the reasons for suspension and discharge are classified into nonpunitive and punitive, slightly more of the control than the experimental cases were removed from school for nonpunitive reasons, such as poor health, employment, transfer, or other circumstances not reflecting misbehavior or poor academic performance. This difference hints at the possibility that the services given to girls by the social agency helped those with circumstantial problems somewhat more than it helped those with behavior problems. This is only the barest of speculations, of course, in view of the minimal difference observed, but it may be worth noting when considering benefits of service programs to high school girls with potential problems.

Taken together, the findings with respect to completion of school can be said to support only an extremely cautious suggestion that the treatment program had any effect. At most, it can be said that extremely small differences in staying in school favor the experimental cases. Since the differences are not statistically significant, only their consistency permits even this cautious conclusion.

Academic Performance

GRADES EARNED IN VOCATIONAL AND ACADEMIC SUBJECTS.   The number of failures can be taken as one indication of academic performance. If the treatment program had any effect, it should be most evident after it had been in operation some time, either because of cumulative influences or because selectively students who perform better stay in school. We know that similar proportions of experimental and control cases drop out. Therefore, unless some factor is operating to differentiate them, similar proportions ought to show failures.

The trends of failures for both vocational and academic subjects are essentially similar. Decreasing proportions of both experimental and control cases are found to have failures between their first and third years, but the decrease is greater for experimental cases. Thus, for vocational subjects, 40 per cent of the experimental cases had one or more failures their first year but only 16 per cent their third year, and this difference is statistically significant. On the other hand, for control cases there were 31 per cent with one or more failures the first year and 20 per cent the third year, a substantial decrease to be sure but the difference does not reach statistical significance. The corresponding trend for academic subjects is to be noted: a statistically significant decrease from 39 to 24 per cent for experimental cases, compared to a smaller decrease, not statistically significant, from 31 to 20 per cent for control cases. It is further to be noted that the record of experimental cases is not as good as that of control cases in the initial year (although the difference is not statistically significant), whereas it is better or equal to that of the control cases in the third year.

The finding is not so clear when academic performance is measured by the number of A and B grades recorded. Such high grades are about equally found for experimental and control cases at each year, with slight tendencies for proportionately fewer A's and B's in the later years, except for a minor countertrend among experimental cases in vocational subjects. None of the differences is statistically significant.

If one is to interpret these findings as evidence of an effect of the treatment program, it must be seen as an effect mediated through the selection process. Rather than conclude that academic performance, as reflected in grades, is directly improved by the program available to experimental cases, it is more exact to say that girls who would earn better grades (especially fail fewer subjects) were helped to remain in school. Such a positive selective effect is, nevertheless, a constructive, if modest, achievement to be attributed to the treatment program.

ADVANCEMENT WITH CLASS AND ASSIGNMENT TO COOPERATIVE WORK-STUDY PROGRAM.   Associated with performance in subjects, but dependent as well on additional evaluations by the teachers, the promotion or detention of a student at the end of each school year and the decision to assign, at the normal time, to the cooperative work-study program are further indications of general academic performance.

A slightly greater proportion of experimental cases than of control cases advanced normally with their classes. Thus, 74 per cent of all the experimental cases, compared to 70 per cent of the control cases, remained in their normal class, whereas 24 per cent of the former and 28 per cent of the latter were held back or reclassified to lower-standing vocational programs, and the same proportion of both groups (2 per cent) were advanced above the normal level for their classes. None of these differences is statistically significant. They can only be taken as a possible suggestion of better performance by experimental cases.

At this high school, students are placed in work-study jobs in the industry for which they are trained when their work is adequate and they are deemed responsible by teachers of vocational subjects and by the guidance counselors. This is a prized assignment since it provides on-the-job experience, apprentice wages, and potential access to the job market after graduation. Assignments are normally made for the second semester of the junior year and continued throughout the last year of high school. Occasionally, students will be assigned for the first time at the beginning of their senior year if they have shown improvement deemed to warrant it, and occasionally they will be dropped from the work-study program if they do not perform adequately in it.

No differences of significance are found between experimental and control cases in the pattern of assignment. For both groups, 48 per cent were never selected. Slightly more of the control than the experimental cases (48 and 45 per cent, respectively) were assigned in their junior year, but a few more of the latter were assigned later. Altogether, half of each group (51 per cent of the experimental and 49 per cent of the control cases) participated in the *co-op* training program.

HONORS AND AWARDS AND SERVICE RATINGS.   Slightly greater percentages of control cases than experimental cases had entries in their records of awards and honors, but in both groups the numbers were few. Only 14 per cent of the former and 9 per cent of the latter were so recognized. Similarly, more of the control cases (65 per cent) than the experimental cases (59 per cent) had at least one service rating, but this difference also is not statistically significant. Such minor differences hardly bear interpretation.

In recapitulation of the findings with respect to the several measures of academic performance, we note the positive selective effect of the treatment program in reducing failing grades in academic subjects.

School-Related Behavior

ATTENDANCE. No consistent or significant differences were found between the attendance records of experimental and control cases. Calculation of the unexcused-absence rate shows that slightly more than one-third of both groups were absent on the average one day a month or less in their initial year; nearly half the cases in school three years later had this low rate of absences. Experimental cases show a slightly better rate for the latter year (49 per cent compared to 43 per cent with less than ten days, not a statistically significant difference). The decrease in unexcused absences in excess of this rate was more substantial for experimental cases than for control cases. It fell from 40 per cent in the first year to 23 per cent in the third year, a statistically significant difference for those with 18 or more days of unexcused absences. This decrease occurs primarily between the second and third years, when a lesser decrease for control cases is also apparent.

As was pointed out in the discussion of academic performance, differences through time for such measures as attendance may be taken as a positive selective effect of the treatment program provided for experimental cases, but since these cases do not differ significantly from the control cases on these measures one must make no claim for direct effects.

TRUANCY. There were 107 problem-potential cases who were truant during the project; 62, or 58 per cent of these cases, were control cases and 45, or 42 per cent, were experimental cases. The difference between experimental and control cases shows the former to have the better record and is substantial enough to take note of, although it does not quite reach the criterion of statistical significance adopted in this analysis. Instances of truancy occur for experimental cases disproportionately in the year of cohort entry, when 42 per cent of them are reported. Truancies in later years are disproportionately greater for control cases: 74 per cent, compared to 58 per cent for experimental cases, but with such small numbers of truancies reported this noticeable difference is not quite statistically significant.

We are probably justified in a cautious conclusion that experimental cases were less truant than control cases as an effect of the social work program. This is an effect that might be expected in view of the weekly schedule of interviews or group sessions, attendance at which was of immediate and constant concern to the social workers. Since these scheduled contacts with the social workers took place during the school day, encouragement to meet the appointment with the caseworker or group leader was tantamount to encouragement to come to school. It is perhaps surprising that more favorable truancy and school-attendance records were not found for the experimental cases. Nevertheless, the effect that does appear must be accepted as a positive achievement of the treatment program.

CONDUCT MARKS. Each student's official school record includes, for each term, a teacher's rating on *conduct*, that is, on appropriate behavior or misbehavior that may or may not subject the student to some form of discipline. We might expect such behavior to be affected favorably as a result of the therapeutic attention to which the experimental cases were subjected.

In each year, the difference between experimental and control cases was minimal and there were no consistent trends that change the relationship between the distributions of conduct marks for the two groups of cases. Significant decreases occurred between the first and third years in the proportions of both experimental and control cases that received unsatisfactory marks for conduct. The selective process operated with equal effect whether the girls did or did not participate in the therapeutic program. However, the major decrease for experimental cases with unsatisfactory conduct marks occurred between the initial and the second years, whereas for the control cases the decrease between each year was more even.

When conduct marks were used as a criterion, no interpretable effect from the treatment program was found for the experimental cases.

TEACHER RATINGS FOR CHARACTER TRAITS AND WORK TRAITS. For each term the student's homeroom teacher, on the basis of reports from all the student's teachers, rated the student on a number of character traits and work traits, and these ratings became part of the official record of the student. Ratings were on a scale from 1 (very poor) to 5 (excellent). The character traits rated were interest, industry, initiative, courtesy, cooperation, self-control, appearance, dependability, and health habits. The work traits were care of tools and equipment, "follows instructions," neatness, speed, attitude, use of English, safety, and workmanship. The records were not entirely consistent in the extent to which all traits were rated but there were usually four or five of each list that were rated. So far as we were able to determine from discussing the ratings with school staff, the teachers varied not only in the meanings and standards they applied but also in the extent to which students were known well enough for judgments to be made. This accounts in part for incomplete ratings for some students and full ratings for others. It is likely that behavior that was noticeably deviant—either negatively or positively—would call the student sufficiently to the teacher's attention so that traits would be rated for her.

With these reservations, the utility of such ratings is obviously limited. Nevertheless, one may assume that students who made up the experimental and control cases had equal opportunities to be rated in the same manner and, hence, any differences that they exhibited had equal chances of being reflected in the ratings. We have averaged the ratings for each year for the comparison of experimental and control cases.

Essentially, the findings for teacher ratings parallel those for conduct marks: no significant differences appear between experimental and control cases, but the latter tend to have slightly higher ratings. Average ratings for both experimental and control cases shift significantly upward between the first and third years, but the shift is approximately the same for both groups of cases. There is no evidence, therefore, of an effect of the treatment program so far as this measure is concerned.

We may summarize the findings on all the measures that have been grouped together as school-related behavior by noting that none of them supplies conclusive evidence of an effect by the therapeutic program. However, the relatively better showing of experimental cases with respect to truancy suggests that the surveillance that accompanies the rendering of treatment services tends to have some effect. This is by no means a trivial achievement, if further research shows that it does indeed occur. Other deviant forms of behavior have often been observed to be concomitants of truancy. An additional conclusion is suggested by the findings with respect to trends on the measures here examined through the three years observed: that there is some tendency for a favorable differential to develop for experimental cases through the selective process. It would appear that if girls remain in school, those with the benefit of the treatment program exhibit somewhat less negative school-related behavior. From the point of view of the school a less deviant population remains and, possibly, educational objectives might more readily be achieved for them. Likewise, a student body resulting from such favorable selective processes might constitute a more favorable context for students who are not deviant in the ways exhibited by the problem-potential segment of the school population.

Out-of-School Behavior

ENTRIES ON HEALTH RECORD.   Matters of health arising from acute circumstances, as well as the results of periodic health examinations by the school nurse and physicians serving the school, are recorded for each student on a health record. Such information covers a broad range of observations, including overweight and underweight, allergies, psychosomatic complaints, and emotional or psychological difficulties. It was considered possible that a treatment program addressed in major part to more positive mental health attitudes and self-understanding might be reflected in such school health records. Since we believed that the records were not sufficiently detailed for refined diagnostic categories, we have taken the frequency of all entries as a rough index of health status. Experimental and control cases were compared on this basis.

Somewhat fewer entries on the health records are found to be made for experimental cases, but the difference from control cases is not statistically significant. There are significant decreases for both groups of cases between the year of cohort entry and the last year observed. It is likely that, in addition to the effects of selection, the older ages of the girls constituting the latter cases would affect this measure. The school health personnel might be less likely to make note of minor health problems for sixteen- to eighteen-year-old than for thirteen- to fifteen-year-old girls, and the girls themselves might be less likely to bring such problems to the attention of school personnel.

ATTENTION OF AUTHORITIES AND AGENCIES. To see whether experimental and control cases might differ in the extent to which they had come to the attention of the police, courts, and other agencies of community control, the potential problem cases were cleared through the Social Service Exchange at the terminal date of the project. However, the appearance of any entries, especially those with explicit reference to the girls themselves, was so infrequent that it is meaningless to compare experimental and control cases on this measure.

When a girl became involved in court proceedings for some offense, and it was known to the school, a notation was kept and this was taken as a further indication of deviant out-of-school behavior. We cannot accept the information as accurate under the more or less informal manner it was recorded, but the data available do not differentiate experimental and control cases in any event. Thirteen of the former (7 per cent) and nine of the latter (5 per cent) were noted to have been involved in court cases.

OUT-OF-WEDLOCK PREGNANCY. Because premarital pregnancy is cause for suspension from school, and a rule made it mandatory that resumption of schooling for unmarried mothers must be in a different school, somewhat more reliable information was available about out-of-wedlock pregnancy than other forms of nonschool deviant behavior. For all the potential problem cases (except five for which data were not available), out-of-wedlock pregnancy was reported for 41 girls, or 11 per cent. Of these 41 girls, 23 (56 per cent) were control cases and 18 (44 per cent) were experimental cases, a difference that favors the latter but is not statistically significant.

On the very limited measures of out-of-school behavior available, we may note, in summary, that only the slightest advantage was found for experimental cases. We find very little evidence, therefore, of effect on these measures of the therapeutic program.

Other Criteria of Effects

Personality Tests

The Junior Personality Quiz was the personality test used throughout the series of test periods in the research. On only two factors was there the suggestion that experimental and control cases differed significantly or meaningfully.

Compared to control cases, scores on the factor designated as Will Control vs. Relaxed Casualness change toward the higher pole of the dimension for experimental cases. Thus we may conclude that the treatment program promoted personality-test responses indicating greater self-control, and persistent, orderly behavior. These traits did not increase for 'the comparable control cases.

Although not statistically significant, slight numerical trends with respect to the factor designated as Adventurous Cyclothymia vs. Withdrawn Schizothymia occur in opposite directions for experimental and control cases. The former increase in boldness, whereas the latter increase in shyness, aloofness, lack of confidence. This is a suggestive difference in keeping with the objectives of the treatment program to which the experimental cases were exposed.

On the other ten factors that make up this personality test no interpretable differences appear between experimental and control cases. We must conclude, therefore, that the treatment program had only the barest effect on personality changes insofar as this instrument detects them.

The Make A Sentence Test failed to reveal interpretable differences and therefore the data will not be presented.

Thus with the use of two standardized measures of personality—one objective and the other projective—only the barest evidence of an experimental effect of the treatment program can be found.

Questionnaire Responses

Three questionnaires were used to detect possible effects at the level of expressed attitudes. The first of these questionnaires asked about general feelings. The minimal differences between experimental and control cases suggest that those girls who had the benefit of treatment may respond slightly less negatively to several questions intended to reflect general self-assessments of their personal situations.

After reviewing data from a second questionnaire that sought to reflect psychological insight and reactions to help, we may report that girls in the treatment program clearly recognized the opportunity to discuss their problems with an adult and, in contrast to the control cases, did not feel that they had been limited in doing so. Experimental cases did not, however, especially attribute benefits to themselves from this opportunity in significantly greater proportions than the control cases. From responses to a number of questions, there was weak evidence to suggest that participation in the treatment program was associated with somewhat greater psychological insight. It is always possible that a superficial attitude questionnaire would fail to reflect so subtle a difference as heightened insight. Indeed, small measured differences might even reflect much greater actual differences.

On a third questionnaire, which asked seniors about their situations and their futures, the major difference between experimental and control cases was the greater recognition by girls who had been in the program that they had been helped by a social worker.

The scant findings from these questionnaires can support only the slightest indication of effect. At best we may cautiously suggest that the pattern of response tends to be somewhat less negative if viewed from the objectives of the treatment program.

Sociometric Data

Sociometric choices were analyzed for those students who remained in school throughout the four testing periods and these data will be considered here. Between the first and fourth test periods, the percentages of control and residual cases naming one or more serious problem students decreases, whereas a greater proportion of experimental cases named one or more serious problem students. Even so, the differences between the experimental, control, and residual cases is not large enough to be statistically significant.

When the sociometric data are considered with respect to outstanding students named by and choosing experimental, control, and residual cases, the trends are similar for both of the potential problem samples (experimental and control cases); no significant differences appear between them. Whether naming or chosen by outstanding students, increased proportions of such students are found at the fourth test period when compared to the first period, and these differences are statistically significant. This is merely evidence, of course, that all students become better known as they remain in school. This phenomenon does not appear differentially to any meaningful degree for experimental and control cases. The same trend, however, is sufficiently greater for residual cases than for either of the potential problem samples so that the differences found between the residual and the experimental and control cases, taken together at the fourth test period, are statistically significant. Although they are not differentiated from one another, both the experimental and the control cases are found to be less likely to name or be named by outstanding students than the residual cases. Slightly fewer of the experimental than the control cases at the fourth testing period are found to name or be chosen by outstanding students, but the differences are small and cannot constitute evidence of a negative result of the treatment program.

With respect to sociometric volume—that is, the total number of students named by or choosing girls in the several samples of the research population—there are no important differences between experimental, control, and residual cases. The trend is for each of the three groups of cases to name more students at the fourth than at the first test period. Likewise, they are chosen by more at the later period, with the residual cases somewhat more likely to be chosen, but not to a statistically significant degree.

The sociometric data do not show evidence of effect from the treatment program. Insofar as the hypothesis that the program would reduce the undesirable associations of the experimental cases is concerned, there is no evidence to support such a conclusion. Nor has there been an evident effect on the level of general popularity of experimental as compared to control cases.

The personality tests, questionnaire responses, and sociometric data have failed to detect substantial differences between experimental and control cases. We must conclude that, with respect to all the measures we have used to examine effects of the treatment program, only a minimal effect can be found.

Conclusion

The measures of effect that have been examined here are objective, in the sense that they are observations external to the girls we studied, as well as self-reports or responses on tests. Such measures constitute, therefore, fairly severe tests of an experimental effect of the treatment program. On these tests no strong indications of effect are found and the conclusion must be stated in the negative when it is asked whether social work intervention with potential problem high school girls was effective in this instance.

However, the evidence is not wholly negative. With due recognition of the very low magnitude of any relationship between experimental or control status of the cases and any of these criteria measured, it may be noted that the direction of many of them tends to favor girls who had the benefit of the treatment program. This may be little basis for enthusiasm, in view of the tireless efforts of able social workers and the splendid cooperation of school personnel in an attempt to help the girls with potential problems, but it is not entirely discouraging. It testifies to the difficulty of changing deviant careers, a difficulty that is apparent whenever serious evaluative assessments have been undertaken. This is certainly not surprising to social workers who have struggled to find ways to be helpful. And it should caution those who like to believe that ways are already known, if but tried, to meet the serious problems of adolescents in their high school years.

Part

Social Work and
Social Workers

Introduction

The selections in this section pertain to social work considered as
a profession and to features of the field's educational enterprise.

"Professionalization and Social Work Today" is the title of the selection by Meyer. In this sociological analysis of the social work profession,
the author highlights similarities of social work to other professions, along
with its distinctive features, problems, and dilemmas. The body of knowledge, the technical competence, and the publicly asserted responsibility
are three characteristics of professions around which the author's comments are organized. Professionalization in industrial society is considered
in terms of increased specialization, division of labor, and urbanization.
The role of authority and responsibility is discussed among the factors
that accompany the development of an occupation into a profession, and
control through the monopoly of services and the prestige of the occupational group are considered as well. The author then analyzes the progress
and problems of social work as a profession, terminating his analysis with
consideration of recruitment, the socialization of professional social workers, places of employment and the professional associations in social work.

The next selection, by McLeod and Meyer, is an empirical study of the values of social workers. In the first phase of the inquiry, the authors derived ten dominant themes from an analysis of writings in social work. These ten value dimensions then served as a guide for the development of a Social Values Test containing 100 attitude statements. The test was administered to three groups of social workers: the professionally trained, students in a school of social work, and a sample of untrained workers. On the basis of selected background information and the test scores of these respondents, it was found that seven of the ten value dimensions were endorsed as predicted; that is, endorsement of the value dimensions varied directly with the degree of social-work training. The major difference among the three groups was between the untrained workers and the others. Additional analyses were undertaken to determine the extent to which value endorsement was a function of selection or of one's present occupational position. After various controls had been instituted in the analysis, it was found that there was still a general training effect, but religion and ethnic factors were also found to be influential. The authors conclude that both training and selection operate to affect the values of social workers, but that training appears to function differently for the subgroups in the sample. The last portion of the report contrasts differences in values between social workers and teachers, revealing that the values of social workers are to some extent distinctive.

In a profession such as social work, in which a significant portion of its knowledge must be drawn from behavioral science, educators and practitioners in social work continuously face the problem of what material to use from the behavioral sciences, and upon what basis. In the next selection, Thomas discusses criteria for selecting behavioral science for use. One set of criteria involves content relevance. The areas of relevance are normal behavior; abnormality and deviation; growth, maturation, and change; and the helping process—for all levels of social work intervention. In addition, it is also proposed that the knowledge have power, by which the author means that the propositions should have been validated, the propositions should have predictive potency, and the variables of the theory should be powerful. A final, essential set of criteria pertaining to the extent to which action may be taken on the basis of the knowledge is discussed in terms of the referent features of the knowledge. Here the author discusses such aspects of the knowledge referents as their identifiability, accessibility, manipulability, cost of manipulation, potency, and ethical suitability. In the final section of the paper types of applicable knowledge are discussed, considering various combinations of the selection criteria. In addition to knowledge that is immediately applicable for direct action and knowledge that is inapplicable, the author identifies three types of applicability intermediate between these extremes.

In her report on the use of case discussion to integrate behavioral science theory into practice, Schroeder addresses the question of whether social work practitioners can begin to use new concepts of behavioral science in practice after having been exposed systematically to the theoretical material. To study the problem, the author instituted a cooperative project located in a large family service agency in which four workers and the author considered the applicability of selected knowledge of social role and small groups. Although there was an earlier exposure to lectures on these subjects and to selected readings, the main focus of the project was upon case discussions with workers to apply the concepts and theory in the diagnosis and treatment of the case problems. Among the conclusions of the project was that it was both feasible and desirable to infuse behavioral science knowledge into practice and that there appeared to be nothing unique about this material in terms of the use of case discussion as a means of application. The workers participating in the project were found to make much greater use of the behavioral science concepts in their analysis of case problems than the nonparticipating staff members, and there was other evidence that the participating workers assimilated and applied the new material.

In the last selection, Vinter discusses problems and processes in developing social work practice principles. Although the assumption that the conceptual tools of behavioral science are essential for developing practice knowledge is implicit in this analysis, the author identifies differences between differences between scientific theory and practice theory. In the connection, requisites of practice principles are presented. Among them are the necessity for the principles to specify the desired ends of action, to be consistent with ethical prescriptions of the field, to draw upon validated knowledge, and to be directed toward specific types of action anticipated to be effective. The author specifies further that in formulating principles of practice, the conditions and course of action must be indicated as well as the anticipated results. Since principles of practice are not typically relevant if they are formulated in the abstract independently of specific change problems, the author addresses himself to the more general universe of discourse that serves as a frame of reference within which principles of practice must necessarily be imbedded. In this context, the author indicates the necessity to formulate practice principles in relationship to some conception of the prime function in a particular area of social work, of the client and the professional practitioner, and of the action and decision issues with which one formulates the principles of diagnosis and treatment. Because the writer indicates how the conceptual tools of social work must be transformed in order to be properly addressed to the action issues of social work, scholars and practitioners who aspire to develop viable theories of practice will find helpful guides in this paper.

29 Professionalization and Social Work Today

Henry J. Meyer

Any discussion of social work as a profession in the United States today must face a number of ambiguities. These we shall meet as we examine some of the central characteristics of professionalization as it appears in social work. There need be no ambiguity, however, about the old question put to social work by Abraham Flexner in 1915. Is social work a profession? [1] The professional status of social work is generally acknowledged. Other questions remain. What kind of a profession will social work become? How will its own professional structure affect its future? How will it meet the demands that society places on it as a profession?

It is to such questions as these that this brief chapter may serve as prologue. Despite the voluminous writings of social workers about professional problems, the analysis in detail of social work as a profession has just started. A number of sociologists and social workers trained in the sociology of professions have begun to mark out the framework of study, to gather together the stray bits of information now available, and to initiate the inquiries that will permit an analysis of social work. [2] In this discussion we shall use these sources as the backdrop for some comments that may help to call attention to issues for social work today.

Professionalization in Industrial Society

It may be useful to characterize briefly the nature of professionalization before presenting a general discussion of the social work profession. [3] The tendency toward professionalization is almost inevitable in a growing industrial society where specialization within an elaborate division of labor must be increased with the shift from agricultural and other primary industries to the factory, trade, services, and technical enterprises. The urbanization that accompanied industrialization has further encouraged the

From the author's chapter in Alfred J. Kahn (ed.). ISSUES IN AMERICAN SOCIAL WORK (New York: Columbia U. P., 1959), pp. 319–341. Reprinted with the permission of the author and the Columbia University Press. Copyright © 1959 Columbia University Press, New York.

development of numerous occupations to serve the city and its people, and it has also increased the social isolation of occupational groups, making them conscious of their separateness and of their interdependency. Specialized occupational knowledge is thus coupled with specialized function for occupational groups in an industrialized society. The occupation becomes, in part, a substitute for the traditional focus of group identification and common interest that the local community used to be. Professionalization is a tendency for occupational groups to acquire the attributes of a community and to seek a favorable position within the larger society.[4] In this process, increase both of authority and of responsibility marks the transformation of an occupation into a profession.

With science-based technology becoming more and more visibly the basis for important functions—not only in production, communication, and distribution, but also in the provision of medical and other services— the prestige of the science-based professions has increased more rapidly than that of professions based on scholarship, such as law and the ministry. The newer professions have clustered around the sciences, and all professions, including law and the ministry, make overtures to science. The hazy line between science and technology has encouraged many occupational groups to aspire to professional status. Almost every cluster of occupations in the economy of industrial society is capped by an occupational group expected to conserve, develop, and apply the fund of basic knowledge required to perform the functions to which the occupations are directed. Such an occupational group is an existing, or an incipient, profession.

The advantages of professional status for those in the profession are real. Prestige is one such benefit, and occupational prestige, in a society where individual statuses tend to be achieved rather than ascribed, is of major importance. Further, however, the command of a socially assigned function by a designated occupational group confers the benefits of partial monopoly. Successful claim to professional monopoly has economic advantages visible in the higher income of professional occupations compared with those unable to claim such an asset. In return for these and similar benefits to individuals who can be considered professionals, the society expects responsible performance of a socially required function.

Efforts to define what is meant by a profession usually emphasize, in greater detail and elaboration, three characteristics: (1) a body of knowledge, of accumulated wisdom, doctrine, or experience; (2) technical competence in the use of this knowledge; and (3) publicly asserted responsibility in the exercise of this competence on behalf of society.[5] Questions about what kinds of knowledge, how much competence, how codified the ethic of responsibility, and the like, constitute the substance of most discussion of whether an occupational group is or is not a profession. Arguments about whether social work—or nursing, or pharmacy, or any other occupation—is or is not a profession have often taken this line. A more productive question asks about the nature of professionalization in social work—or these other occupations—and not whether it is a profession. As Greenwood says, social work must be considered as a profession because it is not otherwise classifiable.[6]

If we accept social work as a profession, it is of some usefulness to differentiate social work among the professions. We may follow Professor Carr-Saunders for this purpose.[7] He identifies four major types of professions in the modern industrial society, and these types are distinguished by the extent to which they are based on a theoretical structure of a department of learning. (1) The old, established professions, such as law, medicine, and theology, are founded on well-established bodies of learning. (2) A second type of profession is based on its own fundamental studies and represents largely the emergence of occupational groups and interests around bodies of scientific knowledge. Illustrations of this type of profession are chemists, engineers, natural and social scientists. The occupational activity of the profession is primarily the development and application of its body of knowledge. (3) A third type makes use of technical skills and establishes as its knowledge base a body of experience derived from the occupational practice. Nursing, pharmacy, and social work are classified among the "semi-professions" on this basis. (4) Finally, a fourth type of profession consists of occupations that aspire to professional status, but consistency of technical practice and the development of a sufficient body of practice theory is so rudimentary that little claim can be made to a theoretical base for the profession. Examples of this type are found primarily in business, for example, salesmanship. Carr-Saunders calls these "would-be professions."

From this classification of professions one should not infer that all occupations that tend toward professionalization will finally resemble the old established professions. Social work might remain a semiprofession. On the other hand, where the scope for elaborating a profession's fundamental knowledge permits cumulative scholarship or science rather than the mere accumulation of recorded experience, the prestige of science and of the older professions provide strong impetus to emulate them. Social workers more often use the medical profession as model than any other.

Other attributes of professionalization are so directly associated with the knowledge base that their use as criteria to classify professions would yield approximately the same results. More differentiating among professions is the extent to which its members seek to validate professional standing by efforts to establish and maintain pre-eminence of the profession's knowledge base, its competence, and its social responsibility. This effort to claim pre-eminence is sometimes referred to, in discussions of social work, as the claim to an exclusive function. But it is the conjunction of competence with knowledge and responsibility, rather than exclusiveness, that gives a profession its authority, even though that authority may, for some professions, be confirmed in law or by other institutional means. One cannot claim health as the private concern of the medical profession or transmission of knowledge as that of the teaching profession. One cannot find an exclusive function for social work in "helping people to help themselves," in social reform, or in humanitarian concern. Paralleling other professions, however, social work lays claim to specialized experience and knowledge coupled with competence for responsible performance within these general areas. Social workers, as well as those outside the profession, may be uncertain about the validity of this claim. This constitutes one of the sources of uncertainty about the status of the profession today.

Some students include as attributes of a profession those sustaining and facilitating institutions that develop as products of professionalization. Educational processes, schools, and apprenticeships; procedures to validate the qualification to practice; associatons for defense or promotion of professional interests, including economic ones; methods of proclaiming ethical commitments and of disciplining professionals to them; the special patterns of the occupational subculture—all these develop with professionalization. The character of these accompaniments of professionalization has a bearing on a profession's performance of its social function. Social work will be affected as a profession by its schools, associations, and occupational culture patterns.

It must be emphasized, in concluding this brief and abstract consideration of professionalization, that any particular profession—such as social work—does not have its character determined exclusively by what the profession itself does. Professionalization is a response in the process of societal change. External as well as internal forces are at play, and one may conceive of professions as institutions for fulfilling social needs or functions. The forms through which the profession carries out its functions, and what these functions are, will be affected by extra- as well as intraprofessional factors. It is in this sense that social work, and other professions, may be said to face demands that must be acknowledged and responded to. A discussion of the profession of social work must try to identify and to take into account some of these demands.

The Social Work Profession Today

It is of some interest to note, as we attempt to characterize the profession of social work today, that much of the information needed is not yet available. The knowledge base for social work has hardly been operationally identified, much less subjected to content analysis. The large literature on practice has not yet provided clear descriptions of the technical competence that social workers may possess. Where social work asserts professional responsibility is likewise incompletely investigated. This is not to say that social work must itself provide knowledge of the sort required. Rather, those social scientists who would understand the profession have to undertake investigations from the outside, looking on social work as a phenomenon for study in the same framework as other professions and occupations. Recent efforts to do just this have made an excellent start, and the discusssion of this section will rely heavily on these works.[8] However, our presentation will be tentative and speculative.

We may conveniently discuss the social work profession by considering the character of its knowledge base, its claim to technical proficiency, and the question of its area of responsibility. We may also refer to some of the structural features of the profession and to some of the ambiguities apparent in social work as a profession today.

We are concerned with the character rather than the content of the knowledge base developed and sought by social work. Two features seem most evident: (1) the emphasis on the primacy of experience in practice, on the one hand, and (2) almost paradoxically, the assertion of scientific knowledge as the foundation for professional competence. These are not unrelated emphases for any profession, to be sure, because scientific knowledge and practice experience are interwoven in the art of a profession; but they are different. Scientific knowledge aims essentially at generalization from theories to specific instances, whereas a body of experimental knowledge seeks to provide the widest possible range of specific instances from which to draw as new instances are presented.[9] Not the choice between them, but how science and experience are to be used, is the unsettled question in social work.

Different segments of the profession show somewhat different attitudes with respect to its knowledge base. Casework, group work, community organization and administration, in that order, are ranged from asserting the need for scientific knowledge as an underlying base to reliance primarily on practice experience. This appears to be true even though casework and group work are well known for the use of the case approach both in teaching and in practice itself. Caseworkers have been more inclined to support and justify their practice decisions by appeal to bodies of theory that claim scientific standing. Thus, psychoanalysis, whatever reservations may be made about it, takes a scientific stance, and casework so understands its use of this body of doctrine and theory. Casework and group work, also, are the fields within social work that have most deliberately imported concepts and terms from the social sciences. Community organization as a field seems least concerned with conceptualizing the theory underlying its activities or with seeking to base it on scientific knowledge.[10]

These differences have historical and situational roots. Casework was developed by emphasis on the individual, his strengths and weaknesses, his psychological mechanisms, and his responses to the social situation.[11] It found in psychology and in psychoanalysis a ready body of ideas about the individual. Its practice setting in hospital, clinic, and agency fostered association with the medical and psychiatric professions, which accept scientific knowledge as basic. Neither group work nor community organization developed in situations where scientific knowledge was highly valued or, indeed, generally available.[12] Since prestige is identified with science, a tendency to give at least apparent support to a scientific foundation is widespread. But throughout all parts of the profession the commitment is ambiguous.

One outcome of this uncertainty is reflected in the educational content of professional training. Curricula of schools of social work, despite efforts to reach common agreements through association and accreditation procedures, mix science-related and practice-derived courses, and there appears to be widespread concern with the problem of the relationship of each to the other. Social work schools find it difficult to identify appropriate prerequisites in underlying bodies of knowledge or sciences. The place of research methods courses, stressing scientific methodology, is uncertain.[13]

Social work is not entirely at liberty to choose whether it will base its claim to professional standing on a body of scientific knowledge. So pervasive is public insistence on science that social work will almost surely have to support its claim to a body of fundamental knowledge by appeal to science. This will require, as a first step, a serious effort to analyze the actual content of what social workers know, where they obtained such knowledge, and the extent to which that knowledge has been or can be subjected to test. This is a difficult task. Social workers will, among other things, have to become more explicit about their assumptions and more articulate about their bases of action. But it will provide a firmer claim to professionalization than at present.

In this task the behavioral sciences can be of service, but they cannot do the job for social work. Like medicine, social work will have to ask its own questions of the social sciences and it will have to choose what is appropriate knowledge from the viewpoint of its own professional objectives. But it will have to respect scientific methodology as a basis for knowledge and tolerate skepticism about its knowledge. It will have to overcome the fear that this will inhibit its confidence to practice and its claim to authority. It must really know what is known and what is not. On this basis social workers, like other professionals, can justify the authority in fundamental knowledge that is a mark of professionalization.[14]

The assertion of competent use of its knowledge base is a second characteristic of professionalization. We have made the point earlier that it is not exclusive interest in an area of social concern, but special competence to work in the area, that characterizes professionalization. In few of the programs employing designated social workers are school-trained, professional social workers predominant. Thus, only in psychiatric social work in clinics and hospitals, in medical social work and the teaching of social work are approximately one-half of those employed as social workers fully trained, as judged by the customary standard of two or more years of specialized schooling.[15] This proportion is approached in some of the family services. But in the largest programs—such as public assistance, group work, and child-welfare work—the proportion is far less. There is no question that what social workers are employed to do is also done by less professionally trained persons. A crucial question is, of course, whether those who claim professional training have competences, based on knowledge, that distinguish them from the less professional or the non-professional. This is a question for which there is no clear, factual answer.

Professional competence involves more than the assertion of knowledge not possessed by nonprofessionals. As Wilensky and Lebeaux imply, development of a professional self among social workers, comparable to that of the established professions, is a part of professional competence.[16] They suggest that the professional social worker, more than the nonprofessional, must exhibit an impersonal and disinterested relationship with his client, an emotional neutrality or objectivity in his concern with the client's problems, an impartiality among clients regardless of personal preferences, and a responsibility for service rather than exploitation. Such norms appear to be evident among trained social workers, but research comparing trained and untrained social workers in these respects is still limited.

The aspect of special competence of social workers that has to do with effectiveness of technique also lacks demonstration in research. It seems likely, but it is not yet demonstrated, that trained social workers have greater skill in counseling, in working with groups and with communities than persons of equivalent experience but less training.

One difficulty in dealing with such questions lies in the fact that what social workers do has itself not yet been objectively described. The actual work of the case worker, group worker or community organizer is reflected primarily through self-supplied reports, or recordings or general illustrations taken from experience. These become the content of the asserted skill of the social worker, with only limited recognition that errors of perception, recall, and reporting as well as other subjective biases, may create inaccurate or enormous presentations. It is suggested that the claim to competence must be accompanied by a willingness to subject the practices of social work to scrutiny in order to see what the content of professional practice really is. Even if social workers accept such a necessity, it is by no means an easy task to observe practice because conceptual, measuremental, operational, and analytical tools for such descriptions are not well developed. Nevertheless, far more could be attempted than is at present if social workers accepted the need to examine directly their technical competence. One indication of professionalization is willingness to make public the professional operations or techniques so that they can be described and tested.

Norms of intraprofessional relations in social work would seem to stand in the way of such a development.[17] These norms protect the profession against outsiders who might question the mystique represented in the "art" of the practitioner, or against the hostile attack on practice skills by those who deny the sincerity and good faith of the practitioner. These dangers exist but they can be recognized and guarded against without depriving the profession of necessary tests of competence.

In a larger sense, the question of special competence is the question of objective evaluation. One should not underestimate the dangers that inhere in disinterested evaluation of effort by social workers or social agencies. Nor should one underestimate the difficulties of making valid assessments. There seems to be no alternative, however, to the necessity that social work subject its competence to test, and there are signs that it is moving in this direction.[18] It becomes more professioinal as it does so.

That component of professionalization that we have referred to as an asserted area for which a profession takes social responsibility in using its knowledge and competence presents again a confused picture for the profession of social work.[19] In its history, social work has long had a double focus: on social reform on the one hand and on facilitating adjustment of individuals to existing situations on the other. These two themes reappear in various forms: as environmental manipulation or promoting psychological functioning, as concern with people through mass programs or casework with persons one by one. Social workers have been conscious of these two approaches to social welfare and have often sought to reconcile them. Mary Richmond, symbol of the case-by-case approach, is reported to have said once to Florence Kelley, symbol of reform in the grand style: "We work on the same program. I work on the retail end of it, but you work on the wholesale."[20] But these two viewpoints are still not integrated, and both are represented by acknowledged spokesmen for the profession.

There is little doubt that those who define social responsibility of the profession in terms of individuals rather than of reform and policy, have the ascendency. Most of the students in schools of social work elect casework as their specialization.[21] Knowledge of the history and the details of social welfare policies is not emphasized in the curriculum as much as "human growth and development." The requirement of a school of social work degree for qualification to membership in the national professional association favors those in private agencies over those in mass programs. This trend is countered, but not balanced, by a growing demand for trained workers in the public programs and by the fact that even in those professions traditionally committed to individual approaches—such as medicine and psychiatry—emphasis on prevention, in addition to amelioration or cure, is forcing attention to public policy and large-scale programs.

Wilensky and Lebeaux suggest that the choice the profession makes in this dilemma will depend largely on the development of its knowledge-skill base.[22] But it also depends on what is demanded of the profession in present-day society. Social work as a profession may not be permitted to abandon either approach, to choose between responsibility for social welfare policy or for direct service to individuals. Expertness in the one may well require expertness in the other for the profession as a whole if not for each professional social worker as an individual. In this respect it may be compared to the medical profession, which has been forced to concern itself with public health and the economics of medical care. Especially as public programs extend further and further beyond income maintenance into family life, facilitating optimum health, planning and providing for services to the aged, and the like, those concerned with the individual must become implicated.

The boundaries of a profession's social responsibility are always unclear because social functions are interrelated and changing. It would seem that social work must look sensitively to its "public image," not simply in terms of its prestige among other occupations and professions,[23] but also for clues as to what may be expected of it. Because positions are available for all trained social workers, the profession should not overlook the fact that there are many other jobs that go unfilled where there is an evident belief that professional social workers should perform.[24] A thoroughgoing study of what tasks the American people, in their communities and in their governmental and voluntary agencies, want the professional social worker to perform is yet to be made. Social work, like other professions, must perceive its area of responsibility as well as define it.

Other Features

We can briefly mention some of the important ancillary features of professionalization of social work. These deserve more extended analysis, and research on them has begun to develop.

The problem of recruitment is affected by professionalization in social work. The professional school is the gateway to the profession. Though they are much concerned with attracting more students,[25] social work schools have, at the same time, built up elaborate selection procedures that reflect some of the ambiguities already indicated. How much emphasis should be placed on personal qualities, how much on intellectual is a continuous question. The bases for appeal to college graduates tend to stress altruistic interests and personality characteristics rather than interest in knowledge and skills. There is evidence that those who become students do differ from others somewhat in this respect.[26] They "like to work with people," "to help others." This is in keeping with the historical background of social work where middle-class persons approached social welfare as a humanitarian cause. Recruitment may be affected also by the relatively low income of social workers and by its relatively lower status among professions.[27] But, as Kadushin points out, this depends on the social level from which recruits come. Negro students and those with working-class backgrounds appear to be increasingly attracted to social work. Recruitment is also affected by the fact that social work is traditionally a woman's occupation. The same appeals cannot be equally effective with persons of such different backgrounds.[28]

During their schooling, future professional social workers begin induction into professional culture, its norms and values.[29] Such induction takes place both in classroom and in the agency where the student begins what is almost a life-long pattern of intraprofessional relationship with supervision. This relationship functions in part as an apprenticeship approach to learning the skills of the profession and in part as a pattern of intraprofessional dependency that carries through from the worker, to the supervisor, to the consultant who is often in a related profession, such as medicine, psychiatry, or law.[30]

During his training period, there is an implicit contest for loyalty and commitment from the student between the school and the agency, but this is less inherent in the system of field placement than in the ambiguities about what constitutes knowledge and competence. One result of spending one-third or more time as a student out of the academic setting is to encourage an early identification with the practical problems of practice rather than with intellectual conceptualizations of these problems. It is to be noted that field work begins for many students concurrently with their first classroom lecture. Another result of this system would seem to be an early and deep-seated sense of responsibility to the client. Also, strong identification with other professional social workers and an immediate sense of being a practitioner seem to result. The total school experience thus points toward an image of the profession that is visible in the first-hand and available models.

For most students this means that social work is equivalent to casework. Most students take their field work in casework, major in casework, and find that they can get financial support for casework. Thus, they go out with casework as the meaning of professional social work and with casework methods as the meaning of professional skill. This is widely recognized as an important influence on the definition of competence and responsibility for the profession as a whole. Taken together, less than 20 per cent of the 1957 graduates majored in other methods.[31] Hence, individual services, rather than mass programs or social policies, are emphasized as responsibility of the professional.

A sizeable proportion of social work students are older than one would find in most other professions. The reasons include the fact that social work schools—unlike law, medicine, and most other professional schools—require a college degree before entrance. Another reason is that women, whose employment history has been interrupted by family responsibilities, may return to the labor market via the school. There is still, too, a sizeable proportion of employed social workers who enter or return to school in order to become trained social workers.[32] Their schooling is often subsidized by public agencies or programs.[33] It is of interest to note that schools do not generally regard the work experience of such persons as a substitute for field placement as a student. The schools tend formally to apply the same training procedures to the inexperienced and the experienced student.

Graduates of the schools enter professional practice frequently as a continuation of their field placement, not usually in the same agencies, but in similar ones. Thus schooling and professional employment tend to merge. They tend to take casework jobs in those social work programs in which they received financial support, predominantly child welfare, mental health service, family service programs, and medical and rehabilitation programs.[34]

The practice of social work by trained workers is almost exclusively in an employment status rather than as independent practitioners.[35] Thus social workers, like teachers, must reconcile professional norms with organizational demands of agency, hospital and clinic, or government bureaus. Bureaucratic demands emphasize specialization, limited responsibility, and conformity to rules. These may encourage conceptions of professional practice in the same directions. The effect of the structure of organizations on practitioners as well as on services is an important area for further study. On the other hand, professional identification can reduce the effects of bureaucracy through emphasis on professional rather than organizational norms and responsibilities and through providing support external to the bureaucracy.[36]

Because a high proportion of trained social workers is employed in hospitals and clinics, the interprofessional team is a familiar setting for the practice of casework and sometimes of group work. Teamed with the psychiatrist and the clinical psychologist, the psychiatric caseworker in particular is in a setting where his specialization must be made more explicit and his competence affirmed. Usually a woman, the caseworker in this team faces problems of sex-role differences as well as differences in professional prestige.[37] In this situation, as in the larger bureaucracy, strong identification with the profession is stimulated as a defense against lower status and prestige.

Perhaps the elaborated system of conferences on the job among social workers, with supervision and with consultants, provides the protection of association with fellow professionals. The widespread local social workers' club and the local chapters of the national association serve a similar function.

Professional associations in social work followed the development of specialties until 1955 when the various separate organizations merged into the single National Association of Social Workers.[38] This association is still young, and within it the special interests of psychiatric social workers, medical social workers, group workers, and other specialties are preserved. If it retains its eligibility requirement, the NASW will in time speak for all school-trained professionals and for these alone. Other associations—such as the American Public Welfare Association—that include both trained and untrained social workers represent wider interests. The even broader National Conference on Social Welfare, whose annual meetings attract about 6,000 persons, is the most diverse of all social work associations. It seems to serve primarily as a forum for the whole range of interests of social workers whether trained or untrained, in whatever field of interest, and with whatever definition of the function and responsibility of social work as a profession. The variety of these associations tends to blur the public image of social work as a profession, but it also enlarges it beyond the image of the social worker as exclusively concerned with the individual case.

The question of the direction that the profession of social work will take is a matter of as lively concern and discussion today as at earlier periods.[39] The old dilemmas pose the issues: scientific knowledge vs. practical experience, person-to-person skills vs. organizational skills, social reform vs. treatment. The strongest emphasis of vocal leaders seems to be on broadening the perception of responsibility, so that the trend since World War II toward a narrow professionalism of individual treatment services will be embraced within the traditional concern with social welfare policies. As one leader recently put it:

> Part of the answer to this dilemma may be in recognizing the fact that greater acceptance in the community involves the status not only of the social worker but also of social welfare as an institution in the democratic society.[40]

He sees progress in this direction as dependent on cooperative efforts of schools, social work agencies, and the professional association.[41] However, it is by no means certain that such cooperation would broaden rather than narrow the profession of social work. In any event, social work is sure to struggle with the concomitants of professionalization for a long time. Such a struggle is characteristic of a vigorous profession.

30 A Study of the Values of Social Workers

Donna L. McLeod

and Henry J. Meyer

Introduction

The profession of social work places great emphasis on what is often termed its *value component*. Social work training involves the inculcation of appropriate attitudes as well as knowledge and skills. The practice of social work itself implies a number of values. That the profession is concerned with this subject is attested by the fact that the Curriculum Study of the Council on Social Work Education devoted a separate volume to the place of values and ethics in the curriculum.[1] While the subject of values is usually included in any discussion of social work practice, attempts to define this area systematically are few, and there have been even fewer published empirical investigations of the subject.[2]

The Curriculum Study, examining the programs of schools of social work throughout the country, noted the paucity of systematic studies and observed that, while values are not explicitly taught or discussed in schools of social work, there is a common core of specific value positions that schools of social work expect their students to hold. For the most part these values are acquired through a combination of selective recruitment and the infusion of course material with value implications rather than through direct instruction. A review of the literature on the philosophy of the profession corroborates the view that there is a common core of identifiable values. Whether or not social workers in fact hold the values espoused by spokesmen for the profession and what precise positions they may hold on such value dimensions are largely unknown.

Thus there are several questions to be answered by empirical study of this area: To what extent do social workers have common values that distinguish them from other occupational groups? What differences are there among members of the profession, and what factors contribute to

This paper was prepared especially for this book. This study was supported in part by a Russell Sage Foundation Faculty Research Grant from the Horace H. Rackham School of Graduate Studies, The University of Michigan.

these differences? How are value differences related to professional practice? What is the relative importance of professional training and of selective recruitment in the inculcation of professional values?

The present study has attempted to delineate and measure some of the relevant value dimensions of social workers in order to begin to answer some of the above questions.

Value Dimensions of Social Work

It is clear from what has been written on social work philosophy that a few dominant themes emerge. Later on we shall outline ten major value dimensions that have been abstracted from the works reviewed.[3] Some of these are more primary or central than others. Some are more concerned with existential questions of what is than with questions of what should be. Taken together they represent an attempt to reduce to minimum elements what might be termed the philosophy of social work in the broadest sense.

We have used the notion of dimension rather than position since each value is viewed as a continuum with poles representing contrasting positions held within our society or by some segment of the population. In many cases both positions are viewed as legitimate or acceptable to some degree by social work as well as by other groups. The hypothesis with which we begin is that social workers as a group are closer than the average of the rest of the population to the pole we state as the social-work value. In the following descriptions, the first-named pole is the value position toward which we believe the profession tends.

I. INDIVIDUAL WORTH VS. SYSTEM GOALS. A primary value mentioned centrally in any discussion of social work values is belief in the worth and dignity of the individual human being, without regard for differentiating criteria, and the importance of maximizing his potential. This might be contrasted with the notion that the goals of the group, state, or system are more important or preeminent.

Florence Kluckhohn characterizes American society as having relatively great concern for individual goals as contrasted with cultures that place primary emphasis on the goals of the lineally or laterally extended group. We can think of cultures that Americans in general condemn for placing little value on individual human life. Viewed from a cross-cultural point of view we are only concerned with a limited portion of this dimension on the side of the individual. Nevertheless, within our society there are those who tend to favor the individual and those who tend to favor the group in situations where conflict of interests occurs. Favoring group goals may sometimes be expressed by defining the needs of some individuals—for example, those who are more productive, healthy, intelligent, or otherwise favored—as having priority over the needs of others.

2. PERSONAL LIBERTY VS. SOCIETAL CONTROL.   Closely allied with the previous value is the right of the individual to direct his life as free from arbitrary external controls as possible. This is often referred to within social work as the principle of self-determination. Contrasted with this is the position that society has a right to exercise controls over individuals to insure its survival and best interests. Everyone admits that personal liberty should not include the liberty to do damage to others. Differences arise as to whether individuals have complete freedom to destroy or do damage to themselves, on the extent to which parents' freedom extends to control over their children, and on the definition of damage to self, children, and others. Questions arise also as to whether society may demand positive acts of compliance as well as impose negative restraints on behavior.

While social work speaks for protection of the rights of the individual and places great emphasis on the principle of self-determination, the complexity of the questions involved and the fact that both poles of the dimension, although conflicting, are also avowed values in social work make it difficult to predict how social workers will stand in relation to other groups on this issue.

3. GROUP RESPONSIBILITY VS. INDIVIDUAL RESPONSIBILITY.   Also central to social work is the belief that the group has responsibility for the welfare of its members. This is contrasted with the position that the individual is responsible for his own welfare, and runs counter to an early American doctrine of individualism committed to laissez faire economics and the survival of the fittest. This latter position, or a modified version of it, still has many advocates in our society, and hence this dimension may be one on which social workers are most clearly differentiated. Williams mentions the clash of humanitarian mores and rugged individualism as one of the important value conflicts in our society.[4]

While accepting group responsibility, social workers also emphasize the development of responsible individuals and the obligations of individuals to contribute to the group. They would not, however, abandon individuals who, for some reason, fail to meet these obligations.

4. SECURITY-SATISFACTION VS. STRUGGLE, SUFFERING, AND DENIAL.   Another basic value in social work is the belief that individuals must have security, acceptance, and satisfaction of basic biological and culturally acquired needs in order to develop their maximum potential. This runs directly counter to a strong religious-cultural theme in our society that stresses the importance of struggle, suffering, denial, and punishment in creating the good man. Often accompanying this latter philosophy is the rejection of biological needs, especially sexual needs, as carnal and representative of the baser aspects of man's nature. According to this philosophy these must be conquered or denied if one is to develop his better nature and become a worthy individual.

This latter viewpoint has its prototype in early Puritanism, but at least a remnant of the philosophy is probably deeply ingrained in our culture. It is suspected that this may represent a real value conflict for many social workers.

5. RELATIVISM-PRAGMATISM VS. ABSOLUTISM-SACREDNESS. Many observers note that social workers have embraced the scientific method and a pragmatic approach to solving problems. They also note that the humanitarianism of 19th-century liberalism, out of which social work emerged, was largely a secular movement in which man's place was elevated. This implies continual questioning of established forms and the acceptance of few absolutes. Social work shares, in this respect, the more general American value of science and secular rationality.

In contrast is a sacred approach to life that accepts many absolute rules for behavior as having superhuman sanction and that does not seek scientific explanation for all phenomena. Since some form of religious-sacred background is a part of the experience of most persons in American society, we would expect many social workers to take a position somewhere between these poles, but with considerable variation among individuals.

6. INNOVATION-CHANGE VS. TRADITIONALISM. Closely associated with the pragmatic approach is a willingness to accept change, as contrasted with an orientation that is committed to the traditional ways of the past. Early social work was primarily committed to social reform and progress. Later, concern with the psychology of individual adjustment drew many social workers away from this earlier position. Nevertheless, social reform is still an important part of the creed of social workers, especially those devoted to community organization and welfare policy. It is expected that social workers generally should be less committed to the *status quo* and more willing to seek new solutions to problems than the general population.

7. DIVERSITY VS. HOMOGENEITY. It is part of our professed American way of life to accept diversity and heterogeneity in ideas, values, and life styles. This diversity is not only to be tolerated, but it is believed to have positive value; it is almost synonymous with democracy. This is especially true in the philosophy of social work. Nevertheless, Robin Williams lists external conformity among the predominant American values. He notes a paradox in that the "heterogeneity of American culture tends to produce a stress upon external conformity."[5]

This tendency can be observed in restrictions that place a premium on conformity to certain cultural norms in residential areas. It is apparent also in dislike of public controversy, a desire to get along, and to squelch those who would rock the boat. The really off-beat individual is viewed more usually with scorn than with interest. Institutions such as un-

American activities committees express Americans' concern with deviation.

The next three value orientations to be described have to do largely with cognitive orientations about the nature of man. They are often mentioned as underlying premises in connection with the other values. It will be useful to examine the extent to which other primary values are dependent on such premises.

8. CULTURAL DETERMINISM VS. INHERENT HUMAN NATURE.   Cultural determinism is the belief that human nature is socially determined and is amenable to change with alterations in the environment. This orientation rejects inherent or biologically inherited personality characteristics, and thus would deny racial or nationality differences attributed to inheritance rather than to culture. It rejects both the notion of natural depravity of man and the notion that babies are born pure and good until corrupted by society.

The contrasting position is that human nature, or parts of it, are inherent or biologically inherited and relatively unchangeable. Questions of the relative influences of heredity and environment have, of course, not been finally answered, and so we would expect some variations in positions. We would expect most social workers to rule out inherent racial and national differences. Bisno notes, however, what he regards as an historical continuity between the theological notion of original sin and the Freudian concept of id.[6] The Freudian influence in social work might run counter to an extreme cultural interpretation.

9. INTERDEPENDENCE VS. INDIVIDUAL AUTONOMY.   The social work position on the relation of the individual to the group is that of a part which is interdependent with the other parts of the whole. This is often mentioned as a premise underlying the value of group responsibility. The contrasting position is that the individual acts autonomously. Persons in our society today can hardly escape the fact of some interdependence. But the question arises as to the degree to which the individual is regarded as free to act and to determine his own fate. The extreme position on the side of interdependence would hold an individual's behavior and the personality organization underlying it to be wholly determined by his relationship with others in the system. This position would tend to assign responsibility for behavior to collectivities rather than to individuals.

10. INDIVIDUALIZATION VS. STEREOTYPING.   Social workers believe that every individual is unique and that people cannot be judged on the basis of one or two facts. This value, coupled with that of the worth and dignity of the individual, underlies the social work principle of individualization, which stresses treating each person as a unique and important human being rather than viewing him categorically as a member of some group. This belief should make social workers relatively immune to stereotyping.

The Social Values Test

In order to investigate hypotheses about the values held by social workers, a test was constructed to reflect the value positions that might be held on each of the ten dimensions described above. The test consisted of 100 attitude statements with ten items relating to each of the 10 value orientations.[7] The items were selected from several hundred on the basis of judgments by a panel of social work educators and social researchers, who were asked to place the statements in their appropriate dimensions. Respondents indicated varying degrees of agreement or disagreement with each statement on a four-point scale.[8] There was an attempt to balance the direction of the statements on each dimension to avoid an "agree" or "disagree" bias.[9]

Although we have used the word dimension in describing these value orientations, we do not claim that the items of the test yielded independent dimensions. The assumption was, however, that the items making up each dimension had some common meaning that was interpretable. Subsequent cluster analysis of items, based on the responses of social workers in the study reported below, indicated sufficient independence of the dimensions to retain all but one of them in revisions of the test.[10]

We report here the investigation of several limited questions about the values of social workers based on the use of this test. The major question considered is whether professionally trained social workers can be distinguished from untrained social workers on any or all of the value orientations espoused in the literature of the profession. A second question concerns the factors, other than professional training, that may be related to differences in value positions among social workers. Data bearing on these two questions come from the study of a sample of social workers who responded to the Social Values Test. The responses of these social workers are compared to those of public school teachers to consider a third question, namely, whether the value dimensions that have been identified distinguish social workers from other professional persons.

The Study of Social Workers [11]

Samples used for this study represent three groups of social workers: (1) fully trained professional social workers, (2) students in social work training, and (3) social workers who had little or no professional training. All together, 293 social workers are included, with approximately equal numbers from each of the three groups.

The professionally trained group represents primarily the membership of a local (Washtenaw County, Michigan) chapter of the National Association of Social Workers. Questionnaires were sent to the entire membership. The response rate was 68 per cent. A few questionnaires were eliminated because respondents did not meet our arbitrary definition of trained by holding a master's degree in social work or equivalent professional training. This sample was augmented by a few respondents who were members of a neighboring (Wayne County) chapter of NASW. The sample of trained social workers received their training in a variety of schools spanning periods of many years. There is no way to know how representative the sample is of all professionally trained social workers.

The in-training, or student, group represents a single school of social work at one period of time. Questionnaires were distributed to the entire student enrollment of The University of Michigan School of Social Work in the spring semester of 1960. The response rate from this group was 71 per cent. Approximately 40 per cent of the sample were second-year students.

The untrained sample came from more diversified sources. Approximately one-half were employees of the Wayne County (Michigan) Bureau of Social Aid. The remainder of the sample was obtained by canvassing agencies of the Washtenaw County Council of Social Agencies for untrained workers, and by the distribution of questionnaires at the beginning of two social work extension classes in neighboring cities. A few of the latter, as well as some of the others included, had previously taken some professional courses in social work. In most cases this training was minimal. Persons with twenty hours or more of social work course credit were excluded from the sample. The amount of training was asked of each respondent so that, in the analysis of data, those with no training could be separated from those with minimal training. Of the 98 respondents in this sample, 68 per cent reported no social work training at all.

In addition to the values test, respondents completed a questionnaire containing information on their demographic and social background, years of experience as a social worker, commitment to the profession, type of employment, and the kind of organizational setting within which they worked. Selected characteristics of the samples are summarized in Table 30–1.

Value Dimensions and Professional Training

The relationship between the level of professional training and the ten value dimensions included in the social attitudes questionnaire is shown in Table 30–2. The scores for each dimension are presented as high and low, divided approximately at the median for the total sample. "High" scores are those in the direction assumed to represent the dominant social work position, and "low" scores are those in the opposite direction.[12]

Of the ten dimensions included in the test, seven were significantly related to level of professional training in the direction predicted. Listed in order of decreasing relationship these are Security-satisfaction, Group responsibility, Interdependence, Innovation-change, Cultural determinism, Individual worth, and Diversity. Those in which the relationship was small or negligible are Individualization, Relativism-pragmatism and Personal liberty.

Table 30–1. **Percentages of Selected Characteristics of Samples of Social Workers**

Characteristics	Trained (N = 103)	In-training (N = 92)	Untrained (N = 98)
Sex:			
Female	66	59	61
Age: [a]			
Under 30 years	13	71	46
30–39	32	16	28
40 or over	47	10	21
Ethnic background:			
Native-born parents	62	82	78
Father's occupation: [b]			
White collar	73	70	54
Blue collar	24	27	45
Religion: [c]			
Protestant	58	72	71
Catholic	11	7	23
Jewish	26	13	3
Religion:			
"Presently committed"	79	72	82
Career commitment:			
Committed to social work	83	59	54
Experience as social worker: [d]			
0–3 years	13	73	50
4–8 years	28	10	27
9 or more years	55	9	12
Social work specialization:			
Caseworkers	84	70 [e]	88

[a] Age not ascertained for 8, 3, and 5 per cent for each sample, respectively.

[b] Father's occupation not ascertained for 3, 3, and 1 per cent for each sample, respectively.

[c] Religion not ascertained, mixed, reported as "other" or "none" by 5, 8, and 4 per cent for each sample, respectively.

[d] Experience not ascertained for 4, 8, and 11 per cent for each sample, respectively.

[e] Students were instructed to report their field placements.

Table 30–2. Percentage of Social Workers with High and Low Scores on Each of Ten Value Dimensions, by Level of Training in Social Work

Value Dimensions	Trained (N = 103)	In-training (N = 92)	Untrained (N = 98)
Security-satisfaction [a]			
High	59	51	27
Low	41	49	73
Group responsibility [a]			
High	63	53	34
Low	37	47	66
Interdependence [a]			
High	59	49	24
Low	41	51	76
Innovation-change [a]			
High	48	54	29
Low	52	46	71
Cultural determinism [a]			
High	53	49	34
Low	47	51	66
Individual worth [a]			
High	53	48	37
Low	47	52	63
Diversity [a]			
High	46	49	34
Low	54	51	66
Individualization			
High	52	47	39
Low	48	53	61
Relativism-pragmatism			
High	44	53	40
Low	56	47	60
Personal liberty			
High	45	52	40
Low	55	48	60

[a] Relationship between training level and dimension score significant at τ of .05.

The same relationships held when the combined samples were classified by number of hours of social work training. A slightly larger percentage of persons with no hours of social work training than of the "untrained" group had low scores, but the differences were negligible. In general, the percentage with high scores increased with increased training.

Examining the dimensions for which significant relationships were found, it is apparent that the major differences are actually between the untrained social workers and the other two groups. Between the fully trained professionals and students in training there are small differences. On two dimensions, in fact (Innovation-change and Diversity) the in-training group had a greater proportion of high scores than the trained group. On the Innovation-change dimension this is not to be accounted for by the preponderance of young people in the in-training group, as might be suspected. The significant relationship between training and value scores on this dimension appears indeed to be caused by value differences between both training groups and the "untrained" social worker. On the Diversity dimension the apparent reversal of the trained and in-training groups is partially a result of our procedure of collapsing scores into a dichotomy. In more detailed analysis, the trained group had a higher percentage of scores in the top quartile, but a lower percentage in the second quartile. With the factor of age controlled, a higher percentage of the professional group was found in the second quartile as well.

Training or Selection?

This leads to the question of whether the relationships observed are primarily the result of social work training or of other characteristics that might differentiate the three groups. All possible selective factors which might account for differences could not, of course, be examined. Some of the background and social factors often associated with differences in attitudes could be examined for their possible relationship to the values included in the test.

One of the more obvious factors that might affect value responses is the amount of nonprofessional education. Sophistication resulting from differences in general education, rather than training in social work, might account for the findings. However, this was not the case when the general educational levels of the three samples were held constant. Similarly, most of the other factors examined showed no significant relation with value scores, and in addition were fairly equally distributed among the three training groups. Only two factors appeared to be strongly related to several of the value dimensions: religion and ethnic background. We will also discuss age as a control factor because the samples vary greatly in age distribution, although no clear relation between age and value scores appeared in preliminary analyses.

Table 30–3 shows the degree of relationship (tau-beta) between training level and each value dimension for the entire sample and for the

Table 30–3. Tau-beta Correlations of Professional Training Levels and Value Dimensions for Entire Sample and within Religious, Ethnic, and Age Subgroups

Value Dimensions	Entire Sample (N = 293)	Religion		Ethnic Background		Age	
		Protestant (N = 165)	Nonreligious (N = 52)	Native (N = 215)	Foreign (N = 74)	Under 30 (N = 123)	30+ (N = 154)
Security-satisfaction	.29 [a]	.33	.05	.29	.27	.28	.25
Group responsibility	.23 [a]	.25	−.02	.18	.27	.16	.19
Interdependence	.23 [a]	.24	−.03	.23	.18	.19	.23
Innovation-change	.17 [b]	.15	−.05	.12	.21	.11	.25
Cultural determinism	.14 [b]	.16	−.04	.09	.24	.10	.17
Individual worth	.13 [c]	.14	.03	.15	.15	.13	.09
Diversity	.11 [c]	.09	−.08	.04	.21	.12	.20
Individualization	.08	.19	−.21	.09	.10	.04	.13
Relativism pragmatism	.07	.04	−.01	.05	.01	.03	.14
Personal liberty	.03	.05	−.15	.03	.00	−.14	.00

[a] $p < .001$
[b] $p < .01$
[c] $p < .05$

training levels within specified religious, ethnic, and age categories. In general, the correlations of training level and value scores do not markedly diminish when these three controls are applied. Within some subgroups, the effect of training appears to be greater than it is for the total sample. There are, however, some exceptions.

Regardless of training level, religious background is related to the first seven of the value dimensions listed. Protestants and Catholics tend to be low on all of these dimensions, and Jews and persons with no religious commitment tend to be high. Catholics are slightly lower than Protestants. On some dimensions Jews are higher than the noncommitted and on others lower.

Because of the small number of Catholic and Jewish social workers included, and because the latter are almost all trained social workers, it is not possible to make a reliable estimate of the independent effect of the training factor within these groups. The relationship can be examined, however, for persons of Protestant background presently committed to this faith. (See Table 30–3.) Such persons include over half of the entire sample (165). This group tends to be low on all seven dimensions, but among the Proestant social workers the correlations between training levels and value scores are slightly higher than for the entire sample on most of the dimensions. Thus, trained Protestant social workers, while lower on value scores than trained Jewish or nonreligious social workers, are not as low as untrained Protestant social workers. In contrast, there is apparently no relation between training and value scores among social workers classified as nonreligious. These persons tend to be high on all dimensions regardless of their training status. The relationships between religion, training, and value scores are so consistent that they are unlikely to occur by chance alone.

Ethnic background [13] was also found to be strongly associated with value scores. It is likely that ethnic background and religion are related rather than separate factors, but the sample is too small to permit analysis controlling these factors simultaneously. Ethnic background was found to be clearly relevant, regardless of the level of training, for the first four dimensions (Security-satisfaction, Group responsibility, Interdependence, and Innovation-change) and less clearly so for the next three. Social workers with one or both parents foreign born tend to be higher on dimension scores than those with both parents native born.

Where it is possible to examine meaningfully the relationship of training level and value responses within ethnic categories, the correlations obtaining for the entire sample are maintained fairly consistently. (See Table 30–3.) However, there are some interesting variations. On several dimensions, training and value scores are much more strongly related within the foreign-parentage group than within the native-parentage group. This is true for the dimensions of Group responsibility, Innovation-change, Cultural determinism, and Diversity. On this last dimension, training is unrelated to value score within the native parentage group. An interpretation of these findings might suggest that foreign parentage may provide experiences that facilitate the acquiring of certain values consonant with those conveyed in professional social work training.

On most dimensions age does not show a consistent relation to value positions. But age does appear to be related to two dimensions. On Group responsibility those persons 30 years of age or older are slightly higher than those under 30, regardless of training level. On the other hand, younger social workers are higher on Diversity than older social workers.

The correlations between training and value scores are generally maintained with the factor of age controlled. (See Table 30–3.) The relation is reduced most for the dimension of Group responsibility. The relationship of training and this dimension is apparently accounted for in part by the concentration of older persons in the trained group. With age controlled, the in-training group scores higher than the trained group on this dimension. It may be that the value of Group responsibility was particularly stressed in the educational setting where the student social workers in the sample were being trained.

Training and value scores are more strongly related in some age categories than in others. (See Table 30–3.) This is most apparent for the dimensions of Innovation-change, Cultural determinism, and Diversity, in all of which the relationship is strongest within the older (over 30) group.

Although the relationship between training level and value scores is maintained, for the most part, when known background factors are controlled, we must be cautious about interpreting the value differences found as caused exclusively by training. Selection on some other basis is always a possibility. In order to establish the effect of training on value formation, longitudinal studies of persons at various stages of social work training should be undertaken.

Present Position or Training?

Factors related to the person's present position as a social worker were examined to see if they, rather than level of training, account for some of the variations in value scores.

While trained social workers who consider themselves "career" social workers tend to be slightly higher on all dimensions except Diversity than those who do not, the number of persons (13) at this training level who are not career social workers is too small to make a reliable analysis. Furthermore, among the untrained group, where career-oriented and non-career-oriented social workers are about equal in number, the noncareer group tends to be slightly higher on most dimensions. Among students there is variation from dimension to dimension, perhaps because the non-career group is quite small (17). In general, career commitment, as measured in this study, cannot be said to account for differences in value scores.

Professional commitment as measured by NASW membership among students also does not account for differences. Students who belong to

NASW are no more likely to have high value scores than those who do not belong.

None of the other factors reflecting the person's position as a social worker—type of specialization, type of work done,[14] perception of agreement among social workers,[15] social work contacts,[16] other professional contacts,[17] or years of experience—showed any clear relation to value scores. The nature of the samples and the kind of information obtained limit the analysis that can be made of these factors.

Summary

Seven of the ten value dimensions, delineated as core values expressed in the literature of professional social work, were found to be significantly related to levels of professional social work training. These relationships varied in magnitude from .29 for Security-satisfaction to .11 for Diversity. The relationships were found to be independent of a number of background and social factors used as statistical controls in the analysis. There was one important exception: professional training was not a significant factor related to the value positions expressed by persons who were not committed to a religious faith. These persons tended to be high on all value dimensions, regardless of their training status.

Religion and ethnicity had strong independent effects on the same values that were related to training. Social workers classified as non-religious, or as Jewish, and those with foreign parentage were higher on value scores than Protestants, Catholics, and those of native parentage.

On the basis of these findings, it may be tentatively concluded that both selection and training operate to produce a professional group distinguishable in terms of certain basic value positions, but that training operates differentially on different groups. As a result, fully trained social workers, though distinguishable from less trained social workers, vary considerably among themselves in their social values.

Comparison of Social Workers and School Teachers [18]

A revision of the Social Values Test [19] was administered to 724 public school teachers in Detroit in 1961. The sample constituted the faculties of 16 schools, 9 of which were elementary schools, 4 junior high, and 3 high schools. Seven of the schools (4 elementary, 2 junior high, and 1 high school) were part of an experimental project intended to improve educational opportunities for children in deprived areas of the city. The remaining 9 schools were selected as comparable working-class or contrasting middle-class schools. Thus, the sample ranged across schools having pupils from all social class levels except the very highest income areas. Although the teachers in these schools cannot be taken as representative of all public school teachers in the city, no obvious groups of teachers were unrepresented.

Because only some items, common to both versions of the social values test, were answered by both social workers and teachers, we cannot compare them on total scores for each of the value dimensions. We have, however, made item-by-item comparisons for each value dimension, using only common questions. On this basis we may consider whether social workers differ from teachers on the core values of social work that have been identified. The comparison is presented in Table 30–4.

Table 30–4. Comparison of Social Workers (N = 293) and Teachers (N = 724) on Identical Items of Social Values Test by Value Dimension

Value Dimensions	Number of Identical Items	Number of Items Social Workers Higher Than Teachers [a]	Mean Percentage Adhering to Value Position of Professional Social Work [b]	
			Social Workers	Teachers
Security-satisfaction	6	6	79	55
Group responsibility	8	7	78	49
Interdependence	6	6	74	40
Innovation-change	6	6	75	57
Cultural determinism	3	3	76	49
Individual worth	6	6	76	54
Diversity	4	4	73	57
Relativism-pragmatism	4	4	70	40
Personal liberty	5	5	52	34

[a] "Higher" means that there is a greater proportion of responses for an item in those categories indicating adherence to the value position of professional social work.

[b] "Value position of professional social work" means the position on the items of a dimension most consistent with the core values expressed in social work literature.

For each of the dimensions (except Group responsibility), every item on which comparisons can be made was answered to a greater extent by social workers than by teachers in terms of the value positions we have described as characterizing the social work profession. Of the total of 48 items, 47 are consistently answered in this way. The comparison between average proportions of social workers and teachers adhering to the value positions of professional social work points in the same direction. Except for the dimension, Personal liberty, approximately three-fourths of the social workers, compared to approximately one-half of the teachers, take the positions hypothesized for the social work profession. If the analysis had been made only for fully trained social workers in the sample, the contrast with teachers would have been even greater. On six of the nine dimensions where they can be compared, over 20 per cent more of the social workers than of the teachers subscribe to the stated value position. Clearly, the value positions of social workers, as expressed in these items, differ from those of teachers.

It would be necessary to sample other professional groups, as well as to establish the validity and reliability of the social values test, in order to conclude that social workers hold a set of distinctive values. We might expect members of some of the other helping professions to be more like social workers than teachers appear to be. We might also expect some nonprofessional segments of the population—for example, educated middle-class women activists in community affairs—to resemble social workers. Further research is required also to determine the extent to which the characteristics of persons selecting social work and admitted into the profession, the type and content of training, and conditions of employment and practice may contribute to any differences that may be found between social workers and members of other professions. It is reasonable to expect that each of these factors plays its part. The evidence from the present data is sufficiently suggestive to encourage such research.

Conclusion

We have delineated the major value dimensions inferred from the literature of professional social work and devised a test to reflect these values. Using the test, we were able to show an association between professional training, together with some background characteristics, and the social values held by a sample of social workers. By comparing social workers and teachers, we have also offered some evidence to support the hypothesis that social workers may hold distinctive values as a professional group.

If these tentative conclusions are substantiated by further research, their relevance for social work education and practice would deserve careful consideration and investigation.

31 Selecting Knowledge from Behavioral Science

Edwin J. Thomas

The knowledge of human behavior so essential to the practice of social work is not an immutable doctrine, complete and correct, but rather is a growing, ever-changing body of provisional concepts, hypotheses, and theories. Confronted by a growing and changing domain of behavioral science, the problem is what to select as the components of social work's conception of human behavior. If social work were an older and more mature profession and if behavioral science were more highly developed than it is, the task of selection might be much easier than it now is. At present, however, social work is still in the early stages of defining its domain of intervention, its techniques, its principles of practice, as well as its conception of human behavior. And behavioral science, for all its vigorous empirical and theoretical effort, is still a long distance from having the established methods, the accumulation of facts, and the powerful theories that have characterized many of the physical sciences. The question of what to borrow from the behavioral sciences is further complicated by the fact that professional criteria governing what knowledge is deemed most useful are not always the same as scientific criteria.

But the task of selection cannot be avoided, however difficult it is. Provisional criteria are needed for selecting potentially useful behavioral science for use in social work. This paper presents a preliminary designation and should perhaps be construed mainly as a scholarly strategy as opposed to a strategy for research, practice, or education. This is not to say, however, that the strategy would not possibly be useful in these other endeavors. The criteria to be discussed pertain to the content and power of the knowledge as well as to characteristics of the referents of the knowledge concepts.

From BUILDING SOCIAL WORK KNOWLEDGE: REPORT OF A CONFERENCE (New York: National Association of Social Workers, 1964), pp. 38–48. Reprinted with the permission of the author and the National Association of Social Workers.

Selection Criteria

Content Relevance

Various scholars in social work have suggested the varieties of knowledge of special relevance to understanding human behavior in the context of social work. Maas has emphasized especially the relevance of knowledge pertaining to stress for individuals, groups, and communities.[1] Towle has indicated the usefulness of knowledge of normality, abnormality, and of maturation, growth, and change for individuals and groups.[2] The curriculum statements of the Council on Social Work Education pertaining to the human growth and behavior sequence have stipulated both the knowledge content (such as knowledge of individual functioning, group processes, and cultural influences) as well as the levels of human aggregation (such as individuals, groups, communities) that should be understood. The comments here draw upon all these conceptions to varying degrees, departing from them largely in that the framework to be outlined is intended to be somewhat more general and comprehensive.

Consider, first, the areas of potentially relevant knowledge. There are four of these, none of which is fully mutually exclusive of the other. They are as follows: knowledge of (1) normal behavior, (2) abnormality, deviation, and atypicality, (3) growth, maturation, and change, (4) research and theory pertaining to the helping process. Most statements of scholars and the profession have acknowledged the importance of the first three areas. The fourth, the helping process, has not always been emphasized as relevant in either the human growth and behavior sequence or, for that matter, in the practice sequences. As distinguished from the principles of practice in social work, research and theory pertaining to the helping process concern what is known in behavioral science about achieving change in people and, as such, are comprised of fact, hypothesis, and theory drawn from both clinical and nonclinical spheres of inquiry. Principles of practice are normative and prescriptive, whereas research and theory pertaining to the helping process are not.

The above four areas of subject matter must be considered for each pertinent level of human aggregation. These levels are those of the individual, the group, the organization, the community, and society. Combining the four subject matters with the five levels of human aggregation results in twenty relatively distinct clusters of potentially relevant behavioral science (see Table 31–1).

Even though each cell of the diagram is not entirely mutually exclusive of the next because of necessary minor overlapping of the four subject matters for any given level, numerous intriguing packages of material are differentiated. For example, consider the group level. In addition to behavioral science pertaining to the normal functioning of groups (Cell 5), which might include the integration and organization, structure, and

Table 31-1. Cells of Behavioral Science Knowledge Potentially Relevant for Social Work

| | SUBJECT MATTER | | | |
Level to which sub-ject matter applied	Normal behavior	Abnormality and deviation	Growth, maturation, and change	The helping process
Individual	1	2	3	4
Group	5	6	7	8
Organization	9	10	11	12
Community	13	14	15	16
Society	17	18	19	20

functioning of groups, three additional pertinent classes of material are indicated. Abnormalities and deviations of groups (Cell 6) would include such topics as the functioning of social groups (such as families, therapy groups, and problem-solving groups) consisting of deviant individuals as well as the atypical and deviating functioning of such groups composed of normal individuals. The area of growth, maturation, and change of groups (Cell 7) might include the developmental processes and phases of families, friendship groups, problem-solving groups, and therapy groups. The area of the helping process (Cell 8) would include research and theory pertaining to achieving change in groups. Research and theory from be-havioral science might be assimilated and collated as they pertain to the helping activities of obtaining and processing information and exerting social influence in order to achieve therapeutic objectives.

It is probably safe to say that of all the cells in the diagram the ones that have received the greatest attention thus far in social work are 1, 2, and 3. Two tasks require attention if the diagram is to be converted into something more than a suggestive skeleton. First, the component subject matters for each cell must be delineated in detail. This is no small job, as the writer discovered when attempting to do this for the helping process primarily at the individual level (Cell 4). In this exploration the behavioral tasks of interpersonal helping were laid forth (obtaining and processing information and exerting social influence) and against them was placed the material from behavioral science that seemed potentially relevant.[5] The second task required to convert the various packages of knowledge into potentially useful information is to assimilate the empirical and theoretical literature pertaining to all the subtopics delineated for each cell. In our endeavors to apply behavioral science to various problems of social work, we sometimes overlook or bypass the necessary step of assimilating knowledge potentially relevant to the area of application. Assimilation is a necessary but not sufficient condition in applying behavioral science to social work. Other selection criteria, to be indicated below, must be made use of in order further to screen the actually relevant content from that merely potentially relevant.

Knowledge Power

For any given knowledge deemed potentially relevant it is desirable to examine the extent to which the knowledge has power. Three features of the knowledge itself may be considered as defining its power:

1. The *validity* of the propositions is determined by the extent of empirical corroboration of the propositions. If the studies of a given domain are not well done, if the findings are inconsistent with what is otherwise known, or if there are precious few adequate investigations of a problem, empirically valid generalizations cannot be formulated and application would therefore be hazardous.

2. Knowledge may be regarded as powerful in terms of its *predictive potency*, which is a function of the formal structure of the theory. For example, a proposition embedded with many other propositions linked by logical relations that make it possible to formulate genuine derivations contains vastly more predictive potency than a proposition that stands by itself or is one among many other propositions not logically related such that when the propositions are combined derivations may be made logically. Other factors being equal, a proposition having predictive potency, as here conceived, is clearly preferable to one lacking such potency.

3. The variable itself may be potent or weak depending on how much of the empirical variance it accounts for in research contexts. Variables known to explain a sizable proportion of the variance (i.e., having high *variable potency*), in researches that have adequately examined the problem, are preferred over those variables that explain but a modest degree of variance, or none whatever, in suitable empirical inquiries.

Consider the research and theory pertaining to the content of what is discussed in therapeutic interviews. On the basis of the writer's examination of the literature pertaining to this problem, reinforcement theory qualifies as being powerful knowledge. Numerous studies have shown that many aspects of verbal behavior in therapeutic as well as nontherapeutic contexts can be impressively altered by the use of positive and negative reinforcement. Reinforcement qualifies eminently as a potent variable; the assertions pertaining to reinforcement have received ample support in research on humans and nonhumans, and the theory is capable of generating logical derivations.[4] To appraise the power of knowledge in any given area of behavioral science it is clear that a meticulous examination of both empirical corroboration and logical structure of theory is required.

Referent Features

The discussion heretofore has pertained to characteristics of knowledge itself rather than to the empirical indicators, or referents, of the variables. A referent pertains to something in the real world and, in this respect, is analogous to the idea of an operational definition in research. Consider the conceptual variable of emotional support, for example. A referent of this variable might consist of an affirmative nod of the head, a warm, encouraging look, a statement of agreement, and so on.

As will become apparent, features of the referents are absolutely crucial in determining whether knowledge—however promising it appears to be in terms of other criteria—is in fact applicable. Some variables have the dubious distinction of having no identifiable referents, except perhaps in some neural substratum (consider Jung's idea of the racial unconscious or Freud's libido). In contrast, consider research and theory pertaining to group size. The size of groups is readily ascertained, of course, by counting the number of people in the group. The action one may take with respect to a variable is obviously greatly determined by the extent to which indicators of that variable can be identified. Clearly, if a referent is not identifiable it cannot be accessible. Thus *referent identifiability* is an important criterion in determining the extent to which knowledge is applicable.

A second referent criterion is *referent accessibility*, which pertains to the extent to which any given referent may be approached in action by a professional helper. The importance of accessibility is that its presence enables one to manipulate a variable, whereas its absence precludes manipulation. Consider the power structure of a family. If this structure is not accessible to the professional helper, he cannot act so as to alter it directly, whereas if it is accessible he may be able to change it. It is important to note, however, that knowledge pertaining to inaccessible indicators need not necessarily be useless. Indirect or complementary action may be afforded with knowledge pertaining to an inaccessible indicator and such action may take many forms, among these being the manipulation of indicators of other variables.

When a referent is accessible and manipulable, i.e., may be altered by a professional helper, the indicator meets the criterion of *referent manipulability*. Direct action is possible with manipulable referents. Group size and group composition are often manipulable referents for various bodies of knowledge and for this reason perhaps as well as any other there appears to be a great interest in knowledge pertaining to these referents in casework and group work. Knowledge pertaining to manipulable referents is thus understandably highly prized.

The therapeutic relationship has long been a principal focus of attention in the practice literature of social work, and for good reason: the interpersonal relationship between the helper and the client is subject to considerable planful alteration. Moreover, the referents of the helping relationship have other virtues, as will be noted below.

Other criteria than the manipulability of a referent must be met before application can readily be undertaken. An important factor in evaluating whether an intervention is practical is *manipulation cost*. Even when a referent is manipulable in principle, its alteration may entail such high costs in labor and money that this intervention would typically be prohibited. Excessive costs, like nonmanipulability, may ultimately be remediable; in the case of costs this depends on how successfully ways may be found to reduce costs. Even though manipulation may have to be foregone because of exorbitant costs, action need not be halted, for again the knowledge may make possible complementary action.[5]

Another characteristic of a referent is its *potency*, which is the degree of influence that a given referent may have in any existing helping context. An indicator may be weak in a helping context even when the variable has high potency in research contexts. For example, a client's attraction to a given helper may affect the client's continuation in treatment less potently when the countervailing forces of time, cost, or effort are high rather than low. Knowledge about weak indicators is of little value unless alternative referents can be found, or unless ways can be discovered to increase their influence through such means as more far-ranging alteration of the indicator or the protection, through insulation, of the indicator's effectiveness from the operation of interfering factors. Indicator potency is nothing other than an operational rendition, in the helping context, of variable potency and, for this reason, indicator potency cannot exceed the hypothetical maximum degree of variable potency. And, clearly, truly low variable potency can be accompanied only by low referent potency.

A final criterion pertaining to referents concerns the *ethical suitability* of any proposed manipulation. The manipulation of a given referent may or may not be consistent with the profession's ethics and society's values. The use of bribes, sexual inducements, or exaggerated claims of therapeutic benefit are ruled ethically unsuitable in most of the helping professions for purposes of establishing a helping relationship, whereas warm acceptance of the client, appropriate support for his entry into treatment, and the use of courtesy and civility are ethically suitable means to achieve a working interpersonal relationship. Clearly, if a manipulation is ethically unsuitable, it should be avoided, in general. Exceptions might be taken to this when the ethical objections are based on incorrectly alleged costs anticipated for clients or others. But even when the objections are mistaken, it might be unwise to proceed anyway with the tabooed manipulation; the conflict and resentment that such action might generate could easily exceed the benefits to be achieved.

Knowledge Resulting from Use of Screening Criteria

When placed against any screening criterion, material drawn from behavioral science may be judged, if sufficient information is available, in any of three ways: (1) It may meet the criterion, in which case there is no difficulty. (2) It may fail critically to meet the standard, i.e., the evidence may indicate that the criterion has, unequivocally and irremediably, not been met. For example, many adequate studies may show that the knowledge is invalid or the variable extremely weak, and so on. (3) The material may fail the criterion noncritically, i.e., the failure may be either equivocal, temporary, or remediable. For instance, knowledge might be judged invalid on the basis of inextensive or weak research, in which case further inquiry might reveal valid knowledge, and so on.

When all the above screening criteria are used in concert it is immediately apparent that any portion of behavioral science may be characterized most complexly. What is most significant, however, are the distinct types of applicability that may be identified:

1. *Material immediately applicable for direct action* is defined by knowledge meeting all of the screening criteria. A large portion of reinforcement theory applies in this way.

2. *Material immediately applicable for complementary or indirect action* is defined by knowledge meeting the criteria of content relevance, knowledge power, referent identifiability, and potency, but failing on the other referent standards. Stated otherwise, such material is characterized by variables having referents that are inaccessible, too costly, nonmanipulable, or ethically unsuitable for manipulation. Portions of research in personality and persuasibility legitimately fall here, in particular problems relating to both the accessibility and manipulability of many personality characteristics.

3. *Material hypothetically applicable for direct action* is demarked by knowledge that fails noncritically on one or more of the screening criteria. An example of such knowledge might be portions of the work done on thought control; neither the ethical objections nor the technical problems of manipulability are necessarily critical, especially when one realizes that therapeutic, custodial, and religious ideologies often function likewise in organizations and elsewhere as means of governing thoughts and action.

4. *Material hypothetically applicable for indirect or complementary action* is stipulated by noncritical failure to meet the standards of content relevance, knowledge power, referent identifiability, or potency, and by failure (of either kind) on the remaining referent criteria. Some of the research conclusions concerning the relationship between ego strength and therapeutic success might be illustrative here (ego strength is mainly nonaccessible to helper manipulation and, therefore, action in respect to ego strength would have to be indirect), but, more importantly, research has not clearly indicated its presumed relationship to therapeutic outcome.

5. *Inapplicable material* is defined by critical failure to meet the criteria of content relevance, knowledge power, referent identifiability, referent potency, or ethical suitability. Portions of knowledge on brainwashing fall here; many of the manipulations of brainwashing would not be

ethically suitable for us and, furthermore, many of the claims regarding the effectiveness of brainwashing procedures have been exaggerated.

Conclusions

Use of explicit screening criteria, such as those noted here, avoids reliance on often-heard, ambiguous standards that can best be characterized as pseudocriteria, for this context. Examples of such false criteria are that the behavioral science lacks clinical testing, has not been integrated with present knowledge, or is mechanical. In general, these standards, when carefully appraised, are (1) so ambiguous as to be meaningless, except possibly as an expression of resistance, (2) wrong, (3) an oblique reference to a criteron elaborated here, or (4) relevant to problems of using knowledge in practice, but not to the selection of knowledge.

The tentative strategy suggested here counters the misconception that almost all knowledge from behavioral science is applicable to social work, or its extreme counterpart that almost all knowledge from behavioral science is not applicable. There are many varieties of applicability.

The present comments suggest that the application of the behavioral science to social work, in any case, is not a direct, simple importation, but rather calls for detailed, thoughtful appraisal of relevance of the content, the power of the knowledge, as well as of many practical considerations relating to the knowledge referents.

32 Problems and Processes in Developing Social Work Practice Principles

Robert D. Vinter

The purpose of this discussion is to consider the problems and processes involved in formulating practice theory in social work.[1] It will focus on the objectives and requirements for this type of endeavor, and some of the means by which such work can be facilitated. Despite the profession's intense interest in methods and techniques of practice, and the large literature on practice, there has been very little analysis of the processes of formulating practice principles. Anyone undertaking this analysis enters relatively uncharted territory, and can be expected to do little more than identify certain of the major issues to be addressed.

An analysis of theory building in social work can be enhanced by making certain distinctions among current uses of the term theory. There are at least three ways in which interest in theory is expressed within the profession. First, there is theory for social work. This consists of formulations, borrowed from the social sciences and other disciplines or developed within our own ranks, that seek to order and explain important phenomena. Thus, we utilize personality theory, small-group theory, and theory about the structure of organizations or community power. Second, there is theory of social work or of social work practice. This includes formulations that seek to account for the behavior of social workers, of health and welfare organizations, or of social welfare as a field of activities and services. Such theory is developed about social work practice, and may be formulated by social workers or by social scientists who find the activities of our profession fit objects for analysis.[2] Third, there is that which we consider practice theory. This consists of a body of principles, more or less systematically developed and anchored in scientific knowledge, that seeks to guide and direct practitioner action. This third type of theory is the present focus of our attention.

This paper was prepared especially for this book.

Actually, there can be no such entity as practice theory, at least not in the same sense that there can be theory for, or theory about, practice. Theory, as commonly used in the sciences, means a set of logically related propositions about reality, the purpose of which is to achieve greater understanding of such reality. In contrast, practice theory is a set of principles directed not at understanding reality, but at achieving control over it.[3] The immediate aim is to effect change in some aspect of personal or social reality, whether this be by modification of the legal structure, or by control of a delinquent's deviant behavior. There is considerable confusion about the essential difference between scientific theory and practice theory, partly because principles of practice may incorporate concepts and knowledge from scientific theory, and partly because these principles sometimes appear as interrelated propositions and directives of a complex form not unlike scientific theory. To confuse propositions directed at explanation with action principles aimed at exercising control over reality, however, is certain to increase the difficulties of interchange between these two intellectual efforts.[4]

Before proceeding, it should be noted that social work is not ready for a grand or unified theory any more than the social sciences are. All discussion here is about specific sets of propositions or principles that refer to delimited ranges of activity. Whatever the seeming commonalities among various intervention approaches useful in social work, we are constrained to consider them as discrete and to accept a multiplicity of practice theories. While it postpones the task of integrating such diverse perspectives, this view seems more appropriate to our present state of intellectual achievement.

Requirements of Practice Principles

The conception of practice theory as a set of action principles implies at least four major requirements. Each of these can be briefly stated here, and elaborated in subsequent discussion. (1) Practice principles must specify or refer to the desired ends of action, the changed behaviors or conditions in which it is intended that effective action will result. In social work we are accustomed to speak of these ends as goals, whether we are referring to particular objectives sought for individual clients, or more general social goals to which the totality of our professional and organizational efforts are directed. (2) Practice principles must be consistent with the ethical commitments that enjoin and circumscribe professional activity. Because of our distinctive value system there are many means we deny ourselves to attain desired ends or goals, even though some of these procedures might be highly effective. On the other hand, there are other means or actions we prefer to employ because they are highly valued. Both goals and ethical commitments are derivative of the profession's general value system, one referring to the ends of action, and the other referring to the means of action. (3) Practice principles should incorporate valid knowledge about the most important phenomena or events with which professionals are concerned. Practice principles for those who are mainly concerned with individuals must be consistent with the known nature of individuals, their personality structures, and their behavioral patterns. Principles for those mainly concerned with legislative action must be consistent with the nature of representative government, the legal and legislative structures, and the like. This component is most likely to be borrowed (and perhaps appropriately restated) from scientific theory and empirical knowledge. (4) Practice principles should direct the professional toward certain types of actions, which, if engaged in, are likely to achieve the desired ends or goals. Such actions must be consistent with the body of ethical commitments that circumscribe our activity, they must be informed by available knowledge about the empirical realities central to the sphere of action, and they should have high probability of effectiveness. To achieve a systematic body of practice theory it is necessary that a comprehensive and logically interrelated set of action principles be formulated, consistent with these requirements.

Good practice principles are action and change oriented. In the engineering professions they direct practitioners toward effective manipulation of physical materials. In the helping professions, particularly in social work, they direct practitioners toward effective intervention in social processes. Well-developed practice principles indicate not only the ends or goals to be sought, but also the means by which these may be achieved. They are, therefore, utilitarian and instrumental.

Frames of Reference

Even the most modest effort in formulating practice principles is shaped by and within some frame of reference. By "frame of reference" is meant that particular universe of discourse employed for perceiving, defining, evaluating, and communicating. The professional who works at stating practice principles is both influenced and limited by his frame of reference no less than the scientist by his basic assumptions, concepts, and values. These frames guide our intellectual efforts however implicitly they may be conceived.

An essential component of any frame of reference is some conception of the prime function of a delineated sphere of social work service. What effects are to be achieved, and for whom, by the provision of such service? To illustrate by reference to my own work, I have proposed a fourfold set of functions that social work serves for the client, the community, and the surrounding society: adaptation, socialization, integration, and consumption gratification.[5] For reasons irrelevant in the present context, I have elsewhere emphasized the integration function of group-work service. A primary purpose of group-work practice, so conceived, is to change the client's relation with his social environment through his participation in small-group life. Some notion of the function of social work service is axiomatic within any frame of reference, but may be derived from ideas about the more general goals of social work and the major functions it can or should serve in this society.

A second essential component is some conception of the client, his attributes, and his status within the sphere of professional practice. In most schemes the client is conceived as a disadvantaged or deviant person who is the prime target of the service (i.e., the one to be changed), in whose interests the service is undertaken, and with whom the practitioner directly interacts. There are, of course, other conceptions of the client: it may be a group or organization or community, or it may be someone who is a beneficiary but with whom the professional does not directly interact. This component also includes some conception of the status of condition in which the person must be in order to merit service as a client.

A third essential component of a frame of reference is some conception of the professional practitioner, of his relation to the client, and of his major activities in providing service. Here are included ideas about the worker and his agency status, his function as a legitimate agent of change, his power, and the resources available to him.[6]

In my own work I have chosen to view the practitioner as one who directly interacts with clients for treatment purposes, intervening in the process of the client group to effect, through it, desired changes among the individual members. By elaborating and combining the second and the third orders of conceptions, I have developed the notion of the group as both the context and the means for that change effected by the worker's intervention in accordance with his treatment goals for individual clients. Several types of decision and action issues that confront the practitioner are defined within this formulation: one set has to do with the clients as targets of service, and another set has to do with the group as a means for changing individual clients. Major diagnostic and treatment principles are specified with reference to these issues, and action techniques are stated in terms of both individual and group phenomena. (These conceptions and their relations with other units for analysis are shown in Figure 32–1.)

All frames of reference currently in use appear to include, if only implicitly, the foregoing components. It is doubtful whether any significant intellectual effort can be advanced except through some ideational context within which events are noted, problems identified, and interpretations and solutions set forth. One value in explicitly presenting the assumptions and issues proposed for a frame of reference is to assure that the most important dimensions of relevant practice situations have been considered. Another value is that of clearly communicating the general conditions under which the action principles should be valid. Specification of the terms of reference for any set of practice principles necessarily reduces their generality, but such delimination in scope is in keeping with the modest level of current attainments.

Emphasis on clarification of frames of reference is not to advocate that one should initially construct a complete framework, which then remains

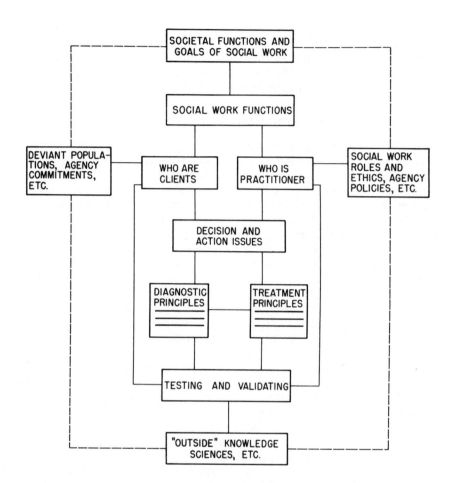

Figure 32–1. Frame of Reference for Developing Practice Principles

unchanged while it is being filled out and principles are being formulated within it. Indeed, there is a reflexive relation between the several components of a practice theory and the processes of its development: each new endeavor tends to introduce some modification or elaboration in the general frame of reference and in all other units of the theory. The framework ought to be sufficiently open so that necessary changes are not impeded by premature closure, and so that knowledge from outside the scheme can be continuously incorporated. (The broken lines in the figure are intended to indicate this openness.) In the long run, it is impossible to attain a systematic set of practice principles unless a consistent and comprehensive frame of reference has been formulated, within which all segments are logically interrelated. It is likely, however, that many professionals will prefer to work in more limited terms, addressing themselves primarily to specific phases of action, or they will prefer to maintain a lower level of abstraction in their intellectual endeavors. Even for such approaches, however, this analysis may be useful in identifying the types of conceptions that are shaped in the background of our thinking.

Formulating Principles of Practice

Whatever the explicitness of the frame of reference, specification of decision and action issues is a prerequisite to formulating action principles. These issues refer to the various occasions for assessment and for planned intervention that are presumed to have crucial significance. The literature of practice reveals a variety of ways by which such issues are identified. Some have to do with determining patterns of client characteristics or behaviors that merit worker attention. Others have to do with the phasing of practitioner activity within sequences of treatment processes. Once identified, these decision and action isues become the bases for prescribing intervention principles.

We have noted that principles proposed for practice should be sufficiently instrumental to guide adequately the overt behavior of practitioners. The requirements cited above can now be restated at a more concrete level as criteria in formulating specific action principles.

First, a given principle of practice should point to the particular conditions under which action is to be undertaken. The practitioner who wishes to implement the principle should be able to recognize the behavioral or social contingencies that define opportunities for deliberate intervention. Thus, a principle may refer to transference phenomena, intragroup processes, organizational communication systems, or whatever. The principle, however, must provide observable cues as to the specific conditions under which it is applicable.

Second, the course of action should be clearly detailed within the statement of the principle. The practitioner must be informed of the particular behaviors in which he can engage if he is to implement the directive phrased by the action principle. Thus, he must respond in a certain manner, or circumscribe others' behavior in these areas, or redefine those aspects of a committee's task.

Third, the particular results to be anticipated from effective implementation of the principle should be identifiable. If the prescribed course of action is followed, what demonstrable outcomes can be expected? [7] With regard to conditions, practitioner behaviors, and outcomes, the problem is one of specifying the manifest phenomena governed by the principle. The referents of circumstance and action must be clear and overt.

All preferred practitioner actions need not have immediately observable outcomes, but the hard core of practice principles should be addressed to concrete behaviors and first-order consequences. Principles that do not indicate the necessary directions of action toward valued ends cannot serve to guide practitioner activity or lay serious claim to professional attention. Indeed, principles that do not impel choices among specific alternatives are largely exercises in rhetoric.

Instead of adequately formulated practice principles, we find reliance on "sensitizing" concepts in much of the literature. Sensitizing concepts orient practitioners to various types of phenomena and underscore professional values and commitments, but do not definitively guide action. They cannot readily be translated into techniques or anticipate outcomes of action. They are essential to practice, but are insufficient to serve as principles. Satisfactory definition of intervention procedures, on the other hand, can lead not only to more concrete and useful action principles, but will also permit their testing and validation.

Codification Procedures

Intellectual effort focused on any delimited sphere of practice generates questions about what events and knowledge to work with. We assume readers are cognizant of the valuable resources to be exploited from the social sciences, and we direct attention here to the potentials of more familiar materials. A major difficulty arises in assessing that which can be found in the professional literature, drawn from practice experience, or extracted from studies of practice. The question of how much validity there is to this knowledge can be dealt with after we have found ways of systematizing it. *Codification* is recommended as a useful procedure for exploiting professional materials in at least two ways: in identifying decison issues to which practice principles must be addressed, and in identifying action courses that have been experientially derived. Codification proceeds, in the first approach, as a review of the literature to inventory practitioner tasks and issues and their relative priorities. Through secondary analysis one can identify the change or service objectives and the dilemmas about means that are currently salient in the field and to which practice principles may be addressed.[8]

In the second approach, codification is directed at identifying existing conceptions of methods and techniques. In a sense, we ask the question: given certain tasks and decision issues, what do practitioners report as their specific means of action? Again, it is possible to inventory and classify techniques contained in the literature of practice, and to gain some assurance that our practice principles are not limited only to the courses of action we have independently generated.

A serious dysfunction of the analysis of practice, whether through codification or empirical study of practitioner behavior, is that it focuses attention on conventional procedures and perspectives. The person engaged in theory construction certainly needs to be informed about these, but he should not be restricted to or by them. He must work from some independent foundation or he will be confined to whatever is already implicit in the literature. He will thus be unable to distinguish fact from fiction, or to discern differences between what practitioners allege they do and the actual behaviors with their real consequences. To get outside the literature, and, to some extent, outside the minds of practitioners, codification can be extended to the literature of other professional disciplines. More important, the codification procedures must be guided by an independent perspective, and they require restatements of the information obtained. A frame of reference provides, therefore, the criteria of a practitioner task, a decision issue or an action technique. It defines some of the terms in which the information elicited must be respecified and reconceptualized. With these safeguards, codification offers a feasible means for preserving the aggregate of professional experience in a form that meets present requirements. At best, however, it is only a prerequisite to more rigorous intellectual activity.

Tasks of Theory Development

The procedures discussed above are among the many steps to be taken in work toward more adequate social work practice theory. These must be accompanied by other activities in an accumulative effort whose main intellectual tasks are four-fold: accurate discernment of decision and action issues, formulation of specific intervention principles, systematizing such principles, and their testing or validation. In this brief statement we have considered only selected aspects of the first two tasks.

It seems likely that professional practice can be significantly improved by the development of new and more effective means rather than by efforts to validate existing methods. A prime function to be served by such intellectual activity, therefore, is to innovate. Recent evaluative studies of practice suggest that advancement of professional endeavor will require both creative formulation of new action courses and more rigorous explication of practice principles.

33 Integrating Social Science Theory through Case Discussion

Dorothy Schroeder

Introduction

The use of social science theory in social work has been a topic of discussion and debate for some years. Historically, the close alliance between social work and sociology waned during the 1920's and 1930's when social workers were attracted by the theories of dynamic psychology, particularly by psychoanalytic theory. They found that these theories improved their understanding of their clients' psychopathology. Ten years ago, however, Helen Harris Perlman remarked:

> . . . the social philosophy which underlies casework, the social auspice which sponsors it, the social aims it preserves, and the social focus it maintains give it its special character. Our modes of functioning and our developing body of knowledge must take their substance and form from consideration of these components. It is not our methodology but the constructive, organized social purposes for which our methods are used which identify us both to ourselves and to others as caseworkers and as social workers too.[1]

Although social workers never lost sight of the profession's social origins and emphases, there has been in recent years a surge of renewed interest in the *social* aspect of social work—most succinctly expressed by the slogan "Let's put the 'social' back in social work." Simultaneously, social science research and theory building have been developed in directions particularly relevant to social work practice.

Social scientists agree that much research still needs to be undertaken in many areas; they have nevertheless been prolific during recent years in

From SOCIAL CASEWORK, 44 No. 7 (1963), 379–385. Reprinted with the permission of the author and the Family Service Association of America.

the production of theory. One of the social work practitioner's frustrations is the extensiveness of social science literature. To keep abreast of it is more than a full-time job for any person; and certainly the amount of literature being printed is more than a practitioner can read in his free time.

In reference to this problem Grace Coyle made the following statement:

> It may perhaps seem to some that such an assimilation of the social sciences is an impossible task, possibly desirable but at any rate beyond us with our limited resources, our relatively short period of professional education, and the pressing demands upon us as practitioners. . . . As the volume and diversity of scientific knowledge increase, the problem of distilling the essentials for application becomes of major importance. . . . Our answer cannot be in closing our eyes to expanding pertinent knowledge or in burying our heads in the sand in which our particular heads now feel most comfortable.[2]

Educators realize that schools of social work must take some responsibility for bringing knowledge and practice together, but there are still many unanswered questions about what knowledge is appropriate and what methods are effective for incorporating it into practice. Since most social science theory has not yet been tested in practice, there is validity in the argument that the first task is to test its utility under clinical conditions. On the other hand, there is equal validity in the argument that if practitioners are introduced to theory through some method that makes it meaningful in relation to their professional practice, they themselves can do the clinical testing and screening by using it in their practice. Within the context of the latter point of view, a project was designed to determine whether the case discussion method might not be an effective means of introducing social work practitioners to social science theory and demonstrating its impact on practice. Practitioners are very familiar with this method: it is used extensively by casework supervisors, for example, and it is used in practice courses in schools and in staff conferences and consultations in agencies. Of all devices for the transfer and application of knowledge in the field of social work, the case discussion method is the one most acceptable to practitioners and the one with which they feel most comfortable.

The project, which was limited to a four-month period, took place in the Family Service of Metropolitan Detroit, a well-established family casework agency with a total staff of twenty-five professionally trained workers providing service in four district offices.[3] The question to which an answer was sought in the project was this: After systematically applying a given set of unfamiliar theoretical concepts to their cases over a limited period of time, will social work practitioners begin to use them in their day-to-day practice?

The backbone of the social work profession is the practitioner who completes his professional career without additional academic education beyond the master's degree. The social work practitioner continues his development by reading; by attending conferences, institutes, and workshops; by participating in professional activities; and by exchanging ideas with other professions.

Any practical plan to accelerate the use of new theory must take into account the mores of the social work culture. If possible, it must also recognize the time pressure under which a sparsely manned service profession must operate. Social workers generally recognize the importance of continuous educational activities, but whatever enrichment is obtained or provided, service to clients always has a high priority.

The Theory

A cluster of theories dealing with social role and small groups was used in the project. Most social workers believe these theoretical formulations hold the most promise for practical use in understanding the individual and his family. In selecting "areas where significant knowledge lies ready for application," Grace Coyle mentioned the following: the concepts of anthropologists on cultural role and cultural conditioning; the community studies and role theories of the sociologists; the work of both social psychologists and sociologists on group behavior; and the contributions of applied economics.[4]

No attempt was made to survey and use all the social-role and small-group theories. Furthermore, the project was not intended to be a clinical test or an evaluation of them. Since the project was time-limited, it was directed toward familiarizing the skilled practitioner with new and potentially useful theories and concepts and toward evaluating his practical problems in utilizing them. With these limited objectives, it was deemed feasible and reasonable to be selective. All the theoretical literature used dealt with social-role and small-group theory, but the criteria for selecting articles, chapters, and books were the usefulness and clarity of the work and the importance of the author.[5] Occasionally a work was selected to demonstrate an author's lack of clarity or to present a specific point of view.

The participants in the project developed their own ideas about the usefulness of the theories. For example, at a staff meeting planned by the project workers, two of them read papers elaborating the idea of usefulness. Elliot Rubin found the concepts of role discontinuity, role conflict, and role pressure particularly relevant because his clients frequently suffered from these kinds of strain. In addition, he emphasized that since problems of this sort have a strong impact on clients, many are ready to recognize them and address themselves to them. Thelma Bernstein stressed the educational function of the caseworker. She differentiated educable from uneducable clients—the latter being unable to reach a clearer understanding of their roles either because the role content is too highly cathected or because not enough neutralized energy is available to permit learning to take place.[6]

Procedure

The four workers selected as the core group to participate in the project appeared to be fairly representative of the caseworkers within the agency. One participant was selected from each district office; no attempt was made to pick the best or the most competent. Four group meetings were held during the four-month period to orient the group to the project; to work out necessary routines; to consider the selection of cases; to discuss and resolve common problems arising out of the project activity; and to help clarify theory and, generally, facilitate the work.

The major activity was the weekly one-hour discussion by the project director and each member of the core group of one of the four cases the participant had selected to be used in the project. Occasionally other cases were brought up for single discussions. During the hour social science theory was used exclusively to develop diagnostic formulations and treatment goals and to identify what additional information was needed for planning the content of future interviews.

This brief outline does not tell the whole story, of course. The workers were well versed and competent in making use of dynamic psychology. It was assumed that even though the case discussions did not deal with this type of content, the participants would continue to use their knowledge of dynamic psychology in assessing ego strength, in testing and observing anxiety reactions, and in making use of the ego-supportive and other techniques known to an able caseworker.

Reading assignments were made throughout the project period. As the workers' knowledge base became increasingly solid, they became better able to integrate the contributions of the various authors and to make more discriminating choices among the concepts applicable to each case.

The staff of the agency had attended a two-day institute on social-role and small-group theory before the start of the study, and although the institute had not been planned as a part of the project, it was particularly helpful.[7] Because of their attendance at the institute, it was assumed that all members of the staff had the same theory base when the project began. This assumption was a pertinent consideration in devising a simple evaluative procedure that called for the participation of the total staff. All caseworkers not actively engaged in the project constituted a control group. Each worker on the staff wrote two diagnostic statements, one at the beginning and one at the end of the project. A content analysis of the statements showed that the participants in the project averaged an increase in the use of social science concepts to the extent of six times that of the control group.

Findings and Conclusions

Selected concepts taken from social-role and small-group theories were consistently applied to the cases of trained and experienced workers in case discussion sessions. The findings in this study have significant implications for practice and education: The workers integrated these concepts into their general knowledge base sufficiently to find them useful and usable not only in the particular cases under discussion but also in other cases as well.

There is nothing unique about social science theory in regard to the method needed to learn it and apply it to practice. Any appropriate and practical theory can be substituted as the knowledge content. In the social work field today, however, there is reason for emphasizing the contributions of the social sciences. Social scientists are rapidly expanding their knowledge through research, and the findings and theory are clearly appropriate for use in social work.

What appears to be happening can be likened to the cultural response of a society undergoing rapid technological advancement. The scientists responsible for the thrust are primarily concerned about pushing forward the claims of their commodity. Naturally, some of them do not have the sophistication necessary to see their contribution in perspective. Others attempt to develop a solid foundation that retains the advantages of established theory while incorporating the new. The social work consumers are responding in predictable fashion. Some overreactors are enthusiastically riding the bandwagon; they can be identified by their superficial and inaccurate writings and speeches. Others, at the opposite extreme, can be identified by their denial of the importance of the new contributions. The solid core of the profession is attempting to find effective ways of bringing about a synthesis of what is good and useful, both old and new—without denying the discomfort and anxiety associated with such rapid movement. These social workers recognize the right and responsibility of the profession to chart its own course.

Grace Coyle referred to an important continuing task as "distilling the essentials for application." An equally important task is making new social science theory available to the skilled practitioner in a way that enables him both to see its meaning for his practice and to familiarize himself with it within reasonable time limits. Once he has acquired this knowledge, it is expected that the accomplished, well-intentioned practitioner will be sufficiently stimulated to continue using the newly found tool and to keep up an interest in its development. This project suggests the possibility of achieving this goal within an agency through the use of a planned period of case discussion supported by several other methods.

A four-month period provided enough time for the goals of the project to be accomplished. The workers tolerated the additional demands put upon them during this period, and they regarded the gains as well worth the effort. The service function of the agency was not notably reduced during the period, even though some released time for the workers was an essential part of the plan.

There was no deviation from the required weekly one-hour discussion of a case with each participant, and, by previous agreement, the participants allowed no other matters to intrude during the sessions. They were able to apply selected concepts diligently and consistently to the case being discussed.

As a result of participating in the project, both the caseworkers and the project director are convinced that social science theories enlarge the knowledge base and enhance the techniques of workers and that the integration of selected concepts from the social sciences with dynamic psychology is possible and desirable.

The project director had a primary responsibility to provide appropriate reading material, build content into the discussions, and maintain the focus of the discussions. Whether the project would have been successful without this leadership is not known. The participants' general feeling was that an informal leader would not have been able to protect the focus of the project and the time the agency had released to them.

Although group meetings were used for orientation, planning, and clarification, case discussions were confined to conferences with individual workers. How effective group case discussions might have been is also not known. As it was, only one case was discussed by each worker each week; it is possible that group discussions would have diluted the impact of the training by requiring each participant to give his attention to a number of cases.

Although no testing devices measured the effect of the institute given before the project began, it is assumed to have been helpful in several ways. The institute provided didactic instruction in some of the basic concepts to be used, and made possible an orderly and systematic overview of the topics that were subsequently dealt with in detail. This academic introduction to the subject seemed to carry continued meaning for the participants, who made frequent reference to the institute content in the case discussions.

The emphasis in this study was on one method of bringing new knowledge into a meaningful context for practice. No analysis was made of the impact of lectures and reading alone. With regard to the content analysis of workers' diagnostic statements, the findings are as follows: the analysis of the first diagnostic statements, prepared after the institute and before the project, showed meager use of social science concepts by the total group; analysis of the second diagnostic statements, prepared at the end of the project, showed a slight increase by the control group and a marked increase by the project participants.

The results of the project show that the case discussion method is a successful addition to lectures and readings. This finding carries significance for educators seeking ways of helping students apply theory to practice.

Notes to Part I, 1

1. The term "behavioral science" is used generically throughout and is intended to embrace what is ordinarily included in both the social and behavioral sciences, excluding here only the policy fields.
2. Because of this focus the paper will not address the related and important topic of the contributions of social work to behavioral science, which is really the other half of the relationship between behavioral science and social work. Among various works touching on this question, the reader is referred to Joseph W. Eaton, "The Relevance of Social Work for Sociology," *Sociology and Social Research*, 43 (1959), 197–204.
3. Gordon Hearn, *Theory Building in Social Work* (Toronto: U. of Toronto Press, 1958).
4. Robert K. Merton, "Notes on Problem-Finding in Sociology," in Robert K. Merton, Leonard Broom, and Leonard S. Cottrell, Jr. (eds.), *Sociology Today: Problems and Prospects* (New York: Basic Books, 1959), pp. ix–xxxiv.
5. Robert K. Merton, *Social Theory and Social Structure* (rev. ed.) (New York: Free Press, 1957).
6. Harriet M. Bartlett, "Characteristics of Social Work," in *Building Social Work Knowledge* (New York: National Association of Social Workers, 1964), pp. 1–16.
7. Werner W. Boehm, *Objectives of the Social Work Curriculum of the Future*, Vol. 1 (New York: Council on Social Work Education, 1959).
8. William E. Gordon, "Notes on the Nature of Knowledge," in *Building Social Work Knowledge, op. cit.*, pp. 60–76.
9. Ernest Greenwood, "Social Science and Social Work: A Theory of Their Relationship," *The Social Service Review*, 29 (1955), 20–28.
10. Hearn, *op. cit.*
11. Alfred Kadushin, "The Knowledge Base in Social Work," in Alfred J. Kahn (ed.), *Issues in American Social Work* (New York: Columbia U. P. 1959), pp. 39–80.
12. Alfred J. Kahn, "The Function of Social Work in the Modern World," in *ibid.*, pp. 3–39.
13. Martin B. Loeb, "The Backdrop for Social Research: Theory-Making and Model-Building," in Leonard S. Kogan (ed.), *Social Science Theory and Social Work Research* (New York: National Association of Social Workers, 1960), pp. 3–16.
14. Henry S. Maas, "Developing Theories of Social Work Practice," in *Building Social Work Knowledge, op. cit.*, pp. 48–60.
15. Kadushin, *op. cit.*, pp. 48–53.
16. Greenwood, *op. cit.*, pp. 24–28.
17. See, for example, Henry S. Maas, "Uses of Behavioral Sciences in Social Work Education," *Social Work*, 3 (1958), 62–69; and Martin Bloom, "Connecting Formal Behavioral Science Theory to Individual Social Work Practice," *Social Service Review*, 39 (1965), 11–22.
18. See, for example, Murray Sidman, *Tactics of Scientific Research* (New York: Basic Books, 1960).
19. See, for example, Joseph W. Eaton, "Science, 'Art,' and Uncertainty in Social Work," *Social Work*, 3 (1958), 3–11.

Notes to Part II, 2

1. James G. Holland and B. F. Skinner, *The Analysis of Behavior* (New York: McGraw, 1961).
2. Adapted from *ibid.*, pp. vii–viii.
3. For aspects of the concept of position, we are indebted to Edwin J. Thomas and Bruce J. Biddle, "Basic Concepts for Classifying Role Phenomena," in Bruce J. Biddle and Edwin J. Thomas (eds.), *Role Theory: Concepts and Research* (New York: Wiley, 1966), pp. 29–30.
4. For many concepts parallel to those presented in Part A, and for types of role conflict and of resolution, see Neal Gross, Ward S. Mason, A. W. McEachern, *Explorations in Role Analysis: Studies of the School Superintendency Role* (New York: Wiley, 1958), pp. 11–21 and 281–319.
5. For the concept of discontinuity, see Ruth Benedict, "Continuities and Discontinuities in Cultural Conditioning," *Psychiatry*, **1** (1938), 161–167.
6. For the concept of role strain, see William J. Goode, "A Theory of Role Strain," *American Sociological Review*, **25** (1960), 483–496.

Notes to Part II, 3

1. This statement is one of the products of a comparative study conducted in five Southeastern Michigan schools, codirected by Robert D. Vinter and Rosemary C. Sarri, School of Social Work, University of Michigan. A statement of the research is presented by Vinter and Sarri in "Malperformance in the Public School: A Group Work Approach," *Social Work*, **10** (1965), 3–13 (Reprinted as selection 27 of this book).
2. Howard S. Becker (ed.), *The Other Side* (New York: Free Press, 1964).
3. Howard S. Becker, *Outsiders* (New York: Free Press, 1963), p. 8.
4. Albert K. Cohen, "The Sociology of the Deviant Act: Anomie Theory and Beyond," *American Sociological Review*, **30** (1965), 5–14.
5. Marshall B. Clinard, *Sociology of Deviant Behavior* (2nd ed.; New York: Holt, 1963), p. 20.
6. David Gottlieb, "Teaching and Students: The Views of Negro and White Teachers," *Sociology of Education*, **37** (1964), p. 345.
7. John W. Porter, "The Heart of the Drop-Out Problem: Early Identification," *Michigan Education Journal*, **30** (1963), 362–65.
8. Aaron Cicourel and John I. Kitsuse, *The Educational Decision-Makers* (Indianapolis: Bobbs-Merrill, 1963).
9. For an evaluation of classroom sanctioning practices, see Harold W. Massey and Edwin E. Vineyard, *The Profession of Teaching* (New York: Odyssey, 1961). General directions are suggested by Amitai Etzioni in his *A Comparative Analysis of Complex Organizations* (New York: Free Press, 1961).
10. Talcott Parsons, *The Social System* (New York: Free Press, 1951), Chap. 7.
11. Kai Erikson, "Notes on the Sociology of Deviant Behavior," in Becker, *The Other Side, op. cit.*, p. 11
12. Burton Clark, *Educating the Expert Society* (San Francisco: Chandler, 1962), p. 180.

Notes to Part II, 4

1. Disability may be defined as ". . . a condition of impairment, physical or mental, having an objective aspect than can usually be described by a physician . . ."; in contrast, a handicap ". . . is the cumulative result of the obstacles which disability interposes between the individual and his maximum functional level." See G. W. Hamilton, *Counseling the Handicapped in the Rehabilitation Process* (New York: Ronald, 1950), p. 17 quoted in Beatrice A. Wright, *Physical Disability—A Psychological Approach* (New York: Harper, 1960), p. 9.

2. Beatrice A. Wright, *ibid.*, p. 373, as italicized by Wright.

3. For example, see Beatrice A. Wright, *ibid.*, pp. 373-377. Similar conclusions are supported by the analyses of the following writers: R. G. Barker, in collaboration with B. A. Wright, L. Meyerson, and M. R. Gonick, *Adjustment to Physical Handicap and Illness: A Survey of the Social Psychology of Physique and Disability* (Bulletin 55, revised 2nd ed.; New York: Social Science Research Council, 1953); L. Meyerson, "Special Disabilities," in P. R. Farnsworth and Q. McNemar (eds.), *Annual Review of Psychology*, 8 (Palo Alto: Annual Reviews, Inc., 1957), 437-457; E. L. Cowen, R. P. Underberg, R. T. Verrillo, and F. G. Benham, *Adjustment to Visual Disability in Adolescence* (New York: American Foundation for the Blind, 1961). An especially revealing study is that of T. F. Linde and C. N. Patterson, "Influence of Orthopedic Disability on Conformity Behavior," *Journal of Abnormal and Social Psychology*, 65 (1964), 115-118.

4. For example, see Beatrice A. Wright, *op. cit.*; Helen H. Perlman, "Family Diagnosis in Cases of Illness and Disability," *Family-Centered Social Work in Illness and Disability: A Preventive Approach* (New York: National Association of Social Work-ers, 1961), pp. 7-21; Eileen Gambrill, "Post Hospitalized Disabled Children," *Journal of Health and Human Behavior*, 4 (1963), 206-10; F. Davis, *Passage through Crisis: Polio Victims and Their Families* (Indianapolis, Bobbs-Merrill, 1963); A. G. Gowman, *The War Blind in American Social Structure* (New York: American Foundation for the Blind, 1957); and Jane Kamm, *A Study of Patients with Orthopedic Disabilities* (Ann Arbor, Mich.: The University of Michigan, School of Social Work, 1956, unpublished Master's thesis).

5. I know of no analysis of the behavioral problems of the disabled from the perspective of role theory, although there have been sociological analyses of specific disabilities (such as blindness) and descriptions of the patient role.

6. For a general treatment of role theory see B. J. Biddle and E. J. Thomas (eds.), *Role Theory: Concepts and Research* (New York: Wiley, 1966).

7. T. Parsons, "Illness and the Role of the Physicians: A Sociological Perspective," in C. Kluckhohn and H. A. Murray, with the collaboration of D. M. Schneider (eds.), *Personality in Nature, Society, and Culture* (2nd ed.; New York: Knopf, 1953), p. 613.

8. S. H. King, *Perceptions of Illness and Medical Practice* (New York: Russell Sage Foundation, 1962), pp. 355-357.

9. Davis, *op. cit.*, pp. 66-67.

10. F. Pine and D. J. Levinson, "A Sociopsychological Conception of Patienthood," *The International Journal of Social Psychiatry*, 7 (1961), 106-122.

11. Wright, *op. cit.*, pp. 345-364.

12. E. Goffman, *Asylums: Essays on the Social Situation of Mental Patients and Other Inmates* (New York: Doubleday, 1961), pp. 66-67.

13. Ruth Benedict, "Continuities and Discontinuities in Cultural Conditioning," *Psychiatry*, 1 (1938), 161-167.

14. Support for these conclusions may be documented with reference to studies

on the effects of sudden change for animals, for humans in natural social situations, and in the psychological laboratory and clinic, but such evidence is far from conclusive. However plausible these effects may appear to be, their postulation must still be considered as hypothesized rather than as clearly demonstrated. The same conclusion pertains to the effects of role conflict, conception conflict and nonfacilitative interdependence, to be discussed.

15. R. M. Williams, *American Society: A Sociological Interpretation* (2nd ed.; New York: Knopf, 1960).

16. H. A. Murray, *Explorations and Personality* (New York: Oxford U., 1938).

17. Bertha Reynolds, *Social Work and Social Living* (New York: Citadel, 1951).

18. See D. Landy, "Problems of the Person Seeking Help in Our Culture," *Social Welfare Forum* (New York: National Conference on Social Welfare, 1960), pp. 127–45; and J. R. P. French, Jr., "The Social Environment and Mental Health," *The Journal of Social Issues*, 19 (1963), 39–56.

19. Beatrice A. Wright, *op. cit.*, pp. 224–229.

20. For an elaboration of this concept and of the conditions that may give rise to it in general, see W. J. Goode, "A Theory of Role Strain," *American Sociological Review*, 25 (1960), 483–496.

21. Problems of role synchrony have not been treated systematically in the literature, although related problems of marginality and so-called reciprocity and complementarity of role behavior have been discussed. For insightful discussions of the problem of marginality and of interaction problems of the disabled, see especially R. G. Barker, *op. cit.*; Beatrice Wright, *op. cit.*; and A. G. Gowman, *op. cit.* For a discussion of reciprocity and complementarity see A. W. Gouldner, "The Norm of Reciprocity: A Preliminary Statement," *American Sociological Review*, 25 (1960), 161–178.

22. A. G. Gowman, *op. cit.*, quoted and paraphrased from pp. 120–121.

23. The "true" degree of handicap is difficult to assess because it requires judgments about the individual's impairment and his capabilities to perform with that impairment. The fact that professionals working with disability often have difficulty making these judgments is one of many factors conducive to generating either asynchronous or invalid role synchronies.

24. Fred Davis, *op. cit.*, pp. 149–152.

25. James Breedlove, "Casework and Rehabilitation," *Social Work*, 2 (1957), p. 35.

26. *Ibid.*, p. 34.

27. *Ibid.*, p. 35.

Notes to Part II, 5

1. Margaret Allen Ireland, *Background Paper on Family Life, Family Relationships, and Friends* (White House Conference on Aging, April, 1960), pp. 25–26.

2. Taken from Joseph A. Kahl, *The American Class Structure* (New York: Rinehart, 1957), p. 66.

3. According to W. Lloyd Warner, et al., *Social Class in America* (Chicago: Science Research Associates, 1949), occupation is the variable that correlates most highly with the prestige rank granted a family by the local community.

4. While these evaluations were subjective, they were based upon two criteria: 1) the evaluation of the social caseworker who interviewed the client, as reported in the record, and

2) the number of types of illnesses reported in the record.

5. Quoted from the record, except for changes to hide the client's identity.

6. Neighborhoods were classified by Mr. Sheldon Siegel, Supervisor of the Department of Services to the Aging, whose position at the agency and experience in Detroit provided him with a great deal of knowledge of the ecological patterns of the Jewish population.

Mr. Siegel also provided help in classifying neighborhoods according to social class characteristics. This information was used then as a check against the occupational varable used to determine social class. High consistency was found in these two variables among the children of the aged. For example, 28 of 44 children classified as middle class lived in middle-middle to upper-middle-class neighborhoods, with none living in either lower-lower-class or lower-upper and better neighborhoods. Consistently different patterns were found in each of the other class groups.

7. See, for example, Talcott Parsons and Robert F. Bales, *Family, Socialization and Interaction Process* (New York: Free Press, 1955), pp. 1–40; or Ernest W. Burgess and Paul Wallin, *Engagement and Marriage* (Philadelphia: Lippincott, 1953), Chap. 1.

8. See, for example, Ernest W. Burgess, "Human Aspects of Social Policy," *Old Age in the Modern World*, Report of the Third Congress of the International Association of Gerontology (Edinburg and London: Livingstone, 1954), pp. 49–58.

9. Ruth Albrecht, "Relationships of Older Parents with Their Children," *Marriage and Family Living*, 16 (1954), 32–35.

10. Gordon F. Streib and Wayne E. Thompson, "The Older Person in a Family Context," in Clark Tibbitts (ed.), *Handbook of Social Gerontology* (Chicago: U. of Chicago Press, 1960), pp. 476–477. See also a number of other recent studies that deal with visiting patterns among extended family members although the parents are not necessarily in the aged group:

Scott Greer, "Urbanism Reconsidered," *American Sociological Review*, **21** (1956), 22 ff; Morris Axelrod, "Urban Structure and Social Participation," *American Sociological Review*, **21** (1956), 13–18; Eugene Litwak, "Geographic Mobility and Extended Family Cohesion," *American Sociological Review*, **25** (1960), 385–394; and W. Bell and M. D. Boat, "Urban Neighborhoods and Informal Social Relations," *American Journal of Sociology*, **43** (1957), 391–398.

11. Evidence for this point of view is presented in Kahl, *op. cit.*, Chapter 9, especially pp. 262–263.

12. In this test and in the analysis that follows, the five cases in which the aged were living with minor children only have been eliminated.

13. Burgess, *op. cit.*, p. 50.

14. This seems consistent with the findings of Streib and Thompson, *op. cit.*, pp. 481–83, who compared mobility patterns with the parents' opinions about the respect their children have for them and the closeness of family ties among the membership of the family of procreation. It disagrees with the findings of E. E. Le Masters, "Social Class Mobility and Family Integration," *Marriage and Family Living*, **16** (1954), 226–232.

15. Streib and Thompson, *op. cit.*, p. 478.

16. For further evidence of this concerning financial assistance, see F. H. Bond, et al., *Our Needy Aged: A California Study of a National Problem* (New York: Holt, 1954). See also Clifford Kirkpatrick, *The Family as Process and Institution* (New York: Ronald, 1955), p. 498, who describes the chief vestiges of this tradition as "a collective guilty conscience."

17. Kirkpatrick, *ibid.*, p. 499, describes four possibilities of an inappropriate relationship:

1. Parents may resist unduly the reversal of roles and insist upon superior moral judgment even when ailing and dependent. Many parents cling to the parental privilege of defining what is right and who decides it, although in other respects they

may gradually permit themselves to be cared for by offspring.
2. Children may push parents toward a transition and reversal of roles—into an armchair while still competent and able.

3. Children may resist the transition and claim dependence long after it is appropriate.
4. The aging parent may push for role reversal.

Notes to Part III, 6

1. C. H. Cooley, *Social Organization* (New York: Scribner's, 1909).
2. E. A. Shils, "The Study of the Primary Group," in D. Lerner and D. Lasswell (eds.), *The Policy Sciences* (Stanford: Stanford U. P., 1951), pp. 44–69.
3. L. Broom and P. Selznick, *Sociology, A Text with Adapted Readings* (Evanston, Ill.: Row, 1955).
4. E. Faris, "The Primary Group: Essence and Accident," *American Journal of Sociology*, 38 (1932), 41–50.
5. R. B. Cattell, D. R. Saunders, and G. F. Stice, "The Dimensions of Syntality in Small Groups: I. The Neonate Group," *Human Relations*, 6 (1953), 331–357.
6. E. F. Borgatta, L. S. Cottrell, and H. J. Meyer, "On the Dimensions of Group Behavior," *Sociometry*, 19 (1956), 223–240.
7. D. T. Campbell, "Common Fate, Similarity, and Other Indices of the Status of Aggregates of Persons as Social Entities," *Behavioral Science*, 3 (1958), 14–25.
8. G. Karlsson, *Social Mechanisms, Studies in Sociological Theory* (New York: Free Press, 1958).
9. *Ibid.*
10. L. Festinger, S. Schachter, and K. Back, *Social Pressures in Informal Groups: A Study of a Housing Project* (New York: Harper, 1950).
11. T. M. Newcomb, "The Prediction of Interpersonal Attraction," *American Psychologist*, 11 (1956), 575–587.
12. G. C. Homans, *The Human Group* (New York: Harcourt, 1950).
13. R. F. Winch, T. Ktsanes, and Virginia Ktsanes, "Empirical Elaboration of the Theory of Complementary Needs in Mate-Selection," *Journal of Abnormal and Social Psychology*, 51 (1955), 508–513.
14. D. Cartwright and A. Zander (eds.), *Group Dynamics: Research and Theory* (Evanston, Ill.: Row, 1953).
15. I. Ross and A. Zander, "Need Satisfactions and Employee Turnover," *Personnel Psychology*, 10 (1957), 327–339.
16. M. Deutsch, "Some Factors Affecting Membership Motivation and Achievement Motivation in a Group," *Human Relations*, 12 (1959), 81–95.
17. E. F. Borgatta and L. S. Cottrell, "On the Classification of Groups," *Sociometry*, 18 (1955), 409–422.
18. S. E. Seashore, *Group Cohesiveness in the Industrial Group* (Ann Arbor: Institute for Social Research, 1954).
19. Cattell, Saunders, and Stice, *op. cit.*
20. L. Festinger, "Informal Social Communication," *Psychological Review*, 57 (1950), 271–282.
21. Festinger, Schachter, and Back, *op. cit.*
22. K. Back, "Influence through Social Communication," *Journal of Abnormal and Social Psychology*, 46 (1951), 9–23.
23. Festinger, Schachter, and Back, *op. cit.*
24. L. Festinger and J. Thibaut, "Interpersonal Communication in Small Groups," *Journal of Abnormal and Social Psychology*, 46 (1951), 92–99.
25. J. Downing, "Cohesiveness, Perception, and Values," *Human Relations*, 11 (1958), 157–167.
26. L. Berkowitz, "Group Standards, Co-

hesiveness, and Productivity," *Human Relations*, **7** (1954), 509–519.

27. Seashore, *op. cit.*

28. A. Pepitone and G. Reichling, "Group Cohesiveness and the Expression of Hostility," *Human Relations*, **8** (1955), 327–339.

29. S. Schachter, "Deviation, Rejection, and Communication," *Journal of Abnormal and Social Psychology*, **46** (1951), 190–207.

30. J. Israel, *Self-Evaluation and Rejection in Groups* (Uppsala: Almquist and Wiksells, 1956).

31. E. W. Bovard, "Group Structure and Perception," in Cartwright and Zander, *op. cit.*, pp. 177–189.

32. M. Deutsch, "An Experimental Study of the Effects of Cooperation and Competition upon Group Process," *Human Relations*, **2** (1949), 199–231.

33. E. J. Thomas, "Effects of Facilitative Role Interdependence on Group Functioning," *Human Relations*, **10** (1957), 347–367.

34. J. T. Lanzetta, "Group Behavior under Stress," *Human Relations*, **8** (1955), 29–53.

35. J. Thibaut, "An Experimental Study of Cohesiveness of Underprivileged Groups," *Human Relations*, **3** (1950), 251–278.

36. A. Pepitone and R. Kleiner, "The Effects of Threat and Frustration on Group Cohesiveness," *Journal of Abnormal and Social Psychology*, **54** (1957), 192–199.

37. M. Sherif and Carolyn W. Sherif, *Groups in Harmony and Tension* (New York: Harper, 1953).

38. A. Mintz, "Nonadaptive Group Behavior," in G. E. Swanson, T. M. Newcomb, and E. L. Hartley (eds.), *Readings in Social Psychology* (New York: Holt, 1952), pp. 190–198.

39. J. R. P. French, "The Disruption and Cohesion of Groups," in Cartwright and Zander, *op. cit.*, pp. 121–134.

40. Sherif and Sherif, *op. cit.*

41. R. L. Hamblin, "Group Integration during a Crisis," *Human Relations*, **11** (1958), 67–77.

42. French, *op. cit.*

43. Hamblin, *op. cit.*

44. French, *op. cit.*

45. *Ibid.*

46. Sherif and Sherif, *op. cit.*

47. Shils, *op. cit.*

48. F. H. Allport, *Social Psychology* (Boston: Houghton Mifflin, 1924).

49. G. H. Mead, *Mind, Self and Society* (Chicago: U. of Chicago Press, 1934).

50. R. L. Gordon, "Interaction between Attitude and the Definition of the Situation in the Expression of Opinion," in Cartwright and Zander, *op. cit.*, pp. 163–176.

51. I. L. Janis and B. T. King, "The Influence of Role Playing in Opinion-Change," *Journal of Abnormal and Social Psychology*, **49** (1954), 211–218.

52. H. H. Kelley, "Two Functions of Reference Groups," in Swanson, Newcomb, and Hartley, *op. cit.*, pp. 410–414.

53. G. Rasmussen and A. Zander, "Group Membership and Self-Evaluation," *Human Relations*, **7** (1954), 239–253.

54. M. Deutsch and H. B. Gerard, "A Study of Normative and Informational Social Influences upon Individual Judgment," *Journal of Abnormal and Social Psychology*, **51** (1955), 629–637.

55. M. Sherif, "A Study of Some Social Factors in Perception," *Archives of Psychology*, **27**, No. 187 (1935).

56. S. E. Asch, "Effects of Group Pressure upon the Modification and Distortion of Judgments," in Cartwright and Zander, *op. cit.*, pp. 151–162.

57. Deutsch and Gerard, *op. cit.*

58. Festinger, *op. cit.*

59. R. Lippitt, N. Polansky, and S. Rosen, "The Dynamics of Power," *Human Relations*, **5** (1952), 37–65.

60. M. Gold, "Power in the Classroom," *Sociometry*, **21** (1958), 50–61.

61. *Ibid.*

62. J. R. P. French, "A Formal Theory of Social Power," *Psychological Review*, **63** (1956), 181–195.

63. J. R. P. French, Jr. and B. H. Raven, "The Bases of Social Power," in Dorwin Cartwright (ed.), *Studies in Social Power* (Ann Arbor: Research Center for Group Dynamics, University of Michigan, 1959), pp. 150–167.

64. *Ibid.*

65. *Ibid.*

66. *Ibid.*

67. B. H. Raven and J. R. P. French, "Legitimate Power, Coercive Power and Observability in Social Influ-

ence," *Sociometry*, **21** (1958), 83–98.
68. French and Raven, *op. cit.*
69. Raven and French, *op. cit.*

Notes to Part III, 7

1. C. I. Hovland, *et al.*, *Order of Presentation in Persuasion* (New Haven: Yale, 1957), pp. 129–157.
2. J. T. Klapper, "What We know about the Effects of Mass Communication: The Brink of Hope," *Public Opinion Quarterly*, **21** (1957–1958), 453–471.
3. H. H. Hyman and P. B. Sheatsley, "Some Reasons Why Information Campaigns Fail," *Public Opinion Quarterly*, **11** (1947), 412–423.
4. P. F. Lazarsfeld, *Radio and the Printed Page* (New York: Duell, Sloan & Pearce, 1948).
5. L. Bogart, "Measuring the Effectiveness of an Overseas Information Campaign: A Case History," *Public Opinion Quarterly*, **21** (1957–1958), 473–498.
6. G. D. Wiebe, "Responses to the Televised Kefauver Hearings: Some Social Psychological Implications," *Public Opinion Quarterly*, **16** (1952), 179–200.
7. Bogart, *op. cit.*
8. I. L. Janis and S. Feshback, "Effects of Fear-Arousing Communications," *Journal of Abnormal and Social Psychology*, **48** (1953), 78–92.
9. Klapper, *op. cit.*
10. E. Katz and P. F. Lazarsfeld, *Personal Influence* (New York: Free Press, 1955), pp. 15–30; E. Freidson, "Communication Research and the Concept of the Mass," *American Sociological Review*, **18** (1953), 313–317.
11. Katz and Lazarsfeld, *op. cit.*, pp. 48–66.
12. Ernest Cassirer, *An Essay on Man* (New Haven: Yale, 1944), pp. 23–41; H. S. Sullivan, *Conceptions of Modern Psychiatry* (New York: Norton, 1947), pp. 14–27.
13. Theodore Newcomb, "Attitude De-

velopment as a Function of Reference Group, The Bennington Study," in G. E. Swanson, T. M. Newcomb, E. Hartley (eds.), *Readings in Social Psychology* (New York: Holt, 1952), pp. 420–430.
14. Katz and Lazarsfeld, *op. cit.*, pp. 48–66.
15. B. R. Berelson, P. F. Lazarsfeld, and W. N. McPhee, *Voting* (Chicago: U. of Chicago Press, 1954), pp. 120 ff.
16. Kurt Lewin, "Group Decision and Social Change," in Swanson, Newcomb, and Hartley, *op. cit.*, pp. 459–474.
17. J. Coleman, E. Katz, and H. Menzel, "The Diffusion of an Innovation among Physicians," *Sociometry*, **21** (1957), 253–269.
18. C. I. Hovland, A. A. Lumsdaine, and F. D. Sheffield, "The Effects of Presenting 'One Side' versus 'Both Sides' in Changing Opinions on a Controversial Subject," in W. Schramm (ed.), *Mass Communications* (Urbana: U. of Illinois Press, 1949), pp. 261–274.
19. W. J. McGuire, "Order of Presentation as a Factor in 'Conditioning' Persuasiveness," in *Order of Presentation in Persuasion*, *op. cit.*, pp. 98–114.
20. A. R. Cohen, "Need for Cognition and Order of Communication as Determinants of Opinion Change," in *ibid*, pp. 79–97.
21. T. N. Ewing, "A Study of Certain Factors Involved in Changes of Opinion," *Journal of Social Psychology*, **16** (1942), 63–88.
22. Berelson, Lazarsfeld, and McPhee, *op. cit.*, pp. 144 ff.
23. A. R. Cohen, "Upward Communication in Experimentally Created Hierarchies," *Human Relations*, **11** (1958), 41–53.

24. A. Leighton, *The Governing of Men* (Princeton, N.J.: Princeton U. P., 1945), pp. 331–332.
25. E. Shils and M. Janowitz, "Cohesion and Disintegration in the Wehrmacht in World War II," *Public Opinion Quarterly*, **12** (1948), 280–315.
26. M. Tumin, "Exposure to Mass Media and Readiness for Desegregation,"

Public Opinion Quarterly, **21** (1957), 237–251.
27. Lewin, *op. cit.*
28. L. Festinger, *Theory of Cognitive Dissonance* (Evanston, Ill.: Row, 1957).
29. J. W. Brehm, "Increasing Cognitive Dissonance by a *Fait Accompli*," *Journal of Abnormal and Social Psychology*, **58** (1959), 379–382.

Notes to Part III, 8

1. F. Thrasher, *The Gang* (Chicago: U. of Chicago Press, 1927).
2. F. T. Rafferty, "Day Treatment Structure for Adolescents," in J. Masserman (ed.), *Current Psychiatric Therapies*, Vol. 1 (New York: Grune, 1961), pp. 43–47.
3. F. T. Rafferty, "Development of Social Structure in Treatment Institutions." Presented at the Annual Meeting of the American Psychiatric Association (Chicago, 1961).
4. M. Sherif and C. Sherif, *An Outline*

of Social Psychology (New York: Harper, 1956), p. 146.
5. J. P. Scott, *Animal Behavior* (Chicago: U. of Chicago Press, 1958).
6. H. W. Polsky and M. Kohn, "Participant Observation in a Delinquent Sub-culture," (Hawthorne, N.Y.: Hawthorne Cedar Knolls School; unpublished manuscript).
7. S. Kobrin, "Sociological Aspects of the Development of a Street Corner Group: An Exploratory Study," *American Journal of Orthopsychiatry*, **31** (1961), 685–702.

Notes to Part III, 9

1. Everett B. Stonequist, *The Marginal Man* (New York: Charles Scribner, Sons, 1957), p. 8.
2. Louis Adamic, *A Nation of Nations* (New York: Harper, 1944).
3. G. E. E. Linquist, *et al.*, *The Indian in American Life* (New York: Friendship, 1944).
4. Kurt Lewin, *Resolving Social Conflicts* (New York: Harper, 1948).
5. Sanford Solender, *The Unique Function of the Jewish Community Center* (New York: National Jewish Welfare Board, 1956), pp. 7, 9.
6. Marian J. Radke and Bernard Lande, "Personality Correlates of Differential Reaction to Minority Group Belong-

ing," *Journal of Social Psychology*, **38** (1953), p. 260.
7. Abraham N. Franzblau, *Religious Belief and Character among Jewish Adolescents*, Teachers College Contributions to Education, No. 634 (New York: Teachers College, Columbia University, 1934).
8. Ludwig Geismar, "A Scale for the Measurement of Ethnic Identification," *Jewish Social Studies*, **16** (1954), 33–60.
9. Daniel J. Levinson, "An Approach to the Theory and Measurement of Ethnocentric Ideology," *Journal of Psychology*, **28** (1949), 19–39.
10. Earl X. Freed, "Ethnic Identification

of Hospitalized Jewish Psychiatric Patients: An Exploratory Study" (unpublished paper, March, 1960; mimeographed).

11. Emory S. Bogardus, "A Social Distance Scale," *Sociology and Social Research,* **17** (1933), 265–271.

12. Radke and Lande, *op. cit.,* pp. 268–269.

13. Margaret Brennman, "The Relationship between Minority Group Membership and Group Identification among a Group of Urban Middle-Class Negro Girls," *Journal of Social Psychology,* **11** (1940), 171–197.

14. Marian J. Radke, *The Meaning of Minority Group Membership to Jewish College Students* (New York: Commission on Community Interrelationships of the American Jewish Congress, 1951; mimeographed).

15. Meyer Greenberg, "The Jewish Student at Yale: His Attitudes toward Judaism," *YIVO Annual of Jewish Social Science,* **1** (New York: Yiddish Scientific Institute, 1946), 217–240.

16. Antonia Wenkart, "Self Acceptance," *American Journal of Psychoanalysis,* **15** (1955), 135–143.

17. Walt Whitman, "Song of Myself," *Leaves of Grass* (New York: New American Library, 1950), pp. 49–96.

18. Lewin, *op. cit.,* pp. 145–146.

19. Arthur J. Brodbeck and Howard V. Perlmutter, "Self-Dislike as a Determinant of Marked Ingroup-Outgroup Preferences," *Journal of Psychology,* **38** (1954), 271–280.

20. Leibush Lehrer, "The Jewish Elements in the Psychology of the Jewish Child in America," *YIVO Annual of Jewish Social Science,* Vol. **1** (New York: Yiddish Scientific Institute, 1946), pp. 195–216; Eugene L. Hartley, Max Rosenberg, and Shepard Schwartz, "Children's Perceptions of Ethnic Group Membership," *Journal of Psychology,* **26** (1948), 387–397; Kenneth B. Clark and Mamie P. Clark, "Emotional Factors in Racial Identification and Preference in Negro Children," *Journal of Negro Education,* **19** (1950), 341–350.

21. Richard D. Trent, "An Analysis of Expressed Self-Acceptance among Negro Children" (Unpublished Doctor's Thesis, Teachers College, Columbia University, 1953), p. 40.

22. David Riesman, "Marginality, Conformity and Insight," *Phylon,* **14** (1953), 125, 241–257.

23. Jack Rothman, *Minority Group Identification and Intergroup Relations* (Chicago, Ill.: Research Institute for Group Work in Jewish Agencies, in cooperation with The American Jewish Committee, 1965).

24. Joshua A. Fishman, "Negative Stereotypes Concerning Americans among Minority Children Receiving Various Types of Minority Group Education," *Genetic Psychology Monographs,* **51** (1955), 107–182.

25. John P. Dean, "Jewish Participation in the Life of Middle Sized American Communities," in Marshall Sklare (ed.), *The Jews: Social Patterns of an American Group* (New York: Free Press, 1958), pp. 304–320.

Notes to Part IV, 10

1. Charles Frankel, "The Family in Context," in Fred DelliQuadri (ed.), *Helping the Family in Urban Society* (New York: Columbia U. P., 1963), pp. 3–22; J. Milton Yinger, "The Changing Family in a Changing Society," *Social Casework,* **40** (1959), 419–428; Harold L. Wilensky and Charles N. Lebeaux, *Industrial Society and Social Welfare* (New York: Russell Sage Foundation, 1958); Reuben Hill, "The Changing American Family," in *The Social Welfare Forum, 1957,* Official Proceedings, 84th Annual Forum, National Conference on Social Welfare, Philadelphia, May 19–

24, 1957 (New York: Columbia University Press, 1957), pp. 68–80; Leon Eisenberg, "The Family in the Mid-twentieth Century," in *The Social Welfare Forum, 1960,* Official Proceedings, 87th Annual Forum, National Conference on Social Welfare, Atlantic City, New Jersey, June 5–10, 1960 (New York: Columbia U. P., 1960), pp. 98–112.

2. Marvin B. Sussman, "The Help Pattern in the Middle Class Family," *American Sociological Review,* 18 (1953), 22–28; Marvin B. Sussman, "The Isolated Nuclear Family: Fact or Fiction," *Social Problems* (1959), 333–340; Marvin B. Sussman and S. B. Slater, "Reappraisal of Urban Kin Networks: Empirical Evidence," a paper presented at the 58th annual meeting of the American Sociological Association, Los Angeles, August 1963; Eugene Litwak, "Geographic Mobility and Extended Family Cohesion," *American Sociological Review,* 25 (1960), 385–394; Eugene Litwak, "Voluntary Associations and Neighborhood Cohesion," *American Sociological Review,* 26 (1961), 258–271; Daniel R. Miller and Guy E. Swanson, *The Changing American Parent* (New York: Wiley, 1958).

3. Talcott Parsons, "The Social Structure of the Family," in Ruth Nanda Anshen (ed.), *The Family: Its Function and Destiny* (New York: Harper, 1949), pp. 191–192.

4. See Litwak, "Geographic Mobility and Extended Family Cohesion," *op. cit.,* p. 385.

5. Norman W. Bell and Ezra F. Vogel (eds.), *A Modern Introduction to the Family* (New York: Free Press, 1960), p. 1.

6. *Ibid.,* p. 1.

7. Eugene Litwak, "Occupational Mobility and Family Cohesion," *American Sociological Review,* 25 (1960), 9–10.

8. *Ibid.,* p. 10.

9. Sussman and Slater, *op. cit.*

10. Litwak, "Occupational Mobility and Family Cohesion," *op. cit.*

11. Carle C. Zimmerman and Lucius F. Cervantes, *Successful American Families* (New York: Pageant, 1960), p. 11.

12. Sussman and Slater, *op. cit.*

13. See Litwak, "Occupational Mobility and Family Cohesion," *op. cit.,* and Litwak, "Geographic Mobility and Extended Family Cohesion," *op. cit.*

14. Phillip Fellin and Eugene Litwak, "Neighborhood Cohesion under Conditions of Mobility," *American Sociological Review,* 28 (1963), 364–376.

15. Phillip Fellin and Frieda Brackebusch (eds.), "Neighborhoods in Transition" (Saint Louis: Saint Louis University, 1962; unpublished manuscript).

16. William J. Goode, "The Sociology of the Family," in Robert K. Merton, Leonard Broom, and Leonard S. Cottrell, Jr. (eds.), *Sociology Today* (New York: Basic Books, 1959), p. 190.

17. Eugene Litwak, "Continuing Family Functions in Urban Society" (unpublished manuscript).

18. William F. Ogburn, "The Changing Functions of the Family," in Robert F. Winch and Robert McGinnis (eds.), *Selected Studies in Marriage and the Family* (New York: Holt, 1953), pp. 74–76.

19. Ernest W. Burgess, "The Family in a Changing Society," in *Selected Studies in Marriage and the Family, op. cit.,* pp. 37–44; see Parsons, *op. cit.,* and Talcott Parsons and R. F. Bales, *Family, Socialization and Interaction Process* (New York: Free Press, 1955), pp. 8–19. See also Yinger, *op. cit.;* and Nelson N. Foote and Leonard S. Cottrell, Jr., *Identity and Interpersonal Competence* (Chicago: U. of Chicago Press, 1955), pp. 95–106.

20. Litwak, "Continuing Family Functions in Urban Society," *op. cit.*

Notes to Part IV, 11

1. C. Chilman and M. Sussman, "Poverty in the United States," *Journal of Marriage and the Family*, **26** (1964), 391–395.
2. T. Parsons and R. F. Bales, *Family, Socialization and Interaction Processes* (New York: Free Press, 1954), p. 10.
3. W. Bell and M. D. Boat, "Urban Neighborhoods and Informal Social Relations," *American Journal of Sociology*, **43** (1957), 391–398.
4. E. Litwak, "Geographic Mobility and Extended Family Cohesion," *American Sociological Review*, **25** (1960), 385–394.
5. Jesse Bernard, *American Family Behavior* (New York: Harper, 1942).
6. Parsons and Bales, *op. cit.*
7. R. F. Bales and E. F. Borgatta, "Size of Group as a Factor in the Interaction Profile," in Hare, Borgatta, and Bales (eds.), *Small Groups* (New York: Knopf, 1955), pp. 396–413.
8. P. E. Slater, "Contrasting Correlates of Group Size," *Sociometry*, **6** (1958), 129–139.
9. B. Mittleman, "Analysis of Reciprocal Neurotic Patterns in Family Relationships," in V. Eisenstein (ed.), *Neurotic Interaction in Marriage* (New York: Basic Books, 1956), pp. 81–100.
10. Chilman and Sussman, *op. cit.*, p. 394.
11. *Ibid.*, where Chilman and Sussman quote from *Poverty in the United States*. Committee on Education and Labor, House of Representatives, 88th Congress, Second Session, April 1964. U.S. Government Printing Office, Washington, D.C., p. 395.
12. R. A. Cloward and I. Epstein, "Private Social Welfare's Disengagement from the Poor: The Case of Family Adjustment Agencies," in M. N. Zald (ed.), *Social Welfare Institutions: A Sociological Reader* (New York: Wiley, 1965), pp. 623–644.
13. W. A. Lutz, "Marital Incompatability," in N. E. Cohen (ed.), *Social Work and Social Problems* (New York: National Association of Social Workers, 1964), pp. 41–52.

Notes to Part IV, 12

1. Robert Cooley Angell, *The Family Encounters the Depression* (New York: Scribner, 1936); R. S. Cavan and K. H. Ranck, *The Family and the Depression* (Chicago: U. of Chicago Press, 1938); T. D. Eliot, "Bereavement: Inevitable but Not Insurmountable," in H. Becker and R. Hill (eds.), *Family, Marriage and Parenthood* (Boston: Heath, 1948), pp. 641–668; T. D. Eliot, "Handling Family Strains and Shocks," in Becker and Hill, *ibid.*, pp. 616–640; R. Hill, J. J. Moss, and C. G. Wirths, *Eddyville's Families* (Chapel Hill, N.C.: Institute for Research in Social Science, 1953); R. Hill, *Families under Stress* (New York: Harper, 1949); M. Komarovsky, *The Unemployed Man and His Family* (New York: Dryden, 1940); E. L. Koos, *Families in Trouble* (New York: Kings Crown, 1946); W. W. Waller, *The Old Love and the New: Divorce and Readjustment* (Philadelphia: Liveright, 1930).
2. E. W. Burgess and P. Wallin, *Engagement and Marriage* (Philadelphia: Lippincott, 1953); E. W. Burgess and S. Cottrell, Jr., *Predicting Success or Failure in Marriage* (Englewood Cliffs, N.J.: Prentice-Hall, 1939); H. J. Locke, *Predicting Adjustment in Marriage* (New York: Holt, 1951); L. M. Terman and M. H. Oden, *The Gifted Child Grows Up* (Stanford, Cal.: Stanford U. P.

1947); L. M. Terman, *Psychological Factors in Marital Happiness* (New York: McGraw, 1938).

3. E. R. Duvall, *Family Development* (New York: Lippincott, 1957).

4. F. L. Bates, "A Conceptual Analysis of Group Structure," *Social Forces*, 36 (1957), 103–111; F. L. Bates, "Position, Role, and Status: A Reformulation of Concepts," *Social Forces*, 34 (1956), 313–321; E. Bott, "Urban Families: Conjugal Roles and Social Networks," *Human Relations*, 8 (1955), 345–384; P. G. Herbst, "The Measurement of Family Relationships," *Human Relations*, 5 (1952), 3–35; R. D. Hess and G. Handel, *Family Worlds* (Chicago: U. of Chicago Press, 1959); M. W. Kargman, "The Clinical Use of Social System Theory in Marriage Counseling," *Marriage and Family Living*, 19 (1957), 263–270; R. Linton, *The Study of Man* (New York: Appleton-Century, 1936); R. Rapoport and I. Rosow, "An Approach to Family Relationships and Role Performance," *Human Relations*, 10 (1957), 209–221; T. R. Sarbin, "Role Theory," in Gardner Lindzey (ed.), *Handbook of Social Psychology*, Vol. 1, *Theory and Method* (Cambridge, Addison-Wesley, 1954), pp. 223–258; G. A. Theodorson, "Elements in the Progressive Development of Small Groups," *Social Forces*, 31 (1953), 311–320; R. H. Turner, "Role Taking, Role Standpoint, and Reference-Group Behavior," *American Journal of Sociology*, 61 (1956), 316–328.

5. N. Ackerman, *The Psychodynamics of Family Life* (New York: Basic Books, 1958); E. Chance, *Families in Treatment* (New York: Basic Books, 1959); J. A. Clausen and M. R. Yarrow, "Mental Illness and the Family," *Journal of Social Issues*, 11 (1955), 3–65; E. J. Cleveland and W. D. Longaker, "Neurotic Patterns in the Family," in A. H. Leighton, J. A. Clausen, and R. N. Wilson (eds.), *Explorations in Social Psychiatry* (New York: Basic Books, 1957), pp. 167–200; F. Cote, T. E. Dancey, and J. Saucier, "Participation in Institutional Treatment by Selected Rela-

tives," *American Journal of Psychiatry*, 110 (1954), 831–833; S. Fisher and D. Mendell, "The Spread of Psychotherapeutic Effects from the Patient to His Family Group," *Psychiatry*, 21 (1958), 133–140; L. L. Geismar and B. Ayres, *Patterns of Change in Problem Families* (St. Paul, Minn.: Family Centered Project, Greater St. Paul Community Chest and Councils, 1959); A. Kaplan and L. Wolf, "The Role of the Family in Relation to the Institutionalized Mental Patient," *Mental Hygiene*, 38 (1954), 634–639; T. Lidy, G. Hotchkiss, and M. Greenblatt, "Patient-Family-Hospital Interrelationships: Some General Conclusions," in M. Greenblatt, D. J. Levinson, and R. H. Williams (eds.), *The Patient and the Mental Hospital* (New York: Free Press, 1957), pp. 535–544; M. L. Moran, "Some Emotional Responses of Patients' Husbands to the Psychotherapeutic Course as Indicated in Interviews with the Psychiatric Caseworker," *American Journal of Orthopsychiatry*, 24 (1954), 317–325; T. Parsons and R. Fox, "Illness, Therapy, and the Modern Urban American Family," *Journal of Social Issues*, 8 (1952), 31–44; C. G. Schwartz, "Perspectives on Deviance—Wives' Definitions of their Husbands' Mental Illness," *Psychiatry*, 20 (1957), 275–291; J. P. Spiegel, "The Resolution of Role Conflict within the Family," in Greenblatt, Levinson, and Williams *op. cit.*, pp. 545–564; L. C. Wynne, I. M. Ryckoff, J. Day, and S. I. Hirsch, "Pseudo-Mutuality in the Family Relations of Schizophrenics," *Psychiatry*, 21 (1958), 205–220.

6. Every family must evolve persistent patterns of expectations and behavior among its members if it is to endure for even a relatively short period of time. In addition, there must be internal role consistency, consistency of family roles and norms and actual role performance, and compatibility of family roles and norms with societal norms. A family in such a state is in equilibrium. When one or more of these conditions are not met the

family is considered to be in a state of disequilibrium or crisis. Two family-crisis periods are described in the larger study; (1) when the patient is in the acute stage of mental illness and (2) when the patient is in intensive, insight psychotherapy.

7. This report covers the last three stages of family organization. The seven role areas are as follows: (1) sexual practices; (2) social activities; (3) household provision; (4) household management; (5) child care and control; (6) authority patterns; (7) maintenance of morale.

8. In two of the cases the patient was hospitalized for a short period of time prior to the beginning of outpatient psychotherapy.

9. Each of the families attempted to hide the patient's symptoms and the possibility of mental illness from other relatives, friends, and neighbors prior to the beginning of treatment.

10. The distinction between family diagnosis and the treatment of the family as a group is an important one. The former often may be necessary while the latter may or may not be the treatment of choice.

11. In one of the families studied, following the beginning of treatment with the patient, the spouse became acutely ill, and finally had to be hospitalized in a psychiatric institution.

12. For a discussion of the criteria to evaluate interaction patterns as well as means to characterize the family as a problem-solving group, see the author's dissertation: *Family Organization during Psychotherapy* (Unpublished doctoral dissertation; Chapel Hill, N.C.: University of North Carolina, 1961).

Notes to Part IV, 13

1. H. J. Meyer, W. Jones, and E. F. Borgatta, "The Decision by Unmarried Mothers to Keep or Surrender Their Babies," *Social Work*, 1 (1956), 103–109; H. J. Meyer, E. F. Borgatta, and David Fanshel, "Unwed Mothers' Decisions about Their Babies: An Interim Replication Study," *Child Welfare*, 38 (1959), 1–6.

2. Unmarried mothers who kept and surrendered their babies were compared on the California Personality Inventory in C. W. Vincent, "Unwed Mothers and the Adoption Market: Psychological and Familial Factors," *Marriage and Family Living*, 22 (1960), 112–118; and C. W. Vincent, *Unmarried Mothers* (New York: Free Press, 1961), Chap. 7.

3. Youth Consultation Service, New York City, from which the present data are obtained as well as data for earlier years. We gratefully acknowledge the cooperation of the director and staff in this research. It was conducted while more extended research on adolescent girls was in progress, supported by a grant from the Russell Sage Foundation.

4. The complete sample is described in Wyatt C. Jones, *Correlates of Social Deviance: A Study of Unmarried Mothers* (Unpublished Ph.D. dissertation; New York University, 1965).

5. Statistical significance in this paper corresponds to satisfaction of the .05 level with a symmetric hypothesis test.

6. See Note 1, above.

7. Vincent, *op. cit.*

8. The MAST (Make a Sentence Test) items, scoring and cross validation are described in E. F. Borgatta (in collaboration with H. J. Meyer), "Make a Sentence Test: An Approach to Objective Scoring of Sentence Completions," *Genetic Psychology Monographs*, 63 (1961), 3–65.

9. R. B. Cattell, D. R. Saunders, and G. Stice, *Handbook for the Sixteen Personality Factor Questionnaire* (Cham-

paign, Ill.: Institute for Personality and Ability Testing, 1957).

10. The scoring categories for the MAST sentence-completion test are listed as follows: 1. Paranoid, 2. Hostile, 3. Assertive, 4. Annoyed, 5. Conventional, 6. Avoidant, 7. Depressive, 8. Anxious, 9. Self-analytic, 10. Hypochondriac, and 11. Optimistic.

The data analysis follows several arbitrary decisions that tend to minimize the possibility of interpreting spurious findings. For example, in the MAST analysis, the variables were dichotomized prior to analysis to give two most nearly equal halves. The 16 PFT variables were trichotomized with the two central scores comprising the *moderate* category, and then

were further dichotomized on the same principle as the MAST. An example of a dichotomy in the form of L vs. MH is the Low group versus the Middle and High Groups.

11. The scoring categories of the Cattell 16 PFT are as follows: A. Warm, sociable; B. General intelligence; C. Emotional stability; E. Dominant, aggressive; F. Talkative, enthusiastic; G. Conscientious, persistent; H. Adventurous; I. Sensitive; L. Suspecting; M. Eccentric, unconcerned; N. Sophisticated, polished; O. Anxious, insecure; Q_1. Experimenting, critical; Q_2. Self-sufficient, resourceful; Q_3. Controlled; and Q_4. Tense, excitable.

12. Meyer, Borgatta, Fanshel, *op. cit.*, p. 3.

Notes to Part IV, 14

1. Such factors as industrialization, urbanization, happiness of parents, personality factors are illustrative of the type of factors which are thought to influence family breakup. Ernest W. Burgess and Harvey J. Locke, *The Family: From Institution to Companionship* (2nd ed.; New York: Am. Bk. Co., 1953), pp. 407–429.

2. William F. Ogburn, "The Changing Functions of the Family," in Robert F. Winch and Robert McGinnis (eds.), *Selected Studies in Marriage and the Family* (New York: Holt, 1953), pp. 74–81.

3. Essentially two types of social-psychological theory have been used to support the view that punishment affects nonviolators. One is typified by Franz Alexander and Hugo Staub, *The Criminal, The Judge, and The Public*, Trans. Gregory Zilboorg (New York: Macmillan, 1931); and the other is typified by Emil Durkheim, *The Division of Labor*, Trans. George Simpson (1st and 5th eds.; New York: Free Press, 1947), Book I, "The Function of the Division of Labor," Chap. 2, "Mechanical Soli-

darity through Likeness," pp. 70–110; and George H. Mead, "The Psychology of Punitive Justice," *American Journal of Sociology*, 23 (1917–1918), 577–602.

4. James P. Lichtenberger, *Divorce* (New York and London: Whittlesey, McGraw, 1931); Max Rheinstein, "Trends in Marriage and Divorce Law of Western Countries," *Law and Contemporary Problems*, 18, No. 1 (1953), 4. Rheinstein, though agreeing that divorce laws have historically embodied the concept of punishment, would not agree that the punishment was intended to prevent breakdown.

5. Irving Mandell and Richard McKay, *Law of Marriage and Divorce* (2nd ed.; New York: Oceana, 1952), pp. 75–76.

6. *Ibid.*, p. 76.

7. *Ibid.*, pp. 77–80.

8. Until recently the only ground for divorce in New York was adultery, which could be prosecuted as a crime by the district attorney in proceedings independent from those constituted by the spouse who wished to obtain a divorce.

9. Harriet F. Pilpel and Theodora Zavin, *Your Marriage and the Law* (3rd ed. rev.; Philadelphia: Lippincott, 1939), p. 363.

10. Durkheim, *op. cit.*, pp. 70–110; Mead, *op. cit.*, pp. 577–602.

11. See Walter C. Reckless, *The Crime Problem* (New York: Appleton-Century-Crofts, 1950), pp. 165 ff. Actually the formulations of Mead and Durkheim as stated in this paper take the variable of social organization into account in a very limited sense. They do not really deal with the factor of power. The effects of public punishment might be directly contrary depending on whether the deviant comes from a high-powered or low-powered group. In this paper there will be no extended discussion of the role of social organization.

12. See Pilpel and Zavin, *op. cit.*, pp. 297–306.

13. See Rheinstein, *op. cit.*, p. 18.

14. Generally speaking, divorce laws are addressed to reducing breakup by opportunity, for they define the conditions under which a married man can take a new spouse.

15. For a discussion of the law as therapy, see Paul W. Alexander, "A Therapeutic Approach," *The Law School, The University of Chicago, Conference on Divorce*, Conference Series No. 9 (February 29, 1952).

16. Max Beckman, "Divorce in Sweden" (Unpublished manuscript, University of Stockholm, 1952).

17. For attempts to express this view, see Robert K. Merton, "Social Structure and Anomie," in Ruth Anshen (ed.), *The Family, Its Functions and Destiny* (New York: Harper, 1949), pp. 226–257. See Talcott Parsons, *The Social System* (New York: Free Press, 1951), especially Chap. 7, "Deviant Behavior and the Mechanisms of Social Control," pp. 249–321. See Nelson N. Foote and Leonard S. Cottrell, Jr., *Identity and Interpersonal Competence: A New Direction in Family Research* (Chicago: U. of Chicago Press, 1955).

18. Talcott Parsons, "Age and Sex in the Social Structure of the United States," in Winch and McGinnis, *op. cit.*, pp. 330–345.

19. Ogburn, *op. cit.*, pp. 74–81. However, Burgess and Locke have pointed out the limitations of such an analysis, *op. cit.*, pp. 713 ff., especially 718.

20. For an illustration of other techniques which are more effective than lectures see Kurt Lewin "Group Decision and Social Change," Theodore M. Newcomb and Eugene L. Hartley (eds.), in *Readings in Social Psychology* (New York: Holt, 1947), especially pp. 334–340.

21. Foote and Cottrell, *op. cit.*

22. See Ernest W. Burgess and Paul Wallin, *Engagement and Marriage* (Philadelphia: Lippincott, 1953), especially pp. 624 ff.

Notes to Part V, 15

1. This conception follows the formulation presented by Philip Selznick, "A Theory of Organizational Commitments," in Robert K. Merton, Ailsa P. Gray, Barbara Hockey, and Hanan C. Selvin (eds.), *Reader in Bureaucracy* (New York: Free Press, 1952), pp. 194–202.

2. Data presented by Wilensky and Lebeaux, based on the Bureau of Labor Statistics study, *Social Workers in 1950*, show that only 16 per cent of all social work personnel held professional degrees. Percentages by fields of service ranged from 4 (public assistance) to 83 (clinic psychiatric social work). There is no reason to believe substantial differences exist today; Harold L. Wilensky and Charles N. Lebeaux, *Industrial Soci-*

ety and Social Welfare (New York: Russell Sage Foundation, 1958), pp. 233–282.

3. A similar analysis is offered in *ibid.*, pp. 245–246, 319–321.

4. *Ibid.*, p. 292; David G. French and Alex Rosen, *Personnel Entering Social Work Employment from Schools of Social Work* (New York: Council on Social Work Education, 1957; mimeographed), p. 11.

5. Lloyd E. Ohlin, Herman Piven, and Donnell M. Pappenfort, "Major Dilemmas of the Social Worker in Probation and Parole," *National Probation and Parole Association Journal*, 2 (1956), 211–226.

6. Committee on Corrections, *Working Paper on the Nature of Social Work Practice in Corrections* (New York: Council on Social Work Education, 1958; mimeographed), especially pp. 10–17.

7. Jeannette R. Grafstrom, "Casework in Public Assistance—Myth, Frill or Goal," in *Selected Papers in Casework* (Raleigh: Health Publications Institute, 1953), pp. 52–66.

8. Alvin Zander, Arthur R. Cohen, and Ezra Stotland, *Role Relations in the Mental Health Professions* (Ann Arbor: Institute for Social Research, University of Michigan, 1957), see Chap. 4.

9. Most studies of personnel turnover have indicated the significance of administrative conditions for professional morale. See, for example the author's "Report of the Personnel Turnover Study," *The Round Table*, 21 (New York: National Federation of Settlements, 1957), pp. 2 and 5.

10. For example, see Dorwin Cartwright and Alvin Zander, *Group Dynamics: Research and Theory* (Evanston, Ill.: Row, 1953); and Theodore Caplow, "Organizational Size," *Administrative Science Quarterly*, 1 (1957), 484–506.

11. Edwin J. Thomas, "Role Conceptions and Organizational Size," *American Sociological Review*, 24 (1959), 30–37.

12. Frederick W. Terrien and Donald L. Mills, "The Effect of Changing Size upon the Internal Structure of Or-

ganizations," *American Sociological Review*, 20 (1955), 11.

13. Thomas, *op. cit.*

14. Richard A. Cloward, "Agency Structure as a Variable in Service to Groups," in *Group Work and Community Organization, 1956* (New York: Columbia, U. P., 1956), p. 246.

15. Thomas, *op. cit.*

16. Cloward, *op. cit.*

17. Robert D. Vinter and Roger M. Lind, *Staff Relationships and Attitudes in a Juvenile Correctional Institution* (Ann Arbor: School of Social Work, University of Michigan, 1958), pp. 20–30.

18. This distinction is drawn from Chester I. Barnard, "The Functions and Pathology of Status Systems in Formal Organizations," in William F. Whyte (ed.), *Industry and Society* (New York: McGraw, 1946), pp. 46–83.

19. This phenomenon has been discussed by Lloyd E. Ohlin, "Conformity in American Society," *Social Work*, 3 (1958), 58–67.

20. Morris Janowitz and William Delany, "The Bureaucrat and the Public: A Study of Informational Perspectives," *Administrative Science Quarterly*, 2 (1957), 141–163.

21. For an analysis of these patterns in the context of a hospital, see Rose L. Coser, "Authority and Decision-Making in a Hospital," *American Sociological Review*, 23 (1958), 56–64.

22. Wilensky and Lebeaux suggest that traditional patterns of supervision impede public acceptance of claims to professional status, and hinder effective relations with other professionals under certain conditions. Wilensky and Lebeaux, *op. cit.*, pp. 237–238. Ohlin, *op. cit.*, points to the role of supervision in professional preparation as another reason for continuing emphasis given it.

23. See Parsons' discussion of this orientation in "The Professions and Social Structure," in *Essays in Sociological Theory, Pure and Applied* (New York: Free Press, 1949), pp. 185–199.

24. A recent survey disclosed that practitioners' major objections to supervision include: "limitations on initia-

tive," "being kept dependent," etc. Robert W. Cruser, "Opinions on Supervision: A Chapter Study," *Social Work*, 3 (1958), 18–26.

25. Albert H. Aronson, *et al.*, *Administration, Supervision, and Consultation* (New York: Family Service Association, 1955); Ruth E. Lindenberg, "Changing Traditional Patterns of Supervision," *Social Work*, 2 (1957), 42–47.

26. Theodore Caplow, *The Sociology of Work* (Minneapolis: U. of Minnesota Press, 1954), pp. 238–244. He also refers to the custom of choosing male executives for social agencies except those associated directly with feminine interests. In this connection it is interesting to note that in the professional literature, the supervisor is typically referred to as "she," while the subordinate practitioner is referred to as "he."

27. In a study of personnel who had left agency positions, the writer found that larger proportions of men than of women cited salary reasons as affecting decisions to leave; larger proportions of those with professional degrees than of those without such education cited problematic staff relations, particularly with supervisors, as affecting departure decisions. Vinter, "Report of the Personnel Turnover Study," *op. cit.*, pp. 3–4.

28. For an elaboration of this point with regard to the mental hospital, see Talcott Parsons, "The Mental Hospital as a Type of Organization," in Milton

Greenblatt, Daniel Levinson, and Richard H. Williams (eds.), *The Patient and the Mental Hospital* (New York: Free Press, 1957), p. 116.

29. Membership agencies are sometimes exceptions to this general rule. Even in such agencies, however, control by clients is exercised indirectly through annual meetings. Lay control of policy does not provide most client members with operating authority.

30. Alvin W. Gouldner, "Red Tape as a Social Problem," in Merton, et al., *op. cit.*, pp. 410–419.

31. Henry S. Maas, *et al.*, "Socio-Cultural Factors in Psychiatric Clinic Services for Children," *Smith College Studies in Social Work*, 25 (1955), 56–75. Roy G. Francis and Robert C. Stone, *Service and Procedure in Bureaucracy* (Minneapolis: U. of Minnesota Press, 1956), Chap. 4.

32. Edwin Thomas, Norman Polansky, and Jacob Kounin, "The Expected Behavior of a Potentially Helpful Person," *Human Relations*, 8 (1955), 165–175, reprinted as Selection 23 of this book.

33. For example, see Wilensky and Lebeaux, *op. cit.*, pp. 245–246; Francis and Stone, *op. cit.*, Chap. 10.

34. Morris S. Schwartz, "What Is a Therapeutic Milieu?" in Greenblatt, Levinson, and Williams, *op. cit.*, pp. 130–145.

35. William Caudill, *The Psychiatric Hospital as a Small Society* (Cambridge: Harvard U. P., 1958).

Notes to Part V, 16

1. See, for example, Milton Greenblatt, Richard H. York, and Esther L. Brown, *From Custodial to Therapeutic Patient Care in Mental Hospitals* (New York: Russell Sage Foundation, 1955); Richard McCleery, *Policy Change in Prison Management* (East Lansing, Mich.: Michigan State U. Press, 1957); Talcott Parsons,

"The Mental Hospital as a Type of Organization," in Milton Greenblatt, Daniel J. Levinson, and Richard H. Williams (eds.), *The Patient and the Mental Hospital* (New York: Free Press, 1957), pp. 108–129.

2. This view has been changing in recent years, with greater recognition of sociocultural conditions impeding

the education of some youth, and concern about their doubtful motivations, especially within the lower economic strata. See Frank Riessman, *The Culturally Deprived Child* (New York: Harper, 1962).

3. For an analysis of such public attitudes, see Elaine and John Cumming, *Closed Ranks: An Experiment in Mental Health Education* (Cambridge: Harvard U. P., 1957), pp. 91–150. See also Julian L. Woodward, "Changing Ideas on Mental Illness and Its Treatment," *American Sociological Review*, 16 (1951), 443–454.

4. For an analysis of contrasting diagnostic systems, their ideological sources and technological consequences, see Rosemary Sarri, "Organizational Patterns and Client Perspectives in Juvenile Correctional Institutions: A Comparative Study" (Unpublished Ph.D. dissertation, University of Michigan, 1962).

5. Robert D. Vinter et al., *The Comparative Study of Juvenile Institutions: A Research Report* (Ann Arbor, Mich.: U. of Michigan Press, 1961), Chap. 9. Certain of the concepts and ideas presented here have been developed in a four-year comparative study of juvenile institutions, supported by NIMH Grant M-2104.

6. Litwak observes that organizational emphasis on impersonal relations and general rules is more likely to occur when the events at issue are uniform rather than nonuniform. Our point is that definitions of the uniformity of events (here human events) vary among people-changing organizations. Eugene Litwak, "Models of Bureaucracy Which Permit Conflict," *American Journal of Sociology*, 57 (1961), 177–184.

7. One aspect of organization-profession interdependence has been the organization's assumption of training responsibilities for the profession.

8. The more prestigious the profession, the greater its capacity to legitimize treatment organizations. One would expect, therefore, to find a scale of pre-eminence within organizations corresponding to the relative ranking of professions in the larger society.

This appears to be the case with respect to psychiatry, whose higher prestige relative to the other professions mentioned is a matter of common knowledge. See Raymond G. Hunt, Orville Gurrslin, and Jack L. Roach, "Social Status and Psychiatric Service in a Child Guidance Clinic," *American Sociological Review*, 23 (1958), 81–83.

9. See Frances G. Scott, "Action Theory and Research in Social Organization," *American Journal of Sociology*, 64 (1959), 386–395.

10. Erving Goffman, *Asylums: Essays on the Social Situation of Mental Patients and Other Inmates* (Garden City, N.Y.: Doubleday, 1961). See especially "The Medical Model and Mental Hospitalization," pp. 321–386.

11. It is recognized that hospitals vary and that increasingly they are assuming characteristics not dictated by professional requirements. See Robert N. Wilson, "The Physician's Changing Hospital Role," *Human Organization*, 18 (1959–1960), 177–183; and Charles B. Perrow, "Organizational Prestige: Some Functions and Dysfunctions," *American Journal of Sociology*, 66 (1961), 335–341.

12. *Salaries and Working Conditions of Social Welfare Manpower in 1960* (New York: National Social Welfare Assembly, undated). See especially Table 18, p. 39.

13. Alvin F. Zander, Arthur R. Cohen, and Ezra Stotland, *Role Relations in Mental Health Professions* (Ann Arbor, Mich.: U. of Michigan Press, 1957). See Chap. 4.

14. See Lloyd E. Ohlin, "Conformity in American Society Today," *Social Work*, 3 (1958), 58–66.

15. For a fuller discussion of these problems, see Robert D. Vinter, "The Social Structure of Service," in Alfred J. Kahn (ed.), *Issues in American Social Work* (New York: Columbia U. P., 1959), pp. 260–265. Editor's note: this paper is Selection V-15 of this book.

16. For example, Lind found that, in two welfare organizations, personnel in the unit with the higher level of pro-

fessionalization spent significantly more time conferring about cases and were also more dependent on colleagues (here including the immediate supervisor). Roger M. Lind, "Organizational Structure and Social Worker Performance" (Unpublished Ph.D. dissertation, University of Michigan, 1962).

17. Blau and Scott present a cogent critique of these and related devices used by treatment organizations. Peter M. Blau and W. Richard Scott, *Formal Organizations* (San Francisco: Chandler, 1962), pp. 189–191.

18. See Amitai Etzioni, "Authority Structure and Organizational Effectiveness," *Administrative Science Quarterly*, 4 (1959), 43–68; and Robert Wilson, *op. cit.*

19. See Zander et al., *op. cit.*

20. Lloyd W. McCorkle and Richard R. Korn, "Resocialization within Prison Walls," *The Annals*, 293 (1954), 88–98.

21. See Goffman, "The Moral Career of the Mental Patient," *loc. cit.*, pp. 125–170.

22. See Dorothy Fahs Beck, *Patterns in Use of Family Agency Service* (New York: Family Service Association of America, 1962), Chart 19, p. 20.

23. J. K. Wing, "Institutionalism in Mental Hospitals," *British Journal of Clinical Psychology*, 1 (1962), 38–51.

Notes to Part V, 17

1. Theoretical frameworks and empirical findings for analysis of self attitudes are provided by Morris Rosenberg, *Society and the Adolescent Self Image* (Princeton: Princeton U. P., 1965); Harrison Gough, "A Sociological Theory of Psychopathology," *American Journal of Sociology*, 53 (1948), 359–366; William McCord and Joan McCord, *Psychopathology and Delinquency* (New York: Grune, 1956); Walter Reckless, *et al.*, "Self Concept as an Insulator against Delinquency," *American Sociological Review*, 21 (1956), 744–746; Walter Reckless, *et al.*, "The Self Component in Potential Delinquency and Non-Delinquency," *American Sociological Review*, 22 (1957), 566–570; Walter Reckless, *et al.*, "The 'Good' Boys in a High Delinquency Area: Four Years Later," *American Sociological Review*, 25 (1960), 555–558; Fred E. Fiedler and Alan R. Bass, "Delinquency, Confinement, and Interpersonal Perception," *Technical Report* No. 6, Group Effectiveness Research Laboratory (Urbana: U. of Illinois, 1959).

2. For example, Gresham M. Sykes and Sheldon L. Messinger, "The Inmate Social System," in Richard A. Cloward, Donald R. Cressey, George H. Grosser, Richard McCleery, Lloyd E. Ohlin, Gresham Sykes, and Sheldon L. Messinger (eds.), *Theoretical Studies in Social Organization of the Prison* (New York: Social Science Research Council, 1960), pp. 5–8; Lloyd E. Ohlin and William C. Lawrence, "Social Interaction among Clients as a Treatment Problem," *Social Work*, 4 (1959), 3–14; and Howard Polsky, *Cottage Six—The Social System of Delinquent Boys in Residential Treatment* (New York: Russell Sage Foundation, 1962).

3. See Erving Goffman, "On the Characteristics of Total Institution," in Donald Cressey (ed.), *The Prison: Studies in Institutional Organization and Change* (New York: Holt, 1961), pp. 15–106.

4. Much of the research on which the solidary opposition model is based involved case studies, and the data collected are such that comparability across institutions cannot be estimated. Even with this approach several observers have suggested that

there is variability in inmates' attitudes and behavior.

5. Donald Cressey has examined some of the characteristics of contemporary prisons which present potential impediments to the development of treatment services; see Donald Cressey, "Prison Organizations" in James G. March (ed.), *Handbook of Organizations* (Chicago: Rand McNally, 1965), pp. 1054–1067.

6. See Lloyd McCorkle and Richard Korn, "Resocialization within the Walls," *The Annals*, **293** (1954), 362–369.

7. See Edwin Sutherland, H. Sutherland, and D. Cressey, *Principles of Criminology* (5th ed.; New York: Lippincott, 1955), pp. 3–250. For examples of personal documents obtained, see Clifford R. Shaw, *The Jack-Roller* (Chicago: U. of Chicago Press, 1930); and Clifford R. Shaw, *The Natural History of a Delinquent Career* (Chicago: U. of Chicago Press, 1931). For a personal report of an admission to a prison see Brendan Behan, *Borstal Boy* (London: Hutchinson, 1958), p. 40.

8. See Stanton Wheeler, "Socialization in Prison Communities," *American Sociological Review*, **26** (1961), 697–712.

9. These organizations are similar to hospitals, residential treatment centers, schools, and universities in having multiple goals which they seek to achieve. They may be classified as *people-changing* organizations in that their major goal is that of changing persons in ways distinctive to each organization. See Robert D. Vinter, "The Analysis of Treatment Organizations," *Social Work*, **8** (1963), 3–15 [see Selection 16]; Robert D. Vinter and Morris Janowitz, "Effective Institutions for Juvenile Delinquents: A Research Statement," *Social Services Review*, **33** (1959), 118–131.

10. Mnemonic labels are used to identify each of the institutions. These labels refer to the characteristic goal of each.

11. See William and Joan McCord, *op. cit*. See also Richard L. Jenkins, "Delinquency as Failure and Delinquency as Attainment," a paper presented at the 26th Annual Governor's Conference on Youth and Community Service, 1957; and Richard L. Jenkins and Eva Blodgett, "Prediction of Success or Failure of Delinquent Boys from Sentence Completion," *American Journal of Orthopsychiatry*, **30** (1960), 741–756.

12. Statements about inner qualities were classified as *character attributes* and were considered to be the most positive responses in accord with our theoretical orientation. The other categories were then ranked from positive to negative accordingly. Examples of character attributes included: "kind and thoughtful," "good personality," and "frank and say what I think." The category, "obedience and virtuous habits," referred to specific mention of conforming behavior, for example: "well-behaved," "doesn't get into trouble," "knows right from wrong," and "doesn't drink or smoke." Responses were coded as inappropriate or indefinite when the respondent was unable to name a quality or stated, "nothing," "don't know," "everything," and so forth.

13. For a report of research on inmate relations completed in conjunction with this project, see David Street, "The Inmate Group in Custodial and Treatment Settings," *American Sociological Review*, **30** (1965), 40–55.

14. Morris Rosenberg, *op. cit.*; Erik Erikson, "Identity and the Life Cycle," *Psychological Issues*, **1** (1959), 111; and Mary Engel, "The Stability of the Self Concept in Adolescence," *Journal of Abnormal and Social Psychology*, **58** (1959), 211–215.

15. See Donald Cressey, "Changing Criminals: The Application of the Theory of Differential Association," *American Journal of Sociology*, **61** (1955), 116–120.

Notes to Part V, 18

1. D. P. Street, R. D. Vinter, and C. Perrow, *Organization for Treatment: A Comparative Study of Juvenile Correctional Institutions* (New York: Free Press, 1966).
2. T. Parsons, "The Mental Hospital As a Type of Organization," in M. Greenblatt, D. J. Levinson, and R. H. Williams (eds.), *The Patient and the Mental Hospital* (New York: Free Press, 1957), pp. 108–129.
3. D. P. Street, *Inmate Social Organization: A Comparative Study of Juvenile Correctional Institutions* (Unpublished Ph.D. dissertation, University of Michigan, 1962).
4. M. Greenblatt, R. H. York, and Esther Lucile Brown, *From Custodial to Therapeutic Patient Care in Mental Hospitals* (New York: Russell Sage Foundation, 1955).
5. H. Rowland, "Interaction Processes in the State Mental Hospital," *Psychiatry*, 1 (1938), 323–337.
6. I. Belknap, *Human Problems of a State Mental Hospital* (New York: McGraw, 1956).
7. H. W. Dunham and S. K. Weinberg, *The Culture of the State Mental Hospital* (Detroit, Mich.: Wayne State U. P., 1960).
8. A. H. Stanton and M. S. Schwartz, *The Mental Hospital* (New York: Basic Books, 1954).
9. N. A. Polansky, R. B. White, and S. C. Miller, "Determinants of the Role-Image of the Patient in a Psychiatric Hospital," in Greenblatt, Levinson, and Williams, *op. cit.*, pp. 380–402.
10. W. A. Caudill, *The Psychiatric Hospital As a Small Society* (Cambridge, Harvard U. P., 1958); W. A. Caudill, F. C. Redlich, H. R. Gilmore, and E. B. Brody, "Social Structure and Interaction Processes on a Psychiatric Ward," *American Journal of Orthopsychiatry*, 22 (1952), 314–334.
11. D. H. Miller, "The Rehabilitation of Chronic Open-Ward Neuropsychiatric Patients," *Psychiatry*, 17 (1954), 347–358.
12. P. Sivadon, "Technics of Sociotherapy," *Symposium on Preventive and Social Psychiatry* (Washington, D.C.: Walter Reed Army Institute of Research, 1957), pp. 457–465.
13. M. Jones, *The Therapeutic Community* (New York: Basic Books, 1953).
14. Belknap, *op. cit.*
15. Caudill, *op. cit.*
16. J. Cumming and Elaine Cumming, *Ego and Milieu* (New York: Atherton, 1962).
17. R. N. Rapoport, *Community As Doctor* (Springfield, Ill.: Charles C. Thomas, 1960).
18. C. Perrow, "Hospitals: Technology, Structure and Goals," in James March (ed.), *Handbook of Organizations* (Chicago: Rand McNally, 1965), pp. 910–972.

Notes to Part V, 19

1. T. Parsons, *The Structure of Social Action* (New York: The Free Press, 1949), pp. 542–552; A. M. Henderson and T. Parsons (Trans.), *The Theory of Social and Economic Organization* (New York: Oxford U. P., 1947), pp. 354–358.
2. F. Tonnies, *Fundamental Concepts of Sociology* (New York: Am. Bk. Co., 1940), pp. 18–28.
3. J. A. Schumpeter, *Capitalism, Socialism, and Democracy* (2nd ed.; New York: Harper, 1947), p. 157.
4. T. Parsons, "The Social Structure of the Family," in Ruth N. Anshen (ed.), *The Family: Its Function and*

Destiny (New York: Harper, revised, 1959), pp. 260–263; George A. Theodorson, "Acceptance of Industrialization and its Attendant Consequences for the Social Patterns of Non-Western Societies," *American Sociological Review*, 18 (1953), 480–481.

5. There are significant exceptions to this remark. James D. Thompson, "Organizations and Output Transactions," *American Journal of Sociology*, 68 (1962), 309–324, has pointed to the need to systematically consider boundary-spanning relations of large organizations, and he has developed a general framework for doing so. There are a number of other works, often in the applied fields, that touch closely on the problems raised here but do not directly relate formal bureaucratic organizations to external primary groups. For an article that covers some of the same issues from a different perspective see Charles Kadushin, "Social Distance between Client and Professional." *American Journal of Sociology*, 57 (1962), 517–531. An approach to external links of organizations through role analysis is represented by Robert C. Hanson, "The System Linkage Hypothesis and Role Consensus Patterns in Hospital-Community Relations," *American Sociological Review*, 27 (1962), 304–313. The more general concept of systematic linkage is found in Charles P. Loomis, *Social Systems: Their Persistence and Change* (Princeton, N.J.: Van Nostrand, 1960), pp. 32–34.

6. Irving A. Fowler, "Local Industrial Structures, Economic Power, and Community Welfare," *Social Problems*, 6 (1958), 41–51; R. J. Pellegrin and C. H. Coats, "Absentee Owned Corporations and Community Power Structure," *American Journal of Sociology*, 61 (1956), 413–419; William H. Whyte, Jr., *The Organization Man* (New York: Simon and Schuster, 1956), pp. 295–296. For a summary of literature and a systematic consideration of theoretical issues see Eugene Litwak, "Voluntary Associations and Neighborhood Cohesion," *American Sociological Review*, 26 (1961), 258–262.

7. The revival of local organizing efforts of political parties—"volunteers," neighborhood units, clubs, etc. —seems evident, expressing in this fashion what an early study of political behavior documented: that to understand how people vote it is necessary to take account of family and friends. See Paul F. Lazarsfeld, Bernard Berelson, and Helen Gaudet, *The People's Choice* (New York: Duell, Sloan & Pearce, 1944), pp. 153 ff. S. Martin Lipset, Martin Trow, and James Coleman, *Union Democracy* (New York: The Free Press, 1956), pp. 67–83, suggest more generally that governmental systems, when under stress, will seek to organize and control primary-type organizations, and they point to the Nazi's development of block clubs during World War II as a case in point. In delinquency-control efforts, there is growing recognition that delinquents cannot be treated as isolated individuals, but must be reached through their significant primary groups, such as gangs. This has led to the development of street-gang programs such as those of the New York City Youth Board. In education there is also increasing concern with the need for closer relations between schools and families where there has been extensive breakdown in the educational process. Thus, the Detroit and the Flint, Michigan, school systems have crystallized these trends into major programs to bring school and family closer together. In Detroit a special, new position has been created—the school-community agent—to facilitate this linkage in low-income areas where educational efforts have had limited success. In fund-raising endeavors the importance of grass-root, primary-group ties is recognized in the efforts of major health foundations to use local neighborhood residents to collect funds in their own neighborhoods.

For a case study of how hospital and local community volunteers coordinate their behavior to maximize goal achievement see Otto Von Mehring, "The Social Self-Renewal of the Mental Patient and the Volunteer Movement," in Milton Greenblatt, Daniel J. Levinson, and Richard Williams (eds.), *The Patient and the Mental Hospital* (New York: Free Press, 1957), pp. 585–593. In the army the close dependence of fighting morale on family stability has long been recognized and was pointed out by Edward Shils and Morris Janowitz as one of the few appeals that made the German soldier susceptible to surrender. See their article, "Cohesion and Disintegration in the Wehrmacht in World War II," *Public Opinion Quarterly*, 12 (1948), 280–315.

It is difficult to think of any major bureaucratic organization that, once examined, does not display *de facto* concern with coordinating its activities to primary groups external to it. Furthermore, there appears to be an increasing awareness and appreciation of such ties.

8. H. H. Gerth and C. Wright Mills (Trans. and eds.), *From Max Weber: Essays in Sociology* (New York: Oxford U. P., 1946), pp. 196–244. Perhaps the clearest statement of this point with reference to the family is made by William F. Ogburn, "The Changing Functions of the Family," in Robert F. Winch and Robert McGinnis (eds.), *Selected Readings in Marriage and the Family* (New York: Holt, 1953), pp. 74–76.

9. For a discussion of reasons why the atmospheres may not be as antithetical as formerly, see E. Litwak, "The Use of Extended Family Groups in the Achievement of Social Goals: Some Policy Implications," *Social Problems*, 7 (1959–1960), 184–185.

10. P. Blau, *Bureaucracy in Modern Society* (New York: Random House, 1956), pp. 58, 62; Julian Franklin, "Bureaucracy and Freedom" in *Man in Contemporary Society*, Vol. 1, prepared by the Contemporary Civilization Staff of Columbia University (New York: Columbia University Press, 1955), pp. 941–942; Eugene Litwak, "Models of Bureaucracy Which Permit Conflict," *American Journal of Sociology*, 67 (1961), 178–179.

11. Elihu Katz and Paul F. Lazarsfeld, *Personal Influence* (New York: Free Press, 1955), pp. 1–100.

12. It is assumed by this statement that both uniform and nonuniform events will be important for modern society in the foreseeable future. Nonuniformity is assumed because, with scientific and technological progress, new areas of ignorance and uncertainty are exposed even though areas formerly considerd uncertain are reduced to uniform predictions. In addition, a society committed to rapid technological change is subject to many unanticipated social consequences that must be dealt with as regular features of urban life. Finally, in a complex society with highly specialized roles and intricate socialization procedures, it is too much to expect that all persons will be perfectly socialized. In the welter of interactions there are always areas of uncertainty.

13. With exceptions as noted in Note 5, above.

14. For a description of such a program see P. L. Crawford, D. I. Malamud, and J. R. Dumpson, *Working with Teenage Gangs* (New York: Welfare Council of New York City, 1950).

The same approach is developing in some school systems where a school-community agent enters family and neighborhood groups in an effort to increase educational motivation of the child by strengthening family life. Similar attempts by industry to influence primary groups relevant to it are not clearly legitimized and hence the detached-expert approach is far less explicit. Even so, there is evidence that community relations experts of some large business organizations operate in this manner in their contacts with key leadership groups in the community. In the military services the chaplain will sometimes act as a detached worker to the families of service men who are accessible, or the public relations officer might perform this function with key community leaders around the army base. Regardless of the present social norms on usage of detached experts, it should be understood that, in principle, any bureaucratic organization can make use of the detached expert. Thus, in Russia, where the norms of political behavior are different from ours, the "agitator" as described by Inkeles tends to operate as a detached worker connecting the bureaucratic mass media with the local primary groups. See Alex Inkeles, *Public Opinion in Soviet Russia* (Cambridge: Harvard U. P., 1951), pp. 67–83.

15. S. Kobrin, "The Chicago Area Project: A Twenty-Five Year Assessment," *Annals of the American Academy of Political and Social Sciences*, **322** (1959), 19–37.

In industry the opinion-leader approach is illustrated by managements' encouragement of executives to join key groups in the community and, through them, to develop a "better business atmosphere." School systems will select opinion leaders in local neighborhoods to help in campaigns for school funds.

16. Katz and Lazarsfeld, *op. cit.*, pp. 1–100.

17. Floyd Hunter, *Community Power Structure* (Chapel Hill, N.C.: U. of North Carolina Press, 1953), pp. 60–114, 171–207.

18. L. T. Empey and J. Rabow, "The Provo Experiment in Delinquency Rehabilitation," *American Sociological Review*, **26** (1961), 679–695.

Because of its high visibility (employment of trained professionals and use of physical facilities) this approach is not as readily used by organizations, such as industries, where there is no clear social mandate for change. Yet there are prototypes in industry that come close to this approach. These are often historically related to paternalistic policies. In its extreme form it manifested itself in the company town. Current variation on this theme is seen in the development, by some large companies, of community centers and recreation centers for the exclusive use of their employees. Provision of executive conferences and seminars at business

schools of universities represents another example.

The Army (especially overseas) may assume the same paternalistic position and provide not only facilities but the context of social relations for dependents as well as for officers and men.

19. William H. Whyte, Jr., "The Wife Problem," in Winch and McGinnis, *op. cit.*, pp. 278–285.

20. Katz and Lazarsfeld, *op. cit.*, Carl I. Hovland, "Effects of the Mass Media of Communication," in Gardner Lindzey (ed.), *Handbook of Social Psychology*, Vol. 2 (Cambridge: Addison Wesley, 1950), 1062–1103; Eugene Litwak, "Some Policy Implications in Communications Theory with Emphasis on Group Factors," *Education for Social Work, Proceedings*, Seventh Annual Program Meeting (New York: Council on Social Work Education, 1959), pp. 96–109; Herbert I. Abelson, *Persuasion: How Opinions and Attitudes Are Changed* (New York: Springer, 1959).

21. It is clear that there are certain advantages and disadvantages in the use of legal authority, and some agencies that have depended almost entirely on legal authority in the past have moved toward other means (e.g., the trend toward treatment of offenders by courts) while others might seek more legal authority to achieve their goals (e.g., raising the legal age at which children must stay in school).

For a summary of thinking on the operation of law in social control, see the hypotheses suggested in F. James Davis, *et al.*, *Society and the Law* (New York: Free Press, 1962), pp. 88–90.

22. Other examples: Schools will refer children to outside medical services that have technical experts available; large business concerns might seek to affect public opinion in areas where they have no clear-cut social mandate by delegating the communication function to other organizations, such as schools, civic groups, or churches, that are in a better position to be heard by those the organization wishes to influence. The delegated-

function approach assumes certain interorganizational relationships and recognizes that once the function has been delegated the agency undertaking the communication will have recourse to the other mechanisms of coordination.

23. Herbert H. Hyman and Paul Sheatsley, "Some Reasons Why Information Campaigns Fail," *Public Opinion Quarterly*, 11 (1947), 412–423.

24. Hyman and Sheatsley, *loc. cit.*; Katz and Lazarsfeld, *op. cit.*, pp. 48–66. Litwak, "Some Policy Implications in Communications Theory with Emphasis on Group Factors," *op. cit.*, pp. 97–101.

25. In this regard the various discussions which point out the advantages of interpersonal relations over mass media as means of exerting influence can be further specified as applying to situations where complex messages must be transmitted. See P. F. Lazarsfeld, B. Berelson, and H. Gaudet, "The People's Choice" in William Peterson (ed.), *American Social Patterns* (New York: Doubleday, 1956), pp. 164–169.

26. Eugene Litwak, "Models of Bureaucracy Which Permit Conflict," *op. cit.* For an alternative formulation see James D. Thompson and Arthur

Tuden, "Strategies, Structures, and Processes of Organizational Decision," in James D. Thompson, Peter B. Hammond, Robert W. Hawkes, Buford H. Junker, and Arthur Tuden (eds.), *Comparative Studies in Administration* (Pittsburgh, Pa.: U. of Pittsburgh Press, 1959), pp. 195–216. For a general discussion of organizational typologies see Peter M. Blau and W. Richard Scott, *Formal Organizations* (San Francisco: Chandler, 1962), pp. 40–58.

27. For a discussion of strains and adaptive mechanisms involving professionals in bureaucracies see Blau and Scott, *op. cit.*, pp. 60–74; David Solomon, "Professional Persons in Bureaucratic Organizations," *Symposium on Preventive and Social Psychiatry* (Washington: Walter Reed Army Institute of Research, 1957), pp. 253–256; William Kornhauser, *Scientists in Industry: Conflict and Accommodation* (Berkeley and Los Angeles: U. of California Press, 1962), Ch. 7.

28. Katz and Lazarsfeld, *op. cit.*

29. The five combinations noted here do not exhaust either the logical or the empirical possibilities. We wish only to cite combinations which can easily be illustrated.

Notes to Part VI, 20

1. For other data and analyses, see U. S. Congress, Subcommittee of the Joint Committee on the Economic Report, *Low Income Families and Economic Stability, Materials on the Problem of Low Income Families*, 81st Congress, 1st Session (1949); U. S. Congress, Joint Committee on the Economic Report, *Selected Government Programs Which Aid the Unemployed and Low Income Families*, 81st Congress, 1st Session (1949); Robert J. Lampman, *The Low Income Population and Economic Growth*, U. S. Congress, Joint Economic Commit-

tee, Study Paper No. 12, 86th Congress, 1st Session (1959); U. S. Congress, Subcommittee on Low-Income Families of the Joint Committee on the Economic Report, *Low-Income Families*, 84th Congress, 1st Session (1955).

2. For a discussion of these measures, see Martin David, "Welfare, Income, and Budget Needs," *The Review of Economics and Statistics*, 41 (1959), 393–399.

3. *Annual Price Survey and Family Budget Costs, October, 1959* (New York: The Community Council of

Greater New York, 1959), pp. 11–12.

4. See Margaret S. Strotz, "The BLS Interim Budget for a Retired Couple," *Monthly Labor Review* (1960), 1141–1157; and with Helen H. Lamale, "The City Worker's Interim Family Budget," *Monthly Labor Review* (1960), 785–808.

5. For a comparison of various estimates, see "Estimating Equivalent Incomes or Budget Costs by Family Type," *Monthly Labor Review* (1960), 1197–1200, Table 2.

6. *Ibid.*

7. Other approaches to the measurement of levels of living and income adequacy are suggested in Robert A. Danley and Charles E. Ramsey, *Standardization and Application of a Level of Living Scale for Farm and Nonfarm Families*, Memoir No. 362 (Ithaca, N.Y.: Cornell Agricultural Experimental Station, 1958). See also Eleanor M. Snyder, "Measurement of the Size of the Urban Population with Chronic Low-Income Status," a paper presented at the 1957 annual meeting of the American Statistical Association, September 10, 1957 (New York: State Interdepartmental Committee on Low Income, 1957).

8. For a subsequent analysis, which also indicates factors associated with the concentration of poverty, see James N. Morgan, "Time, Work, and Welfare," in Michael J. Brennan (ed.), *Patterns of Market Behavior: Essays in Honor of Philip Taft* (Providence, R.I.: Brown U. P., 1965); and Hearings of the U. S. Congress House Committee on Education and Labor,

Subcommittee on the War on Poverty Program, 85th Congress, 2nd Session, April 1964, Part 1, pp. 1732–1736.

9. For additional background on families in these categories, see the following for the aged: Henry D. Sheldon, *The Older Population of the United States* (New York: Wiley, 1958); P. O. Steiner and R. Dorfman, *The Economic Status of the Aged* (Berkeley: U. of California Press, 1957); Gordon J. Aldridge and Fedele F. Fauri, *A Syllabus and Annotated Bibliography on Social Welfare and the Aged*, Vol. 4, *Syllabi of Social Gerontology*, Section 4 (Ann Arbor, Mich.: Institute of Social Gerontology, University of Michigan, 1959).

For nonwhites see: Elton Rayack, "Discrimination and the Occupational Progress of Negroes," *Review of Economics and Statistics*, 43 (1961), 209–214; *The Economic Situation of Negroes in the United States*, Bulletin S-3 (Washington, D.C.: U. S. Department of Labor, 1960).

For farmers see: Buis T. Inman and John H. Southern, "Opportunities for Economic Development in Low-Production Farm Areas," *Agriculture Information Bulletin No. 234* (Washington, D.C.: U. S. Department of Agriculture, 1960).

10. Lenore Epstein summarizes data on the impact of low incomes of children in "Some Effects of Low Incomes on Children and Their Families," *Social Security Bulletin*, 24 (1961), 12–16.

Notes to Part VI, 21

1. Information dealing with the national population was obtained by the Political Behavior Program of the Survey Research Center. The facilities of the Detroit Area Study, an organization associated with the University of Michigan's Department of Sociology and the Survey Research Center, were used in the investigation in Wayne County.

2. A comprehensive report is to be found in Angus Campbell, Phillip Converse, Warren E. Miller, and Donald Stokes, *The American Voter*

(New York: Wiley, 1960). We are indebted to these authors for the use of their data.

3. Professors Daniel Katz and Samuel Eldersveld are analyzing the results of this study. We wish to express our appreciation for the use of their data.

4. The use of terms such as compulsory health insurance, socialized medicine, or socialism was purposely avoided in the wording of the questions in these surveys. The amount of controversy which has centered on these concepts in the past indicated that their use in a study of this type would not aid in any analysis of the medical care problem. It was noted in the Detroit Area Study's survey whether or not the respondent used terms such as the above; 14 per cent of the Detroit residents spontaneously employed the term socialism or socialized medicine in answering the question. Almost all of those Detroiters who used these labels were in decided opposition to governmental participation.

Moreover, it appears that many Americans simply do not know what the term socialized medicine means. In a national poll taken by the Gallup organization in February, 1949, respondents were asked what the term

socialized medicine meant to them. About 40 per cent did not know, gave no answer, or gave incorrect or vague answers. Moreover, of those replying to a question of whether they would approve or disapprove of socialized medicine for this country, nearly as many said they approved it as said they disapproved it. These data indicate that socialized medicine is neither as widely understood nor as widely opposed as its opponents believe it to be.

5. For a summary of some earlier public opinion polls, see Hadley Cantril (ed.), *Public Opinion, 1934–1946* (Princeton: Princeton U. P., 1951), pp. 439–443.

6. In 1952 a representative sample of Greater Detroit's residents was asked: "Do you think that national health insurance is a good thing or a bad thing for the country?" At this time, one-half of the Detroiters thought it was good or very good; 10 per cent said it was fair; and 40 per cent said it was bad or very bad. These data were collected by the University of Michigan's Detroit area study.

7. "Voluntary Health Insurance among the Aged," *Progress in Health Services*, 8 (New York: Health Information Foundation, January, 1959), p. 5.

Notes to Part VI, 22

1. *Poverty in the United States* (Washington, D.C.: House of Representatives, Committee on Education and Labor, 88th Congress, 2nd Session, April, 1964).

2. Cooperating with the project staff were Tom Cook, Ora Hinckley, Lynn Kellogg, Roger Lind, Frances McNeil, Winifred Quarton, Robert Rosema, June Thomas, Jeanne Walters, and Fred Wight.

3. Hans Gerth and C. Wright Mills, *Character and Social Structure; the Psychology of Social Institutions* (New York: Harcourt, Brace, 1953).

4. Allison Davis, *Social-Class Influences upon Learning* (Cambridge, Mass.: Harvard University Press, 1948).

5. W. Lloyd Warner, Robert J. Havighurst, Martin B. Loeb, *Who Shall Be Educated? The Challenge of Unequal Opportunities* (New York: Harper & Bros., 1944).

6. David J. Kallen and Elizabeth L. Navarre, *Status and Ability* (Baltimore, Md.: Health and Welfare Council of the Metropolitan Area, 1962).

7. Urie Bronfenbrenner, "Socialization and Social Class through Time and

Space," in Eleanor E. Maccoby, Theodore M. Newcomb, and Eugene L. Hartley (eds.), *Readings in Social Psychology* (3rd ed.; New York; Holt, Rinehart and Winston, 1958), pp. 400–425.

8. Earl Lomon Koos, *The Health of Regionville, What the People Thought and Did about It* (New York: Columbia University Press, 1954).

9. Joseph A. Kahl, *The American Class Structure* (New York: Rinehart, 1957).

10. Lee Rainwater, *And the Poor Get Children; Sex, Contraception, and Family Planning in the Working Class* (Chicago: Quadrangle Books, 1960).

11. Lee Rainwater, Richard P. Coleman, and Gerald Handel, *Workingman's Wife; Her Personality, World, and Life Style* (New York: Oceana, 1959.

12. *Ibid.*

13. Robert R. Sears, Eleanor E. Maccoby, and Harry Levin, *Patterns of Child Rearing* (Evanston, Ill.: Row, Peterson, 1957).

14. Mildred Buck, "Socialization Differences between ADC Mothers and the Sears-Maccoby-Levin Norms" (University of Chicago, Master's research paper, 1963; mimeographed).

15. Edwin J. Thomas, "Effects of Facilitative Role Interdependence on Group Functioning," in Dorwin Cartwright and Alvin Zander (eds.), *Group Dynamics: Research and Theory* (2nd ed.; Evanston, Ill.: Row, Peterson, 1960), pp. 449–471.

Notes to Part VII, 23

1. Differences in this section were tested by *t* test.

2. All results reported are for responses that were coded as mutually exclusive of one another. All *P* values are from chi-square test. In some cases the theoretical frequencies were too small so that it was necessary to test one category against a combination of others. The statement of the null hypothesis was appropriately modified when this was done.

3. Worby has completed a study in Rochester, New York, which substantially replicated this one. Using a sample of juniors in High School, she varied simultaneously the conceptions of degree of understanding and degree of motivation to help. Her results were almost entirely in accord with those described here with a significant exception: not even in the High M-H condition was H expected to reveal personal information to C. Other data, too, indicate anticipation that an age-status difference will be maintained, independent of motivation to help. See Marsha Worby, "The Adolescent's Expectations of How the Potentially Helpful Person Will Act," *Smith College Studies in Social Work*, **26** (1955), 19–59.

Notes to Part VII, 24

1. A. Weitzenhoffer, *Hypnotism: An Objective Study in Suggestibility* (New York: Wiley, 1953).

2. C. L. Hull, *Hypnosis and Suggestibility* (New York: Appleton-Century, 1933).

3. D. Rapoport, *The Organization and Pathology of Thought* (New York: Columbia U. P., 1951).

4. R. M. Counts and I. N. Mensh, "Personality Characteristics in Hypnotically-Induced Hostility," *Journal of*

Clinical Psychology, **6** (1950), 325–330.

5. D. G. Danskin and F. P. Robinson, "Differences in 'Degree of Lead' among Experienced Counselors," *Journal of Counseling Psychology,* **1** (1954), 78–83; P. V. Gump, "A Statistical Investigation of One Psychoanalytic Approach and a Comparison of It with Nondirective Therapy" (Unpublished Master's Dissertation, Ohio State University, 1944); E. H. Porter, "The Development and Evaluation of a Measure of Counseling Interview Procedures. II. The Evaluation," *Educational and Psychological Measurement,* **3** (1943), 321–350.

6. M. H. Erickson, "The Method Employed to Formulate a Complex Story for the Induction of an Experimental Neurosis in a Hypnotic Subject," *Journal of General Psychology,* **31** (1944), 67–84.

7. L. E. Moses, "Non-parametric Statistics for Psychological Research," *Psychological Bulletin,* **49** (1952), 122–143.

8. It is important to recognize that this analysis is not an analysis of covariance. In this analysis, the matching variable (Recall Time) was obtained under the experimental conditions and was presumably affected by the conditions. In covariance analysis, the matching variable must be measured before the experimental conditions are imposed. The analysis of variance of errors of estimate as carried out here is, in effect, a test of the significance of the difference between the correlation between Amount Recalled and Recalled Time in the Leading condition and in the Following condition. The analysis demonstrates that the correlation is very high in the Leading condition ($-.93$), thus the interpretation that S's are recalling to the limits of their abilities in this condition; it is much lower in the Following condition ($-.63$), thus yielding larger errors of estimate and indicating that other factors have influenced the Amount Recalled, reducing it below the limits of the S's ability to recall as this ability is estimated from the Recall Time variable.

Notes to VII, 25

1. S. Freud, "Turnings in the Ways of Psychoanalytic Therapy," *Collected Papers,* Vol. 2 (New York: Basic Books, 1959), pp. 392–402.

2. A. Hollingshead and F. Redlich, *Social Class and Mental Illness: A Community Study* (New York: Wiley, 1959).

3. S. Harrison, J. McDermott, J. Schrager, and P. Wilson, "Social Class and Mental Illness in Children: Choice of Treatment," *Archives of General Psychiatry,* **13** (1965), 411–417.

4. A. Reiss, *Occupation and Social Status* (New York: Free Press, 1962).

5. *Op. cit.*

6. A. Cohen and H. Hodges, "Characteristics of the Lower Blue-Collar Class," *Social Problems,* **10** (1963), pp. 303–334.

7. Hollingshead and Redlich, *op. cit.*; Suzanne Keller, "The Social World of the Urban Slum Child: Some Early Findings," *American Journal of Orthopsychiatry,* **33** (1963), 823–831; F. Riessman, *The Culturally Deprived Child* (New York: Harper, 1962).

8. Another possible explanation for the discrepancy between the school achievement in children of unskilled workers and the professed expectations of their parents may lie in the difference between the expressed attitudes of lower-class parents and their *actual* expectations for the future. Although these parents may

echo current standards about how they would like their children to succeed in school, they may in fact not believe it possible and convey this by subtle cues to the child. The pessi-

mism is confirmed by the child's observations and imitations of parental social patterns that are incompatible with success in the middle-class school setting.

Notes to Part VII, 26

1. For comments on the value of in-service training, see Kermit T. Wiltse, *Social Casework in Public Assistance* (California: Department of Social Welfare, undated; mimeographed), pp. 28–35; and Ellen Winston, "New Opportunities for Trained Personnel in Public Welfare," *Social Work*, 2 (1957), 8–13.
2. Wilbur J. Cohen, "Current and Future Trends in Public Welfare," *The Social Service Review*, 29 (1955), 251.
3. For example, see Michigan State Department of Social Welfare, *Ninth Biennial Report of the Michigan Social Welfare Commission* (Lansing, 1956), pp. 36–42.
4. The authors know of no research that provides a rigorous evaluation of in-service training or of reduced workloads in public assistance. For a demonstration of staff training in ADC, see Carol K. Goldstein, "Services in the Aid to Dependent Children Program in Illinois," *The Social Service Review*, 22 (1948), 480–489. For a demonstration of the effects of reduced workloads combined with other administrative modifications on investigation and costs, see *Adequate Staff Brings Economy* (Chicago: American Public Welfare Association, 1939).
5. Edwin J. Thomas and Donna L. McLeod, *The Effectiveness of In-Service Training and of Reduced Workloads in Aid to Dependent Children —A Report of an Experiment Conducted in Michigan* (Ann Arbor, Mich.: University of Michigan School of Social Work, 1957; mimeographed document). Editor's note: a full report of this project as well as a sub-

sequent experiment is to be found in Edwin J. Thomas and Donna L. McLeod, *In-Service Training and Reduced Workloads: Experiments in a State Department of Welfare* (New York: Russell Sage Foundation, 1960).
6. The underlying values inferred from the seven items of the test are humanitarian vs. utilitarian approaches to persons, noncoercive vs. coercive methods of change, concern vs. lack of concern for the feelings of clients, use of self as a tool of change vs. nonuse of self, help universally vs. help selectively, motivate by stressing strengths vs. stressing weaknesses, and acceptance vs. rejection of deviant behavior. A high score on this test derived from selecting the first as opposed to the second of the two alternatives of a pair does not of course attest to either the moral good or the efficacy of the implied value, even though these alternatives were the ones highly endorsed by the sample of seventy-five professionally trained social workers.
7. This group was included in the 1957–1958 ADC study which, in addition, evaluated a program of in-service training for supervisors and the effects of modified procedures of work.
8. All results reported may be assumed to be statistically significant at the .05 level of significance. For comparing results for workers Fisher's Exact Test was used; for families, Zubin's *t* test was employed.
9. Knowledge may well have changed but was not reflected on the tests because the tests had to be prepared prior to the training program when some of the details of content had not

been fully developed and the content precluded an easy formulation of objective questions to test the workers' knowledge of an area.

10. Editor's note: for a full report on this technique see Edwin J. Thomas, Donna L. McLeod, and Lydia F. Hylton, "The Experimental Interview: A Technique for Studying Casework Performance," *Social Work*, **5** (1960), 52–59; and for a

more general methodological discussion of the problem the reader is referred to Edwin J. Thomas, "Experimental Analogs of the Casework Interview," *Social Work*, **7** (1962), 24–31.

11. Malcolm G. Preston, Emily H. Mudd, and Hazel B. Frosher, "Factors Affecting Movement in Casework," *Social Casework*, **34** (1953), 103–111.

Notes to Part VII, 27

1. Five contrasting southeastern Michigan school systems are included in this work: a rural community, a middle-class academic community, two industrial communities, and one non-industrial urban community. The implications of differences in type of community will not be reported here but are an important feature of the study.

2. Taken together, these multiple measures resolve many of the deficiencies of previous evaluative studies. See Robert D. Vinter, "Group Work with Children and Youth: Research Problems and Possibilities," *Social Service Review*, **30** (1956), 310–321.

3. The pupil rating form developed in this research has proved to be a sensitive, simple instrument for assessing pupil behavior and change. See Robert D. Vinter, Rosemary C. Sarri, Darrel J. Vorwaller, and Walter E. Schafer, *Pupil Behavior Inventory: A Manual for Administration and Scoring* (Ann Arbor, Mich.: Campus Publishers, 1966).

Notes to Part VII, 28

1. Test developed by R. B. Cattell, J. Beloff, D. Flint, and W. Gruen, Institute for Personality and Ability Testing, Champaign, Ill. For a description, see R. B. Cattell and H. Beloff, "Research Origin and Construction of the I.P.A.T. Junior Personality Quiz: The J.P.Q.," *Journal of Consulting Psychology*, **17** (1953), 436–442.

2. Test developed by Edgar F. Borgatta and Henry J. Meyer. For description, see Edgar F. Borgatta in collaboration with Henry J. Meyer, "Make a Sentence Test: An Approach to Objective Scoring of Sentence Com-

pletions," *Genetic Psychology Monographs*, **63** (1961), 3–65. Also Edgar F. Borgatta and Henry J. Meyer, "The Reliability of an Objective Sentence Completion Scoring Technique," *Journal of Social Psychology*, **58** (1962), 163–166; Edgar F. Borgatta, "The Make a Sentence Test (MAST): A Replication Study," *Journal of General Psychology*, **65** (1961), 269–292.

3. Edgar F. Borgatta in collaboration with Henry J. Meyer, *op. cit.*, pp. 27–46.

4. Gerald Caplan, *Prevention of Mental*

Disorders in Children: Initial Explorations (New York: Basic Books, 1961), p. 12.

5. The .05 level of significance has been accepted for this study.

Notes to Part VIII, 29

1. Abraham Flexner, "Is Social Work a Profession?" *Proceedings of National Conference of Charities and Correction* (1915), 576–590.
2. The work of Wilensky and Lebeaux and of Greenwood mark major steps in this direction. See Harold L. Wilensky and Charles N. Lebeaux, *Industrial Society and Social Welfare* (New York: Russell Sage Foundation, 1958); Ernest Greenwood, "Attributes of a Profession," *Social Work*, 2 (1957), 45–55; Ernest Greenwood, *Toward a Sociology of Social Work* (Research Department, Special Report No. 37, Los Angeles, Calif.: Regional Welfare Planning Council of Metropolitan Los Angeles, 1953). Greenwood has embarked on a program of research on social work as a profession, and some of the results are included in student group research project reports at the School of Social Welfare, University of California. See also Joseph W. Eaton, "Whence and Whither Social Work? A Sociological Analysis," *Social Work*, 1 (1956), 11–26; Herbert Bisno, "How Social Will Social Work Be?" *Social Work*, 1 (1956), 12–18; Otto Pollak, "The Culture of Psychiatric Social Work," *Journal of Psychiatric Social Work*, 21 (1952), 160–65.

   Among relevant discussions of the profession by social workers, see Nathan E. Cohen, *Social Work in the American Tradition* (New York: Dryden, 1958); Nathan E. Cohen, "Social Work as a Profession," *Social Work Year Book, 1957* (New York: National Association of Social Workers, 1957); Ernest V. Hollis and Alice L. Taylor, *Social Work Education in the United States* (New York: Columbia U. P., 1951).

   See also, for earlier studies, Esther Brown, *Social Work as a Profession* (New York: Russell Sage Foundation, 1942); Helen L. Witmer, *Social Work: An Analysis of an Institution* (New York: Farrar and Rinehart, 1942); Robert M. MacIver, *The Contributions of Sociology to Social Work* (New York: Columbia U. P., 1931).
3. The relevance of industrialization as a setting for professionalization, with particular reference to social work, is well documented in Wilensky and Lebeaux, *op. cit.* See also Wilbert E. Moore, *Industrial Relations and the Social Order* (New York: Macmillan, 1951); Theodore Caplow, *The Sociology of Work* (Minneapolis: U. of Minnesota Press, 1954).

   For other references on the sociology of professions, see Robert K. Merton, George G. Reader, and Patricia L. Kendall (eds.), *The Student Physician* (Cambridge: Harvard U. P., 1957), especially Robert K. Merton, "Some Preliminaries to a Sociology of Medical Education," pp. 3–79; William J. Goode, "Community within a Community: The Professions," *American Sociological Review*, 22 (1957), 194–200; Talcott Parsons, "The Professions and Social Structure," *Essays in Sociological Theory* (New York: Free Press, 1954), pp. 34–49; Talcott Parsons, "A Sociologist Looks at the Legal Profession," *ibid.*, pp. 370–385; Talcott Parsons, "Social Structure and Dynamic Process: The Case of Modern Medical Practice," *The Social System* (New York: Free Press, 1951), pp. 428–479; A. M. Carr-Saunders and P. A. Wilson, *The Professions* (Oxford: Clarendon, 1933).

4. Goode, *op. cit.*, p. 194.
5. Cf. Ernest Greenwood, "Attributes of a Profession," *op. cit.*; Robert M. MacIver and Charles Page, *Society: An Introductory Analysis* (New York: Rinehart, 1949), pp. 476–483; R. Lewis and A. Maude, *Professional People* (London: Phoenix House, 1952), pp. 55–71; Ralph W. Tyler, "Distinctive Attributes of Education for the Professions," *Social Work Journal*, 33 (1952), 55–62; Morris L. Cogan, "Toward a Definition of Profession," *Harvard Educational Review*, 23 (1953), 33–50; Abraham Flexner, *op. cit.*
6. Greenwood, "Attributes of a Profession," *op. cit.*, p. 54.
7. A. M. Carr-Saunders, "Metropolitan Conditions and Traditional Professional Relationships," in R. M. Fisher (ed.), *The Metropolis in Modern Life* (New York: Doubleday, 1955) as summarized by A. J. Reiss, Jr., "Occupational Mobility of Professional Workers," *American Sociological Review*, 20 (1955), 693.
8. Particularly, Wilensky and Lebeaux, *op. cit.*, Chapter 11.
9. Cf. Ernest Greenwood, "Social Science and Social Work: A Theory of Their Relationship," *Social Service Review*, 29 (1955), 20–33.
10. The range of evident concern with the type of knowledge base among caseworkers, group workers, community organization, and administrative social workers is reflected in the discussions of these methods in Walter A. Friedlander (ed.), *Concepts and Methods of Social Work* (Englewood Cliffs, N.J.: Prentice-Hall, 1958).
11. Cf. Wilensky and Lebeaux, *op. cit.*, p. 288.
12. For a discussion of the relationship of social work and social science, cf. Grace L. Coyle, *Social Science in the Professional Education of Social Workers* (New York: Council on Social Work Education, 1958); Herman D. Stein, "Social Science in Social Work Practice and Education," *Social Casework*, 36 (1955), 147–155; Donald Young, "Sociology and the Practicing Professions," *American Sociological Review*, 20 (1955), 641–648.
13. Cf. Ernest Greenwood, "Social Work Research: The Role of the Schools," *Social Service Review*, 32 (1958), 152–156.
14. See Alfred J. Kahn, "The Nature of Social Work Knowledge," in Cora Kasius (ed.), *New Directions in Social Work* (New York: Harper, 1954), pp. 194–214.
15. *Social Workers in 1950: A Report on the Study of Salaries and Working Conditions in Social Work-Spring 1950* (New York: American Association of Social Workers, 1952).
16. Wilensky and Lebeaux, *op. cit.*, pp. 298–303.
17. *Ibid.*, pp. 303–308.
18. As an example, see Henry J. Meyer and Edgar F. Borgatta, "Evaluating a Rehabilitation Program for Post-Hospital Mental Patients," *Public Health Report*, 73 (1958), 650–656.
19. See Nathan E. Cohen, "A Changing Profession in a Changing World," *Social Work*, 1 (1956), 12–19; Harry L. Lurie, "The Responsibilities of a Socially Oriented Profession," in Cora Kasius (ed.), *op. cit.*, pp. 31–53.
20. Frances Perkins, "My Recollections of Florence Kelley," *Social Service Review*, 28 (1954), 18.
21. *Statistics on Social Work Education, 1957*, compiled by David G. French (New York: Council on Social Work Education, 1957), Table 10, p. 16.
22. *Op. cit.*, p. 333.
23. Cf. Alfred Kadushin, "Prestige of Social Work—Facts and Factors," *Social Work*, 3 (1958), 37–43; R. Clyde White, "Prestige of Social Work and the Social Worker," *Social Work Journal*, 36 (1955), 21–27; R. Clyde White, "Social Workers in Society: Some Further Evidence," *Social Work Journal*, 34 (1953), 161–164; Norman Polansky, W. Bowen, L. Gordon, and C. Nathan, "Social Workers in Society: Results of a Sampling Study," *Social Work Journal*, 34 (1953), 74–80.
24. See Fedele F. Fauri, "The Shortage of Social Workers: A Challenge to Social Work Education," *Social*

Work Journal, **36** (1955), 47–51 and 61.

25. The Council on Social Work Education has an ambitious recruitment program, and most schools of social work make recruitment efforts of their own as well. See, "Recruitment for Social Work Education and Social Work Practice," *Bi-monthly News Publication* (New York: Council on Social Work Education, 1958), Fourth Special Recruitment Issue, p. 6.

26. See Alfred Kadushin, "Determinants of Career Choice and Their Implications for Social Work," *op. cit.,* pp. 17–27. This article includes an extended bibliography.

27. Because of the large number of non-schooled social workers, it is difficult to find data comparing the salaries of trained social workers with those of other professionals. In a study of starting salaries of June 1956 women college graduates, "social and welfare workers" ranked 8th of 12 occupations reported, lower than home economists, nurses, and teachers, and higher than dietitians, librarians, and secretaries and stenographers. See, *1958 Handbook on Women Workers,* Women's Bureau Bulletin No. 266 (Washington: U.S. Department of Labor, 1958), p. 77. On the other hand, a study of former students in schools of social work who entered employment in 1957 reported beginning salaries of $4,565 for women with a master's degree and $3,905 for women without a master's degree. See David G. French and Alex Rosen, "Personnel Entering Social Work Employment from Schools of Social Work, 1957," in "Recruitment for Social Work Education and Social Work Practice," *op. cit.,* p. 15. Trained social workers earn more income than less trained on the average, and men with equivalent training earn more than women. See *Social Workers in 1950, op. cit.,* p. 17. Salary level may be the best index of prestige between professions and within professions, cf. Ward S. Mason and Neal Gross, "Intra-occupational Prestige Differentiation: The School

Superintendency," *American Sociological Review,* **20** (1955), 326–331.

28. Alfred Kadushin, *op. cit.,* p. 20. With respect to sex ratio, 64 per cent of the former students in schools of social work entering employment in 1957 were women. See David G. French and Alex Rosen, *op. cit.,* p. 11. In 1950 nearly 70 per cent of social work positions were filled by women. See *Social Workers in 1950, op. cit.,* p. 5.

29. See Joseph W. Eaton, *op. cit.,* pp. 13–16.

30. See Frances L. Beatman, "How Do Professional Workers Become Professional?" *Social Casework,* **37** (1956), 383–388; Robert W. Cruser, "Opinions on Supervision: A Chapter Study," *Social Work,* **3** (1958), 18–26.

31. The concentration of students in casework is documented in David G. French and Alex Rosen, *op. cit.,* and in the annually published volumes entitled *Statistics on Social Work Education of the Council on Social Work Education.*

32. The survey by French and Rosen reports that 45 per cent of all men students and 58 per cent of all women students had employment in social work prior to entering professional training. Among women students, two-thirds or more in all age categories above 23 years had such prior employment. Unpublished preliminary tables prepared by David G. French.

33. French and Rosen, *op. cit.,* Table 6, p. 13.

34. *Ibid.,* Tables 8 and 9, pp. 14 and 15.

35. One study concludes, from interviews with 30 caseworkers in private practice in New York City, that they consider themselves for the most part psychotherapists or analysts. Josephine Peck and Charlotte Plotkin, "Social Caseworkers in Private Practice," *Smith College Studies in Social Work,* **21** (1951), 165–197. Development of private practice is sometimes viewed as a sign of professional maturity. See Sidney Koret, "The Social Worker in Private Practice," *Social Work,* **3** (1958), 11–17.

36. For a discussion of agency structure

and bureaucracy, see Wilensky and Lebeaux, *op. cit.*, Chapter 10 and pp. 314–316.

37. The psychiatrist-social worker-psychologist team has been analyzed in detail in Alvin Zander, Arthur R. Cohen, and Ezra Stotland, *Role Relations in the Mental Health Professions* (Ann Arbor, Mich.: Institute for Social Research, 1957).

38. The history of professional associations in social work is briefly reviewed in Nathan E. Cohen, "Professional Social Work Faces the Future, *Social Work Journal*, **36** (1955), 79–86.

39. For a discussion of some factors affecting the ways a profession may change, see Harvey L. Smith, "Contingencies of Professional Differentiation," *American Journal of Sociology*, **63** (1958), 410–414.

40. Nathan E. Cohen, *Social Work in the American Tradition, op. cit.*, p. 346.

41. *Ibid.*, p. 348.

Notes to Part VIII, 30

1. Muriel W. Pumphrey, *The Social Work Curriculum Study, The Teaching of Values and Ethics in Social Work Education*, Vol. **13** (New York: Council on Social Work Education, 1959).

2. Three recent studies of values of social work students should be noted: Barbara K. Varley, "Socialization in Social Work Education," *Social Work*, **8** (1963), 102–109; Lela B. Costin, "Values in Social Work Education: A Study," *Social Service Review*, **38** (1964), 271–280; Dorothy D. Hayes and Barbara K. Varley, "Impact of Social Work Education on Students' Values," *Social Work*, **10** (1965), 40–46.

3. The following are the major sources used: Harriet M. Bartlett, "Toward Clarification and Improvement of Social Work Practice," *Social Work*, **3** (1956), 3–9; Felix P. Biestek, *The Principle of Client Self Determination in Social Casework* (Washington, D. C.: Catholic University of America Press, 1951); Felix P. Biestek, *The Casework Relationship* (Chicago: Loyola U. P., 1957); Herbert Bisno, *The Philosophy of Social Work* (Washington, D. C.: Public Affairs Press, 1952); Werner W. Boehm, "The Nature of Social Work," *Social Work*, **3** (1958), 10–18; Werner Boehm, "The Role of Values in Social Work," *The Jewish Social Service Quarterly*, **26** (1958), 429–438; Nathan Cohen, *Social Work in the American Tradition* (New York: Dryden, 1958); Gisela Konopka, *Eduard C. Lindeman and Social Work Philosophy* (Minneapolis: U. of Minnesota Press, 1958); Robin M. Williams, "Value Orientations in American Society," in Herman D. Stein and Richard A. Cloward (eds.), *Social Perspectives on Behavior* (New York: Free Press, 1958), p. 289.

4. Williams, *op. cit.*, pp. 295–296.

5. *Ibid.*, p. 306.

6. Bisno, *op. cit.*, p. 17.

7. This test was called "Social Work Values Test" and described in a statement (mimeographed) of April, 1960.

8. Answers were scored from 1 to 4, with a score of 4 assigned to the position that was believed most strongly to reflect the dominant social work position. In the study reported here, a questionnaire was discarded if the respondent failed to check more than ten items. Unanswered items (when fewer than ten) were assigned the modal score of the sample for that item, a procedure that tends to minimize differences between subgroups. Less than 1 per cent of all possible responses were not checked, and these, it may be noted, were usually the result of skipping a whole page

rather than failure to respond to individual items.

9. The dimension of Individualization was treated differently from the others by presenting a number of fairly common stereotypes that the respondent could accept or reject.

10. The test has undergone a number of revisions since it was devised in 1960. After item and cluster analyses of responses of 293 social workers, the dimension of Individualization was eliminated because its items failed to form a distinguishable cluster. The other dimensions were retained and a new test (called Social Values Test and described in a mimeographed statement of February 1961) was constructed consisting of 72 items (8 items each for 9 dimensions) of which 59 were selected from the previous test because they were most highly correlated with dimension scores, and 13 items were new. This version of the test was used in the study of school teachers (referred to later in this article) in which responses of social workers and teachers are compared on the items common to both versions. After analysis of responses of both social workers ($N = 293$) and teachers ($N = 724$), the test was revised (in 1962) to consist of 40 items reflecting (by 4 items each) 10 relatively independent dimensions representing the inferred meaning of the manifest content of the empirical clusters of items. Although the meaning of some of the dimensions has changed in the course of test development, it is of note that the content of the value dimensions formulated from the original review of social work literature is essentially preserved. Aside from the selection of items that intercorrelate into relatively independent clusters, the effect of revisions has been to make the test somewhat more applicable to other educated groups in addition to social workers. Further work on development of the Social Values Test is proceeding.

11. This research was conducted in 1960.

12. In the statistical analysis, however, scores were divided into quartiles and a rank-order measure of relationship was applied. (Kendall's $\tau\beta$ for contingency tables.) M. G. Kendall, *Rank Correlation Methods* (New York: Hafner, 1955). All relationships reported are statistically significant at the .05 level unless otherwise noted.

13. Ethnic background here is defined operationally by whether both parents of the respondent were native born, only one parent was native born, or both parents were foreign born.

14. Defined as direct service, supervision, administration, teaching, or research.

15. Respondents were asked whether they thought other social workers would generally answer the questionnaire the same way.

16. Respondents were asked to indicate whether they had contact on the job with trained or untrained social workers or with both trained and untrained.

17. Respondents were asked to name the kinds of professional persons, other than social workers, with whom they had contact on their jobs.

18. The study of teachers making possible this comparison was conducted in 1961 by Henry J. Meyer and Eugene Litwak, The University of Michigan, with the cooperation of William Rasschaert and Carl Marburger of the Detroit Public Schools. Donald Warren and Ronald Feldman assisted in the analysis of data.

19. See Note 10, above.

Notes to Part VIII, 31

1. Henry S. Maas, "Use of Behavioral Sciences in Social Work Education," *Social Work*, 3 (1958), 62–69.
2. Charlotte Towle, "A Social Work Approach to Courses in Human Growth and Behavior," *Social Service Review*, 34 (1960), 402–415.
3. See Edwin J. Thomas, "Behavioral Science and the Interpersonal Helping Processes," a paper presented at the 57th Annual Meeting of the American Sociological Association, August 30, 1962, Washington, D. C. (Mimeographed.)
4. See, for example, L. Krasner, "Studies of the Conditioning of Verbal Behavior," *Psychological Bulletin*, 55 (1958), 158–171; B. F. Skinner, *Science and Human Behavior* (New York: Macmillan, 1953).
5. The above discussion concerning referent accessibility, manipulability, cost, and ethicality was stimulated by the provocative paper of Alvin W. Gouldner, "Theoretical Requirements of the Applied Social Sciences," *American Sociological Review*, 22 (1957), 92–103.

Notes to Part VIII, 32

1. This is a revision of a paper presented at the Annual Meeting of the Council on Social Work Education, Oklahoma City, January, 1960.
2. The most familiar example of such work is offered by Harold L. Wilensky and Charles N. Lebeaux, *Industrial Society and Social Welfare* (New York: Russell Sage Foundation, 1958).
    See also Dorothy F. Beck, "The Dynamics of Group Psychotherapy as Seen by a Sociologist," *Sociometry*, 21 (1958), Parts I and II. Also, John R. Seeley, *et al.*, *Community Chest: A Case Study in Philanthropy* (Toronto: U. of Toronto Press, 1957).
3. This distinction is recognized by Greenwood, p. 25, *passim*. Ernest Greenwood, "Social Science and Social Work: A Theory of Their Relationship," *Social Service Review*, 29 (1955), 20–34. See also Alvin Gouldner, "Theoretical Requirements of the Applied Social Sciences," *American Sociological Review*, 22 (1957), 92–103, especially 93 and 96.
4. Hearn, for example, does not distinguish between practice principles and scientific theory, but seems to assert that formulating principles is merely an "operationalizing" step in the process of theory building. Gordon Hearn, *Theory Building in Social Work* (Toronto: U. of Toronto Press, 1958).
5. This formulation is Parsonian and employed for its heuristic value. See Robert D. Vinter, "Group Work: Perspectives and Prospects," in *Social Work with Groups, 1959* (New York: National Association of Social Workers, 1959); Robert D. Vinter, "Small-Group Theory and Research: Implications for Group Work Practice Theory and Research," in Leonard S. Kogan (ed.), *Social Science Theory and Social Work Research* (New York: National Association of Social Workers, 1960), pp. 123–134.
6. Recent examples of frames of reference that meet most of these requirements include Max Siporin, "Deviant Behavior Theory in Social Work: Diagnosis and Treatment," *Social Work*, 10 (1965), 59–67; Jack Rothman, "An Analysis of Goals and Roles in Community Organization Practice," *Social Work*, 9 (1964), 24–31.
7. Maas presents a discussion of these two criteria taken together, which

yield *if-then* propositions. Henry S. Maas, "Use of Behavioral Sciences in Social Work Education," *Social Work*, 3 (1958), 62–70.

8. A codification effort clearly set within an organizing frame of reference is represented in the work of Ronald Lippitt, Jeanne Watson, and Bruce Westley, *The Dynamics of Planned Change* (New York: Harcourt, Brace, 1958). A more modest example is found in Barbara W. Rostov, "Group Work in the Psychiatric Hospital: A Critical Review of the Literature," *Social Work*, 10 (1965), 23–31.

Notes to Part VIII, 33

1. Helen Harris Perlman, "Social Components of Casework Practice," *The Social Welfare Forum, 1953* (New York: Columbia U. P., 1953), p. 136.
2. Grace L. Coyle, "New Insights Available to the Social Worker from the Social Sciences," *Social Service Review*, 26 (1952), 302–303.
3. The author is indebted to the participants in the study: Thelma Bernstein, Alice Ollie Foster, George Hunter, and Elliot Rubin.
4. Coyle, *op. cit.*, pp. 289–304.
5. The bibliography included the following references: Nathan W. Ackerman, "Group Dynamics. 1. 'Social Role' and Total Personality," *American Journal of Orthopsychiatry*, 21 (1951), 1–17; Nathan W. Ackerman and Raymond Sobel, "Family Diagnosis: An Approach to the Preschool Child," *American Journal of Orthopsychiatry*, 20 (1950), 744–752; Ray E. Baber, *Marriage and the Family* (2nd ed.; New York: McGraw, 1953); Ruth Benedict, "Continuities and Discontinuities in Cultural Conditioning," in Clyde Kluckhohn and Henry A. Murray (eds.), *Personality in Nature, Society and Culture* (New York: Knopf, 1953), pp. 522–531; Dorwin Cartwright and Alvin Zander (eds.), *Group Dynamics* (Evanston, Ill.: Row, 1960), Chaps. 3, 9, 19, 22, 23, 25, 34, 40; Jack H. Curtis, "Social Structure and Individual Adaptation," in Gordon J. Aldridge (ed.), *Social Issues and Psychiatric Social Work Practice* (New York: National Association of Social Workers, 1959), pp. 9–26; Bingham Dai, "Some Problems of Personality Development Among Negro Children," in Kluckhohn and Murray, *op. cit.*, pp. 545–566; Neal Gross, Ward S. Mason, and Alexander W. McEachern, *Explorations in Role Analysis* (New York: Wiley, 1958), Introduction and Part I; Robert D. Hess and Gerald Handel, *Family Worlds* (Chicago: U. of Chicago Press, 1959); Ronald Lippitt, "Group Dynamics. 2. Group Dynamics and Personality Dynamics," *American Journal of Orthopsychiatry*, 21 (1951), 18–31; Talcott Parsons and Robert F. Bales, *Family, Socialization and Interaction Process* (New York: Free Press, 1955), Chaps. 2, 3, 4; John P. Spiegel, "The Resolution of Role Conflict within the Family," in Milton Greenblatt, Daniel J. Levinson, and Richard H. Williams (eds.), *The Patient and the Mental Hospital* (New York: Free Press, 1957), pp. 545–564; Herman D. Stein and Richard A. Cloward (eds.), *Social Perspectives on Behavior* (New York: Free Press, 1958), Section II; Edwin J. Thomas, "Theory and Research on the Small Group: Selected Themes and Problems," in Leonard S. Kogan (ed.), *Social Science Theory and Social Work Research* (New York: National Association of Social Workers, 1960), pp. 91–107; Robert F. Winch and Robert McGinnis, *Selected Studies in Marriage and the Family* (New York: Holt, 1953).
6. Elliot Rubin, "The Application of Social Science Theory in Family

Casework"; Thelma Bernstein, "Some Comments on Worker Role and Client Educability," papers read at a staff meeting of the Family Service of Metropolitan Detroit (1961).

7. The Institute was led by Edwin J. Thomas, Ph.D., Professor of Social Work and of Psychology, School of Social Work, University of Michigan, who also acted as consultant to the project director.

Name Index

Subject Index